BOGART

ALSO BY A. M. SPERBER

Murrow: His Life and Times

ALSO BY ERIC LAX

Faith, Interrupted: A Spiritual Journey

Conversations with Woody Allen: His Films, the Movies, and Moviemaking

The Mold in Dr. Florey's Coat: The Story of the Penicillin Miracle

Woody Allen: A Biography

Newman: A Celebration

Life and Death on 10 West

BOGART

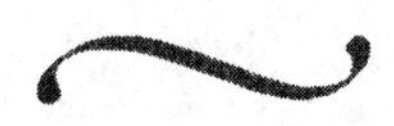

A. M. SPERBER

and

ERIC LAX

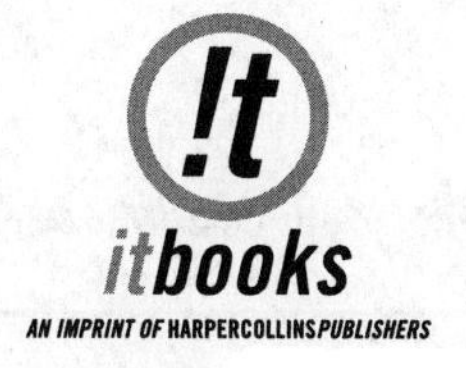

AN IMPRINT OF HARPERCOLLINS*PUBLISHERS*

itbooks

A hardcover edition of this book was published in 1997 by William Morrow, an imprint of HarperCollins Publishers.

FIRST IT BOOKS PAPERBACK EDITION PUBLISHED 1998.
REISSUED IN 2011.

Designed by Blond on Pond

The Library of Congress has catalogued the hardcover edition as follows:
Sperber, A. M. (Ann M.), 1935-1994
Bogart / by A. M. Sperber and Eric Lax. — 1st ed.
p. cm.
Filmography: p.
Includes bibliographical references and index.
ISBN 0-688-07539-8 (acid-free paper)
1. Bogart, Humphrey, 1899-1957. 2. Motion picture actors and actresses — United States — Biography. I. Lax, Eric. II. Title.
PN2287.B48S64 1997
791.43'028'092
[B] — DC20 96-38599
CIP

ISBN 978-0-06-210736-7 (pbk.)

11 12 13 14 15 ID/QG 10 9 8 7 6 5 4 3 2 1

For
Lisa, Alan, and Betty Sperber
and for
Leith Adams and Ned Comstock
A.M.S.

For
Carol Fox Sulzberger
E.L.

A Note to the Reader

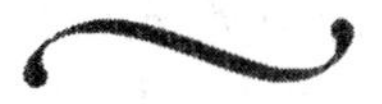

This book is a collaboration between two writers who never met. Ann M. Sperber, who died in February 1994, spent seven years researching the varied aspects of Humphrey Bogart's life and career. She conducted nearly two hundred interviews with people who knew and worked with him, ranging from such well-known good friends as Katharine Hepburn and John Huston to childhood companions from 1905, studio executives, and even a bellman who served Bogart at the Beverly Hills Hotel in 1944. She found extraordinary details of Bogart's early years, and of the lives of his parents and grandparents. In an effort to fully document what it was to be a studio contract player in the 1930s and '40s, she spent a year and a half in the Warner Bros. Archives at the University of Southern California reading every memo, letter, telegram, contract, and script report related to him.

Ann's interest in Bogart developed while researching her 1986 Pulitzer Prize–finalist biography *Murrow: His Life and Times.* Bogart's liberal political views, the FBI's interest in him as early as the mid-1930s, and his participation in the Committee for the First Amendment and its protest of the 1947 House Un-American Activities Committee hearings seemed at odds with the apolitical loner he so often played.

Ann Sperber organized what was literally the quarter ton of research she had amassed into a version of the manuscript that established its direction and set out its themes. After studying what she wrote and the information that she drew on, I was in agreement with her point of view. Over two years I built on her work, adding here, subtracting there, and forming the narrative into a finished piece. The result is something of a hybrid. A book is generally a solitary effort, shaped by the unique voice of its author. In this instance, two people accustomed to singing only solos combined strengths in what I hope is a harmonious duet.

ERIC LAX

Contents

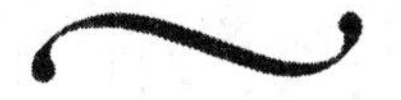

A Note to the Reader vii

1. The House at Seneca Point 1
2. "Young and Handsome as Valentino and Elegant in Comedy" 26
3. Fitting the Bill 48
4. The Portland Rosebud 70
5. "If It's a Louse-Heel, Give It to Bogart" 91
6. The Beginning of a Beautiful Friendship 116
7. Birth of a Hero 135
8. The Black Bird 148
9. "Do Tough Guys Have *Sex Appeal*?" 165
10. "It's Going to Be a Lot of Shit like *Algiers*" 177
11. "The Happiest of Couples" 211
12. Betty 236
13. The Fun Begins 254
14. The Lengthy Good-bye 274
15. The Happiest Time 291
16. After the War 318
17. "A Loathsome Character" 335

18. Mr. Bogart Goes to Washington 354
19. No Mark of the Squealer 389
20. The Boris Karloff of the Supper Clubs 407
21. All the Aspects of a Loser 433
22. The Toy Department 454
23. Beating the Devil 470
24. The Old Bull 490
25. Sunset and Evening Star 509

Acknowledgments 523
Notes 527
Bibliography 601
Humphrey Bogart's Broadway Plays 607
Filmography 613
Index 649

Bogart

CHAPTER 1

The House at Seneca Point

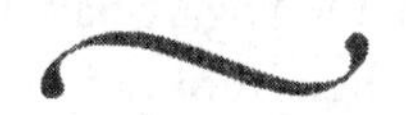

His earliest memories were of the estate where his family summered, and of a sailboat tied to the dock at the end of a stretch of manicured lawn. The elegant two-story Victorian house dominated a curve of land on the shoreline of Canandaigua Lake in western New York State. The spire on the tower room jutted above the treetops on the fifty-five acres of farmland, pasture, and woods, and large high windows stared out over the water. Broad awning-shaded steps led to the lawn that ended at a shale beach, where the long dock sliced into the lake. His father's champion-class yacht was moored there, and he would be a sailor all his life.

A carriage road swept over a little stone bridge to the back entrance of the house, but, like the other homes nearby, Willow Brook was best reached by water. Visitors arrived at a leafy landing on the long, narrow Finger Lake—deep blue in morning, turquoise in the afternoon—gouged out of the hills aeons before by an advancing glacier. The boathouse flanked one side of the four-hundred-foot beachfront. On the other, sheltered by tall stands of ash, oak, and poplar, were the clear-running brook and weeping willows that gave the property its name. It was a showplace, built in 1871 by the owners of the local brewery as testimony to their wealth.

In the last summer of the nineteenth century, Dr. Belmont DeForest Bogart bought the estate for his wife, Maud, then five months pregnant with their first child, a son. Two daughters would soon follow his birth. For the three offspring, Willow Brook was the summer home of their childhood, a place that would figure in both Humphrey Bogart's fondest recollections and his most nightmarish ones.

The Bogarts seemed the model of the solid, successful Victorian family—upper-middle-class New York City people whose comings and goings in the village of Canandaigua were regularly recorded in the local paper: Dr. and Mrs. Belmont D. Bogart had arrived with their little son and were waiting to occupy their summer "cottage"; Dr. B. D. Bogart and children had moved in for the summer and would shortly be joined by Mrs. Bogart; Mrs. B. DeForest Bogart had improvised a studio from an old cabin on the property and was giving much time to her art.

Like the other summer people, they had little to do with the daily life of the town. But as owners of property and householders of substance, they fit easily into Seneca Point, the exclusive lakeside enclave south of Canandaigua for leading locals and for professional families escaping the heat of Boston and New York—a mix of bankers and businessmen, old settlers, clergy, journalists, and academics. Show people were almost unheard of. The only Warner Brothers here were the local steamboat builders.

The colony, usually referred to as the Point, was a little more than halfway down the sixteen-mile-long lake—a secluded Arcadia surrounded on three sides by the grapevine-covered hills that caused the region to be compared with northern Italy. The 142-foot-long sidewheeled steamer *Onnalinda* ferried people from place to place, stopping at any of the sixty-six landings around the lake whenever a white flag was raised, its two decks redolent with the aroma of fresh grapes, peaches, and other fruit headed for the rail spur at the Canandaigua pier, then on to markets in New York, Philadelphia, and Washington, D.C.

The Point was self-contained, protected both by the cliffs and by the owners' corporation, which determined who could move in, and life there was paced to the easy elegance that prevailed for the privileged in those years before World War I. The residents visited, boated, and played tennis; in the evening they played bridge and attended uplifting lectures. On Sundays there were baseball games on the golf course—but only after church. For that, the families would travel by canoe or rowboat to the next point south, where the retired rector of St. John's Episcopal Church in Canandaigua had his cottage. Many of the children would congregate on the stairs, beneath the walls lined with rattlesnake skins. The old priest would recite the service faster than anyone but his wife, who beat everyone through the Apostles' Creed. He was in a hurry to go fishing, and she was in a hurry to fix his lunch so he could. On all days, children went easily between the houses, whose doors were always unlocked. It was a secure, prosperous, homogeneous world, staunchly Republican, though once visited by young Franklin Roosevelt, who developed a cramp while swimming and was pulled ashore by a resident. In later years when New Deal rulings offended local sensibilities, FDR's Good Samaritan was often heard to declare, "I should have let the son of a bitch drown!"

Even in that well-off community, the Bogarts were accorded a certain deference. Dr. Bogart ran a flourishing downstate practice and was known to have inherited wealth. His wife was the renowned illustrator and children's artist Maud Humphrey. It was said in hushed tones that they were DeForests—socially well connected and linked in some indefinable way with one of the oldest and most distinguished names in New York State.

And they looked it. For years afterward people would remember the family, up from Grand Central Station on the overnight Pullman, getting off the train at Canandaigua and boarding the *Onnalinda,* headed for their landing: the doctor, six feet tall and broad-shouldered, immaculate in his heavy suit, boiled shirt, and stiff collar; his handsome wife, nearly as tall, thin, fashionable in starched cottons or flowing silks of gray or mauve, with lavender-ribboned high-heeled high-button shoes that accentuated the tininess of her size-2½ feet, of which she was so proud; the small, dark-eyed boy and his two little sisters Frances and Catherine, all three under the close watch of a nurse in a starched uniform. They swept aboard the steamer, a splendid caravan, the rear brought up by a sour-faced servant couple straining under the weight of abundant trunks and packages.

But there was an underside to the domestic portrait that was generally hidden, though not obscured from those who knew them well. Decades later, Humphrey Bogart would describe for his fans a meticulously proper view of his early life: a weak-willed but charming father; an undemonstrative yet wholly admirable mother; a home life lacking in affection but with plenty of character. "We were a career family," he told interviewers, "too busy to be intimate." Hardly the most comforting of descriptions, but perhaps the best available considering the recollections of his childhood friends. Theirs depict a far harsher reality.

"Dr. Bogart had a violent temper," said Grace Lansing, later Mrs. Gerard Lambert of Palm Beach and Princeton, and a cousin of Woodrow Wilson's secretary of state. She lived nearby with her mother and the shadow of an absentee father, Harry Lansing, the alcoholic scion of a New

York railroad dynasty who had long since disappeared into the wilds of the Adirondacks. Harry Lansing and Belmont Bogart had been hunting friends, and the doctor was attracted to the plump and pretty Mrs. Lansing.

Grace Lambert pitied "those poor children. Humphrey was a month younger than I, very handsome. They were always sent up to the cottage for the summer, with the most *awful* servants. Common people, with loud voices, ignorant. Oh, they were tough! They used to beat them and shout at them, they were *horrible.* And the mother and father didn't seem to notice."

Perhaps because the doctor and his wife were part of the problem. They fought continuously, loudly, and publicly. Both were heavy drinkers, with Belmont, as were many physicians of his time, quietly acknowledged to be addicted to morphine. Maud, for her part, seemed constantly preoccupied with her deadlines, always under pressure and loudly impatient with the needs of her children and household. "She had a short temper," Grace Lambert said. "And she'd flare up—against her children, against anybody. She was always painting, under a set time, so anything that came across this deadline was upsetting to her." When the work was finally done, Dr. and Mrs. Bogart would gather up Mrs. Lansing, and the three would go off by motorboat for dinner in Canandaigua. Next morning, Grace would hear from her mother of how poor, dear Mrs. Bogart had had too much to drink and taken to her bed; but it was all right, Dr. Bogart had given her some pills.

Maud was a hostage to bad headaches, though no one really knew whether they or the drinking came first in a life replete with tension and anxiety. Her son, in his idealized recollections, would describe her as a near teetotaler, hardly venturing beyond a lady-like glass of champagne, a recollection considerably at odds with those of many others, including Grace Lambert: "She drank quite a lot."

Maud also fought a painful skin condition known as erysipelas, a streptococcal inflammation named for the hot, red skin that results. "When the pain began," her son once said, "it lashed her so terribly that her left eye closed and the side of her face flamed. . . . Then my father shot a quarter of a grain of morphine into her to keep her from going insane."

Eventually, erysipelas would be controllable by penicillin; at the time, however, the only relief was through narcotics, carrying with it the dangers of addiction. Belmont Bogart had been snared by drugs in the course of needed medication for a painful leg injury shortly before his marriage, and evidence suggests that Maud was caught as well.

Frank Hamlin, a grandson of the town banker and later chairman of the board of the Canandaigua National Bank, was at the time the smallest of the local boys. He would never forget one day when, in his words, bare-legged and runny-nosed, he stopped off to see his friend Hump Bogart.

Nobody ever bothered to knock on the open doors at the Point, least of all an eight-year-old in a hurry. What Hamlin saw in the hallway, however, made him stop and gape, his greeting locked in his throat.

Dr. and Mrs. Bogart stood on the front stairs, dressed for dinner, oblivious to the boy or to anything besides themselves. The doctor had a syringe in one hand, Mrs. Bogart's extended arm in the other, the summer sleeve pushed back. With the expertise of his profession, he inserted the needle into his wife's forearm, after which she took the syringe and injected him. There was nothing furtive about it, the whole procedure completed with the practiced nonchalance of sophisticates enjoying a pre-supper aperitif.

The scene confused and disturbed the boy. Dr. Bogart was a *doctor,* after all, and doctors used needles. But it also brought to mind bits and pieces of grownups' talk overheard before bedtime. As he stood there trying to make sense of what he'd seen, the couple swept out, unaware or perhaps simply not caring that they had an audience.

Addiction among medical practitioners was to some extent accepted at the time; if doctors liked a taste of their own medicine, it was entirely their business. And early-twentieth-century attitudes to drugs aside, the Bogarts' wealth seemed always to give them a cushioned remove from contemporary mores; they lived by their own rules as surely as Maud Humphrey wore white boots in the rain when custom dictated that one wear only black, a color she deemed "plebeian." Not so easily overlooked, however, was the treatment of the three children behind the lace curtains and the massive front door of Willow Brook.

To adults, Belmont Bogart, whom most everyone called Bogie, seemed a charming, civilized man with an easygoing nature, an outdoorsman who loved hunting and camping and always had time to talk with truck drivers and farmers. His son's contemporaries often saw someone else—a gruff, overbearing grownup who awed them with his physical presence and was quick to resort to corporal punishment for the least infraction. Mrs. Bogart was little better. Faced with a husband increasingly less inclined to work, which made her own deadlines more important, she released her short temper in shouts at her children when they annoyed her or got in her way. She was now in her forties and clinging to the remnants of her youthful good looks. One attempted augmentation, a newly introduced permanent wave, left her hair discolored, unruly, and the subject of unflattering conversation among the other ladies. To Humphrey's friends, she was an imperious, erratic presence, known as "Queen Maud" or "Lady Maud." Mercurial in mood, she was at times a pleasant grande dame paying youngsters the lavish rate of one dollar an hour to pose for her drawings, but at others a shrill, intimidating shrew whose scolding voice carried halfway across the lake.

She was the determining factor in her son's early life.

Maud Humphrey painted angelic children nestling up to Madonna-like mothers in a series of successful books that began in the 1890s with *The Bride's Book.* Her own children, however, seemed little more than biological evidence that she had done her duty as a wife. They knew their place; it was with the servants, to whom they were shunted off in the routine manner of the day, always secondary to her art. In a way, the closest she came to her children was when she had them sit for her. Humphrey was his mother's favorite model, although he was not the original Maud Humphrey baby, as so often later claimed. Her drawings depicted idealized children. And when her own child posed for her, he was removed from the realm of real person with real needs. It was as if in painting a picture of a perfect child, she made her own child, who was the subject, perfect, and therefore perfectly mothered.

"She was essentially a woman who loved work, loved *her* work, to the exclusion of everything else," Bogart would recall. "I don't think she honestly cared about anything but her work and her family. Yet she was totally incapable of showing affection to us."

To her children, she was always "Maud," never "Mother." It was easier, her son rationalized; it was unsentimental, as direct, business-like, and impersonal as Maud was. It also meant a childhood without a kiss or a hug. When she did show her approbation, it was conveyed in a masculine way; long after he was an adult, Bogart still did not know whether her manner was caused by shyness or a fear of seeming weak. "Her caress was a kind of blow," he said. "She clapped you on the shoulder, almost the way a man does."

Humphrey Bogart would eventually come to terms with the mother of his childhood, would even admire her. After all, she was a woman who was famous in her own right, an acknowledged talent in a man's world, and a high-income earner in an age that consigned women to the kitchen. But admiration was as far as he could go: "I can't say truthfully that I loved her." The relationship engendered a streak of distrust that bedeviled his later intimacies with women. Once he was established as a tough guy in films, he gave interviews with super-macho titles such as "I Hate Dames," confessions with more of a basis in reality than the studio flacks who placed them realized.

The classification of dysfunctional families was decades away, but the concept was no stranger to the Bogarts' neighbors on the Point, who were concerned for the welfare of the children. Humphrey's sisters, Frances and Catherine Elizabeth, known as Pat and Catty, were two and three years younger, respectively. (Frances was at first called "Fat" by Humphrey because she was, though she soon grew tall and slender and became Pat thereafter. As an adult, Catherine was called Kay.) Their gentle older brother with his sad dark eyes was protective of them but ill-equipped to cope with the rages of the servant couple who themselves were mistreated by Belmont and Maud, and who vented their resentment on their employers' helpless offspring.

"They were abused," said Grace Lambert. "Everyone worried so about them, but they couldn't do much about it. Those servants were awful."

The worst times were the extended periods, lasting anywhere from two weeks to a month, when the parents would return to the city, leaving the servants in total control. Even though sounds traveled on the Point, allowing others to hear the shouts and cries, Humphrey and his sisters never complained openly. "Wouldn't *dare,*" Lambert said. "They were afraid."

But Grace wasn't. If *he* wasn't going to talk about it, she told Humphrey one day, *she* would. Anyway, she added, the grownups already were. He grew anxious, his eyes troubled beneath the fringe of dark hair: "Don't—don't say that. Don't."

She went ahead anyway—"And it got back to Mrs. Bogart that I was saying things about her servants."

A walkway ran along the lakeshore, a favorite promenade for local families on summer evenings, when neighbor called on neighbor. Grace and her mother were out walking one night when a tall, imperious figure bore down on them out of the gloaming, shouting at the top of her voice. Maud Humphrey Bogart, made even more towering by her high-heeled shoes with the little purple bows, railed at the embarrassed little girl: Oh, *she* knew what Grace was up to, spreading stories about her servants being cruel. Well, she didn't believe it—not a word of it! The eleven-year-old winced, shaken at the dressing-down in front of the grownups. But to Grace's surprise, she saw them turn instead on Maud and berate her. While this comforted Grace, she also knew what would happen to Humphrey.

On another summer's afternoon she had entered the cool, dark hallway of the Bogart house. She often came to pose for Maud, but that day she was just looking for her friend as she made her way up the stairway. The walls of the stairwell and landing were covered with murals, in which Mrs. Bogart, with a sardonic eye, had depicted the comings and goings of the colony.

The house was quiet, except for an odd sound she couldn't quite place: a dull snap at regular intervals that echoed in the stillness. A door on the landing was ajar. Drawn by curiosity, she moved quietly until she saw, outlined against the light from the windows, Humphrey, hunched over, and his father, who held the boy's neck with one arm while the razor strop in the hand of the other came down repeatedly on his back. There was no shouting, no sign of anger, no murmur or struggle from Humphrey, who slightly flinched as the blows landed, his face expressionless. Only the recurring snap as the leather found its target.

Grace quickly fled the house. As she hurried to the carriage road, she passed the little studio where Maud, a cool detached figure in mauve, sat painting one of her famous tableaux of angelic children.

Humphrey Bogart would make his career in film, a medium based on illusion. He was perfectly trained for it, for a good deal about the Bogarts was illusion: the solid Victorian facade that masked alcoholism and drug and child abuse; the distinguished doctor with needle tracks under his boiled shirt; the revered children's artist with no understanding of her own son and daughters. Just as illusory were the Bogarts' pretensions of being Old New York society. The fact was, Dr. Bogart's father had begun as a Canandaigua innkeeper.

Adam Watkins Bogart had always wanted more. With a single exception, his people had been farmers for generations, ever since Gisbert in den Bogart, "Gisbert in the Orchard," had arrived from Holland in the 1600s. They had lived first in Brooklyn—up to modern times there would be a Bogart Avenue there—then migrated in stages to the newly opened farmlands around the Finger Lakes in the lovely, hilly region of western New York known as the Southern Tier.

Adam was ambitious and he was tough, and one way to be freed from slavery to the soil was to run a tavern, a two-fisted job in an area only a generation or two removed from frontier days. By the 1850s, he had saved enough for a lease on the Franklin House, Canandaigua's one hotel, which doubled as the county seat. The town jail was in the basement, a tap room out front was the social hub. Here were farmers gathered on their infrequent visits to town, travelers passing through, politicians arguing and dealing amid clouds of cigar smoke. Adam was in his element as proprietor and host; the appropriate occupation and place for the grandfather of *Casablanca*'s Rick Blaine.

He married a woman of property, like himself no longer young, and like himself eager for betterment. Julia Bogart had the money for the lease on the elegant three-story Jefferson House, the social center of what was then the village of Watkins on nearby Lake Seneca. The brick and stone hotel had been built by a distant cousin of Adam's, who had given his name to the town. Jefferson House had fourteen rooms, each with a fireplace, a two-story balustraded tower, and a spacious lobby with a floor of gleaming black and white Italian tile.

Julia held the lease, and the money, too. Adam minded the business. The younger of their two children, both boys, was given the grandiose name of Belmont DeForest, joining the names of two leading New York high-society families of no relation to each other or the Bogarts, but a clear statement of the parents' aspirations. Only naming the child Vanderbilt Rockefeller would have been more pretentious.

The older boy's name would be obliterated over the years, though not the story of his fate. He was six years old, sliding down the sleek, polished banister of the massive stairs that ascended two floors on one side of the high-ceilinged lobby. Perhaps the father had promised to keep an eye on him. Lost in the pleasure of descent, the boy failed to check his speed. Seconds later, he sailed off the railing and smashed against the bright, hard tiles, dying on impact.

Julia never forgave her husband, although whether because marital rights were not to be denied or, more likely, because she simply wanted another child, Belmont was born a year later. He was two when his mother died in November 1868, after five months on a sickbed, treated by a doctor who had come by every day with useless medications. Her body was interred at Glenwood Cemetery, but not her fury. In the will she wrote just two months before, Julia A. Bogart left her worldly goods to her only child, with specific instructions that the boy's upbringing and financial affairs be in the care of a legally appointed guardian. Adam was left with nothing, not even his son.

He contested the will, charging that his wife was not in her right mind. Local sympathies were with him, but hearings and conflicting family claims dragged on for two years, depleting the estate and embittering Adam. In March 1871, Adam traveled to Newark, New Jersey, to appeal directly to Julia's sisters. Whatever opposition they may formerly have had, they now petitioned the court on his behalf. Wrote one: "He has always thought I was opposed to his having his rights. Now I will say this to you in confidence—Brother Bogart has always been an honorable man with his family. I now think it the best way to let him have his own way and there is not a doubt [that he should be] with his own child." Another stated, "I know his whole mind is on the future welfare of the son" and asked that the money be released "in Brother Bogart's hands so he can go in business and make a living for self and boy. . . . I know [Adam] to be an affectionate father, ever watchful over the interest of the motherless son." Soon after, the court declared all accounts settled, leaving father and son free to go. Adam paid his debts and took his boy to New York City. He did not return to Watkins until he was shipped back in a casket twenty-one years later, to be buried near the wife who hated him.

He had never remarried. Belmont DeForest Bogart grew up alone, a confused, disoriented child who was the object of a custody battle in which one of the litigants was his dead mother.

Not that the boy lacked for material comforts. In the boomtown of 1870s New York, Adam Bogart invested Julia's remaining money well. He made a fortune as a pioneer manufacturer of lithographed tin advertising signs and was determined that Belmont would have not only the name of a rich man's son, but all the advantages as well. He would not have to endure the taproom of the Franklin House, the farmers with their muddy boots smelling of cow dung, and the country politicians with their tobacco plugs and cheap cigars; neither would he have to cater to the patrons of the Jefferson. Instead, he would go to Andover, like the sons of the landed gentry of Canandaigua and Rochester, and then to Yale. He would know the right people. He would be a gentleman.

Belmont learned this lesson all too well. Tall and good-looking, with a thatch of thick, dark hair, he was popular with women and the sons of the best families, an avid huntsman and skilled sailor at the fashionable summer resorts. In a social world attuned to the "Gentleman's C," he made his way easily through Andover and Yale, then the Columbia College of Physicians and Surgeons in New York City; later he was on the staffs of Bellevue, St. Luke's, and Sloan hospitals. Following his graduation from Columbia in 1896 and eased by the right entrées, he launched a prosperous practice that never intruded on the pleasures of a gentleman. He had, on the surface anyway, an ideal life. And perhaps if it hadn't been for the ambulance accident, his son's life would have been very different.

According to newspaper accounts, Dr. Bogart, just months out of medical school, was waiting alongside a city street when a horse-drawn ambulance, top-heavy and balanced precariously on large, spindly wheels, came by. Possibly the horse turned skittish, but without warning the ambulance tipped over and fell on the young doctor, leaving him with massive cuts and bruises, and a fractured leg. The bone, badly set, refused to heal and had to be rebroken and reset. Eventually he learned to walk again, but from then on his health would always be unstable. The use of drugs, prescribed at the outset to alleviate the excruciating pain, became a daily ritual; he would be addicted for the rest of his life.

The accident had a secondary, equally fateful outcome. Two years earlier at an art studio party, Belmont Bogart had met the beautiful, spirited Maud Humphrey, two years younger than he and already famous. Their instantaneous attraction that led to a quick near-engagement was reinforced by the proper social attributes—he had money and position, she was tall and slender with fine features and an independent air that excited him, though not so bohemian as to preclude a good income. But she was also an outspoken conservative as well as a suffragist—her son would call her a laboring Tory—who worked hard for her earnings and for women's rights. Their differences soon led to a break in the relationship.

Now, two years later, she walked into the hospital room and back into Belmont's life. Their reconciliation was as instantaneous as their initial attraction. From that point on, Maud took over. In view of "the impending sufferings" of her fiancé, she told a reporter from upstate, she had decided that she would rather nurse her husband through his trial than visit a fiancé with the chaperons required for a single lady. They were married within a week, a few Humphrey cousins on hand to stand for the bride. "The honeymoon," reported the *Ontario County Times* of Canandaigua, "will be spent in a hospital." They married in June 1898, the bridegroom thirty-two, old for those times, the bride thirty, an age considered well into spinsterhood.

But labels seldom concerned Maud. In her case, moreover, the usual social pressures to marry had been inoperative. Her parents were dead, as were Belmont's; financially, she was independent. Even so, the doctor was a catch; he was rich, he was good-looking, and marriage was still the ultimate success, especially for a woman of thirty.

She was the daughter of a comfortable middle-class family from Rochester's Third Ward, known locally as the Ruffled Shirt District. The Humphreys were proud of their English roots and their lateral connections to the Churchills, connections that make Maud and her children distant relations of Winston Churchill and of Princess Diana. One of Maud's uncles was a prominent lawyer, another the owner of Humphrey's Bookstore, for years a city landmark. Her father John had been a prosperous Rochester merchant.

Maud's determination had sustained her through a bout of near blindness that inexplicably began when she was fourteen and just as inexplicably reversed itself two years later. Her parents died not long after, and she left Rochester at eighteen, going first to New York City to enroll at the Art Students League, and then to Paris, where one of her teachers was James McNeill Whistler. She returned a skilled painter, only to find that men of large affairs, who controlled the fat commissions, weren't about to have their portraits painted by a woman. Children, however, were another matter; the nursery was after all a woman's place. Her best work in any case was in watercolors and in the strong, sure charcoal drawings that would include some of the most insightful likenesses of her son. "The Maud Humphrey baby," he later said, was painted in "water color worked so dry the painting seemed to have been etched."

Maud mined her niche. Her paintings appeared on the covers of such magazines as the *Delineator* and *Buttrick's* as well as in ads and sewing patterns. Soon her work caught the attention of such color printers as Louis Prang of Boston and Frederick A. Stokes of Rochester, who quickly bought exclusive rights to all her color work and kept her under contract until 1900, illustrating popular books of the publisher's invention. It was a lucrative arrangement for them both. Her artworks were printed on finer paper than the text, and were signed and copyrighted so that they could be resold as prints or reproduced as calendars and postcards by other publishers who had made agreements with Stokes. She also illustrated calendars for upstate New York newspapers, generally given to subscribers by their paper boys. A particularly beautiful one, done for the Buffalo *Evening News,* could be cut to form a jigsaw puzzle.

Her books for Stokes brought her immense fame. By the early 1890s, Maud's name was a byword among parents throughout the United States. They called her the American Kate Greenaway, after the beloved English painter whose art graced children's books all over the English-speaking world. *The Bride's Book* did well, but its logical sequel, the *Baby's Record,* seems to have immortalized nearly every turn-of-the-century American infant's first haircut, tooth, word, and step. Among her other successes were *Babes of the Year, Babes of the Nations, Tiny Toddlers,* and *Maud Humphrey's Mother Goose. Little Folk of 1776* and *Children of the Revolution* had tots in the guises of George Washington, Benjamin Franklin,

Betsy Ross, and other early American patriots. *Little Heroes and Heroines* and *Little Soldiers and Sailors* were children's guides to the Spanish-American War. In 1895, when she was twenty-seven, Maud Humphrey's annual income was reported to be $50,000.

As her son later said, "Starving in a garret didn't appeal to her when she discovered she could make $50,000 a year drawing covers for magazines."

Her private sketches were skillful, hard-edged, and uncompromising. The public taste demanded sentiment, and she gave it to them with a vengeance—angelic roly-polies with sausage curls and China-saucer eyes in saccharine poses; Maud Humphrey children would never "cry, drool, get dirty or throw their spinach about," as one critic later wrote, but "sweetly say their prayers for mother, gently toss rosebuds . . . or at most shed a gentle tear." The public clamored for more, and Maud delivered with the skill and detail that earned her her prominence. But she knew what she could do if only allowed to, and beneath the success and brilliant marriage, there ran a deep current of anger.

The Bogarts bought a town house on Manhattan's then-fashionable Upper West Side, a half block from the broad, tree-tented sweep of Riverside Drive along the Hudson. They filled it with horsehair furniture and maintained it with a legion of Irish maids. A year and a half later, Maud gave birth to their first child. They named him Humphrey after her family and DeForest after his father and the presumably rich relations whose connections were always hinted at but never proved. Adam Bogart had died seven years before, all traces of the taproom long vanished. Maud set out to reinvent the Bogarts and make certain that her son never heard anything about his father's forebears beyond occasional obliquely disparaging references. "I know nothing of her background," he said when he was in his fifties. "She never had time to tell me of it, but . . . she was always a little supercilious about Father's family."

For years, Humphrey Bogart's birth date would be a matter of dispute, the official date of December 25, 1899, dismissed as so much studio hype. (A favorite alternative was January 23, 1899, which would have made him a six-month baby.) This is one case where the legend turns out to be the truth; for, while his birth certificate appears to be lost, the *Ontario County Times,* which kept tabs on the region's notables, announced in its January 10, 1900, issue: "Born: at New York, Dec. 25, 1899, to Dr. and Mrs. Belmont DeForest Bogart, a son."

Mrs. Bogart had been out to an exhibit the day before—over Dr. Bogart's objections, according to one biographer. She went into labor that night with a timing that couldn't have been more unfavorable. It was Christmas Eve; Sloan's Maternity Hospital was in midtown, at Fifty-ninth Street and Ninth Avenue, more than two miles south; and it had begun to snow. A hansom cab carried the couple downtown. Maud, now feeling the contractions, was jostled from side to side as the carriage clattered along on its two wheels over the slippery cobblestones on Ninth Avenue while the trains of the Elevated thundered overhead.

Humphrey DeForest Bogart arrived on Christmas Day, with the Black Dutch look of his forebears, the dark-eyed swarthiness that attested to a long-ago presence of the Spanish in the Netherlands. It was six days before the end of the nineteenth and the start of the twentieth centuries. As an adult, he would often refer to himself as "a last century man."

For Belmont and Maud, their New York City facade was the counterweight to their Canandaigua pretense. The family, like their four-story limestone-front townhouse, presented an impressive face to the world. They were listed yearly among the twenty thousand households in *Dau's New York Blue Book*—not quite the Social Register, but "a listing of fashionable addresses," as its publishers proudly put it, giving the names of "prominent residents" of the city.

West 103rd Street, off Riverside Drive, was comfortably upper-middle-class—townhouses of brownstone and limestone arrayed wall to wall, ending in the leafy esplanade of Riverside Park with its broad views of the Hudson. On the semi-rural Drive, moviemakers filmed chase scenes for the nickelodeons, often ending at the domed 150-foot-high Grant's Tomb, which was modeled on the Mausoleum of Halicarnassus, one of the Seven Wonders of the World.

At number 245, broad stone steps led up to the parlor floor and Dr. Bogart's office. He had his world; Maud had hers, in a fourth-floor studio under a skylight, where she usually worked late into the night. When they came together, they often fought. The children cowered in the nursery upstairs, their blankets pulled about their ears in an attempt to block the sounds of their parents screaming at each other and to escape the atmosphere of rage that suffused their growing up.

At age six Humphrey set off on the expected prep school track, beginning at the small Delancey School and at nine transferring to Trinity School, founded in 1709, New York's oldest continuous private school. It was operated by Trinity Church, the wealthy Episcopal parish on Wall Street whose vestrymen controlled many of the levers of power in the city. The school, however, an imposing stone building on Ninety-first

Street, just east of Broadway, was only twelve blocks away from the Bogart house.

By this time Trinity was hardly the charity school that had been its founders' intent, but neither was it an easy ride for the very rich. Run on the austere pattern of the English public schools, it was a boys-only institution, with black-robed masters whose grading weeded out the slackers and sent the rest on to the Ivy League. Humphrey, a new boy among youngsters who had already spent four years together, did not do well. He was an outsider to his classmates and an erratic student, and his dismayed parents and teachers watched his marks yo-yo from near honor levels to barely average to abysmally failing and then up again; his attendance record was dotted with absences. His only consistently good grades were in religion, an inescapable presence at the school, where the day began at 9:00 A.M. with chapel, and where on Friday mornings the Very Reverend Dr. Lawrence T. "Bunny" Cole, headmaster of Trinity, recited the litany over the bowed heads of the kneeling boys.

It might have been the drama that drew Humphrey to ecclesiastical excellence, or possibly a sense of caring that he could not find elsewhere. One of the few boys who bothered with him, a class officer, remembers liking him but feeling that he was lonely "and wasn't happy at home."

During his years of stardom, Bogart reinvented his past and cast himself in the role of a young rebel who stood up to Dr. Cole. The sadder reality was of a boy who tried to make himself invisible. The very few who remembered him at all were to recall a delicate-featured, retiring lad, whose lush curls and immaculate Fauntleroy suits made him an easy mark; "a misfit," said the journalist Doug Storer, a member of the class of 1917, "in the rough-and-tumble world of growing boys. His good looks and his tidiness, plus the fact that he posed for his mother's 'pretty' illustrations, helped earn him a sissy reputation. We always called him 'Humphrey' because we considered that a sissy name. We must have made life miserable for Bogart."

Other than that, he was a non-entity. Athletics were a trial, each gym class an ordeal for the pupil who carried the bruises of his encounters at home. A classmate sometimes paired with him in wrestling would recall his unmistakable fear of being hurt—"you could tell by the look on his face. He'd always lose quickly, just to get it over with." Dramatics, which were held after school, were also shunned. Until he was into his teens, a nursemaid in a starched uniform came to collect him at the final bell, as if he were a small child. Humphrey tried to avoid her, lagging behind as the others rushed for the front door. But she was always there to march him off, his hand imprisoned in her fist, as he cringed under the stares, real or imagined, of his schoolmates.

It was only at the Point that he came into his own.

Though Europe, in the summer of 1914, was about to plunge into World War I, at the lakeshore the elegant Edwardian world of Belmont and Maud Bogart went on placidly, with no thought yet of America's young men fighting and dying in far-off trenches.

For fourteen-year-old Humphrey, however, there were changes only slightly less dramatic than those abroad. The victimized child had grown into a handsome teenager, at about five feet three inches a bit short for his age but attractive to girls. His studied cool and his occasional bouts of moodiness, when he would go off by himself in a silent sulk, only made him that much more interesting.

There was also a new assertiveness that made him a leader of the self-styled Seneca Point Gang, a mob consisting not of gunsels but of future bankers and members of the Federal Reserve Board. His position was consolidated when he fished Arthur Hamlin, the youngest grandson of the local banker, out of the lake, after the three-year-old had fallen off the dock. "I wouldn't be here today if it weren't for him," Hamlin said when in his late eighties.

Bogart would refer to those months as the happiest of his first forty years. As the head of the Gang, he would decide when the boys should go sliding down the waterfalls in the steep, narrow valleys that creased the hills above the Point, or when they should attend the butchering of a steer in a local farmer's barn. He was the first to jump onto the *Onnalinda* or one of the other ferries when it docked, shinnying barefoot up the steamer's side to its top for a plunge into the water, an act prohibited by local ordinance and therefore all the more adventurous. The others jumped, Frank Hamlin remembered; Hump Bogart always dove. For inspiration, they visited a retired sea captain who summered with his sister and who kept them spellbound with tales of past adventures and displays of how to splice a rope or carve. On rainy days, they would gather at the Hamlin house or next door at the Adamses, where the rug by the huge stone fireplace would be rolled back, an old toy box brought out, and, under the leadership of General Bogart, battles of the Crimean War reenacted with correctly uniformed lead soldiers from New York's F.A.O. Schwarz.

In later life he would depict his career as an accident, a job he'd simply fallen into, a part of his self-mythologizing in keeping with a rugged code that saw acting as not quite fit for a real man. Yet those who knew him as a teenager remembered a boy who was slightly stage-struck. In New York, one of Dr. Bogart's patients and friends was the Broadway impresario William A. Brady, a steady source of free passes to plays, the major form of entertainment of the day. But even Seneca Point had its dramatist in residence: Frank and Arthur's mother was Mary Hamlin, an established writer of religious dramas and later author of the Broadway hit *Alexander Hamilton,* which was filmed by Warner Brothers in 1931 and was one of their earliest successful talkies. When Humphrey wasn't playing with his friends at the Hamlin house, he was there to listen to their mother's stories about the glamorous life and make-believe world of the theater.

He staged his own productions, with the Seneca Point Gang as the cast and himself as producer-director. Two poles stood on the beach opposite his house, a line strung between them with a hanging blanket that served as the curtain. For a five-cent admission, parents were seated in chairs and benches set up by the troupe. The dialogue was improvised, but the costumes were real, sent from New York City by William Brady—old discards, stiff and smelly with dried sweat yet somehow touched with magic. The young players' favorites were the cowboy costumes from *Girl of the Golden West,* with leather chaps and outsized boots in which they swaggered. In pants hiked up and a ten-gallon hat down over his ears, Hump Bogart played the male lead, the bandit hero who is redeemed by the love of a good woman.

That same sense of the dramatic had his friend Grace Lansing uncomfortably cast in a lakeside version of *The Perils of Pauline,* the popular new serial that had brought the actress Pearl White to instant stardom as the death-defying heroine whose horrific brushes with disaster thrilled audiences weekly at the movie houses blossoming from coast to coast. Grace, the only girl in a band of boys, was regularly stranded on a raft out in the lake, pushed out of windows, or tied to a stake à la Joan of Arc, a fire set in the underbrush near her feet. "But Humphrey would always rescue me," she said. "Always. Very handsome. He'd go out in a boat and get me off the raft, and he'd untie me from the stake. Well, I survived."

He was acting out the first stirrings of sexual precocity and a new attitude toward women. Until now, he and Grace had an easygoing relationship of pre-adolescence: boating and baseball, playing Indians but not doctor. With the help of a local tutor, Humphrey had built a makeshift clubhouse in the woods where several friends spent the night, the only incident being the arrival of a stray cow through the door. But one day things suddenly changed. "It was," Grace Lambert remembered with a laugh, "sort of my first experience with sex, and it embarrassed me."

They had been walking together, "up the hill, in the wood. And I think he was just feeling his sex; he couldn't have been more than thirteen or fourteen." A summer shower started. Humphrey proposed that they take off their clothes and walk in the rain. To her dismay, without waiting for her answer, he began to strip off his clothes, though Grace resolutely kept hers on. Stripped to the skin, there was no concealing that he had gotten "excited. And he wanted me to sit on his lap! Well, then I knew and I didn't like the idea at *all.* I didn't respond. And then he didn't like *that.*" Sulking, bristling with anger, feeling rejected and embarrassed, he picked up his clothes and "just put them back on," Lambert said. "And then walked home. In silence." It was some weeks before he spoke to her again. Still, she said years later, "he was the most gentle person."

Of all the rites of passage at Seneca Point, the one of overwhelming importance was his maturation as a sailor. Sailing was a birthright on the Finger Lakes, and for Humphrey it had a special significance as one of the few activities that he could share with his father. Belmont first came to Canandaigua for the summer in 1896, shortly after his graduation from medical school, and he immediately established himself as one of the best sailors in the area. The *Comrade,* his champion-class sailing yacht, finished either first or close to it every year in the local club's Commodore Cup. The *Comrade,* Humphrey Bogart would later say, "caught my fancy completely when I was two." Even though Belmont sold the boat in 1903, his son never forgot it. Nor did he forget the pleasure even at so early an age of being on the water with his father, in a boat with so ironic a name. Years later in California, his own fifty-five-foot yawl *Santana* would remind him of his father's marvelous craft.

By the time Humphrey was fourteen, he was handling boats with a skill that delighted Belmont, good yachtsmanship being a suitable activity for every gentleman. Additionally, sailing gave Humphrey independence. Racing alone before the wind or just bobbing at anchor on the turquoise surface in mid-lake, he was for the moment free—free of scolding and of family demands to measure up to being Humphrey DeForest Bogart. He would come to treasure being alone on a boat on the open water where no one, friend, foe, or studio boss, could reach him.

Then suddenly, his summer world vanished. Maud Humphrey took a high-paying staff job with the fashionable magazine the *Delineator* and needed a summer base nearer the city. Willow Brook was put up for sale, and a cottage was lined up for the next season on Fire Island, off the Long

Island shore. Bogart would remember objecting bitterly to the move, with the futile anger of the young and powerless.

He had always looked forward to the Ring of Fire, a Labor Day ritual around the lake, each community touching off a bonfire until a necklace of light rimmed the shoreline, marking the end of the season and the promise of next summer. But after the fires died out in September 1916, there would be only the return to the dark house on 103rd Street, and the ongoing parental warfare.

He was to graduate from school the following June, but his marks would get him nowhere. Under Trinity's tough percent-based grading system, a 60 meant pass, 85 and over was honors, 70 was the minimum for college application. By the end of his sophomore year, Humphrey's average was 58 percent; even so, he was promoted. As a junior, he raised it to 69, still too low to meet the admission minimum The combination of low average and high absenteeism required him to repeat the year.

By now the fearful nine-year-old had given way to a confident teenager with a detached manner toward his classmates and teachers. His sober blue serge suit—the uniform of the older students—was topped by a definitively non-regulation black derby, the symbol of a sporting man. Humphrey may have changed, but his grades hadn't. He raised his average the second turn through the junior year by exactly one point. In the hope that his son's future might be salvaged, Dr. Bogart contacted his prep school alma mater to see if they would take him.

Phillips Academy at Andover, Massachusetts, was then, as it is today, one of the oldest and most distinguished prep schools in the country. Known informally as Andover, it was a school for gentlemen, and "Be a gentleman" was an injunction Bogart had heard since birth.

Humphrey was the first of his father's family born to money and position, and the first with the freedom to repudiate them. He entered the world a gentleman, and so, regardless of his actions, his caste was set. Adam Watkins Bogart rose literally from the muck to make his fortune; Belmont DeForest Bogart assumed the dress and deportment of a patrician but, for all his airs, understood he was wearing a new suit. Humphrey DeForest Bogart was to both the manner and the manor born, but at some level he rejected both. No doubt the transparent strivings of his parents and the chasm between appearance and daily reality in the household helped shape his attitude. The result would be a lifelong tug-of-war between the polite clichés of his parents' world and a gut-level hatred of pretense.

This may have played havoc with his life but it established a sensibility apparent on the screen, which the critic Richard Schickel has described as a "declassed gentleman, a man of breeding and privilege who found himself, as a result of circumstances not entirely of his making, far from his native haunts, among people of rather less quality, rather fewer standards morally, socially, intellectually than he had been raised to expect among his acquaintances. To put the matter more simply, Rick Blaine should not have ended up running a 'gin joint' in *Casablanca,* and Humphrey Bogart should not have ended up being an actor in Hollywood."

He would play tough guys who meet violent ends—in his first forty-five films, by one count, Bogart's characters were hanged or electrocuted eight times, sentenced to life in prison nine times, and riddled with bullets a dozen others—but more relevantly, he played people who have seen what the world has to offer and are not fooled by appearances. The men Bogart generally portrayed are on the surface hardened cases who chafe under the status quo and make a poor fit with society, yet their strength and allure is not so much their anti-establishment air as it is the more dangerous sense that they are familiar with the establishment and know where its rot lies. Raymond Chandler met Bogart early in his career as an actor and wrote, "Bogart can be tough without a gun. Also, he has a sense of humor that contains that grating undertone of contempt." What cements Bogart's appeal is his willingness in spite of all he knows to fight through despair for love, for loyalty, for a sense of having lived up to his code.

The photos of him in his latter teens show a young man with slicked-down hair, center-parted, looking out at the world with narrowed eyes set in a closed, unsmiling face. He had also adopted the slogan that was to keynote his relations with the older generation and with society in general, and which parodied the muscularly upbeat virtues of his class: "Chin down, loose lower lip, nuts to the family." Thanks largely to the man who would become his professional father, he had also found a congenial world away from 103rd Street where he could put that attitude to good use.

William A. Brady entered show business as a prizefight manager and the developer of the Coney Island amusement park, but by the second decade of the new century he had become a noted Broadway impresario who would produce more than 250 plays. The daughter of his first marriage was the actress Alice Brady. His second wife, Grace George, was a star of many of his productions and also of films. The Bradys lived a block away on Riverside Drive, and Humphrey found a close friend in Bill Jr.

Dr. Bogart himself was somewhat stage-struck and he encouraged his son's interest and involvement with the Bradys. Belmont was relatively free of the prejudices that drew strict social lines in New York, as elsewhere. Not only were the Bradys theater people, but William A. Brady was a Jew, and Jews were not considered "gentlemen." In a letter at the time, the columnist and wit Franklin P. Adams wrote to his friend Robert Benchley, who was a press agent for Brady during the fall of 1917, that "while some of my best friends are of the Semitic race, none of them is what you and I would call high-class, let alone Mr. Brady."

Humphrey could not have cared less. His friendship with young Bill meant companionship and access to the best that Broadway had to offer at a time when stars had names like Barrymore and Bernhardt and popular culture meant live entertainment. For a nickel apiece, the two boys could ride the Broadway trolley to Forty-second Street and then catch a matinee in Times Square—the "Crossroads of the World"—and a bustling theater district where playhouses jammed the blocks and huge electric signs proclaimed the latest productions. A fashionable public thronged the streets at show times, and motorized taxis lined up at designated stands, awaiting patrons. Nearby were the nickelodeons and the first of the new movie palaces, and over on Sixth Avenue, the Hippodrome, with lavish spectacles for the larger public.

Bogart would later tell of himself and Bill Brady popping out the lanterns at construction sites with a Daisy air rifle, a story which, in addition to being in keeping with his carefully drawn self-portrait as a part-time juvenile delinquent, might have had some truth to it. There were new summer relationships with girls on Fire Island, a place that turned out to be not so bad after all, and kisses exchanged over hot dogs and tasting of mustard.

In early 1917, however, Dr. Bogart was maneuvering to get Humphrey off to Andover, where he might yet shape up academically. His eagerness seems reasonable enough: Andover put its boys on the fast track to college, the entrance exams for Harvard and Yale always noted on the school calendar. And Humphrey would turn eighteen that year; as far as higher education was concerned, it was now or never for him. Belmont called in every chit available, reminding Andover's headmaster Alfred Stearns that they had been teammates in football, class of '88.

There was a father's genuine concern in his effort, the closest he had ever come to understanding someone who had now become a problem child. Humphrey was a good boy, the doctor assured the headmaster. He just needed to buckle down without distractions. The headmaster met with the candidate; Andover found a slot; Trinity was ready to smooth the transition, men of good will, pulling together in the spirit of the old school tie, to save the lad from himself.

It was a mismatch from the start.

For openers, he began late, a week after the start of classes in September 1917, because he had to take the make-up exams that Andover demanded in New York. He arrived tired and discouraged on a Sunday morning after a long ride in the dark aboard the 3:59 A.M., the only connection between New York and Andover. He'd come alone. Mrs. Bogart was ill, the doctor wrote Headmaster Stearns, and since he had to attend to her, it was quite impossible for him to accompany the boy. Besides, Humphrey really wanted to go up by himself.

Years afterward, Bogart still remembered standing on the deserted platform, dulled by lack of sleep, a disoriented seventeen-year-old in a strange environment trying to find someone to help him with his trunk. Andover might be less than an hour from Boston, but to him it was the far side of the globe.

At Andover, he faced 138 years of Puritan custom. The school day began at 7:45 with morning chapel, and all rules and regulations were spelled out in the pocket-sized *Blue Book* issued to every boy:

> Every absence of the student from recitation, daily chapel, Sunday service, or from his room during study hours, is to be accounted for. . . .
>
> A student absent from town without permission forfeits his connection to the school. . . .
>
> During study hours . . . students are to occupy their own rooms, engaged in preparation of school exercises. . . .
>
> At ten o'clock each student is to be in his own room and to maintain such quiet as befits the usual retiring hour of the community.

This was hardly the regimen for a young man whose playground, a week before, had been Times Square.

He started well enough, with A's and B's, as though to show he could do it if he wanted. Then he tuned out, passing each evening in the room of Floyd Furlow, also from New York, and son of the president of the Otis Elevator Company. "Furlow was witty, very sophisticated, and had not a care in the world—and [had] a larder of good things to eat," a classmate remembered. Two other misfits joined them, one who had been to sea, another from the South African veldt. They talked not of school but of travel and adventure. "Bogart enjoyed *listening* at these sessions," the classmate added. "Didn't *talk* much. Idling away days and nights."

Though Bogart and others later spun tales of high jinks and defiance, classmates remembered only a perennially bored student with few friends in the dorm; a boy who never cracked a book, spoke little, and seemed oddly naive and vulnerable. Although he was a fine sailor and tennis player at Seneca Point, no one at Andover would recall him showing any proficiency in sports.

He was smart enough for the school, but bored by the education. "They made you learn dates," Bogart told an interviewer years later, "and that was all. They'd say, 'a war was fought in 1812.' So what? They never told you why people decided to kill each other just at that moment."

He posed for pictures with the other students. The open, receptive child of earlier years had given way to the turned-off teenager who showed a closed face to the camera, almost unrelated to the world around him. "He lived a life of his own, like no one else's; the mystery man, actually," classmate Arthur Sircom said, "and in the wrong pew at Andover."

Back in New York for Christmas, he found his homecoming preceded by a bad report from Dr. Stearns, regretfully citing Humphrey's "indifference and lack of effort" and serving notice of the withdrawal of his off-campus privileges. His eighteenth birthday was passed in anger and recrimination.

In February, the school placed him on probation. Dr. Bogart pleaded with the administration not to lose faith in Humphrey: he wasn't a bad boy, he had just "given up his mind to sports and a continuous correspondence with his girl friends." He and Mrs. Bogart, the doctor wrote the headmaster, appreciated the school's keeping up the pressure for their son's own good, and they would do everything possible to help him "find himself." Belmont sent a sterner letter to Humphrey with a faintly Dickensian warning: If he did not do better, they would request his dismissal from school and "put you to work"; David Copperfield, taken out of school and sent to the blacking factory. Dr. Stearns had a fatherly chat with Humphrey, after which Humphrey wrote his mother, vowing to do better. But after eighteen years, it was too late.

The axe fell in May. With "great regret," the headmaster informed Dr. Bogart that Humphrey had failed to meet the terms of his probation and it had become necessary to require his withdrawal from the school. Although Dr. Stearns had not been at the faculty meeting where the decision was made, "it was the unanimous decision of those familiar with the situation that it would be unwise for Humphrey to remain here longer. I cannot tell you how deeply I regret our inability to make the boy realize the seriousness of the situation and put forth the effort required to avert this disaster." He hoped, in conclusion, that this would prove a turning point in the young man's life and if he could help in making work arrangements, to call on him.

Maud Humphrey's reply by return mail that Monday—the doctor was "away on business"—was brisk and chilly. She was sending Humphrey $25, with instructions to pack his belongings, ship them to New York—"I believe that is what you ask"—and come home "at once." Humphrey's employment had already been settled, thank you very much, with Mr. Frank E. Kirby, "a very prominent Naval Architect, and now building ships for the Government," who had offered him a shipyard job. "Mr. Kirby," she wrote, "has both brains and influence," and she trusted exposure to so successful a man would help her son come to his senses.

The school, in one last act of forbearance, kept the dismissal quiet. The following Thursday morning, Arthur Sircom was surprised to see Bogart come out of their dorm, a suitcase in each hand. Wasn't it a little early to be going off for the weekend?

"No," he snapped. "I'm leaving this fucking place! For good! It's just a waste of time here."

He turned and walked down the hill to the railroad station, his bags bumping his legs, a forlorn, lost figure. Sircom watched him with pity. "Poor guy," he thought, "you're ruining your life!"

The train for New York wasn't due until 11:15 P.M. No matter. Humphrey DeForest Bogart wasn't staying where he wasn't wanted.

"The bastards threw me out," was all that he would say for some time.

Friday morning he arrived at Grand Central Station and went home to face his family. He never did go to work in the shipyard of the influential Mr. Kirby; instead he chose the sea. The sinking of the British liner *Lusitania* in 1915 by a German U-boat, and its loss of nearly 1,200 lives, a number of them Americans, had brought the United States into the Great War, and U-boats were still the scourge of the Atlantic. On May 28, after four unbearable days at home, he took the train to Brooklyn, presented himself aboard the USS *Granite State,* and enlisted in the Naval Reserve for four years with the provisional rating of seaman 2nd class. At age eighteen, he did not need parental consent, and in any case, he would have had it.

The intervening three weeks until his call to active duty were less strident, not because his parents wanted to enjoy their son before he faced an uncertain future but because his enlistment was the face-saving solution to an increasingly embarrassing problem. Belmont proudly wrote to Andover to announce the good news, asking that the school fathers kindly credit the boy's "patriotic spirit." Humphrey had finally done the right thing.

CHAPTER 2

"Young and Handsome as Valentino and Elegant in Comedy"

At the Brooklyn Naval Base, Navy doctors prodded and poked the new recruit, and examined him for venereal disease. Bogart's medical records list his height variously as 5 feet 7½ inches and 5 feet 9½ inches, missing it equally on both sides; weight 136 pounds; eyes brown; hair light brown; complexion fair; chest 36½ inches; four missing wisdom teeth. Former diseases: mumps and measles. Date of birth: December 25, 1899; home address 245 West 103rd Street; religion Episcopalian. Next of kin and beneficiary in the event of his demise, such payment to be six months' pay at $35.90 per: Belmont D. Bogart of New York.

When Bogart joined up in May, the U-boat war was still intense, but by the time he was called to active service on June 19, 1918, the War to End All Wars was nearly over. On July 2, he reported for duty at the Naval Reserve training station in Pelham Park, New York. On November 9, he received orders transferring him for duty aboard the troop carrier USS *Leviathan,* beginning November 27. Two days after the orders were received, bells pealed at the news of the armistice. Seaman Bogart spent the next six months plying the ocean between America and Europe, ferrying the boys home from France.

Later he would describe shore leave in Paris in great detail to friends, but there were other sights that he rarely talked about—veterans who left arms or legs on the battlefield, others feeble with the aftereffects of mustard gas, and many whose eyes simply reflected the slaughter in the trenches that decimated a generation of young men.

Bogart usually talked about his Navy days in terms of confrontation with authority and the utterance of snappy rejoinders. Yet according to his records he seemed an almost model serviceman, with consistently good conduct reports and high ratings in "Sobriety" and "Obedience" as well as seamanship. Photos show an anonymous-looking young American in uniform, clean-cut, straight out of a recruitment poster.

There are several versions of how Bogart received the wound that scarred his upper lip and caused his slight lisp. In one, his father inflicted it during childhood. Another dramatically put the cause as a flying splinter from an exploding shell during a U-boat attack. The most colorful account was spun by Bogart's brother-in-law, Stuart Rose. In his scenario, reminiscent of a Warner Brothers thriller, Bogart was shepherding a handcuffed prisoner to the Portsmouth Naval Station north of Boston. Humphrey was a genial fellow, the prisoner was so far well-behaved, and the two were getting along fine. When they got off the train in South Station to take a cab over to North Station to continue the trip, the prisoner asked Bogart to light a cigarette for him. As Bogart relaxed his guard to put up the match, the prisoner slammed him in the face with his cuffed hands and made a break; but Bogart, one hand on his ripped lip, the other on his trusty .45, wounded the man badly enough to bring him down while also managing not to shoot anyone else on the platform. The prisoner—hit in either a leg or a buttock—recovered nicely, but the repair of Bogart's wounded lip was botched by a Navy doctor, and three subsequent attempts at corrective plastic surgery failed to lessen both the scar and the nerve damage.

While any of these stories may be true—no definitive cause is recorded—a fairly exhaustive post-service physical accounting of scars and identifying marks mentions nothing about lip scars. The doctors did find four small scars—on the chin, inside left forearm, leg, and back of head—the results of beatings or boyhood scrapes. They also found a pockmark over the right eyebrow, three moles, and in checking for VD, a slight varicocele, or swelling of the spermatic veins, on the left side of the scrotum, a congenital condition so slight as to be of no importance. To the doctors' eyes, however, the upper lip of Seaman Second class Humphrey DeForest Bogart was unblemished, and his record suggests that he had a fairly uneventful career in the U.S. military, free of exploding shells or escaping prisoners.

Bogart's only real problem came up well after the war. On February

15, 1919, he was transferred to the USS *Santa Olivia.* Two months later the ship, making its usual run out of Hoboken, New Jersey, sailed for Europe without him. "Declared a deserter," his commanding officer entered in his service record. Actually, he was merely late for the departure and spent a panic-filled day, then the next six weeks, explaining to one bureaucrat after another that he missed the boat unintentionally. His service file and pay accounts were forwarded to naval authorities in Bay Ridge, New York, for disciplinary action. Eventually the desertion charge was downgraded to absent without leave, and the punishment was entered into his record on June 10: "Neglect of duty—3 days solitary on bread and water," a foretaste of the prison cells he would inhabit in so many films. Even for the time, the sentence was severe; still it was quite preferable to the big red deserter's "R" following him all his life.

Ten days after the sentence was entered, he left active duty, honorably released and still a seaman second class, with a bronze Victory Medal, struck by the Allies and awarded to all connected with the cause. On the back was the inscription "The great war for civilization." An honorable discharge followed.

With a wasted year behind him and nowhere else to go, ex-seaman Bogart returned home, no nearer to an understanding of what he wanted to be, or of who he was.

His family would move in 1925 to a converted brownstone at 79 East 56th Street. Maud "had social aspirations for my sisters," he later wrote, and "had decided that all the better people resided on the east side of the city." But when, in 1919, Bogart returned to the house on West 103rd Street, nothing had changed. His mother greeted him in her usual austere way. "There was no running down the stairs with arms outstretched, no 'My darling son!' Only 'Good job, Humphrey!' or something like that."

Whatever pride she did have for her son ended with feelings for his service. Otherwise, Humphrey was a young man without a college education and with few professional prospects, a situation all the more alarming to Maud because the family's fortune had largely vanished as a result of a disastrous investment made by Belmont in Michigan timberland. Belmont's feelings were more sympathetic than Maud's, but he was often gone for long periods. In addition to his investments faring poorly, his practice had diminished, perhaps because of his morphine usage, and he augmented his income by hiring on as a ship's doctor for cruises.

Over the next year or so, Bogart made an indifferent attempt to join the business world. He worked as a runner for S. W. Strauss and Company, an investment firm with which his parents had dealt and at which they had seemingly pulled a string to try to help him along. A later Warner Brothers biography also had him employed by the Pennsylvania Railroad. By the studio's probably apocryphal account, a supervisor told the young man that if he worked hard and applied himself, he might someday become president of the company. But "when I found out that there were 50,000 employees between me and the president, I quit."

Bogart spent much of what seems to have been his copious free time with friends. He and Bill Brady Jr. were often found at the Playhouse, the Brady theater on West Forty-eighth Street. They were joined by a more recent acquaintance, Stuart Rose, whom Bogart had met during Thanksgiving recess 1917, while still at Andover. Rose, a few months younger than Bogart, was then a dashing cavalryman on leave from the Army and staying with his family, who lived ten blocks north of the Bogarts on Riverside Drive. Humphrey had accompanied his fifteen-year-old sister Frances to a dance to which Rose had come as the escort of a friend. Rose was introduced to the "very good looking and very pleasant" Bogart, but far more attractive to him was Frances, a "very nice tall girl," already about five foot eight, very nearly the height of her brother. After his unit was shipped to France, Rose began a correspondence with her while she attended St. Mary's School in Peekskill, New York. The two would elope in 1924 and be promptly forgiven by their surprised but approving families. In the meantime, he and Humphrey became fast friends.

Where Brady's influence on Bogart was the theater, Rose's was equitation. After his return from the war, Rose taught a class at the Squadron A Armory once a week and gave Bogart lessons. He claimed that although Bogart had not ridden before and was even slightly afraid of horses, he "never found a man who caught on quicker than he did. His body was coordinated beautifully." Rose, Brady, and Bogart were joined on Sunday rides in Central Park by the director John Cromwell, all of them attired in clothes that were somewhere between approximations and parodies of the fashionable riding dress suggested by magazines.

Another Bogart friend was Kenneth MacKenna, who shared an apartment on Waverly Place in Greenwich Village with his brother, the stage designer Jo Mielziner. The apartment was the site for many parties, in which Mielziner recalled Bogart taking an energetic part. Bogart and MacKenna apparently shared a similar taste in women; the recollections of contemporaries were that Bogart often picked up with a girl when, or where, MacKenna left off. (That would change in 1938, when MacKenna married Mary Philips, Bogart's second wife.)

A habitué of speakeasies and of late-night revels, Bogart was well on his way to an aimless Jazz Age life. He may have been lost to one were it not for William Brady Sr. and his family, who were instrumental in the careers of both Bogart and MacKenna. MacKenna took up acting after being encouraged by Brady's wife, the actress Grace George. Brady's daughter Alice, herself a successful actress, urged Bogart to try a show business career. She was slightly older than he and exhibited a friendly though seemingly not romantic interest in him. She suggested he approach her father about a job, and one was soon offered to him as an office boy with Brady's new company, World Films, along with the promise to "give him a chance." Brady informed Bogart that the chance had come when, toward the end of making a picture called *Life,* he fired the director and told Humphrey to take over. Bogart did such a miserable job—"There were some beautiful shots of people walking along the street with me in the window making wild gestures"—that Brady himself had to complete the film.

Since direction evidently was not his forte, Bogart tried his hand at writing and came up with a plot "full of blood and death" that Brady found interesting enough to pass on to Jesse L. Lasky, president of the Lasky Feature Play Company, whose partners were his brother-in-law Samuel Goldfish, later Goldwyn, and Cecil B. DeMille. Lasky, in turn, gave it to his assistant, Walter Wanger, who pronounced it awful and threw it away. Many years later, when Wanger was a successful Hollywood producer and the would-be screenwriter was his neighbor, he liked to say that "Bogart once wrote for me."

If Bogart was daunted by any of this, Alice Brady was not, and she suggested to her father that Bogart be hired as the stage manager for one of his plays. Grace George thought the idea so good that she suggested he manage *her* new play, *The Ruined Lady,* which in late 1920 was about to go on tour. If only because he was beset from two sides, Brady gave him the job and $50 a week.

A company manager normally oversees everything connected with a show except the performances, but in Bogart's case, Brady required that he also understudy all the male roles. The part of the handsome young man, otherwise known as the juvenile, was played by Neil Hamilton, whom Bogart liked to tease about being overpaid for a job that to him consisted merely of repeating lines written by someone else. He learned how difficult this task can be after Hamilton was "taken ill," as Bogart later noted in a press agent's questionnaire asking the specifics of his first stage appearance. According to his friend and biographer Nathaniel Benchley, Bogart, who had never been before an audience, "was unprepared for the almost tangible electric current generated by a house full of people; he was also unprepared for the apparent sincerity of other actors delivering their lines. He was literally terrified when another actor spun on him in a scene that called for a burst of rage."

Joe Hyams, another friend and biographer, quotes Bogart as saying the performance was a Saturday afternoon cast rehearsal, but, even so, he declared that "it was awful. I knew all the lines of all the parts because I'd heard them from out front about a thousand times. But I took one look at the emptiness where the audience would be that night and I couldn't remember anything." In this version, Grace George was taken ill as well—if only from the understudy's ineptitude—and there was no performance. In both accounts, however, the show was scheduled to close that night, and did.

Bogart's unambiguous debut came about in a tryout of an Alice Brady play in May 1921. It was Memorial Day, and after Stuart Rose had marched in a parade and changed into civilian clothes, he picked up Pat and Belmont Bogart and took them over to the Fulton Theater in Brooklyn. Eventually Humphrey appeared as a Japanese butler, wearing a white jacket and carrying a tray of cocktails. He quickly spoke his one line and exited. Rose thought his delivery was terrible, and he was embarrassed for his friend. But Belmont was aglow with pride. He put his hand on Rose's knee and whispered, "The boy's good, isn't he?"

Bogart must have done something right, because in January 1922 he was given a part in another Alice Brady play, a melodrama called *Drifting*. Other than a listing—as H. D. Bogart—as the portrayer of Ernie Crockett, Humphrey was given no mention in the reviews, which was just as well, since they were either poor ("flashy melodrama") or inscrutable ("strangely protuberant"). In June, he took over a minor part in William Brady's production of *Up the Ladder*, which had been running since March. Then on October 16, he opened as the second lead in Brady's production of *Swifty*, with Frances Howard and Neil Hamilton, directed by his friend John Cromwell. Bogart played Tom Proctor, "a young sprig of the aristocracy," whose seduction of a girl in an Adirondack Mountains cabin has led to her ruin. Cromwell later described Bogart as being "a very endearing, ingratiating boy, wholly ignorant of acting," citing as an example his initial question of the director: " 'Which way do I face—

toward the audience?' " Brady Sr. did what he could to help him, including sitting in the balcony during rehearsals and yelling "What?" whenever Bogart mumbled or became inaudible.

Considering the reviews, Brady might better have yelled "Why?" Even Ring Lardner's script-doctoring couldn't save the dialogue, and the acting unfortunately spoke for itself. Only one critic liked the production; the rest panned it. Heywood Broun, the reviewer for the *World,* found it "cheap and implausible." Alan Dale of the *American* cited another actor and Bogart for "some rather trenchant exhibitions of bad acting." But it was the *Herald*'s Alexander Woollcott who wrote the line Bogart always remembered: "The young man who embodies the aforesaid sprig is what is usually and mercifully described as inadequate."

Maud awoke her son the next morning, brandishing the newspapers. "So you wanted to be an actor, eh?" she said, sitting on his bed. "I will read you the reviews."

In a way, they were no worse than the letters from Andover headmaster Stearns, and Bogart determined that, yes, he did want to be an actor. He developed into one, Stuart Rose said, by "observation, integrity, and brains. He had a very strong character." He continued working as a stage manager, and by the time his next break came a year later, in the part of a reporter in the comedy *Meet the Wife,* he was ready. Producer Rosalie Stewart cast him along with Mary Boland and Clifton Webb, who became a close friend. Boland and Webb received excellent notices, and the reviewer for the *World* wrote that "Humphrey Bogart is a handsome and nicely mannered reporter, which is refreshing." The show opened November 27, 1923, and played thirty weeks. This time Maud was impressed, even if she still did not believe that acting was a socially acceptable calling. Belmont's joy was unalloyed.

Steady work with its attendant good salary and a bit of recognition opened the more glamorous Manhattan speakeasies to Bogart—the El Fey, the Dover Club, and such Harlem nightspots as Small's Paradise, Connie's Inn, and the Cotton Club—and it was not uncommon for him to be out until dawn. After one such night toward the end of the run of *Meet the Wife,* an exhausted Bogart blew his lines and forced Boland to ad-lib extensively. Before the final curtain had completely fallen in front of the assembled cast, Boland, furious, told him, "Get this, Bogart—you'll never work in another play with me."

At an earlier time in his career, this might have been a death sentence. But his good looks were now a known commodity that he was able to put to steady use, regardless of the leading body's attitude toward him.

In one of his string of juvenile roles he is supposed to have asked, "Tennis, anyone?" as a means of forwarding the action, but there is no record that he did. (After his death, Hollywood columnist Louella Parsons claimed she heard him utter the line in *Cradle Snatchers* in 1925.) Bogart once told an interviewer that the line was, "It's forty-love outside—anyone care to watch?" but again there is no evidence that the line appeared in any of his plays. Bogart did say that he'd "spoken every bad line except, 'Give me the ball, coach, and I'll get you a touchdown.' "

In September 1924, William Brady Jr. produced *Nerves,* presented by a circle of friends of his and Bogart's. John Farrar and Stephen Vincent Benét wrote the play, the set was by Jo Mielziner, and Bogart and Kenneth MacKenna were in the cast. Also in it was Mary Philips, an attractive newcomer whom Bogart had met backstage during the run of *Meet the Wife,* and who later said, "He must have taken a liking to me." (Occasionally—*Nerves* being one instance—Philips's name was spelled "Phillips" in reviews and credits.) The play, the first act of which took place at a Yale house party and the second in the French trenches of World War I, was a meditation on heroism and cowardice that had the misfortune to open the night after the classic *What Price Glory?* The comparisons were not flattering, but Heywood Broun did write in the *World* that "Humphrey Bogart gives the most effective performance," and the *New York Times* critic remarked that "Mr. Bogart was both dry and fresh, if that be possible."

Bogart later said that his good reviews gave him "a badly swelled head." No cast member saw it more clearly than Mary Philips, who was supposed to walk quietly away during Bogart's delivery of what he considered a particularly dramatic speech. One night, he said, "I noticed her putting a lot of *that* into her walk," so much so that the audience was more attentive to her exit than his expostulation, and after the show he accused her of stealing his scene. Philips, amused instead of chastened, challenged him with a glint in her eye, "Suppose you try to stop me."

"Well," he told Hyams, "I didn't try to stop her, because while I was talking I suddenly became aware that here was a girl with whom I could very easily fall in love." However, it would take five years and a marriage to someone else before that happened. In the interim, Bogart went back to work for the senior Brady as the manager of a road company production of *Drifting,* starring a pregnant Alice Brady. On a Saturday soon after the show opened, she delivered the child much earlier than expected. A new actress had to be in place by Monday. All day Sunday, an assistant manager coached a second prospect while Bogart went through the lines with the long-established Helen Menken, a slender redhead and an accomplished performer who had begun her career in 1906 at the age of six. There was no surprise when the part went to her and no surprise that so solid a professional could learn her lines in twenty-four hours.

According to Bogart's recounting, it was harder for him to handle the eight complicated sets than it was for Menken to remember her role, and the first night some of the scenery fell onto her. She directed her fury at him, and as a result, he said, "I guess I shouldn't have done it, but I booted her. She, in turn, belted me and ran to her dressing room to cry." Within a few weeks they had taken out a marriage license.

The problem was that Bogart wasn't sure he was in love with Menken, a quandary exacerbated by the difference in their professional standing. She was an established success; he was still struggling; and he firmly believed that a husband should support his wife. The license went unused, and his conviction about spousal roles would trouble his marriages for years.

Helen had faith in Bogart's talent and encouraged him. In January 1925 he was cast along with Shirley Booth in the comedy *Hell's Bells,* which ran for fifteen weeks. The reviews were mixed to bad, but Alan Dale of the *American* wrote that Bogart's part was "gorgeously acted." Then in September he opened in another comedy, *Cradle Snatchers,* opposite Mary Boland. After many auditioners proved unsuitable for the role of the young man, Boland, who had not forgotten her threat, said, "Oh, all right, then, get Bogart. I know it's what you have in mind." Once they were together, however, the problems of the past were never referred to. The play, about three society women who amuse themselves in a hideaway with three attractive and willing college men they hire, and the upshot of what happens after their husbands stop by believing they have come to a high-class bordello, had a long run. *The New York Times* reviewer didn't think much of the play but acknowledged that the audience had a good time and mentioned Bogart among the "further pleasing performances." The *World* called it "a raucous and bawdy farce. . . . The company is good throughout, but the honors clearly go to that enormously comical actress Edna May Oliver, to Mary Boland, to Humphrey Bogart, and to Raymond Guion [later Gene Raymond]." Amy Leslie, a leading Chicago critic, was even more effusive: "[Bogart] is as young and handsome as Valentino and elegant in comedy as E. H. Sothern, as graceful as any of our best actors."

He was also by now a serious drinker, a fashionable accomplishment at the time. As much as he enjoyed going to the glamorous speakeasies, he happily passed time in less pretentious places such as Jack Bleeck's Artists and Writers Restaurant on West Fortieth Street, and Tony's on Fifty-second Street, which had a basement entryway, a bar, a kitchen, and little else. The appeal of Tony's was not in its chic but in its clientele of actors and writers, among them Heywood Broun, Alexander Woollcott, and Mark Hellinger, with whom Bogart developed a lasting friendship. He was also drawn there by the generous credit policy of owner Tony Soma, who would carry the bill for years of someone he liked.

The drinking took a physical toll on more than Bogart's liver, and serves as the backdrop for the most credible story of how he got his scarred lip. Louise Brooks, whom he met while acting in *Nerves,* described her first impression of Bogart as "a slim boy with charming manners, who was unusually quiet for an actor. His handsome face was made extraordinary by a most beautiful mouth. It was very full, rosy, and perfectly modeled—perfectly, that is, except that, to make it completely fascinating, at one corner of his upper lip a scarred, quilted piece hung down in a tiny scallop. . . . It was taken for granted that he got punched in the mouth at some speakeasy. When Humphrey drank, he became exhausted and occasionally fell asleep (as in *Casablanca*) with his head in his arms on the table. If he was abruptly shaken awake, he would say something rude and sometimes get socked for it. On one occasion he purposely did not get his split lip sewed up, because he both loved and hated his beautiful mouth." She added that when Bogart went into films, he had a surgeon sew up the scallop, leaving only the well-known small scar. While photographically it was an improvement, "I missed this endearing disfigurement."

Not long after the tour of *Drifting* ended, Helen became the hit of Broadway in *Seventh Heaven.* However well Bogart was progressing, she was far ahead in both acclaim and salary. While that bothered him, it made no difference to her; she was eager to marry him, and she was convinced that, through her friendships with Woollcott and other influential critics, she could advance his career. But Helen's soaring career and important friends were less a help than a problem for Bogart. He had grown up in a household where the woman was the major breadwinner and influence, and he feared he would be cast in his father's role with Helen. Besides, he still wasn't sure he loved her enough to overcome those liabilities.

His friend Bill Brady was by then married to a young leading actress named Katherine Alexander. The couple had an apartment in the east forties, in an area known as Turtle Bay. According to Rose, one night while he and Bogart were visiting there, Bogart told Brady, "God, I don't want to marry that girl."

"If you don't marry that gal," Brady responded, "you'll never get another part on Broadway, Humphrey."

Rose believed that the remark was not quite as cold-blooded as it sounds, but it seems to have found its mark. On May 20, 1926, Bogart and Menken were married in her large apartment in the Gramercy Park Hotel, with Rose as best man. In the register the bride and groom listed their ages as twenty-six. Because of Menken's prominence, Rose said, "everybody in the theater was there." The event itself was quite theatrical because the normally sedate Episcopal ceremony performed by the Reverend John Kent was, in this instance, according to Rose, "almost obscene." Helen's mother and father were both deaf, as was Kent, who translated the ceremony into sign language for the benefit of her parents, and recited it in the warped, sing-song voice associated with Helen Keller. The reporters who were present expected to interview Menken after the service. Instead, Rose said, "she was unstrung by the whole thing. She got hysterics and refused to meet the press. I had a hell of a time calming her down."

It was a foreshadowing of the marriage. "We quarreled over the most inconsequential things," Bogart told Hyams, "such as whether it would be right to feed the dog caviar when people were starving. I contended the dog should eat hamburger and like it. She held out for caviar. What started out to be just a difference of opinion would suddenly become a battle royal, with one or the other of us walking out in a fine rage."

Cradle Snatchers closed a few months after the wedding, its forty-two-week run the longest of the season. In early 1927, Bogart replaced an ill actor in Maxwell Anderson's comedy *Saturday's Children.* Then in June, he joined Roscoe "Fatty" Arbuckle in *Baby Mine.* The 320-pound Arbuckle had been at the height of his film career in 1921 when he allegedly raped starlet Virginia Rappe with a piece of jagged ice during a wild drinking party in his San Francisco hotel room. After she died of a ruptured bladder a few days later, he was tried three times for manslaughter; two juries could not reach a decision and the third acquitted him. But the scandal shattered his career, and *Baby Mine* was one of the many unsuccessful attempts at a comeback he would try until his death in 1933. The show closed within two weeks, and immediately thereafter Bogart accepted an offer to perform in the Chicago production of *Saturday's*

Children. He tried to persuade Helen to accompany him, but she preferred to stay in New York and try out for a new play. They separated; and although there were several attempts at reconciliation, the marriage was effectively over. Helen filed for a divorce and went to London to reprise *Seventh Heaven.* A year and a half after the wedding, the divorce was official. Helen waived alimony.

"I tried to make my marriage the paramount interest of my life," she not altogether candidly told a reporter for the New York *Herald.* "Although my career was a success, I was willing to give it up and concentrate my interests on a home. I was deeply interested in acting, but I felt the managing of a home was something greater. I had planned to make a home for my husband, but he did not want a home. He regarded his career as of far more importance than married life."

Bogart made no public response, but Nathaniel Benchley quotes a letter from Bogart to his friend Lyman Brown, who was a principal in the Chamberlain and Lyman Brown Theatrical Agency, that says in part: "By this time you have probably read in the papers about what an old meany I am. . . . I have tried my very best to keep my mouth shut—and be discreet. Any talking has come from my 'friends' and not from me. Do you suppose the publicity and the divorce will hurt me in a business way—I've tried to do the whole thing as nicely as possible and I don't see why it should, but I want your opinion. . . . When the whole thing is over Helen and I will be good friends. . . . She's a wonderful girl, Lyman."

Many years later Menken acknowledged that "I was to blame for the breakup of our marriage. I put my career first and my marriage second."

In the months following his divorce, Bogart's drinking increased. If he wasn't working, he was touring speakeasies with Brady or involving himself with a succession of chorus girls. The experiences taught him a lesson: "I had had enough women by the time I was twenty-seven to know what I was looking for in a wife the next time I married."

What he envisioned was someone to come home to, but what he looked for was inevitably not what he found. After seeing *The Jazz Singer* soon after the film opened in the fall of 1927, Bogart stopped backstage at a nearby theater to visit the actress Mary Halliday. Mary Philips was also there. This time, they began to date. Philips, herself an accomplished drinker, became his speakeasy touring companion. Mary cared even more about acting than drinking, and she successfully encouraged Bogart to take his profession more seriously than by simply being a member of the Players, the Gramercy Park club for show people that he had joined in 1926. On a weekend country visit with Mary to the well-known actor

Holbrook Blinn, Bogart asked the star how he might make a name for himself. Blinn's advice was that he keep working; a working actor, he said, gives people the idea that he must be good.

Bogart was at a critical point in his professional life. He turned twenty-eight that December, the upper edge of believability as a juvenile. If he was going to have any chance at a continuing career, he had to expand his abilities and land more mature roles, and he hired an agent to help him—though he did little to help the agent. In the press questionnaire for Charles Frohman, Inc., he listed eleven plays in which he had appeared either in New York or in summer stock (including either the one performance or the one rehearsal of *The Ruined Lady* with Grace George) but otherwise provided little information about himself. Yes, Humphrey Bogart was his real name; yes, he began his career with parental approval; no, he was not superstitious. He said his hobbies were golf, contract bridge, and sailboat racing, but he simply drew lines through the spaces for the answers to questions regarding his stage ambitions, his favorite role, and whether he was satisfied with the parts he had played. The space for "What other suggestions have you that would be valuable in securing publicity?" was left completely blank. As for "What have you done in the movies?" the answer, in large letters, was "Nothing." Later that year he was teamed with Helen Hayes in the two-reeler *The Dancing Town* for Paramount. Little else is known about it and a complete copy of the film has not been found.

In April 1928, Bogart and twenty-five-year-old Mary Philips were married at her mother's home in Hartford, Connecticut. She later recalled her new husband as being "a sort of Puritan" who never used "bad language or anything." Bogart told a reporter the day of the ceremony that "Mary is a mixture of New England and Irish, and she furnishes just the sort of balance I need. Marrying her is probably the most wonderful thing that could happen to me." Apparently the only person unhappy about the marriage was Kenneth MacKenna, who had already asked Mary to marry him.

In January 1929, Philips and Bogart were cast in *The Skyrocket,* a predictable love story of a happy couple who become miserable after they strike it rich but happy again after they've lost all their wealth. Their individual reviews were encouraging ("good actors did the best they could," according to the *Tribune;* "Humphrey Bogart contrives both to convince you and make you like him in the role of the cheeky young man," said the *Times*), but those of the play ("a showy counterfeit") were not.

Bogart's loyal friend Alice Brady helped out yet again by offering him a featured role in her already-running new comedy, *A Most Immoral Lady,* produced by William Brady Jr. It ran a respectable 160 performances and soon after it closed, producer David Belasco cast him as a smug young bank clerk in his new comedy *It's a Wise Child.* (Bogart and three others were credited by the *Times* as showing "more than usual vigor" in their acting.) The show, which opened August 5, 1929, was the hit of the season. "Humphrey Bogart, darkly handsome," his "Who's Who in the Cast" write-up went, "has played many stage lover roles, but he resolutely refuses to be referred to as a stage sheik. . . . He is an ardent devotee of golf and the sport of sailboat racing, but is superstitious concerning bridge. He declares that lucky cards avoid the 'East' seats almost invariably."

That summer the Bogarts took a house in Connecticut near where Stuart and Frances Rose also rented. One day Bogart came up to him and said, "You know, I love Mary dearly. But I'm impotent." "Humphrey, you're out of your mind," Rose told him. "You'll get out of this in two or three weeks." And of course, Rose added, he did. But having children was never an issue. Apparently both preferred to concentrate on their careers. They were, however, the godparents to John and Mary Halliday's son John. Some years later when young John was home from prep school, Bogart offered to take him to lunch and then a matinee. There was only one problem. "For God's sake," Mary says he asked her, "what do you talk to a 13-year-old boy about?"

"Religious instruction," she said. And when she later asked the boy what they talked about, the answer was, "He said, 'Listen, kid, there are twelve commandments.' Then he ordered a drink." (The gist of the story seems likely enough, though Bogart was so strictly raised as an Episcopalian, Halliday's recollection of the number of commandments seems inflated.)

Bogart was still in *It's a Wise Child* when the stock market crashed in October. The advent of the Depression was catastrophic for the still largely silent film business, which had already been staggered by the introduction of talkies two years earlier. Attendance fell precipitously. The studios responded by trying to teach silent stars how to deliver a line convincingly, and by scouring Broadway for actors photogenic enough to be successful in movies. In 1930, Bogart appeared with Joan Blondell in a ten-minute musical comedy for the Vitaphone Corporation, a film that quickly disappeared and was not rediscovered until a documentary on Bogart was being produced in 1963. Like *The Dancing Town, Broadway's Like That* is a curious artifact more than a career change.

Bogart's film break came from Stuart Rose, who in 1930 was the eastern story editor for the Fox Film Corporation. His job, and that of his large, mainly female staff, was to read "everything that was published in English" as well as attend every Broadway opening to look for likely film material. Rose's office was in Fox's New York headquarters, at Fifty-seventh Street and Broadway, but the company also owned an old studio on Tenth Avenue, where a casting director "desperately tried to find actors who could talk." The casting director was a good friend of Rose as well as of Al Lewis, an ex–Broadway producer who ran the New York office. The three had been trying without success to find an actor suitable for a talking remake of *The Man Who Came Back.* Finally Rose suggested that they test his brother-in-law.

"Ah, Stu, you're out of your depth," Lewis replied.

Rose persisted, reminding Lewis that Bogart was currently on Broadway, that he played summer stock, and besides, he couldn't be worse than everyone else who had been auditioned. A few days later, Rose was in his office on Fifty-seventh Street when Lewis called. "Get in a cab and come over to 10th Avenue to see this test. It's magnificent." Rose "did and it was." Bogart was then making $500 a week on Broadway; Fox signed him for $750 a week with options and the promise to raise him to $1,000 after a year.

Excited by the prospect of being able for the first time to support a wife completely on his own, Bogart asked Mary to drop out of her play *The Tavern* and come with him to Los Angeles. She refused. She had a contract and a career, and she intended to honor them both. Her resolve matched his. Both were determined to succeed—at acting if not at matrimony. They were a "modern couple," Mary told her husband, and he should feel free to date while he was away, just as she would in his absence.

Bogart sent a telegram to MacKenna in Los Angeles that he was coming out, and boarded the train alone. When MacKenna and some other actor friends met him there and he told them that he had been brought out to star in *The Man Who Came Back,* they laughed and told him that each of them had come out to take the part but that none of them were going to get it. Instead it was going to the silent star Charles Farrell, who would be reunited with Janet Gaynor. Beginning with *Seventh Heaven* (1927), Farrell and Gaynor were the leading romantic team of the period before talkies took over, and the studio's notion was that if Farrell could be trained to speak properly, they could succeed again. Instead of getting the role, Bogart was assigned the task of trying to teach the star to talk.

His reward was to be cast as a rich young man in *A Devil with Women,* featuring Victor McLaglen. Neither the role nor the film amounted to much. By luck he was assigned to work simultaneously in *Up the River,* directed by John Ford and starring Spencer Tracy. The picture was intended to be a melodrama about prison life, but Ford found Maurine Watkins's screenplay "just a bunch of junk" and set to work with comedian Bill Collier to rewrite it. Ford found "there was so much opportunity for humor in it that it eventually turned out to be a comedy. . . . We did it in two weeks." Tracy played a tough convict. With the help of another habitual offender, he aids the romance of the innocent but convicted Bogart, who has fallen in love with a pretty and naive female inmate played by Claire Luce. The confluence of three major talents at the beginning of their careers makes for a still-interesting picture, and during its making Bogart and Tracy began their enduring friendship.

In 1931, Bogart was cast with Charles Farrell in *Body and Soul* (not to be confused with the 1947 John Garfield boxing classic). The two played World War I aviators and fought their own private war on the set. Farrell did not take kindly to director Alfred Stanfell asking Bogart to give him additional diction lessons, and he and Bogart squabbled throughout the two weeks of shooting. When the picture was finished, Bogart invited the six-foot-six Farrell to meet him outside and settle things once and for all. Farrell asked him if he knew how to fight. "I can lick *you,*" he answered with all the contempt of a small dog barking furiously at a larger one. Farrell listened calmly and then said, "It's only fair to tell you that I was a boxing champion in college." As was usually the case when Bogart saw that his needling was about to land him in more trouble than he could handle, he backed off and suggested they perhaps might talk things out. They talked things out so well that they ended up taking a vacation on Farrell's boat and became good friends.

Over the years, Bogart would become notorious for his caustic remarks. His friend the writer Nunnally Johnson felt that Bogart liked to think of himself as Scaramouch, the devilish, boastful coward of the commedia dell'arte, and that his anger was directed at the self-aggrandizement endemic to Hollywood. Nathaniel Benchley pointed out that "his detractors also maintained that he never picked on anyone who could fight back, and this is simply untrue; he more than met his match in John Steinbeck and Lucius Beebe, to name a wildly disparate pair and only two of the several who bested him," including Farrell.

Later in 1931, Bogart was loaned out to Universal and given a small part in *Bad Sister,* starring Bette Davis. He would make more films with her—six—than with any other actress, the last being *Dark Victory* in

1939. (In 1943, each had a cameo in *Thank Your Lucky Stars,* Warners' multi-star salute to itself.) That was followed by *Women of All Nations,* directed by Raoul Walsh and once again starring Victor McLaglen. Bogart's part was so small that he was cut from the prints that were released. For all the splash he had made in any of his other films, his parts in those could just as well have been cut, too. Fox was paying him but had no idea of what to do with him. In *Holy Terror,* a western starring George O'Brien, "I was too short to be a cowboy, so they gave me elevator shoes and padded out my shoulders. I walked around as though I was on stilts and felt like a dummy."

He felt so much like a dummy that he gave up on his sixteen-month film career and in late 1931 returned to New York, where life was no better. Relations with Mary had been strained by their separation and by her subsequent involvement with actor Roland Young, whom she had met on tour. She wanted the marriage to continue, though, and stopped seeing Young. Bogart, accepting some responsibility for what happened, also tried to keep the union alive.

There was trauma in the life of the rest of his family as well. In 1930 Frances Rose endured a difficult twenty-seven-hour delivery, after which she became manic-depressive and in need of frequent hospitalizations. Bogart's other sister, Kay, had become a model for Bergdorf Goodman. Lively and very attractive, Kay shared with her brother a weakness for scotch, as well as a dangerously high capacity. She and Bogart were friendly with writer George Oppenheimer, who co-founded the Viking Press, and Oppenheimer was attracted to Kay. It was not to be. "The trouble with George," Bogart said, "is that he gives out just as Kay's ready to give in."

Maud and Belmont Bogart continued a downward spiral. Belmont's health deteriorated, apparently from his continued use of morphine and other drugs; eventually he was paralyzed and bedridden. They moved from East Fifty-sixth Street to Tudor City, a less expensive apartment complex farther down the East Side. "Then things became really complicated," Bogart wrote. "She had a flat on one floor of the building, Father had one on another. . . . There was no formal separation between Father and Maud. There was never even a thought of divorce. But they just couldn't stand being together for long. Still, he was ill and he was *hers.* So she went over and cooked breakfast for him every morning and was with him for dinner every night. She hired nurses during his attacks, provided the money for his every want, sat with him for hours. Then she went home to her own apartment.

"I never understood the situation, nor did I ask about it. It was their business, and it seemed to work all right. She stood by him to the end, through the years he was paralyzed and bedridden. But she did it in her own fashion."

Soon after his return, Bogart won a part in *After All,* a comedy about British domestic life and manners. The reviews were mixed to poor, but the play survived. Bogart left in mid-run after Columbia signed him to a six-month contract in early 1932, and he returned to Hollywood to appear in *Love Affair.* He had to have felt optimistic that this attempt at films would be more rewarding. He was the second lead behind the popular Dorothy Mackaill in a love comedy filled with triangles and farcical misunderstandings. But reality soon set in. Immediately after it was completed, Columbia loaned him to Warner Brothers, where he was given tenth billing in the Joan Blondell–Eric Linden film *Big City Blues.* Mervyn LeRoy directed the story of a young country boy who finds love and disillusionment in New York City. Bogart impressed LeRoy enough to be kept on for *Three on a Match,* the tale of three childhood friends who reunite in New York, starring Bette Davis, Joan Blondell, and Ann Dvorak. Bogart had sixth billing this time, playing a hired kidnapper named The Mug. Although the film is still surprisingly powerful, his minor part convinced him that he would never make it in the movies, and he returned again to New York.

He discovered that it had become even harder to find work on the stage than in films. Before going to Los Angeles, he had been able to keep regularly employed on Broadway, and while in California he had appeared with Billie Burke in *The Mad Hopes,* a New York–bound comedy. Now with the Depression in full force, theaters were nearly empty. He managed to land parts in five plays, but they rehearsed for a total of twenty weeks, and none ran more than one. In October 1932 he played "a sybarite with the morals of a tomcat" in *I Loved You Wednesday,* a play notable only in that Henry Fonda also appeared in it. A month later, he was in the Theatre Guild production of *Chrysalis.* Brooks Atkinson declared in *The New York Times* that the play was "astonishingly insignificant" and that "Bogart plays the wastrel in his usual style." *Our Wife* opened March 4, 1933, the day President Franklin Roosevelt proclaimed a bank holiday to try to save as many institutions as possible. There were ten people in the audience. In May, he opened in a new play, the Italian comedy *The Mask and the Face,* translated and adapted by W. Somerset Maugham. The 1933 season was abysmal for virtually everyone connected with the theater. Of the 152 plays produced, 121 were flops. At the end of August, only 6 plays were running. Bogart was not in any of them.

Mary found a little more work than her husband, but they only eked out a living. A few months of summer stock in Cohasset, Massachusetts, got them out of New York but further into drinking. When they returned to the city, there was no work for either of them. Their home was a shabby apartment at 434 East Fifty-second Street, near the East River. Their neighbors in adjoining apartments, Mel and Mary Baker and Miriam Howell and her husband, Ralph Warren, became close friends of theirs. Mel, a comedy writer, had the curious habit of taking his food, shaking it up in a paper bag, and then dumping it back on his plate. Mary, an agent, would later represent Bogart.

The three couples pooled their money for groceries and what little entertainment they could afford. Bogart earned a bit of money playing chess as the house player at an arcade, taking on all comers at fifty cents or a dollar a match. He had learned the game from his father and it remained a lifelong passion. Still, whatever he earned was not enough to keep his bar tabs current. Fortunately, "21" and some of the other establishments he frequented had understanding owners who, like Tony Soma, let the accounts stand almost indefinitely. Others, less accommodating, wrote to ask when they might see some payment. In response to one such letter from the Players Bogart wrote:

> To make my position at the moment clear to you, as regards my unpaid dues.
>
> I have not been paying other bills and neglecting my club—the simple truth is that I have not been paying any bills as I have, temporarily no money.
>
> However within the next few weeks I expect to be able to make at least a partial payment.
>
> So if you'll be gentle with me I'll appreciate it.
>
> Sincerely,
>
> Humphrey Bogart

In early 1934 Bogart was given the part of a gangster killed by his girlfriend in an All-Star picture filmed in New York called *Midnight,* released by Universal. It passed unnoticed. Then in May he opened on Broadway at the Masque Theatre in the mystery-melodrama *Invitation to a Murder,* as Horatio Channing, a California aristocrat whose family fortune came from piracy. The reviews were once again poor, but the most important critic in the audience wasn't with a newspaper. Arthur Hopkins, a short man with rounded features who looked more like a banker than the powerful producer-director he was, liked something about Bogart and filed it away in his mind.

After the brief run, Bogart went back to playing chess in the arcade. While working there in the first week of September, he received word to go to his father's apartment immediately; Belmont was critically ill, and he was soon moved to a hospital. Two days later he died in his son's arms.

"It was only in that moment that I realized how much I really loved him and needed him and that I never had told him," Bogart told Hyams. "Just before he died, I said, 'I love you, Father.' He heard me, because he looked at me and smiled. Then he died. He was a real gentleman. I was always sorry he couldn't have lived long enough to see me make some kind of success."

In response to her husband's death, Bogart wrote, Maud "doubled up momentarily as if she had the wind knocked out of her, then straightened and said, 'Well, that's done.' " She did exactly the same when Kay died three years later. Bogart never did understand "whether she meant that everything was a step forward or whether she felt a chapter in her life was finished. . . . But I am sure that if she had outlived us all she would have uttered those words about each of us."

Belmont DeForest Bogart left an estate of $10,000 in debts and $35,000 in uncollected fees. His son vowed to pay what was owed. He also took Belmont's ruby-and-diamond ring and wore it for the rest of his life; it often can be seen in his films.

Melancholy over his father's death, his career stalled, Bogart was haggard, drinking to excess and, many friends thought, near-suicidal. One of these friends was the playwright Robert Sherwood, who, in an effort to help, suggested to Hopkins that Bogart might be good for the part of Boze Hertzlinger, the ex–football player in his new drama, *The Petrified Forest.* Hopkins, the show's producer, remembered Bogart from *Invitation to a Murder* and "sank into one of his silences during which time seemed to stand still," John Mason Brown wrote in *The Worlds of Robert E. Sherwood.* "He thought of more than Bogart's masculinity. He thought of his driven power, his anguished dark eyes, the puffs of pain beneath them, and the dangerous despair which lined his face." These were the qualities required for the part of Duke Mantee, the second lead. The character was unlike any Bogart had ever played, and Sherwood was initially doubtful that his friend could carry it off. Hopkins, however, was confident that he had the right man, and he cast Bogart in the role.

Duke Mantee is an escaped convict, the apotheosis of ruthlessness but also of rugged individualism. Sherwood's description of him could have been drawn from a photo of Bogart: "He is well-built but stoop shouldered, with a vaguely thoughtful, saturnine face. He is about thirty-five and, if he hadn't elected to take up banditry, he might have been a fine leftfielder. There is, about him, one quality of resemblance to [the hero] Alan Squier: he too is unmistakably doomed."

Leslie Howard played Squier, the romantic intellectual who has come to feel that he and his ilk have become as ossified as the petrified forest in the Arizona Desert near where Mantee holds him hostage in the Black Mesa Bar-B-Q. The other hostages are also symbolically petrified: the ex–football player who now pumps gas at the restaurant lived his best years in college; the waitress's aged grandfather spends his days reliving his time as an Indian fighter; his son, a war hero, has retreated into himself; the pompous banker has been eaten by his own success; and his wife, who wanted to be an actress, has instead given away her life to blindly follow her husband. Only Gabrielle Maple is really alive. She works as the waitress in the roadhouse but dreams of being a painter, and Squier sees in her the hopefulness he once had. After secretly making her the beneficiary of his $5,000 life insurance policy, he convinces Mantee to shoot him so that she will have the money to go to France and fulfill her dreams.

At the first tryout performance, in Hartford, the company became aware of how many funny lines there were in the script, and of how compelling Bogart was as Mantee. Audiences literally gasped when he entered with his two days' growth of beard and prison pallor, his shuffling gait and menacing mannerisms. The gangster John Dillinger had recently escaped from prison and his image was fresh in everyone's mind, which added an eerie realism to the play. Mantee's necessary paleness allowed Bogart to play the part without makeup, and rather than put on what would be seen as fake stubble, he allowed his own heavy beard to grow and kept it trimmed in a scraggly fashion. He was so convincing that after the play opened in New York on January 7, 1935, the New York *Post* reported that people asked for seats close enough for them to see Mantee's beard.

The play—and Bogart—drew raves. Brooks Atkinson of the *Times* called it "a peach . . . a roaring Western melodrama. . . . Humphrey Bogart does the best work of his career as the motorized gorilla." To the

World-Telegram's Robert Garland, "Humphrey Bogart is gangster Mantee to the tip of his sawed-off shotgun."

His earnings enabled him to pay off Belmont's debts as well as his own, but there was another tragedy in store. Not long after *The Petrified Forest* opened, Bill Brady Jr. was killed when his country cabin in New Jersey caught fire. According to Hyams, it was the second time in his life that Bogart could remember crying.

The Petrified Forest would be a turning point in his career, though that was yet to be clear; Bogart had seen other good reviews come to naught. Whatever joy he felt was more than counterbalanced by other aspects of his life. The years of disappointment, one failed marriage and another in near ruins, his drinking, the deaths of Brady and of his father, and the attendant need to at last take money seriously so that he could pay Belmont's debts had changed him from a handsome and carefree juvenile into a man in crisis.

Some months into the run of the play, Louise Brooks went to Tony's about one A.M. and saw Bogart in a booth with actor Thomas Mitchell. "Presently, Mitchell paid his bill and went out, leaving Humphrey alone, drinking steadily, with weary determination. His head drooped lower and lower. When I left he had fallen into his exhausted sleep, with his head sunk in his arms on the table. 'Poor Humphrey,' I said to Tony. 'He's finally licked.' "

CHAPTER 3

Fitting the Bill

Jack L. Warner, vice-president and head of production of Warner Bros. Pictures, Inc., was riding in his compartment aboard the Santa Fe Chief as it sped east through a Friday night blizzard in January 1935. A telegram from Jacob Wilk, delivered during the stop in Emporia, Kansas, and damp from the snow, confirmed that he had two seats at the Broadhurst Theater for Monday night's sold-out performance of *The Petrified Forest.* Warner hoped it would make a good film, and Wilk, the studio's New York–based East Coast story editor, was doing his best to make sure his employer obtained the rights.

> HAVE HEARD OTHER NEGOTIATIONS ON FOR PROPERTY STILL TRYING TO STALL SHERWOOD'S AGENT UNTIL YOU HAVE SEEN PLAY

Jack Warner liked to think of himself as elegant. A trim forty-three, he dressed in high-fashion suits and spats. His round face displayed a thin mustache that he considered rakish and a smile that was just a bit too eager. The son of an immigrant Polish cobbler, he wanted to avoid the look of the self-made man that he was, and for the most part he did. Jack and three of his five older brothers, Harry, Albert, and Sam, began their business careers in Youngstown, Ohio, in 1904 with a secondhand projector and an old print of the eight-minute adventure *The Great Train Robbery.* They put on shows with their sister Rose playing the piano and twelve-year-old Jack singing soprano between screenings; "a practice," his son later wrote, "the brothers . . . discovered quickly clear[ed] the room." The next year, with a $150 loan and ninety chairs borrowed from an undertaker, they opened a nickelodeon called the Bijou in Newcastle, Pennsylvania. In the years before World War I the brothers were film distributors in Pittsburgh with branch offices in Maryland and Georgia. Jack and Sam went into production, making several films during and after service in the Army, among them dramatizations of Sinclair Lewis's novels *Main Street* and *Babbitt.* At a time when most producers offered only westerns and slapstick comedies, the brothers' fare was unique. J. L., as Jack was widely known, was a complicated man whose authority was absolute on the Warner lot in Burbank, yet he seemed happiest when reminiscing about the early days in Youngstown and his sometime efforts as a song and dance man.

Warner Bros. Pictures was founded in 1923, with Jack in charge of production, Albert handling distribution, Sam the technical adviser, and Harry the business chief and president. The brothers pioneered sound films. Their experiments with Western Electric in the new medium resulted in *Don Juan* (1926), the first film to have recorded musical accompaniment. Sam died at age thirty-nine, in 1927, the day before the studio released *The Jazz Singer* with Al Jolson. The picture is considered the first feature-length talking movie, but actually it was a silent film with four sound sequences. Its tremendous success saved the company from near bankruptcy, and the next year the brothers presented *The Lights of New York,* this one with talking all the way through. Their *On with the Show* (1929), was the first all-talking movie filmed in color. In 1930, the Warners' assets were estimated to be $270 million.

Warner Brothers' prosperity was based on action pictures, which generally meant machine-gun-punctuated gangster sagas, Busby Berkeley musicals, lachrymose melodramas with a social message wrapped around the gore and, after 1934 when the conservative Production Code was implemented, whatever sex could slip past its tight censorship. But the studio also had some of the finest performers, writers, directors, and cinematographers in the business, and the brothers aspired to something higher. Not that they would drop the formats that had made them wealthy, but Jack Warner wanted both big box office *and* prestige. He wanted class.

Jake Wilk helped them get it. Wilk had a keen sense for commercial literary properties, and he knew from the moment it opened that *The Petrified Forest* was special. The play had everything—gangsters, social significance to spare, the Sherwood name, and the luster of a Broadway hit. Above all, it had the golden-haired Leslie Howard as the idealistic Alan Squier, a writer burned out by the cruelties of life. His appearance in Somerset Maugham's *Of Human Bondage* for RKO had helped turn his co-star, the Warner contract player Bette Davis, into a sensation. Warners wanted some of that sensation for themselves. Howard had already made three films for the studio and enjoyed rare good relations with the management, aided in part by Hollywood's awe of Broadway and a generous new agreement signed the year before.

The tickets were waiting for J. L. at the Broadhurst Monday night, and he left the theater ecstatic. A great play, he cabled back to Burbank on Tuesday morning.

> SUCCESS OF THIS IS DUE TO PUBLIC REACTION TREND AND PSYCHOLOGY OF AMERICA AND WORLD TODAY STOP POSITIVE WONT LOSE THIS

On Friday, Warner held intense discussions about the filming with Howard, who controlled the movie rights along with the director, producer, and writer. Leslie Howard was more than a star; he was a power, whose stature equaled that of director Gilbert Miller, producer Arthur Hopkins, and Sherwood. To Warner's delight, Howard agreed that if J. L. was successful in negotiating the rights, *The Petrified Forest* would be his next vehicle for the studio.

From the start Howard had made it clear that he wanted Humphrey Bogart to repeat the role of Duke Mantee. Privately, he'd given Bogart his personal assurances, but more was involved than simply kindness to a colleague: to a large extent, the play's success depended on the underlying tensions and unspoken clash between the two personalities. Bogart's Mantee was the perfect foil to Howard's doomed, effete hero; the star's insistence on keeping the pairing intact was an act of professional self-interest. Warner, who had an acute eye for talent, agreed, and once the rights were bought, Bogart's name was forwarded to Burbank for inclusion in the casting.

It took six months to close the deal. The acquisition price, $110,000, was divided equally among Sherwood, Miller, and Hopkins; Howard's compensation came as salary for performing in the film. Warners planned to start shooting in mid-September. After performing every night for months, Howard wanted a summer break in Europe. He had approval of both his replacement and any road company and vetoed both, feeling a tour could diminish the audience for the picture. The theater company was well aware that Howard's decision meant the early closing of a smash show, and the final performances were played out by a group of angry actors resentful of being out of work and with no resources for vacations in Scotland.

The Petrified Forest closed June 29. The house was sold out, and the audience, as rapt as on opening night and reluctant to let the moment pass, called for the star, the actors, anyone. In the balcony, Jerome Lawrence Schwartz, a drama major from Ohio State who had hitchhiked from Columbus to see the show, clapped until his hands were red and swollen. As Jerome Lawrence, he would co-author *Inherit the Wind* and *Mame.* He contributed to the tumult as Leslie Howard took the star's solo bow, the cast behind him. Then, with the understated grace for which his public adored him, Howard summoned a surprised Bogart out of the stage-rear lineup to share in the cheers. Stripped of Duke Mantee's menace, he seemed surprisingly young—a short, slight figure, looking at once flattered and flustered.

It seemed his luck had changed. He had no contract yet, but the assurances were solid. Except for the two African American actors, Slim Thompson and John Alexander, no one else from the cast had been summoned to Hollywood. Warners had awarded the female lead to their rising star Bette Davis, ending Broadway star Peggy Conklin's dream of playing Gabby, the fresh, young girl eager for experience, on the screen.

Yet the weeks passed with no word from Burbank. Filming was, of course, still some time away, but in the Bogarts' small apartment off First Avenue, the atmosphere grew tense—not at all improved by the stifling summer, the worst in years. The city baked as dust from the parched Midwest blew through the streets, turning noonday into twilight. Mary, although sympathetic, had a new play, *A Touch of Brimstone,* produced by the eminent John Golden, and was caught up in rehearsals, out-of-town tryouts, and publicity. The Broadway opening was set for September 25. Her co-star was Roland Young, a master of dry comedy. A profile of Mary planted in the *Herald Tribune* never so much as indicated that "Miss Philips" was married. Bogart marked time with a one-week production of *The Stag at Bay,* a melodrama centered on the theft of a formula for poison gas, and a limited-run revival of *Rain* in Skowhegan, Maine, starring the fan dancer Sally Rand, who, in her first dramatic role, credibly played the part of Sadie Thompson.

Then on September 8, he opened *Variety* and read that Edward G. Robinson, a top Warner star and the archetypal protagonist of mobster roles, was to play Duke Mantee in the forthcoming Warner Brothers production of *The Petrified Forest.*

Until two weeks before, the name on the cast list had been Bogart's. Yet for the studio, there was one overriding fact: Bogart was a good actor, but Robinson was a star, a star, moreover, who was guaranteed three films a year at $80,000 apiece but who in the past year had not made a single picture for Warner Brothers. For a cost-conscious studio, paying a bankable actor nearly a quarter of a million dollars not to work was unbearable.

Edward G. Robinson had been synonymous with the mobster image ever since his 1931 *Little Caesar* helped create the prototype of the movie gangster. The film rocketed the actor to fame and taught the studios that crime pays. But the box-office successes that made Robinson one of the highest-paid stars at Warners had also earned him the right to story approval, and months were wasted with stories submitted and rejected by one side or the other. To add to Warners' woes, their contract with Robinson was non-exclusive, allowing him to make pictures elsewhere. In August 1935, Robinson was looking forward to a vacation in Europe; but his agent hinted that, if Eddie got a script he liked, he might decide to stay. A screenplay of *The Petrified Forest* was rushed to Robinson, who knew a great role when he read one. If questions over billing could be worked out, the answer was definitely yes. With the single exception of Bogart, the arrangement seemed an answer to everyone's prayers.

On the night of the announcement, Henrietta Kaye, an attractive and talented sculptor who as a seventeen-year-old had played the juvenile delinquent in *Chrysalis,* was working late in her studio on Fifty-second Street in New York, modeling a clay bust of actor-dancer Clifton Webb. Below her window, the sidewalk was brightly lit and filled with crowds coming and going until all hours to the street's many jazz clubs or to "21" or to Tony's, which was in the building next door. The music from the clubs drifted into Kaye's studio. A light seemed always on behind the large window overlooking the street, and theater friends, toting a bottle for a nightcap, often dropped in to unwind. There was nothing unusual, therefore, in this late-night knock on her door. "It was Bogie, and he was quite plastered—but on his feet and charming and nice."

He stood in the hallway, a half-empty bottle in one hand, a glass in the other. "Mind if I drink and watch?"

She had liked Bogart for the three years they had known each other. They laughed at the same jokes and he treated her as an equal. Moreover, "he had never made a pass at me. I remember fondly the men who did not. He just talked. And I listened."

She turned back to her work as he poured out another glassful and his resentment, beginning with a rambling monologue about his family—

the doctor father, the artist mother for whom he modeled—and ending with the latest downturn of his fortunes: "The reason I'm getting mush-headed is because Eddie Robinson is going to play my part. It's happened before. They buy them and then Bogart is left out in the cold!"

He seemed to have no one else to turn to, and Kaye had a feeling he was separated from his wife. As Bogart talked, she would interject a sympathetic comment, whether just to say "Uh-huh," or more pointedly, "That's too bad, Bogie. Maybe he'll drop dead." Yet despite her affection for Bogart, there wasn't much to say, and she had work to do.

Finally, he stood up unsteadily, and staggered out, clutching his bottle. She felt desperately sorry for him.

His cause appeared lost. Still, he telegraphed Howard in Scotland, whose greatest problem was getting a sailing date. Howard cabled his agent that he expected to arrive in New York September 25; and at the end he added, "BOGART ASKED ME TO APPROVE HIM TELL MR. WARNER YES," which was hardly a ringing endorsement. Certainly it did not dissuade Warners from continuing to try to straighten out the billing with Robinson. Company lawyers had hurriedly drawn up all the papers, and the particulars had been submitted to Hal Wallis, the studio manager and Jack Warner's second-in-command, for his okay.

Then, in the tradition of films and the theater, fate took a hand. In a cable just before sailing, sent this time directly to the studio, Bogart's amiable colleague became Leslie Howard, the demanding star:

> ATT: JACK WARNER
> INSIST BOGART PLAY MANTEE NO BOGART NO DEAL
> L. H.

Howard arrived in New York on September 26. A week later, Bogart had his contract. In retrospect, the switch fulfilled the interests not only of Howard, but also of the studio and their hot property, Bette Davis.

The young actress had survived offbeat looks and nothing roles to show what could be done with talent and an iron will. The year before, she had been the manipulative bad girl who led Leslie Howard down the primrose path in *Of Human Bondage.* Six months later in *Bordertown,* she pinned a murder rap on Paul Muni, going splendidly mad in a performance that had sent New York reviewers wading back to their offices through sixteen-inch snowdrifts to write uniform raves that were followed by great notices nationwide.

For the studio, *The Petrified Forest* meant the reuniting of a winning combination, with the profits for Warners instead of RKO. In publicity releases, Sherwood's brooding, talky disquisition on the decline and fall of the West was reduced to "a gripping tale of love and heroism. . . . The greatest Howard-Davis vehicle that could be procured." Which made Robinson the odd man out. His insistence on co-star billing would make it hard to sell the greatest Howard-Davis vehicle ever if the top credits read "LESLIE HOWARD—EDWARD G. ROBINSON." An obscure actor with an impossible name like Humphrey Bogart posed no such problem.

With twelve days to go before the start of shooting, a Warner typist filled in the few required details on the standard freelance employment form for Humphrey Bogart. It was strictly a one-shot deal, clearly shown by the modest contract, a single sheet of paper with its two sides covered with fine print spelling out the actor's obligations. Tradition has it that he signed a long-term contract, but this was the Warners' minimum artists' agreement, doling out work by the week. Hal Wallis wanted to make as few commitments as possible to an actor whom he had not tested and who had made so little impact in his earlier time at Warners that no one there remembered him.

Bogart didn't mind. From New York he asked only for a guarantee of three weeks' employment at $750 each, the same salary he had been paid in 1932 for *Three on a Match.* The rest he left up to James Townsend in the office of Myron Selznick, the powerful Hollywood agent who looked out for the interests of New York agent Leland Hayward's clients. Townsend signed on his client's behalf. Everything happened with such suddenness that there wasn't even an address for Bogart on the contract.

His hair thinning, his face a mirror of the disappointments of the past five years, at thirty-five he headed once again for the land of youth and beauty. He knew too well that he had been a second choice. Still, he grabbed at what was likely his last chance and pinned his hopes on a single sheet of paper that promised three weeks' work, fifth billing, and a round-trip train ticket with a guaranteed lower berth.

Mary's play had opened to mixed reviews, but the critics loved her. "Her spirit and intelligence irradiate every scene" of *A Touch of Brimstone,* Brooks Atkinson wrote in *The New York Times.* Although recently she had borne the financial brunt of their marriage, now that Bogart was finally in a position to provide for them, he wanted her with him. They argued often and loudly, but even a pleading and storming Bogart was no match for Atkinson. With her career finally on track, Mary was not about to throw it all away for twenty-one nights in a Hollywood hotel as

Mrs. Bogart. By early October the play, proclaimed in newspaper ads as Broadway's "sizzling comedy hit," had settled in for what promised to be a comfortable run. Magazines and theater sections ran pictures of Mary Philips and Roland Young, the newest toasts of the town. Bogart boarded the train alone.

In late October, he reported for work in Burbank at the sprawling, fortress-like Warner compound. The self-contained 135-acre city within a city had sound stages and craft shops where anything from the Neapolitan waterfront to the crumbling stoops and curbstones of New York's Lower East Side could be re-created in days.

Warners was unique in that it was the New Deal studio, with close ties to the administration of President Franklin D. Roosevelt. It engaged not so much in selling fantasy as in conveying the reality of Depression America. The studio had a skinflint reputation, but its money went into a product that put Warners at the forefront of literature of protest, demonstrated in titles such as *I Am a Fugitive from a Chain Gang, 20,000 Years in Sing Sing, Wild Boys of the Road,* and *The Mayor of Hell.*

More than any other studio, Warners reflected a newly urbanized, violent, ethnically diverse, and now impoverished America, its film topics drawn from the headlines of the day. The dramatic rise and fall of lawbreakers was at once a thrill for a penny-counting public and an indictment of a society that had failed so many. In contrast to industry standards that prized the WASP ideal of middle America, Warners' leading men were for the most part short, pugnacious, and defiantly ethnic. Edward G. Robinson, James Cagney, and Paul Muni were anti-heroes known collectively as Murderers' Row.

Of course the studio also provided popular escapist fare: comedies, melodramas, westerns, and, beginning with *Captain Blood* (1935), the costume dramas starring the wild Australian Errol Flynn. But Warners' world was essentially one of dark cities, dark streets, hard rain, and bloodstained pavements. Its quintessential hard-edged, uncompromising, and provocative quality extended even to its musicals: Bebe Daniels in *42nd Street,* singing the love song "You're Getting to Be a Habit with Me," with its drug metaphors; and Joan Blondell in the big finale of *Gold Diggers of 1933,* leading a ragtag troupe of down-and-outers with medals on their shabby coats:

Remember my forgotten man
You put a rifle in his hand
You sent him far away

You shouted hip-hooray
And look at him today.

It was a direct reference to the Bonus Army, the disillusioned World War I vets who the year before had marched on Washington demanding promised pay, only to be attacked by troops ordered out by a government that had replaced its promises with guns and tear gas.

Given all these ingredients, Warners was the perfect place for Humphrey Bogart.

During the bleakest days of the early thirties, the Warner brothers, by begging and borrowing and by paring costs to the core, had managed to keep the studio intact while many companies went into bankruptcy. They survived a federal anti-trust suit that threatened to land Harry in prison. They also survived $31 million in losses for the years 1931 through 1934 and the attempt of some stockholders to throw them out. They were helped, as were the other studios, by putting all employees on reduced pay for two years at the instigation of the Academy of Motion Picture Arts and Sciences. The brothers found it so beneficial to the bottom line that when the stipulated period ended, they refused to rescind the cut.

Their parsimony led to the resignation of production chief Darryl F. Zanuck, who had produced *The Jazz Singer* and initiated the long series of gangster pictures that began with *Little Caesar*. His *Rin Tin Tin* features in the 1920s had kept the studio afloat. Zanuck left to co-found 20th Century Pictures with Joseph Schenck, which, with the purchase of William Fox's studio in 1935, became Twentieth Century–Fox, with Zanuck as the controlling executive.

Hal Wallis replaced Zanuck at Warners, which had survived not only the worst of the Depression but a dip in movie attendance and a devastating back-lot fire. For Bogart, much was still familiar from 1932: the high walls separating the studio from the San Fernando Valley traffic; the sound stages that looked like pastel blimp hangars arranged in a neat grid formation, the alleyways between them as bustling with life as city streets; the writers' low beige building beside the carefully tended quadrangle of executive offices, where Jack Warner and Wallis worked in adjoining suites. Most noontimes, J. L. could be seen seated amid the flowerbeds, gazing at a fountain where a plaster boy held a plaster fish spouting a stream of water into a shallow basin.

Bogart reported for his first day of work on Saturday, October 26, an unprepossessing figure who, instead of driving through the auto gate, arrived by cab and trudged through the street-entrance casting office as if he were an extra. In the caste-conscious little world of the studio, it was immediately noted that the newcomer didn't have a car.

In the front office, no one remembered him. Actor Lyle Talbot asked the casting director, Who was playing Duke Mantee?

"Bogart," came the answer. "He's never been here." Talbot started laughing.

"What's so funny?"

"You better save Jack Warner some embarrassment. Get some stills from *Three on a Match*."

He was assigned a dressing room in the cellblock-like two-story building where the actors changed; bungalows, even for the stars, were a luxury at Warners. Like most of the talent, he had to provide his own wardrobe, and not surprisingly he settled on the outfit he had assembled for Broadway—the shirt, vest, and well-cut trousers that had characterized the gangster John Dillinger. At the payroll department, a three-by-five-inch start-work notice made it official, listing his name, the date, his weekly salary, and in large letters, "MANTEE."

On Stage 8, paint, props, and lighting suggested Sherwood's bleak cafe in the Arizona desert, and the morning was given to filming its patrons going through the motions of their dead-end lives. A little after twelve, the cast and crew broke for lunch. Then at 1:10, Duke Mantee's gang burst through the doorway of the Black Mesa Bar-B-Q. When one of them announced: "This is Duke Mantee, folks, the world famous killer. And he's hungry," he introduced a new screen image. Where Robinson was a swaggering mobster of the white ethnic ghettos, and Cagney a wisecracking gangster, Bogart was a killer with haunted eyes who defied all attempts at context, the unknowable outsider who shared his past and his thoughts with no one.

Carl Schaefer, a soft-spoken Californian then handling coverage in the foreign press, and others in the publicity department immediately noticed that "there was an exciting new guy out there by the name of Humphrey Bogart, and it was obvious he was going to be big." More attention came his way when word got out that Jack Warner wanted Bogart to change his name, but he refused because of his work on Broadway. The incident was Jack Warner's first encounter with the Bogart stubbornness that would irritate him for years.

Little by little, people began to wander by the set, curious about the newcomer. Schaefer and his colleagues would stop by to watch scenes in progress, and were impressed with what they saw. "He *projected.* Some actors, they look pretty good on the screen, but this guy, he was a real personality."

He was also desperate. Beneath the commanding surface, he was insecure and anxious, haunted by a fear of failure and the waiting return ticket to New York. "If I don't make it this time," he told a colleague, "I'll be washed up. I've *got* to make it this time." That feeling of desperation fueled his performance.

The film itself, two weeks in production when he started, was already behind schedule, largely because of Leslie Howard. Company call was generally for nine o'clock, yet it was almost invariably thirty to ninety minutes later before Howard, who was in almost every scene, would amble in, charmingly unmindful of the time ticking off at union scale while everyone waited. Director Archie Mayo was simply outranked by his star. Mayo, a ten-year Warner veteran and former vaudevillian who once sold shirts for a living, had ably directed Bette Davis in *Bordertown* (which with a more serious tone would be the basis for Bogart's 1940 film *They Drive by Night*). Now, however, he was unable to impose discipline. Hal Wallis, alarmed at the meager daily output, sent furious memos to the set, reminding Mayo that the film was expensive enough as it was and demanding that someone have a talk with Howard. There was still no change.

In addition, Mayo, who had trouble handling the confines imposed by the single set, wasted time by overshooting and attempting to find unusual camera angles. One of the dailies showed Bogart in close-up, with the antlers of a moose head on the wall behind him seemingly protruding from his skull. Wallis ordered it re-shot.

To compound the problems, the air conditioning on the soundstage caused the sand imported for the re-created Arizona desert to blow about, bringing on a rash of illnesses and absences. Everyone was exhausted from breathing in the dirt. Bette Davis, pleading a sore throat, skipped a Friday's shooting and declined in this era of a six-day workweek to come in on Sunday to make up time. Howard, too, was disinclined to work on Sunday, as was Genevieve Tobin, playing Mrs. Chisolm, half of the wealthy couple whose car Mantee hijacks. Bogart, however, quietly did whatever was asked.

When Davis sprained her ankle, another day was lost. When the projected five-week production slid into overtime, Wallis's rage grew. How could this happen with a play that took place entirely on one set? And with people like Leslie Howard who knew the play backwards! Jack Warner, in one of his unmistakable blue-tinted memos, joined in railing against the picture's going even further over its already exorbitant budget.

Shooting was finished on November 30, two weeks behind schedule. Howard, both charming and incorrigible to the last, arrived on the set thirty-five minutes late, complaining of not being well and refusing to work until his doctor had seen him.

The studio heads were semi-educated men whose show business instincts could be easily knocked off-balance by someone whose erudition impressed them. When H. G. Wells, visiting Jack Warner for lunch, waxed on about the play's symbolic meaning, an anxious Wallis asked in a memo to producer Henry Blanke if there shouldn't be some kind of foreword to the picture, telling people just what the movie was *really* about. Blanke, a talented filmmaker and the in-house intellectual, was unconcerned. The strength of *The Petrified Forest,* he told Wallis, was that it had something for everyone; so why not let the highbrows read symbolism into it if they wanted and let everyone else just sit back and enjoy the story? Fortunately for Blanke and the picture, Bogart, with an actor's insecurity, had brought a bundle of reviews out to Hollywood saying more or less the same thing. The film was left as it was.

During the last days of production the same self-doubt about the beginning of the film emerged over the question of its conclusion. Depression audiences paid to see happy endings they could not find in the world outside. Overall costs on *The Petrified Forest* had already topped half a million dollars; and what was being offered, instead of the Hollywood convention of evil punished and virtue rewarded, was a finale in which the murderer escaped and the hero was dead in the heroine's arms.

Howard argued to Warner that to change the ending would destroy the picture. "Having carried the story logically to this point, the new end can only . . . satisfy the sap element in the audience and will probably turn the critics against us." Contractually, however, there was little he could do, other than to film both endings under protest and to agree to let sneak-preview audiences and a panel of three arbitrators decide. General counsel Roy Obringer advised Wallis that "Howard should be notified as to the time and place of these previews, in order that Howard will not complain of not having the opportunity to be present and note the reaction of the audience." In the preview for the trade press on the first Monday of 1936, Bette Davis held the lifeless Leslie Howard in her arms as she intoned, "This is the end for which we twain are met." The *Hollywood Reporter* had just one word: "Class!"

That Warner and Wallis eventually chose common sense over convention may have saved the nascent film career of Humphrey Bogart. The trade reviewers loved him. "Humphrey Bogart is the harried, hunted, desperate killer in every move and expression," wrote the critic for *Daily Variety.* His performance was "compelling," said the *Hollywood Reporter.* Bogart and Howard had of course been judged by the standards of the Broadway production—"They repeat the same roles and do them flawlessly," as *Weekly Variety* put it. But Bogart's performance was even enhanced by the film. His underplayed, monosyllabic portrayal, with its suggestion of violence ready to erupt, its economy pared even further in the screenplay, was perfectly suited to the medium. The close-ups caught the desolation in his eyes, the sudden tightening of his scarred lip, and suggested the smoldering fires that propelled the outlaw anti-hero.

When the film opened in February, critics in the general press were hugely enthusiastic. The New York reviewers hailed the film's fidelity to the play even allowing for what *Herald Tribune* critic Richard Watts Jr. termed "a straightforward photograph of a stage play, rather than a genuine motion picture. . . . Mr. Sherwood's brilliant melodrama . . . has been transferred to the screen with care and fidelity and it emerges as a provocative and arresting photoplay."

"Well done, though it defies every canon of cinema lore," wrote Frank S. Nugent in *The New York Times.* "The Warners continue to display their skill at transcribing plays into film." The *New York Evening Journal* found the film "delightfully literate entertainment," the *American* called it "a production of the highest class and most distinguished calibre," the *World-Telegram* "a work of distinction," the *Daily News* "a thrilling and absorbing play." The *Sun* deemed it "painfully real. . . . The Warners, who can make gangster films just a bit grimmer and more realistic than anyone else, have bravely resisted any temptations to concentrate on that angle, or . . . to change the ending."

There was nothing but praise for the cast, particularly Howard, Davis, and Bogart, now welcomed back as one of Broadway's own. "Once more Humphrey Bogart provides a brilliant picture of a subnormal, bewildered and sentimental killer," declared the *Herald Tribune.* "Humphrey Bogart," said the New York *American,* "equals his superb interpretation in the theatre of the gangster character." Thornton Delehanty in the *Evening Post* called his screen Mantee "a brilliant portrait."

For Maud, working anonymously as a commercial artist for the Stonewright Studios, an advertising agency in Manhattan, the reviews meant a new celebrity. The tall, thin woman who sat at her drawing table with long strips of white cloth wrapped around her legs, possibly to control varicose veins, was no longer the forgotten famous artist of a generation ago; she was Duke Mantee's mother. William and Milton Barrie, two young students, ran errands and helped copy the artists' work. They never heard her boast about her son, though she did talk a bit about him. Rather, they had the sense that the two were not close.

Warners hadn't waited for the critics to tell them what they already knew. In December, while the film was still in the cutting room, the announcement to their salesmen that "Leslie Howard and Bette Davis play the leads in this notable production" underwent a little editing by Jack Warner, who with his Parker Pen scratched in a third name: "Humphrey Bogart."

Bogart's special indefinable quality had come through every night in Hal Wallis's screening room, and it convinced Wallis and Warner that Bogart was an asset to the studio. By the time shooting was finished, so were the negotiations to keep Bogart on. In early December, nine days after the close of production, J. L. reminded Roy Obringer: "Be sure and get HUMPHREY BOGART'S contract signed today."

It was signed the next. The twenty-page mimeographed agreement between Humphrey Bogart, "ARTIST," and Warner Bros. Pictures, Inc., "PRODUCER," retained Bogart's exclusive services as "Motion picture and/or legitimate stage actor," including "vaudeville, personal appearances, radio, television, etc." Bogart signed away rights to everything but his shadow and, in the standard morals clause regulating employee conduct, agreed not to "shock, insult or offend the community or ridicule public morals or decency."

The terms, however, were hardly spectacular. The contract ran for twenty-six weeks at $550 each beginning in January, the studio holding the option to extend the term of employment first on a twenty-six-week and then later on a fifty-two-week basis, with increments beginning at $50 a week. If Bogart survived all eight option periods, by 1941 he might make $1,750 a week.

His beginning wage was $200 a week less than he earned as a freelancer in *The Petrified Forest.* His agents had done their best, but Bogart was smalltime; and for all its enthusiasm, Warners clearly was hedging its bets. Despite Jack Warner's bumping him into the announcement to the salesmen, in the screen credits Bogart was still in fifth place, after Genevieve Tobin and the beefy young Warner contract player Dick Foran, who played Boze Hertzlinger, the former football player who loves Gabrielle.

J. L., however, smiled his hearty smile and admonished Bogart to have a little faith. Had he not taken him from obscurity, given him a contract, put him in *The Petrified Forest* in an all-star lineup? It was a catechism that was to become all too familiar. The studio promised to adjust the contract at a later date, the deal sweetened a bit with the lure of a $300 bonus down the line. It was a pittance by Hollywood standards but real money for a debt-ridden actor straight out of Depression New York.

There was one more item in the contract, a leave of absence to play Mantee in the London production set to open in April. Months before, Bogart had promised Sherwood that he would do it, and he happily anticipated a West End opening. Warners was agreeable, provided they had thirty days' notice, with, of course, a contract extension to make up for the time away. For a variety of reasons, however, *The Petrified Forest* didn't play in London until 1942. The summer of 1935 would be the last time Bogart performed on the stage.

On Tuesday, December 10, he signed his name to the long-term contract in the firm, elegant hand that marked him as Maud Humphrey's son, adding in the exhilaration of the moment a small flourish to the "T." In fact, he had just embarked on one of the most frustrating and demoralizing periods of his professional life.

His personal life would not be much better. Mary's play, *A Touch of Brimstone,* had not become the runaway hit anticipated, and closed in December after a respectable ninety-six performances. Soon afterward, she came by train to California. Christmas was spent at the Chateau Elysee, where they celebrated his birthday and his new contract. For Bogart, his long-term deal meant security at last and the ability to finally support a wife.

The problem was, Mary didn't want to be supported. She was an actress, with aspirations no less strong than Bogart's. She wanted her professional life as much as her husband wanted his. She had been offered a new Broadway play, an adaptation of James M. Cain's sensational novel, *The Postman Always Rings Twice.* The steamy, best-selling tale of infidelity and murder had been turned down by the studios as "too hot" for Hollywood. The producers wanted Mary for the female lead as Cora Papadakis, the roadside hashhouse wife who kills her husband to be with an attractive young drifter. It was, she told him, a break from the nice ladies she had always played and a great opportunity. Richard Barthelmess, the silent-movie idol, would be making his Broadway debut as the drifter. Jo Mielziner was doing the sets. Please understand, she begged.

He didn't, and he wouldn't. "This is the first time I've really been able to support you," he argued. "We could never afford to have children before. Stay here and let's start a family. Anyway, the play isn't any good and you're wrong for it!"

For the second time, Bogart found himself married to a woman more successful than he. Now that he could rectify what he felt a wrongful position and assert his manhood, his wife was saying no. In the end, they were both immovable. Bogart's life had become centered in Hollywood as surely as Mary's was in New York, to which she returned and began rehearsals for her play.

The receding tide of the early Depression left Hollywood with five dominant companies: Metro-Goldwyn-Mayer, Paramount, Warner Brothers, Columbia, and Twentieth Century–Fox—studios striking in the similarity of their practices, and even more striking in their differences. MGM's strong suit was the depth of its all-star roster of contract players (its slogan was "More stars than there are in the heavens"), Paramount's was its lush productions, Twentieth Century–Fox's its literary properties. Warners' was its close reading of the national press, and the resulting docudramas were the thirties equivalent of the later based-on-fact television movie.

The minor companies, however, turned out major works, even if they never achieved the stature of the big five. In the 1930s and early 1940s, RKO produced Fred Astaire–Ginger Rogers musicals; comedies with Katharine Hepburn and Cary Grant, such as *Bringing Up Baby* (1938); and Orson Welles's *Citizen Kane* (1941). The studio's overall product, though, was erratic, and there were long periods between successful films, as well as almost constant financial difficulty. Universal began the 1930s with *All Quiet on the Western Front* (1930) and then produced a number of superlative horror films—among them *Frankenstein* (1931) and *The Invisible Man* (1933)—before barely averting bankruptcy.

At MGM, glamour was reflected in all aspects of the operation, from the players to the buildings to the back lots to the limousines that drove the stars from their dressing rooms to the sound stages. In contrast to this Tiffany approach, Warners was a factory—a picture a week, with tight production schedules fixed anywhere between six weeks for a class A product and twenty-one days for the bottom of the line. Actors rode bikes, and their paychecks, along with the technicians', were dispensed blue-collar style every Wednesday at the cashier's office, like workers at the assembly plant gate. Exceptions had to be fought out with the front office; even then they were grudgingly granted and subject to revocation. Warners' practices were enforced by a cost-obsessed management that recycled footage, sets, props, and entire films; the thought of anyone, like Robinson, on salary and not working was almost physically painful.

Part of that ethos was due to financial crises, but even more to the lifetime habits of the Warners themselves. The memories that made Jack Warner a New Deal Democrat in Republican Southern California had also made cost-cutting a way of life. J. L. had been born in the back of a peddler's wagon. His brother Harry had once cobbled shoes. Albert even now picked up in the studio walkways stray nails that might be reused. Cash was held as long as possible. When making *The Jazz Singer* in California, Al Jolson was paid with checks drawn on a New York bank; when he was in New York, with checks from one in California. Jack sat in the screening room until all hours, read every script, and watched each detail; he lived his job and set the pace for everyone down the line. If you were on salary, this often meant ending one picture on a Saturday and showing up for the next on Monday.

Three days before Bogart's new contract took effect, Jack Warner cabled Hal Wallis: "Are we using Humphrey Bogart?" Unhappily for Bogart, the already rapid assembly line was speeded up just as he arrived. A new unit had been formed, devoted exclusively to cranking out low-budget productions. These so-called B pictures, usually directed by lesser talents and more focused on the budget and the clock than on the performances, were given few resources and scant promotion; critics seldom reviewed them. They were the result of simple economics: studios owned theaters, theaters needed product, the product provided a steady flow of cash to the studios. In the glittering first-run downtown movie palaces, patrons got a picture and a stage show. In the neighborhoods, they got a double bill. The second feature hardly mattered; it was a time-filler, meant to give the customers more movie for their money.

The head of the unit was Bryan Foy, a former child hoofer and son of the great vaudevillian Eddie Foy. He was also a composer, a lyricist, and the best low-budget producer on the lot. He had made *The Lights of New York* for $75,000; it earned two million. A likable, gregarious man with the scent of liquor always on his breath, Brynie Foy was a master of turning out something from little in a short time, making some thirty films a year, few of them running over an hour. ("He'd get a script," a colleague remembered, "and he'd say, 'Too fuckin' long.' And the writer would say, 'I don't know how to cut it.' 'You don't know how to cut it?' He takes the script, tears pages out, and says, 'Shoot it!' ")

Privately, Foy would complain bitterly about the films forced on him. But at least he had job security and a decent wage. For Bogart, dumped into the B's from the heights of Robert Sherwood's world, the impact was near-traumatic.

Humphrey Bogart was used, all right. Used again and again. *Two Against the World* was a recycling of a previous Warner feature that starred Edward G. Robinson, with a title borrowed from an old Constance Bennett release. It was ground out in three weeks. Bogart played the cynical manager of a radio station, turning to trash programming on the orders of a venal owner. When the tabloid treatment of a scandal results in the suicides of innocent people, he shoulders the blame, turns on his ratings-hungry boss, and resolves to tell all to the Federal Communications Commission. The ads showed Bogart's face luridly lit opposite display type screaming: "THE COLD-BLOODED GANGSTER OF 'THE PETRIFIED FOREST' FINDS A NEW WAY TO KILL!"

Even in A pictures, Bogart wound up in B roles. In *Bullets or Ballots,* released before *Two Against the World* and starring Edward G. Robinson, he had fourth billing, playing a mobster named "Bugs" ("Beneath a thin veneer of urbanity he was as dangerous as a rattlesnake . . ."), regarded even by his fellow crooks as a "ten-cent thug." The stereotype of the cardboard felon, manufactured for the sole purpose of expiring in a hail of bullets, would dog his career through the thirties.

In *China Clipper* he was Hap Stuart, daredevil pilot, wartime buddy to Pat O'Brien's Dave. Their introductory scene was a triumph of clichés as exposition:

> DAVE:
> Tell me about yourself. We haven't seen each other since that Armistice brawl in the Astor Hotel.
> HAP:
> Golly. Has it been that long?
> DAVE:
> I heard you turned soft and got married. Where's your wife?
> HAP:
> She died, Dave. . . . Pneumonia. I wish you'd known her, fella.

If you could survive seven years at Warners, James Cagney once told a friend, you could survive anything. Thanks to the three-year-old Screen

Actors Guild, actors no longer worked seven days a week around the clock, as they had until the early thirties. But every studio knew how to bend the rules to just within the breaking point. If Warners was a factory, the B unit was a sweatshop.

Isle of Fury was a remake of *The Narrow Corner,* a 1933 Douglas Fairbanks vehicle. The script had been turned down as a possibility for Pat O'Brien. Its implausible plot involved a love triangle on a South Pacific island. Padding in and out were middle-aged extras from the Los Angeles Mexican community with cloth skirts wrapped around their midsections, whom the audience was to accept as Polynesian pearl divers. The major share of attention, both in production and the ensuing ad campaign, went to a rubber octopus.

The picture was shot in sixteen days, the cast and crew working shifts of ten hours or more. It was a punishing schedule for actors driving long distances to work and expected on the soundstage made up and ready to go at 9:00 A.M. The original lead had dropped out three days before the start of shooting. No problem, said the casting office, they'd use Bogart, who was coming right off *China Clipper.* He took one look at the script and protested all the way up to Jack Warner's antechamber. There was nothing to be done. He'd been cast. Contract talent had no say on roles. End of discussion.

Even the story department had called the material "dull." "Good dialogue would help," an editor suggested, but it was a B and no one bothered. Bogart, with a pencil-thin mustache and a pith helmet, went through the motions as the ostensible proprietor of a South Pacific island pearl-diving operation.

The shooting conditions were even worse than the script. Because July 4th fell on a weekday, the company was worked to exhaustion the day before, shooting fifteen hours straight with just two breaks for meals. When the day ended at five minutes to midnight to avoid paying the unions' holiday rates, Bogart, depleted after the non-stop hours under the hot lights, took unit manager Lee Hugunin aside. He saw no reason, he told Hugunin, why the cast and crew should have to work into the night like this—though if he was forced, he added, "I suppose I'd have to do it." The Warner man stiffened in response and declared that the company never forced *anyone.* In his daily report on the film for studio executives, Hugunin included a note: "Humphrey Bogart has been making it rather difficult." It was the kind of friction that would characterize Bogart's relations with Warner Brothers during all his years at the studio.

On July 5, word went out in the afternoon that they'd be running late again. Bogart rebelled. To hell with the studio, he announced. He was going to eat his supper, then he was going home. A frantic call from the assistant director brought Hugunin rushing to the set. Out of loyalty to his colleagues, Bogart agreed to continue. They finished at two A.M. after a seventeen-hour day. At the very late-night break for a snack, the troupe sat amid the debris of struck scenery and props and picked dirt and sawdust out of the food. "Midnight dinner on a filthy set," the script supervisor noted in her report.

These abuses left a lasting scar on Bogart, who during his years of stardom would have written into every contract that he would leave the set promptly at six. He virtually always stuck to this provision, impervious to the pleas of producers and directors. His answer was always the same: "At six P.M., I walk."

There was, however, one bonus for Bogart in the making of *Isle of Fury*. For the waterfront scenes, the studio arranged for a five-day shoot in June on Catalina Island, twenty-six miles off the coast. Their purported South Pacific beach was actually White's Landing, a fashionable mooring spot shared with 125 boy campers from the Pasadena YMCA. The Y promised to keep the kids quiet.

Catalina was a popular boating haven. Its village of Avalon, famous for its nightspots, was celebrated in a popular song whose melody would waft through the cafe scenes in *Casablanca.* The cast and crew were kept as far away from the village as possible, housed in an isolated hotel some miles off and a half hour farther from the shooting site. "This gets away from amusements, vacation atmosphere and night life at Avalon," Hugunin explained primly to the studio, "and keeps the company in a definitely confined area." It also had the salutary effect of saving Warners $50 a day in housing expenses. Direct steamship service to the definitely confined area was available for fifty cents a head, the hotel bar could be closed down whenever the studio ordered, and the extra travel time could be compensated for by moving up the morning call a half hour. "The company will be in bed much earlier," Hugunin noted with satisfaction, "as there is nothing to do."

But for Bogart, the inveterate bar-hopper, the attraction was not the nightlife of Avalon. Rather, it was Catalina itself, with its green hills and razorback ridges that descended to secluded coves whose water was sparklingly clean. In the years to come, Catalina would become an increasingly important part of Bogart's life, a refuge when emotions and events threatened to get beyond his control. For now, however, it was simply a welcome change for him and other members of the overworked troupe, almost all of whom were accompanied by family or friends. Everyone else asked if they could bring someone along. Bogart merely informed the assistant director that he had invited Mrs. Bogart, who had hurriedly arrived in Los Angeles that spring.

In March, Bogart had moved to the Garden of Allah, the rambling hotel and bungalow colony beside Sunset Boulevard that belonged to Alla Nazimova, the Russian actress and silent-film star famed for her interpretations of Ibsen on stage and her haunting, stylized movies. It was an upscale establishment, but the walls were notoriously thin. During playwright Arthur Kober's first stay, he was awakened one night by a sleepy voice asking "Would you get me a drink of water, dear?" Only after he had stumbled to the bathroom and brought back a glassful did he remember he was alone. Even so, the Garden was the residence of choice for homesick easterners, offering a congenial, somewhat boozy intellectuality; a touch of Bohemia amid the palms. The self-contained crazy quilt of villas and planted paths was centered around a swimming pool supposedly shaped like the Black Sea, the area from which Nazimova had come. The Garden was also known for a lifestyle described in those days as "sophisticated," meaning fairly relaxed in matters of alcohol and sex; the bar was open twenty-four hours a day. For Bogart, living there meant daily contact with names and faces from home, including Robert Benchley, the portly, heavy-drinking humorist for *The New Yorker* and comic actor.

One day while he was sitting on the floor in Benchley's villa downing scotch and sodas, the door opened on a slim, stunning woman. Her jet-black hair was brushed austerely back from a seductive gamine face dominated by eyes that were dark as a panther. It was his old Broadway acquaintance Louise Brooks, who had gone on to European stardom in the silents and was now back in Hollywood, a has-been at twenty-nine. Brooks's doll-like features masked a fierce drive for independence. She was an anomaly in Hollywood, a perpetual rebel whose outspoken honesty riled the studio powers. The next day Brooks received a phone call from Mary Baker saying that she and Bogart were having a drink and that he would like Brooks to join them. "Coming from anyone else, the invitation would have meant that two bored people wanted company," Brooks wrote. "Coming from Humphrey, it was nothing less than a declaration of love. Full of curiosity," Brooks came over immediately. Bogart greeted her warmly but then "retreated slowly into gloom and silence and Scotch." To her, it was an act not of rudeness but of self-assuredness. "Being supremely confident of his own attractiveness to women, he scorned every form of demonstrativeness. When a woman appealed to him, he waited for her the way the flame waits for the moth. . . . It was security in sex that preserved Humphrey's ego until his eventual success after he had endured the bitterest humiliation, ridicule, and failure." Little came of the encounter. She and Bogart were too different, she later reasoned; more likely, they were too much alike.

The Postman Always Rings Twice had opened on Broadway in February to generally tepid reviews, some of the best notices going to Mary Philips and her "intuitive artistry" as "the gas station strumpet." The public nonetheless bought tickets, lured by the name of Barthelmess and what passed at the time as sex and violence, two passions far more evident ten years later in the Lana Turner–John Garfield film.

In April the play was still doing adequate business when it moved from the Lyceum Theatre to the smaller Golden Theater. Then, two weeks after the move, it suddenly closed. By the following morning, Mary had packed her bags and was on a plane to Los Angeles. The exact reason for Mary's rejecting the easy travel of a train for a cramped and uncomfortable ride in a small aircraft that kept an erratic schedule and required many fueling stops is unclear. Perhaps she had learned that her husband had found some comfort close at hand during her absence. Whatever the cause, her actions had an urgency about them.

The plane, scheduled to arrive the night of April 26, failed to show up. Bogart spent a sleepless, worried night. The plane was finally traced to a remote field in Oklahoma, where it had made an emergency landing in the middle of a dust storm.

It arrived the next day, and late in the afternoon the couple pulled up to the sweeping side entrance to the Garden of Allah. "Mary Philips has just arrived to be with Humphrey Bogart, her husband," Robert Benchley wrote that night to his family. The Southern California weather, so beautiful the day before, had turned cold and raw, with overcast skies. It was a mirror of the Bogart's marriage.

CHAPTER 4

The Portland Rosebud

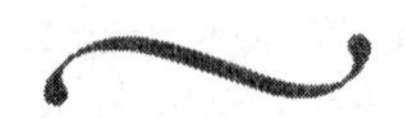

Mayo Methot was nineteen and adorable when she made her Broadway debut in the five-line part of the maid in William Brady's lamentable 1923 Broadway production, *The Mad Honeymoon.* The critics lambasted it, ridiculing everyone in the cast except for the young actress, whose cupid's-bow mouth and large, soulful eyes looking up from under a mass of blond curls reminded many of the screen idol Lillian Gish. George M. Cohan was also dazzled, and immediately signed her to play opposite him as Leola Lane in his new production, *The Song and Dance Man.* For all her youth, Mayo had been a performer since she was six, pushed by an ambitious mother and supported by an adoring sea captain father who spent most of his time sailing to and from the Orient. She had appeared in many productions at home in Oregon, then at eighteen had come East and landed a bit part in a Lionel Barrymore film for William Randolph Hearst's Cosmopolitan Pictures. After several months with a stock company in Massachusetts, she returned to New York and was offered the small role by Brady. Unsure of whether to take it, she telegraphed her mother for advice.

"Take it," she wired back, "and make all you can of it. It may be your chance."

It certainly was. All Broadway was beguiled by "the little blond beauty," as she was called by the New York papers, charmed by her "naive personality and dramatic skill," her touching devotion to her husband

John Lamond, a cameraman at Cosmopolitan Pictures, and her sweet, clear singing voice. The great Cohan himself predicted a brilliant future for his discovery, who was dubbed "the Portland Rosebud."

By the time Bogart met her briefly in the late twenties, the blond curls had been abandoned for the sleek look of the flapper. The West Coast ingenue was now an established Broadway lead whose admirers included critic Brooks Atkinson and producer Arthur Hopkins. The teenage marriage had dissolved in 1927; the rosebud mouth had grown sensuous; the soulful eyes had turned smoldering beneath exotic, arching brows that accentuated her broad cheekbones.

She had also begun drinking. To her colleague Isabel Bunker, she was "a strange girl." Although a loner, Mayo commanded the friendship of those few whom she let close to her. As a performer, she could hold the house in her hands. In the Vincent Youmans hit *Great Day,* she stepped every night into the spotlight in the special silence given off by a theater audience awaiting the big number, and never disappointed them:

More than you know
More than you know
Man of my heart, I love you so . . .

Hollywood had snapped her up in 1930 in the rush to sign for the talkies talent who could actually deliver lines. Once she was there, though, no one knew what to do with her unusual looks. By the time she was thirty-two, all she had to show for her early promise was a string of supporting roles, a fading career, and a dying marriage to one of the two Morgan brothers who owned The Cock and Bull, a popular restaurant and bar on Sunset Boulevard. She was Mrs. Percy T. Morgan when Bogart, at loose ends, ran into her again in early 1936.

In the most popular scenario, they were seated separately at the annual Screen Actors Guild dinner at the Biltmore Hotel in downtown Los Angeles when Mayo, conspicuous in a red gown with a plunging front, smiled at Bogart from another table. After a moment, he realized they had met before and, relaxed by several drinks, wrenched a plaster nude from its decorative perch and presented it to her as the "Oscar for being the most beautiful woman in the room." They danced. They had a nightcap. And so forth.

While they may have played the scene at the Biltmore, their verifiable reunion was a good deal more prosaic. Mutual friends—Eric Hatch, master of the screwball comedy and author of the story and co-writer of the screenplay of *My Man Godfrey,* and his wife Gertie—were in from the East. Bogart dropped by their house in Beverly Hills to say hello, and in the living room was Mayo.

The casual encounter bloomed almost overnight into a liaison, with the Hatch residence as a backdrop—a situation, Gertie Hatch (later Gertrude Hatch Chase) told Nathaniel Benchley, that caused Eric and her considerable unease.

The discomfort mounted as Bogart's affair with another man's wife grew increasingly public. Bogart, however, seemed not to care what people saw or knew. Rather, he appeared focused only on someone who was unpredictable and sensuous, with a wild sense of humor and an inexhaustible love of a good time.

This came at a price. "She was an alcoholic," her friend Gloria Stuart, the blond star of Warners' *Gold Diggers of 1935,* said. "She was very bright, but she was smashed all the time. She'd made a good 'society' marriage, but she just went after Bogart and that was it." He seemed willing to be caught. "I think he found her amusing. She made him laugh a lot. And Bogie liked to laugh."

A very unfunny scene was narrowly averted one night during a party at the Hatches at which Louise Brooks was among the guests. As dinner ended, the doorbell rang and everyone went into the vaulted living room to meet Mayo, "clad," Brooks wrote, "in a sheath of peacock-blue silk. That night, instead of having our usual talk and laughter, we became an audience galvanized by a scene of the most passionate love played out between Mayo and Humphrey without so much as a touch of hands." In time, Mayo got up and put an Argentine tango on the phonograph and danced in her stockinged feet with the slender Russian character actor Mischa Auer. What began as "a burlesque, with him throwing her about and glaring lustfully into her eyes," gradually became a sexual ballet as "her exquisitely persuasive body began to rule his movements, and they danced in the falling arcs, the slow recoveries, and the voluptuous pauses of the true tango." The tension was diffused when the maid announced that Mr. Morgan, having heard about the party, was on his way, presumably to get his wife.

Mayo looked around for her shoes. One was missing. The guests became frantic co-conspirators, rooting about for the missing item—with the exception of Louise Brooks, who sat unconcerned. Suspicious of her inaction, Bogart turned on her. "God damn you, Louise," he shouted, furious, "tell us where you hid Mayo's slipper." Finally Auer, who had hidden the shoe on a ceiling beam that no one else was tall enough to reach, retrieved it and let the lovers make their escape through the back door as the front doorbell rang.

It seems no wonder that Mary Philips dashed across the country in the spring of 1936 to be with her husband. Later accounts had her arriving to find Mayo ensconced at the Garden of Allah, though more likely she was a transient there. Her official address was still the spacious house in the Hollywood Hills where she lived as Mrs. Morgan. For Bogart, as for many others, a passion on the side was one thing; the breaking up of his nine-year marriage was another. Whatever ensued between husband and wife after Mary came out would remain a private matter, but clearly an attempt was made at reconciliation.

That June, Warners exercised Bogart's first option, with a raise of $50 weekly, proof that this time he was in Hollywood to stay. He had been filming almost constantly since Mary's arrival. In early July, with a three-week layoff due him after finishing *Isle of Fury,* he and Mary moved into a small adobe house of their own at 1210 North Horn Avenue, a forty-five-degree tilt of land above Sunset Boulevard. He was still seeing Mayo, however.

Meanwhile, Mayo began divorce proceedings against Percy T. Morgan Jr. The charge was cruelty. Mr. Morgan, she said, would not let her rearrange the furniture in the house.

Mary Baker, the keeper of Bogart's confidences in those years, was convinced that "Bogie didn't really want to marry Mayo. He wanted it to go on as it had been going and to stay married to Mary. But obviously that was not to be." By the time Mayo Methot and Humphrey Bogart worked together in December on Warners' *Marked Woman,* their common future seemed an almost foregone conclusion.

The film was a Bette Davis vehicle, part of a kiss-and-make-up reunion between the studio and the star following her attempt to bolt her contract and the prevailing system by working for other studios on loanouts of her choice. Davis's first picture, *Bad Sister* (1931), with Bogart in a supporting role, was followed by five mediocre movies. Even before *Of Human Bondage,* her career began to take off in 1932, with *The Man Who Played God,* and her troubles with the studio peaked in the mid-thirties. Shortly after she won an Oscar (for *Dangerous* in 1935), Davis accepted an offer from producer Ludovic Toeplitz to make films in England. She complained of being offered middling roles by Warner Brothers, of having to do too many pictures, and of difficult working conditions. Before leaving, she met with Jack Warner and then wrote him a letter, saying in part, "there comes a time in everyone's career when certain things make working worth-while. I am now referring to the very few rights I have asked for."

A performer's "rights," of course, were of no concern to the studio. "Rights" were what the studio owned, along with the performer. When Davis refused to report to work on the ordinary *God's Country and the Woman* in July, Warners suspended her and then pursued her across the sea, insisting on the full execution of their contract with her. The trial in London was a sensation. Davis appeared daily in a red and blue tweed coat and matching beret. After listening to Warners' counsel refer to the actress as "a naughty young lady," a British judge granted the studio an injunction forcing her back to Los Angeles.

Having made its point, Warners didn't underscore it. Not only did the studio pay her legal expenses, it quickly accommodated the prodigal with what was considered the plummy role of the nightclub B-girl in *Marked Woman,* a story based on New York hoodlum Charles "Lucky" Luciano and his gang. "BETTE'S BACK!" the film's pressbook proclaimed.

In a switch from his usual gangster parts, Bogart played a crusading district attorney modeled on New York's crime-fighting Thomas E. Dewey, whom Alice Roosevelt Longworth called the Little Man on the Wedding Cake. Bogart was still a cardboard figure, though, a one-dimensional walking suit set up to be the instrument of Davis's revenge and presumed moral regeneration. Mayo played one of Davis's roommates, a semi-enslaved prostitute referred to as a "hostess" in the restrictive language of the Production Code.

The careers of Bogart and Methot were like the paths of two people meeting on opposite escalators. For the moment both seem to be at the same place. Then one continues up, the other down. Mayo was the one going down. The accumulated disappointment, anger, and alcohol of her six years in Hollywood were evident in her looks. At thirty-three, the once-smooth face was jowly, the pouting mouth now more sullen than sexy, the firm figure of the 1920s given increasingly to fat. On Broadway, distance and the footlights might have veiled the ravages. The camera, however, only highlighted them. The screenplay's description of Estelle, her character in *Marked Woman,* could have been written with Mayo in mind: "Years of night life have already taken their toll of her simple beauty."

Bette Davis, as Mary Dwight, saves Estelle from age discrimination when gangsters take over the club:

VANNING:
Hey. . . . You. Yeah . . . you. . . . Kind of old, aren't you? . . . I need young dames here . . . the kind men go for in a hurry.
MARY:
I thought you said you take care of people. . . . Why don't you give her a break? . . . She can't wreck the place.

Elsewhere, the script directions had Mayo's character "anxiously studying her face in the mirror. . . . With her fingers she pulls the sagging muscles of her chin. She lets them go, and they droop as before. Her eyes fill with a pathetic anxiety." By contrast, Bogart, three years Mayo's senior, was cast as a youthful, sexually desirable man, whose romantic inclinations were strictly in the direction of Bette Davis.

Jane Bryan, a bright new teenage actress then on her second film and playing Davis's younger sister, looked at Bogart and Mayo side by side, and couldn't understand their relationship. "I don't know how he ever, ever married her." She found Bogart "a darling man, always ready with a greeting of 'How are you, kid?' He was extremely professional, as well as very bright and considerate. He was a quiet man on the set. I don't remember him engaging in lengthy conversations or any joviality with the technicians; he was just there, on his marks, ready to go."

Bette Davis was an idol who lived up to Bryan's expectations. "She'd just lost her big lawsuit in England and I think they expected a cowed person to come back on the scene. But she was anything but that. She was terrific. A kind of inner power came through her skin." Davis became a big sister to Bryan off-screen as well, letting the youngster stay overnight in her home when they worked late to spare her the long commute back to what was then the distant suburb of Brentwood. Bryan, who later married the industrialist Justin Dart, returned the favor in 1941 when she held Bette Davis and Arthur Farnsworth's wedding at the Darts' ranch in northern Arizona.

In the film, Bryan visits Davis in New York and innocently gets mixed up with the gangsters. She soon finds herself in over her head and is killed. Davis has gone along with the mob until now, but her sister's murder triggers her rebellion and makes her the marked woman. On the set, Bryan soon had the feeling that she too was as out of her depth. Most of her scenes were with the "hostesses," whose conversation was considerably rawer off-camera than on. "Some of the really tough ladies like Mayo Methot and Lola Lane got a little rough. I honestly didn't understand some of the words they were using." Bryan, a lawyer's daughter who had led a sheltered life, felt embarrassed and uncomfortable. She wanted to leave, but didn't dare: "I just didn't want to call attention to myself."

Bogart, walking by one time, caught the whole scene: the two women talking past the youngster who sat with flaming cheeks, staring at the floor. "He came up and said, 'Girls, I think you're just a little bit too far out in this conversation. I think you ought to pipe down.'" His tone of reproof was made all the more compelling by its coming from a master of the four-letter lexicon. "This was his gentleman side," Bryan said, "not to talk like that in front of a kid."

Mayo did not take the advice well, and railed at Bogart as Bryan stood there. "It was cataclysmic. They were poison to one another." It was an early warning, a clear indication of the differences that were to be the reverse sides of the coin for Humphrey Bogart and Mayo Methot.

Marked Woman did well critically and commercially, but it was Davis's show. For Bogart, it was at least a major supporting role in what was otherwise a time of one-note characters. He had been first a backup to Edward G. Robinson and Pat O'Brien, then later to James Cagney and George Raft, playing men variously named "Rocks," "Bugs," or "Turkey," but otherwise hardly differentiated.

In his second time around with O'Brien, a treacley melodrama called *The Great O'Malley,* he had somewhat more to do as a bitter, jobless veteran driven to crime. One scene in particular came through forcefully, an abrupt change from the saccharine tone of the overall story. The veteran, desperate to feed his family, tries to pawn his medals and wartime pistol. The shopkeeper doles out three dollars for the pistol ("Guns, you can always sell") but turns down the medals ("Ten dollars for that junk?! Why don't you go on relief?"). Bogart's pent-up fury explodes ("The only things left to remind me I was once a man . . . and you call them junk!"), turning his deference into a vicious attack, robbery, and attempted murder. The scene is stark and unsentimentalized.

The publicity department played it for none of what it was worth, and instead stuck to their formula with the ad "AN IRISH COP VS. A GUN-MAD KILLER!"

Finally the opportunity arose to break the cycle. Warners needed an actor who wasn't "ethnic" for the lead in *Black Legion,* the studio's foray into the murky depths of American fascism. Normally the lead would have gone to Robinson, but in this case he was the wrong type. Not that Robinson, who was born Emmanuel Goldenberg, looked particularly

"Jewish," said the studio memos, he just looked "foreign." And they needed "a distinctly American-looking actor."

Like *Marked Woman, Black Legion* was not merely a creation of the Warner story department. The white supremacist network of motorized night riders who terrorized the hard-hit industrial heartland, and who were modeled on the Ku Klux Klan, had been in the headlines all year. There were daily revelations of kidnapping, flogging, and mayhem, and big news stories like this were a staple at Warners.

In the script, based on the true kidnap-murder case that had brought the Legion to national attention, Frank Taylor, a factory worker, is passed over for promotion in favor of a man named Dombrowski. Taylor's joining the band of hooded vigilantes starts a chain of events that ends in the breakup of his family and the murder of his best friend. Brought to trial, he repudiates the other defendants in a dramatic courtroom outburst that exposes the hate group. But there is no happy Hollywood ending. In the fadeout, Taylor is marched off with the others to serve a life sentence. For Bogart, *Black Legion* meant his first leading role in an attention-getting picture.

There is a chilling timeliness about the film, notably in the scene where Frank Taylor, sitting with his young son, flips the radio dial and is riveted by the voice that seems to address him directly:

> Hordes of grasping, pushing foreigners who are stealing jobs from American workmen and bread from American homes. . . . *(Frank reaches for a nearby chair and sits down to listen intently. . . .)* It is to combat this peril, to preserve and protect standards of living which have made American working men the envy of the world that we . . . have raised our rallying cry—America for Americans! . . .
>
> BUDDY:
>
> Pop . . . Can't we get Flash Tyler?
>
> FRANK:
>
> No! Listen to this guy! He's talkin' sense!

Frank and others from the community, some in workshirts, some in suits, gather at a secret meeting in that most American of landmarks, the local drugstore. But rather than a congregation of neighbors, theirs is a fellowship of the fearful, and they are soon caught up in the harangue of the Black Legion recruiter:

> From time immemorial, America, in her generosity and might, has held forth a welcoming hand to the oppressed peoples of

> other nations. . . . In mighty multitudes they have swarmed to our shores . . . and drunk with the impudent power of their stolen prosperity, they are openly plotting to seize control of our government. . . .
>
> Standing alone, you and I are helpless to defend ourselves. . . . *But* if we unite with millions of other red-blooded Americans . . . we are invincible! With fire and sword we will purge the land of these traitorous aliens . . . until once more our beloved Stars and Stripes will wave over a united nation of free—white—one-hundred-percent Americans!
>
> *(There is a wild burst of applause.)*

"*Black Legion* will not stay in its place as cinema fiction," *The New York Times* later commented. "It strikes too hard, too deep and too close to the mark."

Making the film took courage. Hal Wallis proceeded despite threats, concerns over lawsuits, and fears over regional sensibilities. For Bogart, the opening clichéd good-guy scenes notwithstanding, the film was his first opportunity really to act since *The Petrified Forest.* He depicted the moral destruction of Frank Taylor with almost clinical exactness, a preview of his more mature work ten years later in *The Treasure of the Sierra Madre.* His performance even prompted the editorial page of the New York *Herald Tribune* to call the film "as much a story in human disintegration as it is a social treatise." Few who saw the picture would forget the shot of Bogart as the disappointed little man fondling his new gun, casting a giant shadow on the wall. And smiling.

The film's violence leads to murder when Taylor's best friend, Ed Jackson, a cheery guy-next-door type played by Dick Foran (the athlete of *The Petrified Forest*), threatens to go to the police. After being kidnapped by the group in a scare tactic, he breaks free and runs, amid shouts of "Stop him!" Taylor, the hood over his head, shoots, automaton-like, impelled by the mob psychology. Ed falls dead. The frightened Legion members scatter, but one hooded figure remains frozen in place.

Bogart's next scene is riveting. Pulling his hood back, he throws himself on the body with hoarse cries of denial, then suddenly veers in one beat from grief to panic. He twists and scurries hysterically through the underbrush on all fours like a blinded animal, then stumbles to his feet, quickening the pace, eyes staring in unseeing and total fear. Without a break in his stride, he does a full turn and whips off the robe. In a single, seemingly reflexive action, he drops it and plunges forward in the same fluid, emotionally charged momentum. It is a ballet of terror, flawlessly executed.

Comments on the film ranged from the editorial pages of the newspapers to the *Motion Picture Daily,* which labeled the movie "Celluloid Dynamite." *The New York Times* called the picture "cinema at its best . . . [a] quasi-documentary record." Even if the point that decent people could be manipulated through their emotions was made too patly for some critics of the day, it came through with devastating effectiveness, and the picture received much attention.

"For this is the unforgettable, the horrible thing about *Black Legion,*" *The New York Times* continued, "it did happen here! . . . Even though the Warner foreword tried to reassure us by saying the incidents and characters depicted are fictional; we know that . . . Humphrey Bogart . . . is not merely an actor playing a role; he is one of the Michigan men we read about. To see a picture that way is a harrowing experience; but it may be salutary, too."

To some extent, Warners hedged its bets on the movie. The Legion commanders portrayed in the film were penny-ante con men making a profit off the sale of sheets and guns and laughing at their clients; there was nothing about the covert network that in reality reached into the highest levels of law enforcement, the judiciary, and the Michigan statehouse. The studio was uncomfortably aware that the Detroit district attorney, implicated in Legion activities, had been returned to office by the voters of his city, and that recent court decisions had been fairly sweeping on what constituted libel.

On the other hand, Warners reproduced the Legion's ceremonies, including a word-perfect replica of initiation rites and the oath of obedience sworn by Bogart at a secret conclave. ("Before violating . . . my obligation, I will pray to an avenging God and an unmerciful devil to tear my heart out and roast it over the flames of sulfur. . . .") The climactic trial scene, in which Bogart confesses to the murder, is a re-creation of the courtroom confession that stunned the nation, when Frank Taylor's real-life counterpart exposed the group.

Besides the accolades for the movie, the press was unanimous in its praise of Bogart. Archer Winsten in The New York *Post* called his portrayal "dynamic and stirring. The role is one which demands the talents of a Muni or a Robinson. And Bogart has filled it superbly. No more B pix for Bogart!" "His powerful performance," echoed New York's *Morning Telegraph,* "establishes Humphrey Bogart as a star." The New York *Mirror* said "it is exhilarating to watch him," and nationwide, the adjectives were stellar: "Powerful," "superb," "stirring," "compelling," "brilliant." The critic for the New York *American* went so far as to suggest the "dynamic young actor" for the role of Rhett Butler in the upcoming *Gone With the Wind.*

But stardom didn't follow. Despite the raves and the praise for the Warners' courage, despite the critics' urging the public to see the picture as a kind of civic duty, despite the attractions of violence on the screen, *Black Legion,* while it made a healthy profit, was not a runaway hit on the order of Paul Muni's *I Am a Fugitive from a Chain Gang* (1932), or *The Public Enemy* (1931), which had made James Cagney a major star. In promoting the picture, Warner Publicity seemed apologetic: "There's no Paul Muni in *Black Legion,* but there's Humphrey Bogart."

Bogart was not box office. He was a good actor doing a good job, but he was not a screen personality, except within the narrow confines of B-grade clones of Duke Mantee. By the close of his first year under contract, in early 1937, the underlying realities were unmistakable. There were just too many ahead of him in the pecking order. He could work his heart out, but an O'Brien, Cagney, or Robinson action movie would outgross him every time. It was an axiom of the industry: Rave reviews were merely clippings for your scrapbook if the studio saw no advantage in making you a star.

There is an ironic footnote to the success of *Black Legion.* The Warner research department had been meticulous in combing the nation's papers for details and collecting news photos to send on to wardrobe, whose workers ran up faithful reproductions of the pictured black hoods and gowns, complete with sewn-on badges—a white cross on a circular red background with a black square in the center. This turned out to be the symbol of the KKK, covered by United States design patent 68219, issued September 15, 1925, and Warners promptly found itself sued for infringement of copyright by "the Knights of the Ku Klux Klan, a corporation chartered under the laws of the State of Georgia." The case was dismissed the next year, with the Klan ordered to pay the legal costs.

Bogart was naturally discouraged by his Hollywood career so far, and word got back to New York that things had not turned out as expected for him. However, as with most gossip, the rumor was far worse than the fact. The story circulating at Bleeck's and at "21" had two versions: one was that Warners was dropping Bogart's option, the other that he was dropping films. No matter which, a friend recalled, "He was going home, which means that you either have no offers, or only crappy movies." Actually, neither version was true.

He had plenty of work, but the roles assigned him had not progressed. *Kid Galahad* (1937), filmed after *Marked Woman,* is a memorable boxing picture, though not quite a classic like *Body and Soul* (1947) or *Golden Boy* (1939). It has crackling direction by Michael Curtiz, a cast headed by Edward G. Robinson and Bette Davis, and fight sequences that are models of innovative cinematography. But for Bogart, playing a crooked promoter, it meant fourth billing after Robinson, Davis, and a blond six-foot-one mass of muscle named Wayne Morris, who played the Kid and was being groomed to be another Errol Flynn. As in *Bullets or Ballots,* the story ends in a mutually fatal gunfight between Robinson and Bogart. Virtually always, Bogart's various shootouts with Robinson, Cagney, et al., left him instantly dead, while giving his antagonists Pietà-like death scenes in the arms of Davis, Joan Blondell, or Gladys George. In this instance, Robinson, as the hero, gasps his last breath in Davis's arms; Bogart sprawls in the background, a blanket over his remains. This scenario was so commonplace, a reporter noted, that "unfortunately for his curtain-line speeches, says Bogart, the heroes he takes with him to the Land of Shadows invariably survive him long enough to deliver effective last lines. . . . 'It must be a matter of marksmanship,' Bogart ruminates. 'Guess I'll go down to the shooting gallery . . . and brush up.' "

Bogart's big death scene in 1937 was on radio. The *CBS Shakespeare Theater* was an ambitious project of the ten-year-old Columbia Broadcasting System—skillful one-hour adaptations, without commercial interruptions, presented live before an audience, with a full orchestra and some of Hollywood's best talent. It was a summer program in an era before taped reruns, meant to fill in while the sponsors and big-money programs took a break and perhaps to garner some prestige for the network in its ongoing battle with the older, richer National Broadcasting Company. It worked so well that NBC hired John Barrymore to produce and star in a competing series, turning Monday night into what was called the "Battle of the Bard."

For the actors, it meant a change of pace and a chance to read over a live microphone with no orders for another take. From mid-July to the end of August 1937, an astonishing array of talent passed through Columbia's Music Box Theater in Hollywood: Burgess Meredith in *Hamlet;* Leslie Howard and Rosalind Russell in *Much Ado About Nothing;* Claude Rains and Raymond Massey in *Julius Caesar.* Edward G. Robinson delighted both the live and radio audiences in *The Taming of the Shrew,* and Tallulah Bankhead and Orson Welles starred in *Twelfth Night,* with help from Sir Cedric Hardwicke, Estelle Winwood, and Helen Menken.

In June, Bogart was invited to appear in late August as Henry Percy in *Henry IV, Part I.* He was eager to try, and Jack Warner, whose personal permission was required for any radio appearance, gave his assent, "If it won't interfere with his picture work."

It didn't, and he went on with Walter Huston and Brian Aherne. Just why Bogart had been selected was anybody's guess, other than that Hotspur, like Bogart, had a bad temper and a speech impediment. And like most Bogart figures of the time, he dies after one-on-one combat. Except that Hotspur has an exit speech.

Bogart performed relatively well, but he didn't have the skill of a seasoned Shakespearean performer, and he didn't have the diction. By contrast, Huston, whose sister had coached John Barrymore in his great Hamlet, and Aherne, with his English training, rolled through the Elizabethan verse as if they spoke it at home. In addition, they had co-starred in *Othello* on Broadway earlier that year. Bogart knew he was out of his element but plowed onward, stumbling over the Elizabethan tongue-twisters, his voice unable to mask the flat *a*'s and the slurred delivery of too many gangster films ("Ah! I can no law-nger brook thy vaniddy!"). Still, to the radio audience, it was pretty flabbergasting to hear the dying warrior speak the rolling Shakespearean phrases in the accents of Humphrey Bogart:

. . . O, Harry, thou hast robb'd me of my youth!
I better brook the loss of brittle life
Than those proud titles thou Hast won of me
. . . O, I could prophesy,
But that the earthy and cold hand of death
Lies on my tongue: no, Percy, thou art dust,
And food for . . . aaahhhhh (Dies)

It was an earnest try, even if Harry Percy's dying moan was less suggestive of the pains of death than of a bad hangover. But at least he had a chance to work with good material. It was also one of the few breaks in the treadmill of screen roles that had become interchangeable. "You could almost make a card index of the lines they speak," Bogart said.

Never a fashion plate, he paid less and less attention to his characters' clothes, a silent commentary on roles that were off the rack. Hal Wallis, looking at the dailies of *Marked Woman,* shot off two angry memos to director Lloyd Bacon: Would he kindly tell Bogart to be "a little more particular" about his appearance: to close his collar, knot his tie better; and for God's sake lay off those plaids and barber-pole striped ties. And if he couldn't shave close enough, at least use makeup to cover the beard—"He looks dirty."

Bogart was at a low ebb when once again fate intervened in the form of a New York playwright. This time it was the Pulitzer Prize–winner Sidney Kingsley, author of *Dead End,* the indictment of urban poverty recently bought for the screen by Samuel Goldwyn.

Of course, Bogart's was another bad-guy role; but the part of Baby Face Martin, the gangster returned to his old neighborhood only to find his mother's door closed to him and his boyhood love become a VD-ravaged prostitute, went well beyond the confines of the standard movie hood. Kingsley had seen the role as that of "a self-destructive man, finally destroyed by the thing that made him. And a victim of his own success as a gangster."

Sixty years later, in an era of crack dealing, the dialogue could be the same, except the prices would have to be raised: "I'm glad I ain't like you saps," Martin tells an underpaid old friend from the slums. "Starving for what? Peanuts? I got mine, I took it. . . . Look! (*Pulls cuff*) Silk. Twenty bucks. (*Indicates suit*) Custom tailored—150 bucks. And dames."

Kingsley, who "liked him and admired him as an actor," was delighted when Bogart's name came up in discussions about casting the film. Bogart had traveled to New York to see the stage production, and had learned a lot. Martin was played by Joseph Downing, with what Kingsley called a "kind of broken-hip walk" and a habit of nervously sucking his teeth. "All of those qualities were just right for the part. It was wonderful." These mannerisms went into the Bogart repertory. As Kingsley put it, "the mask stuck to the face."

Kingsley, raised in the slums that then bordered the East River, wrote from experience: "I was a dead end kid." But for Bogart, too, the subject struck a powerfully responsive chord, raising memories of the despair-filled early thirties—the walkup apartment off First Avenue that in those days, before the FDR Drive, was only steps from the East Side waterfront, with the moldering tenements and piers side by side with the new luxury housing, the pleasure boats moored off the piers and the slum children swimming in the filthy water.

Director William Wyler had wanted to shoot on location in New York. Although Goldwyn vetoed the idea, a move that detracted ultimately from the film's effectiveness, in every other regard, the production, like all those of Samuel Goldwyn, was strictly first-class, with nothing assembly-line about it. For Bogart, it was a decided change from Warners. The screenplay was by Lillian Hellman, and the cast was headed by Sylvia Sidney, Claire Trevor, Joel McCrea, and Wendy Barrie. Goldwyn also brought in the stage boys' cast to re-create the youthful urban gang that had stolen the show on Broadway and were soon to be known in films as the Dead End Kids.

The movie was expected to be a standout, and Baby Face Martin a choice part. Louella Parsons reported that "there isn't an actor in town who wouldn't do nip-ups for the *Dead End* role, a choice bit of acting in the play." At one point, Paramount's tough guy George Raft had been under consideration, but he worried about his contract and, Kingsley said, "He went around town asking everybody in Hollywood, 'Should I take this part?' " With the exception of Bogart's own talent, Raft's indecision on this and other films in the future would be the greatest boon to Bogart's career.

Yet Bogart almost didn't get to play the part. Goldwyn had asked for him on loanout, a standard industry practice under which contract players were rented to other companies, often at two or three times their salary, with the studio pocketing the difference. But even for a profit, Jack Warner was in no hurry to part with Bogart. He was a recognizable commodity now, and a low-cost, good-drawing talent that could be moved quickly from one production to another. Why should an outsider benefit? Sam Goldwyn's calls to Warner went unanswered, his telegrams ignored, until Warner realized that Goldwyn had something that he wanted in return—the services of the blond star Miriam Hopkins. In late April, the swap was at last arranged. Warners would be paid $10,000 for five weeks, a profit to them of $6,750 over Bogart's modest salary. Hopkins's services drew $37,500 for the same period.

Meanwhile, Bogart's marriage was in the final stage of disintegration. To the end, Bogart clung to the hope of reconciliation; but refusing to settle for halfway measures, Mary left him. By late February 1937, Mayo, pressuring from the other side, had obtained an interlocutory decree entitling her to a divorce, while Mary buried her energy and sorrow in *As Good as Married*, the first of five films she was to make that year.

Baker, the longtime friend of the Bogarts and their faithful go-between, had tried repeatedly to patch things up, but she, too, was out of ideas. Following one last talk with Mary, she went to see Bogart on the Goldwyn lot on Santa Monica Boulevard, one of the few Hollywood studios actually in Hollywood.

They were shooting on the waterfront set. Bogart, dressed as Baby Face Martin, was sitting on some steps, practicing a knife toss under the tutelage of director William Wyler. It had to be just right, the knife slicing downward, neatly impaling an orange peel. Wyler was a perfectionist, addicted to retakes. Baker watched as he repeatedly led Bogart through the motions: flip, stick; flip, stick; flip, stick.

She was getting restive when Wyler finally called for a break. Bogart turned anxiously toward her. They sat down together on the stairs, the imaginary East River below them, the setting so much like the East Side slum streets where they had lived when they were young and broke. There was really nothing more to say. He wasn't the first man to love his wife and want another woman. Nor was Mary Philips the first woman to refuse to put up with it.

"I don't see any solution to this," Baker told him.

His shoulders sagged. "That means I'll have to marry Mayo."

"I guess so, because she won't leave you alone."

Bogart straightened up. Okay, he told Baker. Have Mary get a lawyer, and he'd get a lawyer, and would Baker be a witness?

Baker did as she was asked and a short time later the two Marys went off to New York. Bogart, though, seemed no more enthusiastic about marrying Mayo than he had been about marrying Helen.

On top of all this came a family tragedy. His sister Kay died in New York; Bogart couldn't quite make out the cause in the message left for him on his return home from work. Only that she had died in a hospital operating room, her system undermined by alcohol. (The cause was peritonitis from a ruptured appendix.) Catherine Elizabeth Bogart had lived thirty-five years. "She was a victim of the speakeasy era," Bogart said to friends. "She burned the candle at both ends, then decided to burn it in the middle."

Her death also raised the question of what to do with Frances, whose emotional balance, after several years spent in and out of mental institutions, was at best fragile. The sisters had been sharing an apartment—an alcoholic and a manic-depressive, trying to live together. Frances's psychiatrists told a distraught Stuart Rose that Mrs. Rose could never, in their words, reassume the duties of a wife and mother and that it was therefore better that the couple live apart, with some family member assuming the role of caretaker. Stuart Rose had accordingly set up the two women in an apartment and paid Frances's living costs. But he also had a child to raise, he later told Nathaniel Benchley, and he had sold off assets to meet the hospital bills. Despite a high-paying job as an editor with the *Saturday Evening Post,* he was almost bankrupt. The only answer seemed a divorce, with the stipulation that Frances would go to the West Coast, to be cared for by her brother. (Rose also told Nathaniel Benchley that he paid Frances alimony for almost thirty years, but Mary Baker later told Benchley that Bogart took "full care" of his sister and "resented that Stuart had gotten out from under this.")

Now, of all times, was when Bogart needed the contractual "adjustment" promised by Warners when he had signed over a year ago. "A very heavy expense has descended upon him because of his sister's very serious illness," his agent Noll Gurney wrote to Jack Warner, adding that he needed more than the $50 increments his options promised. J. L. said he'd think about it. A few days later, sitting in Gurney's office at Myron Selznick and Company, Bogart received his answer: No.

He was furious and bitter, his resentment probably deepened by the awareness, if not the full details, of the loan deal on *Dead End* that would enrich Warners and net him not an extra cent. Gurney pleaded with Warner. Bogart, he wrote, was very upset.

> There is no question in his mind but that you are the one motion picture producer to have faith in him and putting him into "PETRIFIED FOREST." . . . Humphrey points out that perhaps your attitude . . . is affected by the fact that after "PETRIFIED FOREST" he did eight or nine unimportant pictures—this was not his fault because "BLACK LEGION" proved that he was worthy of not only your faith in him but that "PETRIFIED FOREST" . . . had justified his being in more important pictures between that and "BLACK LEGION."
>
> I do wish, Jack, that you could see your way clear to reconsider this matter. . . . [Humphrey] has cooperated one hundred percent with your studio, has given nobody any trouble, and . . . has devoted much of his time to the radio and publicity departments.

The answer was still no, and would have been even had the agent written a better letter. Warners, under no constraints to pay, chose not to. Bogart's own agency was the agency of superstars, and it was willing to push only so far for a low-paid contract player. Jack Warner, a shrewd and ruthless judge of his employees' strengths and weaknesses, knew his man. True rebels like Cagney and Davis ran off to New York or London, sought loopholes, and dared court battles. Bogart would simply gripe and grumble and in the end fall into line, driven by his burdensome responsibilities and his overriding need for cash.

That summer, he was once again on loanout, this time to independent producer Walter Wanger. Bogart was cast as a heavy-drinking, outspoken producer in *Stand-In,* an amusing comedy starring Joan Blondell as a struggling actress and Leslie Howard as a Wall Street number cruncher appointed by a bank to run an ailing studio. Director Tay Garnett, who had directed the successful *One Way Passage* for Warners, later said that he'd taken on Bogart as a personal favor, over the considerable reservations of Wanger. More likely, he'd taken him on in self-defense. Over dinner one night with Garnett and Bogart, Mayo, who was fiercely ambitious for Bogart and resentful of the misuse of his talent, shouted at Garnett, "Why can't the best actor in the world get to play anything but heavies? And what the hell are you going to do about it?" Mayo's notion of doing something about it was to throw dishes at him from the supper table, including one or two, just to keep it even, aimed at Bogart.

Bogart's wry observations as the producer got some of the biggest laughs of the picture. Still, his Warner image preceded him. Garnett's assistant, watching Bogart in dailies, said, "You're crazy if you think you'll make a hero out of him—the son of a bitch lisps!" But loaning Bogart to Wanger was really a matter of good business for Warners. They had borrowed Henry Fonda from Wanger for one picture and wanted him for another. They got him, with Bogart thrown in at cost.

When Bogart returned to Burbank a few weeks later, he was assigned to a foreseeable disaster. If *Swing Your Lady,* a "Hillbilly musical," was as far removed as possible from what made Warners tick, it was as close as possible to Paramount's tremendously successful *Mountain Music;* and the Warners were great believers in the old movie adage "If it works, imitate it."

He was to play the lead as a small-time wrestling promoter touring the Ozarks with a dimwit fighter, the plot turning on the gnat-brained wrestler's infatuation with a feisty female blacksmith. Bogart's role was to be the straight man to Nat Pendleton as the lovelorn wrestler and to the Amazon charms of Louise Fazenda, who was also Mrs. Hal Wallis. The rest of the package included synthetic country production numbers and solo turns by "America's Hill-Billy Favorites, the One and Only Weaver Brothers & Elviry." The leading lady was Penny Singleton, later the heroine of the B-movie series based on the comic-strip *Blondie. Swing Your Lady* was considered mild fun for its time. It was also obvious, patronizing, and filled with embarrassing stereotypes. The studio urged it on exhibitors as "the gosh-durndest laff riot. . . . The guffawin'est goings-on since Uncle Rafe got et by the pigs!"

Bogart refused to be part of it, and for once he had the top-level backing of his representatives. Myron Selznick and his associate, the bi-coastal agent Leland Hayward, were the prototype of the all-powerful talent office and the terror of industry executives. Earlier, the two had succeeded in shattering the gentleman's agreement among studio heads, under which they refrained from hiring actors away from each other. Previously, stars whose contracts were up would find the other studios not interested, and holdouts had a way of vanishing from the screen. Now, stars' fees multiplied exponentially, and at one time or another the agency represented, among others, Katharine Hepburn, William Powell, Myrna Loy, Fredric March, Miriam Hopkins, Kay Francis, Henry Fonda, James Stewart, Fred Astaire, Ginger Rogers, and Greta Garbo.

Even though Bogart was still far from being in such company, his persistence with his agents got their attention. Six days before the start of shooting, Hayward phoned Jack Warner's executive assistant, Max Arnow, at his home. In no way, he said, would Bogart play this role. Arnow responded with a prompt order to have Bogart report to him at 9:45 the next morning, and made a note to contact Wallis and J. L.

Bogart reported on schedule to the second floor of the small tile-roofed executive building where Wallis and Warner worked in their adjoining suites. Actors turned down roles all the time, bringing on the professional limbo of suspension without pay, generally lasting until the end of the picture the ungrateful actor had so unwisely refused. It was a hardship imposed industrywide to keep the workers in line and to drive home the point that stars shine only as long as the studios want.

Still, Warner and Wallis were taken aback by Bogart's position. They had never had a flat no from their grumbling but ultimately docile heavy. They knew, too, that while Bogart lived modestly, he needed money. Accordingly, Wallis dangled a $200 carrot. Call it additional compensation, he said; all Bogart had to do was agree to make *Swing Your Lady* and they'd up his salary to $1,000 a week, starting the day he went before the camera.

With the burden of two households to support plus Frances's psychiatric bills, it was an offer he couldn't refuse. But it came at the expense of his self-esteem, a sensibility Jack Warner would trample on many times. The whole matter left him determined never to be financially muscled again, and he resolved to build up a cash reserve he later referred to as "F-Y money."

Despite surprisingly kind reviews, *Swing Your Lady* was a box office catastrophe, clearing barely $24,000 over its costs and adding nothing to either the Warner coffers or Bogart's reputation. "The worst picture I ever made," he said. The film would be remembered largely for the entrance, halfway through the story, of Ronald Reagan, a $200-a-week contract player making his A-film debut with a press card in his hat and the opening line, "I'm Jack Miller, Associated Press." The amiable young sports announcer from Des Moines had tested for Warners three months earlier and had already begun filming B movies.

However difficult Warners' cavalier attitude toward him was for Bogart, the studio was delighted with its property. Bogart had proved his worth as a durable, marketable talent. And so, working as always according to their convenience rather than his, Warners negotiated a new long-term agreement. Bogart looked as though he would soon be more valuable, and the studio jumped in as early as possible to make the best deal it could. By December, Bogart was signed for four more years. He was guaranteed forty weeks' work, starting at $1,100, with an option for an additional two years at $2,000 per week.

In two years he had nearly doubled his salary, with the promise of regular raises to come. It should have been a time of celebration. Instead, Warners chose to observe his new contract with something called *Men Are Such Fools,* a romantic farce so weak that, at one point, Wallis was ready to scrap the whole thing. He probably would have done so if the story about hanky-panky in an ad agency had not already been purchased for Busby Berkeley, Warners' resident musical comedy genius, who yearned for new challenges.

Berkeley should have stuck with choreography. The direction was lackadaisical, and the film, said one reviewer, echoing the sentiments of many, was "depressingly bad." Bogart played a fast-talking account executive, with third billing after Wayne Morris and Warner ingenue Priscilla Lane. In a scene he resisted to the last, Bogart, in a shoulders-to-thigh bathing suit, does a passable dive off the edge of a swimming pool. Commenting on the film, not the dive, *The New York Times* called the result "sad and aimless." It earned a profit of $10,000.

On March 28, 1938, Humphrey Bogart announced his forthcoming marriage to Mayo Methot, the ceremony to be held at sea on the Hatches' yacht as soon as his divorce from Mary Philips became final.

He and Mayo were by now a common sight in the Hollywood clubs and on trips back East. Still, Bogart hoped that Mary would change her mind, and he seemed more resigned than looking forward to marrying Mayo. But any chance for a reconciliation with his wife faded when Philips called Baker from New York, breathlessly happy. Kenneth MacKenna was back in town, and would Baker please pick up her interlocutory decree because she and Ken were getting married.

Six days before Bogart's announcement, Mary opened on Broadway, opposite Roland Young in the comedy *Spring Thaw.* Brooks Atkinson declared it "a pleasure to see Miss Mary Philips again after so long an absence, for surely she is one of the most skillful, as well as one of the most unappreciated, actresses in America."

In August, Mary and Ken MacKenna were married. A week later, on the twentieth, Humphrey DeForest Bogart married Mayo June Methot Morgan. It was the third time around for each. For some, three is a charm. Not for this couple.

CHAPTER 5

"If It's a Louse-Heel, Give It to Bogart"

The marriage was not held at sea, after all, but at the Bel Air home of Mel and Mary Baker on Stone Canyon Road. Gloria Stuart and her play- and screenwriter husband, Arthur Sheekman, had recently come to know Bogart and Methot through the Bakers and would soon become their close friends. Stuart was called on to help Mayo. "She was very broke. She didn't have an appropriate outfit, and Bogie didn't buy her one." Baker asked Stuart if she had something appropriate that would fit, but Methot was much smaller. Finally another friend loaned her a beaded number with a matching hair band, appropriate for garden-party elegance, and so the "something borrowed" traditionally worn by a bride was, in Mayo's case, her wedding dress. Bogart wore a light-colored suit with a darker plaid tie and boutonniere.

Mary Baker planned every detail of the beautifully catered outdoor ceremony, held on the grounds of her home in the high-priced, gated residential area a mile or so west of Beverly Hills. A cordon of studio cops controlled the knots of onlookers gathered to watch the celebrities as they arrived. Cocktails were served on the terraced lawn sloping up to the badminton court, and long tables were set for a sit-down meal for forty or fifty people, which some remember as breakfast and others as dinner. Everyone remembers that there was a great deal of drinking, particularly of Black Velvets, an especially lethal mixture of champagne and Guinness stout.

In two hours, "everyone was blind," said screenwriter Allen Rivkin, and the terraced lawn a hazard beneath unsteady feet. Even so, Stuart was able to see quite clearly when "Mischa Auer took off his pants. Literally opened his belt, dropped his trousers, got up on one of the tables. He had shorts on, and his shirt and necktie, and he was running back and forth on top of the tables. Everybody thought that was terribly amusing." Everybody with the exception of Judge Ben Lindsay, who, Baker told Joe Hyams, looked as though he were about to have a stroke. He had performed the brief civil ceremony, with incidental harp music by one of the guests, Mrs. Walter Abel, there with her actor husband.

The day ended with a monumental fight between the bride and groom. In Mary Baker's view, "It could have been anything. Bogie probably was bouncing with some girl." The upshot was that Bogart promptly collected his best man and host, Mel Baker, then drove off to spend the night somewhere else. According to one friend, they got as far as Tijuana, just across the border from San Diego. Mary, her head reeling, staggered off to bed; soon Mayo fell in beside her and they slept it off. The next day, Bogart collected his bride and sent a rubber plant by way of apology. It was the curtainraiser on the long-running drama billed thereafter as "The Battling Bogarts."

Even before the wedding, the Bogart home on the corner of North Horn and Shoreham in West Hollywood had become an arena for knockdown fights, fueled by alcohol and audible many houses away. Often one of the combatants, usually Bogart, would wind up at the home of screenwriter George Oppenheimer or some other sympathetic neighbor, "muttering about what a shit the other was." Oppenheimer increasingly had difficulty equating the harried heavy drinker with the good-looking, well-mannered boy he knew from their early days.

Noise was what Cynthia Lindsay, a Busby Berkeley swimmer in *Footlight Parade* (1933), remembered. "Noise and screaming and yelling and 'fuck you!' and all kinds of expletives." Lindsay and her husband, actor Russell Gleason, were good friends with writer Betty Reinhardt and her director husband, John, who lived directly across the street from the Bogarts and whose living room Bogart treated like an addition to his own home. Whenever Lindsay was at the Reinhardts', "Bogie was there. He would simply come in as if this was his home away from home. If dinner was ready, he'd have dinner," almost always without Mayo.

Since Bogart seldom showed the effects of alcohol in slurry speech or uncoordinated movement, the best test for telling whether he was sober or drunk was to watch his behavior. "Sober," Allen Rivkin said, "Bogart was great. Drunk, he was a dirty bastard." Cynthia Lindsay agreed. "He was either perfectly charming or totally belligerent, but his belligerence was never against somebody who was either bigger or stronger or more mentally powerful. He would come in and be sweet and charming and then find somebody who looked weak and defenseless and get him. Allen Vincent, a marvelous man [who would win an Academy Award for *Johnny Belinda* (1948)], was often there. He was kind of delicate, and homosexual, and Bogie would just go for him; he would say, 'Why don't you stand up and defend yourself?' And Allen didn't want to fight."

But Mayo did, and the battles spilled out into the street so often that after time the neighbors tended to ignore them. One night, guests gathered at the Reinhardts' were brought to their feet by more than the usual commotion. Cynthia Lindsay gaped at the scene being played out on the Bogart roof, silhouetted in the light of the upstairs windows.

"We heard this ruckus, and there was Mayo with a noose around her neck, running across the top of the building—on a kind of balcony on the lower part of the roof. He was chasing her like a dog on a leash." Others remembered Bogart yelling, "I'm going to hang you!" but no one seemed worried. In fact, Lindsay said, "We were all laughing hysterically; nobody had the feeling that anybody was really going to hurt anyone, because Bogie was chicken."

In Mayo, Bogart had found someone eager to take up his challenge, perennially spoiling for a fight; but unlike her husband, she was quick to move from verbal to physical attack. Mayo may have been short, but she inherited her father Captain Jack Methot's broad shoulders and thick, athletic neck. Her deft right-hand jab was probably from her father, too, and she was quick to use it, without warning and with great force.

To Allen Rivkin, "Mayo was a tough broad," and a jealous wife. He saw the couple at dockside one day, waiting to be ferried to one of the gambling ships then moored outside the three-mile limit. Mayo caught Bogart looking at another woman, and "she slugged him and he fell into the water." On another occasion, Rivkin received a whispered phone call from Bogart, asking him to come over immediately. He did, and found his friend huddled beneath the long, winding staircase in the front hall. "She's throwing bottles," Bogart told Rivkin from his crouch. With a witness present, Bogart thought it was safe to come out. As Rivkin watched, he crept upstairs, looking to the writer like some gangster in one of his own movies, and made it to the landing. Whereupon a door opened and "she reached out and slugged him on the head with a bottle."

Such behavior was hardly unusual. In a small bistro in Laguna Beach, fifty miles south of Los Angeles, the novelist Niven Busch (*Duel in the Sun*) saw Bogart and "a plumpish blond lady whose pictures I'd seen" at the far end of the bar, quarreling in subdued tones. The woman was Mayo, and he watched as the quarrel grew more heated. When Busch turned away for a moment to talk with some friends, "I heard this resounding slap that commanded attention throughout the floor. And I said, 'Oh, Jesus! Bogie has hit this woman.' " He turned to look and saw that it was just the opposite. "Mayo had conked him with a backhanded swipe and knocked him from the bar stool. It was so funny!" Bogart scrambled to his feet and, after he took his seat at the bar, dabbed his head with ice water. By then the quarrel was over and Mayo had become "quite solicitous."

It was a familiar conclusion. Mayo was generally attentive after the damage was done. "Their fights usually ended in bed," Mary Baker said. And Bogart told an interviewer at the time, "I love a good fight. So does Mayo. We have some first-rate battles."

Bogart's friend the sculptor and actress Henrietta Kaye, who had known the Bakers in New York ("She mothered me") and visited them in California, remembered sitting in a garden swing on Sunday afternoons, watching their famous friends. "The Bogarts were always there along with a great many writers like Nunnally Johnson and that crowd. Bogie and Mayo would get very drunk and the group would egg them on. It was part of a big joke"—in the way bearbaiting is a sport. To the young woman, it had all the earmarks of a ritual dance, "something to do with their sex life because they were obviously hung up on each other." But whatever the sexual benefits of their behavior, instead of this being a case of mutual love, it was more a matter of mutual destruction.

Bogart called her "Sluggy," bragged about ducking punches and joked about living dangerously. It was much darker than that. His friends were to call him an abused husband; in reality, he contributed his share of mistreatment. Gloria Stuart and her husband were with the Bogarts amidst a packed house one evening at Slapsie Maxie's, former light-heavyweight boxing champion Maxie Rosenbloom's club on Wilshire Boulevard, which was famous for its comedy revues and billed as the "Laughing Spot of California." As usual, Mayo and Bogart got into a row that escalated until he told her, "You say that once more, Sluggy, and I'm going to clip you."

"Well, I'm saying it once more," she responded.

Stuart watched as Bogart immediately "leaned over and he pushed her into the next table, really *whammed* her. To me, it wasn't funny. I got up and said something about 'You son of a bitch,' and went over to pick up Mayo.

"Of course the whole place fell silent. And he turned to Arthur and said, 'Well, wouldn't you have hit her?' Arthur said, 'Not necessarily.' In the meantime, she was crying. The entire place was silent as I picked her up. Then I led her out, followed by the two men. But she always had a black eye, or wounded cheek or something, and dark glasses. They really had a physical relationship."

The stories of the Bogarts' drinking and domestic violence rapidly became part of the Hollywood lore of the time. They were wholly suited to his rough-and-tumble screen image—Bogart dodging flying bottles; Bogart locked out of the house, spending the night sleeping on the lawn. The news media found it all colorful and amusing because the behavior was understandable, Rivkin said. A real man of that era was a hearty drinker; someone who went out and *didn't* get drunk was "some sort of fairy." But Bogart and Mayo's drinking and fighting were less an amusing mating dance than a matter of a pair in desperate need of help.

On the surface of the domestic drama was a lifestyle that reflected the outward appearance of simple, suburban middle age. Gertrude Hatch Chase called Mayo "a great housekeeper." The house at 1210 North Horn, or 2727 Shoreham, depending on which door was used, was filled with an assortment of cats and canaries, and a quartet of dogs led by a huge black Newfoundland named Cappy. The place even had a name, though not a conventional one like "Northern Light" or "Shore Cottage." It was "Sluggy Hollow." A garden was planted in the back and a gardener engaged, though Bogart liked to putter there in his free moments. For the first time since Bogart moved to Los Angeles, there was also a cook, May Smith, a tall African American of great dignity and talent who soon became one of the family.

A benign influence on the couple was Mayo's mother, Beryl Evelyn Wood Methot, known as Buffy, who came down regularly from Oregon. She was a hearty, intelligent woman and a respected Portland journalist whose self-sufficiency contrasted starkly with her daughter's insecurity. Mayo worshiped her mother and visibly regressed into the role of adoring, dependent child in her presence.

Bogart liked his mother-in-law immensely and in preparation for the visits would lay in cases of beer, her drink of choice. He admired Buffy's independence, her sense of humor, her love of good talk and, perhaps most of all, her ability, like her daughter's, to match him drink for drink, the hallmark of good fellowship in her world and in his. With Buffy, he could play the surrogate son in a bluff give-and-take free of the emotional baggage that to the end weighed down his relations with Maud. Mayo got on with Maud even better than Bogart did with Buffy, Gertrude Chase said. "She was devoted to Bogie's mother, who adored her."

Maud had come for a visit in the late thirties and stayed.

Life in the end disappointed Maud Humphrey—James Whistler's pupil, the society doctor's wife, the once celebrated artist reduced, at age seventy, to drawing sewing patterns for the Butterick Pattern Company on Fourteenth Street in New York. Bogart had long been uneasy about her living alone, but Maud was not about to give up her independence, and he knew it. Whenever someone hinted that perhaps he was being neglectful, his reply was always the same: "When Maud stops working, she'll die."

"And I think I was right," he said in retrospect.

But one day during their frequent telephone conversations, Maud, chattering about her work in a surprisingly youthful voice, broke off after a few minutes. "Oh, I almost forgot to tell you. I'm on strike." Bogart tried to picture Queen Maud with a picket sign. "You don't belong to a union," he managed to get out. "What are you *striking* for?"

Well, she said, no one had come to work that morning, and her best friend, the girl at the next easel, was downstairs on the picket line and she was getting lonely anyway. "So I just went down to be on strike with the rest of them. I've been walking down Fourteenth Street all afternoon."

"That," said Bogart, "was when I insisted she come West for a rest. Temporarily, naturally." Maud never returned to New York, a Victorian transplanted to an alien world. "She thought California a pretty rough place. It had no traditions, no social background."

He took an apartment for her on Sunset Boulevard, two blocks from Schwab's Drugstore, the chapel of the industry. "She joined its congregation," an amused Bogart later said. "She was Lady Maud with a vengeance. . . . Schwab's provided her with the activity she missed in retirement. She . . . made little purchases and then strolled grandly home again."

Even so, there was something sad and ironic about the still-regal woman left behind by time, and witness to arguments between husband and wife even more vicious than those she and Belmont inflicted on their children. The person who had belittled her son's entry into show business would now accost strangers and tell them, "I'm Humphrey Bogart's mother, you know," as if to remind the world—and herself—that she was still someone of consequence.

To her son's friends, however, she was a somewhat dotty presence, always at the house. Gloria Stuart found her a charming but essentially vague figure in the background, little more than the wallpaper. "You'd walk in for dinner, and you'd say, 'How do you do, Mrs. Bogart? Nice to see you.' Then you'd have dinner and play cards and she'd disappear."

Cynthia Lindsay found her "a very jittery lady, rather fey. I don't say 'mad,' but she was a little out of it." Midway through one party, Maud became nervous in the company of so many people and Bogart asked Lindsay to take his mother for a walk in the garden. Lindsay "took her out in the garden and she suddenly leaped into my arms, grabbed my neck and started to scream, which scared me to death. I didn't know what was the matter! Well, it was because a butterfly went by; she was terrified of flying things. So I calmed her down and brought her back in. But there were many mental problems in Bogie's family, and I had a sense that Bogie was just a little unbalanced. Not crazy, just a little unbalanced."

According to Mary Baker, the police often found Maud wandering along the Sunset Strip, aimlessly ambling among the streetwalkers, and would bring her quietly back to her son's door. Frances Bogart had similar problems. She knew she had periods of instability, and like an epileptic who can sense the early warnings of an attack, she did what she could to anticipate their erratic onset. She was a tall, angular, sweet-faced woman dressed always in tweeds and a matched cashmere sweater set, the uniform of the properly reared gentlewoman. But for Frances Bogart Rose, life had come down to watching for the early warnings of the violent episodes and counting on sufficient time to make it to a hospital. "If not," Baker said, "she was in trouble. Straitjacketed and everything else."

Sometimes her seizures made the papers. Among Bogart's friends, the attitude was, "Did you hear what she's done now?" On one occasion, she'd been found wandering down Sunset in her nightgown. On another, with the immense strength that sometimes accompanies derangement, she'd smashed a huge penny scale into a storefront. "The paper would come out, 'Humphrey Bogart's Sister Arrested on Sunset Boulevard,' " Stuart said. "She was an embarrassment and sad. And Bogie was very good about it."

The gentle, melancholy Frances was only a shadow of the vigorous, tennis-playing sister who had been his childhood companion. Even so, according to Joe Hyams, who spent time with them both, "Bogart adored her. He always spoke glowingly of her. She was crazy, but he liked crazy people, being married to Mayo all that time. And occasionally he was a little erratic from time to time; or eccentric, if you will. Unusual. So I always sensed that he was kind of proud of her in a way."

Frances lived near her brother, although her official mailing address of 1210 North Horn, Bogart's house, was indicative of his role as her caretaker. She came and went as she pleased but sometimes visited him in curious ways. Director Richard Brooks was at the Bogarts' one Christmas Eve. Just as it was getting dark, he noticed someone moving outside and told Bogart.

" 'Yeah,' he said, 'don't pay any attention.' It turned out to be his sister. She had come from the hospital. Finally she rang the doorbell. Then she came in and nobody made any comment. She seemed normal and everything else, but she was not well. *Why* was she looking in the windows? To see if everything was all right. Now *those* were the scary things."

Although Bogart harbored resentment at being left with the care of his sister and her child, he accepted the burden unquestioningly and according to his personal code, which was tied to last-century sensibilities. "There was a spirit of duty in the Victorian age," he once said, "which we have largely lost. Whether one enjoyed what one had to do or not, it had to be done, and that was that."

Despite his problems with Jack Warner, work became an anchor for him. In 1938, the year of his marriage to Mayo, Bogart made eight films for Warner Brothers. He was by then part of what was known with some justice as the Warner Family, in which security was assured and life was, if not always pleasant, at least predictable.

Part of the reason was a management style that while it may have encouraged confrontation, nevertheless established a clear and simple chain of command. A tiny group of autocratic, self-taught, dedicated, and above all talented men manipulated the controls in a way that left no doubt as to who was making the decisions and who would obey them. In the process, they continued to turn out fifty-two feature films a year, plus cartoons and short subjects, and they helped create an industry as well as an art form.

Atop the pyramid, of course, was Jack Warner. His formal education may have been limited, but not his ability to read a screenplay and find its weakness, or to know from a one-page synopsis of a submitted property whether it would play or not. Although he disliked actors and distrusted writers, he was a natural editor who loved the cutting room and had a spectacular feel for the pacing of a film. Even though he was outranked by his brother Harry, who as president controlled the purse strings, the studio was Jack Warner's empire and he was its tyrant. The two brothers were as opposite as oldest and youngest often are. Harry was conservative, proper, and a man of his word. Jack was flamboyant, a gambler and womanizer, and a man whose word was as good as his need. After Harry moved from New York to a bungalow on the lot in the late 1930s, their personal differences evolved into hatred as they struggled for control of the studio that benefited from a Harry Warner but required a Jack Warner to succeed. In 1956, Jack managed to grab control of the company in a duplicitous sell-out, buy-back scheme that cut out Harry. Harry died in 1958 at the age of seventy-six. Jack, a gambler on a par with King Farouk, was in the south of France at the time and continued his gaming in Monte Carlo rather than attend the funeral.

"Harry didn't die," his wife of fifty years Rea said after the service, "Jack killed him."

"You know that saying," Jack Warner Jr. said of his father to Aljean Harmetz: " 'Not to know him was to love him.' "

Below Warner were four men who oversaw the daily running of the studio.

In the office across from J. L., constantly bent over his reading, was the bear-like production boss Hal Wallis. His oversized head with its black, slicked-back hair protruded from his broad shoulders seemingly without the aid of a neck, making him seem taller than he was. Everybody snapped to attention when Wallis, usually wearing black-and-white saddle shoes and accompanied by three or four followers, made his frequent visits to the set. His salary grew to $5,000 a week, but eventually he wanted to produce his own films, which he did at Warners between 1942 and 1944. Among them were *Casablanca* and *Now, Voyager*.

Production manager Tennant Campbell "Tenny" Wright, the logistic counterpart and sometime rival of Wallis, had his office in the nearby production building. Wright was a heavyset, red-haired Irishman with a prominent jaw and the flattened nose of an ex-boxer, who raised homing pigeons as a hobby. His early work experience as a circus foreman commanding roustabouts made him uniquely effective in directing the legion of technicians that provided the studio support services.

Wallis and Wright ran two fiefdoms, at once complementary and competitive. Wallis, a former publicist, worked until late at night, screening every frame of A-picture footage. He pushed constantly for tight editing and tight direction to achieve the drumbeat momentum that was the hallmark of a Warner Brothers film. His flood of memos to the directors and producers—then called supervisors—commented on everything from the cutting of a single frame, to the length of Bette Davis's hair, to the lighting, which was invariably too bright for him. He insisted on what he called "sketchy lighting," the chiaroscuro gradations of dark and light that gave a film the distinctive quality that marked it as a Warner product.

Wright broke down the budgets, set up the schedules, cleared the stage space, and lined up the camera crews, grips, and electricians. He assigned the artists who sketched the sets and built scale models, and the carpenters, plasterers, and painters who on demand could create anything from a Washington, D.C., hotel room to a rock-strewn mountain pass. They built the basis for the illusions to be captured on film, transformed by light and sound and editing. Through their work, an actor on a gently rocking device seemed to be driving a car through an outdoor landscape; a slathering of glycerin in front of a camera lens and the wetting down of a simulated building front created a foggy autumn day in New York, all on a windowless soundstage.

While there was none of the decision by committee that is at the center of today's studios, there was always plenty of the jockeying for power found in any corporation. William Schaefer, who went to work for Jack Warner in 1933 and remained his secretary for forty-five years, saw nearly every day that "there wasn't a lot of love between Wallis and Wright." Wright came in early and would always phone J. L. at home with a rundown of what was happening on the lot. Any problems resulted in a call from Warner to Wallis. Wright's method, Schaefer said, was a little bit like the old ward-style politics. "Tenny was a good Irishman with good sources, and that's how the Tammany Hall worked. And I think Wallis resented it."

The company's legal affairs were handled in a similarly personalized manner by Roy J. Obringer, Warners' general counsel, the in-house expert on copyright and contracts who kept the stars in line. Obringer had Tyrone Power good looks, a Cheshire Cat smile, and a dry sense of humor, but his signature at the bottom of a suspension notice meant no money and no work.

Finally, there was Blayney Matthews, Warners' head of security and unofficial pipeline to the upper levels of local law enforcement. A reputed former FBI man, Matthews had worked in the office of Buron Fitts, the powerful Los Angeles district attorney who was the model for the corrupt DA in Raymond Chandler's novels. Matthews took a behind-the-scenes role in anything from fixing a speeding ticket to quashing a charge of statutory rape or vehicular homicide.

The studio security men always wore blue serge uniforms that made them look-alikes of the L.A. police. By the late 1930s, the self-enclosed city they served had its own generators and its own water, gas, and power lines. There were state-of-the-art facilities for film processing and sound, a transportation department that included vintage cars from almost every period, and a vast greenhouse. A huge two-story crafts building was an on-site factory with a machine tool workshop, forge, and foundry that turned out everything from battleship mockups to period furniture, and served as a sometime set for the factory floor scenes Warner writers loved. The studio even ran the twelve-thousand-member Warner Club, a lodge-style fraternal organization with a monthly newsletter and a yearbook giving members' birth and marriage dates and offering health and life insurance. There were twenty-seven hundred employees in the West Coast Studio Division, one of fifty clubs in the United States and abroad. Every one of the West Coast members, from Jack Warner to the lowest gofer, was expected to attend the annual dinner dance at the Biltmore, and any actor's absence was duly noted. "It was always black tie," Ronald Reagan said. "The Warner brothers kind of shut their eyes to the fact that those fellows out on the back lot didn't have tuxedoes. But they would slip in the back door of the wardrobe department and on the night of the dinner, they would all be in black tie!"

Bogart, by the late thirties, had become prominent enough to be included in a Warner Club parody listing the heavy-hitters of the time and sung to a Cole Porter tune:

You're the top, you're a Curtiz flicker.
You're the top, you're a Berkeley kicker.
You're the dulcet tone from the megaphone of Powell
You're a Francis passion, a Kelly fashion,
You're Bogart's scowl. . . .

By the end of 1939, Bogart the long-term contract player had made twenty-five pictures for Warners, but the difference in his roles was still often hard to discern. In *Racket Busters,* a quickie shot in less than four weeks, he played a ruthless mob boss brought to justice in the final reel. Production closed on a Tuesday night, and on Wednesday morning he started *King of the Underworld,* portraying a ruthless mob boss brought to justice in the final reel. In *The Oklahoma Kid,* he was a ruthless gambler gunned down by James Cagney, and seven months later, in *The Roaring Twenties,* a ruthless bootlegger gunned down by James Cagney. After his splash as Baby Face Martin in *Dead End,* he turned up successively as Pete Martin in one film, and Chuck Martin in another. Once a year at least, he wore prison garb. In *Angels with Dirty Faces,* Cagney got an immortal death house scene (pretending to fall apart on his way to the electric chair so that the Dead End Kids wouldn't make him a hero) and Pat O'Brien as the priest had a classic closing line ("All right, fellas, let's go and say a prayer for a boy who couldn't run as fast as I could"). Meanwhile Bogart, as a crooked lawyer, was gunned down yet again by Cagney, dying swiftly in a scene that few recall.

The Dead End Kids were clever, unruly New Yorkers who could drive a director crazy, but they also were gifted comic actors. Bogart liked them and joined in their stickball games between takes. In contrast, Cagney, who had to put up with their scene stealing, reportedly slapped one of them for ad-libbing on camera.

At times Bogart worked two films at once; he alternated shooting on *Virginia City,* a big-budget western, starring Errol Flynn in which he was a bandit chief, and *It All Came True,* a modest comedy in which he was a gangster holed up in a theatrical boardinghouse. For four weeks, he switched back and forth between the leering, pencil-thin-mustached western desperado John Murrell and Chips McGuire, alias Mr. Grasselli, the killer playing guardian angel to a gaggle of aging vaudevillians. It was a difficult part, according to Louis Bromfield, who wrote the story, made more difficult by the screenwriters' inability to decide whether the character was a good guy or a bad guy. "Nevertheless, Bogie turned in one of the best comedy performances I have ever seen."

For Bogart, it meant an almost surreal month, slipping in and out of two worlds that were in themselves illusions—between a dusty Nevada boomtown of the 1860s and a New York brownstone in the 1930s, between the cardboard sidewinder Murrell and the comically tough McGuire alias Grasselli. The Sunday before Christmas, he was Grasselli on Sound Stage 6 from nine to one, playing cards with the old folks ("My goodness, Mr. Grasselli, I can't get over the wonderful way you shuffle and deal!"). Without pausing for lunch, he changed and ran to Sound Stage 7, where, as Murrell, he crouched waiting in a manufactured canyon, with the look, as the screenplay described it, of a wolf sure of its prey ("We can finish off the wagon train easy!").

In *The Return of Dr. X,* his face coated with layers of blue-white makeup, his character was a corpse who comes back to life. "For God's sake," Jack Warner told director Vincent Sherman before they began, "get him to play something other than Duke Mantee." Bogart was Marshall Quesne, a resurrected electrocuted mad scientist with a nasty thirst for human blood. "If it'd been Jack Warner's blood or Harry's," he told journalist Richard Gehman, "I wouldn't have minded as much. The trouble was, they were drinking mine and I was making this stinking movie." He closed with his usual demise on a Wednesday. The following Tuesday he was in a World War I foxhole on Stage 11 for *The Roaring Twenties.* In *Invisible Stripes,* he took fourth billing to George Raft, Jane Bryan, and even, to his dismay, twenty-one-year-old William Holden, touching off a grudge still active in 1954 when the two co-starred in *Sabrina.* Holden proceeded to compound the resentment by his determination, in one sequence, to drive a motorcycle with Bogart as passenger in the sidecar. Bogart objected—"That S.O.B., he'll crack it up!"—but Holden insisted. He promptly ran the bike into a wall. Only egos were injured.

Bogart did the best with what he was given, perhaps comforted by director Konstantin Stanislavsky's axiom that there are no small roles, only small actors. In Bogart's case, it was more a matter of the *same* small role. After twenty-five films, The *Herald Tribune* found him acting with "more force than conviction," while the New York *Post* critic felt his work was growing "standardized. . . . He's always good though it is difficult to keep on being excited about it." Now and then, there were respites from the on-screen thuggery. He was a crusading youth worker in *Crime School* (1938). In *Dark Victory* (1939), he was Michael O'Leary, the love-struck Irish horse trainer nursing an unrequited passion for Bette Davis as Judith Traherne, the socialite horsewoman who dies nobly of a brain tumor in Warners' three-handkerchief classic. (Between scenes as O'Leary, Bogart was doing double duty on the sound stage next door as the heavy opposite a buckskin-clad James Cagney in *The Oklahoma Kid.* Cagney's costume included a white sombrero that made him look, Bogart said, like an outsized mushroom.)

The part of O'Leary "wasn't exactly right for him, but he was jolly good," said Geraldine Fitzgerald, then a young newcomer from the Irish theater, who played Davis's faithful secretary and friend. In the breaks between shots Fitzgerald and Bogart sometimes sat together and talked about life as a contract player. "His philosophy was to do everything, say yes to everything. It was something that he tried to promulgate for new young players. It was important that they should understand. He often said to me, 'Just do everything. You'll find your way. If you don't stick around—if you go away saying, "I must have something good"—you're not really giving it a chance at all.' "

It would later be common wisdom to cite Bogart's Irish stable hand as the apex of miscasting, but Howard Barnes in the New York *Herald Tribune* called his performance "splendid," agreeing with most of his fellow critics that in the words of one, "Humphrey Bogart shows that he can act without a gun in his pocket." The *Hollywood Reporter* proclaimed his performance "lastingly impressive." "Bogart, wonder of wonders, is simply a horse trainer," wrote the surprised Archer Winsten of the New York *Post,* "with a thick but not phony Irish brogue. After a while you stopped expecting him to whip out a rod. . . . You accepted him as a horse trainer. That's acting."

Ronald Reagan longed for Bogart's virile role "because of my love of horses and all, I would have loved to be the fellow in the stable." A proper midwesterner just eighteen months out of Iowa, he was instead cast as an alcoholic society friend of Davis, and was specifically directed to play the role as one of sexual ambivalence. The problem for Reagan was that "the director wanted it to be kind of a—well, as he described it once, a fellow that could sit down in the room while the gals were changing clothes and they wouldn't mind. And I didn't really *see* it that way." There was additionally a certain irony to the casting: Reagan, the small-town Irishman, playing the eastern socialite, while Bogart, the WASP preppie and New York patrician, played the Irish stable hand.

However, the central scene between the stable hand and the lady turns not on love of horses but lust for the woman. O'Leary, with caked boots and ruffled hair, tries to bed Traherne amid the bales of hay in the film's one sexy scene: "I'm as good as some of them that's playing around with you. . . . You wouldn't need to risk your lovely neck jumping horses for excitement. The nights I've laid awake thinking of you." His ardor turns to shock when she tells him she's dying.

"That stable scene is very beautifully played," Wallis wrote in a memo to director Edmund Goulding. "Davis was splendid in it and so is Bogart." Davis later gave credit to Bogart for his help in shooting several difficult scenes: "I thanked God for the help his performance gave me in playing mine."

For Bette Davis, *Dark Victory* was an apt description of her passage through the shooting that ran two weeks over schedule. There were bouts of illness, ending in an attack of hysterics as she struggled with her final scenes. "She cried very heavily," the unit manager reported, "and it was very difficult and very trying for everybody." As single-minded professionals, Bogart and Davis had their differences, but there also was mutual respect. Photographers on the set would catch them sitting together, Bogart chatting, Davis knitting, joined at times by Davis's first of her four husbands, bandleader Harmon Oscar "Ham" Nelson. (Davis publicly battled with the Motion Picture Academy for years over her claim that she named their statuette after Ham's middle name.) In the scrapbooks Davis kept as a kind of acerbic diary, there is a still from *Kid Galahad* of Bogart with Edward G. Robinson. In her strong printing alongside each of her costars is the caption, "Mush mouth Robinson the boy wonder and know it all Bogart the breaker of hearts."

In *Dark Victory,* Bogart finally had a chance for an emotional closing scene. The version previewed to an audience full of stars on March 7, 1939, ended not with the heroine's death but with Judith's treasured Thoroughbred winning the big race and her loved ones getting on with their lives in the spirit of it's-what-she-would-have-wanted. It was a finale, the producers agreed, to "take the edge off Judith's death and leave the theatre with the feeling of entertainment and optimism."

The audience didn't buy it, and Warners, quick to sense the mood, cut the sequence as "anticlimactic." Instead the film ended with Traherne, alone, meeting her death, as she told O'Leary earlier, "finely—beautifully." Also cut, however, was Bogart's close-out, stroking the horse, "tears . . . streaming down his tough face," according to the script directions—"She could have told them. . . . She knew. . . . It's in the breeding. If only the little lady could have been here to see it."

Off-screen, Bogart reportedly cried easily—Mary Philips once said that "he cried at card tricks"—but doing it on command was another matter. The film's dialogue director Irving Rapper, who knew Bogart from their days on Broadway, failed to get him to weep on-camera. Bogart, for all his mastery of acting, came up against an emotional barrier that he couldn't crack. "Irving," he finally said, "I *can't.*"

Dark Victory generated enough momentum to carry Bogart (after other actors had been considered) into the lead of Bette Davis's next picture, *The Old Maid,* once again directed by Edmund Goulding. The 1860s period drama of an unwed mother forced to turn over her young daughter to a married cousin was based on Zoë Akins's Pulitzer Prize–winning adaptation of an Edith Wharton novel. Bogart was to play Clem Spender, a man who dies a romantically early death but whose memory haunts the two women who love him—a figure, Goulding wrote to Wallis, "to remember throughout the play . . . important to our two girls."

Important enough, it seemed at first, to warrant going outside the company for the male lead. Goulding wanted David Niven, whose remake of *The Dawn Patrol* while on loan to Warners had been a hit. Inside the company, George Brent, the other lead in *Dark Victory,* also seemed a good possibility. Instead, five days after the order went out to casting director Steve Trilling to draw up a list, Wallis decided on Bogart.

It was two weeks before the previews of *Dark Victory* but well after the final cut and scoring. Possibly Wallis saw something in the Bogart scenes that he hadn't in those of Brent. Bogart in any case cost less than Brent, and certainly far less than Niven's rental from Sam Goldwyn.

Shooting began on March 15, a Wednesday. By the following Monday the studio executives knew they had made a mistake. The qualities needed for the brash, resentful groom of *Dark Victory* were unrelated to those of the stock nineteenth-century hero who was supposed to ignite the lifelong passion of Bette Davis and Miriam Hopkins. Before the day was over, the rumor on the set was that Bogart was out.

Wallis ordered the footage rushed to the lab for viewing on Tuesday. By Wednesday it was official. A change would require five days of retakes, a fortune by Warner standards, but never mind. George Brent was brought in, a six-foot vanilla foil to the embattled heroines. Studio memos made it clear that, all along, they had wanted an actor "important both [*sic*] in name, performance and appearance."

It was a humiliation. After making more than two dozen pictures without a problem, Bogart was simply dismissed. A Bette Davis biographer reported that on hearing the news, he stalked off the set in a rage. Studio memos referred cryptically to "stress." For Bogart, the bottom line was unmistakable: he'd come up a failure, a character actor who just couldn't cut it as a romantic lead.

In retrospect it is easy to see that the time and the context weren't right for what would become the Bogart image. It would be almost two years before he was again considered for a first-line role in an important picture, and not until *Casablanca,* in mid-1942, would the opportunity come to again play a romantic hero with an important female star.

Nine days after his dismissal from *The Old Maid* in March 1939, Bogart and Mayo joined a pack of Warner celebrities shipped via a Santa Fe Special to Kansas as decoration for the world premiere of Errol Flynn's *Dodge City.* The junket was a studio spectacular, the passenger list filled with stars, press, publicists, and politicians—from Ann Sheridan, "the Oomph Girl," to columnist Ed Sullivan to the publisher of the *Hollywood Reporter* to the governor of New Mexico.

Warners had gone all out to accommodate the guests. There were fourteen Pullmans, two dining cars, an observation car and lounge, plus the

"Gay Lady," a baggage car transformed into a western saloon, complete with cutouts of dance hall floozies. The Gay Lady, it was announced, would "be festively decorated and equipped with slot machines to be operated on a non-profit basis," all proceeds to be donated to the Motion Picture Relief Fund. The publicity department assured Jack Warner that the studio would take "every precaution against moral turpitude."

"Really, it was a saloon," said Jules Buck, who later would become a producer but was then a brash young photojournalist covering the scene. "And if they weren't screwing in the compartments they were doing it in the saloon because Warners had about ten or twelve girls in there. What a trip!"

The Bogarts, four cars down from the Gay Lady, traveled in drawing room A, next to Priscilla and Rosemary Lane, two of three beautiful sisters signed by Warners in the thirties, all three of whom had worked with Bogart. Priscilla, twenty-two, was a golden blonde, Rosemary a wavy brunette; both were great favorites with the press contingent. Bogart, an amateur photographer and hardly immune to the charms of his neighbors, joined the press and the sisters for a photo opportunity in the cleared saloon, borrowing a news camera to snap some photos of his own.

Sometime thereafter, Bob Wallace of United Press International and Buck were hurrying through the train when they stopped short in the vestibule of the Bogarts' car. Bogart was staggering drunk and Mayo was raging, an empty Coke bottle in one hand. A moment later, she smashed it against the paneling and lunged at him with the broken half. As she did, the reporters made their moves.

"Wallace was *big,*" Buck said. "He grabbed her arm. And I grabbed Bogie. Bob was very strong; he forced the Coke bottle out of her hand. She was really screaming at him, stepping on his feet. Bobby hit her. And Bogie, if he knew what was going on, it was a miracle. Thank God I knew which compartment he was in, and I threw him in there."

Out in the corridor, Mayo, still struggling in Wallace's grip, was screaming, "I'll kill the son of a bitch!"

(A studio flack, informed of the event, promptly turned pale. "Jesus! Did you get any pictures?" Buck assured him that they hadn't. "All the actors were protected in that town," he later said. "We really protected all of them.")

The Bogart marriage had grown steadily chaotic. Mayo's drinking, like her husband's, had increased. While Bogart worked constantly, she had landed only two small roles since *Marked Woman.* Her languishing career fed her resentment and increased her need for alcohol, adding greater pressure to a two-year-old marriage that had become a cycle of acrid misrepresentations, stormy arguments, and tearful reunions.

Yet quite amazingly, no traces of his private turmoil appeared in his work, or his work habits—unless, of course, all of it was projected in the burning anger that gave his screen performances that special edge. He clung to his professionalism with an almost obsessive determination: no lateness, no sick-outs, no blowups on the set, the 9:00 A.M. call unfailingly met. The daily production reports that are the diaries of his filmmaking in those years affirm work habits worthy of a teetotaling nine-to-five accountant.

One place Bogart and Mayo could get along was on the ocean. In the late thirties he bought a small powerboat and named it *Sluggy,* and they set out for Catalina whenever his shooting schedule allowed. No crew was needed, just Bogart at the helm, Mayo in the galley or on deck, Dr. Belmont DeForest's son and Captain Jack Methot's daughter, alone together, their demons calmed by the sea.

There were a few other islands of peace and sanity and calm, especially in their relationship with Buffy and in Mayo's easy assumption of the model daughter-in-law to Maud. But the great peacemaker in their lives remained the ubiquitous Mary Baker, the couple's general fixer. A small slip of paper with a few words in Bogart's curlicued, artist's handwriting was found among Mayo's scanty possessions after her death:

> Darling
>
> An afternoon with Baker has convinced me that we're both wrong—and me the worst offender—I love and I love you
>
> Bogie

Despite her pathological jealousy, Mayo shared Bogart's frustration with his one-note roles, and he made the change of pace *Stand-In* (1937) largely at her urging. In addition, she was careful with their money. According to Hyams, it was Mayo who steered Bogart to the firm of A. Morgan Maree, the financial manager and investment counselor to the stars. Maree put him on an allowance and remained his business adviser throughout his career. And it was Mayo who supported Bogart in an actor's inevitable move, a change of agents.

He had always been a negligible quantity at the Leland Hayward agency, where the emphasis, naturally enough, was on stars and not on mid-level players with careers stuck in neutral. In later years, none of

Hayward's many write-ups as either agent or Broadway producer (*South Pacific, The Sound of Music*) would ever note that Humphrey Bogart had once been a client.

"Leland Hayward had just picked him up in New York and got him for peanuts," said agent Sam Jaffe, to whom Bogart turned in late 1938. "And you know what it was like in those days. He was a seven-hundred-fifty-dollar actor and Leland wasn't going to give him too much time. Yet Bogie was very demanding of his agents then. He was already beginning to fight for better roles."

It was Mary Baker, his eternal fairy godmother, now with Jaffe's office, who brought Bogart to the agency whose clients included Fredric March. Jaffe was a small, hardworking man whose understated manner concealed a core of toughness and integrity. He was also well-connected in the family manner common to Hollywood; his sister and partner, Ad, was married to former Paramount head of production B. P. Schulberg and was the mother of writer Budd Schulberg. Jaffe, together with Baker, took on the management of Bogart's career. Within a decade, Bogart would be the industry's highest-paid actor.

In late 1938, however, that prospect seemed as impossible as Bogart being convincing in a romantic lead. He was a well-established nearly thirty-nine-year-old character player with a solid contract and many years ahead of him in safe supporting roles. He was also undersized, rapidly balding, middle-aged—and intent on being a star.

In August, Bogart asked Jaffe to take him on as a client during a lunch at Romanoff's, the fancy Beverly Hills restaurant that catered to Hollywood's elite. Jaffe was a realist who pointed out what Bogart had going for and against him. Still, Bogart's deep determination and striking combination of intelligence and sexual energy impressed him. "Here was a man that read. He had breeding. People think that he was just a drunk and that all he did was have fights. But he always surrounded himself with writers—he admired writing. In that respect he was a lot different than most actors. And he wanted to go forward. He was sincere about getting parts. He was ambitious. And he was going to have a fight on his hands with the kind of company Warners was." Jaffe agreed to pay Leland Hayward half of Bogart's commission for the next several years, and the switch was made. Jaffe knew that "we were going to have trouble, but I felt he had a future. I was one of the few that felt that he could be a leading man."

If anyone at Warners shared that view, he kept it to himself. Almost immediately after Bogart switched agents, he was stuck in the prison-yard potboiler *You Can't Get Away with Murder.* Bogart was disappointed in the assignment and for once it showed, his actions the exception to his otherwise exemplary behavior at work. The unit manager complained repeatedly in his reports that Bogart was "stumbling continually over his dialogue." And why not? These were recycled lines that were by now familiar to the point of numbness. Certainly the end product was nothing for him to look forward to. The ads had the usual lurid head shot and display type that blared, "SIXTY-THREE CENTS WORTH OF ELECTRICITY WOULD END THIS MENACE FOREVER!"

For some critics, the film was evidence of the short-sightedness of the studio. "When you see a picture with such a flatly derivative title as *You Can't Get Away with Murder,*" wrote Bosley Crowther in *The New York Times,* "it is almost impossible to suppress the impish question: 'What about movie producers?' . . . Warners most valuable stock players like Humphrey Bogart . . . are held not so much by five-year contracts, as by five-year sentences."

While his own studio paid seemingly little attention to furthering Bogart's career, other producers, thanks to *Dark Victory,* were looking seriously at him. Walter Wanger wanted Bogart for what he called "a very serious part" in a film starring his wife, Joan Bennett. Warners said no. Darryl Zanuck at Twentieth Century–Fox wanted him for a remake of the 1929 Paul Muni hit, *The Valiant,* and offered to put off shooting until Bogart was available. J. L. and Wallis were not interested. Universal wanted to cast him opposite Mae West and W. C. Fields in *My Little Chickadee* and presented their case to Warner casting director Steve Trilling, who would later be J. L.'s executive assistant. "They have only a temp script," Trilling told Wallis, "but would like Bogart to come over and they will tell him the story. They are so confident in the meatiness of this part that they are willing to abide on his judgment."

But George Raft had just turned down *It All Came True, Virginia City* needed a villain, and Warners needed a workhorse to do both jobs at once. Universal's request was rejected; Bogart's plans, the studio decided, were just "too uncertain."

The most frustrating offer that couldn't be taken came from Lewis Milestone, the director of *All Quiet on the Western Front,* who wanted Bogart for John Steinbeck's *Of Mice and Men.* It was a quality part that hadn't come Bogart's way since *Dead End* and Jaffe pleaded with Warners to loan him out. No, the studio answered, they needed Bogart for *The Roaring Twenties,* and since they didn't know what his assignment after that would be, they were making no commitments. *Of Mice and Men* went on to a Best Picture nomination. Bogart stayed on the assembly line.

"They gave him nothing," Jaffe said. "I mean, what the hell did they do for him? He wasn't getting what he was supposed to, he was being constantly mistreated. Manhandled. Dictated. Belittled." Echoing the *Times,* Jaffe said that "being under contract was like being condemned to jail." Even in various films that would become genre classics, Bogart was relegated to the shadows while the spotlight fell on others. He remained the sidekick (he would later refer to the years he had played "George Raft's brother-in-law") and everybody's nemesis.

The end of the thirties was a time of creative glory for Hollywood: *Gone With the Wind; Wuthering Heights; Jezebel; Mr. Smith Goes to Washington; Bringing Up Baby; Goodbye, Mr. Chips; You Can't Take It with You; Stagecoach; Ninotchka; Dark Victory;* and *The Wizard of Oz* all came out within a short time span. But for Bogart, the coming decade held little promise.

His lack of standing caused problems for Warner publicists, who had to contend with Bogart's low status on the one hand and his desperation for exposure on the other. They did their best for him, but there was only so much they could do. A regional paper such as the Chicago *American* might pick up a release about Bogart paired in *Crime School* with "lovely Gale Page," a radio star making her screen debut, but it was hardly the big time. To Carl Schaefer, who handled the foreign press and admired Bogart's ability, "He was kind of a nuisance in those early days." When a reporter for, say, *The Times* of London was brought onto the set for prearranged interviews with other actors, Bogart would often materialize with a nervously jovial greeting, "Oh, hi, Carl, how are you?"

"He was seen as too obvious and too available. They wanted the Dead End Kids, not Humphrey Bogart. Or they wanted Jimmy Cagney." Usually, though, some kind of deal could be struck so that a few minutes were spent with Bogart before moving on to the main event. Duke Mantee was passé. With B roles in A pictures, Bogart seemed on his way to becoming an upgraded Barton MacLane, the beefy red-headed heavy and king of the B's whose career was less ambiguous than Bogart's.

Bogart's plight was due not just to the studio's myopia. The Catholic Church–backed Legion of Decency's campaign against "immoral" pictures allegedly glorifying crime had caused the Motion Picture Producers and Distributors of America, under Will H. Hays, to adopt a self-imposed code of ethics in 1930. On July 1, 1934, this self-censorship was institutionalized in the Production Code Administration. Its director was Joseph I. Breen, and without the imprimatur of what came to be called the Breen Office, no film could be released.

The regulations were lengthy, strict, and clear. Among them: "Scenes of passion should not be introduced when not essential to the plot"; "The sanctity of the institution of marriage and the home shall be upheld. Pictures shall not infer [*sic*] that low forms of sex relationships are the accepted or common thing"; "Methods of crime shall not be explicitly presented"; "Illegal drug traffic must never be presented"; "Miscegenation is forbidden"; "Pointed profanity (this includes the words God, Lord, Jesus, Christ—unless used reverentially—Hell, S.O.B., damn, Gawd), or other profane or vulgar expressions, however used, is forbidden"; "Ministers of religion . . . should not be used as comic characters or villains."

The impact of the Code had been particularly severe on Warners, whose pictures showed a perceptible shift of tone in the sentimentalization of the anti-heroes who had been their stock in trade. As film historian Thomas Schatz points out, "The hard-edged antisocial type popularized by Cagney and Robinson and Muni had quite literally been outlawed by the Breen Office."

For those stars to continue, their characters needed modifying, with punishment for their worst faults. Though the Cagney-Robinson-Muni characters were still crooked, underneath it all, they were redeemable nice guys: generous, attractive to women, kind to children; bad men who were cleansed in a splendid death scene. But someone had to pay for their crimes, and the Bogart character was perfect. His exuberant wickedness led him to kill and be killed in a violent ending satisfactory both to audiences and the PCA, thereby letting the hero die nobly regardless of his sins. By the late thirties, the notion had become a concept and the concept had a name: the "Bogart role." "The word was," Vincent Sherman said, " 'If it's a louse-heel, give it to Bogart.' "

George Raft had refused the Grasselli part in *It All Came True,* calling it "a Humphrey Bogart part," and thus unfit for any self-respecting star. For *Dark Victory,* there were two kinds of ads. The "class" ads showed Bette Davis alone. The "Group III" ads were "designed for use in situations where 'class' ads have not proven successful," and showed the patrician Davis kissing the commoner Bogart. The understanding was clear among merchandisers of Warner films: Bette Davis was class. Humphrey Bogart was not.

The one incident that more than any other symbolizes Bogart's position at Warner Brothers is how, in 1939, he came to be given top billing for the first time.

In May 1938 he was teamed with Kay Francis in *Unlawful,* a low-budget remake of the 1935 Paul Muni thriller *Dr. Socrates.* Seven years earlier, Francis had reigned as the queen of the movies, and Warners, at great expense, had wangled her away from Paramount. Depression audiences eagerly plunked down their quarters to weep their way through the stylish brunette's travails in pictures such as *Girls About Town, Ladies' Man,* and *One Way Passage,* to be awed by her wardrobe, and to laugh at her occasional comedies. By the late thirties, however, she had been eclipsed by the younger, more dynamic Bette Davis. All Warners had to show for their trouble was a vastly overpaid actress who no longer drew big audiences. Hoping to make her walk out on her $200,000 contract, the studio stopped giving her good leads. Francis had countered with a lawsuit demanding cancellation with full payment. Warners, intent on forcing separation on their own terms, sent her to the Foy unit. Francis, a tough, heavy-drinking woman who had been educated in a convent, gritted her teeth and said she'd scrub floors if that's what it took to continue drawing her salary.

Unlawful was her sixth B picture. "It was a comedown," said Sherman, who was brought in to cobble together a screenplay that could be shot in the twenty days allotted. "She was the highest-paid actress on the lot—and they sent her to Brynie. They thought she'd walk. But she didn't."

Francis and Bogart had no illusions as to why she was there. On the set, they were professionals making the best of a bad situation, with Bogart determined to see his co-star through the process as quickly and painlessly as possible. They got along well. They also had ex-spouses married to one another—in the early thirties Francis had briefly been Mrs. Kenneth MacKenna. Both Bogart and Francis were friends of writer Louis Bromfield and had visited him at Malabar Farm, his new 715-acre home near Mansfield, Ohio. Bromfield, who won the Pulitzer Prize in 1924 for *The Green Bay Tree,* was a prolific writer—he published 34 books in 33 years and also wrote stories that were turned into screenplays—and an ardent farmer with utopian agricultural ideals. Francis, especially, was a familiar sight to the Malabar help, carrying pails of milk into the house in winter while wearing a mink coat.

Francis, said Sherman, "was a nice lady. We got along fine." She and Bogart even helped him out with the script. Writers were officially barred from the Warner sets, but Sherman was there every day, tooling away at the unfinished scenario and trying to make sense of a story about a killer with a Napoleonic complex (Bogart, of course) and a physician (Francis) who subdues him with toxic eyedrops. Director Lewis Seiler, a house director with a predilection for glacial pacing, never bothered to consult the script the night before and arrived on the set each morning not quite knowing what to do. The picture was being shot as it was being written, a routine disquieting to studio hands, who cherished predictability. "Miss Francis, Bogart and the writer worked on the script," the unit manager complained to production manager Tenny Wright. "If . . . the director knew his story and would not depend on the writer to straighten it out . . . we could make a far better showing."

In at least one instance, however, there was a little levity. Arthur Silver of the trailer department wrote a monologue—Bogart as the killer talking of his rise to power—to be used in the coming attractions for the film. It was the usual stuff, Silver said, "how he started on the streets of New York, and how he had to fight his way up and the things he had to do to reach the top of gangland. And towards the end he was to say something like, 'And now I'm king of the underworld, and *nobody* is better than I am!' "

Silver brought the camera to the set and Bogart read the copy. Then without a pause at the end, he jabbed his forefinger at the center of the lens—"*And that goes for you, too, Jack Warner!*"

But the studio had the last laugh. In January 1939 the film was released, its title now *King of the Underworld.* Kay Francis might not have rated the above-title billing of her stardom days, but she had certainly expected, at the least, the first place below the title, with Bogart in second place. That is how the credits had read through the end of filming in August. But the studio was doing all it could to get one more film out of Francis before her contract expired, and a return on the $60,000 they still owed her. When, shortly before the picture's release, it appeared that their efforts would fail, Jack Warner approved a billing change to go with the new title:

HUMPHREY BOGART

IN

KING OF THE UNDERWORLD

WITH

KAY FRANCIS

It was conceivably the first time that the supporting player drew nine times the salary of the ostensible star. Even the usually cynical industry was stunned, as was the press. "It never occurred to us," *The New York Times* commented, "that one day we might be the organizer of a Kay Francis Defense Fund. But after sitting through *King of the Underworld* at the Rialto, in which Humphrey Bogart is starred while Miss Francis, once the glamour queen of the studio, gets a poor second billing, we wish to announce publicly that contributions are now in order. . . . Meaner advantage was never taken of a lady."

By that time Kay Francis had left Warner Brothers, her contract finally completed and with gracious notes exchanged between Jack Warner and her. In September 1938, she announced her retirement. She would make several more pictures—one of them at Warners—but for all intents and purposes, her career was over. For Bogart, the billing was at best meaningless and at worst a cruelty.

That December, he turned forty, a frustrated, middle-aged actor who not only was cast again and again to portray evil on the screen, but who had just been employed as a sort of real-life hit man against another actor. After six years in Hollywood, he had a brawling marriage, two agents who believed in him, and three dependents in various stages of mental illness and/or alcoholism. His large salary notwithstanding, he was in constant need of money and therefore hooked by a studio who had him in what seemed a set pattern for his future: lead roles in minor films, minor roles in big films, and occasional appearances in great ones—but only grooming a horse or toting a gun.

CHAPTER 6

The Beginning of a Beautiful Friendship

Every actor needs a part, every part needs a writer, and no one wrote better for Humphrey Bogart, and for the Bogart character, than John Huston. There was no way, however, to tell that from the first Huston script in which Bogart appeared. In 1938 he played a jewel thief named Rocks Valentine in *The Amazing Dr. Clitterhouse,* a film built around Edward G. Robinson as a psychiatrist who, in trying to understand the criminal mind, turns into a criminal himself. Robinson literally gets away with murder when (yet again) he does away with Bogart. Bogart, who thereafter referred to the picture as *The Amazing Dr. Clitoris,* had no contact with Huston during its making. After all, Bogart's was a stock character and, as Huston later explained, "I was just the writer."

They had become slightly aware of each other earlier on in the Warner Brothers Green Room, named for its apple-green walls. A step up from the commissary next door, the L-shaped room offered waitress service, snowy linen, and comfortable tables, including the big one where writers congregated and at which others sat by invitation only. Bogart was one of the few actors invited, and it was there, Huston said, that they developed "a nodding acquaintance that only grew into something when he did the gangster film [*High Sierra*] that I wrote."

Despite the combined talents of Robinson, Claire Trevor, and Bogart, *The Amazing Dr. Clitterhouse* did only middling business. The most amazing thing about the movie was that Huston even had a chance at the script. Not long before, nearly everyone had been ready to give up on him. The erratic son of actor Walter Huston, he had been variously a boxer, an artist, an actor, and a panhandler. He had also served time in the Mexican cavalry and nearly served time in jail for running down a pedestrian on Hollywood Boulevard. But he found a niche for himself at Warners, where his other work of the time fared better, often in spite of interference. He shared credit with three others for *Jezebel* (1938), which brought Bette Davis her second Oscar. With two others he wrote *Juarez* (1939), a life of Mexican president Benito Juarez, and then watched helplessly as Paul Muni ordered his work rewritten into a ponderous dud. As the lead of the three writers of *Dr. Ehrlich's Magic Bullet,* the bold film with Robinson about the conquest of syphilis, he again watched helplessly as the Breen Office carved out the references to VD.

Dr. Ehrlich's Magic Bullet and *Jezebel* had done well at the box office, though, and by 1940 Huston was one of the studio's choice writers. Tired of biographies and costume dramas, he was eager to do his own kind of story in his own way. Luckily, this coincided with Warners' acquisition of *High Sierra,* the new crime novel by W. R. Burnett. *High Sierra* was purchased within two weeks of publication in March 1940, with a preemptive offer that beat out the other studios. Burnett thought it the best of any of his books since *Little Caesar,* and so did Huston, a self-described "pushover" for the writer's tough, compact, dark-hued novels.

William Riley Burnett was a transplanted midwesterner and sometime screenwriter whose work was mined repeatedly during the thirties. Huston felt, however, that the studios undervalued the depth of Burnett's characterizations, using his stories merely as the basis for shoot-'em-up potboilers. The heavy rewrites endemic to studios generally eviscerated his work and left scant trace of the original; *King of the Underworld* is a glaring example.

In *High Sierra,* Burnett told the tale of the Last Desperado. Roy "Mad Dog" Earldon (shortened in the screenplay to Earle) is a farmboy gone wrong, a burnt-out ex-con with memories of cornfield innocence. A Dillinger-era gangster, he finds on his release from prison that he has become an anachronism. He plots a hotel robbery, but his two novice accomplices bring along a girl, in violation of Earle's professional code, and from that point on, tragedy is unavoidable. He is Duke Mantee mellowed in middle age, and his reawakened humane impulses lead to his being hunted down to his last stand on a mountaintop in the Sierra.

"Take the spirit out of Burnett, the strange sense of inevitability that comes with our deepening understanding of his characters . . . and only the conventional husk of a story remains," Huston wrote to Wallis. "This might easily be the lot of *High Sierra.* On the other hand, if it's done with real seriousness—the seriousness Burnett deserves—I think it could be made into an outstanding picture."

At first Bogart hadn't figured in the plans for the film, although the description of Earldon in the opening pages of the book could fit him:

> His face was swarthy, and his hair coarse, dark and wavy; he had heavy brow-ridges, a thick nose, and a firm wide mouth which at times was compressed into a thin line; his eyes were dark; but unlike most dark eyes, they weren't soft; he gave an impression of virile ugliness.

Even so, he presumed the role was his. In a palliative meant to offset the string of treadmill parts, Wallis had told Bogart to let him know when he found a role he really wanted. When Bogart read Burnett's novella in *Redbook* prior to the book's publication, he immediately wanted to play Earldon and sent a note to Wallis. Wallis never answered.

The reason soon became obvious. The morning Warners made the deal for the book, Wallis rushed a copy to Paul Muni, Warners' current top star and the only actor to fit the description of Earldon better than Bogart. Muni was close to the end of an eight-month leave of absence, on a national tour in Maxwell Anderson's *Key Largo,* and was due back in Burbank in late May. Muni, whose contract stipulated that he would be able to make a long-desired biography of Beethoven on his return, along with an unnamed second film, agreed in a telegram to Wallis that there were possibilities in *High Sierra,* "PROVIDED DON'T BECOME ANOTHER COPS-AND-ROBBERS FILM." His agent, Mike Levee, who also represented Leslie Howard, backed the project. Muni had seven pictures remaining on his contract, and this seemed the perfect vehicle for his reentry.

Some reputations wear better than others, but few have fallen off quite so precipitously as Paul Muni's. One generation's great actor often seems another's ham. At his best, however, he was a performer of immense versatility and integrity. He made a string of popular film biographies portraying Nobel Prize winners and crusaders for justice (*The Story of Louis Pasteur, The Life of Emile Zola*), and assumed varied ethnic identities as a Pole, a Latino, and, in *The Good Earth,* a Chinese peasant. Two of his classic performances came in 1932, as a character based on Al Capone in *Scarface* and as a wrongly convicted man in *I Am a Fugitive from a Chain Gang.* By 1940 he was one of the brightest stars in both Hollywood and New York. At Warners, where stars were just as much a commodity as film stock and sets, he was an independent duchy, with co-producer's privileges and approval rights that extended into the cutting room.

Of all his successes, the most profitable had been *Scarface,* filmed not for Warners but for Howard Hughes. W. R. Burnett shared credit for the screenplay, and for Warners the combination of Burnett and Muni presented the studio with the happy prospect of the best of all worlds: a change-of-pace modern story for its star and a potential gangster-film bonanza at the box office. On March 16, three days after Warners had closed the deal for the book, *The New York Times* announced that Paul Muni would star in *High Sierra,* his "first underworld vehicle since *Scarface.*"

For Bogart, it was like a rerun of the casting of *The Petrified Forest.*

Then reality set in. One writer after another voiced his concerns. How could one write a "sexy, gangster-ennobling picture" that would be acceptable to the Breen Office? And if the sympathetic angle was removed, what was left? A conventional shoot-'em-up with mountains instead of skyscrapers.

Muni or not, Wallis began to have doubts. The finished film would almost certainly have been far different were it not for Mark Hellinger, who stepped in to become the associate producer (Wallis was de facto producer) and, in the process of saving the project, changed the lives of both Huston and Bogart.

Hellinger was a character quite literally out of the 1920s. At thirty-four, he was a nationally syndicated columnist. His short story "The World Moves On" was filmed in 1939 as *The Roaring Twenties,* with Cagney and Bogart as two of the three doughboys freshly returned from the war in France to find that gangsters are the kings of Prohibition. It is Hellinger who tells the audience in a voice-over during the opening credits that everything they are about to see is based on real people and events he covered as a newsman. In 1937, he had become a producer for Warners. Among his credits were *It All Came True, They Drive by Night,* and *Brother Orchid.*

Hellinger was an anomaly in Hollywood, a dapper figure given to tight-fitting suits, dark blue shirts, and yellow ties, the underworld look deliberately cultivated since the days he covered Times Square. He boasted of mob friendships in Los Angeles and drove in a armored Lincoln that had once belonged to the gangster Dutch Schultz. His duties at Warners were so wide-ranging that even the studio lawyers didn't understand them all. He lived lavishly on an eleven-acre estate in the hills above Hollywood and was so good at wangling money that he managed to dazzle even as notorious a skinflint as Jack Warner into footing the bill for his and his showgirl wife's first visit west not by the usual train but in a six-hundred-dollar suite aboard a steamer from New York via the Panama Canal.

Hellinger also had a darker aspect, a sense of foreboding akin to that of Burnett's doomed heroes. There was a quality of desperation in his private life, which despite and because of a family history of heart disease, he propped up with cigarettes, barbiturates, and brandy. Both his parents had died when he was young, and only the year before, his last relative, an adoring brother, had slowly died in his twenties. Hellinger understood Roy Earle.

"What of the superb romance between the man and the crippled girl?" he wrote to Wallis. "And what of the basic character of a man who was born a farmer . . . and wound up as the last of the Dillinger mob? And what of the marvelously phony doctor—and of punks who go fishing to cover their nervousness . . . and of a tough girl who is willing to die for the unattainable love of the strangest of men; a man who uses a gun even as he dreams of the stars. . . . All I ask, Hal, is that you find me someone who has just half the enthusiasm I hold for this grand yarn."

That someone was, of course, John Huston, himself pleading with the studio in those same weeks not to blow the opportunity to make a special picture.

In the beginning their efforts were focused solely on Muni, who contrary to later accounts had no objections to a gangster picture—so long as it was "SOMETHING WORTHWHILE," he added in his telegram to Wallis. And while Huston had been furious at Muni's rewrites on *Juarez,* he was not so furious as to turn away Warners' biggest property, or to pass up the chance to link the star of *Scarface* with his script. He had proposed a revolutionary idea to the studio: Rather than write the conventional screenplay pre-narrative treatment, which inevitably led to heavy rewrites that in turn made the original all but unrecognizable, why not bypass the treatment and, for once, base the screenplay on *the book*? He asked permission to contact Muni, still on tour, to lay out his approach to the material and offer his assurances that this would be no "conventional gangster story." Wallis agreed but told him that the studio would deal with Muni.

A first draft went to Muni in early May, with no immediate response. The rumor on the lot was that he didn't like it. Bogart wired Wallis, reminding him of the note he had left concerning *High Sierra:* "I NEVER RECEIVED AN ANSWER SO I'M BRINGING IT UP AGAIN AS I UNDERSTAND THERE IS SOME DOUBT ABOUT MUNI DOING IT."

Once again, there was no response. Muni had left the door open to a rewrite—even Huston had problems with the script—and his agent was eager to mediate any changes. Burnett, thrilled with the prospect of "such a great actor as Paul Muni," had offered his services at the outset and was now brought in from nearby Glendale to work with Huston under Hellinger's supervision. (Warner ordered the collaboration so the studio could say to Muni if he continued to object, "For chrissakes, what do you want? We got the author on it.") Burnett typed while Huston, who liked to talk out a scene, dictated. "I never had so much fun in my life, John and I working together," Burnett later said. "We laughed most of the time; we could hardly get any work done."

Hellinger laughed less. According to Huston's biographer, Lawrence Grobel, Hellinger was under great pressure from Jack Warner to complete the script, and he would often call the writer to remind him that it was due. On one of these occasions Huston's response was, "Tell him [Warner] to go fuck himself."

Hellinger called again a few hours later. "John, I don't know what I'm going to do, Warner's going to be on the goddamn intercom in another minute."

"Tell him to go fuck himself," Huston repeated when he heard Hellinger's intercom buzz and then Warner asking about the script.

"GO FUCK YOURSELF!" Hellinger screamed.

Huston was amazed, Warner incensed. When Hellinger's contract expired at the end of the year, he was out of work.

By now it was early July and Muni had reported back to the studio. Within a month shooting had to begin or the studio would be in violation of its contract. Huston, working through a massive case of poison ivy—"painted purple and dying to scratch himself," Hellinger reported—pushed with Burnett to finish. On July 10, the revised script went to Muni at his home in Van Nuys. "I am sure you will agree," Hellinger wrote in his cover letter, "that this . . . is a much better job."

At the same time, Muni learned that the studio was reneging on their commitment to make the Beethoven picture. In a volatile meeting described by Muni's biographer Jerome Lawrence, he was told to forget Beethoven. With the world in turmoil, the public wanted some escape. Promises on paper notwithstanding, the gangster picture was now the main event.

Muni reportedly tore up his $5,000-a-week contract. A single sheet of paper was prepared and signed, and by mutual agreement, Muni and Warner Bros. Pictures, Inc., severed relations effective July 17, 1940—

exactly one week after Wallis had sent out the finished script of *High Sierra.*

Though later Muni said he hadn't liked the rewrite, it apparently was never formally rejected. The real issue was the expendability of even the brightest stars whenever they became too uppity. Only three years earlier, an eager Jack Warner had pressured the actor into renewing his long-term contract. But his last two pictures had been losers, and suddenly Paul Muni, like Kay Francis before him, was excess baggage. Six days and several twists and turns later, Bogart began hair and makeup tests for *High Sierra.*

On the surface, the two men could hardly have been less alike. Muni was a product of the Yiddish theater, inclined to the broad gesture and not above chewing the scenery. He was also the man of many faces, who submerged his personality in his roles. Bogart, the New York WASP, deliberately and expertly underplayed to the camera.

But for the studio especially, there were many similarities. Both were New York actors and disciplined veterans of the stage who had proved their versatility; both were dark, intense urban types who had made their breakthrough in gangster roles drawn in part from Depression society and reflective of their own inner turbulence. And both men, though short and slight, had unconventional looks that women found attractive.

In the late thirties, a story making the rounds had Bogart complaining to Wallis about his roles. "Look," Wallis told him, "you want Raft's roles, Raft wants Eddie Robinson's roles, Robinson wants Muni's roles."

"That's simple," Bogart supposedly answered. "All I do is bump off Muni, and we all move up a step."

Though probably apocryphal, the story is nonetheless illustrative of the basic show business truth that, however well intentioned one might be, the way to success is over the bodies of others. When Warner bumped off Muni, Bogart did move up. Now it was Bogart whom Fox wanted for their remake of Muni's *The Valiant.* It was Bogart who eventually would play the Muni role when *Key Largo* was made in 1948. And it was Bogart who would ascend to Muni's position as the number one box office name at Warners.

The studio wasted no time. If you lose a star, why, just make a new one. On July 17, the day Muni and Warners parted, director of advertising and publicity S. Charles Einfeld watched *Dark Victory* in one of the projection rooms, then dictated a letter to Martin Weiser, the master of Warners' publicity stunts.

> Dear Marty,
>
> I want you to give the utmost attention to the building of Humphrey Bogart to stardom in as quick time as possible. . . .

Weiser could sell any movie, build up any actor. He was a genius at bringing whatever project he undertook to nationwide attention. To promote *They Drive by Night,* he had a fifteen-ton big rig driven across the United States for supposed presentation to Ann Sheridan. With it came the good wishes of five hundred thousand members of the International Brotherhood of Teamsters. On it were the painted autographs of truckers, mayors, and members of fan clubs, added at every stop between Chicago and Los Angeles. The empty vehicle became a news item, and before long the whole country was talking about "the Sheridan truck."

Einfeld, a genial round-faced man who loved movies, was the first to sense the star potential of Bette Davis and had a considerable reputation at Warners for spotting rising talent. Muni's departure created a void that had to be filled, and after watching *Dark Victory,* Einfeld urged a move that was long overdue.

"Bogart has been typed through publicity as a gangster character. We want to undo this. For Bogart is one of the greatest actors on the screen today," he continued to Weiser.

> The fellow is a master of technique and can do anything. In "Dark Victory" he showed a type of sex appeal that was unusual and different from that of any other actor on the screen. . . .
>
> Let us see if within the next two or three months we cannot have the country flooded with Bogart art,—and column breaks lauding Warner Bros. for their recognition of Bogart's talent, and predicting great success for him as a star.
>
> This is one of the most important jobs you have before you in the next few months. I know I can count on you. . . .

However deserved the move was, it was made not because it was appropriate but because it was necessary. The events of the last week changed the configuration of Murderer's Row, and a slot had to be filled. Cagney was still in a class by himself; Robinson, the studio agreed, had passed his peak of stardom; young John Garfield, brought in from the Group Theater in New York in 1938 and a dynamo of raw talent, was still unseasoned. Which left Raft as the last body Bogart had to get over before he could claim the part of Roy Earle.

Raft had come from Paramount to Warners in 1938 and had been built into a major star. He was to have spent the summer on loanout to MGM but, because of a scheduling foul-up at Metro, was suddenly at liberty. His salary made him a natural choice for Earle, and he may well have done the part had not Bogart, in perfect gangster fashion, sandbagged him.

Years later, Bogart told a colleague, with mischief in his eyes, how he had talked Raft out of it. "Raft was not a very good judge," actor Bruce Bennett said, "and Bogie was discouraging him—'Oh, you don't want to do that, they're just trying to get your name up there to sell the film.' " Roy Earle, he argued, was just another heavy who gets shot. Heavies died; heroes lived. "So George goes right up to Warner and he said, 'I refuse to be in that picture.' "

Indeed, in the previous months, Raft had badgered Jack Warner for a letter confirming that he would not have to play "out-and-out heavies." He should instead have asked that he be protected from being an out-and-out dolt.

Thus, while Bogart lobbied for Roy Earle, Raft lobbied for a junket to New York and a string of well-paying personal appearances. The studio had held off because the Raft–Ida Lupino–Bogart film *They Drive by Night,* scheduled to open at the end of July, had already been acclaimed as a smash by the trade papers. Raoul Walsh, its director, was up for *High Sierra,* and the studio liked the idea of keeping the winning combination of Raft, Lupino, and Walsh intact. It was Raft's exercising his contractual right to veto a role that cleared the way for Bogart.

The only person conceivably happier than Bogart about this was Huston. "*Everything* was intended for George Raft at that time, and I was not among George Raft's greatest admirers. I thought he was a *clown,* walking around in his white suit with the padded shoulders and form-fitting hips, and bodyguards. He was very much a Mafia type and *liked* to display it. And it turned out, poor devil, he came to nothing. He refused everything that was thrown at him. And he refused *High Sierra.* You know, he was really an *ignorant man.* Poor devil. And I was delighted he didn't do it because Bogie would then play it. And I *knew* Bogie was a fine actor."

In the absence of a bankable star, Warners opted for talent. When Huston went to Hellinger "and I said that I thought he would be lucky to get Bogart instead of Raft," Hellinger agreed. The studio might have pressured Raft, but didn't. On July 22, the day before Bogart's first test for *High Sierra,* Warners granted Raft permission to go to New York. Nine days later, *High Sierra* was assigned production number 324, "Star: Humphrey Bogart."

Raoul Walsh rolled his own cigarettes, and it was said that you could find him just by following the trail of loose tobacco. It was Bogart's fourth film with the director, who was known for his hard-boiled, fast-paced films (*The Thief of Baghdad, The Roaring Twenties, They Drive by Night*). Walsh was as macho as the black patch covering the eye he'd lost years before when a rabbit hit the windshield of his car. The accident ended his acting career but gave him a better one.

Walsh knew exactly the look he wanted for Roy Earle. So did Bogart. Both took their cue from the book. The middle-aged gangster is yanked out of prison by his mobster boss for one last job:

> Roy came blinking out into the sunlight. He had on a neat blue serge suit Big Mac had sent him. He didn't look so bad, except for his prison-bleached complexion. But his coarse dark hair had silvery streaks in it, and his dark eyes were weary and sad. . . . He'd been in the clink nearly six years, and the world outside was now a strange and terrible place.

Walsh had run test after test: Bogart with streaked hair, silvered hair, grayed hair, hair darkened slightly. In his search for realism, Bogart had the sides done in a prison cut, close-clipped, a dark thatch at the top contrasting with its bleak fringe of gray-white stubble. The look harshened the lines in his gaunt face, mute testimony to the art of the jailhouse barber, whose object is not to style but to shear. It set the visual mood for what one critic would later characterize as "the air of a man straining to pick out the melody in a new kind of music that grates harshly on his ears. . . . a man who would just as soon die as try to adjust to a world that thinks this stuff is worth listening to."

For Roy Earle, everything goes wrong: the planned robbery is bungled and ends in a shoot-out and a fiery car crash; the heisted jewels prove too hot and therefore valueless. Roy pays for an operation for a crippled country girl who, cured, becomes an egocentric little tart. In the end, his one option is a dash for the state line, the law chasing him, his only points of reference two creatures as lost as he—a Los Angeles street kid living by her wits and a mongrel pup. Both are with Earle when a police sniper shoots him off the face of the mountain and he dramatically plunges down its side.

Ida Lupino played the waif Marie, who falls for Earle. "It was a damn good role for me and I was delighted to be doing it," she said fifty years later. "As usual, Bogart was a killer and no good and I was in love with him. Perfectly normal and natural for us."

They had met briefly a few months earlier on the set of *They Drive by Night,* the story of truck-driving brothers who haul fruit and vegetables to the big cities and take on their crooked bosses. Recycling the role that had served Bette Davis so well in *Bordertown,* Lupino played Lana, a murderess who goes crazy. Her courtroom mad scene is the high point of the movie. While making the film, Lupino "had just a few words with Bogie because I was so busy in the other scenes. That was a lovely role to do. But it was my first picture at Warners and I was a little nervous, so I really didn't get to know him at the time. But when he was cast in *High Sierra,* I was delighted."

Bogart did what stars almost never do, assisting before the camera as young unknowns tested for the role of the crippled farmgirl. Warners settled on Joan Brodel, a fresh-faced fifteen-year-old, who had been on stage since she was three. In 1937 she began her film career, playing Robert Taylor's little sister in *Camille,* and appeared as the winsome child in a dozen pictures. Warner Brothers signed her in 1941 and changed her name to Joan Leslie. She had been nervous about working with Bogart. "I had heard rumors that he was wild and crazy and a drinker and a swearer—and he was! But he was gentle, just like Walsh. He was against swearing when I was around—'We won't have any of that in front of Joan,' he'd say. 'Not in front of this young lady.' " (Jack Warner also professed a fatherly interest in Leslie. When she turned seventeen during the making of *Yankee Doodle Dandy* in 1942, he had a new car rolled onto the sound stage and presented her with the keys as photographers clicked away. After Warner and the press had left, the car was removed and the keys were taken from her. She never saw either again.)

The filming of *High Sierra* began on August 5. For the next forty-four days, locations alternated among the studio, a mountain fishing camp, and the posh Arrowhead Springs Resort before winding up in the Sierra Nevada of eastern California, in the shadow of Mount Whitney. For the climactic high-speed car chase, Walsh and Hellinger insisted on the real thing instead of the more common and far less expensive key shot projected onto a background screen at the studio to give the illusion of the landscape whizzing by. An action unit was sent to the high country near

Lone Pine, and stunt drivers whipped past the edge of thousand-foot drops as the posse pursued Roy Earle to his last stand high above the timberline. Unit manager Al Alleborn wrung his hands as equipment for the final scenes—Bogart crouched high among the rocks—was brought in by horse and pack mule along a narrow mountain track.

The master stuntman Buster Wiles took the fall for Bogart, skidding as if dead weight eighty-nine feet down the mountainside, past boulders and through underbrush. (He also doubled for the shooter, thus in effect assassinating himself.) Lifelines were stretched out to prevent his sliding into space over the sheer precipice. He landed face down, but because he bounced about five times, he got up and said to Walsh, "I feel like doing that over again."

Forget it, Walsh told him. "It's good enough for the twenty-five-cent customers."

Wiles also doubled for Bogart in the fadeout scene, lying face down in the dirt and mourned over by a weeping Ida Lupino, a few cookies concealed between his fingers to induce Pard to lick his dead master's hand. The dog, which actually belonged to Bogart and whose real name was Zero, yelped on cue and managed to stay hidden in Lupino's basket without wriggling. "I'd open it up between takes," she said, "and he'd sit there with his head up, looking at everything. And when he had to go to the bathroom he'd make a little sound to let me know."

High Sierra cemented a relationship that was key to Bogart's life and career. Unlike most writers, who are seldom around during shooting, Huston visited the sets at Warners several times. He found Bogart unassuming and relaxed, as he usually was with writers. Bogart, who appreciated the craft of writing, was well-read in both literature and current events: he could quote Plato, Emerson, and Pope as well as vast amounts of Shakespeare, he subscribed to the *Harvard Law Review,* and he had a regular correspondence with Supreme Court justice Oliver Wendell Holmes. Bogart and Huston went often to lunch at Lakeside, the actors' country club near the studio, and consumed, Huston said, "more cocktails than one should have at lunch." Huston was amazed that Bogart's intake seemed to have no effect on his afternoon's concentration. "They were three-cocktail lunches, too. Big ones. No ice. And you'd never see that he had had a drink."

Despite later reports, to everyone's recollection Bogart and Lupino got on well. "We were all buddies," Lupino insisted. She was a recent transplant from Britain, a member of a famous theater family, with a background in the London music halls. She found her niche in Hollywood playing what she called "nasty girls" and loving it. "It's much easier to perform those roles. Much easier. Bogie said to me, 'You and I were born to be bad. But we're really saints, Ida.' I said, 'Who? You and me? Impossible. The halos wouldn't fit. Our horns would be enormous!' "

Bogart and Lupino worked so closely that the company dubbed them "Gaffers and Satler," the name of a well-known stove manufacturer. Irving Rapper, the dialogue coach doing his fifth Bogart film (he later directed *Now, Voyager*), said that "Bogie was crazy about Ida." A casual photo of the three taken by the pool at the hotel on location shows Lupino sitting in a chair and Bogart in his bathing suit on his knees, looking as if he did indeed adore her. "It didn't turn out to us being lovers," Lupino later said, "but we did care about each other. Being with him was absolutely heaven and peaceful to me. And, well, I guess he didn't find me too bad." In any case, Lupino's actor husband, Louis Hayward, visited frequently and Mayo was often around. "Ida was in love with [Bogart]," Rapper said, "and she was evidently too charming. Mayo Methot was jealous."

Lupino's judgment on Mayo was more succinct: "A bitch!"

When the third Mrs. Bogart joined them at Lone Pine, the couple's domestic differences were played out before the company. "They should have signed a contract at Madison Square Garden," Buster Wiles said. At one point, Wiles wanted to visit friends in the area, and he asked if he might borrow the Buick the studio had put at Bogart's disposal. Mayo objected.

"She said, 'You can't loan him that car!' He said, 'Will you please keep your mouth *closed*.' Then he said, 'Buster, here's the keys. You take it whenever you want.' " As Wiles drove off, in the rearview mirror he could see the Bogarts still arguing. Wiles felt that "Mayo could be very nice and sweet. But once in a while, when she had a few, she'd get a little irritable," an understatement appropriate to a man who rolls eighty-nine feet down a mountain and wants a retake because he bounced a few times.

Mayo's temper, however, was proving less of a problem than her jealousy, evidenced, among other ways, by a wreath delivered onto the set one day for Mr. Bogart. It was "a good size," according to a Warner employee, nicely mounted on an easel, with leaves of a rich funereal black, a condom hanging from each one. "Well, everyone knew where it came from. They called the florist and he wouldn't tell them and the florist was banned from the lot. But it was Mayo. Oh yeah, it was Mayo."

There is the possibility that it was Mayo who ended the prospect of Bogart and Lupino making more films together. A story later circulated that Bogart so offended Lupino at some point during the shooting of *High Sierra* that she refused to work with him again, yet it is hard to find a reason for believing it.

Lupino, for her part, would remember with special vividness Bogart's coming to her rescue in the heart-tugging scene in which Roy Earle puts Marie aboard the bus to send her out of harm's way. The directions called for her to cry and she couldn't. "I said, 'I'm having trouble, Bogie. I can't make it happen.' And he said, 'Well, just think the way it might really be. You're going to go away with little Pard and you're never either one of you going to see me again.' And oh, I thought—that was it." In another Lupino account, he accomplished the task more brusquely: "Listen, doll, if you can't cry, just remember that I'm going to take the picture away from you." Whatever the method, it worked so well that production had to close down early. "Unable finish," the unit manager reported that afternoon. "Miss Lupino's eyes very weak from crying in scene during the early part of the day."

On other occasions, however, Bogart's temper was inarguably evident. While on location, he was often testy over everything from Walsh's retakes to the stale sandwiches that passed for a catered lunch. Walsh took to calling him "Bogie the Beefer."

Lupino said that the only time she thought Bogart really unhappy was "toward the finish. He wasn't a man that unmasked easily at all."

Bogart's irascibility was more likely over something that had happened in Burbank than over anything to do with the filming.

After five years of waiting, he finally had first billing in a quality production. But he had been awarded that before Lupino's breakthrough in *They Drive by Night,* released during the making of *High Sierra* and on the verge of becoming one of Warners' biggest-grossing films.

On September 18, Hal Wallis sent a query to Jack Warner:

> Don't you think we ought to reverse the billing on *High Sierra,* and instead of billing Bogart first, bill Lupino first?
>
> Lupino has had a great deal of publicity on the strength of *They Drive By Night,* whereas Bogart has been playing the leads in a lot of "B" pictures, and this fact might mitigate against the success of *High Sierra.*
>
> The billing has just gone through with Bogart's name first, and I think we ought to reverse it.

The new billing went out the next day. The company was still at Lone Pine, and was due to return to Burbank that afternoon. Bogart probably knew of the change by then. The front office could be a sieve; and in this case the news probably went out through the typing pool and was all over the lot before the last stencil was cut. Bogart, never one to need an excuse for a caustic remark, certainly had an excuse now. Perhaps coincidentally, the day after the switch, which by then had become common knowledge, unit manager Alleborn reported that "Miss Lupino broke out with a rash. This morning she was unable to work." The studio press release said it was a bee sting. The next day she was listed as ill. The day after, however, the pair resumed work together. In the absence of records no one knows whether Bogart took out his disappointment on Lupino or even if they had a direct confrontation. He knew well enough that she had nothing to do with the decision, and she later insisted that "he never said a word about" the change. "All he said was, 'Well, we've shown Warner Brothers. We're rotten in it, darling, and the audience are going to love us.' That was Bogie. Summing up all the worries and everything."

Worries were something Bogart had plenty of during the making of *High Sierra,* and his billing was only part of them. A month before the credits change he was confronted with a problem that had considerably more far-reaching consequences.

In 1936, while still on his starting salary at Warners, Bogart had supported the striking lettuce workers of the San Joaquin Valley, and he had contributed to the strike fund of Seattle newspaper reporters, then engaged in an acrid battle for job security and above-subsistence pay. By October 1936, the FBI, in a secret report on Communist influence on the Screen Actors Guild, had—without basis—listed Bogart as being one of twenty-one members "with strong CP leanings." It was the first entry into what would become an FBI file of several hundred pages. (The FBI cast a wide net for this list. It included left-wingers like Gale Sondergaard—a Party member—and J. Edward Bromberg, who were later blacklisted; centrist liberals like Melvyn Douglas, James Cagney, and Fredric March; conservatives like Gary Cooper and Robert Montgomery; and active Democrat Pat O'Brien, famous for his portrayals of cops, priests, and the sainted Knute Rockne.)

That the charge of Bogart's supposed Communist Party leanings was groundless was of no consequence. In the summer of 1940 Congressman Martin Dies, chairman of the Special Committee on Un-American Activities of the House of Representatives, swept into Los Angeles to purge

Hollywood of its political sins. The committee was two years old at the time, established, ironically, to investigate the radical right in the wake of the Black Legion disclosures. Instead, the panel had gravitated to more familiar pastures on the left. The problems portrayed so earnestly on the screen in the thirties—the economic violence of the Depression, bigotry, racism, the rise of Nazism in Europe, and labor wars at home—had reflected the social awareness of the film community. Stars and executives donated their names and their talent, their time, and especially their money to a variety of issues in which they thought less about the sponsor than the cause. Actors, writers, directors, and producers of all persuasions mingled in organizations variously titled the Hollywood Anti-Nazi League, or the Motion Picture Artists Committee, or the Motion Picture Democratic Committee. They united in causes ranging from opposition to Hitler, Mussolini, Franco, and imperial Japan (though never to Stalin) to support of the New Deal, civil rights, and the Congress of Industrial Organizations (CIO). The star-studded Committee of 56, headed by Melvyn Douglas and including James Cagney, Joan Crawford, Bette Davis, Henry Fonda, Dick Powell, Groucho Marx, Rosalind Russell, Ann Sheridan, and Jack Warner (probably the only point of agreement ever between Warner and Cagney) launched a campaign calling for an economic boycott of Nazi Germany.

"Everyone is on a committee to free the Scottsboro boys," Robert Benchley had written his family when he and Bogart were living at the Garden of Allah in 1936, "or help the Jews in Germany, or boost the Screen Writers Guild. . . . Last night I went to an anti-Nazi dinner at $20 a plate. . . . It is all very laudable—and expensive."

Dies, a big blond bully from Texas who saw conspiracy everywhere and once tried to prove Shirley Temple a Communist, had no use for the New Deal, organized labor, blacks, or Jews. What he did have use for was publicity, and he saw Hollywood as millions of others did, a place to become a star. He was already a role model to his committee colleagues, among them J. Parnell Thomas, a rotund ex–bond salesman from New Jersey.

In July 1940, John L. Leech, a self-proclaimed "chief functionary" of the local Communist Party, appeared before the Dies Committee in executive session and named Bogart, Cagney, March, screenwriter Philip Dunne, and numerous others as Communists and contributors to the Party. Four weeks later, Leech repeated his allegations before a Los Angeles County grand jury. In a hearing stage-managed by district attorney

Buron Fitts, Leech described secret meetings at the Malibu estate of Paramount Pictures production head B. P. Schulberg, where Bogart and others gathered to "read the doctrines of Karl Marx."

A year before, a trial examiner had characterized Leech as "a pathological liar," a fact noted in FBI records and evaluations but apparently unimportant to Dies. At the same time, the names on Leech's "master list" were, perhaps not coincidentally, almost identical to those in the FBI's four-year-old report. The testimony, promptly released by a district attorney himself eager for publicity, was gobbled up by the media and headlined "HOLLYWOOD STARS ACCUSED AS REDS BEFORE GRAND JURY." In the aftermath, Bogart garnered another entry in his growing FBI file.

Bogart was furious in his denial: "I dare the men who are attempting this investigation to call me to the stand. I want to face them myself."

On Friday, August 16, two days after Bogart's statement, shooting was delayed on Stage 19 at Warners, site of the Tropico Springs Hotel lobby where the holdup scene in *High Sierra* was scheduled to be filmed. "Bogart absent this morning," the notation in the daily production report read, "appearing before the Dies Committee." With Bogart was his longtime lawyer Morgan Maree, a pillar of respectability, ready to testify to the purity of his client's checkbook. Despite Bogart's eagerness to confront Leech and Fitts, when he and Maree were ushered into an unmarked suite at the Biltmore, seated across from them at the narrow table was only Martin Dies, in his trademark vanilla ice cream suit and bow tie, evidence that the committee at its whim could suspend even so basic an American right as facing and cross-examining one's accuser.

Questioned under oath, Bogart denied the allegations: No, he was not and had never been a member of the Communist Party of the United States. No, he had never contributed to the CP. No, he did not know John L. Leech, nor had he ever seen or communicated with him. Yes, he'd been approached once with literature by a "Hollywood pink" and just said no. Except for membership in the Screen Actors Guild, he was not a joiner. The "charges" against him, he said, were ridiculous and completely untrue.

Dies changed tack: Did Bogart, of his own knowledge, know of "any Communistic activities" among actors or screenwriters? No, Bogart answered, it wasn't his place to know who was a Communist, a liberal, or just misguided. "I know of no Communistic activities in Hollywood. No." Then came the inevitable follow-up:

"Do you know any Hollywood actor who is a Communist?"

Bogart knew a fishing expedition when he saw one:

"I couldn't say he is a Communist unless I saw a card." In the secret world of the Party cells, it was the least likely item to be shown.

Blocked, Dies tried another approach. No, of course not, he said—unless Bogart had reason to believe "by conversation" that such a person sympathized with the Communist Party of the United States?

Bogart said he had his suspicions, but again, "No."

"They're not based on any facts as far as you know?"

"Not based on any facts."

Bogart had remained calm all through the session and was even flip at one point. But when, after several more questions, Dies asked if in conclusion there was anything Bogart wanted to add for the record, his anger spilled out: "I've been born an American. I've always been a loyal citizen. I have great love for my country. Anytime I would be called upon I would serve that country. I resent the intrusion and insinuation that I am anything else. . . . I think it's completely un-American [for] a man who has been, as far as I can read in the papers, called a liar to be allowed to testify before a grand jury without the people accused being permitted to have an opportunity to answer those charges. . . ."

The session was over in twenty minutes, but Bogart would never forget it. Dismissed, he drove directly back to the studio and quickly changed out of his slacks and sports jacket and into Roy "Mad Dog" Earle's black suit. Before noon, gun drawn, he burst into the lobby of the Tropico Springs Hotel—*"One move out of you and I'll fill your pants full of lead!"*—snapping out his lines with a ferocity that had more than the usual edge.

The day of Bogart's hearing, *The New York Times* had asked why the grand jury testimony had been released in the first place, adding that "a political belief, however repugnant . . . is not in itself a crime." Those who had been forced to deny Communist leanings were now left to face public opprobrium. "Since no formal charge lies against them they cannot put their cases to a jury and must count on their denials. . . . In a race of that sort the lie . . . has a long head start."

The lie may even have played a part in the Warners decision to give Lupino top billing in *High Sierra.* As far as Warner Brothers was concerned, billing was not to benefit a star's ego but to bring in customers. And who stood to bring in more? A beautiful woman playing a tough character, or a tough guy accused of being a Communist?

A few days after Bogart's hearing, Dies, the credibility of his star witness in tatters, declared that there was "no evidence" connecting Bogart and the others to the Communist Party, and quickly got out of town. "It would be foolish," *The New York Times* commented, "to maintain that there are no Communists or Communist sympathizers in Hollywood. All that is reasonably certain is that precious little Communist propaganda gets into commercial films. What is sinister in the present episode is not the possible drop of Communism in the vast sea of mass entertainment but the misuse of supposedly correct legal machinery."

For Bogart, the man who gave to causes but never joined groups, the episode made him aware that the time had come to choose sides. He had stayed on the sidelines during the thirties and said in a statement issued after his hearing, "I have never contributed money to a political organization of any form. That includes Republican, Democratic, Hollywood Anti-Nazi League or the Communist Party."

Six weeks after his appearance before Dies, he abandoned his neutrality. Humphrey Bogart joined the campaign for the reelection of Franklin Delano Roosevelt and set out on a course of political activism that, in 1947, would involve him once again with the Special Committee on Un-American Activities of the House of Representatives.

CHAPTER 7

Birth of a Hero

The Hitler-Stalin Pact of the late summer of 1939 had divided Hollywood. The liberal to left-leaning committees either disappeared or were reduced to a tiny, die-hard membership as the pro-Soviet left went its own way, rejecting action against Germany with the same passion that they'd supported it before. Now they urged a strict neutrality with no aid to the Allies, and so joined their former right-wing enemies of America First under the slogan "Keep America Out of War."

The more thoughtful, said screenwriter Ring Lardner Jr., were genuinely concerned at the prospect of unprepared Americans facing the Wehrmacht in a one-front war in which the Soviet Union was neutralized and Britain weakened. "It didn't seem likely that America, even with England, could successfully fight against the Axis."

By the spring of 1940, Norway and Denmark were under Nazi occupation, and the Netherlands and Belgium soon would be. Britain was in retreat and France was collapsing. The newsletter put out by the rump remainder of the leftist Motion Picture Democratic Committee called the war "a conflict between two imperialisms which become steadily less distinguishable."

Thirteen months later, as Hitler invaded Russia, the "conflict between two imperialisms" would become the war against fascism, and the calls for strict neutrality changed to calls for a second front. The scars from these volatile currents of ideology would last a long time. In later years much would be written about the unity of wartime Hollywood, but it was a unity of short duration, with fundamental differences only papered over. When push met shove in 1947, there would be those who neither forgave nor forgot.

For Bogart, support for Roosevelt meant support not only of the New Deal but of international involvement, and above all, aid to Britain, which by the fall of 1940 was the last holdout in the West against Hitler. During the Battle of Britain, when German bombers started pounding London, he and Lupino were filming *High Sierra.* "It hit me real hard," she said. "Everything got bombed. My father's theater, our home in Streatham Hill and the church opposite; and at the end of our acre and a half of ground, the United Dairy, beautiful, with rolling green hills. All bombed." She and Bogart discussed what they read in the papers and heard on the news, and it helped, she said, to be with someone concerned with the world beyond films: "It was wonderful to have a buddy I could talk to."

Bogart's joining Hollywood for Roosevelt coincided with the entry of mainstream Hollywood liberalism into presidential politics. Motion picture stars became campaign workers laying the groundwork for the industrywide political mobilization that came with America's entry into the war. As a member of the speakers bureau, Bogart, along with John Garfield, Melvyn Douglas, Claude Rains, and Edward G. Robinson, stumped on behalf of Democratic candidates and against Wendell Willkie, the moderate Republican presidential candidate. Speaking over NBC and CBS radio, he was part of a cast that included Henry Fonda, Walter Huston, Groucho Marx, Douglas Fairbanks Jr., Garfield, and Lucille Ball in a *Salute to Roosevelt,* broadcast twice before the election. Radio specials were run six days a week on the Warner station KFWB, and transcripts of the stars' words were circulated to the state and national committees of the Democratic Party.

A week before the election, Hollywood for Roosevelt took a full-page ad in *The New York Times.* The ad was headlined "Why We of Hollywood Will Vote for Roosevelt" and proclaimed these "the most critical hours of our nation's history." Bogart was listed in the first group of some two hundred names.

His opinions differed from Mayo's and those of his good friends and current house guests, Eric and Gertie Hatch, who had recently arrived in their Rolls-Royce from their home in Cedarhurst, Long Island. "We had driven out to Hollywood, our legal residence," Hatch later explained, "to vote for Wendell Willkie—a sleeveless errand, alas!"

Hatch drew on experience when he satirized the rich. His grandfather had been president of the New York Stock Exchange, and he himself had been an investment banker before he turned to writing.

Dinner was rushed on the night the Hatches arrived. Despite their long trip, they were anxious to attend a sneak preview of *Road Show,* based on one of Eric's books and about to be released by United Artists. The film dominated the conversation, to Bogart's mounting irritation. Concerned over the coming election and the state of the world, he made it clear that he didn't care a whit about *Road Show.*

"Bogie was drinking pretty heavily at the time (as were lots of us)," Hatch later wrote, "and apparently he got to brooding—and drinking—while we were out."

An envelope addressed "Eric Hatch, Esq." was propped atop the dresser in the guests' room when they returned later that night. Inside were three large pages, covered back and front with a large penciled scrawl that somehow retained the elegance of Bogart's penmanship. But while the handwriting was his, he had taken on his wife's voice.

It was less a letter than an outpouring of none-too-sober emotion. ("If they ever repeal the prohibition act . . . I will personally buy you a magnitude of champagne and we will drink it out of my god-damn slipper!"). It was, as well, a brew in which regurgitated traces of the dinner conversation bobbed to the surface, then sank again: politics, patriotism, the war, the movies: "I liked your picture better than Birth of a Nation. . . . what I can't understand is why all the people in your picture talk so Godamn much. . . . in Birth-of-a-Nation nobody said a word and I liked it better. . . . Theodore Roosevelt is just lovely—him and his big stick! . . . could you spare a dime for the boys at Valley Forge who need shoes—they liked your picture too. I have to say goodbye because my Husband Quote (the Son-of-a-bitch) Unquote—says so."

It was signed "Barbara Fritchie," the patriotic heroine of a poem every schoolchild knew ("Shoot, if you must, this old gray head / But spare your country's flag, she said"). Underneath was a P.S.: "One if by land—two if by Sea—lucky one! Barbara."

Hatch, reading through the letter that he later described as "quite some note," looked again at the envelope. At the top Bogart had written, "Vote for Cleveland!!" and at the bottom, "(I too have not been idle)."

Bogart spent November 5 on Stage 19, trying to get through *Carnival,* a cheap remake of *Kid Galahad.* There was a circus in place of the boxing ring, the sluggish director Ray Enright in place of Michael Curtiz, and a screenplay panned even by Warner readers as "a low-budget script written for thrills rather than believability." The only intriguing thing about the film was the question of why Wallis had wanted to make it in the first place. Raft had already turned down the part of the circus manager, for once with good reason. Thus Bogart, concerned with the state of the world, spent Election Day as a circus manager grappling with a hysterical Joan Leslie as a vengeful circus owner feeding the innocent Eddie Albert to the lions.

It was hardly the break he had expected after *High Sierra,* and it is hard to understand why a strong cast led by Bogart and Sylvia Sidney should have been wasted on a property the studio clearly considered inferior. Bogart vented his annoyance on the younger Eddie Albert, who, as a grocery clerk turned lion tamer, had to face the big cats without protection on a set representing the animals' cage. "It was surrounded by tall bars," Albert recalled, "eight or ten feet high, with guys with rifles in case any of them jumped me."

Bogart, using his character's prop cane, gleefully poked at the lions through the bars to irritate them. "He was quite playful," Albert said. "I was frightened enough as it was." The fun backfired, however, when Bogart tried it again on an outdoor set. His bright yellow LaSalle was parked out of camera range but close to the cage. After several jabbings, the lion lifted its tail and sent a stream of urine at Bogart, missing him but hitting the car. This time it was Albert's turn to laugh: "The paint came off—he was quite irritated."

On November 23, one day after the close of filming, Maud Humphrey died after a long and stubborn fight with cancer. She was seventy-two. *The New York Times* ran a brief obituary of the now-forgotten woman. Her uncomplaining code demanded that no one know how ill she was until it was too late. No sooner was she rushed to the hospital than she slipped into a coma. "She died as she had lived," Bogart said. "With guts." His words were a cover for a relationship, or rather the absence of one, that had left both sides emotionally starved. "Cruel as it may sound, Maud was not a woman one loved. . . . For such was her drive that none of us could really get at her."

In her last years, Maud and Humphrey Bogart were like two old fighters who finally acknowledge their mutual admiration and respect but without a trace of intimacy. Throughout her life her portraits of him had been their only common ground. Her last studio was an uncluttered room in her Sunset Boulevard apartment, where she always worked in a freshly laundered smock, holding her pencil with a hand that had lost none of its steadiness.

In typical Maud Humphrey fashion, she had telephoned him one day in a state of fury after a sound truck blared along Hollywood Boulevard, hawking *The Return of Dr. X:* "Who is the vilest fiend in history? Who is the monster who laughs as he kills? Who is the vampire who despoils a woman for his pleasure. . . ."

Maud was livid. Carefully, Bogart explained that the studio had to advertise the film.

"I know," she raged. "*But they might have mentioned your name!*"

After her death he wondered if he had done the right thing in taking her away from New York ("When Maud stops working, she'll die"). He left it to Mayo, the mother-dependent child-woman who had tended Maud lovingly and smoothed the mother-son relationship, to see to the funeral arrangements. And it was to Mayo that Maud left an engraved heart-shaped locket that had been in the family for years, along with a note in her unmistakable handwriting:

> Here is my heart—
> but I had the initials
> changed to M. M. B.
> from M. H. B. so now
> it is your heart

Mayo kept the locket until her death.

That winter of 1940, the Bogarts went east for two weeks of personal appearances at the Strand, Warners' first-run movie palace in Times Square, where *High Sierra* was set to open in a month. As was then customary at Broadway cinemas, the movie was to be followed by a stage show, the two running in succession from ten A.M. until late at night. The Bogarts topped a bill that included Ozzie Nelson and his orchestra, vocalist Harriet Hilliard (the 1950s idealized TV parents Ozzie and Harriet), and the variety act of the "noted Egyptian magician" Galli Galli.

The shows were in essence a holdover from vaudeville, and in fact the Bogarts' appearance was billed as a vaudeville act. "Mr. Bogart," the announcement read, "will be assisted in his sketch by his wife, Mayo Methot, former stage actress." But it didn't particularly matter what visiting stars did on stage. For the audience, it was enough that they were there, the screen gods come down from Olympus, talking, acting, even singing and dancing.

For Bogart, the skit meant a visit to New York, at $3,000 a week for little work. In a perfect example of the closed circle of production and distribution at the time, he was paid by Warner Bros. Pictures, Inc., which was reimbursed by Warner Bros. Circuit Management. Since the Strand was a Warner theater, the corporation paid itself.

After the last show at night, Bogart and Mayo would have a late meal at "21" or Bleeck's. They were a crackling and unsettling presence, reveling in their obstreperousness and leaving bemused customers wondering just how much was staged for their benefit. One night at Bleeck's, journalist Junius Adams saw the couple enter, laughing but radiating tension. Bogart went to the bar, Mayo to a phone booth. She left the door open and launched quite audibly into a long call laced with four-letter words, curses, and vituperation. After a time she stopped, leaned out of the booth and called out, her strong voice cutting through the hum of conversation, "Humph-*ree*! Do you want to talk to Mother?"

While nothing had changed between Bogart and Mayo, there were unmistakable signs of a metamorphosis in Bogart's career. The first night at the Strand, the couple and Mary Baker, who had come east with them, made their way from the dressing room through the maze of narrow corridors to the stage door in the back alley. The blast of wintry air as the door opened was expected. What they saw beyond it, barely visible under the street lights, was not—a sea of faces, arrayed wall-to-wall in the alley and spilling out onto Forty-seventh Street. They were fans, mostly women, waiting in the darkness and the post-Thanksgiving slush, hoping for a glimpse of Humphrey Bogart.

Mary Baker knew then that she had a valuable property on her hands, and wondered how to convince Warners. In retrospect, given the directives of the previous six months, the scene could also have been less a spontaneous demonstration than a deftly staged event showing the fine hand of Charles Einfeld or Martin Weiser. In any case, for the three people at the stage door, it was clear that things would never again be the same.

The good news for Bogart was bad news for Mayo. The scuttlebutt from the publicity department at the studio concerned his image. Now that it was being upgraded, shouldn't he be seen in public with someone younger and more attractive? There was nothing official, only whispers and rumors. On Mayo, the effect of these rumors was devastating. The jealousy that had emerged so powerfully during *High Sierra,* and now fed by growing alcoholism, showed signs of turning into paranoia.

When *High Sierra* was released in January 1941, it more than fulfilled Warners' expectations. The picture had everything, *The New York Times* raved: "speed, excitement, suspense, and that ennobling suggestion of futility that makes for irony and pity. Mr. Bogart plays the leading role with a perfection of hard-boiled vitality. . . . Especially is Miss Lupino impressive as the adoring moll."

Reviewers faced with the more terrifying gangsterism emanating from Nazi-dominated Europe read into the picture a farewell to an era that seemed innocent by comparison. "We wouldn't know for certain whether the twilight of the American gangster is here," the *Times* continued, "but the Warner Brothers, who should know if anybody does, have apparently taken it for granted and, in a solemn Wagnerian mood, are giving that titanic figure a send-off befitting a first-string god. . . . It's a wonder the American flag wasn't wrapped around his broken corpse."

Even those who found the doings unduly sentimentalized were full of praise for the cast, the direction, the taut screenplay, and most of all, the lead. Howard Barnes wrote in the *Herald Tribune* that Bogart's Roy Earle was "one of the finest performances of a fine actor. . . . Bogart. . . . keys the performance of the whole photoplay magnificently. He is at once savage and sentimental; fatalistic and filled with half-formulated aspirations. . . . His steady portrayal, even more than Raoul Walsh's staccato staging, is what makes the melodrama something more than merely exciting."

It was a new kind of screen character—an embattled man equally at odds with public morality and himself. He was a strange mix of ambiguity and integrity, someone who might be on both sides of the law, but whose true allegiance was to the man within, and whose world had neither ideals nor absolutes. John Huston and W. R. Burnett had created the Bogart hero.

The box office figures at the end of January showed that the film had delivered on all counts, and not just in the big cities on either coast. "The picture," declared the Kansas City *Star,* "brings Humphrey Bogart and Ida Lupino to long-deferred and long deserved stardom."

At the close of production Bogart had cabled Wallis, "HOPE WE DID AS WELL AS YOU HOPED WE WOULD," some anxiety mixed with his expressed gratitude for the part. By mid-winter, the overwhelming reaction of both critics and the public had laid those doubts to rest. He had every reason to feel confident when, in early 1941, Warners began casting their newest Broadway acquisition. Irwin Shaw's *The Gentle People* had been mounted to great acclaim and success by the Group Theatre in a production starring Franchot Tone and Sylvia Sidney. Ida Lupino was assigned the female lead and Bogart wanted to play Geoff, the waterfront extortionist who is terrifying to the local men, attractive to their women, and eventually disposed of by the neighborhood's "gentle people" in self-defense. Some read into the story an allegory of collective action against Nazism, a message that was quite acceptable to Bogart. But most of all, it was a prestige project. Like *High Sierra,* it had all the good ingredients—suspense, sex, and violence.

Bogart sent a telegram from New York to producer Henry Blanke that he'd heard he was to do *Gentle People* next: "SEEMS LIKE A GOOD IDEA IS THERE ANY TRUTH IN THE RUMOR OR CAN'T YOU TALK?" Blanke couldn't and didn't. Once again Bogart was in third place, behind Cagney and Raft. Einfeld could enthuse, but Wallis was still hedging his bets. The figures on *They Drive by Night* told it all: the critics might cheer Bogart; his pictures might make money for Warners; but Cagney's and Raft's made more.

Cagney and Raft, however, were not interested, despite the pleas of director Anatole Litvak. Neither was Robinson. Bogart, with a solid hit behind him, bypassed Wallis and went directly to Jack Warner. "IT SEEMS TO ME THAT I AM THE LOGICAL PERSON ON THE LOT TO PLAY GENTLE PEOPLE," he wired Warner, asking for a meeting. "I WOULD BE GREATLY DISAPPOINTED IF I DIDN'T GET IT." J. L. was convinced.

The question is, was Ida Lupino? Her contract gave her the right to do outside pictures and script refusal as well. She didn't particularly want to do *The Gentle People,* hoping instead for the female lead in Twentieth Century–Fox's upcoming *How Green Was My Valley.* Warners management conceded to Lupino on every point possible, hoping to keep their new star away from Darryl Zanuck's studio on Pico Boulevard. They were open to questions of salary, script changes, and even of the leading man. Lupino was thought to want her good friend John Garfield, who was already in line for the secondary role played on Broadway by Elia Kazan. Then came a new twist: "LUPINO REFUSES PLAY IN PICTURE WITH BOGART," the studio cabled Wallis, who was visiting in New York.

The story of Lupino's refusal has had currency for decades. According to a later Lupino biography based in part on her recollections, "Bogart's verbal treatment of Ida [during the making of *High Sierra*] so upset her that she refused to accept an upcoming Warner's assignment." And in an interview three years after the picture's release, Bogart allegedly acknowledged giving Lupino "quite a verbal battering," though omitting the specifics. "He says things to get them off his chest, he explains," the story explained, "and forgets them the next moment. He feels people should accept them in the spirit they're given."

Yet no one connected with *High Sierra* saw anything to suggest animosity between Bogart and Lupino; all the evidence is to the contrary. A possible explanation is that the studio invented the slight as a means of not casting Bogart and shifting the onus onto Lupino. The telegram and two Warner memos that allude to Lupino's refusing to work with Bogart are suspiciously without the usual detail. John Huston was incensed when asked shortly before his death if it was true that Lupino kept Bogart out of the film. He first emitted a strangled "AARGH!," then dismissed the memos with "Ahhh, well, who cares? That's very slim." And Lupino's response in 1991 was, "Warners was absolutely lying. They did not like me at all, they did not like Bogart and they did not like Errol Flynn. The three of us were their gruesome threesome," because the actors' rising popularity threatened the studio's control over them.

Garfield, on the other hand, a dynamic urban type loaded with talent, had strong support from the start, including Wallis, director Litvak, and co-writer Jerry Wald; his agents were also Lupino's. Warner had lunch in his private dining room with those agents the day Bogart wired him. After hearing a litany of complaint, the sum of which was that their clients were not happy, J. L. put "the clincher," as he called it, on the deal for Lupino. J. L. wanted Ida and Garfield—especially Ida—to be happy. At the same time, Henry Blanke reminded him that casting Garfield would end "the problem of convincing Lupino to play with Bogart," if that problem really existed. But the change was not made right away, and with the starting date approaching, Blanke appealed to casting director Steve Trilling. They *had* to begin testing immediately. Couldn't he somehow "straighten out the Lupino-Bogart situation."

The production budget had been released three days earlier, on January 31, clearly specifying Bogart. Lupino would be paid $40,000 against his $16,500. Then the studio formally reversed itself. On February 7, Trilling announced the final cast of *The Gentle People.* Garfield was in. Bogart was out.

The Gentle People, its title changed to *Out of the Fog,* was released in the fall of 1941 to a mixed reception. And whatever the reason behind the rejection of him, for Bogart the experience had been a deep embarrassment.

Warners put him to work opposite George Raft in *Manpower,* as one of two power linemen vying for the affections of Marlene Dietrich, who was on loanout to Warners from Universal. To the casting office, it seemed the perfect solution to the wrangles over *Out of the Fog.* Raoul Walsh was directing, Hellinger producing, and this third pairing of Bogart and Raft was a natural follow-up to *They Drive by Night.* (The plot, however, was closer to a remake of Howard Hawks's 1932 film *Tiger Shark,* in which a Portuguese fisherman played by Edward G. Robinson marries a girl with a sullied reputation out of pity, only to see her fall in love with his best friend.)

But there was trouble even before production began. Raft, in a parallel of Bogart's planting seeds of doubt regarding *High Sierra,* contacted agent Sam Jaffe and tried to convince him that his client was miscast and that the film would hurt Bogart's career. Through various third parties, Bogart heard that Raft had been going around the studio telling executives that Bogart was wrong for the part and that he wouldn't play opposite him. Reportedly, Bogart had earlier complained that playing scenes with Raft drove him crazy. "He reads every line the same way. One two three *pause.* One two three *pause.* How do you compete against that?" By late February, Warners was again weighing other options for Bogart, including a loanout to MGM.

"Raft didn't want the competition," a former Warners' executive explained. "Raft could never figure out why his kind of stardom existed anyway, because he was strictly a caricature of a leading man. Outside of a few pictures he was laughable. And when it came to picking parts, Bogart could read, Bogart was intelligent. He came from the theater. He knew what a play was. But Raft was a bigger star."

The tension came to a head a week later when Bogart, on the lot for a wardrobe test, suddenly found himself in a shouting match with Mack Gray, Raft's stand-in, bodyguard, personal shadow, and live-in companion. Gray had caused the scene, Bogart later complained in a long telegram to Wallis, "AND NOBODY MADE ANY EFFORT TO STOP IT." Raft, nowhere to be seen, refused to continue unless Bogart was dropped from the cast. The studio complied before the day was out. For the second time in six weeks, Bogart found himself thrown off a picture.

"ANY REMARKS AND ACCUSATIONS BY MACK GRAY WHICH WERE ATTRIBUTED TO ME ARE COMPLETELY AND ENTIRELY UNTRUE," Bogart said in his telegram. "I HAVE NEVER HAD ANYTHING BUT THE VERY FINEST FEELING OF FRIENDSHIP FOR GEORGE."

Confronting Raft on the lot, Bogart asked him what he was so angry about? What was he supposed to have said? Raft wouldn't speak to him.

Bogart was hurt, he continued to Wallis. "IT'S THE SECOND TIME I HAVE BEEN KEPT OUT OF A GOOD PICTURE AND A GOOD PART BY AN ACTOR'S REFUSING TO WORK WITH ME."

The studio, however, was more concerned with keeping the bigger of its two properties happy. Bogart got a good weekly salary, but Raft made $60,000 a picture and was already picking up his checks. And so Edward G. Robinson was brought in for Bogart.

In the event, Bogart was well off the film. Raft clearly had problems. Robinson promptly became the butt of unfounded mistreatment that culminated in a fistfight during which Raft, according to a Warner affidavit, "did violently rough-house and push the said Edward G. Robinson around the set . . . directed toward him a volley of personal abuse and profanity . . . threatened [him] with bodily harm, and in the course of his remarks directed and applied to Mr. Robinson in a loud and boisterous tone of voice, numerous filthy, obscene and profane expressions." News photographers had caught the fracas, and for once the studio was unable to conceal the embarrassing behavior of a star. The next day's papers were full of the story. Some executives began to wonder whether George Raft was really worth his cost.

But any solace Bogart might have taken was erased as his own problems grew. Warners hated a vacuum. Actors were paid to *work.* A week after Bogart's dismissal from *Manpower,* a studio messenger delivered the script for *Bad Men of Missouri* to the corner of North Horn Avenue and Shoreham Road. It was a third-string western directed by Ray Enright (late of *Carnival*) in which Bogart was to play the outlaw Cole Younger.

The script came on Thursday afternoon. His orders were to meet with Enright Monday morning. For Bogart, it was the final provocation. He leafed through the script, resealed the package, and penciled a brief note to Steve Trilling on a scrap of yellow paper: *"Are you kidding—?"*

Monday morning, Ray Enright waited. At one o'clock, a messenger returned the script to Trilling, with Bogart's terse note, which concluded: "This is certainly rubbing it in—since Lupino and Raft are casting pictures, maybe I can. . . . Regards Bogie."

Trilling telephoned the house. Mr. Bogart was on his boat in Balboa, he was told. The executive called the marina. Sorry, Mr. Bogart was out cruising and they didn't know when he'd return. Trilling tightly suggested that Bogart call him back as soon as he docked. From his office in the corner of the administration building, J. L. sent orders for a legal notice directing Bogart to report to the studio at 10:00 A.M. the next day.

Tuesday morning, Steve Trilling waited. And waited. That afternoon, a notification went out via registered mail to Sam Jaffe's office. On Wednesday, Warner Legal, in an announcement to department heads, made it official: "Please be advised that Humphrey Bogart's contract has been suspended." It was the first suspension of many to come. Bogart was determined that the studio understand he had stopped being the good soldier and the grateful heavy. Warner management, in their belief that Bogie the Beefer might grumble but would always go along, found instead a new-born rebel.

The suspension, however, meant more than salary withheld; de facto it meant the deep freeze—no scripts, no roles, no publicity, no lucrative radio appearances. Suspension made the offending actor a non-person. That became clear enough as Warners, having recast *Bad Men of Missouri* with the amiable lightweight Dennis Morgan, considered its options of what to do with Bogart. It was a ritual dance peculiar to the industry: an actor, having refused one role, would thereupon declare his readiness to take another. The studio could either take the offender back or keep him or her dangling without compensation for the weeks or even months it took the substitute to finish the picture.

Bogart had declared himself "ready, willing and able" to return to work two weeks after he was suspended. Legal head Roy Obringer put the choice to Warner and Wallis: Should they accept Bogart's offer or continue his suspension? Continue, they said. Sam Jaffe personally appealed to Jack Warner, to no avail.

That May, *Carnival* was sprung on the public, its title changed to *The Wagons Roll at Night.* ("For the millions who cheered *They Drive by Night,*" the ads read). It deceived no one. "*Kid Galahad* in a new set of clothes," wrote one critic. "A bit of carnival color," said the *Herald Tribune,* "does little to fool any seasoned filmgoer into thinking that he is seeing something fresh." Worse still, the audience reaction on opening day amounted almost to a demonstration. At one theater, at least, there was howling laughter at the dialogue and rude, suggestive noises during the love scenes. "Apparently," the *Daily News* reported, "the Strand patrons resented the fact that they had been taken in." The only one to escape unscathed was Eddie Albert, who upstaged Bogart at every turn. "The Strand customers turned out early . . . to welcome Bogart," wrote the *Post,* "and stayed to root for Albert." As for Bogart, the critics who had proclaimed his stardom back in January now found him, as the *Times* put it, "badly hampered in a ridiculously fustian villain role."

It was a bitter spring for him. He hadn't worked in half a year. The promise of stardom following a big hit had seemingly evaporated yet again. It was a pattern that would prevail in one form or another throughout his time at Warners. He would painfully scale the glass hill, only to slide back. Public acclaim seemed always matched with private put-down. He had no way to know it at the time, of course, but this was the point where he bottomed out. His road would never be smooth, but with the unlikeliest of fairy godmothers, he was about to find his way to better fortune.

Louella Parsons, overweight and alcoholic, was the gossip queen of Hollywood and the favorite of her all-powerful boss William Randolph Hearst. Stars and moguls ignored Louella at their peril. An invitation to appear on her radio program, *Hollywood Hotel,* was tantamount to a command, and that spring, Parsons wanted Bogart. Just why she was so adamant is unknown, but he had always been straight with her and perhaps she saw a chance to help a quotable source. Parsons knew he was still on suspension, and she also knew that suspended contract players could not make public appearances. Memos flew at the studio. On the telephone with Warner Publicity, Parsons made it clear that she didn't care about Bogart's status. Was she getting him or not? She had to know—today.

What should they do? an anxious Obringer wrote to J. L. Jack Warner realized he had gone as far as he could go—at least this time.

"Put Humphrey Bogart back on the payroll," he replied.

For Bogart, the reprieve meant more than a return to work: his defiance had paid off. For once, his image was bigger than the studio's will.

CHAPTER 8

The Black Bird

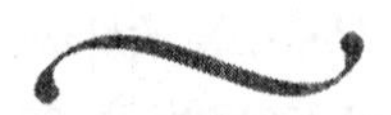

Ten-year-old Max Wilk was addicted to the thrills of *Black Mask* magazine. Free periodicals arrived every day at the Wilk home in the hope that his father Jacob might find something he wanted to turn into a film, and Max, already a voracious reader, looked at them all. But *Black Mask* was his favorite. When he came home from school one afternoon in 1929 and saw the tube with the unmistakable logo, he immediately ripped it open and began to read: "THE MALTESE FALCON, Chapter 1: 'Spade & Archer.' Samuel Spade's jaw was long and bony. . . ."

Max, hooked, tore through the story until he was stopped cold: "To be continued in our next issue." He was furious. When Jacob came home that night, Max was at the door, complaining, "This dumb magazine, they cut the story! I have to find out what happens!"

The next evening, Jacob Wilk told his son that he'd called the *Black Mask* editor and asked for the rest of the story. There would be a two-day delay while Wilk's readers synopsized it; after that, it was Max's.

But it nearly wasn't Warners'. Before they could obtain it, Paramount briefly flirted with an adaptation, then ran into casting problems and gave up. Five months after the last *Black Mask* installment, Warners purchased the screen rights from the thirty-six-year-old author Dashiell Hammett and his hardcover publisher, Alfred A. Knopf, for $8,500. "Well, we bought it," Jacob told Max. "Going to make a movie out of it. But you're responsible. I hope it's a good movie."

Over the next dozen years Warners would film *The Maltese Falcon* three times. The third time, they got it right.

The first version was made in 1931, with Ricardo Cortez as the detective and Bebe Daniels as the mystery woman. It had a general fidelity to the original and did fine at the box office. When it was recycled in 1936 as *Satan Met a Lady,* Hal Wallis had urged the script be improved "by actually making the book." His advice was ignored; the film, with a clumsy script written for laughs, starred Bette Davis and Warren William, and was a low point in the actress's career.

Between this second filming and the successful final one was an attempt, in 1939, at yet another, entitled *The Clock Struck Three.* But *Charlie Chan* screenwriter Charles Belden could not figure out how to write the last half of the story.

John Huston appreciated Hammett as much as he did W. R. Burnett, and when in 1941 Warners offered him a chance to direct his first film (he had directed a location shot for *Jezebel* in 1938), he asked for *The Maltese Falcon.* "The fact was," he said many years later, "that *Falcon* had never really been put on the screen."

Because the prevailing assumption in the industry was that literary properties had to be turned inside out to become cinematic, the previous writers had tried to put their own stamp on the story. Huston was out to challenge that assumption. "I decided," he wrote some years later, "on a radical procedure: to follow the book rather than depart from it." Actually, it was the same technique he had used months before on *High Sierra.* Now the method was in place; and Bogart, just off suspension, was available.

There was only one problem. On May 19, when the cast list was drawn up, Bogart was the number two choice for Sam Spade. The studio's first choice was—who else?—George Raft. But he was not Huston's, whose dislike of Raft had been made clear during *High Sierra.* "Why don't we have *Bogart* play it instead of Raft?" argued Huston in a rancorous meeting with Steve Trilling and Henry Blanke. "But no, it *had* to be offered to Raft!"

To artists concerned only with their own picture, Warners' insistence was mystifying, even given the runaway success of *They Drive by Night.* But in reality the executives' bullheadedness was part of the Hollywood-style chess game in which the studios reduced talent to pawns. Warners had not really expected Raft to take the part. The offer of *The Maltese Falcon* had been made merely for leverage. Jack Warner and Hal Wallis cared about this thrice-cycled whodunit with a novice director only insofar as it was a bargaining chip in pending inter-studio negotiations. Warners wanted Henry Fonda for the Elliott Nugent–James Thurber comedy *The Male Animal.* Fonda worked for Fox. Fox wanted Raft.

The tradeoff was obvious, except that Raft, contractually, was able to say yes or no to the deal. Raft had no interest in *The Maltese Falcon* because, Huston said, "he didn't want to work with a director who'd never directed before. Now *Warners*—I must take my hat off to them—stuck by their guns and stuck by me. They could have put another director in, but didn't." What Huston overlooked was that another director might have led to Raft's changing his mind. The studio was willing to stick by a first-time director only so long as it suited its interest. Huston's greatest asset as a director going into the film was that he scared off George Raft.

The studio went through all the motions of the game. Raft was notified that he was in the film the day the cast list was drawn up. A note accompanying the screenplay when it was sent a week later informed him that "you are to portray the role of 'Samuel Spade.' " The next day, however, in the big corner office in the executive building, J. L. assured Raft, in an ego massaging unusual in Warners' labor relations, that he could indeed turn down the film—if he would only go over to Twentieth Century–Fox and do that studio's picture. They parted on a note of agreement that Raft would go on a "friendly suspension." To protect the studio's legal standing in case Raft didn't close his deal with Fox, Warner told Obringer to have Raft formally ordered to work on *The Maltese Falcon* on Monday, June 2.

The meeting was on May 27. Six days later, word leaked back from Fox that Raft had read their script and didn't like it. Obringer shot off a notice to their recalcitrant star: he had exactly until 5:00 P.M. the next day to close with Fox. Otherwise, he was to report June 4 for *The Maltese Falcon.*

Huston steeled himself for the possibility that he'd have to work with Raft after all. "Just to show his authority, he would be insubordinate on the set," Huston recalled with a laugh three months before his death from emphysema in 1987. He required a portable oxygen tank to breathe and had to pause for bouts of coughing, but he exuded a sense of mischief, and his singular voice was full of inflection. "He liked challenging directors and such. So," he continued, laughing more, "I secretly decided to have a small sap in my pocket, a *sap* being a blackjack. As Raft would always have his two heavies with him, why, if such a moment came, I simply was going to use the sap—*instantly.*" Here he laughed quite loudly. "But I didn't *want* him."

The five o'clock deadline on June 3 came and went without word from Raft. The next morning, Obringer received a call from Raft's agent at the Myron Selznick office, confirming what Raft had told Warner: Under no circumstances would he play Sam Spade.

"I rejoiced," Huston said.

At 4:15 that afternoon, Bogart was on the set, shooting wardrobe and makeup tests. Actually, neither Raft nor Bogart bore any resemblance to the detective as he appeared in Hammett's novel or the first draft of the screenplay. In these, Spade was described as over six feet tall, having a hooked nose and blond hair with a widow's peak that gave him "the look of a rather pleasant Satan," who grinned "wolfishly" and whose eyes glittered "yellowly." But although Bogart was on the set, he was not officially on the picture until the June 5 stenciled roster marked "FINAL CAST" circulated around the lot, headed by Humphrey Bogart as Sam Spade.

The next day, Raft sent a "Dear Jack" letter, reminding Warner that he had promised to cast him only in important pictures. "As you know, I strongly feel that *The Maltese Falcon* . . . is not an important picture." It was true that at $381,000 the *Falcon* budget was modest. Still, even though it was less than the approximately half-million-dollar budget of *They Drive by Night* or *Invisible Stripes,* and nowhere close to the $1 million Errol Flynn epics, it was well over a B budget.

By all indications, Jack Warner's patience with Raft was coming to an end. Why it ever existed had always been difficult to explain. Raft turned down role after role. His on-set disruptions delayed shooting, ran up costs, and created bad public relations. He had been known to take a role, go on payroll during pre-production, and then refuse to shoot while still pocketing the salary. He had even stuck Warners with an unpaid hotel bill in Washington, D.C., following his attendance at President Roosevelt's birthday ball in early 1941.

"He is very likely to report and stall around and then refuse to work," Obringer warned Wallis in late May. Once Raft had nearly physically attacked Obringer, an ill-considered move. "Roy had played a little professional football," said William Schaefer, Jack Warner's secretary, "and he was ready to take Raft on; but then things calmed down very quickly." (Raft's athletic distinction was his reputation as the world's fastest Charleston dancer.) Yet the studio behaved as if Raft were dependability itself, renewing his options and raising his per-picture fees without a murmur.

Schaefer attributed this endless tolerance to Raft's affiliation with gangsters. "It was the only reason. He was never considered a big, big star. He played gangster roles and tough guy parts and he was good for those. He had a certain drawing power for a certain kind of picture. But other than that, why, he didn't have it. And he was always demanding things. Pushing people around. People don't like that."

Certainly Jack Warner had grown tired it. Raft's whining about what he referred to as "dirty heavies" and his insistence on "important pictures" was wearing thin. "I must disagree with you that 'The Maltese Falcon' is not an important picture," Warner wrote in a letter never sent. Just possibly, George Raft was being given enough rope to hang himself, and J. L. was content to watch his career at Warner's self-destruct, allowing Bogart to move up once again.

By the time the negotiations with Raft were over, the casting of the irresistible and duplicitous Brigid O'Shaughnessy had been settled. Initially, Warners had wanted the part to go to twenty-seven-year-old Geraldine Fitzgerald, a luminous newcomer with star potential. Her success on loanout with Laurence Olivier in *Wuthering Heights* and her solid support of Bette Davis in *Dark Victory* caused Archer Winsten of the New York *Post* to call her "unquestionably the finest discovery Hollywood has made among actresses since the last great one showed up." She was one of the few actors on the lot who compelled Jack Warner's respect. The contract he approved obligated her to Warners for only six months a year and left her free to work elsewhere if she wished. In early 1941 her wish was to go back east.

The studio tried to dissuade her. At $1,750 a week, she cost less than Mary Astor, Warners' next choice. She was also eight years younger than Astor, whose career at the studio stretched back to the silents, when she had been a teenage leading lady to John Barrymore. (Other possibilities were Olivia de Havilland, Rita Hayworth and, far down the list, the young Swedish import Ingrid Bergman.)

Fitzgerald did not want the role, nor did she wish to give up her East Coast trip to do a low-budget whodunit with an untried director and Humphrey Bogart as co-star, regardless of how much she had liked him when they worked together on *Dark Victory*. ("There is nothing to be done with her," Steve Trilling wrote Roy Obringer.) Whereas Astor, a Jaffe client and more than friends with Huston, was very interested indeed. In May, Huston and Bogart took her a script, and producer Henry Blanke left one for the weekend, just as a backup. Astor would remember

Bogart and Huston coming to her house. "They both had an excitement that was contagious. I was familiar with the book as a piece of crisp literature. But the idea of putting it onto the screen, *as it was written,* seemed very far out."

Monday, she was on the telephone, calling the script "a humdinger" and saying she'd love to do the part. "I didn't have to be talked into playing Brigid O'Shaughnessy," Astor wrote in her memoir, *A Life on Film.* "She was attractive, charming, appealingly feminine and helpless, and a complete liar and murderess."

The supporting company was drawn largely from outside the studio. Gladys George, the golden-hearted trollop of *The Roaring Twenties,* was Iva Archer, the faithless wife of Spade's partner. Lee Patrick was Effie, Spade's cool secretary (Eve Arden had been the first choice). The English actor Sydney Greenstreet made his screen debut at age sixty as the villainous Fat Man, Kasper Gutman; he was so large at 357 pounds that the studio had to make all his clothes. The brilliant and singular Peter Lorre was Gutman's gay associate Joel Cairo ("Don't try to get a nancy quality into him," Wallis warned Huston, "because if you do we will have trouble with the picture"). Jerome Cowan, the wisecracking reporter from *High Sierra,* was perfectly cast as Spade's sleazy partner. Elisha Cook Jr., who had last shared billing with Bogart on Broadway in *Chrysalis,* played the punk Wilmer.

They constituted Hammett's odd assortment of double-crossers, con artists, and killers in greedy pursuit of a jewel-encrusted statue. Spade himself is caught in the hunt when he is hired by Brigid, who sheds aliases and stories much as a beautiful snake sheds its skin.

At the start of the film, Effie comes into Spade's office.

> "There's a girl wants to see you. Her name's Wonderly."
> "A customer?"
> "I guess so. You'll want to see her anyway. She's a knock-out."
> "Shoo her in, Effie darling—shoo her in."

"I attempted," Huston wrote some years later, "to transpose Dashiell Hammett's highly individual prose style into camera terms: i.e. sharp photography; geographically correct camera movements; striking if not shocking set-ups." A good many things were novel about the production. The camera work, the lighting, the story told largely from the perspective of the often-confused Spade. Oh yes, Huston said in an interview at the time, he was sure someone would compare the innovations with those of

Orson Welles's recently released *Citizen Kane.* But not only did he have his ideas before the release, but Welles himself likely had drawn some of them from the 1919 silent *The Cabinet of Dr. Caligari.* Besides, the truth was there were no new ideas, only fresh ways of adapting old ones.

Huston, using his art background, sketched out shooting angles for each scene weeks before the start of filming. Then he went over the hundreds of sketches with the cameraman and actors, leaving no doubt as to exactly what he wanted. A publicity release proclaimed, "This method of 'designing' motion pictures in advance . . . is not a new one in Hollywood. But this is the first time that the whole operation of preparing the screenplay, designing it, and directing it, has been left to one man—and that man directing for the first time." Having forestalled any charges of copycat direction by Huston's disclaimers, Warner Publicity went on to boast how the production had "real rooms and offices with real ceilings . . . no familiar catwalks, blazing lights overhead. . . . The players . . . say that the whole set-up is refreshingly swell," not mentioning that Welles had used the same device in *Citizen Kane.* Eliminating overhead lights in favor of natural lighting imparted both a gritty realism and a sense of claustrophobia in a story played out mostly in oppressive interiors—the anonymous hotel rooms; the down-at-the-heels offices of Spade and Archer; Spade's seedy bachelor apartment. It was the way ex-detective Hammett saw the private eye: unglamorous, hard-edged, amoral; a man living from client to client and risking life and limb for $25 a day.

Production began on Monday, June 9, in the interior of Spade's office. Cameraman Arthur Edeson's lighting conjured up a gray San Francisco day, with a close shot of a window looking out at the city and the Bay. In the foreground, the big black letters, seen in reverse, read "SPADE and ARCHER." The characters were introduced with the same economy Hammett employed in the book. After Lee Patrick as Effie announced the visitor, the inner office door opened and Mary Astor materialized, demure in the ensemble decided on by Warners—two-tone tailored suit, white blouse, silver fox over right shoulder, pancake black hat tilted over right eye, black suede gloves, bag and shoes: Brigid O'Shaughnessy, alias Miss Wonderly.

Huston, like Hammett, let the characters speak for themselves. Spade was described by Hammett as "what most private detectives would like to be, a hard shifty fellow, able to take care of himself in any situation, able to get the best of anybody he comes in contact with whether criminal, innocent bystander or client." And his client, alias Miss Wonderly, as "tall, pliantly slender, her body . . . erect and high-breasted, her legs long

. . . dark, soft, wavy hair, full lips. Her eyes are timid, childlike at times in their apparent innocence."

Bogart's wardrobe—provided, unlike Astor's and Greenstreet's, by the actor himself—did not vary all that much from his earlier films. Nostalgic recollection to the contrary, Bogart's detective did not wear a trench coat wrapped about him like a latter-day crusader's cape; that came a year later, in *Casablanca.* Instead, he wore the double-breasted pinstripe suit—wide-shouldered, narrow-hipped—that was his virtual trademark and, for a change of pace, a gray single-breasted number. For the economy-minded actor, it meant a bit more mileage from his working wardrobe. Visually, the echo from past films connected Sam Spade to the long line of Bogart killers and added to his aura of moral ambiguity.

Astor struck just the right note as the bewitching schemer. All fragility and helplessness, she engages the firm of Spade and Archer ostensibly to track down the seducer of a non-existent sister. Actually, she wants to trail and kill a rival hunter of the Falcon. By the end of the second day, Huston had shot the long scene that starts the film and had moved on to Spade's apartment: the detective is awakened in the darkness by the ringing telephone and the news that his partner has been found shot to death.

It wasn't brisk enough, however, for Hal Wallis. In viewing the dailies, he missed the rapid-fire pacing of a Warner thriller. He wasn't seeing "the punchy, driving kind of tempo that this picture requires," he told Huston via Blanke in a memo.

"My criticism is principally with Bogart, who has adopted a leisurely suave form of delivery. I don't think we can stand this all through the picture, as it is going to have a tendency to drag down the scene. . . . Bogart must have his usual brisk, staccato manner and delivery, and if he doesn't have it, I'm afraid we are going to be in trouble." It was, Wallis stressed, a matter of pacing. But he was also enunciating a general rule—that whether he played killers or detectives, Bogart was to remain Bogart.

Huston promised to make his lead more "quick and staccato" (he hadn't wanted to start off at too fast a clip, he said), and assured Wallis that, by the midway point, the whole thing would be "turning like a pinwheel." The opening scenes were eventually re-shot, with the familiar Bogart delivery.

In the months following the film's release, Huston would be justly praised for a brilliant directorial debut. He graciously credited the help of director William Wyler, who before shooting began had looked at Huston's sketches and made constructive suggestions, and he acknowledged Henry Blanke for providing what he called the most important advice in his career as a director: "Shoot each scene as if it was the most important scene in the film." The debut was also facilitated by the practiced eye of Hal Wallis and, eventually, at a single, critical point, by Jack Warner. The film's real strength, however, was in the company assembled by Huston and Blanke.

Bogart at forty-two was in top form, young enough to project the vitality of Spade but with the polished skills of a screen veteran. Sydney Greenstreet, in need of extra rehearsal time and nervous at the outset ("Mary dear, hold my hand, tell me I won't make an ass of myself," he said to Astor before his first scene), made the transition from stage to screen with liquid smoothness. He was "perfect from the word go," Huston said, "the Fat Man inside out." The diminutive Peter Lorre, whose whispery voice and ominously gentle manner clothed a rapier wit and a finely honed intellect, had made film history eight years before as the serial child murderer in the German-language chiller, *M.* Behind his baby face was a sense of worldliness, and Huston thought him one of the finest and subtlest actors he ever worked with.

As Brigid, Mary Astor was, Huston said, "the enchanting murderess to my idea of perfection." Evidently she also met other criteria of perfection. Huston was then married to Lesley Black, his second of five wives (shortly before his death he summarized them as "a showgirl, a gentlewoman, a motion picture actress, a ballerina, and a crocodile"), but that didn't prevent an affair with Astor that added liveliness to the filming.

It was something of a Huston trademark. "He had affairs with everybody in the world," script supervisor Meta Wilde said. "I think it was just Johnny's nature. Every woman that came along, he wanted." Wilde, known then as Meta Carpenter, presided over continuity, the screenplay in one hand, a stopwatch in the other, making sure that everything matched from take to take. Familiar in the ways of romantic liaisons—William Faulkner was her lover—she had no problem reading the signals between the director and his leading lady. "There was a lot of chemistry between them. Good chemistry."

Bogart himself remained indifferent to Astor's charms, conditioned after years of playing heavies to viewing his co-stars as colleagues rather than objects of sexual desire. "The ladies like Bogie," Huston remembered, "but he was not a ladies' man."

To Mary Astor, there was an element of sadness about Bogart that was all too visible beneath the blustery surface. "Bogey looked at the world, at his place in it, at movies, at life in general," she wrote in an unedited draft of an essay, "and there was something about it that made him sick, contemptuous, bitter. And it showed. He related to people as though they had no clothes on, and no skin for that matter."

For Bogart, it was easy to regard Astor as lively, entertaining, and one of the guys. In case he ever changed his mind, there was always Mayo in the background, a palpable presence both on and off the set. "Bogie did his best to placate [Mayo]," Huston wrote. "But let her feel there was attention shifting away from her . . . and there would be hell to pay." "She was always taking center stage," he said on another occasion. "She was very jealous of Bogie and wanting to show off. And she was a *bore.* Looked and acted like a bull terrier. Though not quite as pretty."

To Huston Mayo became The Enemy. During all the years Bogart had played the heavy, his personal life had never been an issue. He came in, did his work, went home. *The Maltese Falcon* was a different world. He had a starring role in an ensemble that evolved into a professional family as personalities meshed, and their closeness was heightened by an awareness of creating something new. It was also Bogart's first bonding with a director, both personally and professionally, a beautiful friendship that explicitly excluded Mayo Methot Bogart.

With Huston he could indulge his dry wit and make cracks about his home life. He spoke witheringly of "The Rosebud" in mocking reference to his wife's old Broadway title, which now was as unsuitable and dated as a fashion page from 1924. Divorce, however, did not seem an option. "Bogie was *morbidly* faithful," Huston insisted, "in a way that, seeing him with the Rosebud, I was at a loss to comprehend."

As *The Maltese Falcon* progressed, the movie increasingly meant a social life for Bogart away from home. The troupe took noon breaks for lunch at the Lakeside Country Club—"with drinks" Huston said, "always with drinks"—which had a good buffet and where the Huston-Bogart friendship had first flourished over martinis during the shooting of *High Sierra.*

Mary Astor later wrote that they all sat at a big table outdoors beside the pool. "People from other companies would eye us suspiciously because we weren't in a hurry and would say smugly, 'We're ahead of schedule.' " The conversation was always brisk, the kidding intense. "If you didn't like it, you were ignored afterward." She had once made the mistake of trying to join in "with some kind of naive smart-crack. The kidding was turned onto me unmercifully . . . it was more than I could handle. Tears started popping and I whimpered, 'I just can't keep up with this!' Bogie laughed his head off, along with the rest, and then got up from the table and came around to my place. He wiped the tears away with his hankerchief [*sic*] and said, 'You're okay, baby, take it easy. So you're not very smart [meaning quick with a riposte]—but you know it and what the hell's wrong with that?' "

The joking and clowning provided a necessary release and a chance to unwind. "We had to," Astor added, "for the emotional intensity of the various relationships, the whip-cracking speed of individual scenes, the fountains of words, would have been exhausting." For although virtually all *The Maltese Falcon* was shot indoors on a set, and thus was not grueling in the conventional sense, it was a difficult picture to make. Essentially, it is a series of dialogues punctuated by sudden violence. Three of the protagonists are shady figures searching for a priceless statue that they are willing to kill for, and the story is a tangled mess of plots within plots. At the center of this labyrinth of deceit is the detective, his only guide the twisted track left by his self-admitted liar of a client.

Huston shot the script in sequence, instead of following the customary money-saving method of filming batches of unrelated scenes using the same set. Even so, according to Astor, there were so many twists and reversals in the plot that the actors themselves were frequently lost and would wind up shouting and arguing, "Now wait a minute—he was on a boat, wasn't he? How can he have had time to . . ." Huston, she said, would then pull up a canvas chair "and shut us up and quietly explain it."

Scenes were allowed to run for minutes at a time without a break, the camera moving from speaker to speaker, or speaker to listener, catching reactions, according to a press release, like the eye of "a silent and disinterested spectator." The desired effect, Huston wrote a friend, was that "the audience knows no more or less than [Spade] does."

With the visuals turned into commentary, the eye of the lens was all-important. Edeson's camera, when shot from near the floor, focused upward on Sydney Greenstreet and turned him into an Everest of menace, the visual highlight of a long, unbroken sequence in which Sam Spade meets the Fat Man.

Meta Wilde, whose career with Huston began with *The Maltese Falcon* and lasted to 1985 and *Prizzi's Honor,* described the excitement of that sequence in her memoir, *A Loving Gentleman.* "The camera followed Bogart . . . down a long hallway, and finally into a living room; there the camera moved up and down in what is referred to as a boom-up and boom-down shot, then panned from left to right and back to Bogart's face; the next pan shot was to Greenstreet's massive stomach from Bogart's point of view. The choreography of it was exacting and exciting. One miss and we had to begin all over again. But there was the understanding that we were attempting something purely cinematic, never tried before, and everyone—stars, camera operators, and cablemen—worked industriously to bring it off. . . . After a nerve-racking seven minutes or so, Huston shouted, 'CUT' and 'PRINT IT!' a shout went up and crew members heartily congratulated Bogart, Greenstreet, and Edeson and his camera specialists."

The greatest burden of continuity, however, was on the detective, who goes through the film in pursuit of an unknown goal. Spade had to be coolly self-centered yet reflect a full spectrum of emotion as he peels away the layers to get to a final truth in which everything turns out to be a lie. Bogart sustained the part without a flaw and more than lived up to the expectations of his director, who later said that "he was forever surprising me with how good he was. Practically no direction was required—he was just *excellent.* Two little things that I suggested—I can't recall them now—he picked up and instantly used. The whole experience was a joy. Just everything he did was right. It's instinctive. That really superb kind of timing—not many musicians have it."

Mary Astor appreciated Bogart's technical skill, as well. It "was quite brilliant. . . . A good actor is supposed to 'lose himself' in the character he plays. Instead the character got lost in Bogie, and gained by it. . . . His precision timing was no accident, and he kept other actors on their toes because he *listened* to them during a scene, he watched, he *looked* at them. He wasn't up stage center acting all by himself. . . . he 'related.' "

If any single day could be pointed to as the turning mark in Bogart's film career, a good candidate is June 20, 1941—when the Bogart character finally got to kiss the girl, not the interrupted smooch of *Dark Victory* but a genuine clinch, the certification of his status as a leading man. But like everything in his career, it wasn't easy.

Scene 35, interior. Brigid's apartment. Spade and O'Shaughnessy in passionate confrontation, a fire roaring suggestively, Astor's eyes glistening, her voice, as the script directed, "hoarse and vibrant": "I've given you all the money I have. . . . What else is there that I can buy you with?"

The script direction was specific: "Spade takes her face between his hands, kisses her mouth roughly and contemptuously, then releasing her, he sits back."

The action was straightforward enough, but Bogart couldn't manage it. The cameraman's report of each take is a list of NGA, NGA, NGA—No Good Action, No Good Action, No Good Action. Makeup artist Frank McCoy stepped up to Bogart and wiped his face with a damp chamois; someone made a crack about the fire.

"My goodness, it's nothing but a simple little kiss," Huston finally broke in. "Grab her, kiss her, turn her loose. That's all you have to do!" It took seven takes before Huston ordered a print.

Bogart, half-joking, claimed he was out of practice after years of playing heavies. But there might also have been a prudish self-consciousness about on-screen intimacy, in addition to a physiological problem that Astor talked about only in her final years. Bogart, she said, was what was called "a wetter." His scarred, nerve-damaged upper lip caused an accumulation of saliva in one corner of his mouth, a condition made worse by his nervousness. As far as love scenes themselves were concerned, she said, "he didn't like them." She concluded that, although he was not a kissing type, "Bogie didn't have to kiss the girl. He didn't have to touch her. You knew by the way he looked at her."

A year later when a kiss was called for in *Across the Pacific,* things were no better. "Try not to knock my teeth out next time!" she snapped after the first attempt. Bogart was abject: "I'm sorry, kid."

"Then *I* had to apologize," Astor said, "because he *was* sorry—and embarrassed."

Warners had allotted thirty-six days to shoot *The Maltese Falcon.* Thanks to Huston's meticulous preparation, however, and the guiding hand of Henry Blanke tactfully running interference with Wallis, there was every sign that they could finish early. The professionalism was applauded even by unit manager Al Alleborn: "Fine work this company is doing." Wallis, who screened dailies every night, kept his usual close watch on the smallest details. A bruise on Bogart's cheek after Spade is roughed up looked "phony," and he ordered it redone with adhesive plaster. The hairline on Bogart's now mandatory toupee was "pretty obvious." Peter Lorre's diction was getting sloppy; he was tending to run words together. Mary Astor was becoming just a bit "too coy and ladylike."

Walter Huston made an unbilled cameo appearance as Captain Jacobi of the *La Paloma.* He staggers into Spade's office, mortally wounded, a package containing the black bird under one arm, and drops, lifeless as a felled tree. Word from the set had it that young John, grinning broadly, made his father do take after take, fall after fall, until he was a protesting mass of bruises.

Outsiders were made unwelcome. "We didn't want anyone looking over our shoulder," Astor said, and the cast assured it. A midwestern women's club was greeted by a scene played for its benefit: Peter Lorre swaggering out of Astor's trailer, buttoning his fly and calling back, "Bye, Mary." Studio flacks gave subsequent visitors a wide berth of *The Maltese Falcon* set.

The long climactic confrontation involving all five principals was shot last. It is actually a series of interconnecting scenes that ends in the unwrapping—figuratively and literally—of the Maltese Falcon, as well as the final unwrapping, as it were, of Brigid O'Shaughnessy. The sequence had to come in one smooth flow. It was straight out of the theater, played in real time, beginning with Spade and The Girl entering his apartment to find the crooks waiting, and ending with the detective turning his love over to the cops and probably the hangman.

The sequence consumes almost 20 of the film's 100 minutes and lasts nearly to the end. It is a drama of words propelled by the constant threat of death and betrayal, with long stretches of talk and little overt action. It had to be acted perfectly, so that each climax topped the previous one until the finish. This was going to be the toughest part of the picture. Blanke wrote to Wallis, "One solid sequence of thirty-five pages of script, and every member of the cast is in it," and pleaded with Wallis for an extra day of rehearsal time to go through the entire scene before the cameras rolled. Even though Huston was ahead of schedule, it took all of Blanke's powers of persuasion to wring the time from the cost-conscious studio, and it was an unprecedented step for Warners.

On July 3, they began to shoot. *Scene 114, hallway into Spade's apartment.* "As Spade and Brigid are about to enter the living room, the living room light goes on. Brigid cries out, clings to Spade. Fat Gutman stands in the entrance. . . . Wilmer comes out of the kitchen, a black pistol in either hand. . . . Cairo appears, pointing his flat, black automatic. . . ."

Filming the sequence lasted for over a week, with a day off for the Fourth of July, five gifted actors playing off one another—from Astor's first gasp to Greenstreet's sausage fingers making short work of the cord and paper around the bird: "Now—after seventeen years . . ." to Greenstreet grasping a penknife, first shaving the black enamel coating, then digging, then hacking in total fury—"It's a fake!"

With the villains departed, Bogart and Astor moved into their final confrontation scene—eight pages of dialogue as Spade wrings from Brigid the admission that that she killed his partner: "We've only got minutes to get set for the police. . . . Talk!"

To get it right took three days and into late Saturday night, Astor weeping on the couch, Bogart in a chair, staring straight ahead—"Listen . . . when a man's partner is killed, he's supposed to do something about it." The two actors repeated the scene again and again with the same intensity as the camera angles changed—a close-up on Spade, now on Brigid, then on both in a tight two-shot. Sometime after midnight, Huston got what he wanted. Monday morning, Brigid—"like a sleepwalker" according to the screenplay directions—was led off by the law. It took seven takes to satisfy Huston.

The remaining odds and ends were finished off in another three days, although there would later be the usual re-shoots. Out on the back lot on Friday, July 18, they burned the *La Paloma,* the ill-fated boat of the ill-fated Captain Jacobi. On Stage 19, Spade and the Fat Man faced off one last time. At 2:00 A.M., the picture officially closed—$54,000 under budget and two days ahead of schedule.

One more scene was still on paper. Hammett's ending—and Huston's at the outset—played out where the story had started, in Spade's office. Effie stands by the window, mouth twisted, eyes reproachful:

> "You did that, Sam, to her?"
> "She *did* kill Miles, Angel . . ."
> "Don't, please—don't touch me."

A doorknob rattles in the corridor, Effie goes out to see, comes back, and announces Iva Archer. The story ends on a note of defeat and self-recognition as Spade, with a shiver, accepts Iva, whose seedy amorality matches his own.

> "Send her in."

It was never shot. On the last day of production, Huston and Blanke decided to scrap it. "They feel they can cut the picture without this ending," Al Alleborn reported, "and if necessary they can always get Bogart." In a subsequent meeting with Jack Warner, all parties felt the picture should end where it was. J. L. agreed to a retake of the arrest sequence, properly restaged, and closing on "last looks between Bogart and Astor."

The usual fine-tuning followed, and a week later, they shot the ending that people remember and love. Astor, with Barton MacLane as the police lieutenant at her elbow, moves toward the door, no handcuffs, a fur coat draped gently about her shoulders. Bogart remains momentarily behind with Ward Bond as Tom Polhaus, Spade's buddy on the force, and the statue that has cost so many lives. Meta Wilde penciled in the two-line addition:

POLHAUS:
"Um [it's]—heavy—What is it?"
SPADE:
"The stuff that dreams are made of."

Huston told Lawrence Grobel that the line was Bogart's idea.

Dramatically, the change made sense. Certainly it showed off the stars to optimum effect. But it also altered the nature of the story and of Hammett's hero. In place of an unsavory poetic justice, there were romantic closing images: Bogart, following the cops into the corridor and seeing Astor in the elevator, a condemned soul en route to justice. Her eyes are blank as the elevator's folding gate slashes bar-like shadows across her face. Bogart's look is of longing and regret as the gate closes, and he passes out of the picture, cradling the small black bird.

This final note, rather than amorality, was of honor among detectives. Find your partner's killer even if it means sending over your love; be true to your code even if it means breaking your heart. Spade has done the Right Thing and ends up the ultimate cynic, his gaze directed at some far-off point, and quoting, or rather misquoting, Shakespeare.

In early September, J. L. previewed the final cut. The next morning he told Wallis to reshoot the opening. The audience, it seemed, was confused from the start by Mary Astor's lines. ("That was in New York—I don't know where she met him—She's much younger than I.") Cut the confusion and just tell the audience what it was all about, he said. "Why be so clever, as we have a hell of a good picture."

Huston rewrote, Wallis edited, Huston rewrote the rewrite, and they shot it again: "I am trying to find my sister. I have reason to think she is here in San Francisco with a man named Floyd Thursby. . . ."

This time, there was no confusion. The preview audience loved it. They also loved Bogart. In the aftermath, Jack Warner made some decisions.

The first averted a disaster in the making. A week before, Hal Wallis, for reasons unknown, had changed the title to *The Gent from Frisco.* The morning after the preview, Warner cabled the office in New York to scrap that title; he was changing it back to *The Maltese Falcon.*

The other decision concerned the credits, and ultimately, the course of Bogart's career at Warner Brothers. J. L. took his previews seriously. He watched and listened to audiences closely and passed comments to William Schaefer, taking notes in the next seat. Afterward there was the usual stop in the theater manager's office. There they read through the piles of audience reaction cards, paying special attention to those written by women, the largest and most loyal segment of the moviegoing public.

The billing that had been drawn up in early July carried Bogart's name, as usual, beneath the title. It was just above Mary Astor's, the names in similar type just a little smaller than the title of the picture:

WARNER BROS. PICTURES, INC.

PRESENTS

"THE MALTESE FALCON"

WITH

HUMPHREY BOGART

MARY ASTOR

On the Monday morning after the Saturday preview, the studio mimeo machines were turning out the new official billing, approved as always by J. L. The main title—the listing on the screen—was not affected. For the lithograph to be sent for display in theaters, however, Bogart's and Astor's names were to be enlarged to the same size as the title, in a brand-new layout effective immediately for all ads, cards, posters, and publicity:

WARNER BROS.

PICTURES, INC. PRESENTS

HUMPHREY BOGART—MARY ASTOR

IN

"THE MALTESE FALCON"

BY DASHIELL HAMMETT

Bogart had arrived.

CHAPTER 9

"Do Tough Guys Have *Sex Appeal?*"

Vincent Sherman, behind schedule as usual, was shooting late into a Saturday night in the fall of 1941. A painstaking craftsman and conscientious director addicted to on-set rewrites, he was personally easygoing, and Bogart liked him. Both men had paid their dues in the B's—they had done *The Return of Dr. X* together—and they put in a full day's work without fuss or bother, at least once the film got going. Sherman considered Bogart "a solid professional," even though "he could be a pain, grousing at the start. But then, nobody worked harder."

This time they were making *All Through the Night,* a comedy-gangster-spy hybrid that was yet another George Raft reject. Bogart hadn't cared much for the script, either; but in the course of a long talk, Sam Jaffe had convinced him that it wasn't as bad as he thought.

On this particular Saturday an assistant director quietly motioned for Sherman to come over and told him, "Mayo's in Bogie's dressing room. She wants to see you." Without a word, Sherman went to the trailer. When he opened the door, Mayo was waiting, her hair disheveled, tears feeding streams of running makeup. It was clearly the tail end of an evening of solitary drinking. She staggered to Sherman and threw her arms around him. "Oh, Vince, he doesn't love me anymore!"

Sherman "figured I'd better tell Bogart" and went back to the set, where Bogart and character actor William Demarest were chatting and drinking coffee. The director, distinctly uncomfortable, interrupted them:

"You know . . . Mayo's in the dressing room. . . . She's pretty . . . well, upset. . . . Says you don't love her anymore."

"These frustrated actresses!" Bogart snorted.

Which to Sherman was the underlying problem. "He was going up, and she wasn't getting the roles, and she was a good actress. I think he drove her home later. But he didn't go back to the dressing room."

Maritally that autumn, things were progressing from very bad to even worse, exacerbated in part by the early trade reviews proclaiming *The Maltese Falcon* one of the sleepers of the year and Bogart as a star and sex symbol. "His secretary dotes on him," one reviewer wrote of Sam Spade. "His attractive brunette client . . . succumbs to his dark-eyed charm. . . . [The] wife of his partner flies devotedly to his arms before the victim has had a chance to cool." Warner Publicity touted the new Bogart image. Studio pressbooks, designed to influence exhibitors, pushed the metamorphosis under the banner headline "DO TOUGH GUYS HAVE *SEX APPEAL*?" and pointed out that 75 percent of Bogart's fan mail came from women. "Bogart is one tough guy who really gets 'em!"

Fan magazines took up the theme. "He doesn't know he has sex appeal. . . . But women know it," went part of a story entitled "The Amorous Life of a Movie Killer." At the same time, studio flacks offered up the usual perfect marriage, with "the charming Mayo Methot." There were photos of the Bogarts at home in blissful domesticity, Mayo sweetly pouring tea: "She gave up her career to assure their happiness together."

Privately, she was living in a state of sustained rage. She hadn't worked in two years, and there were no offers. "She had talent," according to Milton Sperling, a producer at that time and later the son-in-law of Harry Warner. "She wasn't a bimbo. But there were so *many* girls under contract." With no work, increasingly she became Bogart's shadow. Warners, via the fan magazines, continued to try to put the best face on it: "To make the marriage last . . . she manages to be with him during every moment he is not actually before the camera." That was the problem.

Actress Marsha Hunt unexpectedly encountered Mayo that November during a radio adaptation of *The Amazing Dr. Clitterhouse,* the 1938 film in which Bogart is a crook and Edward G. Robinson the doctor who, in trying to discern what turned Bogart bad, becomes crooked himself. Bogart reprised his performance as the bad guy, Robinson was back as the doctor, and Hunt played the Claire Trevor role. It was a pro bono appearance, one of a modest half-hour series, with all salaries donated to the Motion Picture Relief Fund.

The pretty, dark-haired Hunt was surprised to find Bogart well-spoken and a bit introverted. He was in every case politer than his wife, who glowered in the background, conspicuously out of place. The fact that she accompanied him "rather interested" Hunt, "because we didn't bring our mates to work. And whether it was a period of making up after a particularly bad time, whether it was jealousy and she just wanted to see whether I would go after her man, I have no idea. But it was curious to see a spouse at radio rehearsals and the broadcast. It was just a job, after all."

Mayo Bogart clearly didn't agree. She sat wordlessly, giving off "a kind of *zaftig,* sultry femininity. Tough. Independent. And not too interested in being liked. You were just aware of that presence. And it *was* a presence." Hunt was not the only one to notice. Harry Ackerman, the producer and director of the program, found the couple to be "like firecrackers together," smoldering on a short fuse when they weren't going off.

They still were able to joke about their differences, at least when they weren't embroiled in them. Stuntman Buster Wiles recalled Sunday mornings off Catalina when he and his buddy Errol Flynn would bring a few of the fish they'd caught to the Bogart boat, where drinks were always waiting. One time Bogart met them with both eyes blackened. "Flynn said to Bogie, 'You look like you've got sunglasses on.' "

Bogart grinned at the two men. "Yeah, that's a right cross from Mayo."

As far as Wiles could tell, "they enjoyed it." And they enjoyed thumbing their noses at the world, if only to convince themselves that all this pain was fun. Invited to the coming-out party of Eric and Gertie Hatch's debutante daughter on Long Island—co-hosted with society friends named Timpson, with the usual pleasure of their company requested—their answer was unorthodox: "We, Mr. and Mrs. Bogart, are so distressed . . . because we really feel it's going to cost too much." Enclosed was a list of expenses:

> Railroad fare, $600. Side trip to Grand Canyon (no sales resistance) $150. . . . Liquor on trip and in Twenty One (God knows!). Breakage (couple of hundred).
>
> So as you can see this trip is really out of the question—please explain to the Timpsons. Incidentally, how well do you know the Timpsons. . . .
>
> Oh, and one more question—what are they coming out

of. . . . And anyway how do Mr. and Mrs. Timpson know our company would be pleasant?

You see, the whole thing's silly.

Love,
Mayo and Bogie

But the laughs were becoming less and less frequent, the confrontations increasingly deadly. To Walter Seltzer, a future producer who at the time was a young publicist for Warners, "It was an ongoing battle. Bull Run." He repeatedly saw Mayo arriving on the set, looking for Bogart "with a black eye and multi-colored bruises on her face." The couple would disappear into the privacy of Bogart's trailer, but the sound of their fighting carried through the thin partitions. "We'd hear noise from the dressing room. Her screaming vulgarities, obscenities. And his share, too; this was not a one-sided fight. Mostly about other dalliances. I was not privy to them, but it was sort of on the grapevine."

At the time it was generally acknowledged around the lot that Bogart was unhappy and available. John Huston's remark that Bogart was "morbidly faithful" to Mayo seems to apply more to his staying in the marriage than to his staying out of others' beds. Yet Bogart's behavior was hardly a cause for raised eyebrows in an industry where monogamy among stars was the significant exception. The basic edict was simple: keep it quiet. Since *The Maltese Falcon,* especially, there had been no lack of young women—extras and bit players—hanging around the set hoping to meet the star and ready, in the approved manner of the day, to discreetly leave a matchbook with their phone number jotted inside. Bogart's follow-up, if only because of Mayo, was commensurately discreet. A dancer who set up an encounter for a girlfriend confirmed that "he never said anything" about his liaisons "or flaunted them in any way."

With one apparent exception. Helen Menken, lovely as ever, was a sometime visitor in Los Angeles and a welcoming friend in New York. Enough time had elapsed to heal old wounds and intermittently revive old embers. "He would cheat on Mayo and go see Menken," Sam Jaffe said. "When he got drunk. Then he'd *tell* Mayo about it, kind of like a naughty boy, doing things just to create a fuss."

Mayo, who knew what it was to be the other woman in a married man's life, felt her position constantly eroding. She was always fearful that there was a successor at hand, ready to take her place as she had Mary Philips's. Once the prime cheerleader of Bogart's career, she was now its chief denigrator. A bitter needler even when sober, Mayo when drunk was a ranting shrew. "She never lost a chance," a friend said, "to remind Bogie how important she'd been and how unimportant he'd been" when they met.

Jaik Rosenstein, a publicist and friend, was there one afternoon when Bogart came home and remarked that it was hot outside. The passing comment set off a tirade: " 'Well, well. Get the great big star. *It was hot all day,* he says. Why don't we call the Associated Press and advise the world by teletype? *Mr. Bogart, the great big Warner Brothers star, says it was hot today. Flash!*' "

However often Mayo came to the studio, there were junkets from which she was now excluded as Bogart enjoyed his new star treatment. Like other Caucasians, he had often gone to Harlem in the 1920s for the music and the shows, and, not incidentally, the beautiful young showgirls. But he had not been back in many years. When, on one of his trips to New York, he wanted to return, a studio publicist asked newsman Allan McMillan to accompany him. A pioneering African American syndicated columnist and the publicist for such stars as Cab Calloway, Duke Ellington, and Ethel Waters, he was happy to oblige.

They took to each other immediately, McMillan said. "He liked a good time, he liked booze and whatnot; one of the nicest men that I ever met in my life. I don't think he had any prejudice so far as race was concerned. He was just like an ordinary guy, even though he was a big star; just an ordinary guy at heart. That's the way he lived."

Bogart came uptown by cab. The first place he wanted to go was the mob-owned Cotton Club, which, for all its black performers, had a whites-only policy for its patrons. McMillan once saw W. C. Handy, the composer of *St. Louis Blues,* turned away at the door. McMillan himself was allowed inside only because he was with both the press and a white movie star. "It was the big thing—everybody wanted to go there. Lena Horne played the Cotton Club, and Cab Calloway and Duke Ellington. They had a big show, a big colored review, and twelve of the most beautiful handpicked colored girls you ever saw in the world—they didn't use the word *black* then. Well, he saw all those beautiful girls and he said, 'This is it!'

"There was a certain girl there in the chorus that he wanted to meet. He was crazy about her. She was beautiful, about five feet two, a great dancer. After hours there were always places where you could go and drink, so we took this girl with us and I think I kept him up in Harlem until about seven o'clock in the morning, when he went back to his hotel. That was a wonderful adventure for her."

At regular intervals after that, McMillan would get a long-distance call from Bogart. "I'm going to be in New York. Leave time, let's get together." And off they'd go to the Harlem nightspots: "Connie's Inn, Small's Paradise, not as big as the Cotton Club, but great shows; Ethel Waters played Small's. There was such glamour to Harlem in the old days! I had any amount of money myself, fifty, a hundred, but he picked up the tabs."

One time, after a night out, Bogart was hungry. It was about six o'clock in the morning, but however tired McMillan may have been, he was reluctant to let Bogart go on alone. "I had to protect him. I knew some of the rough blacks in Harlem. These guys were tough numbers, but they respected me." McMillan took him to Wells Restaurant on Seventh Avenue, an all-night cafe where show people ate breakfast before going home, and still a Harlem landmark. Once inside, McMillan introduced his companion to the proprietor: "Joe Wells, this is Humphrey Bogart."

"Bullshit!" Wells snapped.

Admittedly, at six A.M. on 132nd Street, it demanded a certain stretch of the bounds of probability, but McMillan insisted, so Wells called to his cook, "McMillan tells me that his friend is Humphrey Bogart. Can you imagine that?"

"Tell him, Humphrey, tell him who you are," McMillan urged Bogart, who began to talk like one of his characters. After a moment, the cook nodded. "Yeah, that's Bogie!"

The trade reviews on October 1 of *The Maltese Falcon* were such stuff as dreams are made on. *Variety* called it "perfection." The *Hollywood Reporter* said it would be "one of the most profitable and talked about pictures of the year." According to the *Motion Picture Herald,* "Humphrey Bogart has had no assignment to match this portrayal since *Petrified Forest.*" When the film opened on October 4, the New York dailies confirmed the enthusiasm. "A knockout job, a classic in its field . . . with Humphrey Bogart contributing one of the finest performances of his career," said the *Herald Tribune.* "A brilliant success. John Huston can take a bow," wrote the New York *Post.*

"The best mystery of the year," comparable to the finest of Alfred Hitchcock, said *The New York Times.* "Humphrey Bogart hits his peak. Mary Astor is well nigh perfect. . . . Sydney Greenstreet, from the Theatre Guild's roster, is magnificent." The only dissenting voice was in the *Hollywood Motion Picture Review.* Its reviewer dismissed the film as "a trifle talkative . . . this overlength mystery film with an ordinary draw cast, cannot possibly hold up for preferred playing time."

The impact was all the greater for the critics' being caught unawares. Here was a major movie come to town "on rubber heels," as one of them described it. Warners had been "strangely bashful" about the film's release, said the *Times*—"maybe they wanted to give everyone a nice surprise." The harder truth was that low-budget pictures got low-budget publicity. The studio was content to have a hit on the cheap, despite the pleas of Henry Blanke and even Hal Wallis. "I should think," Blanke wrote to Wallis, "that the company after . . . discovering what they had in their possession would go a little after this picture but . . . it 'sneaks in'—and in spite of all this makes a success."

And a significant success. *The Maltese Falcon* was one of ten nominees for Best Picture of 1941, along with *Citizen Kane, The Little Foxes, Sergeant York, Here Comes Mr. Jordan, Suspicion,* and *How Green Was My Valley,* which won. Greenstreet was nominated in the Supporting Actor category and Huston for Best Screenplay. Astor received the Oscar for Best Supporting Actress, though the prize came for her performance in *The Great Lie* rather than *The Maltese Falcon.* Bogart's keystone performance was passed over altogether.

Nevertheless, his life and career had turned a corner. Only a few months earlier, he had still been Raft's substitute. Sam Jaffe had written to Warners, pleading with them for once to come up with a role made just for Bogart, "because . . . for the past year he's practically pinch-hitted for Raft and been kicked around from pillar to post." Suddenly, he was, as one syndicated writer said, "the white-haired boy of Hollywood." That December, in recognition of his new status, Bogart was invited to appear in a Christmas broadcast with Shirley Temple, the princess of the movies. The gossip columns, prompted by the Warner "planters," played up the image of the good soldier ready to take on another's rejects and make good.

Raft, by contrast, was now considered the man who had slipped on a banana peel. Broadway columnist Ed Sullivan laughed over "Raft's boner." The *Los Angeles Times* reported that the star was "doing a burn over Humphrey Bogart's hit performance." New York *Post* columnist Leonard Lyons spotted Raft in New York at the Strand where *The Maltese Falcon* was playing. As applause for Bogart swept the house, Raft made his only reported witticism: "There but for the grace of me, go I."

Back in Burbank Jack Warner gathered all the clippings under the head, "Raft-Bogart" and sent them to Legal for inclusion in Raft's contract file. In only a few weeks, a studio property had gone from being a big box office draw to being a laughingstock, and for once J. L. didn't seem to mind. Raft would make one more film for Warners and then, his option dropped, depart for other studios, his days as a first-line leading man over.

However routine a movie it was, *All Through the Night* was proof of Bogart's new importance. Rudi Fehr, who would also cut *Key Largo* (and later become head of editing for Warners), was preparing to work on a high-budget B. "Bogart," he said, "made it an A picture."

"With Bogart in your billing," Warners told its exhibitors, "you've got the male star . . . that says *'excitement'* more than any other name in Hollywood."

The picture, with a screenplay by humorists Leonard Spigelglass and Leonard Q. Ross (a pseudonym for the writer Leo Rosten), turned out to be better than anticipated, or than description may suggest: *Guys and Dolls* characters chase Nazi spies while being chased by the police. Bogart is a Sky Masterson–type gambler by the name of Gloves Donahue. After the German baker of his favorite cheesecake is murdered, he and his henchmen set out to find the killer. As far as Gloves is concerned, the Gestapo is just another mob trying to muscle in, even when they frame him for the murder. Among the casting footnotes is the appearance of a corpulent young comedian named Jackie Gleason, whom Jack Warner had signed up for $500 a week after watching his nightclub act.

"You look like the man who came to dinner," Bogart told Gleason, "and ate the guests."

The idea for the story came from producer Jerry Wald's brother Malvin, who in 1936 worked for a neighborhood weekly, the Brooklyn *World.* "The editor was acquainted with several Jewish gangsters who resented the Nazis' holding meetings in Yorkville, the purpose of which was to spread Hitlerism and anti-Semitism. The gangsters would learn where the meetings were to be and tipped off the editor. Whereas the police could do nothing, the gangsters were free to break heads and disrupt the proceedings, and the photographers for the *World* would be on hand to chronicle the attempt to bring Hitler to America."

What began as an unpretentious little comedy—though with a budget twice that of *The Maltese Falcon*—was in some ways a zany dry run for *Casablanca.* The brilliant German actor Conrad Veidt, who the next year would play Major Strasser, here appeared as an icily unflappable Gestapo agent seconded by Peter Lorre. *Casablanca* screenwriters Philip and Julius Epstein touched up the script. The art director was Carl Weyl, who would design Rick's Café. Refugee actors played both Nazi villains and their victims. But a central performer in *Casablanca* was missing. The heroine, a mysterious European woman running from a past she can't explain, was played by the lackluster Kaaren Verne, also the former Mrs. Lorre. Hal Wallis settled for her after he was unable to get his first choice, David O. Selznick's recent discovery, Ingrid Bergman.

The ads featured Bogart with a gun drawn and display type that shrieked, "KILLER BOGART TAKES THE GESTAPO FOR A RIDE!" But *All Through the Night* was principally a spoof, a wartime metamorphosis of the gangster movie. As Wallis's assistant Walter MacEwen noted, "Nazis make swell heavies." The picture is memorable largely for the climax, in which Bogart and William Demarest infiltrate a Nazi meeting. When Bogart is suddenly called to the rostrum as "Herr Mannheimer" and directed to explain just how he plans to blow up a battleship in New York Harbor, he and Demarest find that their assumed identities are those of two hit men from Detroit.

Bogart, in desperation, looks at Demarest, who begins spouting double-talk—"Herr Mannheimer, don't forget, the scradavan is on the paratoot. . . ." Bogart picks up the cue: "How right you are, Herr Schultz, the scradavan is *definitely* on the paratoot. . . . And according to my calculations, until we get on the rillera, keach ran must tantamount—positively—*Heil!*" Lusty *Sieg Heils* follow from the audience as the plaintive voice of the chairman asks, "Would you try to speak a little more distinctly, Herr Mannheimer?"

Demarest had perfected a double-talk routine when he was a performer in vaudeville. Vincent Sherman had intended to use only one line in the film, but at the first screening "the audience laughed at it, and kept laughing. So I put the rest in."

Editor Rudi Fehr, a regular visitor to the set, saw that Bogart had no trouble going along with the double-talk and had a grand time doing it. The two actors "played off each other. They had it worked out, what kind of words to throw in and all that. It was wonderful." Bogart and Demarest enjoyed each other off-camera, as well, and "they laughed at each other's jokes and stories."

It was political slapstick that would have been inconceivable only a year before. In fact, a similar screenplay had been rejected by both Jack Warner and Hal Wallis in 1940. The studio that made *Confessions of a Nazi Spy* in 1939 suddenly backtracked nervously into neutrality. So did all the studios, after attacks by isolationists charging Hollywood (by implication Jewish) with pushing America (by implication Christian) into war. Warners might distribute British propaganda films like *London Can Take It,* and even purchase fighter planes for Britain with the profits; but at the studio itself, the only movie about beleaguered Britain produced that year was *The Sea Hawk,* in which Errol Flynn fights the Spanish and the story is set safely in the sixteenth century. Over at United Artists, Alfred Hitchcock's anti-Nazi *Foreign Correspondent* managed to be filmed without a single mention of either Nazis or Germany.

By 1941, however, the atmosphere had changed. In the space of one year, public opinion had shifted radically, from the strict neutrality summed up by the phrase "all aid short of war," to the current slogan "in the event of war," and in favor of open aid after Congress passed Roosevelt's Lend-Lease Act providing arms to Britain. In the Atlantic, armed American merchantmen ferried supplies to English ports, with orders to shoot back if fired upon. In the new climate, Warners produced *Sergeant York,* with Gary Cooper as the Tennessee-born World War I combat hero who showed that men of peace must sometimes go to war.

Along the coastline of Southern California, with its defense plants and refineries, the Coast Guard beefed up its forces by commissioning civilian small craft to fill in for its own vessels that had been called up by the Navy. Bogart was one of the first to join, volunteering the thirty-eight-foot, diesel-powered *Sluggy* and taking the rigorous skipper's exam. After an inspection at the station in Long Beach, he qualified for the U.S. Coast Guard Auxiliary of Southern California and turned up unfailingly on weekends to patrol the channels off the coast.

For the country, the debate had been reduced to one simple but enormous question: to fight or not to fight. In Washington, Roosevelt's Senate opponents held hearings on the evils of Hollywood, and they bashed the New Deal as well as the ethnic origins of the men who ran the studios. The moguls, subpoenaed to testify, were not cowed. Harry Warner, sitting with the other studio heads, stared down the lawmakers, refused to apologize for making films that dealt with foreign policy or current issues, and upheld what he called the public's right to know the truth. The moralist of the Warner brothers, he believed that films should educate as well as entertain, and he was furious over such charges by isolationist Senators Gerald Nye, Bennett C. Clark, and others that *Sergeant York* was made to "create war hysteria" or that *Confessions of a Nazi Spy* was similarly intended.

"I deny, with all the strength I have, these reckless and unfounded charges," he told the committee. "I deny that the pictures produced by my company are 'propaganda,' as has been alleged. . . . *Sergeant York* is a factual portrait of the life of one of the great heroes of the last war. If that is propaganda, we plead guilty. *Confessions of a Nazi Spy* is a factual portrayal of a Nazi spy ring that operated in New York City. If that is propaganda, we plead guilty. . . . [We deny] that Warner Brothers had been producing a type of picture relating to world affairs and national defense for the purpose of allegedly inciting our country to war. [We deny] that Warner Brothers pictures concerning world affairs and national defense are inaccurate and twisted for ulterior purpose. . . . If Warner Brothers had produced no pictures concerning the Nazi movement, our public would have had good reason to criticize. We would have been living in a dream world. . . . You may correctly charge me with being anti-Nazi. But no one can charge me with being anti-American."

There were calls that autumn for movie censorship, ostensibly to counter violence on the screen. Bogart, responding in the *Hollywood Reporter,* called censorship "the number one enemy of a free democracy" and movies "just as much a medium of public expression as are radio and newspaper." The efforts to control film content went beyond concern about the possible influence of Warner gangsters on the young, he said, and, without naming the Senate committee, labeled it a cloak for other purposes: "There are men who advocate even more dangerous types of film censorship, and if America is to continue to have freedom of press and radio . . . these insidious enemies of freedom must be emphatically discouraged. Because once the movies are gagged, these men will move on to the other means of public expression. We have seen it happen in other countries, and it can happen here."

He had already joined the Fight for Freedom Committee to counter the isolationist efforts of America First. The committee's policy position was "full participation by the United States in the present War." Unlike the right-wing America First, Fight for Freedom was also strongly pro-labor and pro–civil rights. Its members staged programs nationwide to convince the country that Britain and the Soviet Union's struggle was America's as well. "We made speeches all over the place," Gloria Stuart said. The Sheekmans, who had been in Europe when Poland was invaded, had made their way to England and returned to the United States, haunted by memories of what they had seen and in the forefront of the effort to end the presumed neutrality.

All Through the Night completed production in mid-October. Apart from a radio appearance on Thanksgiving Day, Bogart had no work scheduled until January. The first week of December, he prepared to fly to St. Louis to head the list of celebrities that included Melvyn and Helen Gahagan Douglas, Sam Levene, and Linda Darnell, who were scheduled to appear at a Fight for Freedom rally at the twelve-thousand-seat Municipal Auditorium on Wednesday, December 10.

All that changed on the morning of December 7, when the Japanese bombed Pearl Harbor. Studio hands and actors rushed to enlist in the armed forces. Bogart, who had already been in one world war, was too old to fight in a second. Instead, he served at Warners, where rapid adjustments had to be made to avoid tomorrow's movies becoming yesterday's news.

The studio had for some time been in negotiations for *Aloha Means Goodbye,* an action thriller serialized that summer in the *Saturday Evening Post.* It turned on a Japanese plot against military installations in Hawaii, and was viewed as a possible vehicle for Bogart. After some discussion, it was considered wiser to switch the Honolulu setting and change the plot to one against the Panama Canal. "Better shoot it fast," Bogart commented, "before the Canal goes, too."

The fortunes of war smiled on Murray Burnett and Joan Alison, two struggling New York playwrights. In the weeks before Pearl Harbor they had sold an anti-Nazi play to Otto Preminger, but then were told the deal was off. It was too controversial, the producer told them. Given the climate of intimidation created by the Senate hearings, he would never be able to raise the money. Undiscouraged, the writers turned to another anti-Nazi play they'd written that had spent the past year gathering dust on an uninterested producer's shelf. They gave it to an agent to try to make a sale. It had an exotic locale, deep-dyed fascist villains, timeliness, and a love story. Its title was *Everybody Comes to Rick's.*

CHAPTER 10

"It's Going to Be a Lot of Shit like *Algiers*"

The change in atmosphere at Warners the morning of December 8 was immediately evident. The studio grounds had been quickly closed to all visitors "with the exception of the always-welcome press," and everyone on the lot was shocked by the attack and by the continuous radio reports on the magnitude of the devastation. In downtown Los Angeles, eight miles away, long lines formed at enlistment offices, and the drain of one sixth of the film industry's workers into the armed forces began.

As the Robert Taylors, Clark Gables, and Jimmy Stewarts went into service and even combat, causing dismay at the studios where they were under contract, Warners benefited from its offbeat lineup of male stars. They weren't pretty, with the always notable exception of Errol Flynn. More to the point, they weren't young. Though the dashing Flynn was heading into his mid-thirties and still draftable, Cagney, Bogart, and Robinson were well into their forties. Even Dick Powell, the ubiquitous singing juvenile of the past decade, was now thirty-eight.

Thus Warners was perhaps the best prepared of all the studios to shift into wartime picture making. It moved easily from the disguised messages of World War I (*The Fighting 69th, Sergeant York*) to others more openly in tune with America's entry into the war. Projects that had seemed two-fisted before December 7 were now dropped as passé. Jack Warner himself called off negotiations on William Shirer's 1940 bestseller *Berlin Diary* on the grounds that "everyone knows everything that happened there now." A paradigm of the shift is the treatment of two properties the studio acquired, one just before and one right after Pearl Harbor. Their intertwining history constitutes a tale about the ironies of Hollywood and the alchemy of motion pictures.

Two days after the attack, Jack Warner wired Jake Wilk in New York: "JAPANESE SITUATION DOESN'T CHANGE OUR SITUATION ON WATCH ON RHINE OTHER THAN WE MUST GET THIS OUT RAPIDLY."

If any property seemed the perfect fit for the time, it was Lillian Hellman's anti-fascist drama *Watch on the Rhine.* The play, an indictment of American complacency, had been a highlight of the 1941 Broadway season. Warners had begun to close negotiations for the film rights in the late fall. With America actively in the war, there was some fear that the play might have lost its propaganda punch—the phrase was Jack Warner's—but the Broadway box office figures were undiminished and the accolades solid gold. It was a huge commercial hit, the winner of the New York Drama Critics Circle Award as well as the Pulitzer Prize; FDR himself asked for a command performance in Washington. It is hard to conceive of any play that brought more free publicity to its filmmakers, or looked more like a sure thing. Certainly no one at that point would have thought an unproduced play by two unknowns would have been competition for it.

Jake Wilk was so involved in the negotiations for *Watch on the Rhine* that he fell behind in his routine reading of stories and scripts submitted for consideration as film material. His small, paper-crammed office had the antiquated look peculiar to Warner East Coast operations on West Forty-fourth Street. Irene Lee, the West Coast story editor who was on a visit to New York, came in to use part of the company office and rummage through the piles of manuscripts while Wilk glared at her, resentful at the intrusion into what he considered his private domain. The impression Lee got was that "he felt that he owned it. He'd been there such a long time. I think he thought I was a little upstart."

Wilk's sullen mood had no effect on Lee, a pretty, personable, onetime actress with a sharp instinct for what would play. She had acquired some of the best Bette Davis scripts: *Jezebel, The Old Maid,* and *Now, Voyager* by Olive Higgins Prouty, the author of the ultimate tearjerker, *Stella Dallas.* Hal Wallis had brought Lee to Warners and given her his total confidence. She had thirty-five readers on her staff, some of whom, such as Dalton Trumbo and Aeneas MacKenzie, had gone on to screenwriting careers. In her office was a photograph of Wallis, inscribed, "To Irene who never pulls her punches."

Lee never hesitated to go directly to Wallis with something she thought was particularly good, and regardless of how busy he was, Wallis would always see her promptly. The two didn't always agree; she wanted to buy *Gone With the Wind* and Warners turned it down. But, as Lee reflected, so much of discerning what will make a good film is "luck and instinct that not everything I bought was absolutely great either."

The only thing of interest Lee found in Wilk's office was a dog-eared typed manuscript in a dusty three-hole ringbinder, its title, *Everybody Comes to Rick's,* underlined with a double stroke. Down below were the address and phone number of the producers who had left it sitting for a year. "Nobody else was keen about it, but I liked it." She took the script with her back to Hollywood and gave it to Stephen Karnot, one of her several readers who worked for $1.12 an hour, to write the synopsis.

Four days after Pearl Harbor, the play and the synopsis went over to Wallis, who knew anything coming from Lee was pre-recommended. "Hal would give you a quick reaction if he liked it. He liked it." As was the custom, copies were sent to various producers for their reactions. Most of them liked it, too. Warners "also loved a bargain. So they bought it." The price was $20,000.

Not everyone was as keen on the story as Lee. Set in Vichy-controlled North Africa after the collapse of France, it centered on an anti-Nazi Czech millionaire, his American mistress, and her former lover, a night-club owner fleeing his past. In Sydney Carton–like fashion, the nightclub owner gives up both love and the irrevocable letters of transit for his escape in favor of a noble cause. To screenwriter Robert Buckner, the drama seemed "sheer hokum" and its hero "two-parts Hemingway, one-part Scott Fitzgerald, and a dash of cafe Christ." Producer Robert Lord called it "a very obvious imitation of *Grand Hotel.*"

"It was crap," Vincent Sherman said. "But it was a *great* piece of crap—which is often better than real literature." There were obvious and inviting parallels with producer Walter Wanger's 1938 romantic hit, *Algiers,* starring Charles Boyer and Hedy Lamarr. (*Algiers* had been based on the 1937 French film *Pepe le Moko,* starring Jean Gabin, which in turn drew on Howard Hawks's *Scarface.*) Writer-producer Jerry Wald, who had a fine sense for commercial properties and whose credits included *The Roaring Twenties* and *They Drive by Night,* felt a movie tailored along the lines of *Algiers* would "make a good vehicle for either Raft or Bogart."

A good vehicle was just what Bogart needed. He had returned from the Fight for Freedom rallies, buoyed by his receptions in St. Louis and Chicago and by the sense of being a player on the national stage. His stock had gone up in the industry after the open-arms reaction to *The Maltese Falcon,* and he looked forward to getting back to work in a role that would acknowledge his new stature.

All Through the Night had gone into general release with publicity brashly slanted toward the national mood ("the brand-newest twist in big-time action—gangsters vs. Gestapo—*and is it welcome now!*"), and its box office receipts were even better than those of *The Maltese Falcon.* With another hit to his credit, Bogart seemed indeed "the male star that says excitement" that Warner Publicity touted him as. But the fact is, Warners had nothing immediately planned for him.

The studio had wanted a sequel to *The Maltese Falcon,* and Jack Warner sent a query to Jake Wilk, asking if there was a chance Hammett would write a follow-up—without the Mary Astor character, of course, since she presumably received a death sentence, but using Bogart, Greenstreet, and the others. Wilk inquired, but the result was sadly inconclusive. Hammett, alcoholic, ill with emphysema, and worn down at forty-eight, was adapting his lover Lillian Hellman's *Watch on the Rhine.* Besides, he hadn't produced an original work in years (*The Maltese Falcon* was written in 1929) and wasn't sure he could do it. He would try, however, if given a guaranteed payment regardless of the result. Warner was willing to offer a small advance, but the deal foundered when he would not go above $5,000. "IF HE HASN'T CONFIDENCE IN HIS ABILITY TO WRITE AN ACCEPTABLE STORY LET'S FORGET IT," he cabled Wilk. Dashiell Hammett, master of the suspense genre, founder of the "hard-boiled" school of detective fiction, and creator of Sam Spade and *The Thin Man* (published in 1932), never did write another novel. Warner directed Wilk to drop the idea of a sequel "for the time being" and instead to purchase the title *Across the Pacific* to rename *Aloha Means Goodbye,* the substitute Bogart-Astor-Greenstreet in the works.

In retrospect, the careers of Bogart and Huston, separated only by the exigencies of wartime, would seem closely intertwined from *The Maltese Falcon* onward. As 1942 began, however, Huston had his eyes fixed not on a *Falcon II* but on *Watch on the Rhine.* Instead of another exercise in the crime genre, he wanted a shot at the big time, and nothing was bigger than a Broadway hit with a gleaming overlay of topicality.

The studio at first agreed. "We may want Huston to direct the picture," Jack Warner told Wilk. Huston, reportedly, also wanted a crack at the

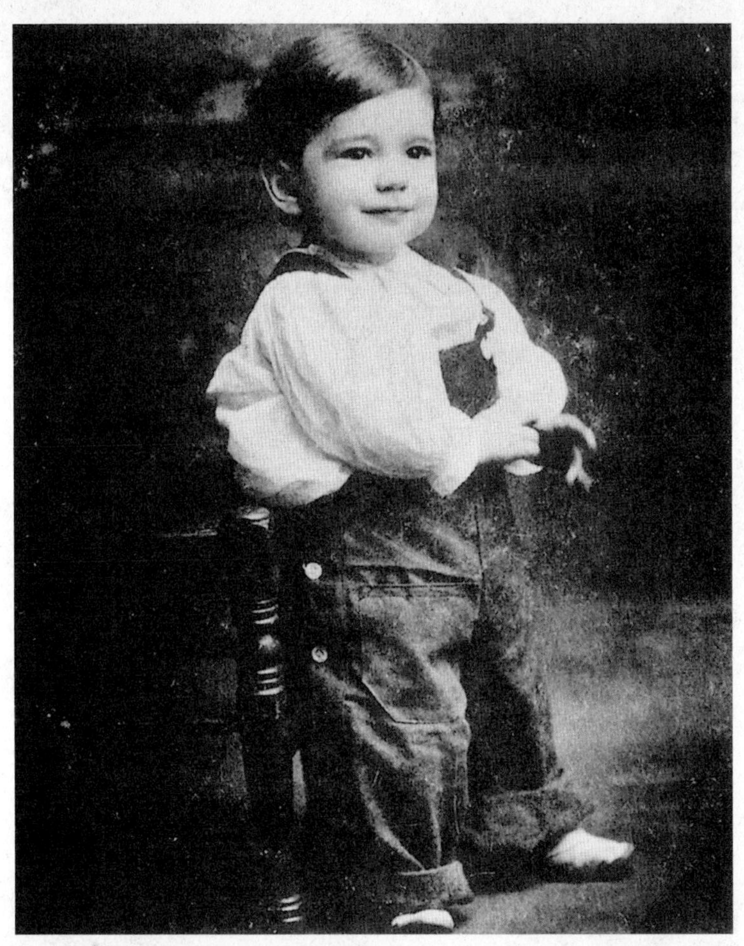

Humphrey DeForest Bogart, age two

Wisconsin Center for Film and Theater Research, Warner Bros. Collection

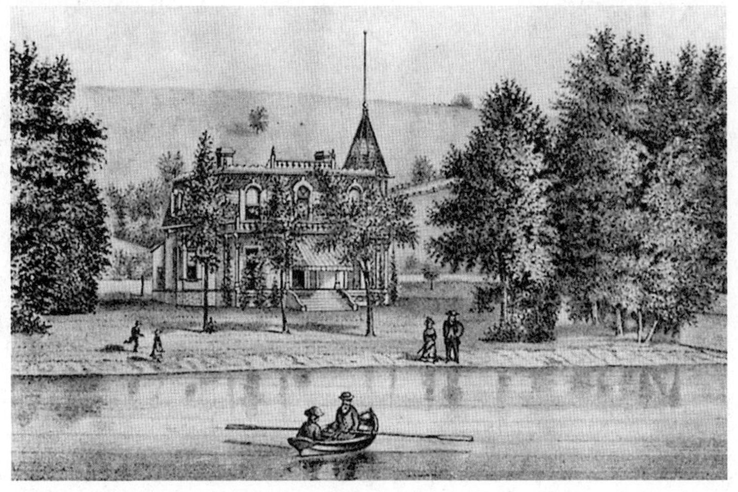

Willow Brook, the Bogarts' summer house on Canandaigua Lake

Ontario County (New York) Historical Society

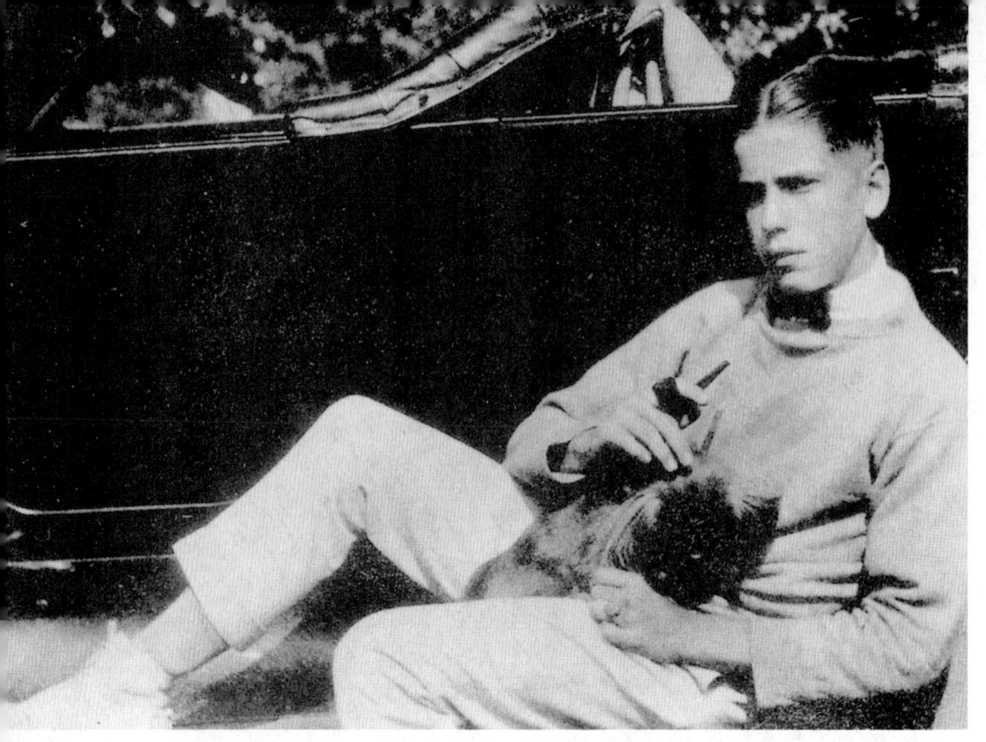

Bogart, around age eighteen Corbis-Bettmann

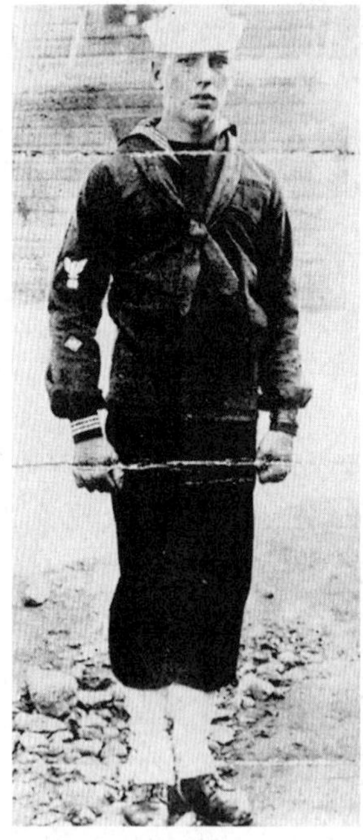

Seaman Second Class Bogart, circa 1919
Corbis-Bettmann

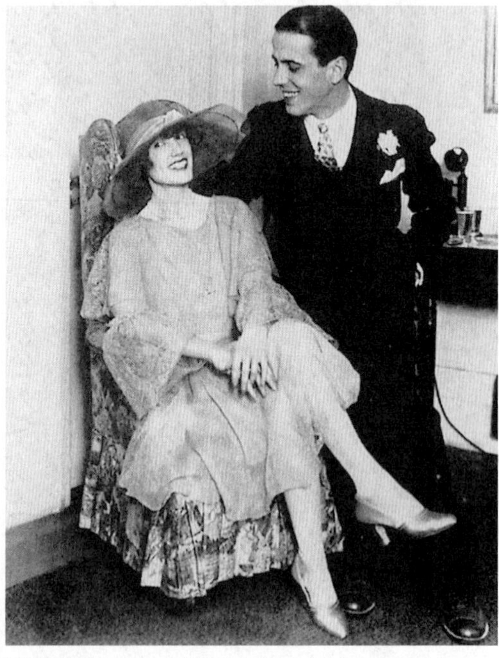

When Bogart and Helen Menken married in 1926, she was a Broadway star and he was a struggling actor. They were divorced within eighteen months but became closer in the years to come. Corbis-Bettmann

With Paul Kelly and Mary Philips in the Broadway play *Nerves* (1924). Bogart and Philips were married from 1928 to 1938.

Wisconsin Center for Film and Theater Research, Warner Bros. Collection

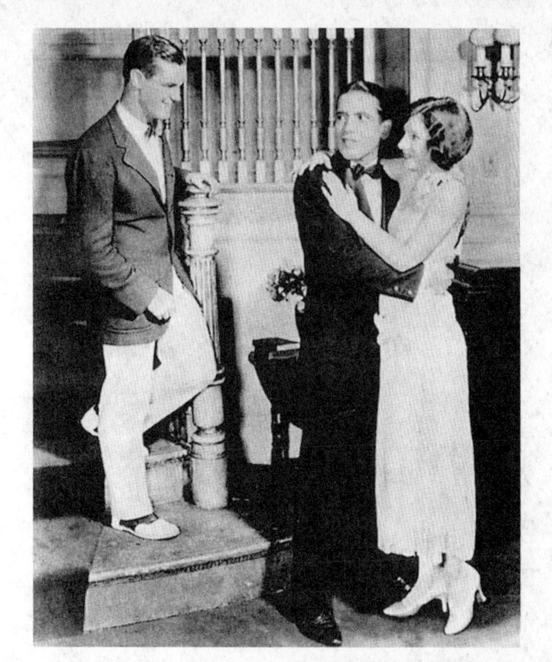

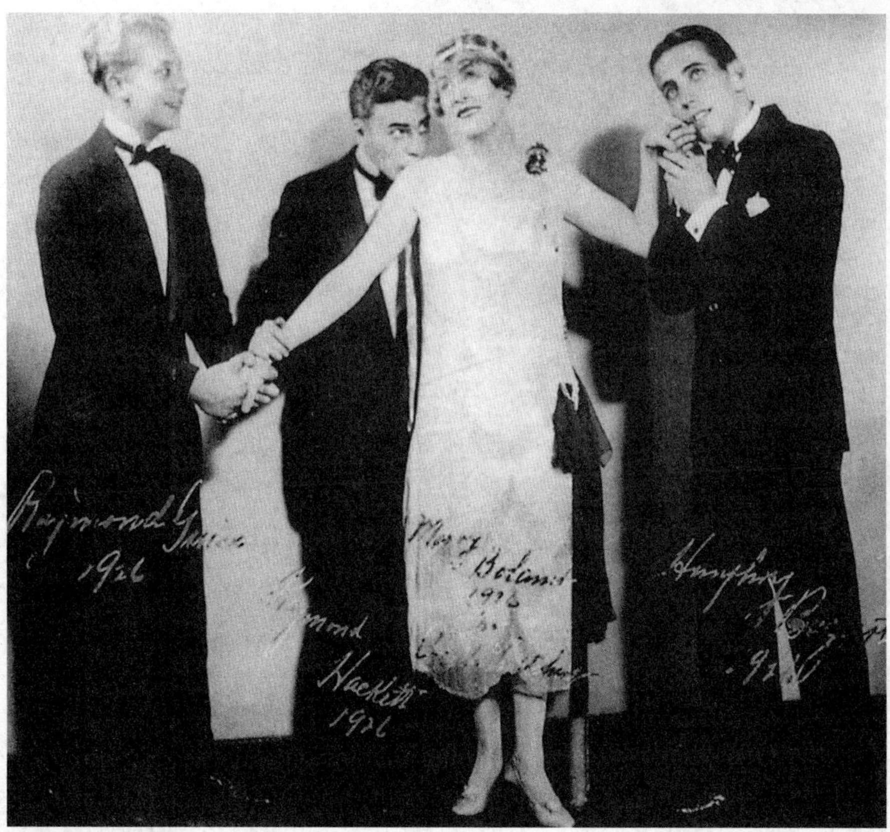

With Raymond Guion *(left),* Raymond Hackett, and Mary Boland in the Broadway comedy *Cradle Snatchers* (1926)

Courtesy of the Academy of Motion Picture Arts and Sciences, Hollywood Museum Collection

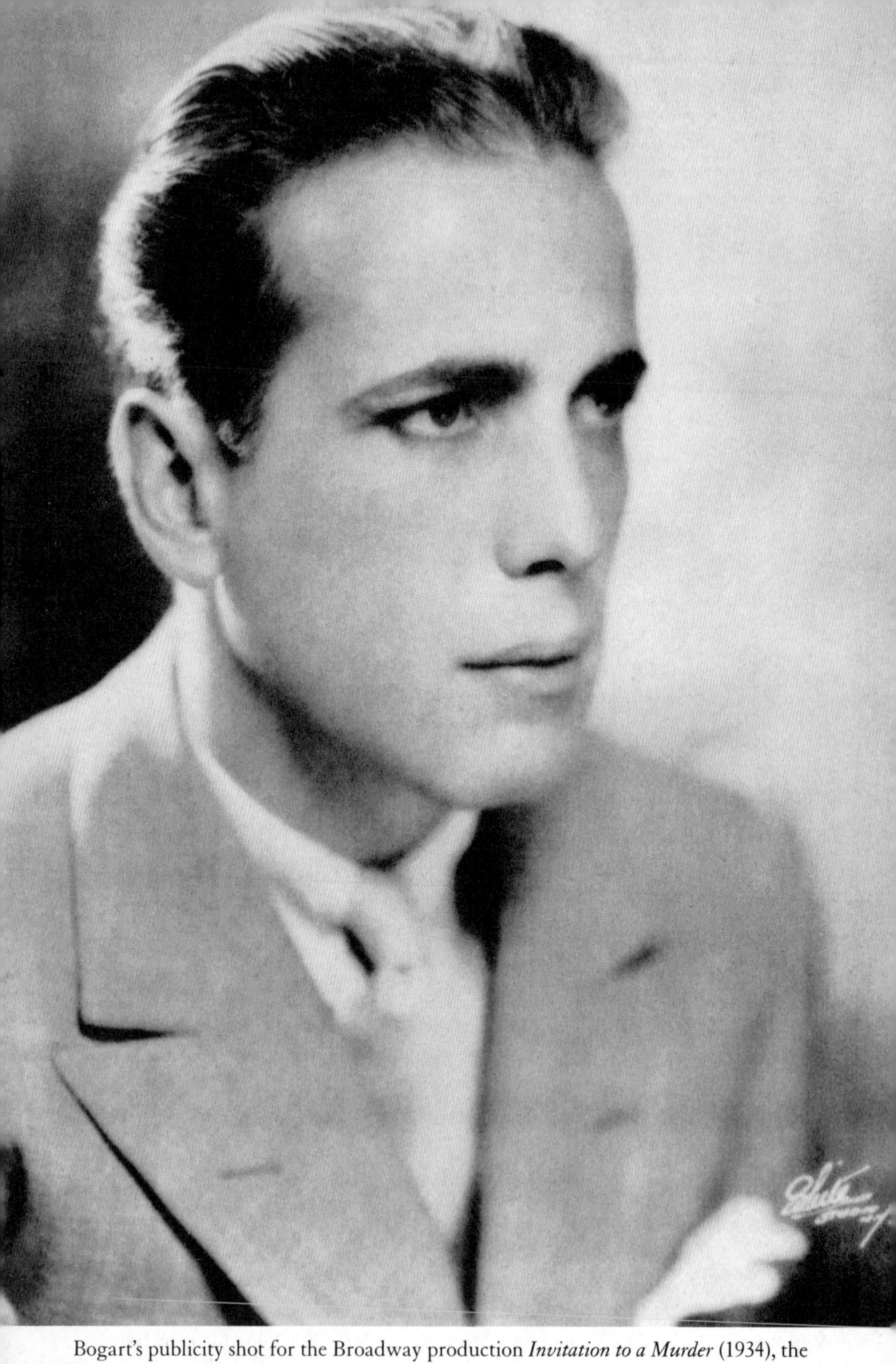

Bogart's publicity shot for the Broadway production *Invitation to a Murder* (1934), the last of his dashing-young-man roles

Wisconsin Center for Film and Theater Research, Warner Bros. Collection

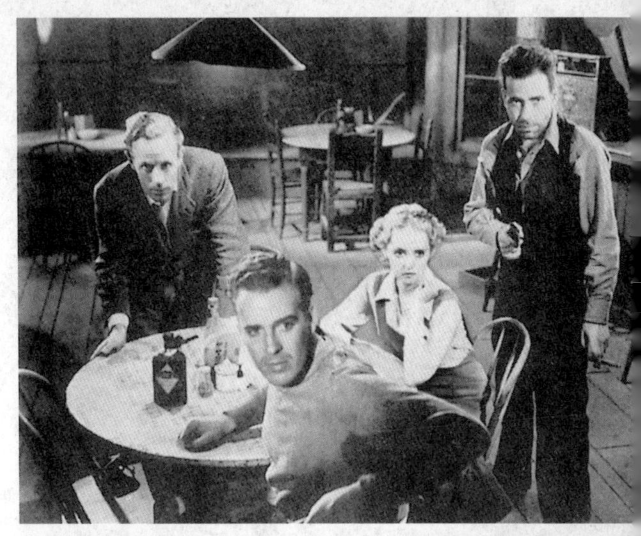

As Duke Mantee in *The Petrified Forest* (1936), with Leslie Howard *(upper left),* Dick Foran, and Bette Davis. Bogart's able playing of the role on Broadway and then in the film established him as a tough guy.
Courtesy of Warner Bros.; © 1936 Turner Entertainment Co.

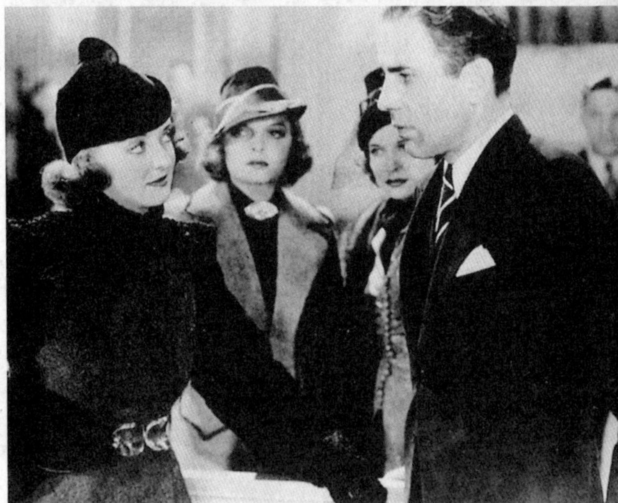

Marked Woman (1937) was one of six films that Bogart made with Bette Davis. Between them on the left is Mayo Methot, whom he married in 1938.
Courtesy of Warner Bros.; © 1937 Turner Entertainment Co.

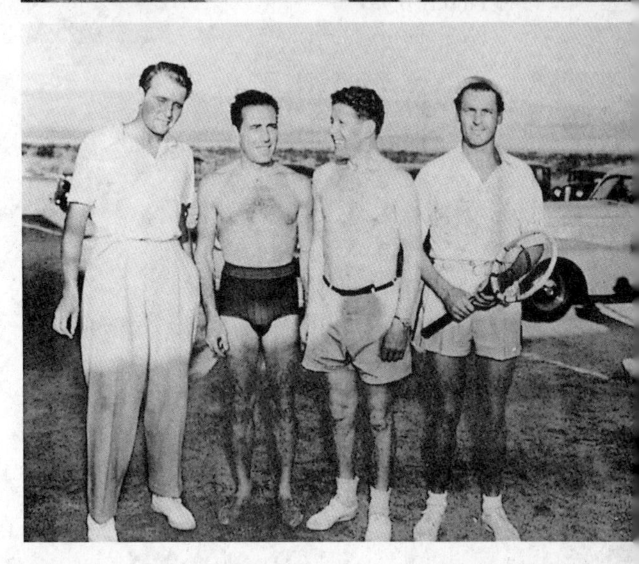

From left to right: Ralph Bellamy, Bogart, Rudy Vallee, and Charles Farrell at the Racquet Club in Palm Springs
Wisconsin Center for Film and Theater Research; courtesy of Warner Bros.

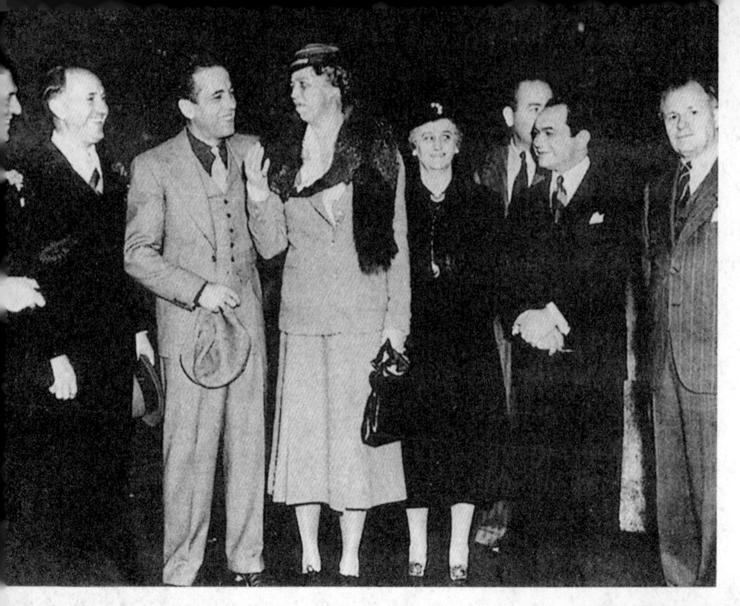

Between Jack Warner and Mrs. Eleanor Roosevelt during a visit by her to the studio. Edward G. Robinson is second from right. Bogart was a staunch supporter of President Franklin D. Roosevelt and campaigned on his behalf.
USC Cinema-Television Library and Archives of Performing Arts; courtesy of Warner Bros.

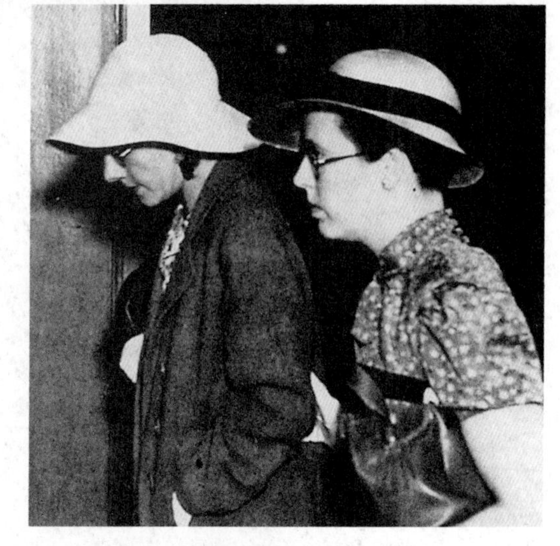

Mary Philips leaving court after her divorce from Bogart became final. With her is their close friend Mary Baker *(right)*.
Corbis-Bettmann

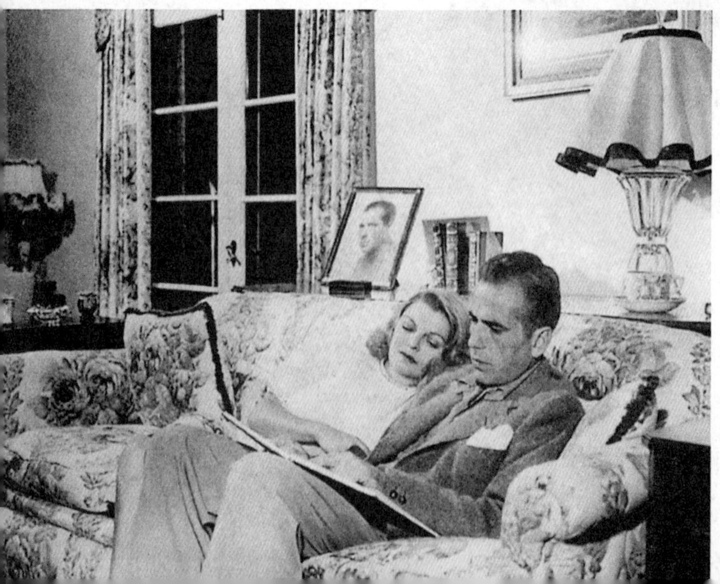

At home with Mayo Methot soon after their marriage. The drawing of Bogart is by his mother, Maud Humphrey, who was a celebrated artist at the turn of the century.
Courtesy of George Eastman House and Warner Bros.

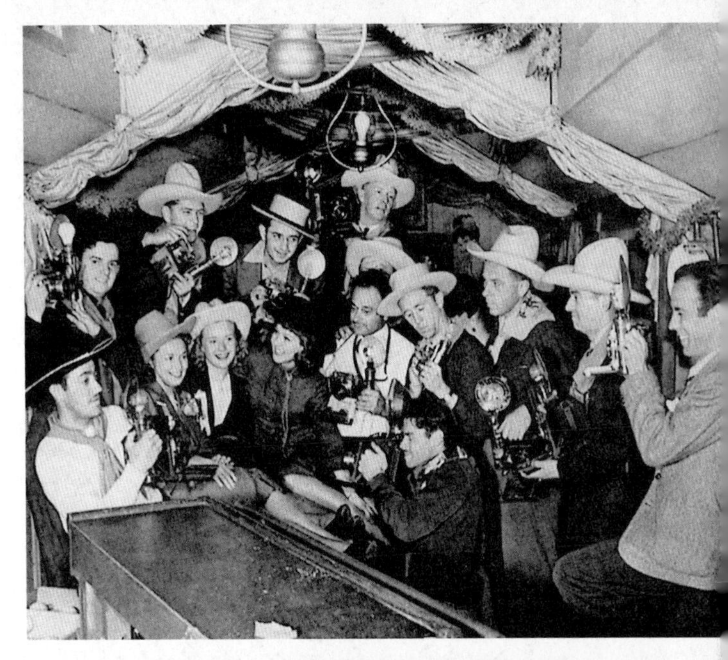

On the Warner Brothers special train to Kansas for the premier of *Dodge City* (1939). Rosemary Lane, Priscilla Lane, and Jean Parker *(from left to right)* are the three actresses surrounded by magazine photographers along on the trip. Shortly after the photo was taken, Mayo Methot, in a jealous rage, tried to stab Bogart with a broken bottle. Bob Wallace *(third from right)* stopped her.

A Delmar Watson Los Angeles Historical Archive Photograph

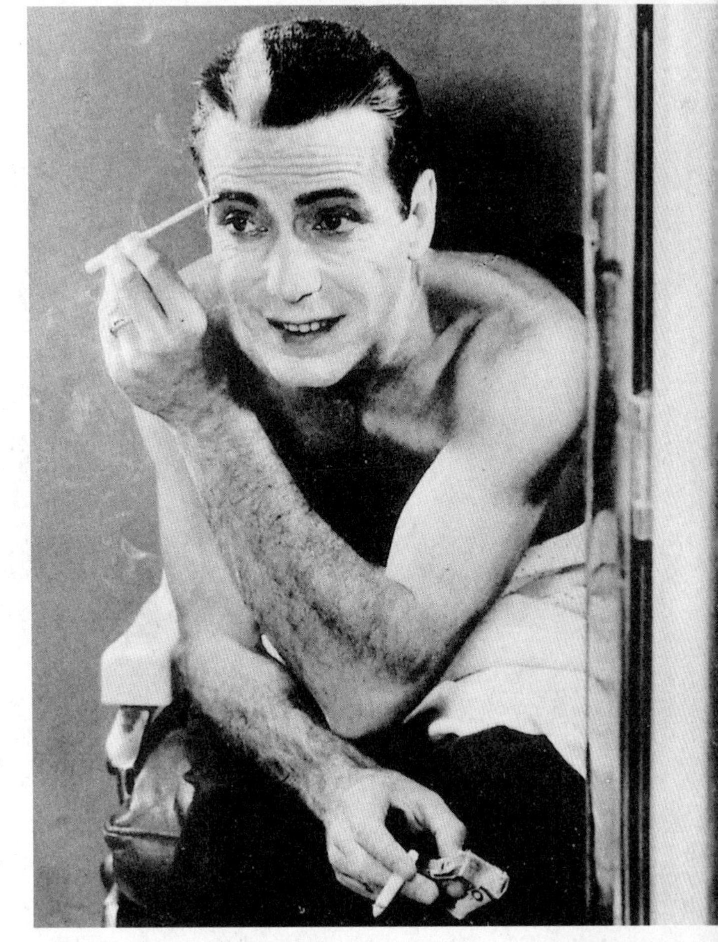

Preparing to play Marshall Quesne, alias Dr. Xavier, an electrocuted, resurrected mad scientist with a taste for blood, in *The Return of Dr. X* (1939)

Wisconsin Center for Film and Theater Research; courtesy of Warner Bros.

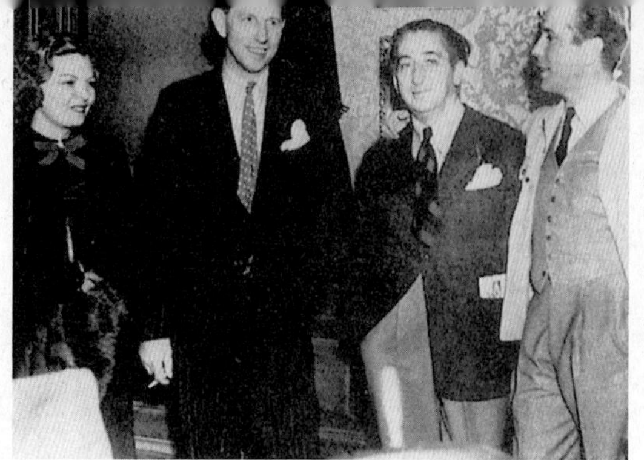

Bogart and Mayo on the set of *It All Came True,* based on a story by their good friend Louis Bromfield *(center left).* Director Lewis Seiler is next to Bogart.

Warner Bros. Archives, University of Southern California; courtesy of Warner Bros.

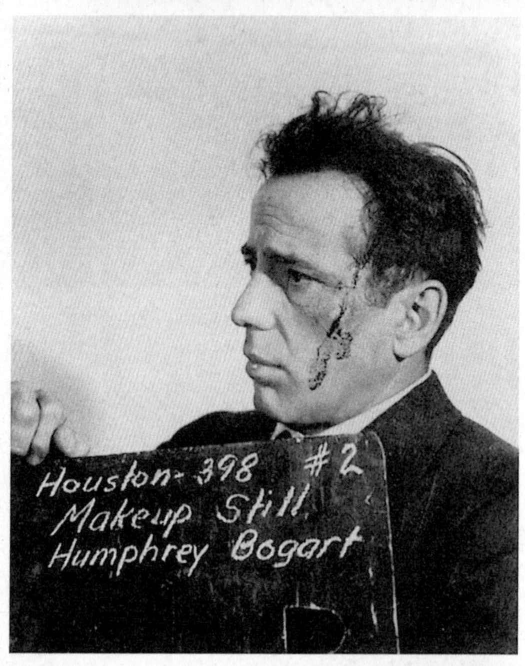

Bogart set the image for the cinematic private eye as Sam Spade in *The Maltese Falcon* (1941).

Courtesy of Warner Bros.

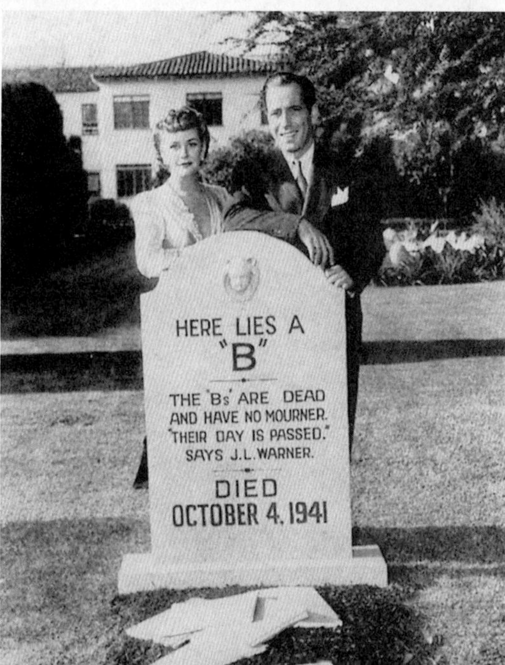

No one was happier than Bogart to attend this "funeral," marking the burial of his and the studio's involvement with low-budget pictures. Ann Sheridan is on Bogart's right.

Warner Bros. Archives, University of Southern California; courtesy of Warner Bros.

screenplay if Hammett's version needed work. The overall effect was to marginalize Humphrey Bogart, who, despite two recent hits and a new contract in negotiation, found himself inexplicably shoved into a third-rate crime movie that his old nemesis George Raft, then in the last months of a dying contract, had suddenly bowed out of. *The Big Shot*, a pallid variation on the aging gunman theme, was a loser from the start. Mary Astor had turned it down. Vincent Sherman was replaced as director at the last instant by Lewis Seiler, who had to be reminded to show up on the set before the actors. Even the producer, Walter MacEwen, admitted needing "a little good luck" and got it with Bogart, who staved off total disaster. Still, when you make a movie about a three-time con, a prison break, and a robbery frame-up, it is hard to expect critics to say anything much nicer than "a reprint of any one of half a hundred gangster films."

To Bogart in those first weeks of 1942, the assignment was confirmation that, whatever the talk of stardom, he was just another warm body drawing a salary. Yet he had come too far to return again to the minor leagues. Even as he began shooting, cursing Jack Warner and Hal Wallis, they were making decisions that set off a chain reaction from which Bogart would for once emerge the winner.

"THE THEATRE AND PUBLICITY DIVISIONS OF OUR COMPANY MUST MAKE NEW STARS," Warner told the New York office in a telegram urging them to promote Gloria Warren after a sneak preview of the sentimental *Always in My Heart* (1942), in which she played Walter Huston's daughter. "WE JUST CANNOT GO ON BEING SATISFIED WITH THE OLD ONES BECAUSE EACH DAY THEY BECOME MORE-UNMANAGEABLE AND LESS BOX OFFICE." In spite of the push, Warren's career did not prosper, but Warner's opinion of his stable of actors was clear.

No one picture was ever produced in a vacuum. As overused as the metaphor may be, the studio schedule resembled a giant chessboard on which the pieces—actors, directors, writers—were moved around by the chief executives, the move of each piece affecting the others.

To pin down the last details for *Watch on the Rhine* in early January, J. L. had reluctantly agreed to some of Lillian Hellman's demands. Her Broadway producer, Herman Shumlin, was to direct. Hammett was to write the screenplay. Neither would be available for some time, but that was the way she wanted it. J. L. had his doubts. He hoped that considering her screenwriting credits—among them *These Three* (based on her play *The Children's Hour*), *Dead End*, and *The Little Foxes*—she would adapt the play herself. Hammett, he said, was not a screenwriter. On top of that, as a pre–Pearl Harbor play, *Watch on the Rhine* became increasingly dated each day, despite its continuing appeal to Broadway audiences. If Hellman and Hammett weren't available, Warner wanted to turn the work over to the studio's best play adapters, Julius and Philip Epstein, and get the film out fast. But Hellman remained immovable, and Warners finally agreed.

The pieces most affected by this were Huston and Bogart. Wallis cabled Wilk to forget about Huston working on the Hellman film: "HE IS SCHEDULED TO DO ANOTHER PICTURE." That other picture was *Across the Pacific,* which, while not the sequel to *The Maltese Falcon,* did reunite the cast. At the same time, *Watch on the Rhine* was put off for months. That left an opening for *Everybody Comes to Rick's,* which Wallis had quickly changed to *Casablanca* in a blatant rip-off of *Algiers.* Not much was expected of it. "Compared to the deep and beautiful Hellman play," one opinion went, "*Casablanca* is a shoddy treatment of the anti-Nazi subject."

It too had begun as a pre–Pearl Harbor story. Murray Burnett, who taught high school in New York City to support his writing efforts, took a European tour with his wife in the summer of 1938. He was twenty-seven. When they arrived in Vienna, they discovered that they had stepped into a Nazi nightmare: "Hitler had invaded Austria and the Viennese were ecstatic about it." The Burnetts lived through a week of anti-Semitic violence, the din of jackboots, and incessant singing of the Nazi anthem known as "The Horst Wessell Song." Burnett, "suddenly faced with reality," was terrified and sobered. When he and his wife left the city, they carried with them valuables kept in trust for Jewish friends and the memory of unbridled fascist hate. By the time they reached the south of France, Burnett "was screaming. We met people, telling them, 'Look what's going on—what's the *matter* with you people?' And they just ran from me. They would turn their backs, they would find excuses; and finally I was left alone. These people did not want to hear this."

One night friends took them to a local nightclub, an oasis of cheer and forgetfulness, where Burnett saw "a black man sitting at the piano. I said to my wife, 'What a setting for a play!' "

Back in New York, Burnett called his writer friend Joan Alison, and together they outlined a play about individual commitment in a time of collective inhumanity. The hero was intended to be a metaphor for a still-neutral America, and the message was that there is no such thing as moral neutrality. The title *Everybody Comes to Rick's,* Murray said, was indicative of the basic theme: "It's a place to go; but underneath, underlying all that, is the fact that everybody, sooner or later, has to come to a decision."

"Unfortunately, all the good people are tied up," casting director Steve Trilling told Wallis as Warners tested for *Casablanca* in February 1942. "[Arthur] Kennedy and Reagan solid till Thursday; Dennis Morgan, [George] Brent and Bogart every day all week." In early January, Warner Publicity had announced Ann Sheridan and Ronald Reagan, the lovers in *Kings Row,* as the leads in *Casablanca,* with Dennis Morgan as "the third member of a starring trio." The story ran in the *Hollywood Reporter* but drew no attention, a trial balloon quickly deflated. It had never been a serious assignment, Reagan said years later; there had been no message from Trilling to come in and discuss the role. "I never had any inkling that anyone had even *thought* of me for that part." Moreover, Reagan was a second lieutenant in the Cavalry Reserve, awaiting active duty and subject to call-up at any time.

By February, in any case, the script was in trouble. The version by the first two assigned writers—Wallis's brother-in-law Wally Kline and his writing partner, Aeneas MacKenzie—was scrapped, and the whole project remanded to the drawing board. Bogart, still on the short list for Rick Blaine, was about to start *Across the Pacific.*

Some later claimed the lead role of Rick Leland in *Across the Pacific* was a warm-up for Rick Blaine, but in December 1941, screenwriter and producer Robert Lord saw the character simply as a profitable recycling of Sam Spade. He urged Wallis to cast Bogart as Leland because "the part is a combination of acid and comedy, a bit like his role in 'THE MALTESE FALCON.' " Lord, who produced several films for Wallis, felt the movie could be "a very big box-office success" if Ann Sheridan played opposite Bogart.

The two had shared billing on six pictures. They were never a romantic team, but they had proved a good combination as examples of the tough-but-tender school and masters of the snappy one-liner. (She had snappy one-liners off-screen, too. A no-nonsense working-class Texan who appeared under her real name of Clara Lou Sheridan in sixteen films, she allegedly hated wearing bras. When pressured at one point by the studio to wear one, she gave in with, "Okay—hammock for two!") Sheridan, however, was tied up in production for *George Washington Slept Here,* and instead the lead went to Mary Astor. With Sydney Greenstreet as the villain, *Across the Pacific* was close enough to being *Falcon II;* even Peter Lorre was in it. Without telling the cast, Huston brought him in for a walk-on scene as a waiter. With Greenstreet and Astor's backs to him, he held the breakfast platter a little too far away, and just brushed Greenstreet's arm as he lifted a coffee cup. After he startled Astor with a sudden kiss on the neck, they turned and broke up when they realized who it was.

The title was from a 1926 Warner silent that starred Monte Blue, brought back for nostalgia's sake in the non-speaking role of Mary Astor's father. Bogart played an American double agent who, single-handed, improbably outsmarts and outguns scores of Japanese soldiers. At this point in the war, American victories were mostly on the screen, and Bogart's exploits allowed audiences to vent the frustrations of the past year, when defeat piled upon defeat and the human losses at Pearl Harbor, Corregidor, and Bataan were still fresh in the public mind. Posters for the film displayed a determined Bogart delivering a powerful sock to the jaw of a Japanese officer. The caption, in huge display type, read: "SNAPSHOT OF A GUY WHO LOVES HIS WORK." An alternative caption was "FOLKS, I'VE BEEN SAVING THIS SINCE DECEMBER 7!"

Like most action films, though, it was essentially an entertainment. Screenwriter Richard Macauley, whose credits included *They Drive by Night,* provided Bogart and Astor with opportunities for banter in *The Maltese Falcon* mode, with echoes of Hammett ("You're good, Angel. You're very, very good.") and a sitcom romance on the high seas:

> "Say, are you getting sick?"
> "I don't know. How do girls usually act when you kiss them?"
> "They don't turn green."
> "Then I'm sick."

The production had the quality of a reunion, and it had been a pleasant shoot despite the scheduling problems that arose when Astor came down with laryngitis, wished Huston good luck in a hoarse whisper, and staggered home to bed with flu and a raging fever.

Bogart's personal problems were continuing to mount as Mayo's drinking and instability steadily increased, as was her physical violence, now oddly foreshadowed by her humming "Embraceable You." Bogart liked to go to the Finlandia Baths on Sunset Boulevard to relax, sweat out the alcoholic toxins, and have a little peace away from Mayo. She, in turn, became convinced that the baths were really a brothel. According to Joe Hyams, one night Bogart came home to find Mayo "waiting for him in the living room, her eyes puffy and glazed. She was humming 'Embraceable You' [and] . . . she lunged at him with [a butcher] knife. He ducked and tried to run for the door. Somehow she stabbed him in the middle of the back." By luck, the blade did not penetrate deeply.

The indispensable Mary Baker, apparently the only woman in Bogart's life whom Mayo was not jealous of, rushed over when she was called immediately after the incident. Baker knew a doctor who for $500 could be relied on for absolute discretion, and he stitched up Bogart. The police were never notified.

After the doctor left, "Mayo smothered [Bogart] with kisses the way she always did after a particularly bad fight. When he didn't respond because the pain was too great she accused him of coming home tired 'because of those girls at the bath.' She was going down to Finlandia to tear the place apart, but Mary, who was still there, quieted her down."

The next day, Bogart, who had a reputation for being chronically punctual, came to the set late. "He was *never* late," John Huston said, who went to Bogart's dressing room that morning. "He was getting dressed, and he had a bandage on—the *back.* It was a wicked stab."

On another occasion of Mayo's violence—she set the house afire—Mary arrived after her call and brought in Blayney Matthews, the chief of Warner Brothers studio police, who helped Bogart put out the blaze. Once again there was no publicity. Hyams writes that Mayo threatened to kill Bogart if he left her, and after the stabbing, Bogart, fearful that she might succeed even if he stayed, insisted Baker and Jaffe take out a $100,000 insurance policy on his life. He was the major source of income for their firm, and he wanted to be sure they were protected against a catastrophic financial loss.

Bogart did not miss any work as a result of his wound, but six weeks into filming, Huston had to leave the picture. Months before, he had applied for a commission in the U.S. Army, and he was called to report with nine days of shooting left. Stage 8 had been appropriately converted to a crumbling plantation in the jungle, and the climax of the story had been saved for last—the hero held at gunpoint while an enemy plane revs up off screen, set to take off and bomb the Panama Canal.

Everyone had known this would be Huston's last film for a while. A story persisted for years afterward, told and retold by Huston himself: how the director received his call-up, announced he was leaving to serve his country, and then walked off the set where Bogart was tied to a chair and guards blocked every exit. The ending in the script was still unfinished, and he left it to incoming director Vincent Sherman to get Bogart untrussed and into his heroics.

But Huston, who liked a good joke, also liked a tall tale. Production records indicate that Huston actually had a week's notice and made provisions for a smooth transition. On April 22, his last day on the job, he sat with Sherman and eased him in as they shot the opening sequences of the final Bogart-Greenstreet confrontation. Huston was too professional to further complicate a production that was already behind schedule and whose leading lady was out with influenza, and he was too desirous of continuing his career to drain his fund of good will at Warners for the sake of a prank.

The transition scene was rewritten two days before Huston's departure. It involved a lone gunman and no ropes on the hero. Bogart's escape was made possible by the time-honored sudden distraction, which allowed him to overwhelm the guard, rush out into the night, and with a burst of fire from his machine gun save the Canal.

There was a disgraceful side to the fun. The officers on the Japanese ship carrying the principals to Panama were dignified. But Greenstreet's gunman—his Wilmer—was a young Nisei, described in the script as "very Americanized, flip and fast on the trigger, with jokes just on the corny side." In other words, a man whose Westernization and loyalty to America were only superficial. The portrayal reinforced the stereotype of the disloyal Japanese at a time when Japanese-Americans, regardless of citizenship, were being rounded up all over the West Coast and interned in camps for no other reason than their ethnic origin. Because of the deportations, most if not all of the actors cast in the Japanese parts were Chinese.

From the first set of dailies, Warners knew that the film was a winner. Everyone who saw the scenes was impressed, no one more than Hal Wallis, who had just become an independent producer. Despite a salary of over a quarter of a million dollars, after eight years of overseeing every foot of Warners' eighteen or so A films a year, Wallis had grown tired of the strain and long hours and of being second fiddle to Jack Warner. In February 1942, he signed a deal to produce four pictures a year for Warner Brothers. The studio's regard for him was evident: Wallis had first choice of all stories and of all Warner contract talent, from director, actors, and writers, through camera crews and stage technicians, down to secretaries and assistants. If he wanted people not under contract to Warners, the studio would do its best to get them. He was given virtual independence, and his fees included 10 percent of a film's gross once it had made 125 percent of the cost of the negative. Despite the generosity of these terms, outsiders wondered whether Jack Warner could accept his ex-lieutenant as an autonomous producer, and if the contract would last beyond the four years agreed upon. (In fact, it would end after two and a half years and nine pictures.) At the time the deal was signed, rumors abounded that Wallis was leaving the company. J. L. insisted nothing had changed: this was simply a reward to a loyal and talented executive.

Wallis had moved with the new job from his office next to J. L. and into a bungalow. Even though he no longer saw dailies on all the films in production, he was still able to keep close track of what was good and what was not, and he had already decided to add *Casablanca* to his small list of personally produced films. The crackling tension he recognized in the dailies of *Across the Pacific,* along with the film's special combination of toughness and comedic overtones, confirmed his decision to cast Bogart as Rick Blaine.

Not long after Wallis signed his production deal, he sat down with Philip G. and Julius J. Epstein, otherwise known as Phil and Julie and commonly known as The Boys. They were lanky, bald identical twins, with a reputation for being the lot's funniest wisecrackers as well as the best adapters of plays. They were masters of the snappy comeback and of gleaming repartee. Of equal or even greater value to the studio was their ability as script doctors. A good but ordinary screenplay became a sparkler after they touched up the dialogue, and everyone knew it. James Cagney demanded that they fix up *Yankee Doodle Dandy* as a condition of his taking the role of George M. Cohan. Their latest credit had been the satiric comedy *The Man Who Came to Dinner,* a Broadway hit that became an even more popular film.

The thirty-two-year-old brothers had hoped to write *Watch on the Rhine* but were happy to be offered this one. "They are anxious to do this script," Wallis's secretary, Paul Nathan, wrote to Jack Warner, "and he is anxious for them to do it." But it was not a case of the Epsteins wanting to do the script because they thought the film would be particularly special; they viewed it simply as an assignment. "You must remember that nobody thought it was going to be anything," Julius Epstein later said. "Warner Brothers made a picture a week, as did every major studio. It was just another picture on the schedule."

Before they were formally assigned to the script, the government asked them to come to Washington, D.C., for three weeks to work with director Frank Capra on the propaganda series *Why We Fight.* Epstein recalled that "we certainly felt we had to go," even though the studio "was quite mad at us. But when we came back, everything was okay. We did a little moonlighting in Washington and wrote quite a few pages."

It was the twins' irreverence in the face of power that gave their comedy its edge. Julius "never took Warner seriously. They were butchers in Youngstown, Ohio, and I'd call Jack Warner, to his face, the Butcher of Burbank." The Epsteins were contract workers in an era when writers spent their careers at a studio, but after several years at Warners, they hoped to get out, because "we were being underpaid and not getting assignments we wanted." Warner knew this, and "knew we would do anything to get out of our contract, so he took it" when the brothers gave him grief.

"We worked only two hours a day," Julius said. "I still work only two hours." (Philip died in 1952.) The concept of concentrated brilliance was foreign to Harry and Jack Warner, who believed in a full day's work—or at least a full day's presence—for a full day's pay. "One day we came in at one-thirty or two and ran into J. L. He was furious. He said, 'Read your contract! Bank presidents get in at nine and you're coming in the afternoon!' We had a half-finished script in our office. We sent it to him and said, 'Have the bank president finish the script.'

"A year or so later, we came in at nine o'clock and sent him a scene. 'This scene is *terrible,*' he told us. My brother said to him, 'How is that possible? It was written at nine o'clock.'

" 'I want my money back,' Jack yelled. And my brother told him, 'I'd *love* to give you your money back, but I just built a pool. However, if you're ever in the neighborhood and feel like a swim . . .' "

Often the brothers—and other writers—wrote only the material needed for the next day, and *Casablanca* was no exception. "Sometimes it was the same day. They said, 'We need another scene,' and we sat down and wrote it. And we'd take the pages to the set ourselves." Asked once if they picked up any ideas while on the set, he answered, "We didn't get any help from actors, the director, anybody."

You mean, the interviewer asked, "You just brought it, said, 'Here,' and then went back to your office?"

Epstein shrugged. "It worked."

It was that irreverent self-confidence, translated to the screen, that Wallis wanted for his new film:

> "And what in heaven's name brought you to Casablanca?"
> "My health. I came to Casablanca for the waters."
> "Waters? What waters? We are in the desert."
> "I was misinformed."

The Epsteins' dryly witty dialogue floated the story and raced it along, but other writers would be added, in response both to the needs of the schedule and the evolving screenplay. Howard Koch was a onetime radio writer whose *War of the Worlds* broadcast on Halloween 1938 by Orson Welles had much of the country convinced that the United States was under attack by Martians. His scripts included *The Sea Hawk, The Letter,* and *Sergeant York.* A liberal activist, he was brought in to strengthen the political and dramatic aspects of the story. Koch changed Rick from an expatriate lawyer on the run from a scandal to a bruised idealist with a hidden anti-fascist past; from the self-pitying drinker that Bogart hated in the role's early stages to the tough cynic who is really for the underdog. For the romantic element, Wallis asked Casey Robinson, the writer of the studio's most successful "women's films" (among them *Dark Victory* and *Now, Voyager*), to come up with love scenes that would complement the plot and provide the story that would make Bogart the symbol of the new romantic hero.

The three sets of writers, working independently, played to Bogart's strengths, and the disparate efforts coalesced with legendary results. "No one," Julius Epstein said, "could have seen what was going to come. *Everybody* now says he wrote scenes for it," he said, laughing. "And it's not my favorite picture. I don't give a damn! Mine is *Light in the Piazza* [1962]; nobody saw it." The months of preparation and rewriting on the movie are documented in excellent detail in *Round Up the Usual Suspects,* Aljean Harmetz's definitive account of the making of the film.

All the basic elements for *Casablanca* were already in the play script of *Everybody Comes to Rick's:* the nightclub setting in a city of danger and ambiguity; the American expatriate hiding from the past and from himself; the amoral Vichy officer and the immoral Gestapo officer; the all-important letters of transit; the gallant resistance leader; and the beautiful heroine, torn between the man she loves and the man she reveres.

Whole scenes, sometimes intact, sometimes reworked, are recognizable in the finished screenplay: Laszlo leading the nightclub patrons in "La Marseillaise"; the hard-edged exchanges between Rick and the black marketeer Ugarte, between Rick and the Vichy prefect, Rick and the Gestapo chief, Rick and Sam. And lines of dialogue that have become touchstones for generations of moviegoers:

> "Think of all those poor refugees, who must rot in this place if I didn't keep them. It's not so bad that, through ways of my own, I provide them with exit visas."
>
> "For a price, Ugarte, for a price."

(The Burnett-Alison version was "I supply these poor people with the necessary exit visas.")

"So, you are not one of those people who cannot imagine the Germans in their beloved Paris?"

"Boss, we'll take the car and drive all night. We'll get drunk. We'll go fishin' and stay away until she's gone."
"Sam, play 'As Time Goes By.' "

By April, the film was taking shape, and Michael Curtiz had been brought in as the director. George Raft was campaigning for Rick Blaine, Warner wrote to Wallis. How about it? Wallis was uninterested. "He hasn't done a role here since I was a little boy. Bogart is ideal for it, and it is being written for him."

It is fortunate for Bogart that Joan Alison was not in charge of casting. An attractive, wealthy divorcée and a decade older than her collaborator Burnett, she had a clear idea of what Rick Blaine looked like. "Both my husbands were wide shouldered and fine athletes," she told Harmetz, "and Rick was my concept of a guy that I would like. Clark Gable. I hated Humphrey Bogart. I thought he was a common drunk."

But Wallis knew his character, and his actor. After years of struggle, Bogart finally had a custom-tailored role, not an off-the-rack item, however well-designed, that others had tried on and slipped off.

Ann Sheridan, Wallis's earlier choice for the female lead, had her role rewritten out from under her. The heroine of *Everybody Comes to Rick's* was Lois Meredith, a beautiful American of the type known in those days as an adventuress. She had dumped Rick in Paris for another man after breaking up his marriage, then arrived in Casablanca only to go back to bed with Rick. Whatever disagreements the Warner writers had, they were united on one point: Lois Meredith might get to France and North Africa, but in no way would she get past the Breen Office.

"Try to get a foreign girl for the part," the Epsteins had advised from Washington, adding, "An American girl with big tits will do."

Warners asked MGM for Hedy Lamarr, the Viennese-born brunette heroine of *Algiers.* Louis B. Mayer said no. They tested the blond French actress Michele Morgan, whose price of $55,000 seemed a little steep, and the black-haired ballerina Tamara Toumanova, who would become Mrs. Casey Robinson.

Wallis, however, already had his sights on another actress. Despite his failure on *All Through the Night,* he was ready to make a second stab at teaming up Humphrey Bogart with twenty-seven-year-old Ingrid Bergman. This time politics helped Warners. Producer David O. Selznick, to whom Bergman was under contract, had been secretly disquieted by talk of Sweden joining the Axis. Apparently the Warners had not heard the rumor, and Selznick was eager to strike a deal before they did and his Scandinavian goddess turned to damaged goods. All the Warner executives knew was that the producer of *Gone With the Wind* and *Rebecca* was suddenly receptive to a loanout.

Bergman's Hollywood career, now in its third year, had shown more promise than success. Selznick had brought her to America in 1939 to star with Leslie Howard in a recycling of *Intermezzo,* the 1936 Swedish romantic hit that had caught the attention of the industry. Since then she had done three films on loanout, getting good reviews but no breakthrough. She was also known to want the lead in Paramount's upcoming adaptation of Ernest Hemingway's *For Whom the Bell Tolls,* a prestige picture beside which *Casablanca* seemed very small potatoes.

Perhaps not wanting to appear overeager, Selznick said he needed to know more about *Casablanca* before agreeing to release his property. In early April, two weeks after their return from Washington, the Epsteins were dispatched to the white-columned mansion in Culver City that was the headquarters for David O. Selznick Productions. Their orders were simple: sell Selznick on the *Casablanca* plot and bring back a yes on Bergman, all on the basis of a partial script marked "TEMP."

"Tell him the story," Wallis instructed them.

"We *have* no story yet," Julius reminded his boss.

"Never mind. Wing it!"

The scene that followed has become part of Hollywood lore. The twins were ushered into Selznick's office, where the producer sat, his buffalo head with its mass of brilliantined curls bent down, intent on lunch.

"He was slurping soup," Julius Epstein said. "Never looked up at us *once.* And I start to tell the story. 'Uh, it's about Casablanca, and the *refugees* are there, and they're trying to get out, and there's letters of *transit,* and a fella has them and the cops come and get him'—

"And I realize I'm talking about twenty minutes and I haven't even *mentioned* the character of Bergman. So I say, 'Oh, what the hell! It's going to be a lot of shit like *Algiers.*'

"And Selznick looked up and nodded. And we had Bergman."

Her casting further changed the heroine's personality. The constraints of the Breen Office aside, audiences would easily have accepted Ann Sheridan as Lois, but not Bergman in the same role. The public Ingrid Bergman of the 1940s was a model of propriety, the star with a wholesome, apple-cheeked appeal that bordered on the virginal. Her image remained that way until 1949, when she left her husband, Dr. Peter Lindstrom. Her affair with director Roberto Rossellini during the filming of *Stromboli* and her subsequent pregnancy shocked the world and led to her being exiled from the United States for seven years. Lois Meredith was "hardboiled, sophisticated. She was a cosmopolitan woman who slept around a lot," Epstein said. But in 1942, "Well, who was going to believe that about *Ingrid Bergman*?"

Lois was tossed onto the scrap heap of discarded characters, and in her place appeared the mysterious Ilsa. Julius Epstein gives credit for the name to Michael Curtiz, who sat in on the story conferences. Born Mihaly Kertesz in Budapest in 1888, Curtiz spoke English atrociously, but he could come up with a new name for a European heroine. His source was in *Journey Through the Harz Mountains* by the nineteenth-century poet Heinrich Heine.

I am the Princess Ilse
And dwell in the Ilsenstein;
Come with me to my castle,
We will be happy there . . .
You will forget your pain,
O heartsick man!

But as *Casablanca* historian Harmetz points out, Ilsa also had an element of danger about her. Much like the Ilse of the poem, she was part lover, part destroyer, an enchantress whose innocence could both beguile a man and lure him to his destruction. Or at the very least, leave him in a railroad station in Paris with his guts kicked in. Bogart completed *Across the Pacific* in early May. After nine weeks of almost solid work, he requested and received a little extra time to rest up before starting his third picture in less than six months. He had discussed everything with Mike Curtiz, he assured Steve Trilling, and most of his wardrobe was ready. Now he just wanted to get aboard his boat and stay there as long as possible.

His new contract, negotiated that January, for the first time guaranteed a four-week vacation. There had been two years left on the old agreement, but the studio yet again sensed a coming rise in Bogart's marketability and wanted to make the least expensive deal possible. The process was an indication of how far Bogart had come. Now it was the studio that behaved deferentially as it dealt with his circle of advisers, which included an agent, a business manager, and a lawyer. Bogart's demands were clear, and most were met. There would be no more options exercised only at the studio's discretion built into the contract. Bogart wanted a straight seven-year deal, just as Clark Gable had at MGM. There would be extra pay for personal appearances for Warners, and permission to do radio appearances when he wasn't working. And, of course, there was the salary. The old agreement stipulated $1,850 a week for 1942. Bogart wanted $3,000. They settled on $2,750. "I sincerely hope," Warner counsel Roy Obringer wrote Sam Jaffe in mid-January, "that Mr. Bogart is now agreeable to executing this contract."

Jaffe did not press Warners on Bogart's having script approval, the central point in his differences with the studio. To put it on the table, Jaffe later insisted, would have been hopeless. "It wouldn't work. At that stage you could not get script approval. All an actor could do was refuse and be suspended." But a few other actors on the lot did have that right; Bogart's problem was that his agent did not have enough clout.

However, Bogart's career had grown under Jaffe's auspices, and he was the biggest client of the firm. Jaffe was hardworking and dedicated, a mid-level agent like most in the business, ready to do whatever he could for his clients. He was not, though, in Leland Hayward's or Myron Selznick's league, able to coerce the concessions that would make their clients happier. Jaffe could reason, he could pester, he could plead; but he couldn't pressure.

On the other side of the scale, Bogart was a star but not yet a major one. The trick to being a successful agent is to know the limits of what can be demanded of the studio. Bogart and Jaffe probably got the best deal they could, but the question of role approval continued to be a festering sore in the relations between Bogart and Warners.

On May 21, four days before the filming of *Casablanca* was to begin, Warners previewed *Across the Pacific* in Washington, D.C. Jack Warner cabled back to Warner Publicity that the film was a smash.

> REACTION OF AUDIENCE . . . CONVINCES ME BEYOND A SHADOW OF A DOUBT THAT HUMPHREY BOGART IS ONE OF OUR BIGGEST STARS. . . .
>
> IN BOGART WE HAVE WHAT I HONESTLY CONSIDER THE EQUIVALENT TO CLARK GABLE.

The preview of *Across the Pacific* wasn't J. L.'s only reason for being in Washington, where the studio had a large office that was the headquarters for its unpublicized lobbying activities. On the night of June 7, Mr. and Mrs. Jack Warner dined at the White House with President and Mrs. Roosevelt. Amid the pleasantries, FDR indicated that he'd appreciate another meeting before J. L. continued on to a family gathering in Miami.

They met again at 2:00 on the afternoon of Warner's departure. The train was to leave at 5:00. By 3:30, William Schaefer was in a sweat as he paced the platform at Union Station. He had been left to cope with the beautiful, headstrong Ann Warner, her cartload of valises and hatboxes, and her sullen repugnance for the coming get-together with the other Warners. By 4:30, Schaefer was close to panic, not quite sure what to do but not about to call the Oval Office. Then, with only minutes to spare, J. L. came down the platform. The luggage was frantically loaded, and the Warner party swung aboard the train as it pulled out of the depot.

Settling into his compartment, the gregarious Jack Warner was uncharacteristically quiet. Normally he would have been overflowing with details after a one-on-one meeting with the president. Finally he became aware of Schaefer's questioning look.

"We talked about a movie I'm going to make."

The movie, Schaefer learned in the next weeks, was *Mission to Moscow,* based on the pro-Soviet best-seller by former ambassador to the USSR Joseph E. Davies. It had been published with covert White House encouragement and was intended—like the proposed film—to create national good will for the Russians; the godless Communists of a year ago were now America's ally. But it was also to be a goodwill offering to the Soviets, as FDR explained to Warner and as Warner explained to his lieutenants. "The Russians," Schaefer said, "were asking the U.S. to start an offensive to take the heat off them, but we weren't militarily prepared to do that, though we were sending them tons of equipment. So to pacify them, Roosevelt evidently thought that making *Mission to Moscow* would help the situation between the two countries."

Roosevelt had shrewdly picked the most pro–New Deal movie mogul to be his silent helper. Not only was Jack Warner politically inclined toward FDR; in addition, like most men who have risen to absolute authority in their own realm but have equal competitors outside it, he always wanted an edge to help him rise above his equals. What better than the president of the United States making a secret request of you? *Mission to Moscow* was more than a film; it was a service to the nation. "It is our patriotic duty to effect its successful completion," he wrote Jake

Wilk, adding a penciled P.S.: "Extremely confidential you know official Washington behind this." To allow for Roosevelt's denial of involvement in the event of trouble, the White House connection remained undocumented. Warner had to pretend that the film was all his idea, even in the face of criticism, and he was a good soldier to his commander in chief. For many years afterward, conservative members of Congress and other anti-Communists accused Warner of being a pawn, maintaining that Roosevelt had bent his arm to make the film. "He always said, no, FDR didn't," Schaefer said. "But Roosevelt naturally did."

The result was a docudrama before the word was coined. *Mission to Moscow* was propaganda purporting to be history. It set out to undo years of demonizing by casting a golden glow over the darkest aspects of Stalin's rule, and it even legitimized the purge trials that decimated the Soviet leadership. For Ambassador Davies, who loved the Soviet Union and privately hated Stalinism ("The purge and the terror here are horrifying beyond belief," he once wrote from Moscow), it was a case of sacrificing some principles for the greater good. He knew Hitler could not be defeated without the USSR's aid. The task, he explained to the journalist Edward R. Murrow, was to keep the Soviets aligned with the Allies by all means possible. *Mission to Moscow* was the wrong film made for the right reasons, and it was a time bomb that would eventually blow up in Jack Warner's hands.

The start date for *Casablanca* had first been set for late April, then postponed to mid-May, then pushed back to the end of the month. Even then the situation was anything but promising. A week before shooting began, Bogart, Bergman, and Geraldine Fitzgerald sat glumly around a table in the Warner commissary Green Room. Fitzgerald was playing second lead to Bette Davis in *Watch on the Rhine,* which was finally in production, her career back where it was in 1938. Her opportunity had come and gone with *The Maltese Falcon,* and despite Jack Warner's personal regard for Fitzgerald, the studio had lost interest in her.

Over lunch, the two *Casablanca* leads vented their own frustration and discouragement. "The whole subject," Fitzgerald told Aljean Harmetz, "was how they could get out of the movie. They thought the dialogue was ridiculous and the situations were unbelievable. And Ingrid was terribly upset because she said she had to portray the most beautiful woman in Europe, and no one would believe that. 'I look like a milkmaid,' she said. I knew Bogart very well, and I think he wanted to join forces with

Bergman, to make sure they both said the same things. He had had such a bad time for years at Warner Brothers." It remains the only memory of Bogart and Bergman's relating to one another off the set.

A good deal has been written about the lack of personal chemistry between two of the screen's most famous lovers. "I kissed him but I never knew him," Bergman allegedly said of Bogart, in a quote that was never confirmed but never denied. Bogart's only recorded comment is a gallant but meaningless "When the camera moves in on that Bergman face, and she's saying she loves you, it would make anybody look romantic." According to Hollywood mythology, Jack Warner, in Bergman's presence, ostensibly scoffed, "Who'd want to kiss Bogart?"

"I would," she supposedly replied.

For all her virginal aura, Bergman reportedly had affairs with her leading men. Not this time. For Bogart, a nine-to-six working actor, the daily sessions were a job that he showed up for on time, did conscientiously, and finished as soon as possible. All that mattered anyway was what appeared on the screen—the only thing Bogart felt an actor owed his public. As it happened, the public, in these same weeks, proclaimed Bogart's new status as a romantic lead.

When filming finally began on May 25, *Casablanca* was a production without a final script, but Warners had no choice other than to commence. The loanout agreement with Selznick specified substantial penalties for keeping Bergman more than the allotted eight weeks. Yet apart from Bogart and Bergman, most of the cast was still not in place; even worse, few of the actors desired were under Warner contracts. Instead, they were an assemblage of outside talent with commitments at other studios. Sydney Greenstreet and Peter Lorre, whom Wallis wanted for the parts of the black marketeers, Ferrari and Ugarte, were taking a leisurely approach in their negotiations. For Victor Laszlo, Wallis had hoped to cast the Dutch actor Philip Dorn, who had played the anti-Nazi leader in *Underground* (1941), but he was on loanout to MGM. Paul Henreid, the second choice, was unenthusiastic and, in any case, not yet available.

The important role of Sam—the pianist, friend, nursemaid, and chorus to the drama—took weeks to cast. At one point Wallis thought of changing Sam to a woman. Suggestions included Lena Horne ("Excellent talent—a very pretty light colored girl"), Ella Fitzgerald, and the singer-pianist Hazel Scott, later the wife of Congressman Adam Clayton Powell. The idea was dropped; possibly because pairing Bogart with a beautiful black female companion would have been generally unacceptable to American sensibilities in 1942.

After it was decided that Sam would remain a man, Wallis wanted Clarence Muse, one of the busiest black talents in Hollywood. He was a good baritone with over forty studio films to his credit, among them *Show Boat* (1936) and *Huckleberry Finn* (1931), in which he played Jim. Wallis also tested Arthur "Dooley" Wilson, a Broadway transplant in his first year at Paramount, in the "Boss, let's get out of here" scene. Wallis rated the result no higher than a grudging "pretty good"; besides, Wilson was a drummer, not a pianist. (In the film, the music was played off-camera by studio pianist Elliot Carpenter.) Nevertheless, the part went to Wilson. Wallis accepted him with one of those sentences that history turns into humor: "He isn't ideal for the part but if we get stuck and can't do any better I suppose he could play it."

For the first day's shooting, the scene was Paris, Rick and Ilsa at the Cafe La Belle Aurore, Sam at the piano, and Elliot Carpenter off-screen playing "As Time Goes By." Four days earlier, the flashback sequence hadn't even existed. Casey Robinson had written it and rushed the pages first to Wallis and then to Curtiz. "The dialogue may be a little flowery," Robinson said in a cover note, "but it fits the scenes, the situations, and what we are trying to get over to the audience in 50 feet [about 33 seconds] of film—namely, an intense love affair between two people."

Julius Epstein said that he and his brother rewrote the scene to improve the dialogue. "The only line of Robinson's that's left, and we fought against it bitterly because we thought it was not Bogart, is, 'A franc for your thoughts.' That was not the character. But the director, everybody, loved the line, so that stayed in."

For weeks afterward, however, the entry under "Script Report" would read "Incomplete." Rewrites dribbled in, subject in turn to more rewrites. Wallis worried over delays, and tempers flared on the set. Curtiz fumed at the sound mixer Francis Scheid on one day and at cinematographer Arthur Edeson on another. Bogart at first sat quietly through it all, playing chess by mail in a match with a partner in Brooklyn named Irving Kovner, the brother of a Warner employee. The match had begun early in the year, the moves noted on the back of penny postcards with a fountain pen in Bogart's distinctive hand. They always began, "Dear Irving" and never failed to include a personal message ("You're too hot-headed—calm down"; "Now I'm in a jam"; "Don't worry I'm playing"). "He is very much interested in the game," Bogart's secretary Kathryn Sloan wrote to Kovner at one point, "and has derived great pleasure from it." It was Howard Koch's idea to incorporate the game into the film. The match was a metaphor for the Rick-Renault (Claude Rains) relationship, he told Wallis, and the "chess-like intrigue which characterizes Casablanca."

The chessboard is part of the introduction to Rick Blaine. The other items in the frame are a half-empty wineglass, a half-smoked cigarette, and a gambling IOU presented for approval to the as-yet-unseen protagonist, which he eventually endorses with a black pencil stroke. His underscoring the bold "O.K Rick" lets the audience know from the outset that this is a thinking man, a sporting man, a drinker, and a strategist who controls his territory. Then the camera draws back for a medium close-up of Bogart, taking a drag with pursed lips, intent on his game, the overhead lighting turning the sockets of his eyes into expressionless black pools.

Peter Lorre as Ugarte tries to work up a conversation with Rick, who sits with his eyes fixed on the chessboard, his answers offhand, his manner contemptuous and distracted. The sequence ends with Ugarte disclosing that he has the travel documents stolen from the murdered German couriers and that he wants Rick to hide them. It is a verbal and emotional duel, the two men maneuvering in counterpoint to the moves on the board.

> "Too bad about those two German couriers, wasn't it?"
>
> "They got a lucky break. Yesterday they were just two German clerks. Today they're the honored dead."

As they talk, Rick moves his king and a castle, protecting both his pieces, a visual subtext to the scripted sparring.

Off-camera, Bogart also played chess against Paul Henreid. "Bogart was anxious to play," Henreid said later, "and I beat the hell out of him time and again. He was a very fine chess player, very fine. I was just a little better."

The Viennese-born actor joined the company a month late. There had been weeks of haggling over the contract and more weeks lost while he co-starred with Bette Davis in *Now, Voyager,* whose production ran consistently behind schedule. Curtiz, shooting on the set for Rick's Café Américain, worked around Henreid as long as he could. He did scenes with Bogart, with Bergman, with Rains—with anyone and everyone except Henreid. Hal Wallis even wrote a scene just so they could hold onto Stage 8. Finally on June 25, Henreid, in his white suit, entered through the doors of Rick's Café. "I reserved a table. Victor Laszlo."

Almost everybody came to Rick's in similarly piecemeal fashion, and the cast consisted of an ethnic blend unprecedented in the Hollywood of 1942, from Dooley Wilson as Sam to the refugee actors. Conrad Veidt, the icily elegant Gestapo major who likes his champagne to be vintage and his caviar very cold, had starred in silents in America and Germany. He had played a zombie in the 1919 German Expressionist classic *The Cabinet of Dr. Caligari,* a blackmailed homosexual in *A Man's Past,* and Vivien Leigh's lover in *Dark Journey.* An actor with chiseled features and the movements of a dancer, he had left Germany with his Jewish wife and listed his citizenship as British. Now, he played exotic villains and Nazis. On the screen, he was the embodiment of the Hitler menace. Off it, he was a gentle, beloved man whom his friends called Mr. Democracy. His circumstances left him depressed but resigned. "There's a time when we win and when we lose," he once told Henreid. "Well, I won very early in my career and now I'm losing. But I had it all and now I do it for the money and for my wife. And we have a good life."

Peter Lorre, born Laszlo Lowenstein, had been a Jewish performer with the courage to satirize the Nazis in their early days in Berlin, before a movie career in which he would portray more than his share of Nazis and other psychopaths. Paul Henreid, himself a refugee, first drew attention as the blond Aryan nemesis in the 1940 British thriller *Night Train to Munich* (first released in the United States as *Night Train*), prompting a flood of letters from women viewers inquiring about "that cute Nazi." Born Paul Georg Julius von Henreid, he liked to think of himself in terms of the old Austrian aristocracy, and his memories were of a family estate in Czechoslovakia. The origins of his father, a banker who raised orchids and Thoroughbreds and who was close to the emperor, are vague, but there were probably at least some ancestors who were Jewish, which would account for the actor's flight from Europe and his abhorrence of Nazism.

Nearly every actor had an exotic backstory. Marcel Dalio, the croupier, had been a great star (*Grand Illusion, The Rules of the Game*) in France. The trembly jowled comedian S. Z. Sakall, cast as Carl the waiter, came from Budapest. Gregory Gaye, the German banker barred from the gambling room, and Leonid Kinsky, as Sascha the bartender, had been actors in imperial St. Petersburg. Greenstreet and Rains rounded out the blue-chip army of supporting players, although Rains's casting as Captain Renault, the prefect of police, had at first been questioned.

"We said, 'There are so many good French actors around, why put an *Englishman* in it?' " Julius Epstein said. "We were absolutely wrong."

The credit for assembling the ensemble properly belongs to Steve Trilling. Epstein, knowing when a plain line would do, said: "It was a marvelous cast."

It was also expensive; Greenstreet and Rains each drew three or four thousand dollars a week, whether they worked or not. Much of the problem continued to be the unfinished script, but Bogart managed to stay calm. He was a veteran of on-set rewrites and of Curtiz's eruptions. "I've been through all this before," he told Koch, who stopped by Bogart's trailer at his urging to " 'relax and have a drink.' He was untroubled, he kept his cool. I can't remember him excited. He came in, looked the rewrite over. If he had any suggestions, he made them. Usually, he didn't. He just did his job and did it very well."

Dan Seymour, a huge young character actor cast as the Arab doorkeeper, recalled Bogart as pleasant and collegial, greeting him mornings on the set with a wry, "Let anybody in you shouldn't've?"

"He always had time for the usual chit-chat between takes," said Leonid Kinsky, "but anybody who led himself to believe that Bogie never worked on his parts was terribly mistaken. He never did any role without serious thinking about every phase of the character he played." And as always, younger colleagues found him helpful. Seventeen-year-old Joy Page played the frightened young Bulgarian refugee, desperate to get herself and her husband to safety, who asks for Rick's help. ("M'sieur, you are a man. If someone loved you very much, so that your happiness was the only thing in the world that she wanted and she did a bad thing to make certain of it, could you forgive her?" / "No one ever loved me that much.") Not only was she frightened by the prospect of her first appearance before the camera, a long scene with Bogart, she was also stepdaughter of the unpopular Jack Warner. Years later she told Aljean Harmetz of quaking in her dressing room, then looking up and seeing Bogart. He told her not to worry and stepped inside. Then "patiently and kindly," he went over the scene with her and remained a protective presence.

Bergman was quick to charm every member of the company. Mike Curtiz, difficult and quirky with actors, called her "Christmas Baby"—possibly, assistant director Lee Katz said, because "Ingrid certainly looked like something you'd love to have for Christmas." Dan Seymour lent her a history of the United States when she needed a primer for her citizenship exam. He was rewarded with an occasional "Ask me a question!" delivered with her incomparably radiant smile.

The difference between the two leads was apparent in their approaches to their work. Bergman often lost herself in the romance of her roles, perhaps explaining her attachments with her leading men. She hated leaving the studio because she found the fantasy before the cameras preferable to the reality of what she felt was a suffocating bourgeois marriage. For Bogart, leading ladies were generally colleagues only, even—especially—in the love scenes that he found more embarrassing than pleasurable. "I don't like them," he once told an interviewer, "maybe because I don't do them very well. It isn't possible to shoot a love scene without having a hairy chested group of grips standing four feet away from you, chewing tobacco. I'll handle that in the privacy of my bedroom, old boy."

"He liked Bergman," though, Leonid Kinsky said. "He respected her because she was a very able actress. But I don't think anything ever took place."

Love on the screen may not have been for him. But his image in *Casablanca* is that of a man desperately in love.

"One thing about Bogart that a lot of people don't realize," Dan Seymour noted, "is that he was a performer. I don't say that he didn't care for Bergman, but he worked with her. Though at the beginning, you felt that they were sort of facing off like two puppy dogs in the neighborhood, marking their territory."

At the start, each, naturally, had been concerned about the other. Bergman later told Nathaniel Benchley that, to prepare for her work, she screened *The Maltese Falcon* again and again. She felt, she said, like a tall Scandinavian woman with a short list of films, and was nervous over meeting Humphrey Bogart. While his career may have towered over hers, in their scenes together he reportedly had to wear three-inch wooden blocks tied to the bottoms of his shoes to make up for the difference in their heights. Years later, she described him as considerate and gentle, even in the late stages of the difficult production when he was apt to snap at anyone else.

It was the professionalism of the two stars that created the magic on the screen, their ability as actors far more potent than the fan-magazine fantasies of offscreen romance. When Bogart finally did become involved with a leading lady, it would turn out to be the exception to the rule and ended in a far more than film-long dalliance.

Whether there was any real feeling between Bergman and Bogart or not, it didn't matter, because Mayo was convinced that her husband had fallen in love with his co-star. When Warner Publicity flooded the columns with items about "the lovely Ingrid Bergman. . . . the Swedish beauty, milky-skinned. . . . one of the most democratic stars in Hollywood," Mayo's response was to phone Bogart at the studio constantly.

Sometimes she would show up for lunch in the Green Room or appear on the set, "always looking like the wrath of God," Lee Katz said. "In fact, looking like somebody you wish would never darken your life."

She was aware of the stares and comments she drew, but was too driven by her demons to stay away, and she haunted Stage 8, a ghost at the feast. Everyone felt bad for Bogart, having to *live* with this woman. Her face was puffy, her body heavy with the weight gained from the drinking that had almost wholly replaced solid food. After she'd stabbed Bogart a few months earlier, her doctor had diagnosed alcoholism and referred her to a psychiatrist, who in turn diagnosed paranoia and schizophrenia. He warned of possible further violence to herself or others and urged that treatment begin immediately. Mayo refused.

Bogart seemed as helpless as his wife, answering excess with excess. Bob William, who had worked for Sam Jaffe before taking a job as a Warner publicist, remembered sitting with the couple one night in their living room. The venom in their mutual vituperation rose with their intake of alcohol. The evening ended with Mayo, in a drunken fury, falling backward and becoming lodged behind the sofa. She continued to shriek as Bogart struck blindly at her, half-weeping in fury and frustration, "You bitch! You filthy bitch!"

The lines of dialogue now so familiar trickled in during the weeks of rewrites: "I *told* you not to play that song!" . . . "Here's looking at you, kid" . . . "If you do, you'll regret it, maybe not tomorrow" . . . "Of all the gin joints in all the towns all over the world, she walks into mine." To the members of the company, it became a daily ritual of learning, discarding and relearning pages, and tempers—Bogart's included—frayed to the breaking point.

His part was the longest, his load of constantly changing dialogue the heaviest, and the cool demeanor of the early weeks gave way to testiness. Bergman recalled him returning from lunch-hour breaks spent arguing with Wallis. There were also arguments with Curtiz, although disagreements with the talented but temperamental Hungarian were unavoidable on even the smoothest-running films. Curtiz stomped about in riding boots and ran his set like an autocrat, his demeanor seesawing between marzipan charm and outbursts of temper in obscenity-laden broken English. This was their fourth picture together—the last had been *Virginia City* in 1940—but the first in which Bogart played the lead. He was more assertive now than when his name had been below the title. "Bogie was certainly short of patience with Mike," Lee Katz said. There were, however, "no pyrotechnics." Bogart just quietly bristled, at times turning and walking off to make his point. Before Leonid Kinsky's first scene as Sascha the bartender, played one-on-one with Bogart, Curtiz was overwhelming the Russian actor with minute instructions when "Bogie just looked at him and said, 'Please, shut up. You can't tell Leonid what to do.' And that was that."

Katz was a Curtiz assistant going back to 1938's *The Adventures of Robin Hood,* starring Errol Flynn. "Mike drove most of his actors crazy. He was from the European school—full of dolly shots and twisting cameras and what have you, very complex on camera moves. So he had a habit, usually, of watching the camera more than the actor. And the actor would realize it." Five years earlier, during *Kid Galahad,* Bette Davis had stopped in mid-scene and snapped at Curtiz: "Mike! Watch *me*! Stop watching the camera!"

But Curtiz was a master craftsman whose broad range can be seen in two of the films he made in 1942: the brilliant musical biography *Yankee Doodle Dandy* and the melodramatic *Casablanca.* He was particularly strong as an action director, and his simple lesson to a younger colleague of how to stage a mob scene with only twenty extras is a classic. Put ten on each side, he said, and then have them run across—"They'll make *soch* a mess!" From his days as a silent-film director he also knew when words were superfluous and how to convey character with a look, a lift of an eyebrow, a nod.

A nod made, according to the screenplay directions, "almost imperceptibly" by Rick is a turning point in *Casablanca.* It signals the orchestra to play "La Marseillaise" and the start of an ensemble scene in which Rick's singing refugee patrons, their backs straight in reclaimed dignity, drown out the German soldiers singing "The Watch on the Rhine." Although it is Henreid, as Victor Laszlo, who commands the cafe orchestra to play the anthem, it is Rick's silent assent they wait for.

The stirring sequence is unmarked by a single line of dialogue, and it marks the hero's return to the battle. "Do it with a full scoring orchestra," Wallis told music director Leo Forbstein, "and get some body to it." The scene was an emotional moment for the company, many of whom had relatives in the concentration camps or dead in the gas chambers. Madeleine LeBeau, who played the layabout Yvonne, had fled France with Marcel Dalio, whose mother was still in Paris, hiding in a basement as Jews were rounded up. Dan Seymour stood at the back, watching the crowd. "I could see their faces. They were crying." A close-up fixed on

LeBeau, her voice heard above the rest of the singing. The displaced citizens of 1942 were singing the hymn of the citizens of 1792 and another German invasion. The original script directed the German officers in Rick's to sing "The Horst Wessel Song," the anthem of the Nazi party; but "Horst Wessel" was under copyright, and copyright infringement—wars and Nazis notwithstanding—was still a violation of an international agreement. Such an infringement, Warner lawyers said, might possibly endanger export of the film in such neutral countries as Argentina, where pro-German sympathies ran high.

In mid-July, seven weeks into the shooting and with only two scheduled weeks remaining, the basic problems in the script were still unresolved. At one point the latest scenario sent out the night before was recalled the next morning by J. L. himself, amid sharp differences about the story's outcome. Every writer favored keeping the ending of the play, in which case Rick would lose Ilsa; but the studio wanted the conclusion dictated by Hollywood convention. "Conferences were taking place all over," Howard Koch said, "arguing about it, with the studio pretty heavily on the side of, We've got Bergman, we've got Bogart, why aren't they going to be together?" The only principal who didn't much care one way or the other, Julius Epstein said, was Bogart, who was only "worried that he wouldn't get to the boat on weekends."

There were other problems: Even if Ilsa did leave with Laszlo, how did they get her to go? Have her turn and run? Not convincing. Lois Meredith had been virtually dragged away. Casey Robinson's brainchild was a quick clip to the jaw, immobilizing the heroine, and then moving her out. But what happened to Rick? Was he arrested?

"Toward the end," Epstein said, "there was chaos—no ending, no knowing what was happening." Bergman appealed to Koch, "How can I play the love scene when I don't know which one I'm going off with?" Curtiz, Koch added, wore a hangdog look and was openly worried. "He kept wanting to *talk* about it. You could see it in his expression." He took his frustrations out on the actors. After one outbreak too many, the gentle Kinsky started to walk off the set, swearing never to come back. Curtiz, for once, was immediately apologetic. "We have no ending for the picture," he said by way of explanation. "Everyone is nervous."

On July 17, with production almost a week behind schedule, the cast assembled for the airport scene. Stage 1 was enveloped in a fog created by what Warner Publicity would describe as "more than half a million cubic feet of vaporized oil." (Because wartime security precluded outdoor location shots at night, it took innumerable requests, meetings, and red tape to be able to film the one inserted shot of plane motors revving up.) In the background on the soundstage, a painted cardboard cutout, creatively lit, served as the plane to Lisbon. *"The outline of the Transport plane is barely visible. Near its open door stands a small group of people."* Actually, it was a group of small people; midgets from Central Casting gathered on the runway to provide the proper scale.

Everyone's nerves were in tatters. "Rick is not just solving a love triangle," Robinson argued to Wallis in a memo. "He is forcing the girl to live up to the idealism of her nature, forcing her to carry on with the work that in these days is far more important than the love of two [but the problems of three] little people." Rick became the deus ex machina, setting all things right: "You're getting on that plane with Victor."

The whole scene depended on Bogart's delivery. It was a four-page monologue with brief interruptions, rewritten for the third time in three weeks and shoved at him the night before to memorize. For Bogart, who learned his lines mornings on the set because he couldn't concentrate at home, it was a double burden, and the last traces of his patience gave way.

The disagreements surfaced over lunch, the specifics vague after half a century. Bogart had one idea of how to play the scene, Curtiz another. Warner publicist Bob William watched as "they wound up shouting at each other—but Curtiz was the kind of guy you would shout at anyway." Unit manager Al Alleborn reported "arguments with Curtiz the director and Bogart the actor." After two hours Alleborn, in desperation, rousted Hal Wallis from his bungalow and brought him back to be the peacemaker. An hour later, the disputes broke out again. Only then, Alleborn recorded, did the parties "finally decid[e] on how to do the scene." The lost time was entered on the production report as "Story conference between Mr. Curtiz and Mr. Bogart."

When the cameras did roll, the magic was back:

> "You're saying this only to make me go."
>
> "I'm saying it because it's true. . . . You belong with Victor. . . . If that plane leaves the ground and you're not on it, you'll regret it. Maybe not today, maybe not tomorrow, but soon, and for the rest of your life. . . . I'm not good at being noble, but it doesn't take much to see that the problems of three little people don't amount to a hill of beans in this crazy world. . . . Here's looking at you, kid."

It was time for the suspension of reality, no questions asked, including the one of how Bogart had managed to put on a belted trench coat while presumably keeping his gun on Rains. Wallis and Koch had solved the problem of getting Bergman away by having Henreid step into the picture—"Are you ready, Ilsa?" But it was the lovers' scene, and it remains the benchmark for renunciation.

Bogart, Huston once said of him, wasn't especially impressive face-to-face; but when the camera rolled, something happened, an almost noble quality took over. The takes of Rick and Ilsa's farewell required several days. Bogart concentrated on Bergman's shining face, his dark eyes made darker still by the black-and-white photography. Arthur Edeson's lighting emphasized the still-boyish profile, and what emerged on the screen was intensity, energy, and magnetism—the requisites of a great movie actor.

Bogart finished August 1, the others two days later. There had been a few remaining scenes to shoot and some retakes. Wallis asked Bogart for "a little more guts . . . more of the curt hard way of speaking we have associated with Rick. Now that the girl is gone, I would like to see [him] revert." Rick's fate following Strasser's death was resolved with Renault's laconic, "Round up the usual suspects." According to the Epsteins, the line had just come to them in a car one night as they rolled along Sunset Boulevard.

Still, it was hard to let go, and it took outside forces to wrap the film. On August 3, two days past the new projected closing date, Bergman, called to the telephone, let out a shriek. *For Whom the Bell Tolls* was definitely hers and Paramount wanted her on location immediately—that night if possible. Warners was already well over the limit of her commitment. Wallis pleaded for another two days, but Al Alleborn had a better idea. Stop the picture. Tonight. Look at the assembled footage and find out if retakes were really necessary. Wallis agreed, and *Casablanca* was closed out.

The final fade-out, however, remained in question. Rick's closing rejoinder to Renault would be recorded in a sound studio as a wild line and later inserted into the soundtrack as the two men walk off into the fog. Long after the close of production, Wallis, dissatisfied with every suggestion, dithered over various versions, one of them being, "Louis, I might have known you'd mix your patriotism with a little larceny." He was intent on just the right punch line and on August 21, he finally had it: "Louis, I think this is the beginning of a beautiful friendship."

With all the talented writers working on the script, it was the producer who came up with the line. "That's Hal Wallis," Casey Robinson said years later. "He wrote that line, and it was marvelous. It was inspired."

It was Wallis, too, who decided on the documentary-style opening—the spinning globe and the black track of the refugee trail dissolving into a montage of masses on the move; the narration was modeled on the popular news series *The March of Time* and spoken by a radio announcer from the Warner station KFWB. The overall effect of tying the film romance to the larger sweep of world events had a payoff that no one could foresee.

Regardless of the production problems, Warners knew early on that they had a hit. In late August, the dour Joe Breen called Wallis in a state of ecstasy after screening the final cut: *Casablanca* was outstanding—one of the best movies to come off the lot—no, one of the best he had seen in years! "I have never heard him rave about a picture as he did about this one," Wallis told Einfeld. Would Charlie *please* start planning "a really big picture" campaign.

Einfeld cabled New York: "CASABLANCA REALLY WONDERFUL . . . BRILLIANTLY DIRECTED GORGEOUSLY PHOTOGRAPHED . . . ONE OF THE HOTTEST MONEY PICTURES . . . BELIEVE ME IT BELONGS IN THE VERY TOP BRACKET."

It had already previewed to raves when, on November 6, Wallis called J. L.'s attention to a front-page article in the *San Francisco Chronicle* mentioning Casablanca as "coming more into prominence in the war picture." In the early morning of November 8, American and British troops invaded the beaches of North Africa, with landings in Algiers and Casablanca.

J. L. quickly sent a telegram to the office in New York to hold all prints, "AS WE CONTEMPLATE MAKING NEW END." Wallis drew up a wish list for two days of retakes and a last-minute update. He wanted Free French uniforms, new sets, plane tickets for Claude Rains, who had gone east. Just as abruptly, two days later, the idea was dropped, and Warner sent another wire to New York:

> WILL DEFINITELY NOT TOUCH PICTURE AS PREVIEWED IT AGAIN LAST NIGHT AND AUDIENCE REACTION BEYOND BELIEF. FROM MAIN TITLE TO THE END THERE WAS APPLAUSE AND ANXIETY. HUNDREDS SAID DO NOT TOUCH PICTURE. MY PERSONAL OPINION IS IF PICTURE IS TOUCHED NOW IT WILL BECOME A PATCH JOB.

Even David O. Selznick urged Wallis and Warner not to tamper with the ending. J. L. soon agreed. "A SMALL TAG SCENE ABOUT AMERICAN TROOPS LANDING . . . IS A COMPLETE NEW STORY IN ITSELF . . . AND WOULD NOT FIT IN THE PRESENT FILM."

A movie had become a news event just in time for its opening, and Warner Publicity didn't miss a beat ("CASABLANCA/ It's more than a town in Africa . . ."). What began eleven months earlier as a plagarism of *Algiers* now seemed a stroke of divine foresight. "Again Warner Bros. have timed the exhibition of an important film to the split second of topical interest," a *Los Angeles Times* columnist wrote. True, the studios were powerful in L.A., but even the Warners weren't running the war as an adjunct to their product. "Casablanca! A magic word," *Film Daily* raved. "A word that will open theater doors wide and keep them open. . . . a word that piques the interest and stirs the imagination. . . . this Warner picture should have the impact of a bombshell."

The New York release was on Thanksgiving at Warners Hollywood, the studio's premiere East Coast theater. It was an appropriate day to open a film that would be helped not only by the critics but by history as well, and the Warners publicity department further adorned the occasion. Veteran fighters of the French resistance marched westward from their Fifth Avenue headquarters to the Hollywood on Fifty-first Street, de Gaulle's Cross of Lorraine raised high above Broadway. There were speeches by resistance leaders and Free French recruiting booths in the lobby, and the ceremony was carried live over short-wave by the Office of War Information, the new propaganda arm of the U.S. government. (The same organization would shortly block the export of the film, under the Roosevelt policy of appeasement toward the Nazi-backed French puppet government of Vichy.)

In a cable from London, General Charles de Gaulle, leader of the Free French forces, requested a print for a special showing to his staff. At home, the country caught *Casablanca* fever. On Broadway, ticket buyers waited in the cold for hours in long lines that snaked past the windows of Lindy's restaurant and around the corner to Eighth Avenue. The studio rushed out press kits with the look of a wartime news bulletin and the headline "THE ARMY'S GOT CASABLANCA—*AND SO HAVE WARNER BROS.!*" Ads asked: "WHAT? You've seen Casablanca only *once*?"

And that was just the beginning. Warner publicist Martin Weiser had gone to San Francisco to prepare for the film's opening there. One morning a friend who was the managing editor of the afternoon *Call Bulletin* rang Weiser's room at the Palace Hotel and told him to get over to the paper immediately. "I want to show you something you'll never see again." The hotel was only a few blocks from the paper and Weiser ran to meet the waiting editor. "He took me into the composing room and showed me the front page of the *Call Bulletin.* There it was, all set, and right across the top—a banner over the masthead—it said: "FDR, CHURCHILL, DE GAULLE MEET IN CASABLANCA."

The picture took in record-breaking grosses and garnered superlative reviews, not only for Curtiz and the principals but for the supporting players, too. Dooley Wilson was hailed as "a find." David O. Selznick acknowledged the boost given Bergman's no longer stalled career in a cable to Wallis and Curtiz: "INGRID IS OBVIOUSLY GOING TO BE WHAT I HAVE FOR SO LONG PREDICTED, ONE OF THE GREAT STARS OF THE WORLD." The only person connected with the film not to gain was Casey Robinson, who was tripped up by his ego. He took solo writing credits only and asked not to be included with the Epsteins and Koch. It cost him an Oscar.

But the heart of the film, as with *The Maltese Falcon,* was Bogart's performance amid an ensemble of wonderful actors. Studio publicity and press reviews acknowledged it. "Bogart and Bergman [played] with brilliant authority and credibility, each passing all previous portrayals," the *Los Angeles Times* said. Warners, *The New York Times* added, had "used Bogart's personality, so well established in other brilliant films, to inject a cold point of tough resistance to evil."

As for *Watch on the Rhine,* for all its thoughtful qualities and high intentions, it is a historical artifact. The picture was finished about the same time as *Casablanca;* but its opening was first delayed so that Warners wouldn't have two major anti-Nazi films playing at once, then delayed again in favor of *Mission to Moscow.* Despite fine reviews and Oscar nominations for Best Picture and Best Screenplay, by the time it was released in the fall of 1943, its moment had passed; and unlike *Casablanca,* it has not held up over time.

Casablanca made Bogart; Bogart made *Casablanca.* Whether in a white dinner jacket or in a trench coat and snap-brim fedora, he became a new and timely symbol of the post–Pearl Harbor American: tough but compassionate, skeptical yet idealistic, betrayed yet ready to believe again, and above all, a potentially deadly opponent.

Along with Errol Flynn, Bogart was emerging as the quintessential Warners leading man. If only by a necessity caused by the age of its stars, the emphasis at the studio now was not on youth but on sophistication and the wisdom that comes with maturity. Exuberance was replaced by a melancholy that overlay even the most action-packed story. In Bogart's portrayals there was a wryness born of experience, hints of a troubled past not shared with the audience, and an essentially dark view of the world appropriately in keeping with the times.

More often than not, the Bogart hero would be a man without a country. In *Across the Pacific,* he played an Army intelligence officer cashiered in a bogus court-martial to lend credibility to his attempt to infiltrate a Japanese espionage ring. In *Casablanca,* he was an American who could not return to his country, for reasons left to the audience's imagination. In *Action in the North Atlantic* (1943), Warner Brothers' salute to the wartime merchant marine, he played a former skipper who had lost his command. In *Passage to Marseille* (1944), which was adapted from the novel *Men Without Country,* Bogart played an anti-fascist journalist who is framed by a corrupt government and sent to Devil's Island and who escapes. In *To Have and Have Not* (1944), he would appear as yet another American expatriate in a hostile environment. All these men were forerunners to the wanderers and expatriates and loners—the Fred Dobbses and Charlie Allnuts and Philip Queegs—that would mark his work in the post-war years and early fifties.

CHAPTER 11

"The Happiest of Couples"

Four weeks after finishing *Casablanca,* Bogart traded Rick's white dinner jacket for the navy pea jacket of Joe Rossi, first mate of the freighter *Sea Witch,* a liberty ship ferrying supplies to the beleaguered Soviet Union through submarine-infested seas, in *Action in the North Atlantic.* Romance and intrigue were replaced by a political tract in the two-hour docudrama about the supply convoys, and the desert of North Africa was exchanged for the arctic waters off Murmansk (although the supposed Russian port was actually the pier in Santa Barbara). But it was the same Bogart character he had played in many earlier pictures, just differently dressed.

He had accepted this assignment before making *Casablanca.* It was a role he could walk through, but he didn't particularly mind. He liked Lloyd Bacon, the director of *42nd Street* (1933) and a long string of Warner hits. In fact, Bacon had directed Bogart seven times before, more than any other director.

And he was happy to be done with the action in North Africa. The ending just didn't ring true, he said to a studio publicist. "Miss Bergman is the kind of lady no man would give up willingly, even to the tune of a lot of high sounding philosophy." Still, he was "rather proud of his love scenes with Ingrid Bergman," reported Hollywood columnist Sidney Skolsky. "Incidentally, he has yet to see himself on the screen in *Casa-*

blanca." Months after its release, Bogart would still be claiming that he hadn't seen the picture. "I haven't been allowed to," he told a friend.

No one could tell whether he was joking, but as truth or fiction it was a telling comment on his marriage. Once again, it was necessary for him to learn his lines on the set, because there was no peace at home. For the first time, however, his domestic turmoil was having an effect on his work and on others in the cast.

"You son of a bitch! You just don't know your lines!" Bernie Zanville shouted at Bogart, before he remembered that he was just a low-end contract player on his first picture and that he was yelling at the star. Zanville had stood by for days, cowed and apprehensive, as Bogart held up production with daily complaints about the script. "I hate this dialogue," he would announce, whereupon a writer would scurry to the set to make changes. Eventually, Zanville realized what was happening. It wasn't just the ponderous propaganda of *Action in the North Atlantic* or John Howard Lawson's windy script. It was Bogart himself, unable to pound the lines into his head.

After Zanville's outburst, Bogart laughed, said he was right, and a friendship began. Zanville was a Brooklyn cantor's son, new to the business and an easy mark for practical jokes. Warners, anxious to rename him ("You couldn't have a guy named *Bernie Zanville,*" a studio worker said), came up with the usual list of white-bread choices, from Brick Bernard to Zane Clark. Bogart suggested Dane Clark, and it stuck. Bogart had previously told the young actor that the studio had decided to call him Jose O'Toole, the South American–Irish sensation, which sent him racing to Jack Warner in indignant protest while Bogart and his friend Raymond Massey howled. Another time, in one of the movie's many disaster scenes, Clark started to run through the only partly simulated flames of a shipboard fire. Bogart had convinced him that actors did their own stunts. A horrified assistant director stopped him: Didn't he know that there were stuntmen? Out of the corner of his eye, Clark could see Bogart laughing.

The film, full of special effects, dragged on until the Friday before Christmas and closed forty-three days behind schedule. Jerry Wald, producing his last movie before going into the service, developed ulcers. Was it fear of the Army, the unit manager wondered, "or the making of this picture?" Bogart and Mayo hoped to spend the holiday with Louis Bromfield on his farm in Ohio, but the studio wanted their star closer to home if more work was suddenly needed. The Bogarts reluctantly canceled their plans and sent Bromfield, a descendent of Daniel Boone, a coonskin cap for Christmas. In return, he gave them a picture of Malabar Farm, "to make you homesick," he wrote. "We miss you both very much at this holiday season; everyone here sends much love and more and more success for the New Year to you both—our favorite couple."

In January 1943, Bogart and Mayo went on location to Brawley, California, a place for which few people were ever homesick. He was on loanout to Columbia for *Sahara,* a grim, gritty war film about desert survival, and Brawley, in the Borego Desert of the Imperial Valley just north of the Mexican border, was an eminently suitable locale. The valley, almost all of which is 235 feet below sea level, has an extreme climate. Even in mid-winter it was hot, with temperatures in the nineties. Bogart and his colleagues, deliberately unshaven, played a tank crew stranded in the North African wasteland. The company was put up at the Planter's Hotel on the edge of the city limits and forty miles from the location. Brawley, ringed by corporate farms that produced alfalfa, cotton, and sugar beets, was the center for growers in the region. Their farmhands were mostly illegal aliens who were overworked and underpaid and whose protests for better conditions led to bloody clashes with the grower-backed police.

Because Brawley offered little diversion in the evenings, Bogart regularly invited colleagues up to his suite for drinks. The German actor Kurt Krueger, who played a downed Nazi airman, spent congenial nights in the star's sparsely furnished rooms. Bogart enlivened the occasions, and "couldn't have been more outgoing." Krueger shared a ride to the location one day with Mayo, who sat beside him, carefully cradling a thermos. Why, he asked, was she bringing coffee when there was always coffee on the set? Mayo threw back her head and let out a peal of throaty laughter. "Coffee? Hell, no! Bogie needs his ice-cold Martinis."

Bruce Bennett, who played one of Bogart's tank crew, and his wife, Jeannette, had driven down from Los Angeles in their four-door sedan, and on the first day off from shooting, they set off with a picnic hamper for a lunch across the border in Mexicali. After they had gone two or three miles, Bogart and Mayo popped up in the back seat and cheerily asked, "Well, where are we going today?"

The couples regularly played darts in the hotel courtyard after the day's shooting, or met for dinner. Bennett was an anomaly among actors. Born Herman Brix, he was a graduate of the University of Washington, and in the 1928 Olympics was the silver medalist in the shot put, an event in which he set the world record several times. Bogart enjoyed his company, and Bennett, somewhat to his surprise, found Bogart well-educated and likable, "a sincere person who at moments let people see the *real* Bogart. He was a very good conversationalist who had no tolerance for people who were phonies. He'd call someone who didn't particularly know what he was talking about a 'conversation barber.' He did not believe in idle conversation. If it was meaningful or humorous, it was fine. And he had a very good sense of humor." Theirs was a business based on publicity, Bogart once told him, "so I do an awful lot to stir things up."

But there was nothing feigned about his domestic situation. Bennett easily saw that "Mayo was a very unhappy woman. We knew she was a talented actress in New York, that she couldn't get started here, couldn't make the grade. She and Bogart were constantly needling each other. She would say, 'You don't do anything in front of that little black box—you're not acting—you're posing and making faces!' And he'd say, 'Well, it seems like we do pretty well with it, so go back to New York and work for pennies!' "

The arguments continued into the nights. Shouts pierced the walls of their suite, punctuated by the crash of breaking glass and the thuds of shoved furniture. Bogart would stumble onto the set the next morning, unsteady, quarrelsome, and hungover. "He would have to take a while before his mind cleared and he got down to work." Just as on *Action in the North Atlantic,* he would start the day with disputes and questions. Long after the film was finished, director Zoltan Korda, the brother of the London-based Hungarian film magnate Alexander Korda, complained about Bogart's behavior, mystified by why he argued every morning. "Don't you realize what was going on?" Bennett told him. "He was learning his *lines.*"

"My God," Zoltan replied. "If I'd known that, it would have taken a load off my mind."

"It drummed the dialogue into his head," Bennett added. "Then Mayo would come out on the set with a thermos of martinis and he'd drink a couple and—'all right, I'm ready.' And being the consummate actor that he was, he did a remarkable job. The martinis were the hair of the dog. Mayo and he would be fine—and then they'd fight the next night."

The one interlude of quiet on location came when Bogart was in Burbank filming a cameo spot with comedian S. Z. Sakall as part of Warners' studio showcase, *Thank Your Lucky Stars.* The unimaginative three-page skit with Cuddles Sakall intimidating the fearsome Humphrey Bogart was a quick replacement for a much better original idea. Bogart had been scheduled to sing and dance in a zoot suit with Ida Lupino and Olivia de Havilland, as a jive trio called "The Rhythmaniacs." Unfortunately, the *Sahara* schedule was such that Columbia couldn't release him when the actresses were free.

The Bogarts' nightly fights continued through the four months of filming that ended in April. In August, they would celebrate their fifth wedding anniversary. Bogart looked forward to spending part of the intervening time on the *Sluggy.* He was not scheduled to work again until sometime in May, when *Passage to Marseille* (the studio spelled it without a final *s*) was due to start. The picture, a potential blockbuster that would reunite Wallis, Curtiz, and most of the principals of *Casablanca,* had been in preparation for six months. In addition to the more recognizable talent, Wallis had lined up *Casablanca*'s art director Carl Weyl, its editor Owen Marks, and the master cinematographer James Wong Howe, who had been Wallis's first choice for *Casablanca.* The story was by the team of Charles Nordhoff and James Norman Hall, whose trilogy of *Mutiny on the Bounty, Men Against the Sea,* and *Pitcairn Island* formed the basis for the Clark Gable–Charles Laughton *Mutiny on the Bounty.*

Bogart was to play a French newsman who denounces the 1938 Allied sellout at Munich that permitted German annexation of the Sudetenland of western Czechoslovakia. In return, he is framed for a murder by an appeasement-minded government anxious to silence him, and sent to the hellish penal colony Cayenne in French Guyana. This man without a country who feels at the time of surrender that France is getting exactly what it deserves ends up giving his life for *la patrie.* The Casey Robinson–Jack Moffitt script dealt more closely than any other contemporary film with the taboo subject of French fascism. Sydney Greenstreet, cast as Duval, the army major who is sympathetic to the Vichy government, so hated the part that he did everything possible to avoid it.

But the day before the close of production on *Sahara,* an entirely different script arrived for Bogart at the hotel in Brawley. The title on the cover read *The Pentacle,* and the screenplay was about a man who kills his wife just after their fifth wedding anniversary. Bogart called Burbank and spoke to Steve Trilling, now Jack Warner's executive assistant, who assured him that the studio hadn't switched pictures; it was simply a film that they wanted him to do before *Passage to Marseille.* Bogart told Trilling to forget it. The writing was dull, the motivation weak; besides, he didn't like the part. J. L. immediately wired back: Was this the cooperation Humphrey had promised when he signed his seven-year contract? And just where would Bogart be if he, Jack Warner, had not brought him out from New York for *The Petrified Forest*? "AFTER ALL, HUMPHREY, IT WAS OUR STUDIO THAT MADE IT POSSIBLE FOR YOU."

Warners agreed to rewrite the story and Bogart agreed to do the picture. A start date was set for May, and *Passage to Marseille* was moved to June. The following day the cast and crew headed home. Just before leaving, Bogart stopped by the Bennetts' room with a set of liqueur glasses, brightly colored and beautifully made, that he had bought in Mexico. As he presented the glasses to the young Jeannette Bennett, he told her almost wistfully, "You shouldn't be in this environment. You're too nice a person."

He spent the next weeks on the boat at Newport Beach, awaiting the promised rewrites on *The Pentacle.* They were not forthcoming. Then, five days before the scheduled start date, a motorcycle courier drove up to the dock with a new screenplay. The script opened with the fifth wedding anniversary celebration and well-meaning friends toasting "the happiest of couples." In private, however, the happy couple were anything but:

> "I want a divorce . . . *I don't love you any more.* . . . I not only don't love you, but . . . I can't stand to be with you or near you. . . ."
>
> "Well, I'm not going to divorce you. . . . I'll make the rest of your life as miserable and hopeless as you've made mine. . . ."

Steve Trilling was halfway between the dining room and the projection room when Bogart called to tell him, "I will not do it as it is." Three months after the new contract and the handshakes and the promises of cooperation, Bogart and Warners were back into the familiar pattern of the actor digging in his heels, and the studio alternately threatening and cajoling. "We are reluctant to believe that said message expresses your true attitude," general counsel Roy Obringer wrote.

Without the contractual right of script refusal, Bogart was on shaky ground. By early May, the picture's title had appropriately been changed to *Conflict,* and the company tone had turned belligerent, with threats to hold Bogart accountable for damages. Jack Warner threatened to replace him in *Passage to Marseille,* and showed that he meant it by sending out feelers to Charles K. Feldman, the powerful agent for Jean Gabin. The big, blond, burly costar of the World War I classic *La Grande Illusion,* Gabin was known as the French Spencer Tracy. "Let Bogart know I mean business," J. L. told Hal Wallis, whom he had meet with Gabin. At the same time, Warner continued along a softer path toward his reluctant star in an almost daily bombardment of letters and telegrams. "DEAR HUMPHREY," one went, "YOU MUST REMEMBER THIS; AM DEPENDING ON YOU AS THE REGULAR GUY I KNOW YOU ARE."

Bogart was conveniently out on his boat whenever a cable or call came in, with one exception. The conversation was preserved because the studio had the call transcribed by a stenographer. On May 6, Bogart picked up, expecting Trilling: "Hello, Steve." A different voice, no less familiar, replied. "This is not Trilling, Humphrey." It was Jack Warner, calling from New York. "This is nothing personal," he continued. "I'm running a big business and try to call the shots for the good of all concerned."

"This is personal between you and me, Jack. I am more serious than I have ever been in my life and I just do not want to do this picture. If you want to get tough with me, you can, and I know how tough you can get, but if you do get tough and do the things you say you will, I will feel that I have lost a friend. I ask you as a favor to me to take me out of this picture, for I feel very strongly about it. I am very sorry I ever gave my word to you that I would do it, for if I had stopped for a minute I would never have agreed. . . . I just can't do it!"

For half an hour, J. L. and his top male star argued past each other. Neither gave ground. Bogart asked outright for suspension. Technically, he was already on it, but that was not what Warner wanted. The argument turned into a battle between a question of authority that had to be asserted and a matter of personal feeling that begged to be considered. The coercion was clearly audible beneath J. L.'s even tone as he said, "Don't make the mistake some people have." He didn't threaten people, Warner went on. But then, he'd seen others talk just like Bogart and, for his information, one of them was now trying to get a job as an extra.

They ended at an impasse.

"Turn your dogs on me."

"You're making an awful error."

"What are you doing, frightening me? . . . Why don't you burn this script up and forget it?"

"I've burned up hundreds of scripts . . . but I know you can do a great job. . . ."

"Well, I'm sorry, Jack, but I can't do it."

"Well, I have said everything I can. Goodbye and good luck."

Almost immediately after hanging up, Warner shot off a letter to Hal Wallis: "If you can get Gabin for MARSEILLE, by all means do so. With the rest of the cast, the great story you have and Mike directing, I know we will have a really important picture."

Given the cost of *Passage to Marseille,* the move seemed self-defeating. Though Gabin, as a Frenchman, was a more appropriate choice for the role and a huge box office draw in France, he was not a particular asset in America, and certainly not on a picture that would cost over $2 million and would lack the winning combination of *Casablanca.*

If Warner's reaction seems excessive under the circumstances—he had battles with stars all the time—one explanation for his fury may be that Bogart was merely caught in the squeeze going on at the same time between the head of the studio and its top producer. Hal Wallis had come through brilliantly in the first year of his production deal. All the studio's top hits—*Casablanca; Now, Voyager; Watch on the Rhine*—were his. He had, in truth, succeeded all too well. Warner, increasingly obsessed with receiving the creative fame accorded his producers, watched Wallis's triumphs with jealousy.

Not long after J. L.'s phone call to Bogart, rumors (probably factual) had Wallis talking to Darryl Zanuck about the possibility of moving to Twentieth Century–Fox. Warner telegraphed Wallis his demand for a public denial, "AS CAN'T TRUST YOU WITH BIG IMPORTANT PICTURES AND HAVE THIS GOSSIP." "PER 'DAILY NEWS' ARTICLE 23RD, I RESENT AND WON'T STAND FOR YOUR CONTINUING TO TAKE ALL THE CREDIT," he later wired Wallis, and followed with a telegram to Charles Einfeld in Publicity: "WANT YOU INFORM ALL PRODUCERS DIPLOMATICALLY IN GIVING STORIES OR INTERVIEWS THAT I SHALL BE DEFINITELY ACCREDITED AS EXECUTIVE PRODUCER OR IN CHARGE OF PRODUCTION. SICK, TIRED EVERYONE ELSE TAKING ALL CREDIT AND I BECOME SMALL BOY AND DOING MOST OF WORK . . ." To leave no doubts whatsoever as to where things stood between himself and Wallis, Warner made his case clear: "STOP GIVING ME DOUBLE TALK ON YOUR PUBLICITY. . . . I WILL TAKE LEGAL ACTION IF MY NAME HAS BEEN ELIMINATED FROM ANY ARTICLE OR STORY . . . AS BEING IN CHARGE OF PRODUCTION."

All of which suggests that the real issue was that *Passage to Marseille* was a Wallis film, and *Conflict* was not. The message was quite clear. If Bogart could do a film for Wallis, he could damn well do one for Jack Warner.

Wallis's initial reaction was to try to accommodate J. L., and by ordering rewrites for Gabin, he seemed ready to drop Bogart. A week after the Warner-Bogart standoff, Sam Jaffe, urged on by the studio, pleaded with Bogart to do *Conflict* as a favor. Warner, in New York on business, asked him to be reasonable—"DEAR HUMPHREY: WHY DON'T YOU PLAY THE GAME. . . ." Obringer confided to Warner that "confidentially believe Bogart weakening and we should just continue the pressure. . . ." But the result of all the lobbying, threatening, and pleading was delivered in a phone call from Jaffe to Trilling: "Bogart has not changed his mind."

An angry J. L. immediately wired Feldman to ask if Gabin was taking the part. As for Bogart, pressure changed to punishment. Whether or not he did *Conflict,* they were going ahead with *Passage to Marseille,* presumably with Gabin, and Bogart would "just have to stew in his own juice." But by the end of May, Warner was stewing, too. Gabin sent word that he wasn't interested, and Sydney Greenstreet, scheduled for both films, talked of pulling out.

On Thursday, June 3, the front page of the *Los Angeles Times* carried the headline "LESLIE HOWARD ON PLANE SHOT DOWN BY FOE." The commercial flight from Lisbon with thirteen passengers and crew had crashed in the Bay of Biscay after being attacked by German fighters, apparently under the impression that Winston Churchill was aboard. There was little hope of recovering the bodies.

Bogart had not been in touch with Howard for some time. In 1939, the British actor had left Hollywood and returned with his family to England. Too old for military service, he devoted himself to making films and propagandizing for the Allied cause. He had been on his way to London after a speaking tour in neutral Spain and Portugal. He had intended to return three days earlier but had stayed on in Lisbon to attend the opening of a new, pro-Allied film. In the end, the self-indulgent, tightfisted, and sometimes arrogant Leslie Howard was a true hero, closer to the characters he portrayed than anyone would have thought.

For Bogart, however, Howard had long been a model. Howard's support had made the difference between stardom and struggle for Bogart, and his death confirmed Bogart's own belief that what he did had little use or importance. A movie was a movie, nothing that mattered very much. Later that day, Steve Trilling received a call from Bogart. He'd do their movie, he said; he'd do whatever they wanted.

Neither film was an unqualified success. *Conflict,* released two years later, opened to mixed reviews but with solid performances by Bogart as a wife-killer, Alexis Smith as the sister-in-law he is in love with, and Greenstreet as the family friend and psychiatrist who traps the murderer.

Passage to Marseille, for all its high expectations, was entangled in a web of flashbacks and overlaid with a too heavy rhetoric. The romantic subplot with Michele Morgan left the public cold.

There had been some apprehension at the studio that portraying Cayenne, the controversial convict-labor French penal colony on the Caribbean coast of South America, might cause problems; a 1940 Warner film on the subject was tied up by continued protests from the French consulate. But the objections this time came from a wholly unexpected quarter and for a very different reason. At the climax of the film, a German plane attacks the freighter carrying Bogart and strafes the passengers on deck. Bogart, with a movie-lucky machine-gun burst, brings down the plane as it returns for another strafing run. Then, enraged, he wipes out the German crew as they emerge from the floating wreckage. Church groups who thus far had kept silent on the mass murder of Jews in Europe protested against the celluloid killing of "helpless men." Some state censorship boards threatened to cut the sequence altogether.

At the suggestion of the Office of War Information, the scene was eliminated from the export prints. For domestic distribution, however, Warners stuck to their guns, keeping the sequence and its follow-up: Victor Francen, as a humane French officer, reproaches Bogart. Bogart in turn points to the corpse-strewn deck, a dead cabin boy in the foreground, and says, "Look about you, Captain, and tell *me* who are the assassins." (Among the teenagers who tested for the cabin boy's role was Marcel Ophuls, whose 1970 documentary *The Sorrow and the Pity* is the definitive study of the political divisions in wartime France.)

The actors drew good crowds to the picture, but Bogart, who allowed his creeping baldness to show in the action sequences, said later that anyone could have played his role. Making a follow-up to *Casablanca* required more than using most of the same cast.

On August 20, the Bogarts spent their fifth anniversary on the set of *Conflict.* Mayo, unusually trim in shorts and a flowered shirt, gave Humphrey a hand-carved chess set and a board inlaid with the initials HDB. He gave her a pair of gold earrings. The studio publicity department ground out stories of the Bogarts' "long and happy marriage," which, of course, was neither.

Its deterioration was steady. Rose Hobart, a Broadway friend playing the unwanted wife in *Conflict,* provided a sympathetic ear between takes as Bogart expressed his concern about Mayo's downward slide. "He knew that she had talent, and that she was ruining herself." Hobart was one of the busiest character actresses in Hollywood, and to her and Bogart's amusement, she was playing his wife for the third time. She found Bogart a cordial and welcoming but deeply unhappy man. His mood was not improved by the picture. "He *hated* it," she said, but his sense of humor was unaffected. The movie opened with the couple arguing over having mutton for dinner. "Only at Warner Brothers," he told her, "would you kill your wife over a cold hunk of lamb."

Between takes, he retreated to his chessboard. "He must have had three games going," Hobart said. "Which is another thing no one realized—how *smart* this guy was. He had a talent, he knew he had to work on it, and he knew what a shit town this was." Hobart enjoyed working with him. "He was right there *with* you. He wasn't being Bogart, or making faces. He was in character. That makes the difference. And when we shot the thing where he *did* kill me, he was scary—he really was. I screamed bloody murder."

The most interesting part of *Conflict* is a scene that was never filmed, a two-page sequence proposed by Bogart partway through the filming that is a revealing look into his feelings. "I got the idea from Bogey some weeks ago," screenwriter Dwight Taylor wrote in a memo to producer William Jacobs. "I really think it will be *sensational*." In the sequence, the Bogart character, having disposed of his wife, is seen chatting with a bartender.

> "Have you ever been married?"
> "Yes sir. Three times."
> "How did you get rid of them?"

Then he launches into a monologue. Wouldn't it be nice, he speculates, if women could be put up in bottles like liquor, or were, say, just a few inches high—

> "Then you could carry them around in your pocket and take them out when you needed them. . . . as soon as you wanted them lifesize, you could kiss them or tickle them or something. Then when they got mad and started bawling you out, you just blow on them and they get small again and you can put them back in the bottle."

The scene ends with the bartender rejecting the idea—"There's something just too darn *good* about it." Trilling also rejected it, responding with, "We do not want to shoot this."

By 1943, Bogart's extra-marital life was the subject of what Warner publicist Bob William called "quiet gossip" among a small circle of studio personnel. Under the guise of personal appearances in New York, he made surreptitious visits to his first wife, Helen Menken. In Los Angeles, most of the rumors involved Verita Thompson, a tiny, pert brunette and former Arizona beauty queen who came to Hollywood to make her way as an actress, and stayed on to make toupees. William remembered her being referred to as " 'Bogart's gal.' She had a little freckled face. Bright, and, I thought, very attractive."

She had been Verita Peterson when Ann Sheridan introduced her to Bogart at a wrap party on a Warner sound stage in 1942. In the years to come, Verita would be his personal hairdresser, fashioning the toupees that were essential for preserving the illusion of youthful middle age. Nearly half a century later she would maintain that they were lovers. "It's just this thing that happens between two people. You never know when that spark is going to hit."

Like Bogart, she was caught in an unhappy marriage. "He'd tell me all *his* problems, I'd tell him all *my* problems." Her husband was a technician who spent his days at one studio or another, and their house was conveniently close to the Warner lot. Bogart "would call me from a phone booth or whenever he could get to a private telephone and we would meet somewhere. You can always manage to get together if you want to do it." She claimed that some nights he would show up drunk and half-clad on her doorstep when Mayo had thrown him out. How her husband reacted, she didn't say.

Thompson called Mayo "a firecracker. She'd cut your throat for two cents. She was a likable person. But she was *tough.* And divorce wasn't real attractive, if you were a leading man on the screen. Didn't look so good for Warner Brothers Studio. We always met in secret, not like now. They would have killed him—they would have killed *me.* Those days were *rough*! It's hard to explain that to people. They just can't imagine what it was like." As for Bogart, he was a "very kind and wonderful lover. He didn't think of *himself* all the time. Very gentle and sweet. Not like some of these pigs."

She also claimed that he arranged for the studio to employ her in the unionized makeup department. But though she was a visible presence in Bogart's life, in the extensive Warner records for the years 1943 to 1950, her name is listed only once, under "Hairdresser."

Few people recall hearing of the relationship, William explained, because "it was not an open secret; it was a kind of inside thing." Sam Jaffe added, "I didn't know much about her; I was just aware that there was such a girl. She would come and touch up his hair. Well, he *might* have, you know. What the hell. These girls were easy prey, and he was depressed and sad and upset with his marriage and his studio problems, which were constant. So he probably had what you call a slap and tickle. He might have stopped by, he might have slept over. So what? She was inviting him, so what the hell."

Whether or not the relationship with Thompson was intimate, Mayo was becoming more and more disturbed. Gloria Stuart recalled a dinner party one night at the Bogart's house on North Horn Avenue, with herself, her husband Arthur Sheekman, and Mel Baker as the guests. Though Mayo was nowhere in sight, she was a presence nonetheless. "She was upstairs in the bedroom with a gun, and here we were having dinner below. I kept saying to Arthur and to Bogie, 'This is dangerous—I don't want any part of it. I want to go home.' And Bogie kept saying, 'Oh, come on. You know she's just kidding.' Finally Mel said, 'I don't know whether she's kidding or not, *she's got a gun*!' The three of them got up from the table and went upstairs. She had locked herself in the bedroom and she yelled, 'I'm going to plug you through the door!' She didn't—but the games these people played!"

Another time, Mayo tried to slash her wrists. Because the studio management's only concern was to keep things quiet, they had her talk to a publicist instead of to the psychiatrist she so clearly needed. Jaik Rosenstein found Mayo in tears. "I don't know what I'm going to do," she cried as she clutched him with bandaged arms. "I know he's running around on me." Rosenstein's advice was that if she wanted to drive her husband into another woman's arms, this was the way to do it.

In 1940s Hollywood, such problems were covered up or fixed, but seldom resolved. Mayo, ill and alcoholic, was simply told to pull herself together. Bogart's comment on the slashing was that it was "not very deep," and his reaction was to retreat further into the cynicism that helped him keep his problems at arm's length. With his mother and sister, he had already battled two household cases of mental illness. He appeared determined to deny the third.

"My wife is an actress," he told Rosenstein. "She's a clever actress. It just so happens she's not working right now. When an actress isn't working, she's got to have scenes to play. And I've got to give her cues."

Yet Bogart could no more ignore her stormy challenges than she could stop baiting him. Verita Thompson believed that he feared Mayo might try suicide in earnest, or that one of them might seriously injure—or possibly kill—the other. Still, he couldn't stop pushing the buttons. "He took pleasure," a close friend said, "in goading his wife."

Nonetheless, according to Thompson, his role in Mayo's deterioration "weighed heavily on him. He hadn't been blameless; he wasn't just the victim of a bad marriage. There was something in him that made him needle people, provoke them; and his wife had been awfully sensitive to such provocation."

Bogart's own stability at the time was precarious. He no longer could cope with the punishing cycle of heavy workdays, heavy drinking, and sleepless nights. By 1943, there were indications that Warners' iron man, the consummate pro who was always on time and ready to work, was beginning to rust. During the filming of *Passage to Marseille,* unit manager Eric Stacey reported, "Humphrey Bogart suffering from a very bad hangover and being unruly and hard to manage; Mike [Curtiz] said he lost an hour to an hour and a half."

Art Silver of the trailer department was called one hectic morning after Bogart arrived on the set drunk and upset. "He says he likes you," Silver was told, and a soothing presence was needed.

"Bogie was weaving. And to make matters worse, Mayo appeared and she was smashed. I heard somebody say that he had slept in the car all night. So they put his moves on the floor and I said a few words to him, nothing much. I was there like an aspirin tablet. Finally they said, 'Okay, we're ready to shoot.' I said, 'My God, how can you shoot this?' Somebody gave Bogie a little shove, and he went out to his mark and he said his lines like he was absolutely sober. Then he turned around and said, 'Cut. Print.' Somebody got Mayo off the set, I don't know how. She was in terrible shape. But the man did his job. He was miraculous."

The incidents piled up and sometimes required Jack Warner's intervention. "You know," J. L. said to him on the set one day, "you're acting like an ass. You're costing us a lot of money for no damn reason." On another occasion, Warner was called to the lot in the early morning. Locked out of his house by Mayo, Bogart had made his way to Burbank and slept a few hours in his dressing room. He had then found a bicycle belonging to the studio and, still in pajamas and obviously drunk, refused to get off it until Warner appeared.

On an Easter morning, studio publicist Arthur Wilde was delegated to pick Bogart up at home at 4:00 A.M. for a sunrise service at the Hollywood Bowl. At midnight, however, Mayo called to say that he was out drinking.

Finally, Wilde found Bogart at the home of one of his friends, "drunk as a skunk and unshaven and smelling badly." Once at the Bowl, however, he went out on the stage and read the Lord's Prayer, moving the huge congregation as well as the assembled clergy to tears. They gathered to congratulate him as he came off, but his only response was to turn away and ask, "Where can I puke?"

The Bogart who had previously controlled his excesses was now becoming disturbingly reminiscent of another Warner star, John Barrymore, who a year before had died an alcoholic's death.

In the summer of 1943 Warner Brothers was at its most successful. Two years earlier, the B unit had become a casualty of the times—Bogart, who survived it, was photographed with Ann Sheridan by a mock tombstone for the B movie—and the studio was turning out fewer but more costly pictures for record audiences. Warners seemed to have the perfect sense for what would most please. Its string of hits included *Yankee Doodle Dandy, Casablanca,* and *Watch on the Rhine,* as well as Irving Berlin's *This Is the Army,* and they would gather five of the eleven New York Film Critics Circle nominations for Best Picture.

Mission to Moscow opened in Washington, D.C., with a screening for the top names in government, the diplomatic corps, and the press. Roosevelt was "delighted" with the film. A promotional trailer set to go into every theater was previewed for an invited audience that included Soviet ambassador Maxim Litvinov, who clapped loudly at the end. J. L. wired Charles Einfeld that "[AMBASSADOR] DAVIES TOLD ME ON THE PHONE THAT WARNER BROS. ARE REALLY THE NEXT PRESIDENT!"

The critics were generally appreciative. The *Hollywood Reporter* hailed the studio for its "courage and patriotism." In a telegram sending his greetings to a Moscow conference on American and British cinema, Jack Warner called on the film industry to create mutual understanding. He expressed confidence in the "RUSSO-AMERICAN GOODWILL WHICH IS SO VITAL TO THE WORLD'S FUTURE," and promised "THE UTMOST EFFORT TO PRESENT AN HONEST PORTRAYAL OF THE USSR, WORTHY OF OUR GALLANT FIGHTING ALLIES."

But the reception for *Mission to Moscow* was not unanimously positive. *Life* magazine, among others, labeled the film a whitewash. In *The New York Times,* Suzanne LaFollette, niece of a progressive Wisconsin senator, called it "totalitarian propaganda for mass consumption." Nevertheless, business was brisk. "NATURALLY PICTURE IS CONTROVERSIAL," J. L. assured Einfeld, "AND THAT'S WHAT MAKES IT A BIG HIT." What with the wartime alliance firmly in place and the blessings of the White House hovering over the picture, any criticism seemed little cause for concern.

As the war turned in the Allies' favor, Bogart felt the frustrations common to his age group, whose members had been too young for the last war and were too old for this one. Classified I-A-H by his draft board, he was physically fit but, at forty-three, unlikely to be called up. At Warners as elsewhere, the younger men had gone off to combat while the older stars fought the war on celluloid. For Bogart and the other overage male stars, the only option was such good works as Army base tours, public service broadcasts, and filmed War Bond appeals. He even bused tables at the Hollywood Canteen, the converted livery stable on Cahuenga Boulevard just off Sunset where screen idols mingled with servicemen en route to combat in the Pacific.

Shortly after Pearl Harbor, the Hollywood Victory Committee was formed. The industrywide organization provided talent for the USO from a roster of more than fifteen hundred actors and actresses who donated their services to do camp shows, make hospital visits and radio appearances, and go on cross-country War Bond tours. Though only a small minority got to travel overseas, in the fall of 1943 Bogart applied for permission from Warner Brothers to do so. His contract stipulated a four-week vacation, he reminded the studio, adding, "I would like to spend my vacation entertaining the troops."

All tours outside the United States were set up in cooperation with the War Department. The Hollywood Victory Committee and the USO made the arrangements and the studios supplied the talent—once they had firm assurances that their million-dollar properties that were being sent into the war zone would return within a specified time. Bogart, like Errol Flynn, was to be away for a maximum of eight to ten weeks.

There were the usual well-publicized preliminaries to the tour, such as the photos of Bogart, stripped to the waist, getting his necessary inoculations on the set of *Passage to Marseille.* Other preparations were more covert. Unknown to Bogart, the War Department, through its Office of the Provost Marshall General, ran a loyalty check on him. The investigators relied on the customary unnamed sources and gathered data from neighbors, the Screen Actors Guild, and local police, as well as from the files of federal agents working in the Los Angeles area. In the midst of a war being fought against fascism, with the Soviet Union as a major ally and Axis sympathies ostensibly the prime concern, the War Department seemed interested only in Bogart's possible Communist connections.

He was clean on all counts. To the surprise and amusement of military intelligence, the legendary tough guy emerged as an almost stodgy citizen, a man of "excellent character," who never missed a day's work because of any misbehavior or excesses. "His only fault is his violent temper and his quarrels—with his wife.

"Allegations that Subject has been connected with the Communist Party did not appear to be founded on fact," the report on him ended. The question remains whether all entertainers going into a sensitive war zone were subject to such a background check, or whether the backwash of the 1940 encounter with Martin Dies had become a permanent part of Bogart's national security profile.

That November, he and Mayo began a ten-week, thirty-five-thousand-mile tour of West and North Africa and Italy. They entertained thousands of GIs, playing at least two shows a day, with visits to hospitals shoehorned in between. It was a small troupe—Bogart and Mayo, actor Don Cummings and accordionist Ralph Hark; they called themselves the Filthy Four. At their first stop, in Dakar, Senegal, they performed before a huge audience on an outdoor stage constructed of twigs, native style. A local orchestra greeted them with twenty choruses of "As Time Goes By."

They had no clear idea of what to do, no formal act in mind when they left the States. Bogart took his cues from the audience and he improvised a tough-guy composite from his catalog of Warner heavies. Mayo, accompanied by Hark, sang blues numbers and show tunes. "My wife," Bogart told a reporter, "is the only real entertainer here." That, as entertainment, their show was fairly primitive hardly mattered. To these audiences of young men in their teens and early twenties, what counted was that Bogie, the embodiment of manly cool and incontrovertible toughness, was in their midst. News of his coming spread quickly. Even German propaganda broadcasts took note, citing the appearance of the gangster Humphrey Bogart as evidence of a breakdown in American morale.

In Casablanca, soldiers recognized Bogart on the street and continually asked him, Where is Rick's? The city itself was nothing like the Warner back lot, especially in December. "No heat or hot water and colder than the hinges [of hell]," Mayo wrote her mother, "but we have good warm clothes and we sleep in long underwear. You should see us."

Bogart added his usual P.S. ("All our love Pal") but it was Mayo who took care of the family correspondence, invariably beginning "Buffy Darling" and signed "Your Baby." She wrote her mother two or three times a week, the letters brimming over with the filial language of an eight-year-old and revealing the two personalities in the fractured psyche of Mayo Methot Bogart: the hard-drinking, two-fisted, middle-aged virago and the submissive, mother-fixated, and insecure little girl.

The Battle of North Africa was over, but the Battling Bogarts traveled on, a trail of Bogie-Mayo stories following them across the continent. They worked hard, though, and put in extra time talking with enlisted men as well as officers, sharing a cigarette with lonely youngsters who asked for more mail from home and wondered when Ann Sheridan would arrive. In a token of the approaching season, a grateful infantryman made up a special Christmas greeting ("Joyeux Noel/Afrique '43") from the forces in French North Africa to "Mr. and Mrs. Bogart—With great appreciation and thanks for what you've done for us soldiers."

The front had moved to Italy and in December the Bogarts flew to Naples. The city was now secured as a major base of operations, but the fighting was heavy to the north in a brutal hill-by-hill campaign. The Bogarts were put up in a building reserved for officers. "It is very muddy, rainy and cold but we are in real soldier clothes and warm," Mayo wrote Buffy. "You should see your daughter in my real soldier suit. Strictly GI." The soldiers were eager to see them, but the audiences in Italy, where the body count rose by the hour, were quite different from those they had played to in Africa.

Whenever a movie star or other celebrity performed in Naples, the Army used the thirty-five-hundred-seat San Carlo Opera House, near the waterfront. Despite German bombing raids every evening, the building was untouched. Bogart's appearance had been widely anticipated as the highlight of an otherwise grim Christmas. Instead, he later said, it was one of the worst experiences of his life.

It was an odd setting—performers in uniform, the audience in combat fatigues, and around them the gilded nineteenth-century opera house where the kings of Naples had been entertained. The interior was a cream and gold birthday cake of galleries and boxes, its gilt now fading and cigarette burns marring the red plush upholstery. Bill Mauldin, the cartoonist historian of the GI's war, was then covering southern Italy for the Army daily newspaper, *Stars and Stripes,* but made his way north to see Bogart.

Mauldin was among the throng in the house "packed with these lean, mean fighting machines, these guys down from the front—all wearing their helmets, a pretty scruffy-looking lot. Well, he came on stage—Mayo wasn't around anywhere—looking somewhat the worse for wear. They had made something of a name for themselves with their drunken fights, and I think he had a shiner. He looked bad. Not drunk, but suffering. He came on stage and started right off with his gangster routine: 'Listen, you guys, I'm formin' a mob to take back to the States—any of you guys want to go with me?'

"They just stared at him. They were all combat-fatigue cases, for God's sake. They all had the flu, trenchfoot, they were exhausted. Most of them were from units that were down to fifteen, twenty, twenty-five men. And they weren't getting rations, or very poor rations. They weren't getting proper clothing. Their feet were wet all the time because they weren't getting proper footgear. They were bitter about the rear echelon because they *knew* why they weren't getting stuff—it was being stolen and sold on the black market, a perfect *Catch-22* scene.

"This was sort of our own re-creation of Valley Forge, what was going on up there in the mountains. And these guys—they weren't *hostile* to him, they just didn't see the humor in it, so they stared wearily back at him. It was all an actor with a hangover needed.

"You could see him sort of wilt. He'd pulled this joke—and there was absolute silence. For an actor to get no reaction at all like that is worse than if they'd booed him. Being a trouper, he stood up there and did his best with what he had, and they were very polite. They appreciated his taking the trouble to come. But they *knew* that they were never going to get home. They were just trying to *live*—trying to survive. There was no rotation yet, and every one of these men knew the only way he was going to come down out of those hills was feet first. Even so, they applauded stuff and even chuckled a couple of times at some things, and he bulled his way through. But it was a bad moment."

Years afterward, when they got to know each other better, Mauldin asked Bogart if he remembered that night at the San Carlo. "Jesus Christ, do I remember it! I wish I could forget it! Those *eyes.*" They were the eyes he remembered from World War I, aboard the *Leviathan* and the *Santa Olivia,* bringing the troops home from the trenches in Europe.

But Bogart was a quick study, and the Italian tour continued on a surer if somewhat chastened note. "He picked up on it," Mauldin said, "and he was great with them." The Bogarts visited bases in the southern peninsula, doing their two shows a day in the open—and thus often in the rain—and many times adding a third show at night. "We work pretty hard all day long," Mayo wrote home. "I'm pretty tired when we get back to wherever we're billeted for the night. It is all wonderful though and I think we're doing a little bit to help those lonely hard working tired guys."

The Bogarts moved around, never knowing their destination. Sometimes they went by transport plane—one of Mayo's letters was datelined "flying somewhere over Italy"—other times in Army trucks or jeeps, bumping along dirt roads turned to ice-caked mud tracks in a chilly, nonstop rain. Closer to the lines, they played to smaller but no less avid audiences, performing on a platform of boards thrown across two truckbeds. In the light of headlamps, Bogart did his act, while Mayo, accompanied by Ralph Hark, sang requests and numbers from her 1929 Broadway hit *Great Day:*

Without a song the day would never end
Without a song the road would never bend
When things go wrong a man ain't got a friend
Without a song. . . .

"It's all pretty well blown up, but Bogie and I have the situation well in hand," Mayo wrote to Buffy. At one stop, the GI audience serenaded them with "White Christmas." Mayo quietly broke into tears.

In tent hospitals they sat by countless beds, talking with casualties by the light of gasoline lanterns. If people knew the half of it! wrote Mayo to her mother. "I'd like them all to take a walk through a field hospital. I've never seen such courage. No matter how badly they are hurt they have a smile and are so glad to see someone from home." But she almost lost her composure as she watched her husband, with what conviction he could muster, reassure a young triple amputee that his girl back home would still be waiting, then adding a P.S. to a letter at the anxious boy's request.

Mayo was at her best in those weeks—tireless, caring, and needed once again. The young patients responded instinctively to the broad-faced woman with the bright eyes, the warm smile, and unfailing humor.

The couple quarreled, made up, quarreled again, gave raucous parties for the soldiers, and coped with the shortage of fresh food. "When I get home I'm going to eat lettuce like a rabbit," Mayo wrote Buffy. They coped with the shortage of decent liquor, too: "All we get is plenty of lousy cognac that tastes like fried oil but we drink it." Their fighting, like their drinking, was accepted. One day they were packed into a jeep; and as Mayo sang at the top of her voice, Bogart turned back and yelled,

"Someone hit her with a wrench!" Everyone laughed, Mayo loudest of all.

"We spent our New Years Eve [of 1944] drinking the fried oil," Mayo wrote in another letter home, "and made our own fireworks. We have had a million laughs and I have never enjoyed anything more in my life. Bless you angel and we both wish you a happy new year."

In the middle of war, there were encounters with familiar faces. Sam Jaffe's young brother-in-law, Phil Gersh, wangled a short leave, scrubbed off the dirt of the hills, and turned up one evening at the hotel in Naples. Despite his ablutions, "I guess I looked lousy. I sure felt lousy, sleeping on the ground in tents." The desk orderly called the Bogart suite while fixing the soldier with a fish eye, then reluctantly allowed Gersh to go up when Bogart instructed him to do so. As soon as Bogart saw Gersh, he told him, "Look, kid, why don't you stay here? Let me talk to these guys." But it was not so easy to billet an enlisted man in officers' quarters.

Naples, known as PBS, for Peninsular Base Section, was run by an Army bureaucracy obsessed with appearances and a military caste system that consigned the fighting men to the lowest class. A dogface who came in off the front line, weary and bedraggled, received a welcome matching the chill of the Naples winter, and the Army's VIP hotel was the headquarters of the deep-freeze greeting. Although it had little to boast of compared to its peacetime splendor, the hotel had three things Gersh said field soldiers never saw—"rooms and bathrooms and beds." And it was off-limits to anyone below lieutenant colonel.

Bogart talked to the officer in charge. The answer was still no. The skinny, exhausted Corporal Gersh stood there as the noisy argument escalated, Bogart's voice carrying above the others: "But that's my *manager.* My manager, damn it! I want a bed. Put him in *my* room!" Finally, after Bogart threatened to quit the tour, a cot was installed in the little sitting room. "The hell with them," Bogart steamed after it was over. Gersh sank into the first bed he'd seen in months and minutes later was asleep. He woke in the very early morning to the sound of gunfire—not the enemy, but Mayo and Bogart, back from a performance. "And both loaded. The troops always gave them guns. And they started shooting at the ceiling—and it started falling down." Fortunately they were on the top floor. "But a lot of generals came running—oh, it was something!—and they took the guns away."

On a quieter night in Caserta, just northeast of Naples, Captain John Huston of the Army Signal Corps, along with Lieutenant Jules Buck and the English thriller writer Eric Ambler, camped out on couches in the

Bogarts' sitting room. Huston and Buck, the brash young photographer of Warners' pre-war days, were in Italy shooting footage for what was to become *The Battle of San Pietro* (1945), the wartime classic and landmark of documentary filmmaking.

They had been on the front line under fire for four days, Huston said, when "word was telephoned through to me that Bogart was coming, and I would be at liberty to come back and see him." The friends were reunited in a vast and drafty palace that had once been home to the Italian air force and now housed Fifth Army headquarters.

Bogart and Mayo were in the bar. "You still shooting pictures, kid?" he asked Buck. Then Huston and Buck introduced the Bogarts to Ambler, whose *Background to Danger* had been George Raft's finale at Warner Brothers.

It was evident to Buck that the Bogarts had been drinking for some time, and that "*she* was really tanking up." The reunion slowly soured as Mayo watched her husband pal it up with Huston. There had never been any sympathy between the director and the woman he contemptuously referred to as The Rosebud, and her sense of exclusion grew as she downed shot after shot.

Before long, Huston said, "Mayo decided she wanted to sing." She pushed her way unsteadily between tables to the middle of the floor, then started in:

More than you know
More than you know
Man of my heart, I love you so. . . .

"She sang off-key," he continued, "her voice was unsteady—she just couldn't sing. It was *embarrassing.* There was a piano in the bar, sort of off to one side. Somebody tried to play along, but it didn't help. She had no voice. She had nothing much of anything."

The Bogart road show was scheduled to go on until mid-February, held over two weeks by popular demand. Instead, in the first week of the month, it abruptly ended. Perhaps it was inevitable that Bogart would clash once too often with the authorities at PBS, Naples.

"He was raising hell," Huston said. "And Bogie *loved* to raise hell. Of a completely harmless nature. I mean he loved to cause ructions and make noises—almost a little boy quality, that was. You know, beating the drum, marching around the room. You see a *kid* doing this.

"Well, there was a general who was next door to this suite that Bogie had, and Bogie was up there with a bunch of the fellows, enlisted men and so on, getting smashed. So the general knocked on the door and asked them to quiet down, and I think Bogie suggested that he fuck himself. Which did not go down well, and Bogie was not all that politely asked to get the hell out of Naples."

In any case, his return was long overdue. The studio had expected the couple back in mid-January and had twice scheduled the start of his next film, *To Have and Have Not,* to coincide with his supposed arrival in Burbank.

The Bogarts had every reason for satisfaction in the knowledge of a job well done. Their jackets were patched with insignia presented by grateful servicemen from the coast of West Africa to the hills of southern Italy. Their domestic squabbles notwithstanding, while on tour they were closer than they'd been in years. Before leaving, Bogart wrote and asked Buffy to join them in Los Angeles: "We'd like you to come down—20 cases of beer, Butch!" And Mayo added, "So you can see your son and I are very lonesome to see you."

The flight home to a U.S. air base took two days in Army transport planes that were short on heating and amenities and long on stops for refueling. They were both more worn by ten weeks of non-stop work in grueling conditions than either cared to admit. By the time they landed, still in Army clothes, they were exhausted and querulous. They checked into the Gotham, the Fifth Avenue hotel used by Warners personnel, where a short time later a visitor found them, still in battle khaki, screaming at each other and throwing lamps, furniture, and anything else they could lift.

An aunt of Phil Gersh had heard news of their arrival from Sam Jaffe, who was also at the Gotham, and thought she might get their autographs. Instead, she found herself an unwitting witness to domestic warfare. "The place was a shambles," Jaffe said, "and there was Mrs. Gershe [that branch of the family apparently used the additional *e*] standing there with her autograph book, looking on in horror and amazement." She was still standing there when Bogart rushed past her and disappeared out the door. In former days, his fights with Mayo usually ended in the bedroom. This time he was nowhere to be found. Mayo called Jaffe's room repeatedly and with increasing hysteria as the hours passed. She'd driven Bogie away, she blubbered, and he'd probably been killed in traffic.

He appeared the next morning, deadly calm. His manner was deliberate, his control an icy contrast to Mayo's frenzy. Where had he been all night? she asked. He seemed to take pleasure in telling her exactly where he had been: with Helen Menken. Then he picked up the phone and talked to Jaffe. The agent was well aware of the ongoing relationship with Menken, but he was a manager, paid to handle his clients' careers, not their morals. Still, even though he had little use for Mayo, whom he called "a slut," Jaffe didn't like what was happening between the couple. "He played with her emotions. I know he did it, because he told me so."

He tried to play with Warner Brothers, too. Traveling back under Army orders, he had informed the authorities that he wished to stay in New York rather than continue on to Los Angeles. After the rigors of the tour, he wanted a little vacation before returning to work. From Warners' perspective, Bogart had asked for a vacation and had had it; how he spent it was immaterial. *To Have and Have Not* had been on the books since mid-December. Bogart was its star and it was time for him to start shooting. Bogart, for his part, made it clear that he didn't care about the new film. He was tired and wanted to relax.

Jack Warner was livid. Obliging the War Department was one matter. Indulging the whim, as he saw it, of an egotistical star was quite another. "THIS IS UNCALLED FOR," he cabled to Abe Lastfogel, the William Morris Agency head now running the camp shows from USO headquarters in New York. Bogart wasn't on some Mediterranean cruise; he was under Army orders, and if he wouldn't return on his own, it was up to the Army to get him back.

In language particular to Hollywood contracts and the Fugitive Slave Act of 1850, J. L. Warner reminded the USO that Bogart was to have been returned February 1; and if it couldn't live up to its word, it was going to find "terrific opposition against important stars going abroad." Lastfogel, visualizing his program going down in flames, assured Warner that nothing like this had happened before. Washington was equally disturbed about the "Bogart matter," he said, and added that he had forwarded J. L.'s wire to the Pentagon.

A blizzard of telegrams promptly set in to and from Burbank, New York, and Washington. Their single objective was to strong-arm one lone actor into going home. The Army did its part by issuing orders for Bogart's return; the Warner office on West Forty-fourth Street struggled to obtain cross-country passage, no easy matter in wartime, with civilian transport tight. Jaffe was drafted into the effort to get Bogart on the train. Throughout, Jack Warner assured everyone that it wasn't the money the studio was losing that he cared about, it was the fundamental principle of control basic to the underpinning of the studio system.

Mort Blumenstock, Warners' harassed New York publicity director, pulled strings and finally came up with accommodations on the Twentieth Century Limited for Thursday night, the 10th. Wednesday morning, he located Bogart at the Gotham and then, with some trepidation, reported the result to Burbank: "HE ABSOLUTELY REFUSES TO LEAVE."

By Thursday morning, Bogart had disappeared again. Don't bother to try to find him, Burbank cabled New York, the USO was working on it. Then a few hours before departure time, Bogart telephoned Blumenstock's office. Blumenstock told him that his "whole professional existence" depended on his getting on the train that night. "BELIEVE HAVE SCARED HIM ABOARD CENTURY," he wired Warner, "AND WILL CONFIRM TO YOU WHEN I HAVE HIM ON TRAIN AND TRAIN IS IN MOTION."

At the last, as always, Bogart's desires succumbed to his insecurities. He and Mayo appeared at Grand Central Station, where Blumenstock was waiting, tickets in hand. Arrangements had been made with the Chicago office for the change of trains there to take place under close supervision. Blumenstock saw them aboard and lingered as the train picked up speed to make sure no one jumped off, then cabled confirmation to Warner. The whole procedure suggested less a star returned from serving his country than an extradition. "They treated him like a criminal," Jaffe said. The choice, however, had been Bogart's.

Four days later, the Bogarts arrived at Union Station in downtown Los Angeles, where they were swamped by a hoard of reporters and photographers. Mayo, tight-lipped, wore a fresh corsage. Bogart, by her side, remained expressionless, blinking in the glare of the popping flashbulbs. The war was "grim and dirty," he told the press, "and there are no heroics."

Steve Trilling had wired Bogart en route to ask if he might stop off at the studio before going home, "AS THERE ARE MANY THINGS TO BE ACCOMPLISHED WHICH HAVE BEEN HELD UP AWAITING YOUR ARRIVAL." Both he and director Howard Hawks were anxious to see him, if only briefly. There were questions of the script and casting to be discussed, as well as a new girl, a protégée of Hawks's, that they were excited about.

CHAPTER 12

Betty

The girl was so pretty that Earl Robinson, who had been asked to look out for her on the four-day train trip from New York to Los Angeles, felt compelled to write his wife en route "to reassure her that there was nothing in this." Robinson, a popular composer, had been called out to Hollywood by agent Charles K. Feldman to work on a proposed film. Feldman told him he would have company—just a kid, really, whom he was thinking of signing up. She had never been on her own before, and would Earl keep an eye on her?

She came down the long platform at Grand Central Station to board the Twentieth Century Limited in early April 1943, a leggy, long-haired, simply-dressed teenager wearing a gardenia corsage, her mother by her side. No one would have recognized her as the high-fashion blonde with the smoky-eyed stare on the March cover of *Harper's Bazaar.* Robinson saw no "starring qualities" in the nevertheless attractive girl, but then he was there with his wife and "I wasn't looking for them." Rather, she seemed more a schoolgirl with a crush on movies, and since Robinson had "a New York attitude toward Hollywood," his opinion of starlets was low, even if they *were* good-looking. "I thought Hollywood was unreal, and I lumped her in with that. Which was stupid on my part." Even so, he found the eighteen-year-old "honestly friendly," and was comforting to her mother, Natalie, when she "sort of latched on to me, thinking that I could be a guardian, I guess. I was thirty-three then."

The pair spent the day in Chicago while awaiting the departure of the westbound Super Chief. As they ate together that evening, Robinson "figured she was making as much as I was, and could afford to pay for herself," and so he suggested that since they each were on Feldman's payroll, they go Dutch treat. She thought it entirely fair, and Earl Robinson began revising his opinion of Betty Joan Bacal, soon to be known as Lauren Bacall.

For the Feldman office, the girl whose professional name was Betty Bacall was just one more promising face, a minimal investment made in the wake of a few phone calls and a one-page commitment to a screen test. Feldman hadn't even met her when he was in New York a couple of months earlier. His visit was taken up with what at the time seemed more important things. There were meetings about a film he was making, talks with the Conover Agency for a group of mannequins to back up Rita Hayworth in Columbia's *Cover Girl,* plus screen tests for big-name models and for an exciting brunette named Ella Raines, who was being groomed for presentation as the latest discovery of director Howard Hawks.

Betty's childhood friend Gloria Nevard called her "a determined young lady with a will of iron." The two had been roommates and best friends at the Highland Manor School for Girls in Tarrytown, New York. Both were children of divorce, raised by working mothers who instilled character in their daughters and who "were special ladies, unusual for their time. Very independent, and very strong." Both girls studied dancing and performed in school shows. Betty had been born Betty Joan Perske, but she later shucked the surname of her long-vanished, deadbeat father and took on her mother's.

Even at Highland Manor, she was strikingly pretty, with long blond hair, and she acted in school productions. Despite the breakup of her parents' marriage, Betty was the focus of a large Jewish family, with a circle of adoring aunts and uncles and a grandmother who had emigrated from Romania with her small children. Their actual name was Weinstein-Bacal, but the immigration officer at Ellis Island apparently wrote down only the first half, and so the family became the Weinsteins. After her divorce, Natalie Perske legally became Natalie Bacal, and Betty, who was eight, became Betty Bacal.

One of Betty's uncles had loaned her mother the money for the expensive boarding school. The Weinstein-Bacals were raised on the verities of hard work, night school, and the conviction that in the new land nothing was beyond reach if you worked for it. Betty had learned the value of persistence by the time she was enrolled in boarding school.

When one morning the students were served bowls of overcooked cereal that had congealed into a lumpy, unappetizing mass, the other children managed to swallow it, but she refused to. Told to stay in her seat until she ate it, Betty sat alone in the empty dining hall all morning, her back ramrod straight, the cereal untouched. However, once back in the safety of her room, she cried throughout the night. The episode was a hint of the determination and emotion that would be evident in her career.

After Betty finished at Highland Manor, the family decided she would attend Julia Richman High School in New York. She wanted to be an actress and after high school she took classes at the American Academy of Dramatic Arts on Fifty-seventh Street, but the lessons ended a year later because tuition money ran out and the scholarship program was closed to women.

She then embarked on the beginner's hard road, working variously as a garment center model, a theater usher, and a vendor of show business guides in front of Sardi's restaurant, the social center of the theater community. She learned that it didn't help to be a shrinking violet and it didn't hurt to be young and pretty to make oneself visible.

She also learned that it didn't help to be Jewish. She was sixteen when she landed her first job as a model. One day another of the girls asked, "What are you?" Not knowing the girl meant ancestry rather than religion, she answered, "I'm Jewish."

"Oh—but you don't look it at all."

Soon afterward, Betty was fired, ostensibly because she was too thin for the designer's clothes.

When Nevard visited her in the city, she already seemed a part of the Broadway scene. At Betty's insistence they lunched at Sardi's, its walls covered by portraits of the celebrated clientele. Horrified at the prices, Nevard ordered what seemed the cheapest item on the menu, then flushed with embarrassment when the waiter brought a plate on which there was only a squat cylinder of tuna fish, still in the shape of the can. At the theater where she ushered, Betty took Gloria backstage to meet the actors, among them Vincent Price and Kirk Douglas. Betty also knew Burgess Meredith. Bacall, who had never really known her father, was especially attracted to leading actors who were older.

She had a distinct flair for comedy and a special quality, on stage and off, that made people take notice. Arthur Sheekman and Gloria Stuart, on the East Coast shepherding his new play *Franklin Street* through out-of-town tryouts, were delighted with the tall ingenue whose entrance in high-button shoes, flat hat, and spaced-out look, raised a laugh every time she came on. To Stuart, "She was darling. Very ambitious and talented and very good in the play." Joyce Gates, who was also in the cast and became a lifelong friend, agreed. "She was strikingly good-looking, with a lot of humor. Very ambitious. And single-minded."

The production, directed by the Broadway giant George S. Kaufman, folded in Washington, D.C., but the tall blonde left a lasting impression. She was the only member of the cast Kaufman wrote to after the closing, hoping "there will be another, or maybe this one all over again," even if he did address her as "Peggy." Through her network of her older and more influential friends, she was introduced to fashion editor Diana Vreeland, the arbiter of taste for millions of women. Enchanted by Bacall's looks, she put her into the pages of the January and February 1943 issues of *Harper's Bazaar* and then onto the March cover. The February issue, which came out just as Feldman was ready to leave New York, misspelled her name "Becall."

Nancy Gross "Slim" Hawks, the wife of Feldman's partner and client Howard Hawks, had seen the shot of Betty and two actresses modeling blouses while leafing through the magazine in Los Angeles and had promptly urged her husband to sign the striking young woman. Others had noticed her, too—David O. Selznick and Howard Hughes both made inquiries about her, and Columbia wanted to put her under contract. The difference between the Hawks and the Columbia overtures was that Hawks was offering a personal contract which guaranteed that, if the screen tests worked out, he would use her in one of his films; Columbia's offer was only the regular studio contract that promised servitude and assignment to whatever project and director the studio wanted. So she accepted Feldman and Hawks's proposal of an expenses-paid trip to California, under the assumption that she would quickly know whether or not she had a future in Hollywood.

Hollywood was invented for people like Charlie Feldman (born Charles Gould in 1904). He was a lawyer who became an agent and an agent who became a producer. In the course of his career, his over three hundred clients included John Wayne, Gary Cooper, Greta Garbo, and Marilyn Monroe. For a man who expected to make a living in show business, he did things that would crimp a lesser talent's ability to operate, such as marrying the golden-haired actress and former showgirl Jean Howard, who was avidly courted by tyrannical MGM head Louis B. Mayer. Howard's beauty so obsessed Mayer that he not only barred Feldman from his studio, he tried to have him barred from others; on the other hand, Feldman was the only agent with whom Darryl Zanuck, Twentieth Century–Fox's head of production, dealt personally. He was a devoted believer in the star system and the high salaries stars command. "No one ever heard of Ali Khan until he married Rita Hayworth," he once said, "and no one ever heard of Prince Rainier until he married Grace Kelly." He backed up his belief by getting his clients unprecedented deals. He negotiated $150,000 for Claudette Colbert, whose studio salary had been $2,500 a week, for *It Happened One Night* (1934). He did the same thing for Irene Dunne to play in *Magnificent Obsession* (1935), at a time when she had been making $60,000 a year under her studio contract. He raised John Wayne's fee to $750,000 a picture plus a percentage of the profits, and claimed he was the first agent to get a piece of the take for his stars. He also was the first agent to make package deals, bringing together script, star, and director, all usually clients of his. He gave Woody Allen his first screenwriting and acting jobs, on *What's New, Pussycat?* (1965); and the dozen other films he produced ranged from *The Glass Menagerie* (1950) and *A Streetcar Named Desire* (1951) to *The Seven Year Itch* (1955) and *The Group* (1966).

His partner, Howard Winchester Hawks, born in 1896 and the son of a wealthy paper manufacturer, had a degree in mechanical engineering from Cornell University, which made him a formally educated man in a business run by high school dropouts. He was also something of a daredevil. At age sixteen, he was a race-car driver and pilot. He also was attracted to films and worked during the summer vacations of 1916 and 1917 in the prop department at Famous Players–Lasky. After college and service in the armed forces in World War I, he became a designer and pilot for an aircraft company before returning to Famous Players–Lasky in the script department, where he did largely uncredited work on dozens of screenplays.

The critic and film historian David Thomson wrote, "Like Monet forever painting his lilies . . . Hawks made only one artwork. [Its theme is] that men are more expressive rolling a cigarette than saving the world." The males in his pictures value honor, and adversity is countered with persistence. The mutual needs of men and women despite their joyous incompatibility created a dark side to the funniest of his films, showing that life is entirely worth pursuing even in the face of its inevitable disillusionment. A clear love of language pervades his movies, and his characters often speak in rapid, overlapping voices that add pace, humor, and a sense of real conversation. He directed more than a dozen classic movies that play as beautifully today as when they were made decades ago: *Bringing Up Baby* (1938), *Twentieth Century* (1935), *Air Force* (1943), *Scarface* (1932), *Only Angels Have Wings* (1939), *His Girl Friday* (1940), *The Big Sleep* (1946), *Red River* (1948), *Gentlemen Prefer Blondes* (1953), *Rio Bravo* (1959), *Man's Favorite Sport?* (1964), and *I Was a Male War Bride* (1949).

Hawks was also "a chronic liar and compartmentalizer, a secretive rogue, a stealthy dandy, and a ruinous womanizer." Meta Wilde, later John Huston's favorite script supervisor, began her career in the thirties as Hawks's secretary before becoming his script supervisor. She found him "cold and ruthless" as well as "austere and unapproachable. It was *Mr.* Hawks, and he would say, in that chilly tone, 'Ye-e-es?' Once in his office—there was a long walk to his desk—a young actor came to see him. Howard was bent over the desk as the young man walked the whole way to it. When the actor got there he just looked up and said, '*Well?*' "

As his secretary, Wilde worked unlimited hours while also ferrying his children, delivering payoffs to his bookies, and steadying his put-upon first wife, Athole Shearer, the sister of Norma Shearer. There were also the long, icy silences, his bigotry, and the underlying misogyny that would destroy his three marriages. His cruelty emerged in a neutral monotone, his anger crystallized in frost. One day in the 1950s, William Faulkner turned his great sad eyes on Hawks's third wife, Dee Hartford (later Cramer), and commented in his soft drawl, "Miz Dee, I wouldn't want to be a dawg, a hoss, or a woman around Mr. Hawks."

Both Hawks and Feldman had the souls of gamblers and a minimal concern for sexual fidelity. But both were also imaginative, loyal, and dedicated to their clients and actors. They lived lavish, outsized lives, often at the expense of others, but in Hollywood that hardly made them unique. The movie business was perfect for them. And, at least for a while, they would prove perfect for Betty Bacall.

Bacall and Robinson were met at Union Station in Los Angeles by a Feldman underling, who drove them first to the office of Hawks-Feldman Productions on Wilshire Boulevard in Beverly Hills and then on to the Claremont Hotel in Westwood Village. That evening they had dinner with Feldman and Robert Ritchie, MGM's onetime Vienna representative who had discovered Hedy Lamarr and Luise Rainer. Feldman wanted him to appraise his prospective acquisition.

Lunch the next day was with Feldman and Hawks at the Brown Derby.

Hawks, in later interviews, would say that in a sweater and gabardine skirt, the sexy young woman of *Harper's* looked to him like "just a kid." He would claim, "I said, 'Fix her up with a tour of the studio so she can say she's been here, and then send her back home.' " As with many Hawks recollections, that account is more colorful than accurate. The Feldman office records clearly detail the money laid out and the promises made before bringing the "kid" to California: a test within a stipulated time and, until then, a modest stipend to cover her expenses. The morning of her arrival, the Claremont's manager, Mrs. McCall, called the agency to ask how the room bills should be handled. Feldman instructed her that both Bacall and Robinson would be paying themselves.

Betty Bacall was not the highest priority for Hawks and Feldman. That distinction went to Ella Raines, whom they had brought to Los Angeles two months earlier. Unlike Bacall, who was imported quietly and housed modestly, Raines was accorded all the perks of a prospective new film sensation. The instructions from the office were that she was to have deluxe accommodations at the Beverly Wilshire Hotel near the H-F office or, if it was full, at the Beverly Hills Hotel. In addition, a public relations man was always to accompany her and make sure that she had the best of care.

Her screen test left everyone ecstatic. The great screen lover Charles Boyer wanted to use Raines in his next film, and Hawks was certain she was star material. The list of actresses who had already played Hawks's heroines included Katharine Hepburn, Rosalind Russell, Frances Farmer, Barbara Stanwyck, and Rita Hayworth. He prepared to launch his latest find, and asked his own publicity agent to break the story of her discovery.

Not that Bacall was neglected. Besides the meals out with Feldman and Hawks and meetings in their office, on the Sunday after her arrival Feldman and Jean Howard invited her to their Beverly Hills home for lunch. Feldman invariably asked his wife for her impressions of new talent—John Wayne, she once told him, seemed "just a great big good-looking cowboy," which was to the point. Of Bacall Howard said, "She just sounds like a tough kid to me. I think she's very *pretty.*"

As it happened, the immediate plans of Hawks and Feldman called for a "tough kid" from Russia. Hawks had a per-picture directing contract with Warners, and he and Feldman in partnership had just signed a production deal with the studio to make the war movie to end all war movies—a multi-national, possibly multi-studio extravaganza that would celebrate the principles contained in the 1942 Declaration by the United

Nations (not to be confused with the Charter of the United Nations signed in San Francisco in 1945), and recently reaffirmed at Casablanca.

Battle Cry, unconnected with the Leon Uris war novel and the subsequent 1955 film, was to be a One World celebration scripted by Hollywood's top writers, with an all-star cast. It would be a composite of sequences depicting everything good and fine about the freedom-loving nations standing up to fascism, an amalgam of music and narrative, history and drama; the American sequence was to include *The Lonesome Train,* Earl Robinson's twenty-seven minute cantata about Abraham Lincoln. Hawks meant it to be the greatest action picture of all time.

Neither Bette Davis nor Claudette Colbert, the two great stars approached so far, had accepted roles. But Betty Bacall, with her wide cheekbones and exotic Tartar looks, was a natural for the Russian episode. Writers brought in from New York were already drafting that portion of the screenplay at the Beverly Hills Hotel; her entrance would be by parachute into a field where she would conveniently meet a soldier. Given the later political climate, it is interesting to speculate on how Betty Bacal's life might have turned out if she had begun her Hollywood career in a movie segment titled "Diary of a Red Army Woman."

While she waited for her future to be decided, Betty called the Feldman office three or four times a day to remind them that, even though their calendar was studded with names such as Cary Grant, Ingrid Bergman, and Marlene Dietrich, she was there, too. Other days there were meetings with her mentors about *Battle Cry,* all logged in the office daybooks, her name misspelled as it was in *Harper's Bazaar.* "Friday: Becall + Robinson Brown Derby 6PM very important. . . . Monday: Howard Hawks and Becall + Robinson here."

"It was just natural" that she and Robinson would be paired, he said, "because we were both there under the same circumstances." Robinson, a close friend of the folk singer Woody Guthrie and a member of the musical left, was also being tested for the planned film. He was an engaging performer, and at Feldman and Hawks's urging he showcased his talents to the industry elite at parties in Beverly Hills and Bel Air. Betty was usually along and to Robinson's pleasure would join in as he played the piano. "She had a good voice and was very musical. We got toured around Hollywood by Charlie. I would sing songs of mine and Betty would chime in." One that she particularly liked was "Porterhouse Lucy the Black Market Steak," a spoof on the joys of rationing.

About three weeks after she arrived in Los Angeles, a memo was passed down the line at Warners from the office of J. L.'s executive assistant Steve Trilling: "Mr. Hawks will direct the following test on Monday April 26 for BATTLE CRY: Shooting at 10:00 A.M.—BETTY BECALL." Assisting would be Charles Drake, a veteran of Hawks's *Air Force* who was about to begin work with Bogart on *Conflict.* The scene to be shot, however, was not from the still uncompleted *Battle Cry* but from a popular Broadway play titled *Claudia.* It was a role Betty knew well and had nearly understudied.

Late Sunday afternoon, she went to the Feldmans' and spent the night. Jean Howard, seeing that "she was nervous and frightened, did what I could, without holding her hand. She knew that she was with friends. My nephew drove her over to Warners to do her test." In sharp contrast to the usual rushed assembly-line test whose lack of production values had ended many an aspirant's dream of a Hollywood career, Bacall was given the care of a great director; Hawks paid attention to every aspect of makeup, lighting, and photography. A still that survives from that morning's test shows a dreamy-eyed girl with wavy hair falling to her shoulders, the light picking up the bone structure of the perfect, strong young face.

On May 3, 1943, using her legal name, Betty Bacal signed a four-page, single-spaced document putting her under personal contract to Howard Hawks, starting at $100 a week, with options up to seven years and a maximum of $1,500 per week. Hawks in turn retained her exclusive services, along with the right to sign her over to any other major producer, a clause whose significance would only later be apparent. For the time being, she was the protégée—and the property—of one of the most accomplished American directors, a man who lived in baronial splendor, played the horses, seldom paid his bills, and was always in need of ready cash.

By the end of May, Betty Bacall had gone from transient to resident of Beverly Hills and had applied for a driver's license. A monthly budget had been set up by the Feldman office, based on a net salary of $80.40 a week and a monthly allowance of $35. Once allotments were made for rent for a small Beverly Hills apartment, phone bills, groceries, clothes, car payments and upkeep, and dental work, and 10 percent was deducted for the purchase of War Bonds, she was left with $4.80 a month to do with as she liked. After Natalie Bacal signed away any and all rights to her underage daughter's earnings, she was brought west by Hawks-Feldman to share the furnished apartment at 275 South Reeves Drive that was within walking distance of the agency.

In June, Hawks, his lawyer, Natalie Bacal, and "Betty Bacal, a minor" appeared before a Superior Court judge and obtained approval of the contract. A savings account was set up for the minor, with her mother as trustee. For the rest, Natalie was content to step back and let her daughter's mentors decide what was best for her career. Jean Howard thought that "she was pretty solid, good material. And a real *mother*. Not a stage door type."

Then came the months of transformation. To begin, there was the speaking voice. Feldman had recently had to give up on a young model already making $350 a week at the Conover Agency. She was considered one of the most beautiful girls in New York, possessed of grace, charm, beauty, and refinement—and a high-pitched voice. Feldman paid for coaching and was ready to sign her up as soon as she improved. She didn't.

Later allegations notwithstanding, Betty Bacall had no such vocal problems, though her speech did have the unmistakable inflections of her home town. Her delivery, Jean Howard said, was simply "faster and harder" than the low, modulated tones of the heroines of Howard Hawks. Warner publicist Bob William, whose sister had gone to Julia Richman High School, recognized her and was immediately aware of her "real New York accent." Another Warner employee would remember "a low voice. But Howard wanted it very, very low, so that it wouldn't be squeaky on screen."

Hawks later insisted that "she had a little thin, reedy voice," casting himself once again in the role of miracle worker. But her achieving the timbre Hawks desired was more the result of her own effort than of his alchemy. Each day Bacall drove up either Benedict Canyon or Coldwater Canyon Drive, both of which connect Beverly Hills with Mulholland Drive, the ribbon of road that overlooks the city on one side and the San Fernando Valley on the other. She would stop at a deserted spot and read Lloyd C. Douglas's biblical novel *The Robe* aloud, deliberately making her voice lower, more masculine, more sexy, an exercise suggested by Hawks.

One day, Hawks later said, his secretary left a message: "that girl" had asked to see him. "And when she came over she talked 'way down, you know. She'd changed her voice. And—what the hell, you *have* to notice a girl like that."

Jean Howard agreed. "It was a great voice. It had that individuality."

Next came the question of style. She was sent to the manorial Hawks property on Moraga Drive in the hills of Bel Air; she later wrote that the huge single-story ranch house filled with antiques was "the most beautiful house I had ever seen." Dee Cramer, who was married to Hawks from 1953 to 1959, agreed. "The style was not to be *believed*." The estate included barns, a gardener's cottage, a fleet of trucks, and a racing stable filled with Thoroughbreds with names like "The Bride," "She Does," and "Break-up."

The young actress was put under the supervision of Hawks's wife of three years, the fashionable, trend-setting "Slim," one of America's best-dressed women. The second Mrs. Hawks, about twenty years younger than her husband and only seven or eight years older than Bacall, soon became her role model. The two became almost interchangeable. To Dee Hawks Cramer, who knew and admired her predecessor, "Slim *was* Lauren Bacall. I mean just mannish, striding around with these great clothes and able to say four-letter words trippingly. And the *wit* was not to be believed. Betty really emulated Slim—she *became* Slim." The metamorphosis made no sense to Jean Howard. "I knew that Betty was impressed with Slim, and wondered why. Because I thought Betty was much better than Slim, actually—more of a person, and real."

Dressed in Slim's clothes and placed in settings of elegance and taste, she was photographed at the Hawks home by John Engstead, whose glossies had set the public images of Carole Lombard, Claudette Colbert, and Marlene Dietrich. The results were the classic poses—the lowered head with its sweep of smooth, fair hair, and the sultry upward glance later dubbed "The Look"—that became the trademark of Lauren Bacall.

By late July, it was clear that *Battle Cry* had insurmountable problems. It was too complicated, there were too few writers available and too few stars committed; more to the point, it was too expensive. Jack Warner told Hawks and Feldman that the negative costs alone were estimated at four million dollars, nearly double the original figure, and that he was not prepared to spend that kind of money, even though he had already paid H-F Productions more than $92,000. By mid-August, all parties had agreed to shelve the project and move on to another story. The subject was not yet specified, but Hawks's name was money in the bank, and Warner was ready to guarantee Humphrey Bogart as the star.

Hawks, meeting subsequently with J. L., said he had right of first refusal on the novel *To Have and Have Not* by his good friend Ernest Hemingway. The literary rights were currently held by Howard Hughes, but if Warners was prepared to reimburse him, there could be a deal.

The novel was one of Hemingway's less popular, and originally no one in Hollywood was especially excited about the property. Warners had rejected it shortly after its publication in 1937, but in 1943 the story was suddenly the answer to everybody's problems. The studio wanted to put *Battle Cry* behind them and cut their losses, while Hawks, being dunned by the IRS for back taxes, needed the $100,000 directing fee his contract guaranteed. An agreement had been worked out to keep his home out of the hands of the government by paying it in stages out of Hawks's Warner earnings. In less than a week the novel was bought by Hawks from Hughes and resold to Warners. One slice of the profits went to H-F Productions, and another part of Hawks's fee was apportioned to Uncle Sam. By September 7, all was set to move forward on *To Have and Have Not.*

Ann Sheridan was the first actress discussed for the female lead opposite Bogart. She was one of Warner's hottest stars and, as she proved six years later in *I Was a Male War Bride,* fully matched the self-assertive profile of the Hawks heroine. But when Warners suggested that they might want a new face, Hawks and Feldman seized the opportunity to provide one. Hawks asked that Bacall's April screen test be run for Jack Warner, who liked the clip tremendously. If she got the lead in the new film, Warners was to share her contract.

Hawks and Feldman launched a quiet campaign to increase Bacal's visibility by introducing her at celebrity-studded evenings in their homes or those of other influential people. Hostess Elsa Maxwell, the friend to the well-connected, gave an intimate, exquisite luncheon for her, which was acknowledged with a small mention in Hedda Hopper's column in the *Los Angeles Times.* Bacall was unaware of the Warner dealings and knew only that her kind hosts had arranged something special in honor of her nineteenth birthday.

For all their kindnesses, her closest allies also posed dangers, and she dealt with them much as she had with the porridge incident at boarding school: with outward determination but inner turmoil. Feldman, his glamorous wife notwithstanding, was known to have many affairs. At least some people thought he wanted to include Bacall among them. Earl Robinson was certain. "Charlie was sweet on Betty. He was trying to make her and she resisted him." Jean Howard was equally convinced he wasn't. "He did *not* make a try, I can tell you that for sure. Betty, really, was not his type. She was a little tough, maybe. A little too . . . Jewish. I don't like to say that, he didn't have a *prejudice* against them, but I know that he never had affairs with them."

Hawks's prejudice was completely open. Anti-Semitic barbs studded his conversation, and they shocked his protégée. She noticed that Feldman was the only Jew ever invited to Moraga Drive and wondered if Hawks knew about her own background. She reasoned that, as Feldman's partner, he must. But mindful of how she had lost her first modeling job, she was both intimidated into silence and full of self-reproach for not standing up to the benefactor who was offering her the American dream along with his slurs. "She had a dilemma about being a Jew, with Hawks, in among that bunch of anti-Semites," a friend said. "She had the guilts about that."

Whatever Hawks's prejudices, there were hints, subtly or not so subtly conveyed by third parties, that Mr. Hawks wanted to be more than simply a business associate. Joyce Gates, Bacall's friend from the failed Kaufman show, had also come out for a screen test and was staying with her mother at the Beverly Hills Hotel. Betty told her all that was going on. "She was careful. And very scared."

Yet she managed, unlike so many others, to avoid the complications of the casting couch. Among those who seemingly fell into sexual liaisons was the much-publicized Ella Raines. Betty was at the Feldman's one day when he asked his wife to bring him a key that he had left on his dressing table. Jean Howard made it a rule never to probe through her husband's things, because "if you look for something, you're going to find something you don't want to see." She found the key next to a tie clip she had never seen before. "I looked at it," she said fifty years later in a voice still steely from the memory. "It said: 'For Keeps. E. R.' That told me there was a lot of stuff going on. But it was just one of many things with Charlie. Poor girl."

Jules Buck, the photographer and later producer who married Joyce Gates and knew both Raines and Bacall, said, "Ella was very sweet, but they were totally different persons. Betty was a force. She was pushing herself, seemingly *without* pushing herself. Ella was retiring. She did not have the charisma that Betty manufactured." Raines never fulfilled the promise of her test. Part of the problem was her first assignment. Universal's 1943 naval movie *Corvette K-225,* with Randolph Scott and produced by Hawks, was designed to show off military hardware and Canada's participation in the war, not a sexy actress. In the eight-year career that followed, she never made another film for Howard Hawks, and the slot for the next ideal Hawks woman remained wide open.

The bulk of the contractual details on *To Have and Have Not* were settled that fall, but the question of the leading lady was still unresolved. Even though weeks earlier Roy Obringer had noted the possibility of Bacal appearing in the picture, the studio had cooled on the idea, a shift not uncommon in a business in which enthusiasms wax and wither overnight. *Old Acquaintance,* the newest Bette Davis movie, showcased blond, eighteen-year-old Dolores Moran, who, unlike Bacall, was already on the Warner payroll. As for Betty, Jack Warner said, they would make a deal when and if they used her, "but we're not obligated to do so."

H-F Productions was so eager to get the production contract signed, Bogart pinned down, and the IRS off Hawks's back that the clause in the draft agreement on the film covering Bacall's possible appearance was dropped by mutual consent. Trilling paraded the tests of "our various young people" before Hawks and promised J. L. he would do his best to talk the director out of using "Betty Becall."

Despite his urgent need for money, Hawks did not give up. In October, he took Bacall onto the set of *Passage to Marseille* and introduced her to Bogart. A few polite words were exchanged. A slight figure in his convict's uniform of loose trousers and cotton shirt, Bogart seemed friendly enough, but there was no clap of thunder, she later wrote. He would remember seeing a pretty walking prop that could either help or ruin a film, and he wondered if she could act.

As 1943 ended and Bogart and Mayo were off entertaining the troops in Italy, tests of both Dolores Moran and Bacall for the part of Marie were scheduled, to be shot under Hawks's supervision. The sequence was a key scene between Marie Browning and Harry Morgan, the Bogart character.

Moran went first, testing the Friday before New Year's Eve. Bacall was scheduled for Monday afternoon. In her memoir *Lauren Bacall by Myself,* she describes rehearsing all weekend, with stock company player John Ridgely taking Bogart's place. Hawks had them play the scene repeatedly so that the casting would turn out his way, not Jack Warner's. On Monday there was another hour and a half of rehearsal before shooting began. The next day, Hawks, Trilling, and Feldman viewed the film with J. L., and all knew they had their leading lady. On Wednesday in a meeting with their business manager, Feldman and Hawks declared that the newcomer had great potential as a motion picture personality, and H-F Productions formally took over Hawks's contract with Betty Bacal.

Even in the early drafts when Marie was called Corinne, the role had been clearly angled toward H-F's client. Screenwriter Jules Furthman, a veteran of two films with Hawks and three screenplays for Marlene Dietrich, the classic *Shanghai Express* (1932) among them, seeded his dialogue with explicit references ("That lynx-eyed, long-legged mess of peaches and cream") and telltale giveaways ("You must have caught her awfully young. She doesn't look a day over nineteen") that make it evident he was using Bacall as his model.

It was originally a lesser role, that of a waif-like young hooker with a direct manner and a fondness for drink. The flashier role was that of Helen Gordon, the hero's ex-wife and former lover, "a sleek, beautiful New Yorker of twenty-five," who was independent, worldly, and adept at sexual banter: the Hawks woman incarnate. When she loses out in the end to the younger woman, she departs with her head high ("insolent as ever," according to the screenplay), and leaves a pearl necklace for her rival. In those early drafts, the Bogart character had to contend with several women, among them a Cuban cafe owner and an American girlfriend, as well as an ex-wife.

But the "sleek, beautiful New Yorker" could no more pass the censors at the Breen Office than could *Casablanca*'s Lois Meredith, and gradually the number of women was whittled down to two. The role of Helen Gordon was reduced to the secondary character of Helene de Brusac, the spoiled wife of a French Resistance leader, and virtually written out of the picture. Hawks helped to build up the role of Marie Browning, turning the rum-addicted waif into the Hawks ideal—outspoken, self-assured, sexually aggressive, at once young and ageless. The way was clear for Betty Bacall. Dolores Moran, who was assigned the part of Helene, would remain a feature player.

Jack Warner found Jules Furthman's complicated draft of the script, finished in late 1943, too long and too talky, and he directed the author to cut it down and put in some action. Even then, the love scenes needed work. Eventually three more writers would be added, one of whom was William Faulkner. Alcoholic, "out of print and broke," as his lover Meta Wilde put it, he knocked out Warner screenplays to support his household in Mississippi. A small, neat man with dark eyes, thinning hair, a shy manner, and a pipe perpetually between his teeth, Faulkner was back in Hollywood after a six-month leave of absence, and his old friend Howard Hawks had put him to work. It would later be fashionable to downgrade Faulkner's screenwriting as journeyman's work done of necessity. But Jack Warner measured writers not by whether they were literary giants but, like all his employees, in terms of their commercial value. Faulkner, J. L. said, was "a hell of a writer."

Though Jules Furthman was continuing to revise his own script, his work had to be done over by Faulkner. This meant that the writers often stayed just one step ahead of the shooting, but that was no problem for Hawks. He was happy with on-set rewrites, usually done in close collaboration with the actors.

Yet it was actually two lesser talents that the studio signed in December for what Trilling called "the polishing required" who were to come up—

at least in first draft—with the most memorable scene in *To Have and Have Not* and one of the most memorable in American movies. Many have laid claim to writing it. Slim Hawks was one. She had lent her stylish facade and even her nickname to Marie, and in her memoirs she describes her husband, pencil and pad in hand, jotting down her mots at night, to use them in the morning. Credit for the whistle scene, however, belongs elsewhere.

Cleve F. Adams was a mystery writer and sometime Feldman client with a dozen books and three hundred magazine stories to his credit; Whitman Chambers had one original author's credit for a low-budget production called *Sinner Takes All.* The first week of January the two men were set to work building up the part of Marie and in the process created a new scene, only hinted at in the early drafts. Each worked alone but followed the same line of thought, possibly prompted by Hawks and whatever he had perceived in his last test of Bacall. A week later, they handed in a few pages of typescript establishing the sexually aggressive female and the intrigued male. It began with banter and ended, at the woman's initiative, in each other's arms.

> (*She sits on his lap, puts her arm around his neck and kisses him.*)
> "Why did you do that?"
> "I just wanted to see if I'd like it."
> "Did you?"
> "I haven't decided yet."
>
> "You're not very hard to figure, Harry. . . . Sometimes I know exactly what you're going to say—most of the time—the other times you're just a stinker."
>
> "Tell me, Harry—do you know how to whistle?"
> "No."
> "It's easy. You just pucker up your lips—" (*Which Morgan does. He grabs her and kisses her thoroughly. When he releases her, her eyes are sulky. She steps back.*) "I said—it's easy. You just pucker up your lips—and *blow!*"

Nineteen days later came the rewrite, with a nickname for the hero and the bitterness changed to sassy good humor:

> "You know you don't have to act with me, Steve. You don't have to say anything, and you don't have to do anything. Not a thing. Oh, maybe, just whistle. You know how to whistle,

don't you, Steve? You just put your lips together and blow." (*She exits.*)

There would be more attempted changes; at one point the scene was even set aside. And possibly it was Hawks himself who did the final touchup. Still, in a production loaded with great names, the big scene was written by two obscure writers whose names never made it into the credits.

By the end of January 1944, all that was missing was Bogart and a script that wouldn't cause problems in Washington, D.C. Furthman had kept the Cuba setting of Hemingway's novel, but there also remained an unflattering portrait of a dictatorship potentially upsetting to America's good friend, the Cuban strongman Colonel Fulgencio Batista. Hawks offered to go to Havana to attend a high-level meeting brokered by Hemingway. The director, Trilling informed Warner, "felt he could get this all clarified . . . with these top men, with whom Hemingway is very friendly, probably Batiste [*sic*] himself."

Two weeks later, for reasons unrecorded, the trip to Cuba was abandoned, most likely because at some point in the discussions, the U.S. government threatened to withhold the picture's export license. To avoid further trouble, the setting was eventually changed to French Martinique. A greater problem was Bogart, whose prolonged absence in Italy meant two postponements of the start date while the company was in place and being paid—no one more than Howard Hawks, who collected $3,000 for every week of overtime.

"We want to be ready the day he returns," Jack Warner said of Bogart. Whether Bogart was ready was immaterial.

He arrived in Los Angeles worn out from the rigors of the tour and of Mayo. Home again on North Horn Avenue, she was fascinated with the handguns they had brought back and repeatedly took them into the back yard to fire round after round into the hillside.

The new start date for the film had been pushed back two weeks—the result of more script problems rather than of studio generosity—but there was hardly any time for rest and recuperation. Hawks and Trilling needed Bogart for conferences on the picture, and the Red Cross needed him for *Report from the Front,* a short requested by the Office of War Information. The six-minute pitch was to be played in movie houses across the country, followed by ushers with collection plates. It required a spokesman just returned from overseas to provide the needed credibility, and preferably not a comedian, no matter how much time he devoted to the troops. Bob Hope had made the last appeal, to little effect; audiences were unstinting with their laughter, but not with their money.

Six days after his return, Bogart, in trench coat and snap-brim hat, reported to the shooting site outside the Warner crafts building, where he was to emerge from a dummy plane and meet the press, played by a half-dozen extras from Central Casting. He knew the four-page script and had even made a few rewrites, changing the ending from a polite query ("Will you make a donation . . . now?") to a command ("Make a generous donation. . . . Now!") Then, after two hours of lining up and with the cameras ready to shoot, he refused to continue unless Mrs. Bogart was included. Producer Gordon Hollingshead, chief of shorts for Warners, had no choice. Filming was postponed for a day and Bogart recorded the voice-over instead.

The next morning, Bogart emerged from the doorway of the dummy plane, then turned and brought out Mayo—gallantly, deftly, as befitted his wife and companion, for better and for worse, of almost seven years.

At one point in the two intervening weeks before shooting on *To Have and Have Not* began, he met his co-star at the door of Howard Hawks's bungalow on the lot. This time she registered: a lovely young woman with blue-green eyes, as tall as he was, maybe taller. He told her he had seen her test, and she would always remember his verdict: "We'll have a lot of fun together."

CHAPTER 13

The Fun Begins

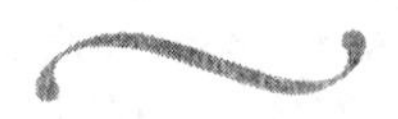

The fun began at 9:00 A.M. on February 29, 1944, a leap year Tuesday, when the company of *To Have and Have Not* gathered at Warners for the first day of production. The problem was, only thirty-six pages of the screenplay had been written.

For a less resourceful director, the abrupt changes in the film would have been traumatic, but Hawks was above all a great improviser. Roles were switched, cast lists overhauled. Actors who had been wardrobe-tested only weeks before were suddenly without a part. The research department dropped the Spanish references and boned up on their French. Dan Seymour, the Arab from *Casablanca* signed to play a Cuban revolutionary, read the pages brought to him by messenger and immediately phoned his agent. "My character's not in this script!" he exclaimed. "Here they've got 'Dan Seymour—Captain Renard' and he's a French Vichy police chief who runs the island of Martinique. What's going on?" The agent called back a few minutes later. "Hawks says you can play a Frenchman as well as you can play a Cuban."

The first day's shooting started with the lead-in to Marie's entrance: a hotel hallway, an open door, and the first of her two opening lines: "Anybody got a match?" Bacall wrote that during rehearsal, she shook with fear—her head, her body, the hand holding the cigarette. "Hope we don't hear her knees knocking!" the sound mixer whispered to Bogart. The cameras rolled. The first try was a false start. Second, NGA—No Good

Action. Bogart tried to joke her out of her nervousness. Then she "realized one way to hold my trembling head still was to keep it down, chin low, almost to my chest, and eyes up at Bogart, [which] turned out to be the beginning of 'The Look.' " The third take was a print. The dailies showed none of the nervousness. Instead, there was the enduring image of the beautiful young woman in the doorway—coolly appraising, supremely self-assured.

That Thursday night, the Bogarts attended the Sixteenth Annual Academy Awards, held for the first time at Grauman's Chinese Theatre on Hollywood Boulevard. It was a sober wartime affair with no tuxedoes, and Bogart wore his familiar dark pinstripe suit. Mayo was in a street-length flowered silk dress under a full-length mink, a corsage of white gardenias on one shoulder and a single gardenia in her hair. Warners had nearly two dozen nominations, among them Best Picture, Director, Screenplay, Actor, and Supporting Actor. *Casablanca* was pitted against *Watch on the Rhine,* and Bogart, with his first nomination for Best Actor, had to contend with Paul Lukas, who repeated his Broadway success in the Hellman drama.

In keeping with the spirit of the time, the proceedings were crisply military in tone, from a leadoff Army short (*Motion Pictures on the Fighting Front*), to the patriotic presentation mounted by the Hollywood Victory Committee. Lena Horne, Betty Hutton, Red Skelton, and Ray Bolger played in front of a ten-tier bleacher filled with two hundred men and women in uniform. The climax to the whole production was the descent of a huge American flag.

At 10:15 presentation of the major awards began, broadcast over a short-wave hookup to a worldwide GI audience. Sidney Franklin of MGM, the producer of the 1942 winner *Mrs. Miniver,* opened the envelope with the winner of Best Production and announced *Casablanca.* There was a surprised gasp from the audience, followed by long and loud applause and then laughter as Jack Warner raced Hal Wallis to the podium to claim the statuette. Warner got to the podium first. As Aljean Harmetz described it, "there was nothing Wallis could do except go back to his seat and listen to Jack Warner joke with Jack Benny, master of ceremonies for the evening. Almost as an afterthought, according to one reporter, Warner thanked Wallis and the movie stars, although he couldn't quite remember who all of them were." A few minutes later, Wallis received the Irving Thalberg Award, "for the most consistent high quality of production by an individual producer . . . during the preceding year." The choice was not a hard one. Of the eight awards Warner Brothers won that night, seven went to Wallis movies and the other to Wallis himself. "Every Wallis movie that was released in 1943 won at least one award," Harmetz points out, "and Wallis had, single-handedly, tied 20th Century–Fox for first place. But Jack Warner had taken the credit."

Casablanca won in almost every major category—Michael Curtiz for Director, Phil and Julie Epstein and Howard Koch for Screenplay, Claude Rains for Supporting Actor. The film seemed as if it would sweep every award when George Murphy, standing in for James Cagney, broke the seal on the envelope for Best Actor. Bogart had been surprised by his nomination and did not really expect to win, but neither did he expect the roar of approval as Murphy announced Paul Lukas. It was a sentimental response to a dark-horse choice. Lukas's twenty-five-year Hollywood career had been fading, and everybody loved a comeback.

After the ceremony, Wallis's secretary asked Warner's secretary, William Schaefer, for the Oscar. Warner's response "was to refuse even to allow Wallis to be photographed with the statue." Warner was not entirely out of line, however. While there was not a rule on who accepted the award, until 1948 it was generally done by the studio head. More important was the larger issue of Wallis's success and Warner's inability to cope with it.

That night speeded the dissolution of the Warner-Wallis partnership. By the end of the year, Wallis would be gone from the studio. The Bogarts' difficult marriage was coming to an end as well, hastened by the attraction between Bogart and Betty Bacall. In Bogart's first several encounters with Bacall there had evidently been no more than his usual consideration for a younger colleague. When Dolores Moran blew her lines on the first day, she was similarly put at ease with a quiet, "Take it easy, Junior, you'll get it."

But there were soon indications of something more between the two leads. Regardless of her youth and nervousness, Bacall's strong showing in the dailies marked her as a talent of stature, a strong personality and performer who could hold the screen, in vivid contrast to Moran, whose scenes were cut back as Bacall's grew in importance.

"Moran just didn't come through," Walter Surovy, the Viennese actor cast as a French resistance agent, said (he is listed in the credits as Walter Molnar). "She was a beautiful woman—and dull. In Vienna we would say, no *schmaltz.* But Betty was not only beautiful, she was just *marvelous.*" Married to the beautiful diva Risë Stevens, Surovy was a capable judge of *schmaltz.*

"Betty *was* special," Dan Seymour agreed. "She had a sense of timing. And, of course, Howard Hawks knew exactly what to do with her." Marcel Dalio, the croupier of *Casablanca* now playing a Martinique hotel owner, followed her every move and intoned with Gallic appreciation to those nearby, "O-o-o-oh, watch out for *her.*"

She had a combination of naïveté and knowing, of sugar and steel, and Bogart, intrigued, tested her sense of humor and capacity for being teased. He later recounted a story conference early in the film, Hawks deep in discussion with the actors and the inexperienced young woman adding her two cents' worth. Bogart couldn't resist. "An *excellent* suggestion, Miss Davis," he said, referring to her as if she were another vastly more accomplished Bette. He watched her nostrils flare, her head go up, her face grow taut. Then she burst out laughing.

Seymour noticed that "at first, she got a hell of a heckling, from Bogart and everybody else. Here's a new kid on the set, Hawks's protégée. But this kid was ambitious. She knew what she wanted and she was a hard worker. And she was really a lot of fun. She had a great sense of humor. Bogie loved to sort of wise her up. He was the leader of the pack. They saw that this gal knew what she was doing, and could take it."

Bogart's pranks included, on one occasion, handcuffing Bacal to one of the portable dressing rooms and making a great show of trooping off to lunch. "Of course we came back and took them off again, but she played along. She was a good sport, and she was *smart.* I can still hear Marcel Dalio saying, with that accent of his, 'Oh, she's so nice, Da-nee! She's *such* a nice woo-man!' "

But Seymour sensed something else behind the foolery. "I think Bogie wanted to make her feel at home. He realized this kid had never done a picture before, that this was a big break. Here you're a leading woman to Humphrey Bogart—but you're nineteen years old, you've got the lines to think about, and you know you have to get a characterization; it's a rough deal. So I think he took the pressure off her, making her one of the bunch. And she knew how to handle it."

The change in their relationship was so gradual as to be unnoticed by the crew at first and possibly by the stars themselves; Bacall later called it "almost imperceptible." Meta Wilde, the script supervisor working on her fourth Hawks film, saw no indication of a growing attraction during the first weeks of shooting. "It was all so new to Betty. She wasn't used to what a sound stage looked like or what a camera looked like or what sound people were going to do. She had to concentrate. So I think it was some time after they had been acting together that the chemistry started."

In Bacall's account, she was sitting in her dressing room, joking with Bogart, when he leaned over, put his hand under her chin, and kissed her. He then pulled a matchbook from his pocket and asked her to write her phone number on the back.

He had never had a relationship with a leading lady, or with any woman so much younger than himself—a quarter century younger, to be precise. In an industry that regards young females as so many toothsome morsels, he had preserved a demeanor of absolute correctness. He was aware in an age that some would call innocent and others repressed that his co-stars were often teenagers with the faces and bodies of women. (Joan Leslie, required to greet the hero with a rush of affection in *The Wagons Roll at Night,* was instructed by director Ray Enright, "Imagine he's bringing a big doll for you.") To Bogart, unlike many other Hollywood men of power, that meant they were to be left alone.

Betty Bacall, though young, was above the age of consent. And unattached. Four weeks into production, they shot the whistle scene. "The way they did that scene, we *knew* things were happening," Dan Seymour said. "He had that sort of smile you can still see on the screen."

To Walter Surovy, "It was like an explosion. They looked at one another like—well, did you ever go into a party and there was somebody who was fascinating to you and it was fatal? It happens. So I believed from the beginning that this was going to work."

"She's wonderful," Bogart said in a later interview. "She has a point of view. Startles me sometimes. I blink, and realize that she is looking at things with younger, clearer eyes, and that she knows more than I do. And I say, 'Look here, how does she know more'n me?'—and I realize why. She's smarter'n me, that's all."

Bogart was not the only one on the set to fall for her. "She was different looking, with an animal quality and great eyes," according to Fred De Cordova, who went on to a career as a prominent television producer but in 1944 was a young dialogue director just in from New York. "I found her fascinating, totally fascinating." He had called her at the home number wheedled out of a friend in the contracts department and asked her to dinner. It was not a good night, she told him. Ten days later he called again. Once more it was not a good night. He called a third time, "not giving up easily in those days. And a male voice answered the phone. I said, 'Hello, this is Fred De Cordova,' and Bogie said, 'Isn't there any way you're going to get the hint that Betty and I are together, and to stop bothering us with these silly phone calls?' I said, 'I think I've got the hint.' And that was that. And done in his best way—like, 'Listen, sweetheart, you're *bothering* us!' "

On the set, the two became inseparable, walking hand in hand for all to see. "They really were smitten with each other," Joy Barlowe, a Warner dancer taken on for the cafe scenes, said. "Just crazy about each other. You could tell by the looks. He always had his hand on her shoulder. And he called her Baby. They were always disappearing. That was when directors told the company, 'Okay, take a break, be back in fifteen.' And the rest of us, we'd be right back there. But they would disappear into one or another of their dressing rooms, and sometimes fifteen minutes ran a little longer. But we just thought, 'Oh, what the heck.' And they'd come out looking very happy, a little mussed up but nothing that you couldn't fix. I mean, they weren't *obscene* about anything."

Walter Surovy, watching them emerge in disarray, was reminded of the romantic comedies of his native Vienna and thought it perfectly delightful but not worth much comment: "Being European, I found it nobody's business." Others shared his attitude, Meta Wilde said. "They would go into his dressing room at the lunch hour and we would wait until they got ready to come out." Bacal would gaze up at the famous star "like a smitten movie fan [and he] responded in predictable male fashion, a malleable wad in the hands of the newcomer."

To Barlowe, "Bogie was more serious. Betty was pretty giggly—and silly. But cute. And funny. And Bogie got a little more giggly because of her." On the set, Wilde added, Bogart would swing along singing the nonsense hit "Mairzie Doats" in a raspy cigarette baritone, certainly not minding anybody seeing that he was in love with Betty and that she was in love with him.

Inevitably, the relationship affected the production. "Bogie had a lot of power," Barlowe explained. "He had a lot of know-how about cameras and angles, and because she was new, if he didn't like something he'd say, Is that really necessary? Or, Could we eliminate this? He'd even block *himself* out to get her right."

Hawks, in later interviews, insisted that Bogart's suggestions made his job easier. "I might have been in some trouble, using a brand-new kid like that. . . . And well, Bogart, he just fell in love with her. Without *that,* I'd have had a hell of a time."

Actors loved working for Hawks because he was an imaginative and talented craftsman of boundless versatility. He was known as an actors' director because he would discuss the material scene by scene, and when he rewrote, as he did throughout shooting a film, he took his cues from the company and used the script as a point of departure.

Dan Seymour described how "we'd sit down every morning, Marcel Dalio, Bogie, Betty, everybody. Hawks would say, for instance, 'You know the essence of the story, Bogie?' And Bogart would say, 'Yeah, I know the essence. It stinks.' So Hawks would say, 'Bogie, you say so-and-so to Dan.' Then he'd turn to me: 'What are you going to say to *him?*' I'd say, 'What the hell do you *want* me to say?' And he'd say, '*Answer* him. Do what the character would do, that's all.'

"They had a secretary writing it all down, and we'd do it again, and rehearse it. Then Hawks would look at Faulkner and ask, 'What do you think?' And Faulkner would reply, 'I think it's all right. It'll play, it'll play.' And that's how the whole show was done."

"The script was all there," one associate of Hawks said, "but every scene was sort of manufactured. That's how Howard made these actresses sound so good—'*You* say it.' And out would come this sort of marvelous spontaneity and the overlapping dialogue, which was so ahead of its time. That was his specialty."

"A good director," Bogart told an interviewer on the set, "is like a good psychiatrist. He builds up the confidence of his players until they forget their fears and inhibitions. Once you have that confidence [in a director], you're not afraid to take chances."

Neither, of course, was Hawks, whose casting was a leap of faith and a mix of the proven and the untried. On the one hand were Bogart, Walter Brennan, Dalio, and Seymour. On the other were Betty Bacall and composer-pianist Hoagy Carmichael, a close friend of Hawks who had never made a movie and whom Bogart later called a surprisingly excellent actor. Indeed, he told a friend, it was just a bit disturbing to see how easily Carmichael did it. "A great deal easier, I assure you, than for me to sit down and write 'Stardust.' I don't like to have my chosen profession made to look quite so simple."

Bogart also realized that Carmichael was "very, very serious" about his screen work. He found him at his mirror one day, studying the lines around his eyes. Carmichael had gone to bed early the night before and was now worried that the wrinkles might not correspond with those of the previous day. Another time, he had come up with the idea of chewing on a match—new to him, anyway, though not to the cast. The next day Bogart handed him a box of multi-colored kitchen matches. They were actors' "mood matches," Bogart solemnly assured him, color coded for use with various frames of attitude.

The atmosphere on the set spawned irreverence and a relaxed mood. Aldo Nadi, a former Italian fencing champion playing the Vichy captain's bodyguard, had insisted on the star treatment and his own chair. That didn't play well with Bogart.

"Nadi didn't have one word in the whole picture," Seymour said, "and he was a real schmuck. First day, he brings a chair with his name on it. So Bogie says to me, 'Sit on the chair and break it.' " Seymour weighed close to three hundred pounds. "Everybody sat in that chair! First Bogie would sit down on it as hard as he could, then *I'd* sit down, until finally we broke the thing. And Nadi was all upset. So Bogie said to the property guy, 'Bring him one of the *regular* chairs.' "

Once the cameras rolled, Bogart was all business. "He used to kid me, but when he did a scene with you, he held it together. It was give and take—you gave, he gave it back to you. And the scene played, it had motive. I've worked with a lot of big actors. Most of them were worried how they looked more than anything else and they wouldn't play the character. But with Bogart, every time was a characterization. He'd play to *you,* not to some camera over there. And he expected you to play to *him.*"

As an example, Seymour cited the scene at the bar where tough guys Sheldon Leonard and Seymour are trying to question Walter Brennan, playing Eddie, the old drunk. Bogart comes in to talk, and first he, then Seymour, picks up a bottle and sets it down. "That wasn't rehearsed. It just happened because we were working together. And when you've got a director who lets you play with it and feels that you know what you're doing, then it works out beautifully. But you could only do that with a good actor like Bogart."

Such an approach meant an almost stately pace of filming in a studio where an A production was given no more than six weeks and where front office tempers boiled if schedules lagged. But Hawks had the huge successes of *Sergeant York* and *Air Force* behind him; even more important, he was the quintessential WASP among the immigrants. He set his own rules with a lordly nonchalance that at times could intimidate even Jack Warner.

One day during rehearsals assistant director Jack Sullivan sidled up to Hawks and whispered something. Hawks smiled, got up, quietly thanked Sullivan, and walked off the sound stage, leaving the cast and crew puzzled. Bogart got to his feet and asked Sullivan what had happened. The assistant director whispered something to him. Bogart smiled, and went back to his seat.

A minute later, a crack of daylight flared at one end of the darkened sound stage and Jack Warner strode in with the gossip queen Louella Parsons. "How come you're not working?" he asked. "Where is everybody? I want Miss Parsons to see what's going on." Jack Sullivan took him aside and whispered yet again. Warner turned several shades of deepening red and hustled a confused Louella off the set. The company was dismissed, everyone but Bogart and Sullivan still unclear as to what had happened.

When they came outside, Hawks's car was gone. It was a power play in which Jack Warner for once came in second. Hawks ran a closed set, and even Warner himself couldn't come on without clearance. There had been no fireworks, simply the exercising of quiet, unquestioned authority, an authority of which, up until then, no one had been more mindful than his young protégée.

Meta Wilde watched with interest. "Betty would sit on the floor at Howard's feet and look up at him adoringly, like a little girl—which she *was*—and listen to Howard like he was God; which I think he thought he was at times. She was his creation. He trained her and gave her the right to a career. He *made* Lauren Bacall."

Hawks was not a man to cross. He was a tall, lanky midwesterner with pale blue eyes set in a long, aristocratic face, and smooth gray hair; he beguiled women and was sometimes called the Silver Fox. He spoke in an even, controlled monotone, never raising his voice, and was unfailingly polite if also aloof. He kept a tight rein on his emotions, his private life, and his set. At a price, of course. On his nightly drive home from the studio in his earlier days, punctually at six o'clock he would stop his car at the same corner, roll down the window, and throw up.

The tight control extended into his home. There was the glittering circle of friends that included Ernest Hemingway, Gary Cooper, and Cary Grant. And of course there was the Moraga Drive estate, overseen by his wife. The couple lived a life that on the surface seemed more scripted than real, as if they were characters in a Howard Hawks movie. At one point, Slim had had an inkwell made from the hoof of a favorite horse that had died, inscribed: "To the Silver Eagle of the American turf/from a slick chick."

Mrs. Hawks, a tall, elegant presence, beautifully dressed, would come almost every day, always in the company of her dark gray poodle. Its fur had black highlights, and its nails were done in a bright red. Dan Seymour thought it "very handsome-looking. And the biggest ham there was. She would put it on the café bar and it would walk up and down, sort of showing off. The nails were so long, you'd hear them tapping. It was really funny, but that's the way the upper class lives. She would talk with her husband first, then she'd go over to Betty and they'd go somewhere and talk. They were very thick, though Betty was her own gal."

The budding affair with Bogart and its intimation of divided loyalties threatened to alter Betty's adoration of Hawks. On the set, he was a patient mentor, creative and understanding in his use of fresh talent. But he was also proprietary, a latter-day Pygmalion who was not about to permit any interference with what he considered his creation. His feelings were a matter not of romance but of control and self-interest.

"Howard was cold—icy cold," Dee Hawks Cramer said. "He never got involved with his stars, the girls he created, because he was always finding new girls. I'm sure it was a business deal. Very cold-blooded. A commodity," in much the same category as a valuable brood mare or a particularly promising filly.

For the first several months, Betty Bacall knew only his beneficence. Then one night in late April, about two weeks before the end of production, she was commanded to come to the Hawks home. In her memoirs, the mature Bacall relived the terror of that confrontation: her mentor telling her in his quiet voice that she meant nothing at all to Bogart; that she was throwing away her big chance; that he, Hawks, was washing his hands of her and that he would send her to Monogram, a B studio on Hollywood's so-called Poverty Row that ground out product with titles like *Sarong Girl* and *Woman in Bondage.* She tearfully assured him that she would do better, then drove home and cried all night.

The next day, Bogart picked up the pieces and quieted her fears. She was much too valuable to Hawks and there was no way she would be sent to Monogram, he told her. Howard was simply jealous, that was all. Bogart also assured her of his feelings for her. She calmed down, but Bogart did not. What followed, according to studio records, was an angry confrontation between the two men, which threw the production into jeopardy amid clear indications that Bogart was threatening to walk. Jack Warner, called in as the peacemaker, asked Bogart to his office for a "personal talk to smooth over everything."

A summons to meet with Warner was usually cause for dread. His corner office was built for intimidation. Steps led down from the doorway into what seemed a pit, lit by a triple row of recessed ceiling lights that worked entirely to Warner's advantage. Along one wall was a huge mural of the United States. Sitting elevated behind the big black desk in the farthest corner and facing the visitor on the diagonal, Jack L. Warner loomed like a living bust on a dark pedestal.

But Bogart was now a money star and the balance of power was different from that in 1937, when he came to ask for an extra few hundred dollars. Sam Jaffe and Bogart's lawyer and business manager Morgan Maree had been pushing for a renegotiated deal. *To Have and Have Not* was two weeks behind schedule. Warner seized on the blowup with Hawks to use the one inducement that had always worked with Bogart—more money. Naturally, Warner told him, the wartime wage controls made a contract change a problem. But if Humphrey would put the new deal aside for a moment and just cooperate and finish the picture, well, the studio would gladly forgo the usual layoff deductions and thus add at least $33,000 to his salary. All this was done, Obringer wrote, in the hope that Bogart "would be a good boy and get in and pitch."

Bogart agreed. Hawks made no more threats. Filming continued. The following Monday, the first of May, Bacall, in a clinging black satin sheath held together at the bare midriff by a single plastic ring, stood beside Hoagy Carmichael at the piano, and sang "How Little We Know," the song that he and Johnny Mercer had written for her.

Maybe I'm only supposed to stay in your arms awhile,
As others have done.
Is this what I've waited for?
Am I the one?...

Some later accounts alleged that the actual singing was done by a very young Andy Williams, dubbed in for Bacall. But studio memos and production reports make it clear that the voice in the film is her own.

As she sang, across the lot in the executive building, the last touches were being put to the agreement converting Howard Hawks's discovery into the newest Warner star. In a final step, her backers granted legal permission to change her name: "In this connection her professional name is now Lauren Bacall."

That same April, Mayo turned forty. The last vestiges of her beauty were gone. She had let herself go, the cardinal sin in the movie colony, and was a squat, unkempt figure with lackluster hair pinned carelessly back with a cheap barrette. Stately, thin Lauren Bacall was the disaster that had been waiting to happen.

At first Bogart tried to make a show of life as usual. The couple celebrated Mayo's birthday at the home of their old friend Mischa Auer. Mayo sported the costly bracelet watch her husband gave her, and the Russian actor cooked dinner. It was an evening of good friendship and laughter, the three remembering how Auer had dropped his pants at their wedding reception.

The studio publicity department kept churning out stories about the happy, scrappy Bogarts in an attempt to shore up the image of the faithful husband in the face of rising, though still discreet, gossip. "It has been apparent since their return from a USO overseas jaunt that things have not been going well," Louella Parsons wrote. "Bogey has been seen more and more in the company of his bachelor friends . . . and at dinner minus Mayo who has heretofore practically been his shadow." When it became clear that something had to be said about Bacall, Warner Publicity head Alex Evelove and his staff dished up the relationship as an on-the-set flirtation, the sort of harmless attraction between a leading man and his leading lady that could add a bit of spice to a film's PR ("the star studied Miss Bacall's pert and pretty face, topped with the tawny blond hair . . .").

Bacall has written of furtive meetings on street corners, at the trailer home of boating friends of Bogart, even at her apartment, where a disapproving Natalie Bacal kept her distance. As in *Casablanca* days, the company always knew when Mayo was on the lot. It took only one ring from the gate saying she was coming through to make the two leads quickly unclasp their hands and move just a bit apart. Mayo, fighting back, tried to use the telephone as a weapon. Bogart told Joe Hyams about being called to the phone on the set to hear Mayo, her voice dripping acid: "Hello, lover boy. How're you doing with your daughter? She's half your age, you know."

It was a repeat of the Bergman situation, except that this time, Mayo wasn't imagining things. Bogart's tardiness or absences from home increased, and whether Mayo called friends, agents, or the studio, she always got the same answer: "He's out with the cast." On the set, wags began to refer to Bacall as The Cast. One day, after hearing that Bogart was out on his boat with "the cast," Mayo sped down to Newport, determined to have a confrontation. A short time later, Mary Baker received a call from the harbor police telling her that Mrs. Bogart was creating a disturbance. Mary drove down and found Mayo chasing around the docks, looking for her husband, while weary harbor cops tagged behind.

Early in the filming it was evident that Warners had a future star. Martin Weiser, put to work building up Bacall's image, found her a publicist's dream. She was eager to cooperate and quick to show her appreciation. Unlike most leading ladies, she wooed the flacks in the publicity department, and her efforts served her well.

"The *loveliest* young girl," Weiser enthused more than forty years later. "She'd come maybe two or three times a week. Knew our first names. We loved thinking up publicity for her. Lana Turner was the Sweater Girl; Ann Sheridan the Oomph Girl. So we called her The Look. Her head would go down and she'd look up, sort of. She was play-acting and getting away with it. *But you knew that she knew*—and it was funny and great."

The studio had assigned a photographer to shoot stills to be used in the ad campaign. One of the photos would be the basis for the poster artwork and for the publicity, and that single shot would define the movie to the public. The natural place to take the pictures was on the set during filming, but directors often didn't want publicity cameramen underfoot. When the set was unavailable, photographers could use a photo gallery atop steep wooden stairs behind New York street, but getting an actor to go up there was difficult, Weiser said. "When a picture is finished, the star wants to go on vacation. Or he has another picture waiting. Or they'd promise to come in the gallery, like Errol Flynn, and then say, Can't do it. Though there was that other type you could count on, like Ida Lupino, or Bette Davis."

Weiser approached Bogart to see if he could talk him into helping get a good photo for the ads. "He looked at me and smiled and said, 'I know, you want me to come in the gallery. You know I hate posing for stills, and I don't like coming in the gallery. Why don't you use one of my pictures? They all look the same. Just don't retouch them.' He would not approve any stills that had been retouched. 'I don't want to look like Van Johnson,' he'd say. In the early days we wanted to retouch that little cut on his lip. He refused. 'No, no, no, that's me! That's the way I am! Don't retouch those stills!' And we didn't."

Bogart's "no" to Weiser was gentle, "but he meant it." Weiser's only hope was to set up a gallery somewhere in a corner of the set, wait for a break in the shooting, and pray that he would be cooperative. Either that or get someone to persuade him.

The next time Bacall came in, Weiser had a proposition, sweetened by the realities of studio life. Her great promise notwithstanding, she was still a newcomer and an unproved quality, a leading lady whose credits were below the title; only Bogart's name was to be above. Originally, she had been listed after Dolores Moran. Weiser therefore suggested an arrangement that might work to their mutual benefit.

Even though she was in this picture, he told her, it didn't mean that the ads were going to use a shot of both Bogart and Bacall. "I hope they do, for *your* sake, but at this point nothing has been done. In the past it's always been a big head of Bogart, or Bogart doing something with a gun. It's possible that you might not be in the ad at all. Your name would have to be there, but it may not show. So maybe you can help me." Weiser told her of his plan to shoot on the set during a half-hour break. If she would bring Bogart over, "We'll get the shots *with you.* Not him alone. Do you think you could do that?

"Leave it to me," she said. "He'll come. I know he will."

A few days later, assistant director Jack Sullivan phoned Weiser about a coming break. The publicist, his photographer in tow, rushed to Bacall. A few minutes later, she and Bogart walked up, hand in hand.

Weiser's idea was for Bogart to grab Bacall and pull her toward him until they looked as if they're about to kiss. "I showed them just how I wanted Bogart's hand to go around her back, with his thumb on her shoulder. Then I shot it with speed lights. They could stop a bullet in action, and to me, this was an action shot. It wasn't posed. 'Don't worry,' I told them. 'You're not really posing. It's like making a movie, because it's so fast. You can move, but we don't know what we're getting, so we'll have to do it many times.'

"We shot again and again and again. I even stepped in and took Bacall in my arms to show him what I wanted. 'I know exactly what you want,' he said, and then he did it *perfectly.* He loved this girl and he was *enjoying* this. When I knew I had what I wanted I told them, 'Thanks very much.' And he said, 'No no no no, I think you need another shot—how about *this?*' And then, 'How about *this?*' Then, 'You gotta have a kiss shot.' And so he kissed her. Half the shots were of the back of his head and I knew I'd never use them, but they were enjoying themselves. So—what does it cost? It's just more film."

The next morning, Alex Evelove glared at Weiser over a desktop piled high with proofs and read him a lecture on wasting money: "You've got the back of Bogart's head, and you're shooting up her nostrils. You *need* this?" Weiser, citing Bogart's history of avoiding the gallery, argued that one good shot made it all worthwhile. Evelove, half out of weariness, finally said, "You may be right. But let me know about these things." Weiser exploded. "I *didn't* know about these things. *Bogart wanted more shots!*"

Years later Weiser said, "He was so happy in the arms of Bacall. *Very* happy. And she played it beautifully. What an actress! And the shots! You can't take a bad shot of Betty Bacall. New York picked out the one which I knew they would." It has Bacall with her arms around Bogart's waist while he tightly grips her upper arms. She has a sultry look; his is one of deep passion. "It became a whole campaign," and a movie poster classic as well.

After sixty-two days of production, *To Have and Have Not* wrapped shooting on May 10. There were more publicity photos, and the company worked through dinner, ending with the closing scene of the cafe orchestra playing as Marie and Morgan—"Slim" and "Steve"—walk out the door to the waiting boat and happiness together. Bacall and Bogart, however, went off in separate directions—Bacall to dinner with the Hawkses, Bogart presumably home to Mayo. Bacall would later write of the feeling of emptiness, watching him drive away. The studio released the story that Mr. and Mrs. Bogart were going to spend some time at Newport, aboard the *Sluggy*. "There you will find Mayo busily engaged with a four-burner shipmate preparing meals for Humphrey's fabulous appetite whetted by salt air."

Only two facts disturbed this idyllic picture. Bogart and Bacall continued to meet in secret, and Mayo had broken her foot. A boarding accident on the boat, said studio publicity. Falling down drunk, Bogart told Bacall.

He had been working without a break since the spring of 1943 and was physically and emotionally exhausted, though Warners seemed unaware of his condition. He had expected some time off. Instead, the studio immediately sent him a new script, based on the best-selling *God Is My Co-pilot*, a religion-drenched recycling of wartime clichés. Bogart was assigned to play a Bible-thumping aviator.

Absolutely not, he told the studio, setting off the usual round of orders and recriminations. This was now the familiar story of his career: a big hit soured in the aftermath. "Our pal Bogart doesn't think *God Is My Co-Pilot* is big enough for him," Steve Trilling wrote to Jack Warner. "Apparently he would rather play the Co-pilot."

Jack Warner wired from New York, recalling their "lovely talk," the fake goodfellow tone not hiding the customary reproaches—"IS THIS

WHAT YOU CALL BEING A REGULAR GUY?"—amid the usual litany of all that Warners had done for him. In a P.S. to Trilling Warner added, "THIS IS REALLY A TOUGH WIRE AND I MEAN TOUGH BECAUSE I AM SICK AND TIRED OF THESE UNGRATEFUL PUPS ANNOYING MY INDIGESTION AND AM NOT GOING TO GIVE ANY MORE THAN ONE STOMACH I HAVE ALREADY GIVEN."

Bogart's response was to offer to tear up his contract. "YOU SPEAK OF MY SUCCESS AS IF YOU ALONE WERE RESPONSIBLE FOR IT. I FEEL THAT I HAVE HAD SOMETHING TO DO WITH THAT SUCCESS. . . . YOU ARE USING THE BOX OFFICE VALUE I FORTUNATELY HAVE AT THE MOMENT TO BOLSTER A PICTURE BY FORCING ME INTO A MEDIOCRE PART. . . . YOU HAVE ASSIGNED A DIRECTOR IN WHOM I HAVE NO CONFIDENCE. . . . I HAVE WAITED ONE SOLID YEAR FOR A CHANCE TO GET A FEW UNINTERRUPTED WEEKS TO GAIN BACK MY HEALTH AND PREVENT A BREAKDOWN ONE AND ONE HALF WEEKS AFTER THE START OF IT THE WIRES AND THE THREATS AND THE SAME OLD STORY START AGAIN. . . . I AM TIRED OF THE STUDIO'S ATTITUDE THAT I AM A HALF-WITTED CHILD."

Roy Obringer sent off the usual suspension notice. Less than three weeks after completing one of his biggest films, Bogart was barred from working at Warners and, without Warners' permission, at any other studio as well. Sam Jaffe, who tried to smooth things over, was also banned from the lot. He was unable to "control" his actors, Obringer chided. Jaffe said that he was sorry, but Bogart didn't work for him—he worked for Bogart.

Bogart's single bright spot in that summer of anger and frustration was Bacall, a source of glowing youth and optimism in what must have seemed the desert of his middle age. Film and real life had melded. They called each other Slim and Steve, the nicknames of their characters, taken from the nicknames Howard and Nancy Hawks used for each other.

"Bogart was enchanted with her," a friend told Joe Hyams. "I think he was fascinated by this unformed thing which he could make into the perfect wife. And she wanted to be Mrs. Bogart." As Mary Baker put it, "She courted him as much as he courted her."

Bacall has written of driving at any hour to meet him on the boat or at a spot on the highway to Newport Beach. She had, she said, so much to give—"all the love that had been stored inside of me all my life for an invisible father." Age mattered not at all. "I was older than nineteen in many ways, and he had such energy and vitality he seemed to be no particular age." Bogart wrote her letters that were touching in their tenderness and vulnerability. She was his last love, he wrote, and even if he lost her, he would love her and watch over her all his life. He wished he were younger, so that there might be more years ahead of them.

At the same time, his sense of obligation held him back. Mayo was, after all, his wife, and she was physically and mentally disintegrating. He knew, too, that he had not done much to help her. Each of them tended to attack weakness, and in that way they had been too well matched for their own good. Now, though the marriage had been destructive to both, he had a future and she did not.

"I don't want to break this marriage up," he told a friend, "but I like [Betty's] youth, her animal-like behavior and don't-give-a-damn attitude."

He had been raised on a few bedrock certainties: the Victorian spirit of duty, the personal need for responsibility, for doing what had to be done. He had demonstrated his adherence to this code by taking on his father's debts, as well as the burdens of his aging and ailing mother and of his manic-depressive sister. That same code now had him at war with himself. Happiness was within his grasp, but seizing it meant abandoning his responsibility to Mayo. If he cut her loose, he could save himself. But he would also cut her lifeline.

That June, a three-car motorcade made its way down the coast to Huntington Beach for a sneak preview of *To Have and Have Not.* Jack Warner, Steve Trilling, and Charlie Einfeld were in the lead, followed by Howard and Slim Hawks, with the writers Faulkner and Furthman riding behind. Audience reaction exceeded all expectation. Einfeld said that it would be a bigger hit than *Casablanca,* and that Bacall was a combination of Garbo and Dietrich. Like the heroine of Warners' *42nd Street,* she had gone on stage an unknown and come off a star.

Her handlers immediately began to jockey for position, and each side—Warners and H-F Productions—defined its interest in what was now a million-dollar property. The studio's consent to Hawks's co-starring her had not come without a price. Warners' insistence on a split of her contract with H-F was a reasonable request back in January, when all Hawks had to go on was a promising screen test. Now, the bill was due. The two sides agreed to pool their interests, each with a claim on "the minor's services," as the court put it, for two photoplays a year. The deal affirmed Hawks's "continued interest" in the joint property, but it was so complicated an agreement that the studio itself was unclear as to where

Hawks's jurisdiction ended and its own began. A sheaf of documents was drawn up in the fall. Betty signed. Then her mother signed. Warner's newest sex symbol was still a minor, and every move had to be approved by the cooperative courts.

Bacall might have been the biggest comer since Garbo, but she was also the bargain of the century. She was still under contract to Hawks; while negotiations went on that summer he generously raised her salary to $200 a week. She had made $125 a week during filming, the total sum of her services coming to $1,687.50 plus overtime of $85.92, payable to Howard Hawks. The publicity buildup and what passed for Hollywood reporting would omit the fact that Bogart, at $2,750 a week, had starred opposite a leading lady whose pay for the entire picture came to a little over half his weekly salary.

However underpaid Bacall was, she was, on the other hand, still special and protected. She was as much Hawks's property as the studio's and he would do all he could to protect his investment—which hadn't yet returned a dividend. The new arrangements did provide Betty with a Warner salary and a $5,000 bonus, but for Hawks, there was no immediate windfall nor any up-front money for assigning rights in the property he had so carefully developed. He twice approached Jack Warner about sharing the costs of the year he had needed to train Bacall, and for her mother's expenses. H-F lawyers presented a bill for $4,900, not excluding sixty-eight cents paid to the Los Angeles county clerk for document registration fees. J. L. declined to pay it. This was strictly Hawks's investment, he said, and the studio *had* after all put the young lady in an important picture. Besides, H-F Productions was due 20 percent of the gross on *To Have and Have Not* (though only after Warners deducted what they had paid to H-F for *Battle Cry*.)

That summer Charlie Einfeld's crew in Publicity geared up to sell Lauren Bacall as the screen's hottest new attraction. On the cover of the thick press book was Weiser's shot, with its strong suggestion of stand-up sex, emblazoned with the banner: "BOGART—IN LOVE WITH THIS KIND OF WOMAN!" A two-page centerfold was filled with a collage of syndicated columns and splashy picture stories under the headline: " 'THE LOOK' BLANKETS THE COUNTRY WITH PUBLICITY BREAKS."

Publicists knocked out releases that reinvented her past: Miss Bacall was from New York City and had been named Lauren after her grandmother—a bit of fantasy that would have amused Sophie Weinstein. "She is the daughter of parents who trace their American ancestry back several generations," the copy continued, hinting at society connections and presumably taking the curse off her real origins. Elaborate posters and lobby cards were printed: "WARNERS TEAM A GREAT STAR AND A BRILLIANT DISCOVERY."

But the great star was on suspension and the brilliant discovery was rushing off to assignations with him, often in Newport, where she stayed with friends on their boat. Bogart entered some small sailboat races and won two, which, she said, "gave him more of a kick than any movie could have done." And the peace of the water invigorated him. "This is why I love sailing," he told Bacall. "The sea—the air—it's clean and healthy and away from the Hollywood gossip and leeches."

In late August he slipped her aboard the *Sluggy* while Mayo was being treated for her broken foot. The rendezvous was disrupted by Methot's unexpected return. Bacall writes of nervously crouching in the head while Bogart and sympathetic friends talked Mayo off the boat.

The wrangling with the studio continued. Warners offered Bogart a way out of his suspension by going on loanout to Columbia in a western for the talented Sam Wood, director of *Goodbye Mr. Chips, A Night at the Opera, Pride of the Yankees, Kings Row,* and *For Whom the Bell Tolls.* Wood, eager to have Bogart, drove down to Newport to talk with him aboard the *Sluggy,* and Bogart, after months of inactivity, was ready to work. Sam Wood was a hotshot, he told Trilling in a phone conversation in late July. If the script was good, he might be interested. Only one thing held him back: What was Howard Hawks going to do? Trilling said he didn't know. Nothing was set. Just some plans for a story with a detective background. Now was Bogart going to Columbia or not?

Hawks, however, was not at work on merely "some story." He was winding up negotiations for the screen rights to Raymond Chandler's 1939 novel, *The Big Sleep*—"a highly censorable detective yarn," Trilling informed J. L. Unlike the Sam Wood film, it had a part for Bacall.

Bogart played for time. He would wait until Sam had more to show, he told Trilling. He loved to work, but he could wait. As things turned out, he would have to wait quite a while. At the peak of his popularity, he was suddenly facing one of the longest suspensions of his career.

That fall, Warners prepared for its biggest release since *Casablanca.* The circumstances surrounding its stars were rich with irony. Its sex symbol was an inexperienced nineteen-year-old; its celebrated male lead was sitting in limbo on a boat; and his fast-disintegrating marriage was being peddled to the press as a model of contentment by a studio desperate to apply damage control.

"He and Mayo have common interests," an interviewer for *Life* gushed. "Both are unpretentious and their pleasures simple and childlike. . . . Aboard their cruiser the Bogarts lead a clear-eyed, ruddy-cheeked life."

"In five years," Mayo told the reporter, "we're going to retire and become beachcombers." Then, looking at Bogart she added, "That is, if Pa can keep his hair and teeth that long." She was smiling as she said it. To the man from *Life,* it seemed the usual earthy humor of the battling but fun-loving Bogarts. In fact, it was a declaration of war.

CHAPTER 14

The Lengthy Good-bye

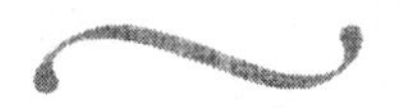

There was a flimsy cease-fire before the hostilities on North Horn Avenue reached a crescendo in mid-October 1944, following the start of production on *The Big Sleep*. Bogart and Bacall did not see each other from late summer until early autumn. He had counseled caution after the near disaster on the *Sluggy*, and by mutual agreement the affair was suspended, contact limited to the flowers that arrived on Bacall's doorstep the day she turned twenty. Mayo, tearful and abject, had sworn to cut out her drinking. Bogart, though restless and resentful, finally agreed to one last attempt to save the marriage.

He explained his reasons to Bacall when they met again on October 10, the first day of shooting on *The Big Sleep*. He professed his love for her and told her how many times he had wanted to call; but Mayo had promised to reform, and he owed her the chance.

"I said I'd have to respect his decision," Bacall wrote, "but I didn't have to like it."

Hawks initially had been uninterested in another pairing of Bogart and Bacall. *His Girl Friday* (1940), with Cary Grant and Rosalind Russell, and *Ball of Fire* (1941), with Gary Cooper and Barbara Stanwyck, two of his best films, were fast-talking, funny love stories with an edge, and he wanted to get back to comedy. His next production was to be based on the Broadway hit *Dark Eyes*. The screwball plot about two Russian aristocrats had been bought by Warners with the hope that

Marlene Dietrich would like it—or even better, that Greta Garbo, who had not made a picture since *Two-Faced Woman* (1941), would want to do the flip side of her ardent-Communist role in *Ninotchka* (1939). The film had been on the books for months, set to go pending the completion of *To Have and Have Not.* Hawks's director's fee was to be paid up front, and H-F Productions and Warners were to split the profits.

But Garbo and Dietrich remained as elusive as their screen images. More important, there were fears that the screenplay would offend Russian sensibilities by even *seeming* to debunk a valiant ally. Amid memos about "bad taste" and "political dynamite" (this last in reference to a satiric portrait of a red-baiting senator), the project was shelved, ostensibly because of casting problems, actually because of Hollywood fears of political incorrectness. Only in 1944 could a movie studio fear being censored because it might be viewed as anti-Soviet.

Hawks and the studio talked of another screwball comedy. Various possibilities were discussed, and various leading ladies were sounded out—Ginger Rogers, Jean Arthur, Ann Sheridan, Barbara Stanwyck. They all wanted their vacations first, though, and Hawks was eager to get started. For a time it seemed as though Hawks considered every option except that of using the actress he had under contract.

At the time, *To Have and Have Not* was going through two previews and drawing uniform raves for the Bogart-Bacall combination, especially for Bacall. Hawks, if only because he was out of options, bowed to the inevitable. Like its predecessor, *The Big Sleep* was to be a compromise, a way out for Howard Hawks, who once again passed up the movie he wanted in favor of the one that was at hand.

Shooting began on a Tuesday. By Wednesday of the following week, Bogart had packed his bags and moved out of 1210 North Horn.

Mayo was an addict left to fight her habit on her own. She had tried going cold turkey and for a while had managed with difficulty to stay away from the elaborate bar set up in the corner of the den, with its brass-studded bar stools, its big mirror, and the rows of polished glasses reflecting the light from the ship's lamp on the opposite wall. But it took more than determination to overcome a chemical dependency, compounded now by anxiety at the thought of her husband spending every day with her twenty-year-old rival. Bogart came home one day to find her messily drunk in the den, and the screaming fights resumed. Bogart, depressed, sometimes joined in the drinking, but other times just disappeared into the night.

On October 19, 1944, Warner Brothers announced in a statement carried nationwide by the Associated Press that Mr. and Mrs. Humphrey Bogart had decided to separate after six years of marriage. "I believe the public will realize that this is of deep concern to us," Bogart said through his studio, "and will respect the fact that we both feel too deeply about it to discuss it."

"He is regretful," Alex Evelove wrote in a memo to Jack Warner, "but feels there was no other way."

A constant parade of celebrities passed through the Beverly Hills Hotel on Sunset Boulevard, so bellhop Ken Leffers wasn't particularly impressed when room service sent him off with a glass, some ice, and a bottle of beer for Humphrey Bogart, who had just checked in. Room 207 was one of the smallest suites, near the lobby. Bogart met him at the door, took the order off the tray, and set it down. Then he pulled out a handful of change from his pocket, carefully counted out the cost of the beer, and handed Leffers a nickel tip. "He could have made a mistake not giving me a quarter," Leffers later said, "but I doubt it."

Bogart arranged for Bacall to come unnoticed to the hotel. She would write of slipping through a side entrance late at night for a tryst that soured when Bogart, anxious and disheveled, answered the door to find that Bacall had brought along a girlfriend whom she wanted him to meet.

Mayo dialed the hotel incessantly, but Bogart refused her calls. Ill and isolated, she had as her only trump card her rapidly deteriorating physical condition, and she played it in a telegram to their close friend Louis Bromfield at the Gotham Hotel in New York. "SIT TIGHT" was the response; and Bromfield and his secretary, George Hawkins, set about contacting Bogart. Hours later, man and wife were on the phone. She promised to enter a hospital. Buffy Methot, down from Portland, was at once peacemaker and nurse, caring for her daughter and smoothing the rough spots. By mutual consent, a few days later a cleaned-up and sober Mayo went to the Beverly Hills Hotel and presented herself at the door of suite 207, a penitent seeking absolution. Ken Leffers, making a delivery sometime later, found the couple seated at a small table on which was a miniature wedding cake.

On November 1, less than two weeks after the Bogarts had separated, the press announced their reconciliation. News photographers snapped the couple at a nightclub on the Sunset Strip—Bogart in his pinstripes, smiling his crinkly smile, lifting a glass with a here's-looking-at-you-kid flourish, and Mayo in a flowered silk dress, blushing, her hair waved and burnished, a cluster of white flowers on either side.

"Mayo and I have decided to try it all over again," he told reporters. "We're returning to our normal battling."

"I love him," she announced. "In fact, I adore him."

"Both said they had dismissed their attorneys," the Associated Press story read, "and that there would be no divorce."

On the set of *The Big Sleep,* Lauren Bacall applied ice packs to her eyes swollen by crying. After a week with no scenes to play, she had returned the last day in October and was sitting in Makeup when Bogart came to tell her he'd moved back. Mayo, he explained, was ill and needed him.

The news media were kept off the set that day. Hawks said nothing. "He'd be glad when this picture was over," Bacall wrote later.

Up to that point, filming had gone reasonably well. Bogart had slipped easily into the character of the world-weary, hard-boiled detective Philip Marlowe, in command of his role from the first line on: "My name's Marlowe. General Sternwood wanted to see me." Domestic chaos notwithstanding, he turned up ready to go every morning at nine, showing the professionalism that always commanded the respect of his directors, including the demanding Howard Hawks.

"Howard raved about him," Dee Hawks Cramer said. "Bogart had everything—excellent background; stage experience, which Howard was in awe of; humble, didn't have airs. An ordinary guy. But a professional. And *on* the set, in spite of the drinking." Regis Toomey, a veteran of Hawks and Frank Capra movies, played Marlowe's friend in the DA's office. "Bogie always knew his lines, knew what he was doing all the time. If he wanted anything changed, he'd note it in his script before we got to it and he'd ask the director, 'Would it bother you if we did this?' And usually the director would agree with him."

William Faulkner again kept pace with the needs on the set. He was joined by Leigh Brackett, a bright, diminutive, blond-haired woman who wrote dialogue tougher than anyone else's. With *The Big Sleep* she began a career that would include three more Hawks films and an early draft of George Lucas's *The Empire Strikes Back.* Toward the end of the year, Jules Furthman was brought in to help with the problematic ending. It was, in Hawks's fashion, a close-knit company, with everyone viewing the rushes together. The script evolved through the regular interplay among the writers and the director and the actors. Hawks told Dee Cramer that Bogart was "inspired" on the set. "He brought so much to it. Totally prepared, wonderful ideas, and Howard *loved* that."

In one scene—an antique bookshop fronting for a porn operation where Marlowe tries to gain access by posing as a customer—Bogart, his hat pushed back, glasses on his nosetip, lent the part a nerdy fussiness. His cue was from Chandler's text, but he laid on a comedic gloss that was his own (and that in retrospect can seem to mock a forties stereotype of a homosexual). Hawks, untroubled by such concerns, loved the relaxed way it came about. "We were just playing around," he said later, "just playing around."

As always, Bogart was helpful to supporting players. At the end of her scene as a cabby flagged down by Marlowe in a follow-that-car sequence, Joy Barlowe was supposed to reach into a vest pocket and hand Bogart her card. ("Call this number."/"Day and night?"/"Night's better—I work during the day.") Simple enough, but her driver's gloves continually interfered with her cleanly grabbing the card.

Barlowe, concerned by the delay she caused, "could see everyone saying, 'When is she going to get that card out?' Or, 'Where did they find *her*?' I was so nervous that he'd say something and I'd be kicked off." Instead, Bogart quietly suggested that she keep the card above the visor. It worked. "He had that much patience, and who was *I* to him? He was crazy about Lauren Bacall and I was just another nineteen-year-old little chubface. But he took his time, said 'Try it that way, honey,' rather than saying, 'Could you get somebody else, she's holding up production.' He was so kind about it, and I was so relieved, that it was a breeze."

Regis Toomey, viewing the rushes one day before lunch, watched one of his scenes with Bogart and hooted, "Oh, shit!" To Toomey, his performance was "wooden. It wasn't a terribly important scene, but it was the two of us, and there was something there that moved the plot." Hawks asked Bogart's opinion. Bogart shrugged; "Oh, it was all right." When Hawks told him that Toomey was unhappy, Bogart quickly suggested they shoot it again. To Toomey, "This was unusual for a star, because he might have said, 'What the hell does how Regis feels about it have to do with the picture?' " The stage had already been cleared for the next scene, and there was a wait while it was reset, but neither Hawks nor Bogart complained. After the cast saw the retake, Bogart complimented a grateful Toomey. "It was a simple thing, but I remembered it. He never gave you the impression that he wanted to be regarded as a star. Anything but. He was one of the cast."

It was the congeniality, the kidding, the small amusing incidents that most of the actors would remember. Martha Vickers, the teenager playing Bacall's nymphomaniac younger sister, was supposed to simulate an orgasm in a scene that was discarded in the editing. The problem was, Vickers was a total innocent who hadn't a clue what an orgasm was, let alone how to go about simulating one. Hawks, for once, was stumped. It was left to Toomey, the product of a strict Irish Catholic upbringing, to explain what was wanted.

"This girl didn't know *anything.* I asked, 'Are you a virgin?' 'Uh, yes.' 'Do you know what an orgasm is? Mr. Hawks wants you to be having an orgasm here.' 'No, I don't know what it is.' 'You don't know what an *orgasm* is?' 'No.' " After Toomey explained, "She got the idea all right. Howard liked the scene very much. 'Reg,' he said, 'if I ever have to explain an orgasm again, I'll have you come and do it.' And Bogie just laughed and laughed."

The afternoon of Monday, November 6, shooting wound up early. "Mr. Bogart slated to make an electioneering speech," unit manager Eric Stacey noted in his report.

The 1944 election, in which Franklin D. Roosevelt ran for a fourth term, would be the last instance for many years to come of Hollywood liberalism triumphant and in sync with Washington. Industry activists under the banner of the Hollywood Democratic Committee (HDC) spearheaded voter-registration drives, fielded their own candidates, and supported an open foreign policy. They favored pro-labor laws and "full rights for all racial and minority groups." This last was in part a response to increasing tensions in Los Angeles, which was changing from a big small town of transplanted white midwesterners to a sprawling multiracial urban center with all the attendant problems: unemployment, housing shortages, job discrimination, racial hostilities, and a rise in Klan activity. The year before, in the "zoot-suit riots," mobs of servicemen had torn through the streets assaulting Latinos while the police looked on. The HDC called for an investigation.

Studio front offices competed to stage media events for national politicians and issues. Jack Warner's private dining room was turned into a war room, where Roosevelt supporters planned strategy and studio executives worked on advertising and publicity. Industry Republicans, centered at MGM, staged a rally at the hundred-thousand-plus–seat Los Angeles Memorial Coliseum for FDR's challenger, New York governor Thomas E. Dewey, the model for the hotshot prosecutor of the old Warner crime movies. The multi-star spectacular was directed by Cecil B. DeMille; Ginger Rogers, the vice-chair of Hollywood for Dewey, called the event "a mobilization against the New Deal." Three weeks later, Hollywood for Roosevelt, co-chaired by Jack Warner, Sam Goldwyn, and Katharine Hepburn, honored FDR's running mate, Senator Harry Truman, at the cavernous Shrine Auditorium. Afterward, at a fund-raising dinner for the National Democratic Committee at the Ambassador Hotel, stars and producers were entertained by Groucho Marx and Danny Kaye dancing in drag to Gene Kelly's choreography, and by Judy Garland singing "The Song of Checkbooks."

Bogart was on the program committee. As his private problems drove him from home to hotel and back again, the Democratic National Committee had difficulty reaching him to ask if he would make a five-minute broadcast on behalf of FDR. Once they did, the answer was easy—"available almost any time."

On a Saturday night in late October, Bogart read a script he had approved, about "a man named Roosevelt," and poured scorn on Republican opposition to voting rights for GIs serving overseas. The guys he'd met in Africa and Italy, he said, thought about the future—"about the peace and international relations, about jobs and security"—when they weren't busy trying to stay alive. "And I learned just how cockeyed Republican Senator Robert A. Taft was when he said—and I quote: 'they were out of touch with the country.' It seems to me that if a man is ready to *die* for his country, he's not exactly out of touch with it."

It was Rick Blaine campaigning for FDR, and Bogart was one of the Democrats' most powerful assets in what promised to be a tight race. Jack Warner, in New York for a visit and to meet with party leaders, was asked by national committee chairman Robert Hannegan to loan them Bogart for a special broadcast on election eve.

The committee had planned a live, hour-long political spectacular to air on all four major networks, a parade of stars, public figures, and ordinary citizens. It was an unparalleled use of the medium in a final effort to reach the undecided. Its creator, Norman Corwin, CBS's top writer-producer, the poet laureate of the airwaves and celebrant of the New Deal, wanted Bogart as the anchor.

Corwin saw in him a "magnetic quality, so very American. He had universal appeal. He didn't have big biceps. He didn't have a jutting jaw. He wasn't Dick Tracy. But he had manly qualities. He was tough without being aggressive, a guy you would want to sit down at a bar with, to say nothing of inviting into your home."

After Warner had given his approval, Corwin stopped by North Horn Avenue. Bogart was "cordial and amenable. No frills; just very straightforward. He said yes right away when he was asked. There were no ifs, no conditions, no saying, 'Well, if I like the script . . . ,' no feeling that you had to run it by his agent. He was quite articulate on political matters and glad to be part of this effort, because we had to make sure FDR *won.*"

Over thirty stars went on the air the evening of November 6. There were songs by Earl Robinson and "Over the Rainbow" lyricist-composer E. Y. Harburg. Judy Garland sang "You Gotta Get Out and Vote." Remote pickups from across the country added the voices of public leaders and carefully selected plain folks—soldiers, farmers, housewives, office workers—who praised the New Deal and blasted the "big money boys." Vocal effects created a "Roosevelt train" ("All aboard for tomorrow!") that achieved a bandwagon momentum as a string of celebrities—Rita Hayworth, Gene Kelly, Lana Turner, John Garfield, Claudette Colbert, and many more—declared themselves with all the fervor of the faithful at a revival. Corwin "had them lined up in the studio, feeding to a mike—'*I'm* Groucho Marx! *I'm* Linda Darnell! *I'm* Jane Wyman!' I know it sounds crude today, but it had shape, and it had rhythm, and it had a kind of fetching energy."

It was a New Deal show all the way, the accent on jobs, social justice, the peace to come, racial equality, and hopes for the United Nations. Clarence Muse, who had almost played Sam in *Casablanca,* sang the "Free and Equal Blues" with Earl Robinson:

I went down to the Saint James Infirmary
And I saw some plasma there
And I ups and asks the doctor man
Was the donor from Asia, Africa, America or where?

James Cagney, Danny Kaye, Keenan Wynn, and Groucho Marx made up a barbershop quartet:

The old Red scare
It ain't what it used to be
Ain't what it used to be
Ain't what it used to be. . . .

Bogart, at the microphone throughout, held it all together as the broadcast switched between coasts in a buildup of speakers—Roosevelt's special envoy Averill Harriman, the prominent Republican civil rights lawyer Bartley Crum, and finally FDR himself, introduced not by Bogart but by a woman who was the youngest voter in America, herself introduced by the oldest voter in the country. Bogart, to the manner born, segued easily among the patricians. To Corwin, "this wasn't a character he was playing. He was playing Bogie. And he did it supremely well."

In the next day's returns, Roosevelt topped Dewey by some three million votes, of which at least one third, the NDC told Corwin, were swing votes captured by the Monday night broadcast. The Dewey forces inadvertently added to the program's effect. In the hope of cashing in on the huge audience expected for the Democrats' show, the Republican National Committee had purchased the time slot following the broadcast. However, at the last minute comedian Jimmy Durante, under conservative pressure, dropped out of the Corwin show. His sudden departure left the script five minutes short, and the broadcast ended at 9:55. The networks filled the dead air with organ music. America turned off its radios and went to bed.

As a New Deal pageant speaking for the liberal wing of the party alone, the program also revealed hidden fissures in the organization; Corwin himself later said that the show "was rather radical" for the 1940s, a notion shared by others at the time. For instance, when the planning began, Jack Warner had been entirely cooperative. He both authorized use of Bogart and gave blanket permission for all Warner employees to "make public appearances or do anything else that will help anyone on the Democratic Party ticket." Within a week, however, he had become wary of the production and of an agenda he could not control, and wired publicity head Alex Evelove, "KEEP MY NAME OFF IT."

Warner, adept at sensing political change, was aware of the deep undercurrent of right-wing feeling in Hollywood. After the election, a small group of conservative industry people gathered to assess the damage from Roosevelt's election. Calling themselves the Motion Picture Alliance for the Preservation of American Ideals, they had organized earlier that year to ferret out "un-American ideas" allegedly existing in the film business. The organization had supporters in Washington and Sacramento and saw Martin Dies's House Committee on Un-American Activities as its champions. Its members included stars, directors, producers, and writers: Sam Wood. Walt Disney. Clark Gable. Gary Cooper. Many were from MGM, but the executive committee also included the suave, handsome Casey Robinson who had contributed so much to the success of *Casablanca.* As the war neared its end, the liberal Hollywood coalition that it had so far held together was now coming steadily apart. The coalition's hopes were pinned on the reelected commander in chief, an aging man in visibly failing health, and the Motion Picture Alliance wanted to exert its influence wherever possible.

Mayo grew complacent following Bogart's return. Mistaking a skirmish for the entire war, she quickly slid back into her old habits. One morning at three o'clock, Bogart stumbled to the phone and called Bacall. "I miss you, Baby," he said before the receiver was torn from his hand. Bacall stood paralyzed as Mayo's voice suddenly pierced the line—"Listen, you Jewish bitch, who's going to wash his socks?"—and screamed obscenities at her rival.

On December 4, the news media announced that Humphrey Bogart had again left home. "This time, he says, his separation from his wife of six years . . . is final." Mrs. Bogart, Louella Parsons reported, had retained the noted lawyer Jerry Giesler. "It's hard to break up a marriage of six years," Bogart told the columnist, "but we have had so many fights I believe it is the right thing to do. . . . She can have anything she wants if she will let me go—and I believe she is too sensible to want to hold me."

Privately, it wasn't so simple. "I don't want a big settlement," Mayo told Hedda Hopper, Parsons's chief competitor. "I want him because I love him."

During their marriage, she had often seemed the stronger of the two, domineering and intimidating. His longtime friend Clifton Webb was appalled by the term "battling Bogart," despite the documented black eyes and domestic disruptions. "Why, any woman could walk all over him. The man's a softie and—I might add—a very gallant one." "Mayo," said a friend who asked for anonymity, "will never in the world let any girl walk off with Bogie. She'd rather hang for murder than see someone else his wife." But now the woman everyone knew as Sluggy seemed to implode. She broke down in tears during every phone call as she told her story to reporters.

As Mayo increasingly retreated from reality, Buffy once again arrived from Portland. Against all advice, Mayo kept trying to reach her husband, getting Buffy to front for her when he wouldn't take her calls. Bogart's affection for his mother-in-law was undiminished; and as gently as he could, he told her that he wasn't coming back. Mayo kept flailing.

"What can I do?" she cried when Hedda Hopper called. "He hasn't come home and he tells me he won't come home. But it is *his* home and I want him in it. I don't want to do anything to hurt him." Buffy took the phone in mid-sentence. "Mayo isn't capable of making any decisions at this time. She's very upset." End of call.

"There is no fight in Mayo these days," Louella Parsons told her readers.

Boozy, plump Lolly Parsons had always had a soft spot for the Bogarts. Their first separation had been her exclusive. Her insistence in 1941 that he appear on her nationally syndicated radio show broke the impasse between Bogart and Jack Warner and got him off suspension. But as power-hungry as Parsons was, and however ruthless she might be in getting a story, she was shaken by the sound of the once-feisty woman weeping uncontrollably over the phone and begging her to call Bogart and ask when he was coming home.

When Parsons reached him at the Beverly Wilshire Hotel, he played it straight. Nobody loved the gossip queens. They were at once the guardians of studio-imposed morality and violators of basic privacy, regarding stars as their performing seals. But in a business where careers could be wrecked by a single story, Bogart liked Parsons the most.

The marriage was all over, he told her, asking that she please make Mayo understand. "I've tried to tell her through her mother, but Mayo won't listen. I'm not going home. I can't go on with the battles we've had for six years, and I want a new life."

In the tumultuous weeks between his first and second flights from home, he was punctilious about meeting his obligations on the set. Only after he moved out and was alone in his hotel room, able to mull over the past and future without distraction, did the doubts and fears surface.

He worried for Mayo, who had often threatened suicide and whose whole life had become an exercise in self-destruction; although he wanted a new start for himself, he felt he had failed her. Besides the question of dividing up the marital assets, there was conscience money to be paid. Obviously he would be generous, but it would be a new obligation, touching off his lifelong fears of going broke. Then there was the matter of Bacall's youth and his being a quarter of a century older. His wives had always been contemporaries. Now he was taking on a girl whose entire life span was less than the difference in their ages. She would want children. He was childless despite three marriages.

For Bogart at forty-four, the future was more intimidating than the past and all its problems. In their stolen moments together, Bacall found him "hypersensitive," his usual humor replaced by a flaring temper. She was in love with a man, as she later put it, who was turning his life upside down. And about to do the same to a film.

Jack Warner raged at the delays and Hawks promised to do better, but the pressure to finish filming forced cuts in a story line that had become too complicated to follow. Raymond Chandler's *The Big Sleep,* like Hammet's *The Maltese Falcon,* is the tale of a detective lied to by his clients and left to find his way through a deadly maze. Successive drafts had remained remarkably close to the book, with Hawks adding some bright banter for Bogart as Marlowe and for Bacall as the daughter of the dying millionaire.

November in Los Angeles was wet and chilly. Hawks came down with the flu, missing days of shooting, and production fell ever further behind. Peter Godfrey, a second-stringer on the Warner payroll, was set to take over as director in the event the schedule slid too far. A week after Bogart's return to Mayo, Bacall contracted a heavy cold that turned to laryngitis. John Ridgely, cast as the smooth-talking gambler Eddie Mars, was also out with the flu, and two of the cast's killers hobbled about on injured ankles.

On the back lot, street sets were soaked by rain, despite the tarpaulins laid over them, and the time needed for them to dry added to the delays. On top of the physical problems were others more personal. The last Friday of the month, unit manager Eric Stacey made a note for production head Tenny Wright: "Mr. Bogart overslept this morning."

He came in over an hour late, hollow-eyed and bleary, starting a pattern documented in the unit manager's reports.

"Dec. 14th . . . Company waited for Mr. Bogart one and a half hours, from 9:00 to 10:30 A.M. . . .

"Dec. 15th . . . Mr. Bogart delayed the company for one full hour in the morning. . . .

"Dec. 20th—Thirty minute delay . . . It was necessary for Mr. Hawks to speak to Mr. Bogart for a half hour and straighten him out relative to the 'Bacall' situation, which is affecting their performances in the picture."

The front office, for once, was unable to handle the problem. This wasn't Flynn or Barrymore being unprofessional. This was Humphrey Bogart, their workhorse. Ironically, the success of the October release of *To Have and Have Not* in New York compounded the difficulties. The film had broken records at Warners' Hollywood Theater at Fifty-first Street and Broadway in New York and was "THE TALK OF THE TOWN," the New York office wired Burbank, topping *Casablanca,* and playing to capacity amid absolute "FUROR CREATED BY NEWCOMER LAUREN BACALL." She was, Jack Warner said, a "box office sensation." The publicity breaks so carefully planted months before had now bloomed in the pages of *Look* and *Collier's,* on page one of *The New York Times* drama section, and on the cover of *Life,* as well as in columns by Walter Winchell, Earl Wilson, and Louella Parsons. The entire studio rejoiced over J. L.'s "sensational new girl."

But it was by no means easy for a youngster barely out of her teens to be catapulted into the glare of stardom. A writer for *Silver Screen,* on *The Big Sleep* set for an interview, watched a studio publicist walk over to the new sensation, trying to make the introductions. "She gave this woman a tolerant glance and asked, speaking pure Bogart, 'Well, what creep wants to talk to me now?' "

Bogart rested a hand gently on her shoulder. "Look, Baby, don't get to be a character quite so fast."

Nonetheless, her success led to a shift in the balance of power on the set. Hawks's erstwhile Galatea was suddenly a star in her own right, involved with an even bigger star. The mighty director began to feel his authority diminish.

"He sensed he had lost. The girl he invented was no longer his," Bacall wrote. Dee Hawks Cramer said that he was convinced Bacall and Bogart were "siding together against him. He had very strong views on how a scene should be shot, and he was getting conflict. She was not his package anymore and he didn't like the way she was acting."

Thursday, December 21, Hawks edited footage, but no scenes were shot and no pages credited. "The company lost quite a bit of time," Stacey reported, "due to conferences regarding the story and discussions with Mr. Bogart, Hawks, and Lauren Bacall." Off the set, Bogart tried to talk about the divorce with Mayo, but she wasn't listening. His depression was evident. "There have been several instances," Stacey noted, "when Hawks has had to take him to one side and talk with him at great length because he was dissatisfied with his performance, which was no doubt caused by his domestic troubles."

On the day after Christmas, everything came to a head.

The cast had worked until noon on Saturday, December 23, before closing down for the holiday. Tuesday, everyone was back on the set, except Bogart. That morning, Mayo had gotten her wish. Her husband had come back home. Though not in the way she wanted.

On Christmas, he'd given Bacall her present—a gold watch—but spent the day alone. It was his forty-fifth birthday. His life was stuck in neutral, his wife would not divorce him, and a hotel room had become his home. All in all, the perfect circumstances for a breakdown and uncontrolled bingeing. No one knows just how long he drank that Christmas night or if he stopped off anywhere before arriving at the door of 1210 North Horn.

On Stage 19, the company waited for Bogart. When assistant director Bob Vreeland phoned the Beverly Wilshire a little after nine o'clock, the room clerk said Mr. Bogart had left. Fifteen minutes later, a frantic phone call came from Mayo. Her husband had shown up at the house, "very drunk." Bogart drunk was nothing new; not so Mayo sounding terrified. After informing the front office, Vreeland and Stacey raced off for the Bogart house, followed by Warner's top cop, Blayney Matthews, and his second-in-command. The scene was straight out of *Conflict.*

Others, notified by Warners, also arrived at the house. Among them was Sam Jaffe, whose assistant had already called a dependable, discreet doctor to come over to administer a sedative. Bogart, however, had passed out—"in very bad condition and sleeping by the time we arrived," Stacey noted euphemistically in his report to Wright. While everyone was waiting in the living room for the doctor to arrive, Bogart suddenly appeared, red-eyed and unshaven. "The atmosphere," Stacey reported, "became extremely strained. . . . Bogart himself kept asking, 'Are we holding a wake?' " The unit manager, feeling his presence was no help, departed, leaving the studio cop in charge. Bogart had always liked Matthews, he reasoned; let Blayney handle it.

"I really do not feel that Bogart's condition can be straightened out overnight," the report to Wright concluded, "since he has been drinking for approximately three weeks and it is not only the liquor, but also the mental turmoil regarding his domestic life that is entering into this situation. I would imagine that the smart thing to do would be to have a psychiatrist handle Bogart and report directly to you or Mr. Warner regarding his ability to return to work."

Back at the studio, Howard Hawks tried to shoot around his missing star and had to settle for a few close-up shots before finally sending everyone home. "There is absolutely nothing the company can shoot without Mr. Bogart," Stacey noted. With no scenes credited, the production shut down to await Bogart's recovery and return. "THANKS FOR NOT SHOWING UP TODAY," a furious and frustrated Jack Warner wired him.

Wednesday morning, Hawks faced an empty set. The otherwise blank production sheet has a single line: "The company did not work today . . . account illness of Mr. Bogart."

Hawks had always been a law unto himself, indulged by a studio that knew it had a winner. Its forbearance, however, was wearing thin, and

Hawks grew belligerent in return. It was evident to Meta Wilde that Hawks "was very angry. Jack was pressing him, and Howard didn't *like* to have anybody take him to task. He didn't want to have anybody challenge him about how he was doing *anything*—how much money he was spending, how long it was taking."

Delays were now in their second month. Filming lumbered along from day to day and rewrite to rewrite; by December the script was a dog-eared mass of pages marked "Temporary," scribbled over and crammed with newly dated inserts. A quarter of the film remained to be shot. With the company immobilized by Bogart's indefinite absence, Hawks sat down with Leigh Brackett and Jules Furthman and began slashing the script. Faulkner had already posted his last pages from the train carrying him back home, with a cover letter to Warners story editor James Geller:

> The following rewritten and additional scenes for THE BIG SLEEP were done by the author in respectful joy and happy admiration after he had gone off salary and while on his way back to Mississippi. With grateful thanks to the studio for the cheerful and crowded day coach which alone saved him from wasting his time in dull and pointless sleep. With love,
>
> WILLIAM FAULKNER

In the weeks of struggling to shorten the screenplay—Faulkner telescoping, Brackett rewriting Faulkner, Hawks rewriting both—they had more or less been faithful to Chandler, even retaining the denouement in which Marlowe escapes murder by committing murder. Through all the rewrites, it was the one scene that had remained in place and that they saw as essential to the story's symmetry.

That Wednesday, however, Hawks was out of options. Now all he could do was rip out and cut and hope to make things better in the editing room. He took out eleven scenes, almost thirteen pages. "It was the sort of thing Howard would do, like a spoiled child," Meta Wilde said. "A sort of gut reaction: 'The hell with it. Here goes. Twelve pages. That what you want? Okay!' "

The always expert Furthman began carpentry on a new, foreshortened ending, tailored to a bullet-ridden climax; but it had been drastic surgery, and however neat the splice, the cuts made an already confusing plot incomprehensible.

At one point Hawks sent Chandler a telegram asking whether the Sternwoods' chauffeur, Owen Taylor, was murdered or a suicide. "Dammit I didn't know either," Chandler later wrote to his English publisher

Hamish Hamilton. "Of course I got hooted at." Having heard about Jack Warner's response when he saw the cost of the seventy-five-cent wire, Chandler added that "Warner called Hawks up and asked him whether it was really necessary to send a telegram about a point like that."

Nearly a year after the production supposedly was finished in January 1945, all concerned with the picture agreed that some additional scenes were necessary. Those scenes more than compensated for the plot problems, and the genius of Hawks—the style and pace of the film, the blend of crisp performances, photography, sets, and music—made *The Big Sleep* a classic and one of Warners' biggest-grossing films. Chandler, who liked it, was particularly impressed by Hawks's direction and Bogart's performance. He wrote a friend, "You will realize what can be done with this sort of story by a director with the gift of atmosphere and the requisite touch of hidden sadism. Bogart, of course, is so much better than any other tough-guy actor that he makes bums of the [Alan] Ladds and the [Dick] Powells. As we say here, Bogart can be tough without a gun. Also he has a sense of humor that contains that grating undertone of contempt. Ladd is hard, bitter, and occasionally charming, but he is after all a small boy's idea of a tough guy, Bogart is the genuine article. Like Edward G. Robinson when he was younger, all he has to do to dominate a scene is enter it."

Despite Chandler's reaction, Dee Cramer felt that for Hawks "it was the most confusing picture he ever made. The individual scenes—which were Howard's forte anyway—were brilliant, but the plot got out of hand. He always hated the picture because he lost track of it." Though publicly Hawks was proud of *The Big Sleep,* privately it brought up memories of acrimony and resentment toward his star.

If Hawks never forgave Bogart, the studio did. On the Tuesday that he failed to show up, the Cost Department began adding up the losses, just in case Warner decided to present a bill. It was an unlikely ally, production manager Tenny Wright, who pointed out that until now Bogart had always shown up on time, that he had not had a day off through the entire picture, and that the fault—with a director continually behind schedule—had not been his alone.

Bogart made things easier by coming back to work on December 28 after only two days away, "apparently in good shape." The events of that lost Christmas weekend had been a catharsis, and he was now on his second wind, if not relaxed, at least recovered.

In the midst of his greatest personal crisis, Bogart completed the creation of the character of the modern private detective begun with Sam

Spade in *The Maltese Falcon.* Alistair Cooke wrote that the hero as embodied by Bogart is "a direct descendant of Sherlock Holmes. . . . a depressed, eccentric bachelor of vast, odd knowledge . . . which in the moment of resolution slices through the butter of the surrounding confusion. . . . As a Victorian bachelor-hero, Holmes must be asexual. Bogart too is a lone wolf, but with a new and equal stress on the noun. His general view of women implies that he was brought up, sexually speaking, no earlier than the twenties. Hence he is unshockable and offhand, and, one gathers, a very devil with the women, who is saved from absurdity by never having to prove it."

The underlying appeal of Bogart as both Spade and Marlowe is not so much that he is tough (with or without a gun) as that he is romantic. He makes these characters desirable and remote, both too cynical and too honorable to be true anywhere but in the fantasies of his audience. These contradictory qualities already existed in the fictional characters, but Bogart enhances them by what is most special about him as an actor: his suggestiveness, his ability to project a sense of something going on beneath the surface. His characterizations advance the story as much as the plot does. Robert Mitchum did the same in *Farewell, My Lovely* (1975), based on another Chandler novel, as did James Dean in his few films.

Eventually Spade and Marlowe would devolve into caricature. There is no peril that can make the handsome and fantastic James Bond sweat, no pain that can break him. But as the critic Judith Crist pointed out, when Spade or Marlowe "got hit they hurt and they needed time to recover; when they killed they flinched and were gnawed by regret. Above all, they did what they had to because they were men, in the head and the heart and not exclusively in the groin."

At the end of *The Big Sleep,* Marlowe's reward for fighting his way through a labyrinth of lies and brutality, for being shot at and beaten up, for killing to avoid being killed, is to wind up with Lauren Bacall in his arms, telling him that whatever the problems of life, there is "nothing you can't fix." In December 1944, fighting for his own survival, all Bogart wanted was the same resolution for himself.

CHAPTER 15

The Happiest Time

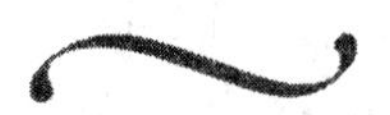

In January 1945, Humphrey and Mayo Bogart settled into what their lawyers called an "armed truce." The Christmas weekend had shattered the last of Mayo's illusions of reconciliation, but she wasn't quite ready to let go. Mrs. Bogart was resting, her attorney Jerry Giesler said, and for the moment would make no decisions regarding a divorce.

When it came to legal hired guns, none had more firepower than Giesler. It was he who, with Blayney Matthews's help, had gotten Errol Flynn off from a charge of statutory rape, and kept Busby Berkeley out of prison after a drunk-driving accident that killed three people. On the complicated laws regarding adultery then prevailing in the state of California, Giesler was a particularly formidable opponent.

Warners' swift action on the morning of December 26 had kept the crisis under wraps, but rumors abounded. The Bogart-Bacall affair was in danger of becoming a public relations disaster just when *To Have and Have Not* was scheduled for national release. The studio quickly concocted a plan to cash in on the publicity while neatly separating the lovers and avoiding any further chance of scandal. Put Bacall on a train to New York, Charlie Einfeld was urged, "so that we don't get a situation here that this tremendous publicity turns into notoriety."

For Bacall, the junket to New York—in 1945 the entertainment capital of America—held out the additional hook of Hometown Girl Makes

Good. "Seems everybody on main stem knew Bacall when," Einfeld advised, "so let her be pretty down to earth."

Unfortunately for Einfeld, Bogart indicated that he, too, planned to go to New York.

The Big Sleep was wrapped up in mid-January ("Mr. Bogart's personal troubles again being the cause of Mr. Hawks's slowdown"). The production in roughly equal measure ended on its own and was shut down from the top, thirty-four days behind schedule. Immediately after he finished shooting, Bogart was set to board the Super Chief with Louis Bromfield and his secretary, George Hawkins, for a two-week visit at the Bromfield farm in Mansfield, Ohio. From there he'd proceed to New York and await Bacall's arrival.

Bogart's last day before the cameras, January 12, was particularly hectic. There were process shots on Stage 5, retakes with Bacall on Stage 12, and a trip to Stage 1, where Arthur Silver, using Hawks's cinematographer Syd Hickox, was to shoot a special trailer for the movie. The effort and expense to produce a mini-production like this was spent only for the biggest stars. The trailer was like a short subject, with a scene of Bogart entering a book-lined set that was a mockup of the Hollywood Public Library and saying, "I'm looking for a mystery yarn; something off the beaten track."

Though Silver had written hundreds of trailers, he had never before directed one and set to work without much competence. Before long Bogart said, not unkindly, "I've got to get out of here. I'm going to direct. I think it's going to be great." Bogart set all the camera moves, established the action, and decided how he and the other actors were going to say their lines. Silver was grateful. "He did it for me—and he got out. I said, 'I couldn't do it this good. Thank you. And have a good trip.' "

In New York, Gary Stevens, a young publicist with the Blaine, Thompson Agency, which oversaw radio publicity for Warner Brothers, anxiously waited Bogart's arrival. Except for *The Milton Berle Show,* nothing had been arranged, because no one knew exactly what Bogart was going to do, and knowing exactly what their star was going to do was important to the studio.

He arrived Monday, January 29, and immediately fulfilled Warners' worst fears. Mayo had finally agreed to a divorce, but the terms had not been settled. Only days before, Warners' New York publicity head Mort Blumenstock had begged columnist Earl Wilson to hold off on Bogart-

Bacall until the divorce had been worked out. But that evening, Bogart, a white flower in his lapel and seated at his corner table at "21," saw Wilson at a nearby table and called him over, along with George Frazier of *Life* magazine. Expansive after numerous martinis, he talked non-stop as he passed around snapshots of "Baby." "I'm in love again—at my age," he gushed.

Notepads were whipped out. Did he intend to marry the young lady? "You're goddamn right!"

The next morning, possibly conscious of the use Jerry Giesler could make of his words, he backtracked. Reporter Inez Robb of Hearst's International News Service found him in his suite at the Gotham, badly hungover. ("I chose this Oxford gray suit to go with my complexion.") Yes, Mayo had agreed to a divorce, but he was still a married man. "Mayo's a fine girl but we couldn't make a go of it. Hell, just say it was a clash of personalities." On the mantelpiece, dominating the room, were three large photos of Bacall, although he insisted that the divorce had nothing to do with her. "She's a swell kid, and I'm afraid I've made it kinda tough for her by shooting off my big face. . . . I've probably loused up everything."

At the Warner Brothers headquarters on West Forty-fourth Street, Blumenstock read the papers, downed aspirin, reported to Burbank, and phoned Bogart continually, even threatening to bring Mayo east if he didn't shut up. "I POINTED OUT TO HIM," Blumenstock wired Einfeld, "THAT IF HE CONTINUED TO TALK THE WAY HE DID I WAS GOING TO BRING THAT OTHER PARTY TO NEW YORK POSTHASTE AND THE SITUATION WOULD REALLY BE SNAFUED. HE REALIZED THAT WAS SERIOUS. . . ."

Bogart was drinking heavily, prey to his own insecurities as he waited for Bacall to arrive on Friday. To Inez Robb, he'd joked about the difference in their ages—"I'm held together with platinum wire, glue and hair tonic I take internally. I'm well preserved, don't you think, for an old guy?" Beneath the jaunty bravado, he worried that he might be an appendage to Bacall's PR blitz and that he might lose the twenty-year-old, who would soon have New York at her feet.

Gary Stevens took Bogart to the studio on Broadway and Fifty-third Street for his appearance on Milton Berle's show, in what would later be the Ed Sullivan Theater. Stevens, the future general manager for Warner television, had a solid record for placing studio stars on network radio and for being able to include free plugs for Warner films. Bogart, however, had been the first major star he was assigned to shepherd, and his instructions were simple and clear: "Do anything he wants." The initial contacts between the two men had been perfectly pleasant. Because Bogart was chatty and no mention was made of the stories in the papers, Stevens was unprepared for what happened when they arrived at the studio.

"Bogart came in with a trench coat buttoned up to his neck, like a character out of his own movies; all he needed was fog in back of him and Sydney Greenstreet laughing on the side somewhere. He walked up to Berle, whom he'd never met, and said, 'Let's establish the ground rules. If you open your mouth about Baby, I'll knock your teeth in.' Berle thought it was a gag, but Bogart was *glaring,* and he realized that the guy was serious. But they got along okay on the program."

A few nights later, there was an even more disquieting scene.

Except for the Berle incident, Stevens had found the actor "very co-operative, very affable, very benign, in a sense; a little shy." He seemed to have no ego. He got no thrill from autograph seekers and was uncomfortable with strangers who pounded him on the back with unwarranted familiarity. All in all, Bogart was well-bred, educated, and articulate—at least until alcohol took hold of him. Then, Stevens found, "he was a definite Jekyll and Hyde. As soon as he got a few drinks under his belt—where one drink was too much and twenty were not enough—he became raucous. He became nasty. He became vicious. He became dictatorial."

One night at the Gotham the alcohol and the stress of waiting for Bacall became an explosive combination. That afternoon, Stevens had accompanied Bogart to "21," where he had had a sandwich and a couple of drinks. There were more drinks after they returned to the hotel.

Back in his suite, Bogart rubbed at his neck and shoulders. "Jesus, I'm tense," he told Stevens. "I've got to get a massage." Warners had a masseur on payroll for the top executives, and when Stevens called the office to ask if he could come over for Bogart, the answer was, "Look, anything this son of a bitch wants, *do* for him. We don't care what it costs us, but stay with him."

Twenty minutes later, the masseur and his portable table were at the door. Bogart requested a strong massage and asked Stevens to call room service for more drinks. Forty minutes and several drinks later, the massage was over and Bogart invited Stevens to stay for dinner. When Stevens began to politely refuse, Bogart interrupted. "No! You're not going home! You're with me!"

With the Warner admonition "*Do anything he wants*" still ringing in his ear, Stevens settled in. Bogart showered with the bathroom door open—"the fastest shower that I've seen a man take. Less than forty-five seconds. No soap, nothing. Grabbed the towel and came out. Then he finished a drink and said, 'I don't know, this neck of mine and shoulder—*where the hell is that guy with the massage?*' "

You just had the massage, Stevens told him.

"*I know!* He gave me some kind of light massage. Get that son of a bitch back!"

When Stevens pointed out that it was after seven P.M. and he had no idea where the man lived Bogart began to yell.

"Well, goddamn, you get him back here! I want him here! I need a *real* massage!"

Stevens tracked the masseur down at home in Brooklyn and asked him to return. The man picked up his portable table, got on the subway, and an hour later he was again at the Gotham at Fifty-fifth Street and Fifth Avenue. After an hour's strenuous massage, he departed.

Bogart continued to drink but wanted none of the steak dinner he had ordered, and he yelled at Stevens to get the table full of untouched food out of the room. His fury grew. He demanded that Stevens make reservations at El Morocco. A minute later he changed El Morocco to the Stork Club, then Toots Shor's. Five minutes after that, he decided he wanted a nap.

"He must have been on his eighth or ninth drink at this time," Stevens later said, "and I don't think he had a quarter of a pound of food all day."

Sometime after ten, a calmer Bogart turned to Stevens and told him, "I'm not going to be able to sleep—these pains—and I don't want to start taking aspirin with the drinking. That bastard you had up here, get him on the phone and get him back."

Reluctantly, Stevens called Brooklyn. Now it was the masseur who yelled at him.

"Look," Stevens explained, "I'm only telling you: he's a Warner star, I'm a messenger boy, and he wants a massage."

Bogart, hearing the argument, joined in. "What the hell's going on? You tell him to get here, or I'm going to call Jack Warner and have your goddamn fucking job taken from you!" By now he was in a world of his own, alternately threatening and moaning—"I'll get them on the phone, what the hell's the number—they can't do that to me—I came in here to do them a goddamn favor, to promote the picture, and my neck is killing me."

Stevens, whispering into the phone, told the masseur to forget the subway and take a taxi. Bogart drank through his third massage of the evening, which was delivered and received with mutual cursing. Then, Stevens said, he reverted to his kinder self.

"When he got up, he was appreciative. He went to his pants pocket where he had some rolled up bills and gave the guy two or three twenties. So the guy wasn't unhappy." No wonder. In 1945, it was the equivalent of a week's pay.

When the Twentieth Century Limited with Lauren Bacall aboard pulled into Grand Central Station on Friday, the platform was packed with clamoring, adoring fans who were undeterred by record-breaking snow and sleet. A cordon of police swept the Bacall party—the star, her publicist, her mother, and her dog—into a limo for the half-mile ride to the Gotham. More reporters and photographers were waiting in suite 801, where the young actress fielded questions with the aplomb of a pro. "BACALL HANDLING HERSELF BEAUTIFULLY," Blumenstock cabled Einfeld. "WITHOUT A DOUBT MOST INTERESTING PRESS TURNOUT EVER GIVEN A HOLLYWOOD ARRIVAL."

Upstairs in 901, Bogart sat by the telephone nursing a hangover after a night out with Louis Bromfield and George Hawkins, who had come to New York with him after the stopover in Ohio and were staying down the hall. Anxious not to oversleep and miss Bacall's arrival, he had dragged himself from bed, ordered breakfast, stripped, and gone into the bathroom for a shave, the front door ajar for room service. Moments later he heard a female voice say, "Has Miss Bacall arrived yet?" and turned to see a reporter, who in turn saw all of Bogart. Later he would swear it was Inez Robb. Robb always denied it.

Whoever it was, "I'll say this for her," Bogart said later, "her eyes never left my face. That's what I call reporting."

For Bacall's sake as well as his own, Bogart wanted to keep a low profile. It was *her* moment, *her* press conference, but he resented the circumstances that had put him in a secondary role. Here was an older man sitting alone while downstairs his young bride-to-be was getting her first taste of fame. It didn't take much imagination for him to identify with Norman Maine, the alcoholic actor-husband of the heroine in *A Star Is Born,* the Hollywood tale of a screen hopeful whose career takes off while her spouse's fades into obscurity.

He rang Bacall's room often to ask when she was coming up and to complain that "fucking Warner Brothers are running your life!" When she finally arrived, he was sitting on the couch alone, tears streaming down his face. "He thought I might have changed my mind," she later wrote, "that after thinking about it, I'd decided against marrying him." She was jarred by the depth of his insecurity and surprised that he, who had always seemed the stronger, needed reassurance.

Peter Lorre was also in town, staying a few blocks uptown at the Sherry Netherland, when Bogart called him. Lorre offered to come to the Gotham, but Bogart said he was feeling kind of sentimental and wanted to go over to the Astor Hotel on Broadway between Forty-fourth and Forty-fifth streets, a favorite place for a drink when he was a young actor. Bogart also asked Gary Stevens along. Stevens had often chaperoned Lorre on his visits to New York, and had even found him bedmates when necessary. "Gary, you've got to help me," Lorre would complain. "I can't get to sleep."

The three took a table near the bar. Stevens, more familiar with Lorre than with Bogart, knew from him about their friendship, the pranks they'd played on Michael Curtiz, and the nights Bogart slept off a drunk at Lorre's house. He also knew that Bogart often loaned Lorre money without thought of repayment, because Lorre's fees, however great, could not keep pace with a high lifestyle and a draining drug habit. In fact, at the evening's end Bogart reached into his pocket, peeled off a wad of bills, and handed them to his friend. Bogart's feelings about Lorre were obvious to Stevens: "He *loved* Peter—really loved the guy."

Bogart sipped his drinks quietly, his mood nostalgic. When he was a young actor on Broadway, he said, he'd come to the Astor bar all the time. "I'd sit down with agents and other actors, hoping I could get some kind of decent break." His thoughts were obvious. He was talking about the early twenties. Before Bacall had braces on her teeth. Before Bacall was even born. It suddenly became evident to Stevens that he and Lorre had been asked along to provide reassurance for Bogart's doubts about the age difference. "If I could get just five good years out of this," he said. "Anything after that would be a bonus. I know it isn't easy. I know it isn't going to last."

Lorre quickly broke in. "Oh, Bogie! Don't *talk* that way! I think you could get more happy. I think everything's going to be all right with her. I *like* her!" To Stevens, it was like something out of *Casablanca:* " 'Oh, Rick, I got to get *out* of here! You *must* help me, Rick!' But I always felt that Lorre was also doing it to ingratiate himself further. Because that's what Bogart wanted to hear."

Apart from Bogart's and Bacall's ages, there had evidently been some question, too, about the difference in their backgrounds. When she had brought up the matter of her being Jewish, Bogart waved it aside—Hell no, *she* mattered to him, not her religion. Why even ask? Basically, they were both agnostic. "He couldn't really understand my anxiety," she wrote. But privately, to Mary Baker, he "worried about her being Jewish, because she wanted kids and he worried about half-Jewish kids."

His reservations may have reflected the bred-in-the-bone prejudices endemic to his class, time, and society. Lee Gershwin, who had known his mother in Hollywood, recalled the stiff, social anti-Semitism of Maud Humphrey. By contrast, colleagues such as Dan Seymour and Art Silver had always found Bogart open-minded, sympathetic, and, as Seymour put it, "very respectful as far as Jews were concerned."

If, even for a 1940s liberal, Jews in the family may have been another matter, Bogart certainly behaved as if it were not a personally difficult issue. During these weeks in New York, he broadcast over CBS for the American Jewish Committee, and in the same period, he also wrote articles on tolerance, supported the Jewish cause in Palestine, and on public service programs denounced "racist bunk." Singer Lena Horne said he "raised hell" when homeowners on North Horn passed around a petition trying to get her out of a house she had secretly rented. She and Bogart did not know each other, but after the incident with the neighbors, "he sent word over to the house that if anybody bothered me, please let him know."

For Bacall, the two weeks in New York were an unmitigated triumph. Her picture was on every news wire and in every newspaper and magazine. "FOR NEWCOMER WITH ONLY ONE FILM APPEARANCE TO HER CREDIT LAUREN BACALL RECEIVING ONE OF BIGGEST RECEPTIONS EVER ACCORDED STARLET," Blumenstock telegrammed Burbank. Warners packed her days with interviews and photo sessions, from ten-thirty in the morning until six at night, but left Bogart and Bacall alone in the evenings. "What they do after six o'clock," Blumenstock told an inquiring reporter, "is entirely their affair."

Those evenings Bogart showed her his New York—the celebrity crowd at "21," the newspaper crowd at Bleeck's, old friends from the theater. Upon meeting Bacall, Helen Menken was gracious and welcoming and full of kind words for Bogart, maintaining that the failure of their marriage had been her fault.

During the intervals between interviews and dinner, Bacall's friends came to the Gotham to share their common memories and a few moments of her fame. Her boarding school roommate Gloria Nevard was working as a guide at NBC and acting in soaps; like Betty, she was engaged to a man considerably older than herself. The two young women talked enthusiastically about their lives and loves. "Betty was all excited about the movie and everything. I was tongue-tied. It was *so* exciting!"

They continued talking in the bathroom while Bacall soaped herself in the tub before changing for dinner. "She told me she was going to be married, but I knew I couldn't open my mouth because it wasn't official yet." For Nevard, the contrast between the cool sexpot of the stories and photos flooding the media and the starry-eyed Betty Bacal sloshing in the tub, going on about Bogart like a teenager with a crush, was startling. "She was so in love. She was just completely transported." Meanwhile, in the living room Nevard's mother and Natalie Bacal commiserated unhappily over their daughters being involved with older men.

Certainly for Natalie Bacal, Bogart's being a thrice-married forty-five-year-old heavy drinker, without even the saving grace of being Jewish, seemed a less than ideal match for a daughter not yet twenty-one. Bogart was even older than two of Betty's uncles. "Christ!" Bogart told his bride-to-be after meeting her extended Weinstein/Bacal family, "You've got more damn relatives than anyone I've ever seen."

Charlie Einfeld arranged a Washington, D.C., appearance for Bacall at a National Press Club luncheon. It was a one-day job with every member of the capital press corps in attendance. But Bacall said no, she didn't want to leave Bogart. Blumenstock offered to fly her down and get her back by six o'clock. She still refused. Didn't like airplanes, she said. Blumenstock, at an impasse, cabled Einfeld: "BACALL VERY DETERMINED NOT TO GO TO WASH."

Jack Warner sent off a telegram of his own. "DEAR LAUREN: VERY SURPRISED TO HEAR YOU DECLINED TO GO. . . . I THINK YOU SHOULD PLAY BALL. . . ." He asked her to cooperate and hoped she had a lovely time. (He deleted a phrase and kept it in reserve: "I think it would be much wiser for your future if you would play ball.")

"I wanted to be with Bogie," she later explained, "and had his backing. . . . I took on his tone with them very early on."

Jack L. Warner had a tone of his own, which he always used with young stars suddenly aware of their power. (A wire from New York to Burbank read: "WE HAVE TRIED TO ARRANGE WITH REGARD TO BACALL HAT SIZE.") Warners' hidden agenda in the junket was that it would separate the lovers for at least a day. "PERSONALLY THINK WASH TRIP

WOULD ACCOMPLISH JUST WHAT YOU ARE MOST CONCERNED ABOUT AVOIDING," Blumenstock wired Einfeld. In the end, Bacall did go to Washington and wound up in a photo that hit every paper in the country: perched atop a piano, her lovely long legs draped over the side, with Vice-President Harry Truman at the keyboard.

For Warner Publicity, the two weeks Bogart and Bacall were together in New York were alternately a PR agent's dream and nightmare. The studio's precautions notwithstanding—separate suites, chaperoning by mother and press agents—the publicity men remained haunted by the question of appearances and the possibility of something going wrong. A studio publicist was with Bogart and Bacall whenever they stepped out of their rooms. Jack Diamond not only handled Bacall's publicity, he was a trusted friend of the couple. He also, however, passed on to the studio whatever Bogart told him in confidence, a fact that would emerge only years later, when studio records were opened.

There was a collective sigh of relief from Warner Brothers when Bogart and Diamond left New York in mid-February for a week at the Bromfield farm before continuing to Los Angeles. The following day, Bacall and her mother also boarded a train for Mansfield, where the party spent a pleasant, bucolic week. At the end of their stay, Bogart and Bacall accepted Bromfield's invitation to be married at Malabar Farm.

In later years, friends who asked Bogart about the happiest time in his life would always get the answer: "When I was courting Betty." He moved back to the Garden of Allah, populated with the companions of his younger days: Gloria and Arthur Sheekman, Robert Benchley, actor Louis Calhern and Calhern's ex-wife Natalie Schafer, and actress Shirley Booth, with whom he'd played in *Hell's Bells.* Dorothy Parker was also there, along with the rest of the brilliant, boisterous writers' group that made the place part literary circle, part college dormitory.

The Sheekmans' daughter Sylvia was the Garden's "resident child." The ten-year-old was adept at mixing martinis for guests who came to her parents' bungalow for gourmet dinners put together with pooled rationing cards, the invitation lists reading like a Who's Who of the gifted. For Sylvia, "It was like the Algonquin West. The electricity that flowed from one person to the other, and the spark of good conversation. The intelligence and the accomplishment and the brilliance—all of that was there. A mix of New York and Hollywood, enormously urbane people."

One of her favorites was the family friend she knew as Uncle Bogart, who had moved into Villa 8, the so-called actors' villa. He always greeted her with a quick hug and a "Hey, kid." He chatted with her as she mixed martinis, or he would sit her on his lap and talk about things that interested them both. Over a non-gourmet dinner of chicken pot pie and guacamole with tortillas during the second week of March, he introduced a new friend, someone who seemed terribly glamorous and was at least in her twenties. The ten-year-old suddenly felt awkward. "The way she moved, everyone fell under her spell. I didn't know who this person was, who had him totally. I just had the feeling that he was mad about her."

Always polite and mindful of her duties, the young hostess asked the newcomer how she liked her martinis. "She gave me that wonderful look and said, 'Just pass the vermouth over the glass.' And I thought that was *so* stylish. She was treating me as an equal. She didn't condescend, she didn't patronize me. I adored her from that moment on."

It was a small gathering that evening: songwriter Arthur Schwartz, the composer of *Cover Girl,* Rita Hayworth's latest hit musical; Adrian Scott, an upcoming writer and producer known for his radical views and fresh from his first big screen success, an adaptation of Raymond Chandler's *Farewell, My Lovely* called *Murder, My Sweet.* With him was his pretty wife, the actress Anne Shirley. For Bacall, it was a new world, one which she entered skillfully and unobtrusively.

Bacall was so cool, so self-possessed, that as far as Sylvia Sheekman was concerned, "butter wouldn't melt in her mouth. She knew that she was in the company of old and valued friends who'd been through a lot together. She was in a way like a blank piece of paper; whatever anybody wanted to write on it, they could. She had no problem with her ego. She just loved this man and was glad to be there. I felt awash with admiration for her."

The ten-year-old was not alone in her feelings. Dorris Bowdon Johnson, another friend from the past and the wife of screenwriter Nunnally Johnson, agreed that "everybody adored Betty. She was pretty, she was quick-witted, and sharp. Bogie was bedazzled by her, obviously, and for good reason."

Bogart took Bacall down to Balboa for a weekend on the boat. An enthusiastic letter with yacht club letterhead to his friend Louis Bromfield—"Dear Father Bromberg," it began—showed a newfound exhilaration and an un-Bogart-like joy in living. He had felt that something was wrong in his relationship with Bacall, he wrote in mock seriousness, and now it was all clear: "She's too old for me—and I'm too young to be married." That week there had been several high-profile marriages between celebrities of disparate ages, notably a seventyish conductor and a twentyish socialite. Fine for those old geezers, he continued, "but what of me—a child I say—a baby—?"

He had just told "Lauren," he wrote, that she might get herself arrested for contributing to the delinquency of a minor, "getting me down here on this boat and doing 'God Knows What' to me. 'Marriage,' she keeps saying—!"

He signed it, "Puzzled / H. DeF. Bogart Jr."

It was Buffy Methot who smoothed the final break with Mayo, as she once had smoothed the marriage. While being sympathetic and supportive, she also gently forced reality on the child who had never grown up. "She must make up her mind that her marriage has ended," she told Louella Parsons, "and readjust her life."

By mid-March, the lawyers had finally worked out a settlement. Jerry Giesler declined to give the press a figure but did say that Mrs. Bogart had received a good deal more than the community property decreed by law. Rumors had it that Mayo's settlement included the house at Shoreham and North Horn, two thirds of Bogart's cash assets, his life insurance, and his investment in two Safeway Supermarkets. He was buying himself out of the marriage. He also felt he was defaulting on his duty. Mary Philips MacKenna saw Bogart on the night the agreement was reached and found her former husband "despondent and miserable. The end of the marriage bothered him, even though he felt he was doing the right thing."

"MRS. BOGART NEVADA-BOUND," the headline in the March 15 Los Angeles *Examiner* announced. Mayo went by train to Las Vegas to begin the six-week residence required for a Nevada divorce. The actor Victor Mature met her at the home of mutual friends, where she was trying to keep up appearances. She was "very nice and pleasant but distressed. She seemed a very unhappy lady." Two weeks after arriving, she returned to Los Angeles, unable to keep her commitment. Her mother and her lawyer persuaded her to leave, she once again took the train to the desert and the countdown began anew.

This time she stayed. On May 10, wearing dark glasses, a sober suit, and the ever-present white flower in her hair, Mayo Methot Bogart appeared before a deputy county clerk. After charging "great mental suffering" in the otherwise boilerplate complaint that was heard in private and then sealed, she was granted a divorce from Humphrey Bogart, who had offered no contest. "Bogey and I are the best of friends," she told the waiting press. "He is a very nice guy. It was a very pleasant marriage."

The two had met a few times in the final stages of the negotiation, almost always with their lawyers present. After May 10, in contrast to his other wives, he had no further contact with her.

Two weeks earlier, he had begun work on *The Two Mrs. Carrolls,* a chiller starring Barbara Stanwyck, produced by Mark Hellinger, and directed by Peter Godfrey. In an instance of stunning miscasting, he played a psychotic artist in the English countryside who paints portraits of his wives as the Angel of Death before dispatching them with a glass of warm, poisoned milk.

In June, Bacall was set to start *Confidential Agent,* based on Graham Greene's Spanish Civil War spy novel, starring Charles Boyer as the hero and Peter Lorre as a particularly unsavory fascist. It was her first film under a new arrangement that made her entirely the property of Warner Brothers, the result of negotiations begun by Howard Hawks and Charles Feldman immediately after the closing of *The Big Sleep.* Within three months, Hawks, Feldman, and Warner Bros. Pictures, Inc., concluded a million-dollar deal in which the studio purchased the corporate stock of H-F Productions. In return, Warners received a few defunct story rights, a two-picture deal with the young actress Ann Blythe, a contract with writer Leigh Brackett, and the script of the long-defunct *Battle Cry.* But the centerpiece was the asset listed in first place under "Artists": the rights to Lauren Bacall.

Hawks, Slim wrote later, had a dream of his ideal woman. "Until Howard got to Betty Bacall, there hadn't been an actress to make that dream come alive on the screen." The problem was, ideal and real seldom match.

"It was a business deal," according to Dee Cramer, who heard the story countless times from Hawks. "By that time Howard said, 'Oh-oh. I see nothing but trouble trouble trouble for my little star.' Howard spent money like water. Slim spent money like water. And they had a chance to sell the corporation. Howard was fed up; he had had enough of Bacall. When he talked about her, it was in belligerent tones—she just got too big for her britches. But it was really the money. Howard and Slim needed it desperately, since it was all going out the window. So a chance to make a million dollars tax-free was really the motivation. By then Howard couldn't have cared less about Bacall personally. He was on to the next project."

Throughout the negotiations, Warners insisted on one essential clause:

a waiver of the rule limiting the number of pictures that Bacall could make a year, a rule that stood as her only shield from the casting treadmill of the Warner player. Hawks agreed to the deletion. In April, while Mayo killed time in Las Vegas and Bogart and Bacall proceeded with their wedding plans, Warners and H-F drew up papers expressly eliminating "any limitations or restrictions whatsoever as to the number of motion pictures in which the services of Miss Betty Bacal may be required."

For Bacall, who through her first two films had been protected by a mentor who put her in roles carefully tailored to her unique abilities, the change would be disastrous. When, before the deal was consummated, Bacall's lawyer asked to see her contract and its assignment to Warner Brothers, Roy Obringer sent exactly what was requested: "All the documents relevant to your desired examination." The waiver agreement was omitted. After all, no one had asked for any departures from the contract. The waiver would come as a surprise to Bacall after the deal was done.

That spring, however, Lauren Bacall's life was the embodiment of a fairy tale. Even the most hardened industry observers were impressed. "A situation which happens once in a lifetime," Obringer wrote to Warner counsel Ralph Lewis, "where you have a personality develop overnight and become a terrific box office value." A new Warner contract was in the works, at a starting salary of $1,000 a week. There was also a $5,000 bonus, the result of a petition by the studio to lift the wartime wage controls to permit its star to take her rightful place. "Miss Bacal must now support her new position . . . with the dignity and appearance generally current with other stars in the industry with whom she must compete," Obringer wrote in his petition to the IRS. What was omitted from *this* letter was how grateful the studio was for the wage controls. Otherwise it would have had to pay its new star much more.

The wedding date was set for May 21 at Malabar Farm. Earl Wilson, visiting Hollywood, found Bogart afflicted with last-minute jitters. "Something terrible's going to happen. Maybe the guy that's supposed to marry us won't show up. . . . Or I'll louse it up by dropping the ring.

"Baby," he continued to the columnist, was not a bit nervous. "She comes up to me every day and crouches and holds up four fingers, three fingers, whatever it is, and says, 'only four more days,' 'only three more days!' That tigress, I have the feeling of a mouse that's going to be torn up by a rabbit."

His jitters showed in private, too. Once, on the boat, lying at anchor in Balboa, he'd gone into a rage touched off by heavy drinking. Then he took the skiff and left his frightened fiancée to cry the night away. Mayo or no Mayo, she realized, life with Bogart was not going to be easy.

The studio granted the couple time off to be married, and Hellinger arranged to shoot around Bogart during his absence. The plans included a stop in Chicago for an appearance before cheering fans at an "I Am an American Day" rally in Soldier Field. After the wedding, there would be a honeymoon weekend in Los Angeles and a return to the set. At Union Station on Friday, May 18, the two stars posed for news photographers before boarding the eastbound Super Chief. Bogart, dressed in his ubiquitous gray, was high enough on the train steps to smile down at his beloved, herself in a conservative suit, tailored blouse, and corsage. For the couple's protection, Warners had arranged for a private car to drive them down the ramp past a crowd of screaming, jostling fans.

Every step of the proceedings was planned to fit a two-day schedule. The couple arrived in Ohio on Sunday and had samples taken for the required blood test. The results normally required a five day wait, and Bromfield had called Bogart in Los Angeles shortly before their departure to say he wasn't sure they would get around it. But a moment after he hung up, the local doctor's wife, one of his neighbors on the party line, had phoned to say, "About that blood test, Louis—I think Doc can fix it up in half a day."

Monday morning, the bride and groom went into Mansfield for their license. Ohio law mandated that the bride be a resident of the state. Bacall, a kerchief tied over her hair curlers, gave her address as Rt. 1, Lucas, Ohio, the address of Malabar Farm. To Hope Bromfield, a pretty, ash-blond teenager and the second of the three Bromfield daughters, Bacall was like someone from another world—"Really good-looking, with a tart kind of humor. She could be quite sarcastic when she wanted to be, but funny. She kidded George and Daddy quite a bit—and Bogart. A sort of amusing, vivacious kind of person. I remember thinking of her as an adult, and of myself as a child."

The wedding was a family affair, with very few guests. George Hawkins was to give the bride away. The Bogarts were still everyone's favorite couple, no matter who the other half was. "Louis loved Mayo," a family friend said. "He really liked her." But Bogart was the continuity.

The ceremony was held in the high-ceilinged entrance hall of the main house. In front of the patterned green-white-gold wallpaper that lined the spacious hallway were clusters of ferns and white snapdragons, gathered and arranged by Bromfield. The paneled sliding doors were open to the living room and dining room beyond, with its wide windows and French crystal chandelier. At the grand piano in the corner, Hope Bromfield waited for the signal to launch into the bridal chorus from *Lohengrin.*

A little after noon, the wedding march began, but quickly stopped when a last-minute attack of nerves sent the bride scurrying to the toilet. Then, to the familiar strains of Wagner, Bacall, with George Hawkins at her side, began the descent down the broadly sweeping staircase—tall and erect, holding a bouquet of white orchids, a pink, belted suit setting off her deep tan, the long blond hair combed out and falling to her shoulders, a touch of lipstick the only noticeable makeup.

Bogart, in a gray flannel suit with a white carnation pinned to its lapel, was waiting at the foot of the stairs. Bromfield, his best man, towered above him. Judge Herbert S. Schettler, who would officiate, watched with the small group of guests that included Natalie Bacal, Bromfield's elderly mother, Mary Bromfield, the Bromfield daughters, the family cook, and a boxer named Prince, who quietly padded in and settled himself across the judge's feet.

The ceremony was a simple, three-minute affair. The judge, reading the improvised service from a loose-leaf notebook, addressed the couple as "Humphrey" and "Betty Joan." Bogart, wet-eyed, spoke his responses softly but with precision. The bride's familiar low voice was even huskier than usual. She gave him a mesh band of yellow gold; hers was a wide carved band to be worn with an emerald-cut chrysoberyl that he had given her in January. After they were pronounced man and wife, the groom swept the bride into his arms and kissed her lightly on the cheek. The Associated Press wire service reported that the bride said, "Oh, goody!," returned the kiss, and then kissed Hawkins. Bacall mounted the stairs and tossed the orchid bouquet, which was caught by fourteen-year-old Hope.

Outside, the battalion of reporters and photographers who had turned the simple country wedding into a media event waited impatiently. "Every photographer in the world was there," said *Life* photographer Ed Clark, who had flown in from Los Angeles that day. "God, there was just a swarm of us. And everybody was griping because we couldn't get in, like 'Who the hell do they think they *are*?' "

Clark, a soft-spoken man and master photographer, knew Bogart slightly. He and his colleagues from the magazine spent a lot of time on movie sets shooting pictures for a regular feature called *Life Goes to the*

Movies. Bogart apparently remembered Clark, because, to his surprise, when Bogart opened the door after the ceremony, he called Clark over and asked him in. "The other guys, they were *livid.* Especially the guy from *Harper's Bazaar.* But it wasn't just me, it was *Life.* We had the entree; everybody wanted to be in *Life.*"

Clark found the atmosphere inside the house relaxed. "Bacall was coming down the stairway; Bogart was cool, smoking one cigarette after another, drinking one martini after another. But very calm, collected. He knew exactly what he was doing." So did Clark. "Hell, I'd covered ten thousand weddings. I just said, 'Stand here, give him a bite of cake,' " and in minutes *Life* had its wedding shots.

Then the press stampede began, with the others snapping pictures of the newlyweds and shouting questions about their plans. Eventually everyone moved outside for group portraits of the wedding party. Apart from the bride's mother, there were no Bacals or Weinsteins at the wedding. It was not her Uncle Jack or Uncle Charlie, by Bacall's account her surrogate fathers, who escorted her down the staircase and gave her away, but her husband's friend's Anglo-Saxon secretary. The stereotypes were preserved. With the national media present, there was no intimation that America's blond sex goddess was a Jew.

Neither was there the drunken chaos of Bogart's marriage to Mayo. No one dropped his trousers, and the groom did not drive off with his best man. Rather, the new Mr. and Mrs. Bogart spent the night in a front room with flowered wallpaper, ceramic roosters, and Audubon prints. The next morning, they departed for Chicago, another train back to Los Angeles and, beginning Monday, another workweek on the set and business as usual.

But in fact, nothing was the same. While the newlyweds were putting their small world in order, the larger one was changing forever. The little man who played the piano at the National Press Club while Bacall swung her legs over the side was now president of the United States and, though few knew it, in control of history's first atomic weapon. Just five weeks before the wedding at Malabar, Ed Clark of *Life* had been in Warm Springs, Georgia, covering the sudden death of Franklin Roosevelt. (One of his most memorable pictures was of a black soldier, an accordion in his hands and tears streaming down his face, intoning the spiritual "Going Home" as the president's coffin was moved onto the slow train back to Washington.) With victory in Europe that May, the alliance FDR had helped form to win the war began to show its cracks; and those cracks soon would have a dire effect on Hollywood.

In April of 1945, the German concentration camps across Europe had been opened to the media, confirming earlier reports of gas chambers, mass torture, and systematic genocide. Newsreels showed the dead piled up like cordwood, the surviving barely alive—a fleshless scarecrow population in the tens of thousands, tattooed, disease-ridden, and hardly recognizable as humans. A shocked General Dwight Eisenhower, intent on confirmation by impartial American eyewitnesses, had immediately requested that delegations from Congress and the media travel to the sites. On behalf of the film industry, Jack Warner asked to come along, "to visually record and educate the American people to the bitter fruits of race hatred." The War Department's refusal came directly from General George Marshall, the Army chief of staff and Ike's superior, who pleaded an inability to enlarge the original list, already put together on "extremely short notice." The rejection of Warners was ironic in light of later neo-Nazi claims that the atrocities had been a hoax produced by Hollywood.

During a month-long, Pentagon-sponsored junket through the ruins of Europe that July, a dozen industry leaders including Warner, Darryl Zanuck of Twentieth Century–Fox, and Harry Cohn of Columbia finally saw the horror firsthand. It was a momentary sideshow in a schedule otherwise given over to hobnobbing with generals and heads of state, but its effect was profound. There were no cameras at the camp in Dachau, outside Munich, to capture the images of the last five thousand inmates, about one eighth of the former population. The visitors were shown the gassing sites, the wooden shelves where the prisoners were warehoused at night, the places where medical experiments on the living were carried out, and the made-to-order furnaces to burn the dead. The studio bosses gaped, confronted by scenes beyond the imaginings of any of their wartime films, and certainly beyond anything permitted by the Breen Office. The evidence before their eyes was a silent reproach for the pitiful inadequacy of their pictures.

"HOW LONG HAVE I BEEN TELLING YOU," Harry Warner asked in a cable to his brother, "TO MAKE A PICTURE SHOWING THE ATROCITIES?" But in downplaying the Holocaust, the studios had followed the lead of the news media and the government; and J. L. Warner was not about to question the judgment of the State Department, the War Department, and his good friend Franklin Roosevelt. Still, what he saw had a tremendous effect on him.

That August, Bogart and an invited group of Warner employees gathered in Projection Room 5 for what had been billed as an off-the-record briefing on the European trip, but Jack Warner kept putting his notes aside and returning to "that Dachau thing. Many will die who were still there. . . . We went into the gas chamber. . . . they'd bring these hundreds of thousands of people—give them a towel, soap. . . ."

Despite the souring of East-West relations, Warner had tried while on the trip to enter the USSR. The Soviets were eager to welcome the distinguished visitor from Hollywood who was the producer of *Mission to Moscow,* and the powerful diplomat Andrei Gromyko tried to cut through the bureaucratic knots and rush a visa to the traveling executive. The papers somehow never caught up with him.

"And [now] . . . everybody's accusing the Russians of being bad guys," Warner told his audience. "Don't want to let anyone in. Well, what the hell, they just got through being stunned by the killing of twenty-odd million of their own people. . . . The only people who are *really* doing things to create another war are those newspapers . . . that are printing stories . . . about get ready for the next war with Russia. It's ridiculous! . . . Start a war with what and who against? . . . The world can't *stand* another war."

Warner Brothers was going to fight this junk, fight the lies and the hate, he said. Warners would show these warmongers up, mobilize opinion, produce films to counter the forces who would divide and conquer. "It's a racket . . . to keep labor, religion, everybody in turmoil, black against white, white against black, Negro, Jew against Catholic, Christian. . . . that's what Hitler was successful in doing. . . ." The audience was galvanized. It was J. L.'s finest hour.

Wednesday, August 15, the sound stage for *Confidential Agent* was silent. The unit manager made a laconic entry in the daily report: "Company did not work . . . A/C holiday—end of war."

Like the rest of the nation, Los Angeles was in an uproar, celebrating the victory over the Japanese and the end to World War II. Motorists, uncaring about gasoline rationing, cruised Hollywood Boulevard, honking their horns. A happy, jostling mob thronged the intersection at Hollywood and Vine, the crossroads of the movie world. To one witness, "It was like Times Square on New Year's Eve, only with the sun out. And more guys in uniform getting banged."

Others celebrated in different ways. Jack Warner sent telegrams of congratulations to the White House, Winston Churchill, the military brass, Eleanor Roosevelt, and Ambassador Joseph E. Davies, the guiding spirit behind *Mission to Moscow.*

In a steel shed in the Philippines, three thousand Marines had just settled down to a preview screening of *The Big Sleep* when word of the war's end came over the PA, followed by momentary silence. Then a roar of three thousand rifles went off, sending bullets ricocheting and MC Gary Moore diving under a seat.

The war's end gave a new dimension to political Hollywood. At a celebrity-packed meeting at the pseudo-Egyptian temple that was the American Legion Hall on Highland Avenue, the Hollywood Democratic Committee voted to merge with the eastern-based Independent Citizens Committee of the Arts, Sciences, and Professions, a liberal, ostensibly non-partisan organization for which the Hollywood division, abbreviated to HICCASP, became the marquee. Its agenda included civil rights, economic rights, abolition of the House Committee on Un-American Activities, and "mutual understanding, friendship and cooperation among the great powers."

Bette Davis was among those at the Legion Hall, eulogizing Roosevelt in a ghost–written speech and saying "our right arm is gone." Bogart was not there. It was a working night; besides, he hated meetings and committees. Even so, he had agreed to join the HICCASP executive council, and his name was prominent in the full-page ad that appeared in the trades. ("*Will You Follow Through for Franklin Roosevelt? He believed in the unity of the Big Three . . . a lasting world peace: . . . WANT TO JOIN US?*")

Being a signatory to the ad was the antithesis of the Bogart image, of the loner who went his own way. He played the cynic on- and off-camera so well that many thought of him as apolitical, even after he'd gone on record with HICCASP in early 1945. The bags of hate mail that had arrived following his broadcasts for Roosevelt in the previous November were instrumental in his decision to be more engaged in politics. Some of the letters had objected to an actor voicing opinions ("you cheap sissy have the asinine impudence . . ."); but others with no signature and no return address were straight out of *Black Legion,* dripping with ethnic slurs and accusing him of "contaminating the air of free America."

Bogart, insulted and furious, sent a telegram to his ex-brother-in-law Stuart Rose at the *Saturday Evening Post,* asking if he would like to buy an article in which the actor made his views clear.

"If you'll write it," Rose replied, "not get some God-damned press agent to write it for you. And I'll know when I read the first paragraph."

It had appeared in February, a three-page piece titled "I Stuck My Neck Out." Its contents had been kept from everyone, the studio included.

> On the evening of November 6, 1944, I exercised the privilege granted me by the Constitution of the United States and guaranteed by the Bill of Rights. I voiced my choice for the presidency. Right out loud and over the radio, I said I hoped F.D.R. would be elected. . . . In the weeks since I exercised that simple and fundamental prerogative of American citizenship, my mail has increased tremendously and my lexicon of epithets has grown accordingly. . . .

It was Sam Spade talking the language of the Founding Fathers, Bogart revealing a side of himself previously known only to a few intimates. Until then, he had hidden his literateness from the public, the press and, at times, himself, like some effete and shameful secret.

The founders of the republic, he wrote, hadn't seemed particularly worried about actors expressing their opinions.

> But, of course, there wasn't a Hollywood when they drafted the Declaration of Independence, the Constitution and the Bill of Rights.
>
> I've made myself tolerably familiar with those great documents. In none of them can I find a clause prohibiting actors from exercising any of the rights or privileges they affirm and guarantee. I do find in them ringing affirmation of the equal rights of all men.
>
> "All men," I take it, includes actors, along with industrialists, laborers, conservatives and liberals, blacks and whites, Christians and Jews, Protestants and Catholics . . .
>
> The less caustic of my . . . correspondents have softened their verbal shots with the explanation that actors . . . exercise considerable influence on the public. Let's give ourselves a break and say we have some influence. . . . That doesn't give us an edge on the family physician, the parish pastor, the local newspaper and national magazine editor or any other individual who pulls his weight in society. . . .
>
> I'd hate to think that an ailing Democrat would cancel an appendectomy . . . because he suddenly discovered his surgeon was a Republican. . . . Or that a Republican housewife would struggle along with a plugged kitchen sink rather than call in a Roosevelt Democrat plumber. . . . Personally I've never known of honest political opinions affecting a surgeon's skill, poisoning a farmer's vegetables or influencing an actor's performance.

> Hitler's Nazis, it is true, have some novel ideas along that line. They've banned much of the finest German music because the composers were something less than 100 per cent Aryan. They've burned the paintings and books of many of their greatest masters because the artists and authors did not agree with the Nazi political philosophy. They've even banned some actors for similar reasons. . . .
>
> In this country of ourselves, a person is not required to earn citizenship privileges. He can be born into them—as I was—or acquire them through simple process of law. We are given a priceless "free ride" on the liberty earned by the blood and courage of our forebears. Only I don't believe in free rides, and that is why I am likely to have a permanently sore neck. I believe we must pay our freight in this democracy by working with all our intelligence to keep it a living, vital force. That, to my way of reasoning, includes our voicing our considered opinions on issues of the day, even on who we think should be our next president. . . .

The trade papers, he said in closing, seemed fearful that actors, by speaking out, might hurt the box office,

> thus bringing in fewer dollars for this reasonably well-nourished motion-picture industry.
>
> I've never had an aversion to money. I'm downright fond of the stuff. But not fond enough to earn it by keeping my mouth shut when I want to express my honest convictions. . . .
>
> It may be a moot question what good, except to their own souls, actors, painters, musicians and members of kindred artistic professions may accomplish by participating in politics. We may be giddy dopes or impractical dreamers. . . . Only I seem to recall a distinguished gentleman by the name of Ignace Paderewski, who was not only the world's greatest concert pianist but prime minister . . . of his native Poland. . . . Winston Churchill, whose voice and dramatic delivery qualify him for stardom in almost any role, is listed in his current biography as an author. He seems to have done all right in politics. . . .
>
> George Washington was a country farmer and surveyor. . . . Benjamin Franklin was a printer, author and scientist. . . .
>
> Paul Revere . . . was better known in his own time for engraving and silver and gold smithing than he was for horseback riding. And Thomas Jefferson was a right smart violin player. There may pos-

> sibly be a few die-hards who still insist the country would be better off had Jefferson stuck to his fiddle playing, but I doubt any American can be found who wishes Paul Revere hadn't left his engraving to gallop around the countryside yelling that the redcoats were coming. . . .
>
> If that doesn't exactly make a case for actors, it does make a case for equal opportunities and equal rights of citizenship. All we actors want is our share of them. . . .
>
> Personally, I'm going to keep right on sticking my neck out, without worrying about its possible effect upon my career. I love doing it. You meet so many interesting people that way.

The article, in retrospect, has an unintended twist. Bogart mentioned, in passing, the French actor Talma—a tragedian, friend of Napoleon, and political adviser. "He died in 1826. Give us time and we [Hollywood] may produce a prime minister or President yet."

Many Americans believed that the end of the war would be the beginning of a time of prosperity and peace. Instead, the first chill of the Cold War set in. The differences among the Allies put aside in wartime reasserted themselves, and East and West fell back into old habits and familiar slogans. The change in the political environment in Hollywood was stark. Wartime positives gave way to film noir–like ambiguity, with no one certain of the outlines of the new mise-en-scène.

Despite J. L.'s notion that the Russians were not inclined to another war, by mid-summer of 1945, Warner Brothers had begun to compile a list of writers known to be left-wing, however profitable their scripts had been for the studio. Generally these were the scenarists for the anti-fascist action films showcasing Bogart, Garfield, and Flynn, and the thought for the present was merely to steer the writers in other, hopefully more neutral directions—or in the words of one memo in August, "away from subject matters in which too much of the pink tinge might show through."

In October 1945, what was to be called the Studio Strike changed Jack Warner's politics. The previous spring a jurisdictional dispute between two unions, the long-entrenched International Alliance of Theatrical Stage Employees (IATSE) and the new Conference of Studio Unions (CSU), had divided Hollywood's sympathies. At stake was control of Hollywood's army of technicians. The IATSE, with sixteen thousand members, had, despite a record of ties to organized crime, considerable leverage with the studio heads, who knew that a walkout by IATSE projectionists could darken every movie theater in the country. The CSU "was everything that IATSE was not: militant, leftist, and honest."

The origin of the conflict occurred in 1937, when seventy-seven set dressers—the interior decorators of movies—formed their own union to negotiate a five-year contract with the studios, at a time when the IATSE was intent on swallowing every craft guild. Two years later, the IATSE demanded that the studios recognize a new set dressers' local under its umbrella. The studios refused, saying that they already had a contract with the independents, and the IATSE backed off after the studios agreed that henceforth they would not negotiate with any other outside group on behalf of the dressers. When the 1937 contract expired in 1942, the dressers joined with the local painters' union, a loose affiliation of model builders, illustrators, and designers headed by Herbert Sorrell, under the auspices of the CSU. By 1945, Sorrell, who was now the head of the CSU and who had been a guiding force in the successful 1941 cartoonists' strike at the Walt Disney studio, represented nine unions with nearly ten thousand members. After he proposed a new contract on behalf of the set dressers, IATSE president Richard Walsh warned that his men would strike if the studios negotiated with the CSU.

Sorrell appealed to the War Labor Board that his union had a right to be the dressers' designated agent, regardless of the 1939 deal between the IATSE and the studios, and the board agreed. The studios claimed impartiality and ostensibly tried to avoid conflict, but many thought that they preferred to work with the IATSE. When in March of 1945 the CSU called its locals out on strike against all the studios to demand recognition, the IATSE sent groups of men to break through the pickets. The Screen Writers Guild gave unenthusiastic support to the CSU, and the Screen Actors Guild rather unhappily voted not to. Even so, few observed the picket lines; and although to many Sorrell was a Communist provocateur, the Communists supported the pledge of the American Federation of Labor not to strike during the war. Other guilds refused to support the strike for the same reason.

After the war ended and the pledge was lifted, there was a ripple effect throughout the industry as labor groups picked sides. The Congress of Industrial Organizations (CIO) supported the strikers; the Teamsters did not. The studios sided with the IATSE and hired replacement workers. The acrimony grew, and what had been a dispute between the unions turned into a studio lockout. In the early fall, the CSU, in the hope of finding an opening in the producers' united front against it, singled out Warners for mass protest.

The union's choice of the studio synonymous with liberalism, the one that had been Roosevelt's film arm and executor of New Deal policies, was an odd one. A special representative of the Soviet motion picture industry, in Hollywood briefly the year before, had wanted to visit only Warner Brothers—the film company, as he put it, "which is most progressive in all respects." Jack Warner's files even contain a photograph of the VIP luncheon in 1942 held by the studio in the executive dining room for Mme. Litvinov, wife of the Soviet ambassador.

Thus no one expected the scene on Friday morning, October 5, as hundreds of strikers massed before the studio walls in a scene straight out of a Warner protest film; except this time, instead of Paul Muni or James Cagney battling the back-lot heavies on a sound stage, it was happening for real on West Olive Avenue, just outside the auto gate. As Warner and other executives watched from the roof of the studios, strikers in work clothes jeered the IATSE workers driving in and overturned three of their cars. More IATSE members arrived and the fighting increased. At noon, Burbank police chief Elmer Adams ordered the crowd to disperse, in the name of the people of the state of California.

Rose Hobart, just back from a long USO tour and unaware of what was happening, stopped en route to the Warner lot and joined a crowd of onlookers across the street. The studio, with its high, blank walls, looked like a fortress under siege. Still photographers patrolled the roof. A moment after Hobart asked what was going on, a line of Burbank police and studio guards carrying fire hoses advanced from inside the gate toward the street. A blast of water slammed into the pickets.

"They turned the fire hoses on those people, just opened up the hoses. I thought, *They can't do this to us!* Here I'd just got back from touring the Aleutians—this was ridiculous! I couldn't make any sense of what I'd come back into."

In the pre-dawn hours the following Monday, the violence escalated. Then as the American flag was raised over the lot at six A.M., a phalanx of club-wielding assailants poured out the main gate, falling upon the strikers.

The Warner Brothers family was breaking up in what the union would call Bloody Monday. Dance director LeRoy Prinz, trying to get past the line, was knocked senseless and woke up in the studio infirmary. A striking technician had his jaw broken. Out on Olive Avenue, Blayney Matthews—bluff, likable Blayney, the fixer and nursemaid to the stars—waded into the middle of the melee, directing the men with the truncheons. Warner loyalists saw the strike as an attack on the studio. "Blayney was *fearless,*" an executive later commented. "He stood up to the leaders of the strike and went right into the middle of them all where he could have gotten killed!"

Arthur Silver of the trailer department, finding the entrance blocked by three overturned cars, parked in a public garage and walked back. "And on the street before we came up, there was a *huge* truck, open in back. There must have been fifty goons in it, stripped to the waist, with leather bands; I had never seen anything like it in my life. These men were monsters! And they were ready to go in to bust the strike."

After being advised to "get the hell out of here," Silver went home. That night, he received a call from J. L.'s executive assistant Steve Trilling. "Mr. Warner wants you to come to the studio. How are we going to win the strike if everybody stays out? We can't make the rank and file come in, but if the executives and department heads don't come in, we're lost."

"So I came in and I stayed at the studio. Dave Weisbart, a top cutter, and I took a big suite of offices. Henry Blanke and some of the people from the prop department were able to bring in beds. It was a wild two weeks. Nothing but crap games and card games at night, and the best of food. Every night the police at the auto gate would tell us when the pickets left so we could drive home and see our families. Then we'd come back at twelve o'clock and the parties would be going on. Some of the guys would get girls in there, and some of the actresses would come in. Those parties were wild!"

The Battle of Burbank, as it was known, had liberal Hollywood up in arms. Hundreds of telegrams of protest arrived at the studio. HICCASP and the Screen Writers Guild denounced the violence "perpetrated by hired thugs and police" as a "violation of American civil liberties." Steve Trilling, who obviously had not been in Russia, wrote that the strikers' siege resembled the one at Stalingrad. The studio collected depositions from non-strikers protesting that it had been singled out and was only trying to keep its doors open. Both sides overreacted. The studio with the slogan "Combining good citizenship with good picture making" became, in union handbills, "The Beast of Burbank."

Despite official Screen Actors Guild neutrality, actors gave the studio a wide berth, anxious for both their reputations and their safety. Peter Lorre had shut down *The Verdict,* the last production on the lot. Frightened of the violence, but even more of being called a scab, Lorre refused to continue, despite threats and pre-dawn calls from Trilling.

In late October, the National Labor Relations Board announced that the set dressers were entitled to be represented by whomever they wished. The studios and the IATSE backed off, but the differences were left to fester. The IATSE claimed the strike was Communist-inspired, as did the Motion Picture Alliance and the California legislature's version of the Committee on Un-American Activities. Telegrams protesting the strike were sent to Blayney Matthews, the man with the FBI contacts, asking for background checks of people on the studio-compiled list of those who had honored the picket line. Meta Wilde, whose contract ran only from film to film, told the studio she wouldn't work against the strikers. It took months and a personal appeal to Matthews before she was hired for another film. A few years later, named as a Communist by Lee J. Cobb, Rose Hobart was summoned before an investigating committee and confronted with, among other bits of "evidence" regarding her political views, a blowup of herself outside the Warners gate the morning of October 5. She never made another film.

In early November, Steve Trilling wrote to Jake Wilk that "The Dove of Peace has now alighted on the fortress of Burbank. So—business as usual." But in fact, business at Warners fundamentally changed. Until then, liberals had an ally in Jack Warner, but to him, the strike was an attempt by ingrates to tear down all that he had built up. In its aftermath, he turned to the right. His political realignment strengthened the underlying anti-communism endemic to Old Hollywood and would lead to a cataclysm for Humphrey Bogart.

CHAPTER 16

After the War

Following their return from Ohio, the Bogarts stayed at the Garden of Allah and returned to their separate films. He finished *The Two Mrs. Carrolls* in June; she wrapped up *Confidential Agent* in August. On the surface, *Confidential Agent* looked like a class act: Charles Boyer as leading man; a story by Graham Greene; and a strong supporting cast. In addition, Herman Shumlin, director of the Oscar-nominated *Watch on the Rhine* and producer of such great Broadway hits as *Grand Hotel, The Corn Is Green*, and *The Little Foxes*, came in from New York to direct.

But the movie's assets were mostly on paper. The cloak-and-dagger story about Spanish Loyalists and Fascists in pre-war London was no longer timely. An even greater weakness was the director himself. A spectacular talent on Broadway, he was out of place in Hollywood. *Watch on the Rhine* had owed much of its success to Hal Wallis, who backed up Shumlin and translated his instructions for the puzzled crew. Now Wallis was gone, and even by the studio's own assessment, Shumlin had much to learn about motion pictures. Hot-tempered and inflexible, he substituted bluster for expertise, and it showed on film.

In a stark contrast to the tender loving care of Howard Hawks, Bacall, improbably cast as a British aristocrat, was left on her own with veteran actors. The disastrous result was a direct consequence of the selling of her contract to the studio.

"It was wrong casting from the start," Bogart later wrote. "Betty shouldn't have been in it. She didn't want to do the part." Shumlin, however, had insisted on a big-name star and lobbied for it to be her. He came to regret his choice. Accounts of fights between the director and his leading lady appeared in the papers, and a visiting midwestern columnist picked up some unscripted dialogue between the two. Shumlin: "You can keep your cool if you *think* cool." Bacall: "The only way I keep cool is with my clothes off!"

"Betty wouldn't take anything from anybody," according to Dan Seymour, once again in the supporting cast. "Sometimes she'd just stand there, with her arms crossed, looking at Shumlin, with an expression that said, 'Drop dead.' "

The studio was no happier than the stars with the myriad takes, the endless delays, and a director who wasn't shooting close-ups of their million-dollar property. "Let the audience *see* the girl," J. L. roared after one screening. The nadir came one night when for some reason the sound stage door was left open. The script called for a gun to fire somewhere in the background. The prop man wanted to use sound effects. Shumlin wanted live ammunition. The prop man said it was too dangerous. Shumlin insisted.

The prop man came out with a gun loaded with real bullets and warned everyone that they would ricochet. One caromed out the door and through the window of a nearby bungalow that happened to be that of Harry Warner, who was sleeping. Warner's angry emergence in a felt hat and a bathrobe made of what looked like an Indian blanket that hung past his ankles marked the end of using live ammunition.

"A great part of my time was spent in defending or trying to explain your ways," producer Robert Buckner wrote Shumlin. "I often deeply regretted your quick-tempered, arbitrary manners. They did not make my days any easier." Nevertheless, Warners, which had invested heavily in the picture, tried to convince itself it had a hit. Jack Warner, determined to showcase Bacall in a serious drama and certain that *Confidential Agent* would further her career, decided to hold up the release of *The Big Sleep* and shove the new film into its slot.

Perhaps Charlie Einfeld, the master spin doctor and creator of Bacall's publicity, might have been able to save the picture, but he had left the studio to work independently. His successors tried to persuade the public that Graham Greene's bleak tale of a tired, middle-aged ex–freedom fighter and a jaded society woman won over to his cause was a rerun of *To Have and Have Not*, even though its one dip into sex—a quick kiss between Bacall and Boyer just before the fadeout—was pallid. Yet the advance publicity hyped romance ("Watch her lips answer the call when

Boyer whistles for Bacall") and ballyhooed the story as "The Fusion of 2 hot metals!" To add to the troubles, production ran so late that the publicity department in New York had to show rough footage instead of a finished film to the magazine editors and writers they were hoping would do feature stories about it.

Arthur Silver, readying the trailer in his office on the lot in Burbank, picked up a call from a Warners publicity man in New York. The publicist, who had just seen the rough cut, was in a panic: "*Stop everything!* We're going to lose our asses on this picture! We've got a girl who said, if you want something all you have to do is put your lips together and blow, a guy who's supposed to be the hottest lover on the screen, *and they hardly have an embrace*! We've got to *do* something!"

To Silver, the solution seemed clear: spice up the trailer. "They had written some crud line, something about 'The Lover Meets The Look.' So if New York wanted it that way, what I had to do was get some hot clinches." When he asked Shumlin to shoot Bacall and Boyer embracing, Shumlin refused: "I'm not changing *one word* of this script. Not a word! I think it's wonderful." Fortunately, Bogart was visiting the set and suggested that Silver explain the problem to Bacall, who readily agreed to cooperate. So did Boyer, who was actually relieved. "I was woor-eed about that," he told Silver in his famous accent.

The company was scheduled to work late that night, and a plan was hatched to sneak in the shots whenever Shumlin took a break to go to the toilet. According to Silver, assistant director Art Lueker "hated Shumlin" and agreed to shoot four or five clinches from different angles. Lueker, Bacall, and Boyer did as they were told, and Silver put the embraces into the trailer. "Of course it was a complete fraud, because in the picture itself, there was almost *nothing*, but in the trailer, it looked like the hottest movie that was ever made."

No hotted-up trailers, though, could undo the damage to Bacall.

The first sign of trouble came with the screening of *Confidential Agent* for the trades. "Bacall," said *Variety*, "fails to measure up." The critic for the *Hollywood Review* agreed: "Confidentially, it stinks. . . . [Bacall's performance is] like a phonograph record that has become stuck on a turntable."

Overall, however, the reviews of the film were surprisingly positive. In New York, the *Times* and the *Herald Tribune*, respectively, dubbed the picture "engrossing" and "savagely exciting." But the *Times* went on to say that Bacall's performance "comes close to being an unmitigated bore," and the *Herald Tribune* faulted her "tiny range of expression." The *Times* decided she had been "pushed too far too fast. . . . She is not even the interesting personality which careful direction made of her in *To Have and Have Not.*" It was a theme that carried through many reviews: Bacall needed Hawks and Bogart to make her look good. The public was no kinder. At the Strand in New York, dialogue raised snickers never intended by Shumlin, and the audience laughed uproariously when Bacall, wearing a tight sweater, told Boyer, "I have my points."

It seemed that all the reviewers who had ever said a kind word about Bacall were now trying to put distance between themselves and their earlier enthusiasm. Having acclaimed a goddess, they were delighted to bring her down to earth: "Miss Bacall starts out brusquely and surly and she ends that way"; "Extraordinarily inept . . . might be a high school girl giving an impersonation of herself"; "The noise she makes is that of a bubble going poof!"

Bogart and Bacall were on the boat in Balboa when the early notices came in. "I watched Betty's reactions," he later wrote, "not knowing at first how to help her. She was badly hurt. Nobody but myself really knows how she took this beating, what she went through in the shock and surprise of it." The only thing to do, he decided, was to kid her about it, "and pretty soon we got to the point where she was kidding about it too. She has a sense of humor. She has a sense of values, too, and she has guts."

As though attracted by the scent of failure, the Hollywood Woman's Press Club announced that Bacall was among its nominees for Most Uncooperative Player of the Year. (The group's "Sour Apple" was eventually awarded to Greer Garson.) Bogart defended her against those who "went out of their way to knock her just as they had built her up.

"Betty went from what was practically oblivion to the spotlight of world attention. Then . . . before she had time to catch her breath, she took a panning that would have staggered even a seasoned star. The plain fact of the matter is that Betty was lauded for one picture out of all proportion to her deserts and panned for another that wasn't by any means her entire fault. She admitted freely that she wasn't good in the picture and that's a pretty hard thing for a kid to do after she has been shot right to the top.

"There are very few really great actresses on the screen. There are great personalities and I think Betty is one of these. . . . Now she's out to show them. She won't quit until she does that, and I'm backing her all the way."

Years later, Bacall wrote, "Thank God I had Bogie."

Only a few critics put the blame where it most belonged. "The fault is not Miss Bacall's," the New York newspaper *PM* said, "but rather her studio's and her sponsor's—for propelling the girl into a star situation for which she is so palpably ill equipped." A Chicago columnist noted that "They are calling her 'The Fizzle' instead of 'The Look.' Well, surely it was up to her bosses—to her director and producer—to see that the role was right for her and she be properly guided." And New York *Post* critic Archer Winsten stated the obvious: Bacall was not some ersatz back-lot actress. "She is unique in every respect." Warners now appeared before the industry as a studio that had not properly cared for one of its star properties.

The one critic who liked Bacall's acting and sympathized with her anger over her reviews was the one who was in the best position to judge. Graham Greene wrote in a 1979 letter to the London *Sunday Telegram*, "I also as the author of the book resented those cool notices. This remains the only good film ever made from one of my books by an American director. . . . [Some] thought that a young American actress should not have played an English 'Honourable'. However the Honourable in my book was only removed by one generation from a coal miner. . . . Her performance was admirable."

Although Jack Warner's decision to pull *The Big Sleep* in favor of *Confidential Agent* initially seemed wrongheaded, doing so allowed the studio time to make fundamental changes in *The Big Sleep* to protect its investment in a contract player whose stardom hung in the balance. As the *Los Angeles Times* said in its review of *Confidential Agent,* "There's still promise in 'The Look.' "

Other than sneak previews, *The Big Sleep* had played only for GIs in jungles: the Philippines on V-J Day and on Okinawa, in a valley littered with the charred hulls of Sherman tanks. In the winter of 1945, Charles Feldman, dependent on Warners Brothers' continuing good will and having sold the studio a million-dollar actress now facing an abrupt devaluation, had a plan to control the damage.

Feldman had always been uneasy about Bacall's role in *The Big Sleep.* To him it was hardly more than a bit part that had been beefed up through a few post-production retakes back in January. That November, with the film a make-or-break prospect for Bacall, Feldman wrote a long letter to Jack Warner, outlining a way to protect both his client and the studio's financial stake in her future. What he proposed were entirely new, one-on-one scenes with Bogart and Bacall, loaded with provocative banter.

He wanted to highlight the "insolence" that had endeared Bacall to both the critics and the public. Feldman was certain that Bacall's performance would justify the expense if J. L. would approve the new filming. Although it would be costly, he pointed out that another Bacall failure would be even costlier. If she got the same reviews on *The Big Sleep* as she had on *Confidential Agent*—"which she definitely will receive unless changes are made"—Warners might lose one of its most important assets.

The same thought had occurred to J. L. and he approved the new expenditures. Philip Epstein was called in for rewrites and new copy. Although Howard Hawks, in a final battle of egos, had broken with the studio a few months earlier, an extra $10,000 persuaded him to return for six days of shooting. Another old grudge was patched up as well after what Louella Parsons reported as a "frank talk" between Hawks and the two stars. In January 1946, Bogart and Bacall began shooting for the third time on *The Big Sleep*. Some scenes were retakes, others came out of Epstein's typewriter the weekend before and were doctored by Hawks to recapture as much of Slim and Steve as possible:

> "You got a touch of class, but I don't know how far you can go."
>
> "A lot depends on who's in the saddle. . . ."

When it was released in August 1946, *The Big Sleep* turned out to be all that Feldman and the studio hoped for. Even though no one knew exactly what the story was about, no one particularly cared. "Whether you understand it or not," one critic wrote, "*The Big Sleep* is as exciting as they come." Yet despite enthusiastic reviews, the damage done to Bacall could not be erased. *Variety* declared that Bacall was "redeemed," but most reviewers held back. "Miss Bacall is okay in the same type of role she originally scored in," was typical. "Her film career," the *Hollywood Reporter* announced, "is still to be decided."

Whatever the reviews, *The Big Sleep* fixed Bogart and Bacall as icons of American pop culture. "The love song of heroine Bacall and hero Bogart is wailed on a police siren," wrote Cecilia Ager, the screen critic for *PM*, "the counterpoint of a phantasmagoria of violence, mist and confusion." Even so, Bacall's career foundered. It would take years, she later wrote, to get even halfway up to the dizzying heights from which she had fallen.

Personally, the damage was far more devastating. When Bacall signed her Warner contract at the age of twenty-one, she placed the hottest new career of the decade in the hands of the studio. The studio, in turn, immediately put expediency before the best interests of the actress, a blunder for which she nearly paid with her professional life. Not surprisingly, Bacall felt betrayed. She would never again trust Jack Warner; and the permanent climate of suspicion exacerbated the uneasy relations between Bogart and the studio, setting the stage for the departure of the star who had come to symbolize Warner Brothers.

For the Bogarts as a couple, however, these were the times Bacall remembers as the happiest of her life, and the months of late 1945 and early 1946 were a period of contentment for Bogart. Not long after their marriage, he and Bacall moved to Kings Road, into a three-story house that hugged the slope of the hillside above Sunset Boulevard. Its amenities included a large blue sunken Roman bathtub and an awning-shaded deck looking out over West Hollywood. The staff at North Horn Avenue—cook, butler, and gardener—followed Bogart by both choice and necessity. Mayo had finally sold the house and moved back to Portland.

The change in Bogart was evident and fundamental. "In his earlier marriages," Gloria Stuart pointed out, "he'd always been the loved one. With Betty, *he* was the lover." He gave her a bracelet with a small gold whistle, a memento of her signature scene in *To Have and Have Not.*

Bogart cut back on his drinking. Instead of the battleground of the past, friends visiting the home found a comfortable family routine, and gave Bacall the credit. "He was a changed man with her," Sam Jaffe said. "He was very happy." John Huston, returned at last from the war, said Bogart's life was "improved by Betty's presence. Oh, boy, was she good for him! Open and hearty and direct. With humor—and a kind of bravura quality. Insulting and tropical. I just loved her from the word go."

"Betty was *marvelous* with him," another friend added. "She would quiet him, she never let him get away with his sometimes nasty temper, picking at people when he was in the mood that came on with booze. She'd say, 'Shut up, Bogart! I don't want to hear any more out of your mouth—that's the end of it!' "

Acquaintances describing the new Mrs. Bogart used such words as "energy" and "panache." In a hallway after a dinner party, thinking herself unobserved, screenwriter Philip Dunne watched as she twirled a large lavender cape—"going V-R-R-R-O-O-M-M-M! As though she were a toreador! It was fascinating to see the way she sort of *commanded,* the way she walked; her boldness about presenting herself. And yet I always had the feeling she was saying, 'Here's little Betty—here she is, a big movie star and a glamour girl. It can't really be me!' "

Quick-witted and unintimidated, she was more than equal to the demands of a difficult if loving husband. A friend described them as having "a kind of *Thin Man* relationship. Very tart. Give and take. But done with a lot of warmth and humor. You got the feeling he adored her and she worshipped him."

It was something of a paradox—the middle-aged man and the startlingly knowing girl-woman whom he called Baby, who was at once a surrogate daughter, the quieting mother figure he had never known, and a real love. "They *liked* each other," said Evelyn Keyes, the Columbia star who had just married John Huston. "They complemented each other perfectly. We're not talking about love, that's not the issue—though he was in love with Betty. They *respected* each other. There was an age difference, but Betty seemed to have a maturity, more than I did. And they watched out for each other. They *did* have all the money in the world, so they had all the help, all the comforts, but I'm talking about just an understanding of one another."

They had a new addition to the family, a puppy named Harvey, after the invisible rabbit of the popular Broadway and film comedy; it was also one of Bogart's names for Bacall when they were courting. Harvey was a wedding present from the Bromfields; his sire was the stately Prince, who had padded in during their marriage ceremony. Harvey had been escorted to California by Max Wilk, the boy who in 1929 had persuaded his father to buy *The Maltese Falcon.* Sixteen years later he was now Private First Class Wilk, and he couldn't get a ticket home, because returning veterans packed the cross-country trains. He visited Warners' Chicago office, hoping someone there could help, and he was quickly given a compartment aboard the Super Chief. Or rather, Harvey was. It was indicative of the clout Warner Brothers had in those days: the only way Private First Class Wilk could get an accommodation home was as chaperon to Humphrey Bogart's dog.

Two nights and a day later, Wilk and Harvey arrived at the Bogarts' house. Even though it was only about eleven A.M., Bogart had an iced pitcher of martinis in his hand. " 'We had a hard night,' he explained. 'Baby is asleep. She is hung over. We were at the Hellingers' house last night. She'll love the dog. Come outside, sit under the tree.' So we sat under the tree. I think I had a martini. I think I had more."

Wilk knew Hellinger and his parties. "His big kick was to get people drunk. I felt it was a kind of sadistic way to spend an evening."

" 'You know,' Bogart told me, 'I'm very glad to meet you. I really respect and admire your father. He's the only man at Warner Brothers who knows *anything* about anything.'

"Then *she* came out, looking like death warmed over. But when she saw the dog, she fell madly in love with him."

At Christmas, Bacall threw a surprise forty-sixth birthday party for Bogart. Almost as he came in the door, Bacall handed him a drink and asked that he take a look at the tub; something was wrong with it. When he walked into the bathroom, Mark Hellinger, Raymond Massey, Nunnally Johnson, Arthur Sheekman, Robert Benchley, and the gang from the Garden greeted him, scrunched together in the blue Roman bath, glasses raised, yelling "Surprise!" Bogart was "like a kid," touched that people cared so much about him.

A week or two earlier, the couple had driven to Balboa with New York *Herald Tribune* writer Thornton Delehanty for the realization of a lifelong dream of Bogart's.

The Marconi-rigged yawl *Santana* was an aristocrat of the sea, fifty-five feet of mahogany, teak, polished brass, and sail—a championship racer with below-deck quarters as roomy as speed allowed. A small crew could bunk in the main saloon, which was painted a cheery white and trimmed with mahogany. There was a tiny galley and, in the stern, a cabin where two could comfortably sleep. The boat had been built in 1935 for the heir to a California oil fortune, and then was owned by a succession of actors that included George Brent, Ray Milland, and, most recently, Dick Powell, forced to sell because of a sinus condition. Bogart paid him $50,000. The yacht was well-known in the sailing world and was considered "a delight to the seaman's eye. Her decks run long and clean. . . . There's no sign of the seams . . . just a flawless white skin, smooth and hard as a ball bearing."

Powell took his final trip on the *Santana* with the Bogarts and Delehanty, an overnight shakedown cruise to Catalina. Bogart happily puttered in the engine room, put up sails despite the windless day, and ran fore and aft, furling, unfurling, and making fast. At dusk they reached the island and moored in a quiet cove, where Bacall busied herself in the galley producing what Delehanty later described as "an enchanting mess of liver and potatoes and salad" and Bogart looked blissful under a two-day growth of beard. "He's the ugliest handsome man I've ever seen," Bacall told Delehanty. The next day the group headed home, the wind up, the sails puffed to perfection as *Santana*'s long, lean bow sliced neatly through the waves. "Bogie," Bacall wrote later, "was in love." *Santana* was the only serious rival Bacall has ever acknowledged.

More than the motor craft he previously owned, *Santana* connected him with one of the few happy memories of his childhood. To be out on the water was to be loved, to be safe, to be out of reach, whether of abusive servants and parents or an impatient studio executive. "I don't use the boat to drink on or chase dames on," he later told a reporter. "I use it to get away from things. Hemingway said that the sea was the last free place in the world, and I respect it and love it."

It must have seemed to Bogart in late 1945 and early 1946 as though his life was nearly perfect. A new long-term contract was in negotiation. He and Bacall moved again, this time to a hilltop house with a vast yard and swimming pool purchased from Hedy Lamarr. Hedgerow Farm, despite its Beverly Hills postal address, was not in the city itself but up Benedict Canyon, which leads from the shaded flats south of Sunset Boulevard to the crests of the hills separating Beverly Hills from the San Fernando Valley. The move was Bacall's idea, an upscale nudge to a husband inclined to be close with his cash. "He didn't like to spend money," Sam Jaffe said. "She got him to, and she made a home for him."

A magazine described the sprawling, whitewashed, single-level house with bay windows and eight large rooms as "comfortable, luxurious, but not ostentatious." There was walnut paneling in the living room, and a fireplace surrounded by a carved English mantelpiece. In back, a huge lawn stretched out to the garden, swimming pool, and spreading shade trees, all enclosed by a picket fence. The Bogarts settled in with fourteen chickens, eight ducks, and, of course, Harvey, who loped about the hills by day and returned at night with ticks that were plucked by Bacall. "If he comes home when we're in the midst of entertaining guests," Bogart said, "Betty goes into her veterinarian act."

The public loved it—Slim and Steve settling down in the post-war dream of a home, a family, and a steady job. The image was replicated again and again in fan magazines: the Tough Guy and the Sexpot as just plain folks, puttering about the house, relaxing in the den, feet up on the coffee table, listening to the radio.

That summer, he knelt in the courtyard of Sid Grauman's Chinese Theatre and impressed hand- and footprints in a carefully laid square of wet concrete. He had shot all that day, then left the set in the late afternoon after changing into what he called his lucky shoes, the oxfords he wore in *Casablanca* and *The Big Sleep*. Yet while his most famous films had been shot in Burbank, he had come from the Columbia lot in Hollywood, where he was making *Dead Reckoning* for Harry Cohn, on loan-out after a year away from Warners. Both Bogarts in fact had been idle, due partly to delays caused by the strike, and partly by role refusals. But none of that mattered during this interlude. Grinning happily, Bacall's arms around him as the flashbulbs popped, Bogart dug a finger back into the cement and added the inscription: "Sid—May You Never Die Till I Kill You."

The balance of power between stars and studios shifted as the motion picture industry underwent major upheavals following the war. There was also a change in moviegoing habits as middle-class families moved to the suburbs. The captive wartime audience was replaced by an affluent, mobile population with autos galore and gas cheap and plentiful; films were now increasingly just another leisure business competing for the consumer dollar. On top of these changes was television. Film executives thought they might control the new medium, but they had no more chance of doing that than they would of putting a genie back in its bottle. That didn't stop Harry Warner from still hoping.

In the early 1950s Richard Dorso, who, among other accomplishments, was one of the first syndicators of television shows, was invited to Warner Brothers for lunch with Jack Warner, with whom he often played tennis, and some other executives. Harry Warner, who had never met Dorso, joined the group. After a few minutes of general conversation, Harry looked over at Dorso and asked, " 'Who's he?' Before anybody could stop me, I said, 'I'm in television.' And Harry jumped to his feet. '*Television!*' He turned to Jack, 'What's *he* doing here? Television! That's our enemy! You, with your relationship with Harry Truman! I told you to tell him to stop television! It would hurt us! And he wouldn't listen to you! It's your fault!'

"*Stop television?* Now that's the kind of ignorance that prevailed."

When World War II ended, Warners was in need of stars. Cagney had left in 1942 and Flynn was sinking into alcoholic middle age. The studios were suddenly dependent on a shrinking pool of big-money talent, and newcomers were less willing than their Depression-era counterparts to be tied down by long contracts and fixed salaries. Stars—Burt Lancaster and John Wayne among them—formed their own production companies and struck deals with studios that gave them a share of the receipts. Bogart did not yet have that luxury, but he was now a money player whose presence on the screen guaranteed business, and whose absence from it could hurt the studio. Warners' own distributors would tell the studio, "We want a Bogart picture." *The Big Sleep* set new box office records, but its success only emphasized that, retakes aside, this newest Warners bonanza dated from January 1945.

By 1946, one fact was clear to Jack Warner: the studio needed Bogart more than Bogart needed the studio. Roles were offered but rejected. Suspensions were meaningless. Unable to get any projects going with Bogart and Bacall, Trilling sniffed to J. L. about "two of our most important stars" turning "super critical."

Warners provided much to be critical of. It came up either with tired recycles of W. R. Burnett stories or such wild miscasting as starring Bogart in a biography of Will Rogers, or as Captain Horatio Hornblower, the swashbuckling British hero who outsmarts the French and Spanish in C. S. Forester's Napoleonic wars epic. With each refusal, the studio warned of sanctions and sent strongly worded telegrams, but Bogart stayed out, knowing Warners would have to come around. The stock company he was so integral a part of had broken up—Wallis was gone, Hawks too—and the studio was trying to redefine itself. In this new environment, Jack Warner's threats took on a hollow ring. Yet in J. L.'s view, he was now being faced down by the hirelings he had helped to greatness.

On one occasion, a rejected script was redelivered to the Bogart house, arriving during dinner. Fred Clark, the Jamaican butler, took the package inside while the Warner courier waited. A minute later, the studio employee heard an unmistakable voice yell "No!" A moment later, Clark reappeared with the packet and the two receipts, unsigned. He politely handed them back and said with some disdain in the crisp accent of the British upper class, "Mr. Bogart does not want the script."

The only way Warners seemed to be able to get Bogart to appear in one of its films was by letting him perform first on radio. On October 14, 1946, Bogart and Bacall broadcast an adaptation of *To Have and Have Not* on *Lux Radio Theatre.* Hosted by William Keighley, who directed Bogart and Robinson in *Bullets or Ballots,* the show was the glamour hour of the airwaves. Warners publicity considered *Lux* a "plum." It also paid handsomely. Knowing that, the studio withheld its consent for Bogart and Bacall to appear until the couple agreed to shoot a cameo for the upcoming Warner Brothers comedy *Two Guys from Milwaukee.* The deal gave the studio the benefit of the Bogarts' film appearance in return for the two picking up $10,000 for an evening's work. (Some months before, the studio had decided to keep Bacall off the air, according to a confidential memo, "because of her earlier attempts when we were unable to use her because of slurred diction and delivery.")

Judging by the thunderous applause that welcomed the couple, the studio audience didn't give a damn about diction. Bogart was his usual adept self, and Bacall proved a natural for the medium. The Whistle Scene re-created the electricity generated on the screen, and it was followed by Humphrey Bogart letting out a peal of good-humored laughter.

The national mood was reflected in the 1946 elections, as a conservative backlash swept the country. For industry liberals, this was supposed to have been a year of consolidation in which Hollywood was solidly fixed on the new political map. Warner's cartoon genius Chuck Jones designed ads promoting HICCASP's candidates, and Bogart headed a list of endorsers ranging from the late president's oldest son, James Roosevelt, to screenwriter Dalton Trumbo. Bogart's name was on the program committee for a star-packed dinner at the Beverly Wilshire Hotel that supported more openness on nuclear research. Against the hush of a rapt audience, ex-captain Ronald Reagan read aloud from Norman Corwin's *Set Your Clock at U-235*:

> *Now we are in it together . . .*
> *The secrets of the earth have been peeled, one by one,*
> *until the core is bare:*
> *The latest recipe is private, in a guarded book, but*
> *the stink of death is public on the wind from*
> *Nagasaki . . .*

Bogart was also among the sponsors of an open forum on *The Challenge of the Post War World to the Liberal Movement* held by the feisty left-of-center magazine *The Nation* at the Ambassador Auditorium. At home in Benedict Canyon, evening gatherings were a combination of strong opinion and strong drink. The regulars were described as "liberal thinkers, writers, newspapermen, intellectuals, men who talk and argue." An exception was Louis Bromfield, a frequent visitor to Los Angeles, who had turned increasingly conservative. He and Bogart would often end up in heated disagreement. Bacall, half-joking, put up a sign: "Danger!! Alcohol and Bogart at work! Do NOT discuss: Politics—Religion—Women—Men—Pictures—Theater—or anything else!"

Bromfield was the one backing a winner. In the primary election that spring, a liberal-supported statewide ticket had been defeated and a new virus had been injected into the political process. HICCASP reported its candidates "immobilized" by "redbaiting." That November Jerry Voorhis, one of its congressional stars, lost his supposedly safe seat to the political unknown Richard Nixon after a campaign charging Voorhis with voting "the Moscow line." In Wisconsin, a similar tack worked for another unknown, Joseph R. McCarthy. In the state capital of Sacramento, HICCASP was denounced as a Communist front.

Hollywood liberalism slowly withered. Neither star endorsements nor the invocation of FDR was enough to stem the tide. Instead of leading the way, Hollywood had been shown its place. Its activists, no longer national players, were remanded to playing make-believe in an already unreal world. On the set of *Dead Reckoning*, directed by John Cromwell, co-star Lizabeth Scott watched Bogart pause at times, look off into the distance, smile sourly and say to no one in particular, "Isn't this a *stupid* way to make a living?"

Scott was a discovery of Hal Wallis. Her high cheekbones and shoulder-length blond hair led columnists to dub her "The Threat." She had initially been tense about working with Bogart but instead found him "warm, charming, delightful." In one scene, as an ex-paratrooper in pursuit of a friend's killers, Bogart was to pull two oversized hit men out of a closet. "He said to the crew, 'Hey, you guys, you've got to help me out.' They put them on a little platform with four wheels, and he pulled them out with such ease and strength, it was really something to behold when you saw it on the screen."

He never shot past six o'clock, ate alone in his dressing room on the contents of a lunch pail from home and a bottle or two of beer, and followed that with a half hour's nap. For all the calm of his day, his discontent was often evident to younger colleagues. Scott was always aware of it. "Not that he didn't want to be an actor, that he didn't enjoy the fame, the success, the material aspects; but that somewhere within himself, he thought he should be doing greater things."

Richard Brooks, later the director of *The Blackboard Jungle* (1955) and *Elmer Gantry* (1960) but then a young writer breaking into Hollywood, had the same reaction when he met Bogart in late 1946. Brooks, just out of the Marines, had written *The Brick Foxhole*, a novel about homophobia in the military. Bogart gave it to Mark Hellinger, who backed off the subject but told the author, "If you ever get out alive, come see me."

They met at The Players, the popular restaurant on Sunset Boulevard owned by writer and director Preston Sturges. Brooks came in to find

Hellinger waiting at a corner table with his wife and the Bogarts. The actor, impressed with the novel, was gracious. Brooks tried to think of an appropriate response and told him, "Well, you're a very important man now, Mr. Bogart—"

A snort cut off the compliment. "Hell, I've been playing George Raft's brother-in-law for years!" Then Bogart launched into a diatribe about his early days at Warners. Brooks thought the actor seemed uncomfortable with praise, and that his past rejections were more vivid than his present success. There was also a dour, hardheaded understanding of what his fame was all about. His pragmatism had been evident in a telegram to Jack Warner after the success of *To Have and Have Not*, in which he pointedly referred to "the box office value I fortunately have at the moment." Bogart seemed never to believe in his publicity, his write-ups, or the permanence of anything.

Brooks, who soon joined the circle of Bogart's closest friends, understood that, to Bogart, pessimism was a realistic attitude. "From his own experience he knew that the people with the power loved you as long as you could make a dollar for them. That was the bottom line. Were you successful? And were your movies successful? Without that, you were gone, they wiped you off the slate. You never existed."

During the winter of 1946, Bogart and Bacall went to San Francisco for location shooting on their first co-starring film since *The Big Sleep*, almost two years before. Bogart had given the galleys of a novel, *The Dark Road*, to producer Jerry Wald. He was attracted by the central role of a man framed for his wife's murder who pursues her killer while being pursued by the police. There was also a role for Bacall as the woman who believes in him. The book's author, David Goodis, was on the Warner Brothers payroll and a client of the Jaffe office. (In 1960 François Truffaut adapted another Goodis novel, *Shoot the Piano Player*.)

The story, retitled *Dark Passage*, reflected the mood of its time. Events unfold in an atmosphere of paranoia and the constant threat of disaster. Its harassed hero struggles in a web of malice, misinterpretation, and betrayal. "He is always certain that he'll be caught the next time he moves or speaks," Wald wrote Warner, "but something drives him on."

There were later spin-offs, notably the 1960s TV series *The Fugitive* and the subsequent 1993 film. But the studio was at first reluctant and proceeded only after heavy lobbying by Bogart and Wald, the producer of a string of hits from *Across the Pacific* to *Mildred Pierce*. Wald was the champion of both the tried and the off-beat—he later urged Warners to make *Rebel Without a Cause*—and he prodded J. L. to give him the go-ahead on the one project that Bogart would accept without argument.

Bacall's role was a factor in Bogart's decision, though by no means the determining one. Wald and director Delmer Daves even talked at one point of replacing her with the auburn-haired Swedish newcomer Viveca Lindfors. Far from protesting, Bogart said he'd take any female star they suggested. He proposed Bacall for roles that he thought suitable but never made his consent conditional on the employment of his wife.

It was a pleasant shoot, regardless of the rain, fog, and onlookers with autograph books. Daves, a former screenwriter—he contributed to *The Petrified Forest*—was a genial blond bear of a man who enjoyed working with his stars. Reporters streamed in and out of the Bogart suite at the Mark Hopkins. Across the street at the Fairmont, the dance band played "Bogey Man Boogie" in honor of the visitors. At the Golden Gate Bridge, 1,500 fans so tied up traffic that the highway patrol had to be called in.

Dark Passage is notable for a storytelling device in which the protagonist becomes the camera; the audience watches the initial events unfold through the eyes of the fugitive. The ambitious undertaking required a camera of a new handheld kind that could approximate the motions of the unseen hero. He is made visible in stages, appearing first in bandages—he conveniently meets up with a plastic surgeon—that are finally unwrapped to disclose Bogart's face.

"I can just hear Jack Warner scream," Bogart said. "He's paying me all this money to make the picture and nobody will even see me until it's a third over."

The new film rolled smoothly toward the wrap, and a new Warner contract was successfully concluded after months of haggling that at one point had Bogart ready to pull out. Finally, he and Jaffe presented terms that were non-negotiable: a fifteen-year contract; one picture a year for Warners at $200,000 per picture; approval of scripts and directors, with blanket approval for a short list that included Howard Hawks, John Huston, John Cromwell, Delmer Daves, and Michael Curtiz; and permission to do one film a year for another studio.

"The proposition was a matter of take it or leave it," Thornton Delehanty reported in the New York *Herald Tribune*. "The studio took it. Bogart and Jack Warner shook hands . . . and agreed that henceforth they would love each other like brothers." Considering how little Jack and his brother Harry loved each other, that wasn't saying much.

The sixty-seven-page document—the longest agreement for a screen actor on record to that time—had to be ratified by a full meeting of the board of directors of Warner Bros. Pictures, Inc. It was a far cry from the days of *The Petrified Forest* or his first $200 contract with Vitaphone. In Burbank, Warner photographers caught a smiling Bogart signing the contract. Bacall was by his side, with Sam Jaffe, Mary Baker, and Morgan Maree lined up behind the couple like proud godparents.

On Christmas Day 1946, Humphrey Bogart turned forty-seven. He was the king of Hollywood; his 1946 salary of $467,361 was the highest in the world for an actor. He had a beautiful young wife, a new home, and a fat contract. The year ahead looked full of promise. Part of that promise was spelled out in the closing pages of the contract. It referred specifically to "the screenplay . . . based upon the literary property entitled 'TREASURE OF THE SIERRA MADRE' " The script had been on the Warner shelves for years. It had occasionally been considered as a film during the war, only to be returned, with the entry on the report usually reading "Awaiting a new writer." But at last the studio had found the writer it wanted, and for some months the blank space had been filled with a new entry—"Awaiting John Huston."

CHAPTER 17

"A Loathsome Character"

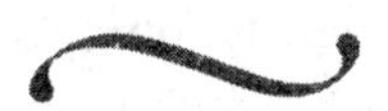

By the end of 1946, Bogart was considered a serious romantic lead and acknowledged as a top box office draw. After a dozen years of playing characters that were, almost without exception, the studio's choice, he was at last in a position to take on any role he wanted. He exercised this freedom by choosing to play a loser driven by greed into mindless, homicidal paranoia in *The Treasure of the Sierra Madre.*

The grim fable of three drifters in 1920s Mexico and their soul-destroying quest for gold marked a striking departure from the heroic leads usually accorded a male star, as well as from the gritty Warners socio-dramas and gangster stories of the thirties. Fred C. Dobbs is a laborer, panhandler, prospector, and, ultimately, a would-be murderer of little redeeming value—the very sort of man who, when played by Bogart in earlier films, was killed by Edward G. Robinson or James Cagney in the final reel. The thugs named Bugs or Turkey, however, were secondary characters, scapegoats who took the punishment for the equally bad but redeemable hero. Dobbs is central to the story; without him, the moral is lost. "Wait till you see me in my next picture," Bogart gleefully yelled to New York *Post* critic Archer Winsten on the sidewalk outside "21." "I play the worst shit you ever saw." Which was part of the appeal: "He's a man prepared to take big risks," John Huston said of Bogart a few years after the film was released. "He'll go out to the racetrack and bet ten dollars while others are betting hundreds. At poker he plays cautiously. But when the stakes are really huge he's a high-flying gambler."

The script was adapted from a joyless tale of back-country Mexico, first published in Berlin and written by a German expatriate claiming to be an American. The author, who called himself B. Traven but whose real name appears to have been Ret Marut, was a recluse with a vast underground following who had become famous by pursuing anonymity. He was thought to be a former actor, polemicist, and revolutionary who had fled to Mexico following the failed Communist uprising in Munich and the short-lived Bavarian Soviet Republic after World War I. Early inquiries about film rights invariably brought the reply that the author sold them only to"non-capitalist countries." He had reportedly escaped being executed by a firing squad in Germany and was deported from Britain as a Communist. Ever on the lookout for enemies, he took on numerous identities while turning out a string of novels of uncompromising bleakness that were admired by readers around the world. His books have sold 25 million copies in more than thirty languages.

The Treasure of the Sierra Madre had its genesis in a nineteenth-century ballad by a minor German poet, about three Americans prospecting in a foreign land—"They coveted gold and riches/Three wild fellows, sunburned and weatherbeaten." The ballad was a great favorite in the days of dramatic recitations and therefore arguably familiar to Traven the ex-actor: The three partners strike it rich. While one goes off for wine to celebrate, the other two decide that half the gold is better than one third, and plot his murder. The first man returns with the bottle but declines to join in the drinking. After the wine is gone, he is set upon by his knife-wielding partners. "I guess I had that coming," he says as he dies. "You see, I poisoned the wine."

The poet called his three Americans Sam, Will, and Tom. Traven changed them to Howard, Curtin, and Dobbs, and he both fleshed them out and made them more allegorical. Howard is the worldly old prospector who knows that nothing lasts. Curtin is young, and his character is still unformed by either decency or hardness. Dobbs, the weakest of the three, is the eventual victim of his own fears and cynicism.

In the film, only one murder is committed: Dobbs, having tried to rob Howard and murder Curtin, is himself robbed and killed by bandits. Howard, the counterweight to the two younger men, goes to live with the Indians as a healer. Curtin, following his brush with death, finds life to be more important than riches. Their hard-earned gold dust is dumped as worthless sand by the bandits and returned to the elements in the violent sandstorm in the final sequence, amid the loud laughter of the two survivors over what they see as a great cosmic joke.

The last scene was the contribution of John Huston, whose first post-war film broke every studio rule. There was no love story, no women (barring a well-disguised and unbilled Ann Sheridan sauntering across the screen as a hooker), and no happy ending. The Mexico of B. Traven was not the exotic Technicolor tourist fantasy of most movies, but instead a grim landscape of dusty oil towns, ramshackle villages, and scrub brush. The closing scenes play out against a desiccated terrain that is a symbolic desert of the heart and mind.

All of which looked lush to Bogart, who told his friend Thornton Delehanty that the picture offered "top acting possibilities." At forty-seven, he was at the peak of his ability, confident and ready for a new and demanding role. He could scarcely wait to start filming. "He considers *The Treasure of the Sierra Madre* one of the best screen plays he has ever come across," Delehanty wrote in the *Herald Tribune.* "He has unbounded admiration for Huston, both as writer and director, ever since they worked together on *The Maltese Falcon.*"

After making *The Maltese Falcon,* Huston had urged Warners to acquire the property when the rights became available in 1941. For years Huston's agent Paul Kohner had wooed Traven by mail and through their correspondence had learned a great deal about the writer. He also had become Traven's film agent, although the two had never met. When Kohner learned that an independent producer who had been granted an option could not come up with the money, he called Huston on the Warner lot and asked if he could get the studio to make an offer. A deal for the rights and for Huston to direct was struck within an hour. For the activist and film buff Traven, Warners was the ideal studio and Huston the perfect adapter.

For all that, the film was nearly made without either Huston or Bogart. Warners wanted to shoot the movie immediately, and the studio's first choice for Dobbs was Huston's father, Walter, who six years later made an Academy Award–winning Howard. John Garfield's name came up for Dobbs, as did Edward G. Robinson's. Kohner learned that Traven's surprising choice for Howard was Lewis Stone, best known as Judge Hardy, Mickey Rooney's father in the white-bread Andy Hardy series that was MGM's celebration of Main Street USA.

Warner Brothers executives recognized the book's potential from the outset. They saw a superb action story with three great roles for their tough guys, something, one said, that might "go down as one of the greatest pictures of all time." J. L. blessed the project and Hal Wallis wanted to bring the author to Hollywood. But filming, set to begin in early 1942, bogged down in a morass of detail after the legal department insisted on clearing world rights. Traven vainly protested by mail that his publishers were either dead or in concentration camps, but Legal remained convinced that even with half the world in flames there might be someone out there ready to sue for copyright infringement. It was finally Jack Warner's insistence that kept the project from the dead file.

By that time, Huston had been called into service, and "All the time I was in the Army I was afraid that they might let someone else do it." Indeed scripts were drafted and other directors were considered. At one point production looked so certain that Tenny Wright readied his carpenters, and the film would have been made had not the Breen Office found the subject derogatory to Mexico and thus potentially offensive to a wartime ally.

Once out of the Army, Huston immediately set to work on the script. He completed the screenplay in early 1947, after months of work and many suggestions from Traven by mail. Shortly after finishing, he and a small group from the studio went to Mexico to scout locations. Bogart, who was finishing *Dark Passage,* looked forward to a six-week break before starting the new picture with his old friend.

At the same time another project with another old friend came along for Bogart. Like Huston, Mark Hellinger had gone off to war, in his case as a correspondent in the Pacific from 1943 to 1945. He had subsequently become one of the film industry's hottest independent producers. *The Horn Blows at Midnight* (1945), with Jack Benny and directed by Raoul Walsh, was broadly funny, but Hellinger's forte was his hard-edged action pictures. *The Killers* (1946) and *Brute Force* (1947), were well-written, shot with a new post-war realism, and drew mass audiences as well as critical praise. *The Naked City,* his upcoming production, was to be filmed not on a back lot but, in a radical departure for Hollywood, on the streets of New York.

After Hellinger's very successful treatment of Ernest Hemingway's "The Killers," Hemingway sold Hellinger the rights to his best short stories, including "The Snows of Kilimanjaro." In early 1947, Hellinger and Bogart agreed to jointly produce one film a year with Bogart as the star, and the actor became a director and shareholder of Mark Hellinger Productions. The result was the Dream Team of that era: the top tough-guy star, the leading tough-guy producer, and the supreme tough-guy novelist. Both MGM and Columbia were interested in financing the venture, as was David O. Selznick, Hollywood's blue-chip independent producer. Ben Hecht, co-author of *The Front Page* and screenwriter of *Wuthering Heights, Notorious,* and *Spellbound,* declared through an intermediary his interest in working on a Bogart picture.

For Bogart, the career-long contract player, the deal meant independence, a producer's status, and a separate artist's contract that guaranteed a minimum per-picture fee of $199,999. It also meant an earning potential beyond anything in his Warner contract: a share in the profits of his work and the benefit of IRS rules that allowed him to keep 75 percent of that share as capital gains. With *High Sierra* in 1940 Mark Hellinger had improved Bogart's career. Their partnership promised to improve his life.

At Hellinger's art deco compound in the Hollywood Hills, writers, stars, and star-struck mobsters mingled in alcoholic conviviality. Regulars included the Bogarts, Richard Brooks, and John Huston, who provided uncredited writing on the screenplay of *The Killers* during his last months in the Army. (Huston's credit was omitted because technically he was under contract to Warner Brothers. After the screenplay was nominated for an Oscar, Hellinger and the others wondered what they would do if it won. Huston supposedly said, eyes twinkling, "Let us pray that it doesn't win.") At the walnut-paneled bar, drinks were dispensed by the insecure, desperately accommodating host who constantly questioned the loyalty of those who loved him.

Even though he had the high regard of much of the film industry, Hellinger could never convince himself of his success. To Richard Brooks, it seemed as if he greeted each new day as though some fresh catastrophe were imminent. Hellinger was effervescent in the daytime, edgy as evening came, and constantly active. Nights when he was alone at home, he telephoned friends and became suspicious of their activities if no one picked up. In the background his wife, Gladys Glad, wandered through the house, the shades drawn and the lights dimmed to soften her fading looks. A tall, fair-haired wraith who had once been Broadway's most beautiful showgirl, she was by now boozily remote.

Hellinger was on his own self-destructive course. He answered the warning signals of his failing heart with a punishing workload and the steady ingestion of two quarts of liquor a day. A heavy drinker himself, Bogart was not about to lecture a friend on his lifestyle. In fact, he credited Hellinger for teaching him how to drink. For many years, Bogart in the course of an evening would mix martinis with beer with Drambuie. Finally Hellinger told him that that was drinking "like a kid." Under such expert tutelage he switched almost exclusively to scotch, calling it "a very valuable part of my life."

Bogart admired Hellinger's creativity, his uncanny eye for talent, and, perhaps the rarest commodity of all in Hollywood, his cheeky independence. Hellinger was generous with his time, his wallet, and his energy, an innovator and doer whose handshake was his bond.

They were each New Yorkers but of opposite types. Bogart was a WASP from the Upper West Side of Manhattan, Hellinger a Jew from the outer boroughs who displayed a Broadway gloss and was sensitive and close-mouthed about his origins. For both men, the tough show business exterior masked an overriding need for love that they had trouble accepting. Each was essentially a pessimist, aware that the pendulum of fortune swings two ways, and conscious of the chasm at one's feet. But their bleak view of life was balanced by a wry sense of humor. Hellinger once subsidized a writer whom he barely knew, keeping up a flow of funds until the author completed a manuscript that turned out to be a violently anti-Semitic diatribe. Hellinger wrote one last check and sent it off, not because of the man's writing, he said in his covering note, but because "even a no-talent bastard has to eat."

Bogart's friendship with Huston, which began with a nod in the 1930s, was by now a strong tie, both on the set, where Huston was his favorite director, and in daily life. "He had this *enormous* respect for John," their friend Jules Buck recalled. "After all, John made him a star." Some wondered, though, if the respect was invariably reciprocal. Huston was fond of Bogart, but at times Huston, always the *director,* acted as if his fondness was tempered by a sense of superiority. The friendship was genuine, however; and while Huston held Mayo in contempt, he adored the new Mrs. Bogart. His own new marriage, in mid-1946 to Evelyn Keyes, created a close foursome; Keyes considered the Bogarts "nice guests and good hosts, with a joie de vivre about them." The couples enjoyed suburban pleasures at the Bogarts' Benedict Canyon house or at the Hustons' home in the San Fernando Valley, with its collection of horses, dogs, and a chimpanzee who flirted with Bogart and peed in the guests' martinis.

Both wives were considerably younger than their husbands, but according to Keyes, "Everybody I knew was married to an older man." Indeed, at times the ages seemed reversed as the two men bounced around under the influence of scotch and gin while their spouses watched. Although alcohol brought out Bogart's tendency to make cutting remarks,

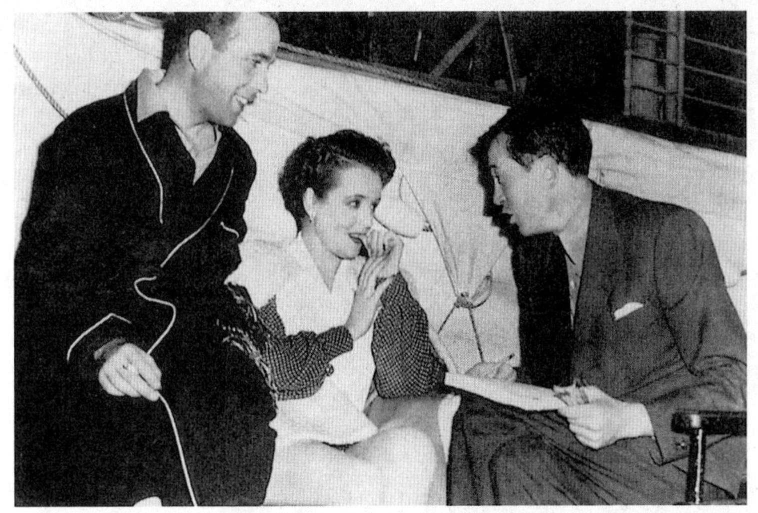

Bogart, Mary Astor, and John Huston during the making of *Across the Pacific* (1942)

Warner Bros. Archives, University of Southern California; courtesy of Warner Bros.

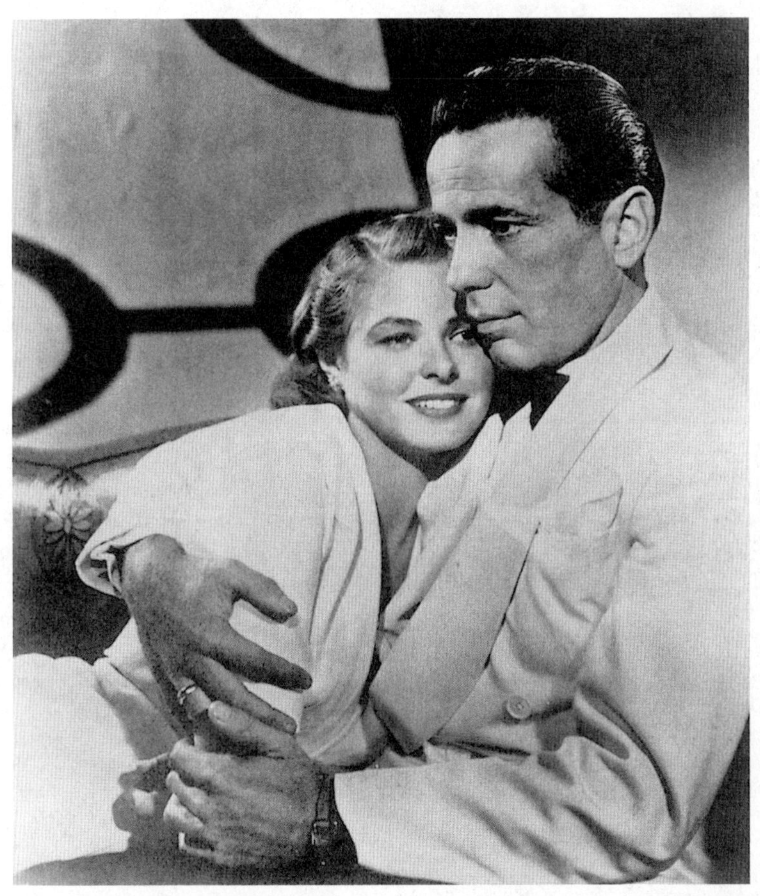

Casablanca (1942) turned Bogart into a romantic leading man and made a star of Ingrid Bergman. Courtesy of Warner Bros.; © 1943 Turner Entertainment Co.

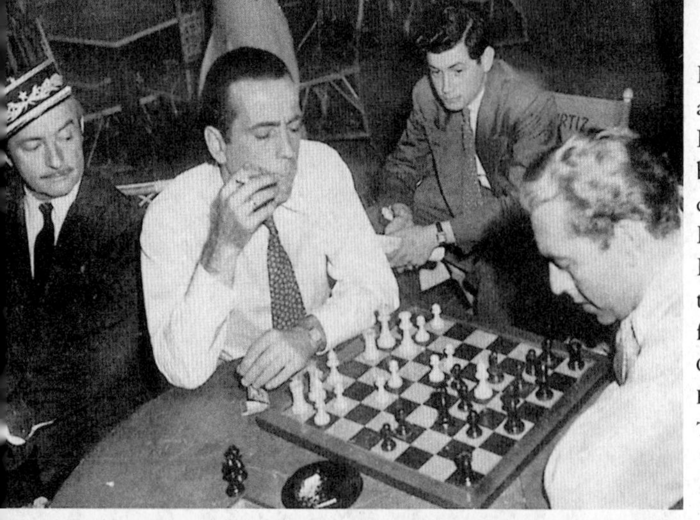

Bogart loved to play chess and was quite good at it. Paul Henreid claimed to be better. Claude Rains, in costume as Captain Louis Renault, watches over Bogart's shoulder between takes of *Casablanca.* The fourth man is unidentified.
Courtesy of George Eastman House and Warner Bros.; © 1943 Turner Entertainment Co.

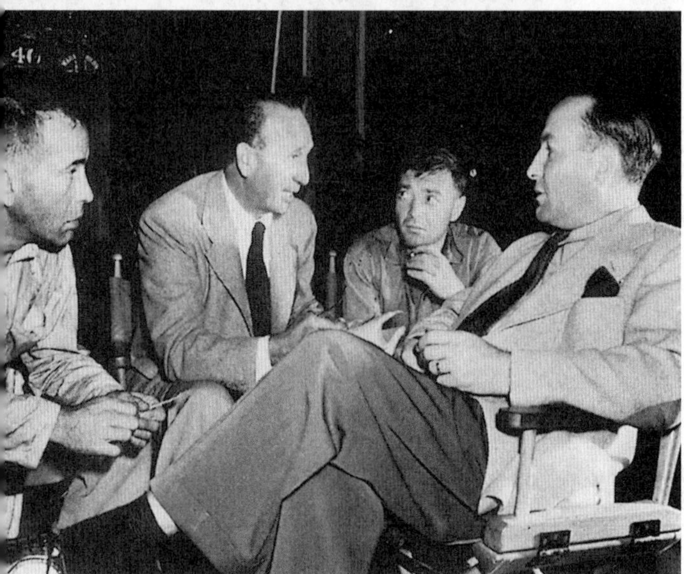

With director Michael Curtiz, Peter Lorre, and Hal Wallis *(right)* on the set of *Passage to Marseille* (1944)
Warner Bros. Archives, University of Southern California; courtesy of Warner Bros.

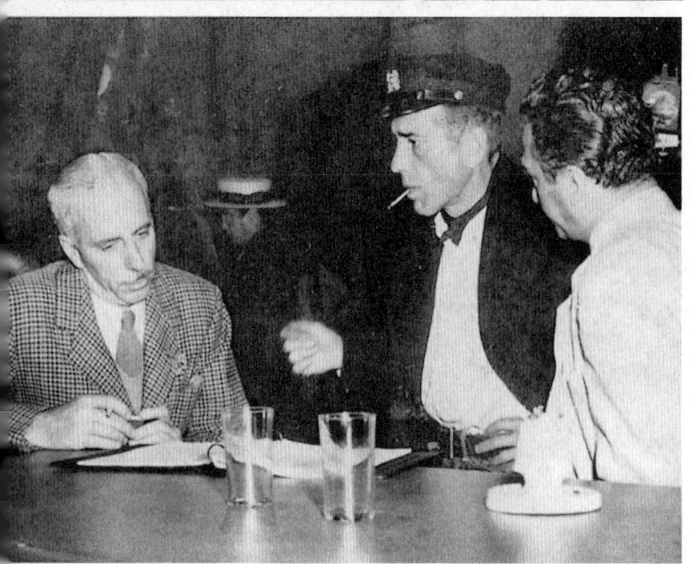

Bogart dressed as Harry Morgan in *To Have and Have Not,* with director Howard Hawks *(left)* and Marcel Dalio (1944)
Courtesy of George Eastman House and Warner Bros.; © 1945 Turner Entertainment Co.

Bogart and Mayo at the sixteenth annual Academy Awards presentation, March 2, 1944, at Grauman's Chinese Theatre in Hollywood. Bogart was a Best Actor nominee for *Casablanca.* He was also about to fall in love with Lauren Bacall, with whom he was working on *To Have and Have Not.*
Courtesy of the Academy of Motion Picture Arts and Sciences

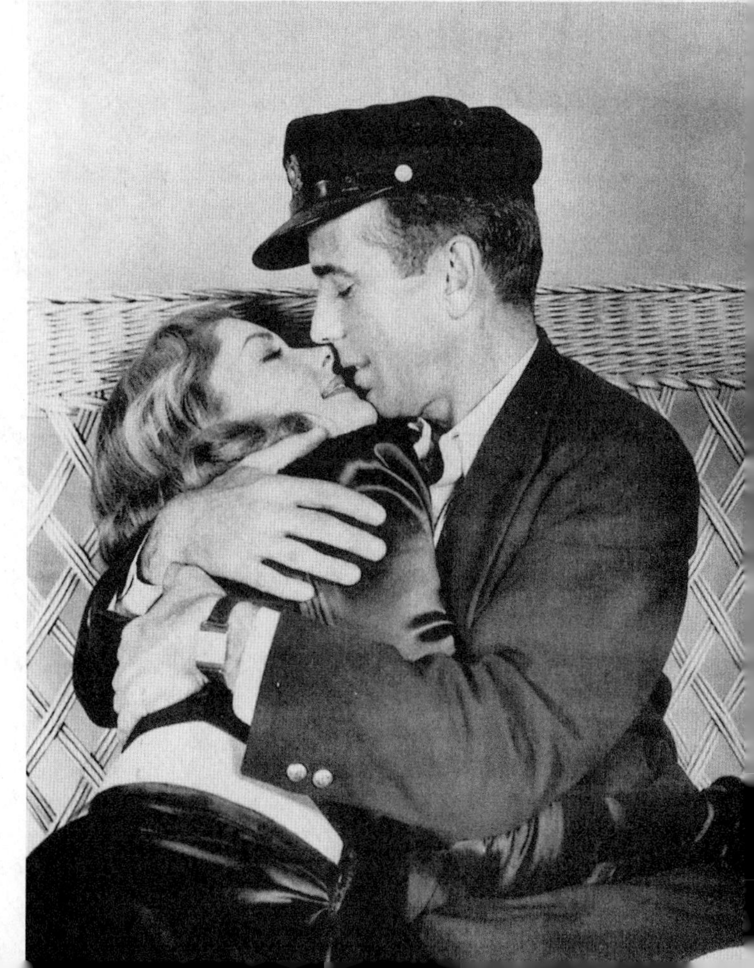

In this publicity shot for *To Have and Have Not,* the evident affection did not need to be staged.
Courtesy of George Eastman House and Warner Bros.; © 1945 Turner Entertainment Co.

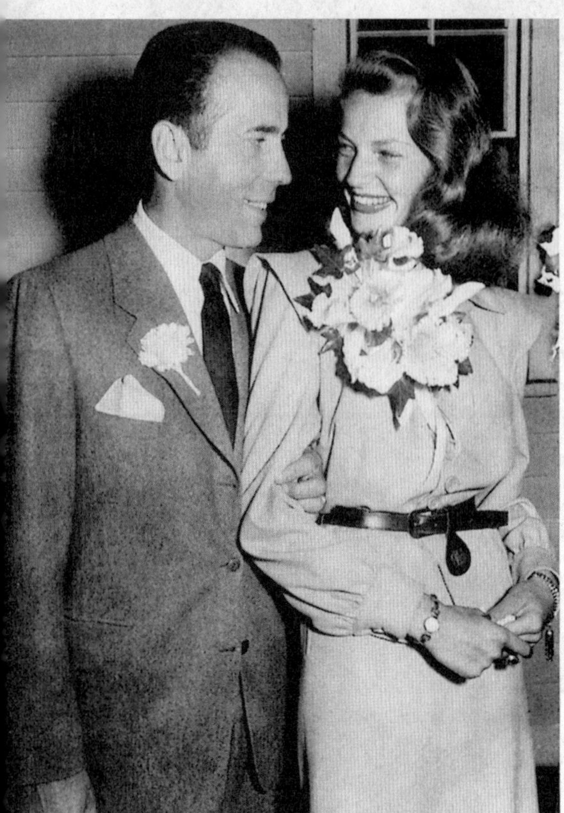

Bogart and Bacall immediately after they were married on May 21, 1945

Corbis-Bettmann

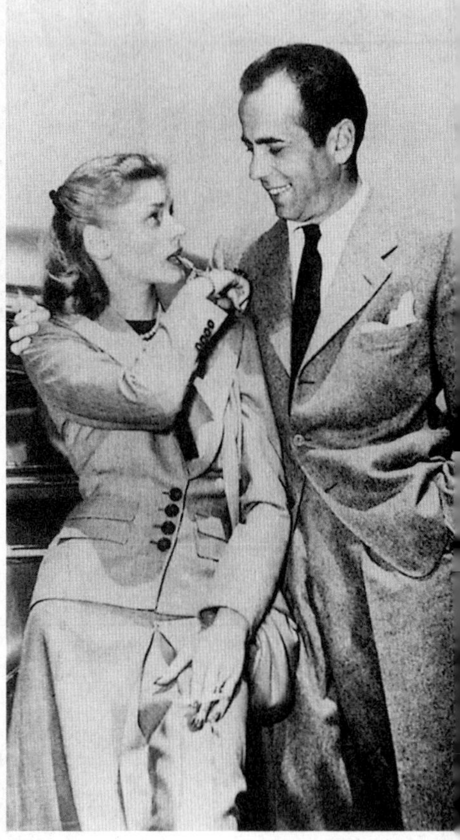

Lauren Bacall wearing the gold whistle Bogart gave her in memory of their famous scene in *To Have and Have Not*

Courtesy of the Academy of Motion Picture Arts and Sciences and Warner Bros.; © 1945 Turner Entertainment Co.

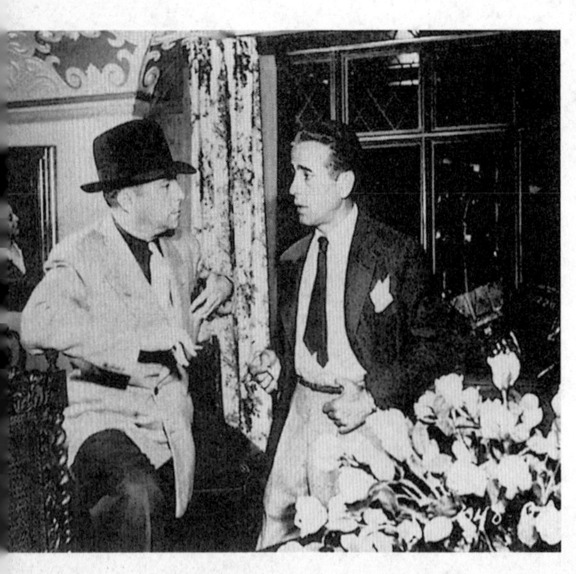

Bogart with Mark Hellinger, his friend and future business partner, during the making of *The Two Mrs. Carrolls,* probably summer 1945

Courtesy of Warner Bros.

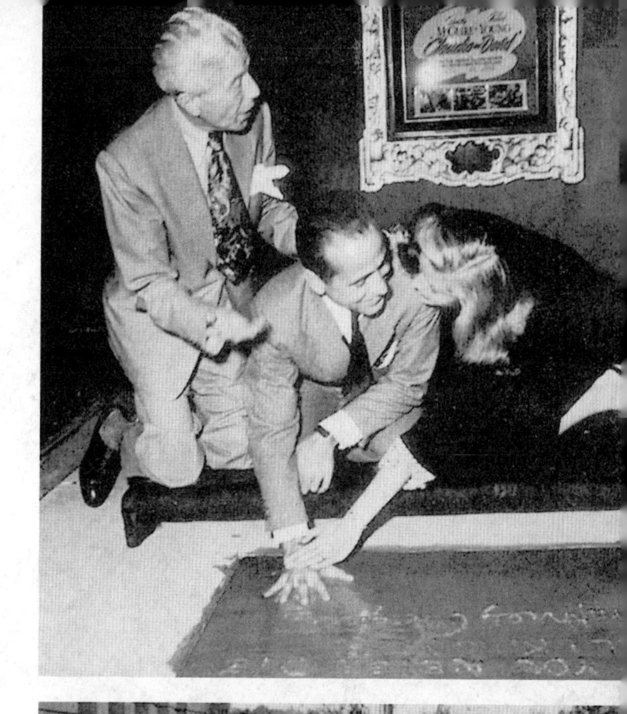

Bogart's note to Sid Grauman *(left),* in concrete along with his hand- and footprints, read "Sid, may you never die till I kill you." Bacall helps out, about a year after their marriage.

Courtesy of Warner Bros.

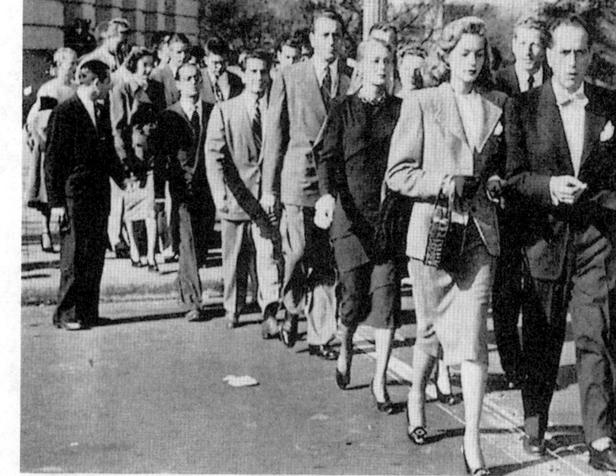

Bogart and Bacall leading the Committee for the First Amendment to the House Committee on Un-American Activities hearings in Washington, D.C., in October 1947. Behind Bacall is June Havoc. Danny Kaye is between Bogart and Bacall. Bogart became the lightning rod for criticism of the group.

Archive Photos

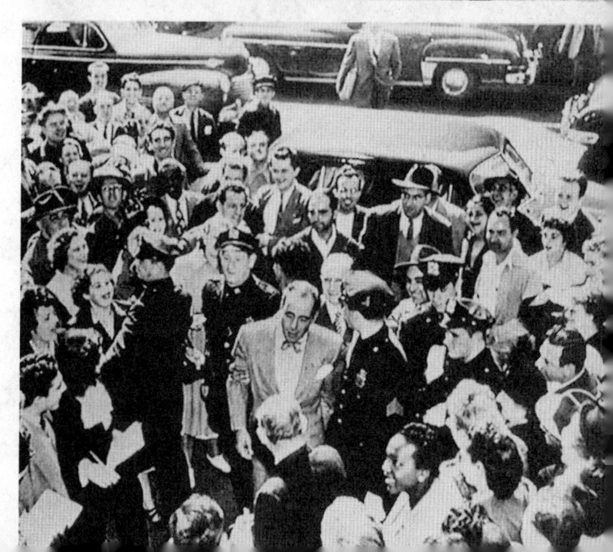

Bogart is cheered by several hundred fans in New York City as he goes to court to defend himself in the matter of the panda incident (1948).

A Delmar Watson Los Angeles Historical Archives Photograph

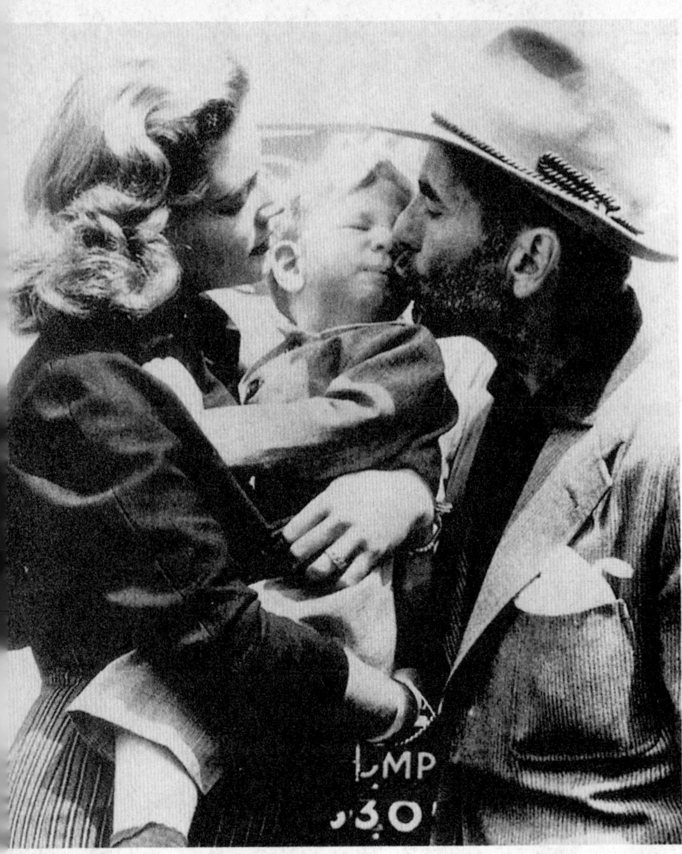

After six months of shooting in Africa, Bogart and Bacall were reunited in London with their son, Stephen, for the completion of *The African Queen.* The beard was grown for his role in the movie.
AP/Wide World Photos; Hearst Newspaper Collection, Department of Special Collections, University of Southern California Libraries

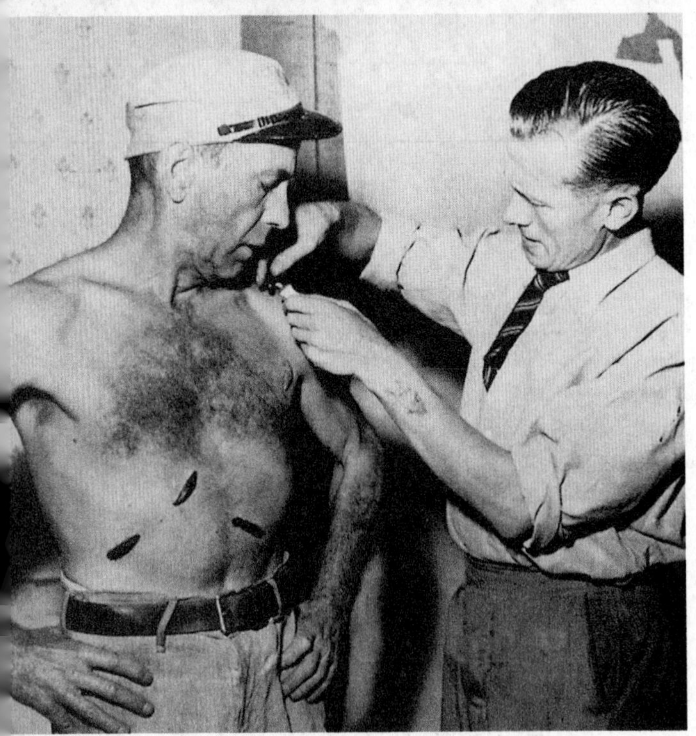

John Huston, a stickler for verisimilitude in *The African Queen* and all his other pictures, wanted the character Charlie Allnut to be covered with real leeches. When Katharine Hepburn urged Bogart to agree, he answered, "You try it first, kid." It took several attempts for the makeup artist to find an adhesive that would hold the rubber ones that were used.
Photo courtesy of Paramount Pictures Corporation and Horizon Management, Inc., Romulus Films, Ltd., and CTE (Carlton) Ltd. Print courtesy of the Academy of Motion Picture Arts and Sciences. *The African Queen* © Horizon Management, Inc. © 1951, © renewed 1979

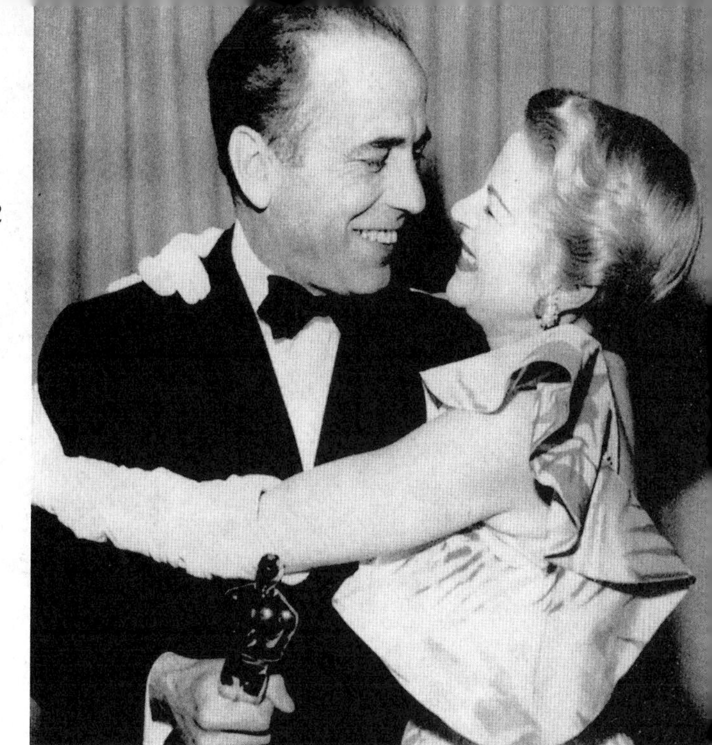

Claire Trevor, who had won an Oscar for her performance in *Key Largo,* with Bogart after he won Best Actor in 1952 for *The African Queen*
Archive Photos

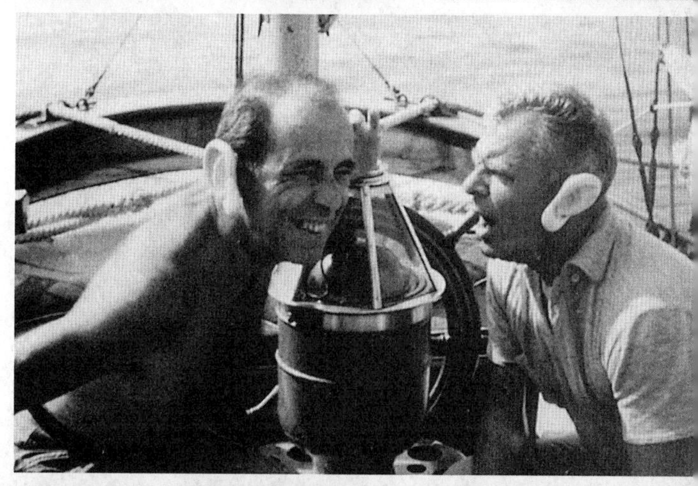

Bogart was an excellent sailor and was on the ocean nearly every weekend he was in Los Angeles. His skipper was Carl Peterson. He ran a tight but playful ship.
Courtesy of Mr. and Mrs. George E. Roosevelt Jr.

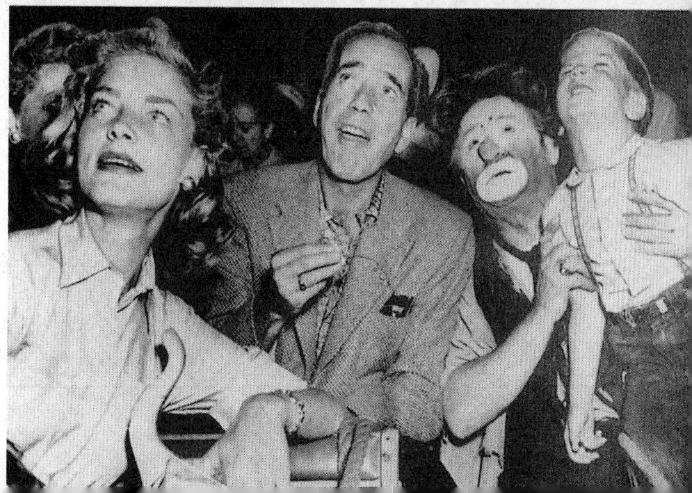

Clown Otto Griebling joins the Bogarts at the circus in September 1953.
Hearst Newspaper Collection, Special Collections, University of Southern California

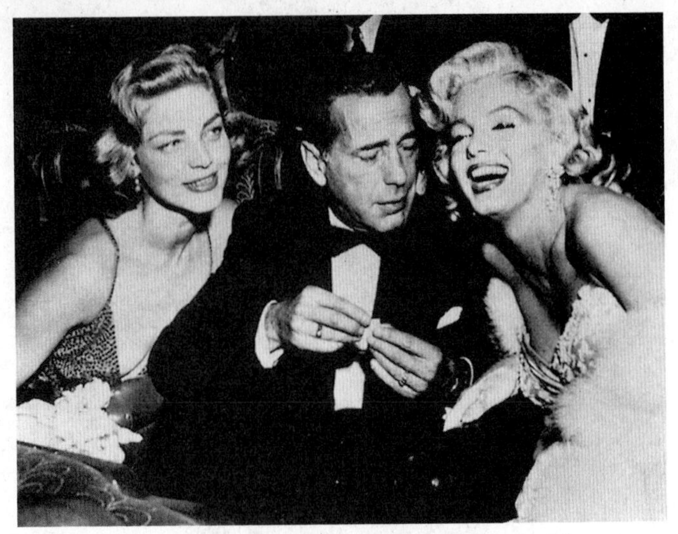

After Bacall and Marilyn Monroe completed *How to Marry a Millionaire* (1953) Archive Photos

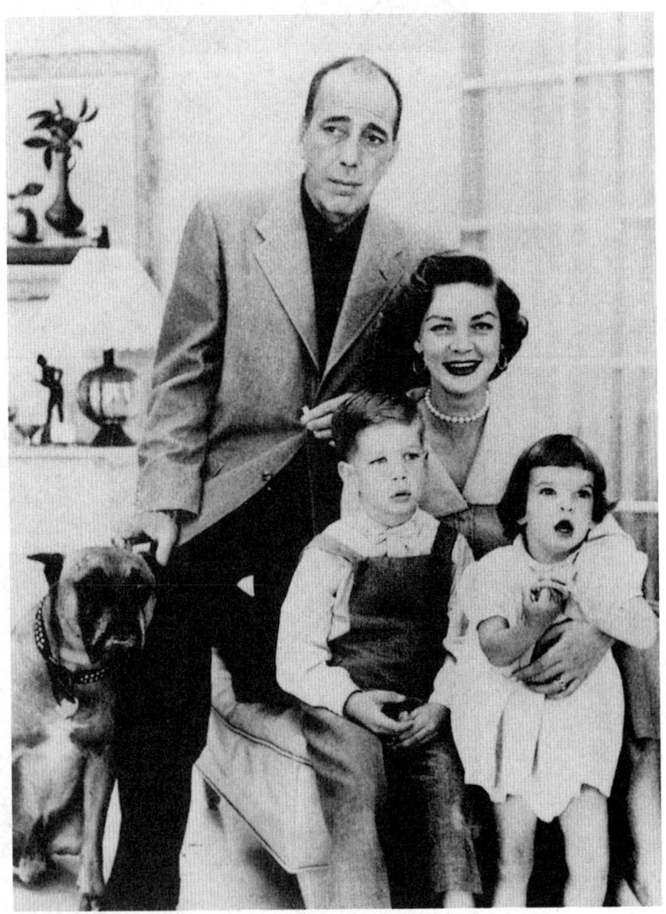

With Stephen and Leslie, circa 1955 Archive Photos

they didn't bother Huston, who also enjoyed putting people on. "Bogie liked to drink and insult people and then smile," Huston said. "He had a *wonderful* time within himself."

To Keyes, "these were John and Bogie's boyhood days. They acted like a couple of kids all the time. John was a big game player, so everyone around him played games. They also smoked a lot, which they later paid for [Huston died of emphysema], and they drank a lot. I remember conversations of John and Bogie the next morning—'Oh! did we do *that?*' '*Oh,* do you remember this?' 'Can you *believe* we did . . . ' That's childhood, isn't it? They didn't act older; they didn't *know* they were older. They just had fun."

The fun could take odd turns, as it did one evening at the Hustons, when screenwriter Charles Grayson, Ida Lupino, and her Warner executive husband, Collier Young, were invited over. Bogart and Huston had dipped heavily into the liquor supply. Shedding their jackets and shoes, they decided to play football—to Keyes's combined amusement and horror, in the living room, with a Ming vase. "It was sitting there, gorgeously, by the fireplace, and Charlie Grayson picked it up and *threw* it, and somebody didn't catch it. Everybody roared with laughter. You don't think that Bogie and John are going to cry or scold because a Ming vase gets broken! They continued flopping over the couches and chairs, leaping around the room as drunk as they could be. They thought it was hilarious and they weren't feeling much pain."

Eventually Bogart did. In order to get better traction on the floor, he had removed his socks as well as his shoes, and the shards and splinters from the vase cut his feet in many places. Bacall plucked out the pieces, saying in a caring voice, "Oh, *honestly,* how could you do such a thing?" Meanwhile, according to Keyes, "Ida Lupino sat and watched. Staring. The stillest person in this whole thing. Just looking on with utter *amazement.* But they thought they were frightfully witty, Bogie and Johnny, and they had big conversations about it the next day, still enjoying it, even with Bogie's Band-Aided feet."

Over the years, the identity of the man who called himself B. Traven became part of the mythology surrounding *The Treasure of the Sierra Madre.* In his 1980 autobiography, Huston wrote of vain attempts to meet Traven while scouting locations in Mexico. Then one morning Huston, who never locked his door, awoke in his Mexico City hotel room to find a small, shy man standing by his bed, saying he was Hal Croves, a translator empowered to speak for Traven. Huston wrote that additional meetings convinced him that the unprepossessing visitor couldn't possibly have been the genius who had written *The Treasure of the Sierra Madre*, but that was camouflage. According to Warner Brothers' records, after sending home the group from the studio, Huston headed to Traven's return address in Acapulco given him by Kohner "to confer with the author, if possible." (Kohner became convinced that Croves and Traven were the same man, and Croves admitted this was so shortly before his death in 1969.)

Traven's letters show that he was delighted with Huston's draft; it was, the author wrote, "as close alongside the book as a picture will ever allow." The two then worked further on the script, riding in the foothills of the Sierra Madre between sessions. Huston not only arranged for Traven to be on the set during filming and receive a $500 weekly stipend under the alias of Croves, had also planned a jungle expedition with him once the picture was completed. Huston left for Los Angeles with a promise from Traven to send his further comments along. Traven also promised to recover Huston's pick-pocketed wallet, and told of spreading handbills all over Acapulco. "You'd be surprised if you were here and saw the immense propaganda," he wrote Huston, referring to the multitude of notices, "it's the talk of the town. . . . My love to Evelyne [*sic*] and a poke in the ribs to you." The letter was signed "H. C." The ongoing charade was just another game for Huston, but it allowed Traven a disguise, however transparent, and it enabled Huston to maintain the fiction of "the spook in Mexico," as Warner executives called the ostensible front man.

In Traven's long letters to Huston, written in a mixture of German grammatical constructions and American slang, he suggested scenes that have become touchstones of the film. For instance, early on the partners travel into the interior to begin their prospecting on a train that is attacked by bandits. Dobbs fires at the leader—the gold-sombreroed man who is in the end to be his murderer—but he misses and the outlaw escapes. Traven's suggestion was "a sort of duel between Dobbs and Gold Hat. . . . this I think Bogart could well express by his face and gestures without any dialogue save a few words." Huston was captivated by the idea and responded, "From that moment on, their destinies are paired in some mysterious way."

It was a key moment in Bogart's performance—Dobbs, smoking gun in hand, peers out the train window and makes eye contact with his adversary, and his fate. From there, Traven wrote, there was a clear plot line to the scene where the two men meet for the last time "and Dobbs, recognizing Gold Hat, recognizes that he has arrived at his journey's end, that this time he cannot escape, from the expression of his face. Bogart can do that as few others."

Another of Traven's suggestions was for Huston personally. While they were in Acapulco, Traven had watched Huston spread cash around, generously, nonchalantly, with hardly a glance at the recipient. "I was just thinking," he wrote Huston in Burbank, "why don't you yourself play the Man in the White Suit? . . . You would be most natural in the part." Near the beginning of the film, Dobbs, who is broke, shuffles up to a prosperous gringo in a white suit at whom he doesn't look and whose face is not shown. "Hey Mister," he asks, "will you stake a fellow American to a meal?" The man casually hands him a peso. Later, Dobbs sees a white-suited American getting a shoeshine (White Suit's face is hidden by a newspaper) and uses the same line with the same result. But on the third occasion, when Dobbs sees White Suit on the street and tries again, he receives nothing but scorn. "Such impudence never came my way!" White Suit lectures the shambling bum. "Excuse me, Mister," Dobbs says abjectly, "I never knowed it was you. . . . just looked at your hands and the money you gave me." White Suit then hands him a peso and says, "Do me a favor, will you? Go occasionally to somebody else. . . . This is the very last you'll get from me. Just to make sure you don't forget your promise, here's another peso. But from now on, you have to make your way through life without my assistance."

Traven was convinced that "Bogart will be a great Dobbs. He will draw the public as no one else." But he was not so certain about Walter Huston, his Dobbs of six years ago, now cast as Howard. The elder Huston was sixty-three, which Traven felt was too young and too robust for the grizzled old man. "You know as well as I do that Howard, not Dobbs, is the soul of the picture," Traven wrote, and to that end he asked, could John please make his father look "over seventy." That was accomplished by having Huston play the part minus his false teeth, and Traven soon put his reservations about the casting aside. "Howard steals the picture in spite of us. . . . it will be Walt's picture. . . . Don't let Humphry [*sic*] know." Bogart, who had not worked with Walter Huston since the radio broadcast of *Henry IV* in 1937, already realized that the picture would belong to the master. "First he is a gentleman," Bogart told an interviewer, "then an actor, and what an actor! He's probably the only performer in Hollywood to whom I'd gladly lose a scene."

Though the parts of Dobbs and Howard were quickly cast, there remained the other two central roles—the prospector Curtin, and Cody, the intruder who horns in on the partners' strike and dies defending the camp. Two "very strong likelihoods," Huston wrote Traven, were Ronald Reagan as Curtin and Zachary Scott as Cody, but they were eventually assigned to other productions, and the role of Cody went to Bruce Bennett, who had worked with Bogart in *Sahara* and *Dark Passage.* The larger role of Curtin would take longer to fill. Barton MacLane, the perennial Warner heavy, was cast as McCormick, the crooked American contractor. For the bandits, Huston wanted to avoid the usual faces from Central Casting and chose Mexican star Alphonse Bedoya as Gold Hat and other Mexican actors for the lesser roles.

The locations for *The Treasure of the Sierra Madre* were extensive. Some scenes were to be done in Burbank, others in the California mining country in the mountains near Sacramento. The bulk of the picture, however, was to be shot in Mexico, at sites scouted and photographed during Huston's trips with art director John Hughes, the designer for *The Petrified Forest* and *They Drive by Night.*

During pre-production, Huston went to Tampico to film some shots that did not require the actors. Everything seemed in order. The script had been cleared with censors in Mexico, a prerequisite for filming there. So Huston was unprepared when a party of officials drove up, ordered him to stop and demanded that all footage be turned over to the Mexican government.

A local newspaper had charged that the company was out to malign Mexico; and when word reached the capital, Huston was ordered to stop shooting until what he had already filmed could be examined. In response, the staff of Warners' Mexico City office pulled strings and the mayor of Tampico interceded. After two days of standing by in the street with cameras ready to roll, Huston was told he could continue; the government, Warners was informed, had found nothing construed as offensive to the dignity of the country. In Huston's more colorful retelling, the two days became two months and his savior was the artist Diego Rivera, whom Huston claimed made an appeal on his behalf to the president of the nation.

The first day of production was March 17, on the Warner lot. Drawing on hundreds of photographs taken on the scouting trip, John Hughes had reconstructed the plaza in Tampico with dazzling fidelity. On Stage 22 Dobbs and Curtin, out of work and out of luck, shared a bench and commiserated on their ill fortune. ("Cigarette?" / "Thanks.") To cast

Curtin, Huston had gone outside Warners for Tim Holt, who had so effectively played the destructive son in Orson Welles's *The Magnificent Ambersons* (1942). The actor's father, cowboy star Jack Holt, appears briefly alongside Walter Huston at the fleabag Oso Negro, where Huston as Howard spins tales of fabulous gold strikes. The others listen and dream of treasure but ignore his warning that "gold's a devilish sort of thing. . . . I know what gold does to men's souls."

On the sidelines awaiting his scene was thirteen-year-old Bobby Blake, cast as the barefoot street urchin who pesters Dobbs into buying a share of a state lottery ticket; a sure winner, the boy points out, because the numbers add up to thirteen. (As an adult Blake played the lame killer in Truman Capote's *In Cold Blood* and the detective of TV's *Baretta* series.) Blake, watching Bogart perform, was drawn to him "like a moth to light. He was unjazzy. Un-Hollywood. Very gentle."

Their first scene together was on a cafe set. Dobbs, spending on a cup of coffee much of the remaining money panhandled from White Suit, tries to shake off the determined boy. ("State Lottery, Señor?"/"Beat it.") Dobbs ultimately buys the one-twentieth share of the ticket that will bring him treasure and death, but not before throwing a glass of water in the boy's face to try to drive him off. Huston, Blake later said, "made him do it several times, and he didn't want to. He was being nice to me. But boy, when the camera turned, he threw that water and he threw it hard, because he was a professional, and that scene was supposed to be what it was supposed to be."

Blake was a street-wise kid from Nutley, New Jersey, who, starting out in the *Our Gang* comedies, had spent almost half his life in movies and loved the Warner tough guys. "I got to work with Eddie G., I got to work with Greenstreet, the whole gang, but Bogart was probably more special than all the rest. I used to watch him like a kid watches a father. You know, you watch your father shave so *you* can learn how to shave. Bogie used to take his script to the dressing room and he would read lines into the mirror. I would watch him with the door open a crack; I was like two feet tall; nobody was going to pay attention to me scooting around there. He'd look in the mirror and he'd get a line and he'd rub his ear. Another time he'd do something with his lip. And then he'd take a pencil and he'd cross out a couple of lines. The first time I was scared. But then after a while it seemed like Bogie didn't notice, or he didn't care. I remember even once or twice putting my fingers on the door to make it move. I was fascinated by him cutting his dialogue. I thought, 'Wow, he doesn't want to talk.' "

The result was to pare down the lines to the essentials, to get the sound of everyday speech and sharpen meanings. For instance, Dobbs yielding on buying the ticket share was written, "Give me the twentieth so I don't have to look at your ugly face any longer." Bogart changed it to, "Give me a twentieth so's I don't have to look at your ugly face."

After Bogart got his lines the way he wanted them, Blake said, he would go and talk to Huston. " 'John, I don't have to say this. Let the kid say it,' meaning Tim Holt. Or, 'Let the old man say it.' He was not like the other actors. Jimmy Cagney was flashy on the set. Edward G. Robinson had a very erudite kind of quality about him. But Bogart—it was almost like he was the prop man. Very quiet, but he also was the center of things. He wasn't pushy or flashy. And he wasn't giving interviews between takes. He was just this little almost fragile man: his pants were too big for him and his shirt was too big for him, and his shoulders only came out about an inch beyond his ears, but he was tremendously commanding.

"When I went on the set to read for the part, John Huston and Bogie came over. John was very colorful, and he was a big, tall man, arms gangling all over the place. He looked down at me and he was nine thousand feet in the air. Then he reached down and got me under the arms and he picked me up and threw me up in the air and held me like he was weighing me. He said, 'I don't know. I . . . I think he'll do all right. What do *you* think, Bogie?' And Bogie kind of grumbled something down his throat, and that was it. I had the part."

When it came time for Blake to film his first scene, "Huston just assumed that I was going to hit the marks and it was all going to come out fine, but my asshole was so tight you couldn't have got a dime up it with a sledgehammer." Bogart—"sensitive and warm"—made the difference. "He wasn't an overt, gee-whiz-sonny-don't-worry-I'm-going-to-help-you kind of guy; those are only words anyway. Instead, you got the *feeling* that things would be all right, and the feeling was much more important. I was frightened that I was out of my element, but Bogie was very helpful, because he was so good. When he elbowed me, he really elbowed me; and he really threw that water. But you could just tell it was going to be okay. You knew that when you were near him you were safe."

On his last day of work, Blake looked for a memento of his time with Bogart. On the cafe set where Dobbs had thrown the water in the boy's face, the glass was still on the table, next to Dobbs's empty coffee cup. Making sure no one was looking, he snatched them both.

Sunday evening, April 6, the company, along with Bacall and Evelyn Keyes, boarded what was to be a direct, nine-hour Pan Am flight to Mexico City. Warner Brothers had arranged for a reception at the airport and had lined up limousines to whisk everyone off to the location in time for brunch. Instead, a ground fog kept the plane circling between repeated passes at the field, and the sudden sharp ascent after each aborted landing made stomachs heave. Finally, running low on gas, the flight was redirected to Veracruz, an hour away. The passengers shakily disembarked as the plane refüeled. "As many of the party as could ate breakfast," one of the crew noted in the Production and Progress Report. Eventually they arrived in Mexico City, where they were met by a crush of bands, pretty girls with flowers, newsreel photographers, and civic notables. Home for the next two months was the luxury Hotel Reforma at San José de Purura, the fashionable spa 140 miles from Mexico City.

Huston shot in the back country under an unrelenting sun for almost eight weeks, a rigorous routine that left him energized and Bogart exhausted. "We had nice quarters—sure," he told a unit publicist with some humor. "But John didn't make any shots around that beautiful little resort village where we stayed. No. He had to go up into the hills. I mean MOUNTAINS! If he saw a nice *close* mountain to photograph, then that mountain was no good. If we could get to a location site without fording a couple of streams, walking through a nest of rattlesnakes and scorching in the sun, then he said it wasn't quite right. We called him 'Hard-Way Huston.' "

When Huston couldn't find what he wanted, he created it, as he did with the locale for the final and fatal meeting with Gold Hat. Dobbs stumbles onto a water hole, stoops to drink, and sees the reflected face of his killer. A site near a ruined hacienda was perfect. That there was no water hole was immaterial to Huston. He ordered a pit dug; prop men planted shrubs and cactus around the edge; and giant drums of water were carted in and drained into the pit with a garden hose.

"He's just a mite teched with genius," Bogart said. "You have to be a mite teched to be a genius, I guess."

However exhausted Bogart may have been, he didn't lose his fondness for playing jokes on other actors or the crew. When, one day, the still photographer seemed to be taking shots exclusively of Tim Holt, Bogart turned to unit publicist Bob Fender and demanded to know exactly *who* the star of this picture was! Fender, seeing his job vanish, broke out in a sweat until Holt and Bogart, laughing, told him there was no film in the camera.

There was also considerable amusement over the presence of a hairdresser for a movie about three bums. Nevertheless, each morning at seven, Betty Lou Delmont made sure the stars were properly disheveled. Applying what she called mud shampoos, she carefully matched the grime from one day to another. Wigs made to various lengths suggested the passage of time for men out in the wild without benefit of a barber, and in Bogart's case they were essential. "You know that he has practically no hair left," producer Henry Blanke noted during pre-production. Male pattern baldness, a problem for Bogart since the thirties, suddenly became acute during *Dark Passage* when his hair fell out in patches. Joe Hyams reports that the condition was exacerbated by hormone treatments that Bogart underwent in 1946 because he wanted to have children. Doctor-ordered vitamin B_{12} shots helped the hair grow back, and the wigs did the rest, though not always perfectly. In a scene early in the film, Dobbs spends much of one of White Suit's pesos on a shave and haircut. As he leaves the shop, his hair slicked down, the join in the back is evident. In May, however, writer Charles Grayson reported that Bogart was "growing a fine new crop of hair."

For the visiting Americans, certain sights and sounds remained vivid long after the close of production: all-night shoots lit by lamps attached to huge generator trucks that had been brought up along the widened forest trails; the call on the set for *"Silencio"* followed by *"Listo Señor Bogart"*; the local extras—serape-clad farmers and their wives and children from the nearby Indian village—gathered in the darkness beyond the perimeter of light, the silence broken only by the call of a night bird and the chirp of crickets.

For the villagers, the studio largesse of ten pesos, or two dollars, a day was a godsend, and the community welcomed the visitors in a formal ceremony presided over by the serious young mayor; Huston made an appropriate response. At the end of each day, the extras were thanked in Spanish for their splendid cooperation, and the town treasurer made sure that the promised pesos were evenly distributed.

Raul Perez Herrera, the young local doctor who also served as the company medic, took the Americans around to nearby villages. Everywhere they saw malnourished children with swollen bellies and bowed, stunted legs. Herrera, like Belmont DeForest Bogart, was a graduate of Columbia University. "Once he sees that we in the troupe are all right," Bogart wrote, "(and what the hell could we need after seeing those kids?), he plunges into his work. . . . Sometimes he reports for morning call without having had a wink of sleep." The company took up a collection for a mobile medical unit, and Bogart made the presentation, while Warner Publicity churned out upbeat releases about village kids provided with fresh milk. But everyone connected with the film knew that the gesture was no more than a palliative.

Throughout the production, a quiet, self-effacing figure in faded khaki would arrive promptly every morning, stand to one side all day, and leave only after the last scene was shot. He was listed on the staff sheet as "adviser." "We have a lad on the show," the auditor reported to Burbank, "who goes by the name of Hal Croves—the mystery character—he is alleged by some to be Bruno Traven." He made good copy for publicist Bob Fender, who drew up long interviews with Croves sounding forth on his friend and employer, the celebrated author, who, he maintained, ran a goat farm somewhere near Oklahoma City. There evidently was also some contact with Bogart, to whom Traven later sent a story idea, addressing him informally as "Bogey." By all indications, Traven played his role as the humble facilitator to the hilt. Bacall, in her memoirs, makes no mention of the pale-eyed little man with graying sandy hair who hovered at the edge but never participated.

Partway through the shooting, Bruce Bennett arrived to play his finely tuned ensemble piece as the intruder who forces his presence on Bogart, Holt, and Huston. He quickly noticed the "wonderful understanding between the three of them as to their characters." Bennett saw the same camaraderie between Bogart and Huston. "They were very close. You sensed that everything was right between them." Holt, a quiet, self-assured presence whom Bennett found "not particularly entranced with the motion picture business," kept to himself. The elder Huston was genial and down to earth, a grand old man of the theater.

Bennett joined in whenever the two Hustons and Bogart went sightseeing. In a nearby town they stopped to hear guitarists play mournful tunes on the steps of the old Spanish church. Walter hummed along in the wisp of a voice that made "September Song" a classic and then sang old ballads in the car all the way back.

"As a performer he was outstanding, absolutely beyond comparison," Bennett said. "John pretty much let him do what he wanted, although John was very much that way anyway. He *always* tried to get the actor's interpretation of the scene before he gave any direction. He might compress it, or rearrange it physically, but he didn't interfere with the nuance of it. When the director of photography would say, 'Now if he can just come a little closer and face *this* way, we can get this on-camera,' John would snap, 'Stop it, don't do that. I want him to play the scene the way he wants to. If we have to change the camera to get it, we'll change the camera—we don't change the actors.'

"Of course Huston was full of mischief. As this character trying to horn in on their gold mining, I come in there with my burro and sit down. They give me some food to eat and there's a discussion around the campfire about whether they should let me stay or not. Close-ups were taken, and in mine I'm supposed to be eating—I'm very hungry. There was a stew or something that the other three had supposedly made and I was really *eating* it. Huston stood by the camera, Bogart next to him, saying, 'Cut! Now do it again and this time *this* way.' Well, he did it about three times before I caught on—the camera wasn't even running. They had shut it off after the first take and were trying to keep me eating. The minute I wised up it was 'Break for lunch!' "

After nearly two months on location, Huston and Bogart's friendship became strained as the film fell behind schedule. There were constant logistical and language problems, then came the so-called planter's rain. The film, begun in mid-March, was meant to close in early June. On July 4, Bogart was to sail in the Honolulu classic, the great trans-Pacific yacht race from California to Hawaii that had been suspended since the attack on Pearl Harbor. It was the biggest sailing event on the West Coast, and for Bogart the fulfillment of a dream. He had lined up a seven-member crew for the *Santana,* and had invested $15,000 in new sails, rigging, and rebuilt storage areas. Huston had assured him at the beginning of production that they would finish in time. Instead, by mid-May they were two weeks behind, with scenes yet to be shot in California. Huston's cheery complacency increased in direct proportion, it seemed, to Bogart's growing restiveness.

"Out to make a fucking masterpiece, right, John?" he muttered, while trying to get Huston to guarantee that he would be free in time for the race.

"He didn't usually bellyache about things," Huston said many years later, "but he loved his boat, and that's what that little contretemps was about. His boat. He wanted to be done—quite rightly. He wanted to join the big race. He was *down* for it. And he wanted to know when we would finish, and could he keep this very important engagement? Well, I at first thought that he could, then I—*I* didn't know. And then he got to *haranguing* on the subject." The irritation boiled over during a dinner in the hotel dining room. "He got a bit loud," Huston said, "and I just reached across the table and took him by the nose."

"He grabbed Bogie's nose," one of the diners recalled, "and twisted it, *all* the way around. And big tears came and streamed down, but Bogie didn't let out a grunt; he didn't move; he just—took it."

"Well," Huston said, "it's hard to do anything if your nose is between somebody's fingers."

To Evelyn Keyes, who left Mexico early and heard of the incident only after the company returned to Los Angeles, "it was like Big Daddy and a child. It's the way John would treat his children Anjelica and Tony—'*It's not amusing any more, behave yourselves!*' And Bogie took it the same as the children—as all of us did! When John spoke, you paid attention."

It was Bacall, Huston said, who finally stepped in. "She said, 'John, you're hurting him.' I knew I was. I stopped it. And that's all there was to it. Shortly after that, Bogie came to me and said, 'John—let's, for God's sake, be like we used to be.' And we were." Characteristically for their relationship, it was Bogart who apologized.

On the evening of May 30, the crew packed up the cameras, lights, and sound equipment, and everyone headed back to Mexico City. "Hal Croves" was persuaded to come along for one last night with the company before they returned to Los Angeles. There still remained four days of back-lot shooting, another ten days in the mountains of California's mining country, and then twenty-six more on the sound stages in Burbank.

Bedoya and two actors brought up from Mexico, this time flanked by bandits from Central Casting, besieged the camp, first on location at Kelley's Rainbow Mine in Kernville, then on Warners' cavernous Stage 7. ("Badges? . . . I don't got to show you any stinkin' badges!") Walter Huston danced the "goatish kind of jig" called for in the script as the old man, suddenly aware that they've struck it rich, mocks the two amateurs blind to the gold beneath their feet. Bogart had still to film the crucial scenes of Dobbs's descent into madness, revealing gold's ability to warp and destroy.

After seventy-six days of production, and no end in sight, the word was that Jack Warner had had enough of rushes with characters talking in Spanish, costs running over budget, and his leading man looking like a grimy slob. Huston struggled to shape up. Scenes were shot so far out of sequence that the story line jumped back and forth by as much as fifty pages at a time. Against this background, Bogart had somehow to sustain the intensity and paranoia that is the thread of Traven's tale—the metamorphosis from down-and-out working man to the obsessive, greedy maniac, driven by conspiracy theories, who shoots his friend at point-blank range. The secret of good acting, Bogart had once said, was in the concentration. Now that belief was put to the test.

Helga Smith, a UCLA undergraduate allowed on the closed set courtesy of Blayney Matthews, sat and watched Bogart film the final disintegration of Fred C. Dobbs as he ranted, gun drawn, at Curtin—"I know you for what you are. . . . Oh, you're not putting anything over on me. . . . I'm doing this to save my life."

The young woman saw more than she expected. "As soon as the word 'Cut' was said, he would go back, always to the same area, where the lights were dimmed, fling himself onto a chair with his arms flopping to either side, and then just go wild. He simply went berserk. Whoever was around him, he'd scream at them—you had to get out of his way because his arms would sort of flail around—saying, 'Get out!' or 'What do you want?' "

Smith, fascinated, watched as streams of profanity tumbled out nonstop—" 'goddamn,' 'bitch,' 'fuck,' things like that. He would repeat and repeat his cursing, then quiet down a little bit before starting again. In the takes, he was perfect—they never had to cut or redo something because of his actions. Within seconds he was just a different person. It was like watching twins. He really had to have some power to pull himself together to put on such a good performance. He was out of control, but he knew perfectly well what he was doing. It was simply . . . the *intensity*."

Matthews had told her it was one reason the set was closed. Also, he said, Mr. Bogart didn't want a bunch of strangers staring at him when he was losing himself in this difficult part.

"If you're shooting a sequence," Bruce Bennett explained, "you've got to remember and you've got to think and carry through, bit by bit. And if you're trying to sustain that mood, it's like somebody's intruding on your thoughts; and you're likely, very likely, to bark at them—though for the most part Bogart was remarkably free of that sort of thing. Remember, he was in almost every scene. He's the film."

In the last two days of production Bogart, worn out by the hundred days of filming, faced his last and toughest scene: the isolated Dobbs, his partner's almost-murderer, panics over the disappearance of the body and rants in the disjointed ramblings of a madman. Huston spent a morning on rehearsals, then filmed in the afternoon. Bogart was tired. One shot required eleven takes.

Not every critic was ready to accept the famous tough guy as a terrorized, soliloquizing psychotic. Humphrey Bogart, *Time* declared after the film opened in January, couldn't quite eliminate the existence of Humphrey Bogart. Nevertheless, while the main kudos predictably went to Walter Huston, *Time* joined *The New York Times,* the *Hollywood Reporter,* and virtually every other major publication in declaring that Bogart had given the performance of his career—and this, as the *Reporter* put it, in the role of "a loathsome character that few leading men would play."

On July 22, Bogart was released from the film. Henry Blanke viewed the rough cut with Jack Warner and on August 1, J. L. sent a lyrical telegram to the office in New York: "THIS IS DEFINITELY THE GREATEST MOTION PICTURE WE HAVE EVER MADE." *Life* would call the picture one of the half dozen of recent years "which genuinely deserve to be called 'great.' "

For all the cheering, there was one dissension—a letter to the editors of *Life* signed by Hal Croves and datelined San Antonio. "Croves" had turned up on Stage 7 in the last weeks of filming. He was listed as an adviser but left after two days for reasons now unknown, though a likely explanation is that the $500 weekly stipend was slashed to $100. It was production head Tenny Wright's decision, but Traven, embittered, blamed Huston, and the letter slapped at Huston for "paying me a lousy $100 a week," thereby allegedly showing his low esteem of Traven. "Never again will Mr. John Huston have an opportunity to direct a picture based on any other of Traven's 14 books. Traven does not need Mr. John Huston."

Paul Kohner, who had shepherded the project for years and even advanced Traven money from his own pocket, advised the mercurial writer to see a psychiatrist; Traven terminated their correspondence. Twenty years later, the two men finally met face to face and embraced. "This could have happened long ago," Kohner said. The frail, aged man smiled sadly: "I know."

Bogart finally returned to the *Santana* in the late summer of 1947. He told reporters he planned to organize an ersatz race to substitute for the Honolulu Classic he missed; it would be called the Bogart Also-Ran. Then he and Bacall sailed to Baja California on a long, loafing cruise to unwind from the stress of his work in the film. On his return he found a paranoia that made Fred C. Dobbs seem the model of rationality.

CHAPTER 18

Mr. Bogart Goes to Washington

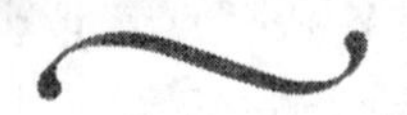

Immediately following the 1946 elections, the Chicago *Tribune* launched an incendiary two-week-long series alleging a Communist takeover of Hollywood, with Franklin Roosevelt as the instigator. Robert Rutherford McCormick, publisher of the *Tribune* and the New York *Daily News,* had been arguably the most implacable and, since his papers had a circulation of more than five million, the most powerful of the enemies of FDR. McCormick "carried on crusades against gangsters and racketeers, prohibition and prohibitionists, local, state, and national politicians, Wall Street, New York, the East and Easterners, Democrats, the New Deal and the Fair Deal, liberal Republicans, the League of Nations, the World Court, the United Nations, British imperialism, socialism and communism." But McCormick's greatest animus was reserved for Roosevelt, whose international policies he felt were anathema to George Washington's philosophy of no foreign entanglements and whose social programs he was convinced debased individualism and fostered collectivism.

The *Tribune* had a history of finding that film studios were hothouses of corruption. In 1907, an editorial proclaimed that nickelodeons appealed "to the lowest passions of childhood. . . . Wholly vicious, they should be censored and suppressed. . . . no voice [can be] raised to defend the majority of . . . theatres because they cannot be defended." The chief perpetrators of the moral and political subversion in Hollywood were easy to name. The 1946 series wrote darkly of "Russian-born"—a euphemism for "Jewish"—studio heads who had purportedly delivered an unsuspecting public into the hands of the Kremlin. The list incorrectly included the Warner brothers—Harry was born in Poland; Albert in Baltimore; and Jack in Canada—but several other studio heads had, in fact, emigrated from Russia, including Louis B. Mayer of MGM, whose family had moved to Canada when he was a child, and Joseph Schenck, co-founder of Twentieth Century. Schenck had come to America at age sixteen along with his twelve-year-old brother Nicholas, who became the head of Loew's, Inc., the holding company of MGM and operator of the Loew's theater chain. Of course, all were Jews, regardless of birthplace, and that was the real point. Mayer—all the studio bosses—were as much Communists as Karl Marx was a capitalist; they were among the most successful businessmen in America, and in general their politics were conservative. Mayer was for many years the head of the California Republican Party. Jack Warner was one of the few Democrats.

As further evidence of the Red threat, the *Tribune* series called *Mission to Moscow* "one of the greatest propaganda triumphs of Hollywood Communists and fellow travelers. . . . The 'Thought Commissars' had everything in the way of a vehicle to glorify Russia and promote the particular type of communism for which Dictator Stalin stands."

McCormick's views were hardly unusual in a time when restrictions on where Jews could live were exceeded only by those on blacks, and his views were shared by many members of Congress. In addition, a large portion of the populace found the liberal social and geopolitical changes of the century an affront to the past and a threat to the future. For them, anti-communism served as a mask for religious and cultural xenophobia.

The House Committee on Un-American Activities promised that a "top priority" of the new Congress in January 1947 would be an investigation of Communist influence in Hollywood. That spring, a traveling House Un-American Activities Committee panel was back at the Biltmore Hotel on Pershing Square in downtown Los Angeles, where Bogart had been summoned before the Dies Committee in 1940. Its purpose was to take testimony from a string of cooperative Motion Picture Alliance witnesses who were eager, in the words of William Randolph Hearst's afternoon Los Angeles *Herald-Express,* "to tell what they know about communist infiltration in the film industry."

Poor health had forced Martin Dies to return to East Texas in 1944, and the HUAC chairmanship had passed to Democrat John Rankin of Mississippi. Proclaiming that the committee's inspection of the film capital would uncover "the greatest hotbed of subversive activities in the United States" and "one of the most dangerous plots ever instigated for the overthrow of the government," Rankin was a rabid anti-Semite who felt that wherever Jews had prominence, disreputable acts and communism were sure to be found. On the House floor, where discourse was normally conducted civilly, he would refer to his colleague Emanuel Celler as "the Jewish gentleman from New York." When Celler took exception, Rankin asked in a honeyed voice of innocence, "Does the member from New York object to being called a Jew or does he object to being called a gentleman?"

Now, with the House in Republican hands, Rankin was replaced as chairman by the pugnacious J. Parnell Thomas of New Jersey. (Thomas's real surname was Feeney, but after his father's death he had taken his mother's maiden name in an effort to appear less obviously Catholic or Irish. He also began attending Baptist services, though he sometimes said that he was an Episcopalian.)

At the committee's closed hearings in Los Angeles in May, Jack Warner was a reluctant and rattled witness. He was asked: "The charge is often made . . . that *Mission to Moscow* was made at the request of our Government. . . . Now, is such a statement without foundation?" His answer was, "No, it is not without foundation." It was the first time he acknowledged that Roosevelt or members of his administration had urged that the film be made. Following that, in an attempt to show his sincerity as an anti-Communist, Warner identified writers he called un-American, among them the Epstein twins. Then he begged his inquisitors not to make his testimony public.

In no time, Thomas's staff leaked the transcripts to the press, which had a field day: "FORCED TO MAKE PRO-RED MOVIE"; "WHITE HOUSE PRESSURE PUT ON"; "FILM RED HUNT WILL EXTEND TO GOVT. MEN." A Chicago *Tribune* editorial charged Roosevelt's purpose had been to "make himself the American Stalin." In concluding the proceedings, Chairman Thomas declared himself "amazed" by the revelations and called for an inquiry to be held in Washington, D.C., "to give the American people the full facts and information of this dangerous situation."

Initially the *Los Angeles Times* defended the film industry and even had kind words for *Mission to Moscow:* "Both Warners and the Office of War Information, which warmly supported the project, were aware that this film 'went overboard' for Russia. . . . there ARE some Communists among Hollywood writers and actors. Writers and actors, in common with most creative persons, tend to sponsor underdog causes. . . . Some of them frankly admit to being party members. . . . But the assertion that leftists control Hollywood or its output is sheer nonsense. The content and form of motion pictures are controlled by producers and high studio executives. In the main this group is about as left-wing as [General Motors chairman] Alfred P. Sloan."

Within a week, though, the paper had swung fully behind the investigation, declaring that the House panel had "just begun to scratch the surface."

At the Federal Building in downtown Los Angeles, Richard Nixon, the freshman congressman who was the committee's newest, brightest member, announced that subpoenas were ready to be served. Two months later, he told the Associated Press that the "red network" was about to be uncovered and promised to name names. "It will be sensational," he said.

Although there were certainly some Communists working in the movies, the promise of names was always greater than the number of names revealed. Like Senator Joseph McCarthy's later claim that he had a list of 205 card-carrying Communists in the State Department—a figure that turned out to be entirely specious—so, too, was the Thomas Committee's announcement of "hundreds" of prominent movie-industry Communists.

Forty-one writers, actors, producers, and directors were subpoenaed to appear before the Committee in Washington. Of them, nineteen immediately made it clear they would not cooperate and were tagged the "Unfriendly Nineteen" before they left Los Angeles. Thirteen were writers: Alvah Bessie, Bertolt Brecht, Lester Cole, Richard Collins, Gordon Kahn, Howard Koch, Ring Lardner Jr., John Howard Lawson, Albert Maltz, Samuel Ornitz, Waldo Salt, Adrian Scott, and Dalton Trumbo. Most of the other six were writers who had moved on to producing and directing: Herbert Biberman, Edward Dmytryk, Lewis Milestone, Irving Pichel, and Robert Rossen. The only actor was Larry Parks, who earlier in the year had won an Oscar nomination for *The Jolson Story* (1946).

The first reaction within the film community was indignation, even among many conservatives. Louis B. Mayer's initial response to the HUAC hearings was, "Nobody can tell me how to run my studio." The Hollywood left and liberal center, which had fragmented over the past two years, coalesced in a last stand of the old Rooseveltian alliance. Screenwriter Philip Dunne (*How Green Was My Valley*), director William Wyler (*The Best Years of Our Lives*), character actor Alexander Knox, and John Huston held an urgent lunchtime meeting at Lucey's restaurant across the street from the Paramount and RKO studios on Melrose Boulevard—"the place," Dunne said, "where you could get better lunches than at the commissary."

"The whole town was taking cover," Huston said later. "We said that there ought to be some representation—that it was time that somebody speak up, and that if it could be orchestrated, why, so much the better."

The group devised a strategy, agreed on an informal steering committee, and were joined by Anatole Litvak, the director of *The Amazing Dr. Clitterhouse* and *Confessions of a Nazi Spy,* which had earned Warners the sobriquet of "premature anti-fascism," the derisory right-wing term for sympathy with the Soviet Union before it became the United States' wartime ally. At Dunne's suggestion, they named the new organization the Committee for the First Amendment. Nearly fifty years later, in *Constitution* magazine, Dunne wrote:

> Obviously the Constitution, in particular its First and Fifth amendments, was important to those in the entertainment media who were accused of membership in the American Communist Party. But it was also of crucial importance to those of us who were not communists, but were convinced that the procedures of the House Committee, purportedly aimed at communists, in fact constituted a threat to fundamental liberties guaranteed by the Constitution to us all.

The liberals' 1946 election debacle severely weakened the Hollywood Independent Citizens Committee of the Arts, Sciences, and Professions (HICCASP). The group was split by ideologies, and in a move that took it farther to the left, it merged with other groups to form the Progressive Citizens of America. Bogart was nominated for the new executive board but, in an anomaly for someone of his stature, was not elected. The Committee for the First Amendment attracted many members of the film community who shared the old HICCASP ideals. Huston called Bogart, who immediately signed on. "Betty was all for it too," Huston said. "She was, I think, more politically minded than Bogie."

To help the CFA raise the money to buy ads, telephone volunteers led by Joyce Buck and Jane Wyatt (later the all-understanding mother on *Father Knows Best*) called scores of likely donors. Checks arrived from every sector of the community. Publicist Charles Einfeld, formerly of Warner Brothers, was an active supporter. Others, particularly agents dependent on the studios, requested anonymity. Charles Feldman gave $10,000, but it came in the form of several smaller checks and the CFA was not allowed to use his name. Agent Irving "Swifty" Lazar's donation was annotated "$50 (no name)."

Philip Dunne was a prime mover in organizing the committee. He and his wife, the actress Amanda Duff, had recently moved to Malibu and had so far been unable to get a telephone installed, although, he said, "down the block was a bookmaker that had ten phones. When Amanda complained to the phone company, she was told, 'They pay their bills.' She said, 'So why don't you give us a chance to pay ours?' "

While they waited, Dunne used the phone at the home of his neighbor Isobel Lennart, who later wrote the play and film *Funny Girl.* Lennart, in New York on business, had left the key so the Dunnes could take care of the house for her. Dunne itemized his calls so that he could properly repay Lennart. When she returned, he told her about the committee. "By the way," he added, "in organizing this thing, I used your phone." Lennart's face turned ashen. Dunne thought it was on account of the phone bill. Years later she told him she was a member of the Party.

In late October, a full-page ad appeared in the industry trades and in several of the Los Angeles papers, 140 signers on record in their opposition to the hearings. Bacall and Bogart, given the alphabetical order, were near the top:

> **We the undersigned,** as American Citizens who believe in constitutional democratic government, are disgusted and outraged by the continuing attempt of the House Committee on Un-American Activities to smear the Motion Picture Industry.
>
> We hold that these hearings are morally wrong because:
>
> Any investigation into the political beliefs of the individual is contrary to the basic principles of our democracy;
>
> Any attempt to curb freedom of expression and to set arbitrary standards of Americanism is in itself disloyal to both the spirit and the letter of the Constitution.

Some of those listed already had firsthand experience with the curbs. Katharine Hepburn had publicly protested the May hearings at a rally honoring former vice-president Henry Wallace, a critic of U.S. foreign policy and a prospective third-party candidate for president. Hepburn, secure in her Yankee roots, told more vulnerable colleagues like Edward G. Robinson who were of immigrant stock to let her handle the tough assignments. "I said to Eddie: 'Don't! You let *me* do it because—God! I'm practically the American flag! They can't say *anything*!"

The Los Angeles *Herald-Express* tried. In a follow-up story in October it carried head shots of the actress, captioned, in boldface type: "AT WALLACE HOOPLA IN A RED GOWN." "They could attack you in a cheap way," she later said.

Still, with the expertise gained in the FDR campaigns, industry liberals felt that they might prevail. Billy Wilder's favorite co-writer, I.A.L. "Izzy" Diamond, turned his abundant wit on the chairman:

> The words of Parnell Thomas are
> designed to make you think:
> *"The guys who write the dramas are*
> *as red as red-hot mammas are,*
> *and even their pajamas are*
> *adorned with Russian mink."*

"The Hollywood people being 'investigated' by the Thomas-Rankin Committee are citizens," the Americans for Democratic Action proclaimed in an ad. "If *their* civil liberties can be taken from them, the civil liberties for all Americans no longer are guaranteed.

"It doesn't take burning fagots to stage a witch hunt. Blazing flash bulbs and klieg lights will serve."

"The damn thing snowballed," Dunne said many years later. "Everybody was indignant."

"What we objected to was prior restraint," Gene Kelly stated. "I was appalled."

So many people wanted to come to CFA meetings that the gatherings had to be held in the largest homes available; lyricist Ira Gershwin's huge living room was a favorite meeting place. The crowd on October 9 at William Wyler's house on Summit Drive in Beverly Hills contained an all-star cast: Bogart and Bacall, Danny Kaye, Judy Garland, Rita Hayworth, Edward G. Robinson, and Gene Kelly, hobbling about on an injured ankle. (Other supporters included Groucho Marx, Frank Sinatra, Paulette Goddard, Fredric March, George S. Kaufman, Archibald MacLeish, Jerry Wald, and Walter Wanger.)

Outside in the dark, dim figures were seen noting license plate numbers. The identities of those who tipped them off about the meetings stayed guarded in the records of the county sheriff's office and in Bogart's growing FBI file.

The HUAC hearings into Communist influence in Hollywood opened on October 20 in Washington, D.C. Initially, there had been talk of a ban on microphones and cameras in fear of a "circus" atmosphere, but only the most naive could believe that anyone on the committee would have been willing to forgo so much publicity. Cabell Phillips of *The New York Times* noted that "the Hollywood investigation . . . is one toward which the committee has been pointing for several months . . . designed for maximum impact on the public consciousness. Its substance is that Communists have elected the film industry as the principal vehicle for poisoning the American mind." Three days before hearings, it was announced that all media would be admitted. "WRAPS OFF," the Los Angeles *Herald-Express* reported. There was full radio coverage, and the infant television networks sent live transmissions to Philadelphia and New York. The press tables accommodated ninety reporters, and newsreel cameras were mounted on the raised committee dais so they could shoot over the shoulders of the members and into the pit where the witness stand was set up. Witnesses' attorneys, it was ruled, would not be allowed to testify, make statements, or cross-examine other witnesses.

The committee had deliberately chosen the largest, most intimidating space available to hold the hearings. The ornate, wood-paneled, marble-lined Caucus Room in the Old House Office Building could seat almost four hundred people. Its crystal chandeliers were outfitted with high-watt bulbs to supplement the klieg lights and boost picture quality; they also raised the heat and the glare in the packed room. Chairman Thomas, who needed to sit on a District of Columbia telephone book topped with a red silk pillow to be visible above the rostrum, called in the cameras on Saturday the 18th to film his "opening statement" before an empty chamber and thus lift the curtain on what *Variety* called "a Congress-eye view of Hollywood that Barnum might have staged." (Thomas had a flair for dramatic presentation: as a new congressman in the mid-1930s, he introduced a bill calling for the public hanging of kidnappers.)

Jack Warner and MGM head Louis B. Mayer were the first witnesses of note, testifying on alleged Communist infiltration into the movie business. Warner, expecting only to document his and his brothers's patriotism, was amazed when, following his prepared statement, the committee's chief investigator, Robert E. Stripling, fired off hostile questions regarding *Mission to Moscow.* What had been Warner's patriotic duty in 1942 was regarded nearly as treason in 1947.

Jack Warner Jr., home from the Army and sitting in the audience, watched his father twist under the questioning, surprised that he hadn't better protected himself. "It's obvious he should have expected it because

Warners got a lot of criticism from the conservative right. The old America Firsters. The war was over now, but they hadn't changed."

J. L. sat blinking in the glare of his own klieg lights—Pathè News, recently bought by Warner Brothers, was among the newsreel cameras—and panicked. He reeled off names of writers he said had been fired for slanting their copy, some of whom were on the payroll, others of whom had been gone from the studio for years. He listened to his May testimony, read back to him, about alleged Communists at Warners; then denied they were Communists, just "un-American." He had originally named sixteen allegedly Red writers, then said it wasn't sixteen but twelve, and that he had been wrong about the Epsteins and two others (all four of whom in fact were known for their criticism of communism). The man who had sent his personal greetings to the Russians in 1943, who had kept the photo of the luncheon for Mme. Litvinov, who had himself tried just two years before to get to Moscow, now suggested a "pest removal fund" to send "ideological termites" to Russia if they preferred it there. (Immediately after Warner's testimony, cables went out from Burbank to the distribution offices to destroy any and all material relating to *Mission to Moscow,* "AS UNDER NO CIRCUMSTANCES DO WE WANT ANY BOOKINGS THIS SUBJECT.")

But the committeemen, with a bigger target in their gunsights, wanted to know about FDR's connection to *Mission to Moscow.* J. L. backtracked on his May testimony and tried to cover for Roosevelt. "I want to make a correction," he said. It was not Ambassador Davies who asked him to make the picture. "My brother contacted Mr. Davies after reading *Mission to Moscow.* . . . My brother made the deal with Mr. Davies to make it, and it was at my brother's suggestion. . . . I am rather surprised I said what I said, but I want to stand corrected, if I may." (Harry was not subpoenaed by the committee, and there is no record of how he felt about J. L.'s explanation.) J. L. went on to call the charge of White House pressure "a fantasy," and defended not the film but its intention to reassure an ally in the war's darkest days, amid fears of a separate peace. His composure returning, he added, "If making *Mission to Moscow* in 1942 was a subversive activity, then the American Liberty ships which carried food and guns to Russian allies and the American naval vessels which convoyed them were likewise engaged in subversive activities. The picture was made only to help a desperate war effort and not for posterity."

Stripling asked whether, under current circumstances, it wasn't "dangerous" to produce a "propaganda picture [that] portrayed Russia and communism in an entirely different light than what it actually was?"

"I am on record about 40 times or more that I have never been in Russia. I don't know what Russia was like in 1937 or 1944 or 1947, so how can I tell if it was right or wrong? . . . The war was on. The world was at stake . . . and when you are in a fight you don't ask who the fellow is who is helping you."

"Well," Stripling continued, "due to the present conditions . . . don't you think that was dangerous . . . ?"

Warner, his hands gripping the table, asked how "I, you, or anyone else could know in 1942 what the conditions were going to be in 1947. . . . Our reason for making the picture . . . was to aid the war effort."

"I think he got angry," Jack Jr. said, "because the administration had asked him not to tell and he couldn't betray that. And yet he was being crucified, in a small sense. These were our allies. Hell, there were a lot of Russian Army people in United States military headquarters during the war; it was one war for one reason. But we were hung up. The Justice Department didn't do a thing. They'd all changed. All the men that he used to know were gone."

Jack L. Warner, minus his usual bounce, made his exit, followed by his counsel and his son. In the car, he sank back in the seat, soaked in perspiration. "Jesus, I couldn't even get a laugh out of them," he lamented.

"He couldn't get a laugh!" Jack Jr. later marveled. "These men weren't there to laugh."

Warner put the best public spin he could on his appearance. "HAPPY EVERYTHING OVER," he wired publicity man Mort Blumenstock in the New York office. "GOOD FEELING HERE AMONG RIGHT THINKING PEOPLE. THERE WILL ALWAYS BE SO MANY BUMS." He did not specify whether the bums were on the witness stand or on the dais. To Benjamin Kalmenson, Warners' head of distribution and one of his oldest and closest associates in New York, he was more realistic: "EVERYTHING WORKED OUT AS GOOD AS CAN BE EXPECTED. HOPE YOU FEELING WELL. WISH I COULD SAY SAME."

As the week went by, the charges piled up as a string of so-called friendly witnesses testified to Hollywood's supposed sellout to the enemy. The Motion Picture Alliance, on the side of power at last, paid back old grudges. Director Sam Wood called three of the people subpoenaed by the committee—Dalton Trumbo, Donald Ogden Stewart, and John Howard Lawson—"agents of a foreign country." Walt Disney said the

Communists had tried to take over his studio. Actor Adolphe Menjou, a self-styled expert on communism, called on America to "arm to the teeth." Robert Taylor, Greta Garbo's heartthrob in *Camille,* complained of being cast in a wartime pro-Russian movie. He said he wouldn't work with Communists and urged the studios to "fire every last one." After his testimony he strode down Capitol Hill, flanked by District of Columbia police and a pack of adoring fans.

"Farce," Stefan Kanfer has written of the period, "is tragedy out for a good time."

Witnesses fed the committee names based on rumors, suspicions, and casual conversation. John Cromwell, Bogart's director on *Dead Reckoning,* was fingered for an after-dinner remark that capitalism was doomed.

Leo McCarey, director of *Going My Way,* said he wasn't popular in Russia because of one character ever-present in his films.

"Bing Crosby?" asked the committee counsel.

"No," McCarey answered, "God."

A bemused Gary Cooper, his long legs jutting from beneath the witness table, talked of scripts that weren't "on the level" but declined to name any name. So did Ronald Reagan. As president of the Screen Actors Guild, he stated the then-centrist position that acknowledged some Communists among the membership but discounted their influence. The best answer to communism, he said, was to "make democracy work," which drew applause from the onlookers despite admonitions from the chairman.

The revelations of the friendly Motion Picture Alliance witnesses were amplified in headlines nationwide—"HOLLYWOOD NAMES ITS REDS"; "EXPOSE RED WORK IN MOVIES"; "UN-AMERICANS HOLD FILM JOBS"; and, regarding L. B. Mayer's testimony, "STUDIO MOGUL TELLS CUTTING OUT ALIEN IDEAS." Meanwhile, the nineteen uncooperative subpoenaed men were flayed in the press while they waited their turn to testify. Some of the Nineteen were Party members, others were not. Whatever the case, no major studio had ever hesitated to employ them.

Several were colleagues from the old days at Warners, able writers whose unabashedly patriotic wartime action scripts provided good workaday roles for the Warner tough guys, box office success for the studio, and renewed options for themselves. John Howard Lawson, writer on *Action in the North Atlantic,* was in fact a leading Party member and had admitted his affiliation in an article in *New Theatre* magazine in 1934. Albert Maltz (*Destination Tokyo, Pride of the Marines*) and Alvah Bessie (*Hotel Berlin,* original story for *Objective Burma*) were called as well. Howard Koch, a co-writer on *Casablanca,* was under fire for his work on *Mission to Moscow,* an assignment he had never wanted.

Before they even had a chance to speak on their own behalf, these so-called unfriendlies were regarded not as witnesses but as felons, already tried and convicted by the press and the committee. It was the fact of "headline publicity, day after day, new lists of names!," Dunne said later, that led the Committee for the First Amendment into a second, activist phase. "That was the engine. That's what motivated us. That and calls for censorship."

At a CFA meeting at William Wyler's house, Dunne and some other members made a pre-arranged call to the Nineteen and their lawyers in a Washington hotel room. "They said, 'The following names were mentioned today,' then reeled off the list of all kinds of names coming from these dinky witnesses, these crazies, these right-wing grotesques."

That night, Gene Kelly said, "We decided to bring this thing out in public, this miasma of fear and oppression. And we decided we'd charter a plane—all these movie people chartering a plane!"

To Bacall, there with Bogart, the phone call from Wyler's home had been a promise of help. She turned to her husband: "We must go."

Despite the prominent names supporting the CFA, industry approval was hardly unanimous. Howard Hawks was appalled. "It's wrong! They should keep their feelings to themselves—this is what makes Hollywood look bad!"

"Howard *hated* it," Dee Hawks Cramer said. "He was violently non-political, and every time something came up on the Bogarts' going to Washington, he would just throw up his hands."

Jack Warner, despite his own mauling by the committee, was in a rage over the CFA delegation—many of whom were under contract to his studio—going to protest and perhaps make matters even worse for his business. "All we do for them," he complained to his son, "and here they're trying to cut our throats!"

Mark Hellinger called in Jules Buck, who had written for him and was among those going. "How can you go on this trip with a bunch of Commies?" Buck realized at once he was a surrogate for Hellinger's anger at Bogart.

"What are you talking about? What Commies?"

"Well, uh—you know the CFA's a Commie group."

"But your friends are on it."

"Yeah, I know they're on it—they're crazy! Bogie's making a mistake!"

"It's his *right* to make a mistake!"

Yet Hellinger had hired Albert Maltz, one of the best-known of the Nineteen, to write the final draft for *Naked City.*

The CFA leadership was frankly and agreeably surprised to land Bogart as one of the delegation. A declared liberal but a non-attendee of the protest meetings in recent months, he was going simply as a foot soldier. "Just one of the enlisted men," Huston said, "though it took a little nerve to even be a member of the flight." But for Bogart, there was also the memory of 1940 and the broad, smug face of Martin Dies, whose inquisition had led the press to question his loyalty to his country.

He and his colleagues didn't like the way things were going, Bogart told a reporter, his anger evident; and they had simply decided to do something about it. "We said, 'All right, if the orphans [bastards] want publicity, let's give them publicity!' "

Actress Marsha Hunt, who played Mary Bennet in *Pride and Prejudice,* noticed "a kind of tense fervor" about Bogart in response to the trip. "He and Betty were angry. I didn't have the impression that they were going to oblige a friend who had said, 'Hey, come on.' No, I had the feeling that they were there out of conviction, and very strong conviction." Richard Brooks sensed that Bogart had a pessimistic, even fatalistic, view of the trip. To Brooks, it was almost like watching a Bogart character: the skeptical idealist out to do the right thing but expecting nothing. "In all the good causes he was always there. About Washington, I think he was afraid that they were *all* going to get hurt. He knew beforehand. He didn't know *how,* or what method would be used. But I think he knew it was like Don Quixote. Nothing was going to happen; they were fighting a lot of windmills." They were all alike, Bogart told Brooks—Hollywood, Washington, wherever, and he repeated what he had said the year before: "The people with power loved you as long as you could make a dollar for them. After that, you were gone—they wiped you off the slate. You never existed." Then he added, "They're going to kill you *anyway;* when the time comes, they'll get *you*!"

The roster for the flight, released the last weekend of October, included Danny Kaye, Gene Kelly, Paul Henreid, Evelyn Keyes, Jane Wyatt, Marsha Hunt, June Havoc, Geraldine Brooks, Richard Conte, and Ira Gershwin, as well as the Bogarts, Dunne, and Huston. A number of independent producers, notably David O. Selznick and Walter Wanger, worked quietly behind the scenes to back the effort. Charles Einfeld put his personal assistant at the CFA's disposal.

By common agreement, Huston and Dunne were the designated

spokesmen, but Bogart was their ace in the hole. "We needed him for name value," said Henry Rogers, later one of the top public relations men in Hollywood but then a young publicist risking trouble by handling PR for the trip. In the lineup of stars, Bogart was the biggest, and thus a magnet for the media. Dunne called his presence and marquee value "essential."

Howard Hughes—an aviator, film producer (who became a blacklister in the 1950s as head of RKO), and, most importantly in this instance, the head of TWA—chartered a plane for them at the knockdown fee of $6,300. "I think it was John Huston who wangled that," Dunne said. "Possibly Howard wanted something from him." But Hughes had scores of his own to settle. A few months earlier he had been brought before the Senate War Investigating Committee regarding expense money he had allegedly lavished on Elliott Roosevelt, one of FDR's sons. The younger Roosevelt was named part of a team designated to select a new reconnaissance plane and ended up picking Hughes's. Although there was the matter of Hughes being paid $60 million for planes he never delivered, the real goal of Republican committee chairman Owen Brewster of Maine was the same as J. Parnell Thomas's: to vilify Roosevelt and his administration. The Republicans' behavior could be seen as the latest manifestation of the time-honored political practice of demonizing one's enemies, and specifically as an attempt to quash liberalism and eradicate the New Deal. Hollywood was less a political threat than it was a high-profile face to draw attention to a political cause.

The departure was set for 7:00 A.M., Sunday, October 26, which would enable the CFA to stop along the way and still be present for the resumption of hearings on the twenty-seventh. Before the flight left, however, members of the CFA did one last thing to help make their case. *Hollywood Fights Back* was to be a nationally broadcast radio program not unlike the 1944 election show for Roosevelt, with Norman Corwin once again in charge. On Friday, the writers for *Hollywood Fights Back,* veterans of the old Hollywood Democratic Committee and HICCASP, wrote the script at Music Corporation of America headquarters in Beverly Hills. Working on the script with them was Jerome Lawrence, the former college student who had hitchhiked to New York from Columbus, Ohio, in 1935 to catch the final Broadway performance of *The Petrified Forest.* Now a top radio writer, he was outraged by the hearings and wondered, "What the hell was the war *for,* if this is happening all over again?" Lawrence and the others sat at secretaries' desks that stretched around the circle of the agency building's rotunda. Dunne, Huston, and Corwin edited the copy while others worked the phones, booking stars to participate.

Lawrence wrote Bogart's remarks, which were perfectly in character: "This is Humphrey Bogart. Is democracy so feeble that it can be subverted merely by a look, or a line?" A chunk of a just-published New York *Herald Tribune* editorial was added: "The beliefs of men and women who write for the screen are . . . nobody's business but their own. . . . Neither Mr. Thomas nor the Congress in which he sits, is empowered to dictate what Americans shall think."

The piece was taped on Saturday, one of twelve recorded segments in what would be mostly a live show featuring forty-three speakers, beginning with Charles Boyer and a puzzled, earnest Judy Garland saying in the voice of Dorothy that she didn't much like what was going on and was not sure she was in Kansas anymore. Then Myrna Loy. Burt Lancaster. Paulette Goddard. Melvyn Douglas. William Holden. Lucille Ball. Fredric March. Van Heflin. Robert Ryan. Jackie Gleason. Kelly, Kaye, Bogart, Bacall, Hunt, Henreid, Huston, as well as Democratic U.S. senators Elbert D. Thomas (Utah), Harley M. Kilgore (West Virginia), Claude Pepper (Florida), and Glen H. Taylor (Idaho). John Garfield, Frank Sinatra, and Helen Hayes were brought in by remote from New York—these were Broadway and Hollywood's best, from Ethel Barrymore to Robert Young. For his statement, bandleader Artie Shaw proclaimed: "The only really creative people are free people, and that goes whether you create on a typewriter or a clarinet or a motion picture screen. . . . [The House] Un-American Committee wants . . . to approve the notes we play and the words we say. . . . When freedom goes, most of the good things of American life go with it. Better get off the bandstand, Mr. Thomas, nobody's dancing!"

ABC, the newest of the networks, agreed to carry the show nationally at 1:30 P.M. Pacific Standard Time, 4:30 P.M. on the East Coast. By then, the delegation would be airborne, well on their way to Washington.

Before they left, there was a meeting at Chasen's restaurant for a final briefing, and a warning. "Most of our troops were sort of political innocents," Dunne said later. "We told them, 'This is very dangerous stuff—you can't *choose* the people whose rights you're going to support. It's the rights that are important, not the people. And look out, because what these really are, are trials for treason—that's what it amounts to.

And a verdict will be handed down and the punishment will be administered by the blacklisters.' "

In one respect, Dunne himself was almost as innocent as his troops. "We did not think there would be a blacklist. But there might be; and we were going to head it off." (Ring Lardner Jr., too, did not foresee the enormity of the hearings. "We thought we were winners. We didn't anticipate that our careers would be wrecked.")

In the back room at Chasen's, William Wyler, unable to fly because of a wartime ear injury, gave them last-minute pointers: avoid the movie star look—no fur coats, no big hats, and no slacks. For the women, well-tailored suits, white gloves. For the men, suits and ties, no sports jackets, no casual attire. "It was not *quite* role playing," Marsha Hunt said, "but we were to be suitably dressed and pulled-together, because doubtless there would be pictures taken."

The trip was timed to coincide with the appearance before HUAC of Motion Picture Association of America president Eric Johnston, who had publicly expressed his disapproval of government censorship and the blacklisting of writers. His letters critical of HUAC to members of Congress had been reprinted in full-page ads in *The New York Times* and the *Washington Post.* Privately, he had met with the Nineteen and their lawyers and told them, "We share your feelings, gentlemen, and we support your position." (He had also said that he and his associates "are embarrassed by the fact that Jack Warner made a stupid ass of himself" in his testimony in both Los Angeles and Washington.) The members of the CFA were among many who took Johnston at his word. "The Motion Picture Association of America had promised us over and over there would be no blacklist, and no censorship," Dunne later said. "We were there to reinforce that, a bunch of working people, showing that the producers had the support of those who actually made the movies."

The Committee for the First Amendment were going to Washington specifically in support of Johnston, although its members also felt that the rights of the Nineteen were being abused. (The Nineteen had their own agenda and their own support system, notably the Progressive Citizens of America, which, on the same day that the CFA flew east, met in New York to bolster the spirits of subpoenaed artists.) Still, the reality of the new political climate was such that Dunne, Huston, and the others saw that the dividing line between the CFA and the Nineteen would blur in the public's perception. Because the CFA based its stand on the rights guaranteed in the Constitution rather than any one partisan political perspective, it was able to attract some conservatives as well as moderates and liberals; but all of them knew that there would be accusations of fronting for the left.

During the meeting at Chasen's before their flight, they asked themselves the question they felt their government had no right to. "We requested," Huston said, "that if there were any Communists among us, to speak out; that it wouldn't make any difference. But just to speak out, to declare themselves. And no one did."

Early on Sunday morning, October 26, the travelers assembled at Burbank airport. Flashbulbs popped as the delegation lined up at the ticket counter. Everyone had arisen before sunup, and Bogart looked as though he needed more sleep. With Bacall beside him and wearing a topcoat over his gray suit and bow tie, he told reporters, "We are against communism and everything it stands for, but we feel the present investigation is a screen to obtain censorship of motion pictures and newspapers." Then they boarded the four-engine Lockheed Constellation, cheered on by well-wishers who had come out in the cold morning to gather behind a chain-link fence to see them off.

Not everyone came along wholeheartedly. Paul Henreid, himself later a victim of the blacklist, said, "It was stupid. I didn't want to have anything to do with it." His wife, however, was a volunteer. "She said, 'You will lose all your friends if you say no. You are not working, you have time, you can fly.' And so I flew, against my better instincts and for my darling companion of my life and love, Liesel. She is still happy. I am not."

But that Sunday everyone was energized by the excitement. There was "a sense of holiday, with a mission," Marsha Hunt said. The seventeen-hour itinerary included stops in Kansas City, St. Louis, and Pittsburgh, ostensibly for refueling; but since the Constellations were designed for non-stop cross-country flights, the landings were really planned to generate publicity, with press conferences and speeches on the tarmac.

The airline, whose ads proclaimed it "The Route of the Stars," was well versed in the care and feeding of celebrities. Within TWA, the name for special trips such as this was Goldplated Flights, and a double crew saw to the comfort of the guests. On board, the passengers, pilots, and attendants shared a general conviviality. Danny Kaye emerged from the cockpit in a pilot's uniform, buttoned the wrong way, and asked, "Has anybody got a road map?" Airlines were then prohibited from serving alcohol on domestic flights, but many of the passengers had brought their own, and drinks were freely passed along in paper cups. The atmosphere was a combination of crusade, wrap party, and bus on the way to summer camp. The passengers sang the full Frank McHugh–James Cagney repertoire: "When Irish Eyes Are Smiling" and "Galway Bay," and they sang barbershop quartet. Almost everyone joined in, but not Bogart, who normally loved to sing. "He had a very attractive voice and enjoyed using it," Jules Buck said. "It was baritonish. In pictures he lowered his voice an octave." Instead, Bogart quietly sipped a drink as Huston's hollow baritone filled the plane with "Oh my daa-a-a-rling Clementine." When Huston fumbled over the words to "Galway Bay," Kaye came to his rescue.

The camaraderie, which continued throughout the flight, was reinforced when everyone listened to the radio broadcast of *Hollywood Fights Back.* Marsha Hunt joined the others crammed into the cockpit and backed up into the aisle as "we clustered around and heard the program we had recorded. It was a Who's Who. We all made note that the announcer had caught the fever. When the broadcast ended he said, 'This is the *American* Broadcasting Company.' And boy! how he shot that word *American* out. We cheered away. It was lovely."

"We were on a high," Jules Buck said, "high adventure. It was very good to get the hell out of Hollywood and show them in Washington that we meant business." But the tension was almost as high as the adrenaline. There was "a mingling," Hunt said, "of laughter and concern about what we'd need when we got there." There were constant miniconferences in the narrow aisle as small clusters consulted, broke up, and regrouped.

Marion Hirlman Stevenson, one of the flight attendants who had boarded at Kansas City during a crew change, watched the high spirits but saw the seriousness beneath. "It wasn't fun and games, and it wasn't a part in a play. It was their livelihood. It was serious business."

In the tail section, publicist Henry Rogers conferred with Huston, Dunne, and David Hopkins, son of FDR's closest adviser, Harry Hopkins, who had spent his boyhood in the White House and knew the ways of Washington. They agreed that others in the group would refer any tough questions to Huston and Dunne, to reduce the chances of a gaffe and to ensure that the delegation spoke with a consistent voice. There was some concern about Bogart, who considered himself politically sophisticated; he was their biggest draw as a speaker, but what if he went off half-cocked? Huston smiled and said he'd talk to Bacall. If it was necessary, "She'll get him to keep his mouth shut."

The question had also come up: *What will we do if they slap us with subpoenas?* And what if they were called and asked the big question: *Are you now or have you ever been . . . ?* They agreed at the start that there would be no compliance, and Dunne drafted a statement to be read to the committee: "I respectfully decline to answer that question on the grounds that the information is privileged under the First Amendment of the Constitution."

Then they would call a news conference; and after Supreme Court justice and Dunne family friend Felix Frankfurter put them under oath, they would answer all questions to make it clear that they would reply to any inquiry from the press but not from the government.

"That was the compromise," Dunne later said. "Really kind of cockeyed, but that's what we agreed we'd do."

The flight reached St. Louis in the afternoon and Pittsburgh after dark, in a pouring rain. Marsha Hunt recalled the shiny look of the landing field, the crowds waiting in the night.

"They had been standing in the chill rain. Huston and Dunne were our main spokespeople, but these people were not to be denied. They wanted to see Betty Bacall and they wanted to see Bogart, and they wanted to see Danny Kaye, and Gene Kelly. I remember talking to those crowds. I wanted them to have their faith in films restored and to understand that we on that flight held no brief with communism or even interest in it. That was not the point. The point was freedom of thought, of expression; and the public mustn't be taken in."

A little after ten P.M., the plane landed in Washington. The CFA had asked the press that there be no runway interviews and that questions be saved for a news conference that would follow at the Statler Hotel. They might as well have asked the tide to stay out. Jules Buck was amazed by the response. "We came in to an *enormous* crowd. Jesus Christ! I'd never been in something like that!"

They were led into a waiting room and bombarded with questions as they scrunched together on the hard banquettes. The large windows were full of the faces of fans gaping from behind the glass, jostling each other for a better look, turning the room into a giant goldfish bowl. To Buck, "It felt like being on exhibit. It had been a long trip, you understand, and we were worn out."

A formal statement was read: "We do not represent any political group or party whatsoever. We are simply Americans who believe in constitutional democratic government. . . ." To the press corps, they seemed weary and travel-worn. Predictably, the ground rules notwithstanding, Bogart was immediately tagged the leader of the group.

No, he said as they filed to waiting cars, they hadn't been subpoenaed, they were just upset at the way the hearings were being conducted. Their group represented five hundred artists and technicians in Hollywood. "We feel that our civil rights are being violated."

"He led the tired delegation to a hotel," a reporter wrote. "He said he hoped to meet with friendly Senators and Representatives tomorrow and 'take their advice' on his next move."

The news conference at the Statler later that evening drew an overflow crowd. The members of the Washington press corps filled the seats and sat in window bays or on the floor. Huston and Dunne took questions from a dais bristling with microphones and cables. They hadn't come to attack anyone, Huston said. They were here to defend their rights as citizens. They were not planning to make a scene, but they did intend to consult with members of Congress about HUAC's abuse of power, and they hoped eventually to see the committee "legislated out of existence." Then Bogart took the microphone and went on the offensive. The last week's testimony was "supposition and hearsay," he said, and criticized the committee for not even questioning the allegations while at the same time muzzling the lawyers for the accused. "That just isn't right."

The CFA members hoped that their news conference and presence in Washington would be the main news story the next day. But for all their well-intentioned fervor, they were amateurs up against a canny pro. Parnell Thomas, in a swift countermove, announced the arrest of a Soviet agent with alleged ties to Hollywood. His promise of a bombshell regarding the agent's activities grabbed the bigger headlines on Monday morning: "SURPRISE WITNESS PREDICTED TODAY TO TIE IN SOVIET WITH MOVIE REDS / Chairman Thomas Indicated New Revelation Will Shock Nation."

Besides the evidence that HUAC was not about to be upstaged by what it regarded as a bunch of liberal interlopers, the CFA had other, internal problems. Before leaving Los Angeles, Dunne and Huston had instructed everyone that there should be no contacts with the Nineteen, not even one's friends. There should be nothing that could imply collusion, to indicate that they were really there to support a buddy more than a principle. The hope was to deprive Thomas of any further ammunition to use against them.

Still, the leadership did not want the two groups tangling each other's lines. At two A.M., Huston and Dunne took a cab to the Shoreham Hotel for a secret meeting with some of the Nineteen and their lawyers, "so," Dunne said, "our actors wouldn't be involved" if news of the meeting ever got out.

The choices for the Nineteen were tough. To answer "no" to the question of past or present Communist involvement could mean perjury; to answer "yes" meant acknowledging HUAC's right to pose the question and therefore lay the groundwork for further queries and the demand for names. Huston and Dunne advised the witnesses to use a strategy much like their own. Respectfully decline to answer, citing the First Amendment, and then sit down. "I doubt very much if anyone or anything would have gone crazy on that," Dunne said later, "because I think in court it would have been sustained."

Huston suggested a preemptive move: "If you *are* Communists, why don't you say so, on the steps of the Capitol Building, to the press? And then go in and refuse to testify?" But to Lardner and the others, the strategy still meant answering questions under duress, not to mention staking their all on the fragile premise that any movie company, in 1947 with the Cold War raging, would keep openly acknowledged Communists, past or present, on the payroll. "Phil Dunne and John Huston," Lardner later explained, "were more or less taking the position that it would be wrong for the movie companies to blacklist anybody. Therefore anybody had a right to belong to anything he wanted, including the Communist Party, and therefore you should state it. Our two objections were, you should state it only when you wanted, at a time and place of your own choosing, and that you should avoid it because it would just make for trouble."

The Nineteen and their legal team, unconvinced that a First Amendment argument would suffice, told Huston and Dunne that they had settled on a different strategy. His lawyer, Ring Lardner said in later years, "insisted that we maintain that we were *trying* to answer. He said, 'Look, there's a possibility that you're going to get indicted and charged for this. . . . The only point of fact we could argue is whether you were or were not deliberately refusing to answer. . . . So therefore you should say that you are trying to answer the question in your own way.'

"It didn't work."

Monday the twenty-seventh was a sunny and mild Indian summer day. The CFA left their topcoats at the hotel and marched two abreast to the House Office Building, Bogart and Bacall in the lead and reporters and photographers fore and aft. No one, in or out of government, was immune to Hollywood. The syndicated columnist Jack Anderson, at the time a young legman for Washington pundit Drew Pearson, saw venerable congressmen thrown off balance by the visitors, Bogart particularly. To the politicians, it wasn't a matter of a short, balding man trying to get a point across. This was Rick Blaine and Sam Spade, the embodiment of their manly fantasies, and they were suddenly the guys in the black hats.

"He intimidated them," Anderson said, "and they resented it."

Outside the Old House Office Building, traffic backed up as the delegation posed for photographers, the Capitol dome behind them like a stage set (three of the women with furs, despite Wyler's admonition). Bogart stood front and center in his familiar tough-guy stance, thumbs looped in the waistband of his trousers. According to Dunne, "Not only was he parked there, he parked *himself.* And John and I were in the back, where we felt like stage managers."

The one face absent was Gene Kelly's. He had deplaned in Pittsburgh the evening before to spend the night with his parents. He arrived in Washington Monday morning and missed out on the group shot—which, given subsequent developments, might very well have been providential.

The Caucus Room was already filled to overcapacity as the stars pushed their way through the crowd to reach the seats held for them in the back. The committee, watching the stirring of the spectators straining for a better look, waited with visible annoyance to begin.

Despite its promises of new and shocking information, HUAC had so far produced very little. If anything, the hearings had created a backlash. Conservative papers, put off by Thomas's high-handed methods and his silencing of respected lawyers, had begun to question the committee's tactics. Worse, the show was getting dull. A week of friendly witnesses was beginning to draw yawns from columnists, and there were hints that the majority of the media might just unplug their mikes, pack up their cameras, and find a more interesting mud-wrestling match. According to *Daily Variety,* the committee's one trump card was "the hope of conflict."

To keep its audience, HUAC needed a fight. Thomas arranged one.

As of Sunday night, Motion Picture Association of America president Eric Johnston was to have been the leadoff witness, speaking for the producers who paid him $100,000 a year to run their organization. Suddenly, there was a switch. Johnston, the professed critic of both blacklisting and HUAC, was rescheduled for the afternoon. Instead, the committee called John Howard Lawson, the first of the so-called unfriendlies. The CFA members had taken their seats expecting to show silent support for the spokesman for their industry, but the shuffle turned them into a backdrop for the Nineteen and made them party to the imminent, by now expected confrontation. "Thomas pulled a fast one," Dunne said ruefully. "It was a very smart maneuver on his part." (The ballyhooed Soviet agent and surprise witness did not materialize.)

The conservative New York *Sun* had predicted considerable gavel banging, "since those who are stated to be revealed as communists have already indicated their intention to resist the committee," and the tension in the room was evident. Thirty-one Capitol policemen were stationed around the room, officially to provide security. One of them jumped when a flood lamp exploded with a soft *plop,* showering nearby spectators with glass.

Two motions—to quash the subpoenas and recall earlier witnesses for questioning—were denied with quick raps of the gavel. The first witness was called.

Everyone in the back rows knew Jack Lawson. An ambulance driver for the Red Cross in World War I and then after the war publicity director for the organization in Rome, he had gone on to become a dramatist, with nine plays produced on Broadway. He came to Hollywood in the late 1920s, and in 1933 was first president of the Screen Writers Guild. (His 1949 book, *Theory and Technique of Playwriting and Screenwriting,* was much consulted in the 1950s and '60s but is now out of fashion.) Heavyset, emotional, warmhearted, and dogmatic, he was the guru and doctrine enforcer in Party circles from the late thirties until 1950. Lawson's screenplays, however, indicated little more politically than an abhorrence of Franco and Hitler.

Most of the friendly witnesses who had testified during the first days of the hearing had read an opening statement. Lawson asked that he be allowed to read one and passed the text to the dais:

"Rational people don't argue with dirt. I feel like a man who has had truckloads of filth heaped on him. . . . The so-called 'evidence' comes from a parade of stool pigeons, publicity-seeking clowns, Gestapo agents. . . ."

Chairman Thomas put down the copy. "Request denied."

Lawson exploded. To call him a hothead would be a charitable understatement in any circumstance. But here the committee, as well as most of the press, had spent a week vilifying him and now he was being refused his say. A shouting match erupted between the chairman and the witness: "Answer directly!" . . . "I'm not on trial here." . . . "You're inquiring into freedom of the press." . . . "You're just making a big scene. . . ."

Their voices, swelled and distorted by the PA system, rose to the accompaniment of hisses, boos, and clapping from the onlookers. Lawson's conduct, along with that of some of the others who later testified, was consistent with the attitude of strident dissent that was the foundation of his political views. It also foreshadowed the theatrically disruptive behavior of Abbie Hoffman and Jerry Rubin and the rest of the "Chicago Seven," who a generation later were tried on charges of inciting a riot at the 1968 Democratic National Convention.

Dunne noted dryly that "both Thomas and Lawson were doing the same as the other, yelling and screaming. Jack was directly attacking the committee as a lot of fascists. Now that invective may have been correct, but still, this was a congressional committee. And that, in the end, got the rest of Congress mad."

To many, the words were barely intelligible, more like amplified barking as the tempers clashed. Pounding his gavel, the chairman, his head and bull neck flushed scarlet, and Lawson, ten feet away, tangled in what one paper, heretofore sympathetic to the unfriendlies, called "a fishwife brawl."

Director Edward Dmytryk, one of the Nineteen and then one of the Hollywood Ten, was seated near the front. Instinctively he turned toward the CFA delegation, thinking "This isn't what they came for." From his position at the back, Philip Dunne looked down the rows and wondered, "Who's going to be knocked off by this?"

Bogart rose from his seat, tense, his tongue nervously curled to one side of his mouth. Nearby, Danny Kaye and actress June Havoc had also got to their feet. Bacall, seated, stretched her neck in an effort to see past the sea of heads. By now, no one was taking notice of the stars. The audience was mesmerized by the drama being played out at the front of the hearing room.

Evelyn Keyes felt a sense of horror. "The bank of camera lights, so bright. And the seats were dark. And this *gavel* being hit, near the microphone, drowning out John Howard Lawson's voice. Gaveling these Americans. And they were not allowed to speak. The gavel kept getting *louder,* just noise. That was for our benefit. I glanced at Betty's face, and Bogie, and Danny Kaye. We were all very somber."

Lawson was asked, Was he now or had he ever been a member of the Communist Party?

Deathly silence, then: "That question is in no way related to this inquiry, which is an attempt to get control of the films. . . ." *Bang!* More arguments, then the chairman's voice: "Stand away from the witness stand!" Lawson protested as blue-coated Capitol policemen moved in from both sides. He stepped down, hitched up his trousers, and strode up the aisle to the sound of a contempt motion being read out, along with the contents of a supposed Party card and a nine-page recitation of membership in so-called fronts, including the Hollywood Democratic Committee.

Regardless of the merits of the case, it was, as a PR exercise, a disaster. A principled stand came across as bluster, and both sides looked bad. The liberal Republican New York *Herald Tribune,* a staunch HUAC opponent, reported that "Mr. Lawson . . . screamed at the committee and was screamed at by the committee." For the actors, who knew when a show wasn't playing well, it was a dismaying start. But to the press and public, the CFA put on a united face: an American citizen, one of their own, had had his rights trampled.

That afternoon, fifty reporters crowded the suite at the Statler as the stars awaited turns at the microphone. Henreid, arms folded, lounged against a wall. Bogart, chain-smoking, sat on the floor. Danny Kaye, by his side, chewed his fingernails. Next to him were John Garfield and Phil and Julie Epstein, who had come down from New York with another protest delegation. The windows inexplicably remained shut as heat and cigarette smoke added to the closeness of the room, fueling tempers already riled by the events of the morning.

No one, they made clear, was going to back down. "We stuck to the same principle," Dunne said later, "even after Jack Lawson and his people had put on that unholy show." Bogart charged "a censorship of fear by Congress." Gene Kelly called Lawson's treatment "a denial of free speech. . . . What if he *is* a communist?" Bacall asked a reporter how he'd like it if Congress investigated the press.

But they were outsiders, unprepared for the Washington scene or press corps, actors coping with an unfamiliar role and finding that they didn't know the lines. Bogart rubbed his cheek in the manner known to millions as he groped for the name of his congressman—"God, I'm a dumb Joe—wait—I'll find out"—and smiled the famed lopsided smile as he told *Life* White House correspondent May Craig, "As politicians, we stink." In later describing the session, he said with some accuracy, "We muddled through."

Gene Kelly said he had missed the morning session. Garfield talked of Roosevelt. Danny Kaye quipped that "this whole procedure is as if I came out before an audience of 5,000 people and before I'd said a word the audience shouted, 'You stink!' " He paused for the expected laugh but got no reaction. "Tell a joke, Danny," a voice snapped deadpan from the back. The stars were light-years away from the easy coverage of promotional tours and fan magazines.

"These were political reporters," Evelyn Keyes said. "They weren't *trying* to make you look good. It was a touchy time. People were taking sides. And we were there to complain about our government! So you got hard questions. But I also felt they treated us like little children who were out of their depth. We were movie folk. Tinsel Town people. It was like, 'Upstarts. What do *they* know?' "

To seasoned journalists, the visitors seemed decent, pleasant people, well intentioned but not well informed about the workings of their government. *Life* writer Sidney Olson called them the "Lost Liberals," bereft of Franklin Roosevelt and in search of a new center of gravity. Still, the undertow of the Cold War was evident in some of the questions.

"Either you're for the commies or you're against them," a Canadian reporter yelled out.

"It's being for the Constitution or against it," Dunne answered quietly.

When the group returned to the Hill that afternoon, it was hard to find seats among the rows packed with spectators who had come to see the stars. Therefore, many missed hearing Eric Johnston, their purported champion, testify under questioning that personally he would fire Lawson if the communism charge was true. Johnston said that the motion picture producers intended to do everything they could to keep movies free of both subversion and government censorship. He criticized the committee for making unproved allegations and challenged them to name specific instances of Communist propaganda in films. "Unless this evidence is presented and we are given the chance to refute it in these public hearings, it is the obligation of the Committee to absolve the industry from the charges against it." Then he urged that Communists be exposed because "an exposed Communist is an unarmed Communist," but that they be exposed "in the traditional American manner." In closing he reminded the members that "I have never objected to your investigating Hollywood. I told you we welcomed it, and we sincerely do."

For the Nineteen and the CFA, friends like Johnston made enemies superfluous. "The mistake we made was to expect anything else," Samuel Ornitz, one of the Nineteen wrote. "First [Johnston] made all the beautiful liberal speeches and then delivered the good old coup de grace." The CFA, too, was shocked by Johnston's about-face.

Tuesday brought more confrontation. Dalton Trumbo, screenwriter for *A Bill of Divorcement* and *Thirty Seconds over Tokyo* and later of *Spartacus* and *Exodus,* was followed by Albert Maltz and Alvah Bessie. Bessie pointed out that while the committee was trying to get him to disclose his political affiliation under threat of being cited for contempt of Congress, at that very moment Dwight Eisenhower was refusing to say whether he was a Republican or a Democrat. All three witnesses were loudly defiant, engendering the same high-decibel interchange between them and the chair that had taken place on Monday. There were also the same yelled dismissals, the security men moving in, the recital of the alleged record, and the contempt citations. As plainclothesmen yanked at his elbow, Trumbo leaned one last time into the microphone and declared, "This is the beginning of American concentration camps!" The high drama over, the writer returned to his seat beside his wife and sat composed and elegant, drawing on a cigarette in a long-stemmed holder.

The Hollywood delegation felt a chill—"a kind of disbelief," as Marsha Hunt put it, "that this was my own government." They also sensed the sympathy shift away from the unfriendlies as the focus changed from their words to their demeanor.

After the final gavel of the morning session, the CFA delegation, led by Bogart and Bacall, delivered a signed petition addressed to the Speaker of the House, calling for redress of grievances: "The procedures adopted by the House Committee on Un-American Activities violated the civil liberties of American citizens. . . ."

The draft had been typed up in the office of Representative Chet Holifield, one of the few Southern California liberals to survive the sweep of 1946. It seemed the ideal tactic—dramatic yet with a constitutional gloss, attention-grabbing yet high-minded, and in contrast to the lowbrow antics of the chairman. They presented themselves as a troupe of citizens in the American tradition, grass-roots folk who just happened to be celebrities, calling on the Congress of the United States for an end to the abuse of power.

Frank Capra couldn't have done it better—and only in one of his movies might it have worked. Mr. Bogart could go to Washington and petition Congress for redress of grievances, but nowhere was it written the Speaker of the House had to come out to accept it and be caught in a photo-op with him; and The Honorable Joseph William Martin, Republican from the Commonwealth of Massachusetts, didn't. The Speaker, the group was told, was unfortunately unavailable. "Joe just brushed it aside," Dunne said.

So the delegation, followed by the press, dutifully filed into the House Clerk's office, where a bewildered functionary accepted their petition as flashbulbs popped and cameras clicked. Huston made a short speech about "an intolerable situation"; they were given a receipt, and walked out, not sure what they had gained other than a lesson in Washington reality.

They also tried to see Richard Nixon, the only Californian on the HUAC panel. Someone in his office told them the congressman had flown to California the day of their arrival. In Los Angeles, William Wyler tried to reach him, but Nixon had vanished.

A few days later, Representative John Rankin, in an effort to clearly show who were the people behind this un-American dissent, waved a copy of the CFA's petition and told his fellow committee members and the audience, "I want to read you some of the names. One of [them] is June Havoc. We found out from the motion picture almanac that her real name is June Hovick. Another one was Danny Kaye, and we found out his real name was David Daniel Kamirsky. [Actually, it was Kaminsky.] Another one here is John Beal, whose real name is J. Alexander Bliedung. Another is Cy Bartlett, whose real name is Sacha Baraniev. Another one is Eddie Cantor, whose real name is Edward Iskowitz. There is one who calls himself Edward Robinson. His real name is Emmanuel Goldenberg. There is another one here who calls himself Melvyn Douglas, whose real name is Melvyn Hesselberg. There are others too numerous to mention. They are attacking the Committee for doing its duty to protect this country and save the American people from the horrible fate the Communists have meted out to the unfortunate Christian people of Europe."

Back at the Statler after delivering the petition, Bacall dictated a piece for the Washington *Daily News:*

"Perhaps I'm the girl whom some Americans remember as having said a certain line in a certain picture. If I am, and you know me, then let's forget about it for the moment. . . ."

She paced the hotel room in her stocking feet, talking away, her long legs moving in quick strides, as a hunt-and-peck typist took her words down.

"I attended two sessions of the hearings and it frightened me. . . . I don't want to alarm you, but I think you should be aware of the dangers. . . . When they start telling you what pictures you can make, what your subjects can be, then it's time to rear up and fight! It starts with us, but I'm sorry to say it won't end with us. . . ."

At one point during dictation, the door opened a crack and Bogart stuck his head in. Wasn't it time for supper? Bacall shooed him out and went on speaking.

Wednesday the 29th the Committee for the First Amendment left Washington on the first leg of a five-city return trip. In Philadelphia, they taped interviews for airing over local radio, and Bogart reminded the listeners of WIP that their city was the birthplace of the Constitution and the Bill of Rights. His comments and those of the others were monitored by the FBI. Transcripts were forwarded to the Bureau in Washington and the Los Angeles field office under the heading: "Communist Infiltration of the Movie Industry."

The delegates had mixed feelings about their effort. Bogart thought they had done fairly well. The Washington press, he told a Philadelphia interviewer, was both tough and intelligent and for the most part had agreed with their position. As for the remaining five percent, they would think the same no matter *what* you told them—"I discount those."

Other CFA members, however, were nervous. When the charter flight approached La Guardia Airport for the New York City stop and was put in a seemingly endless circling pattern, a kind of paranoia overtook them. "Don't you believe the field's *that* crowded," Marsha Hunt said. "We are being punished. We are being put in our place."

The airport news conference was given mixed reviews. Broadway columnist Ed Sullivan of the *Daily Mirror* drew attention to the name painted on the plane—"*Star of the Red Sea*"—as though the word "Red" bore some dark connotation. "He took a slap at us," Henry Rogers said, "and his column was very powerful in those days."

Once the group was in Manhattan and in the warm embrace of "21," their mood turned more upbeat. The general feeling, according to Marsha Hunt, was "There! It's over and we did what we could." On the way in, the cabby driving Huston and Bogart half-turned toward the back seat and in a scene straight out of a Warner Brothers movie said, "You're right. No congressman's gonna tell *me* what to think!"

As the chartered plane flew west the next day, word came in that the hearings had been suspended without explanation. On the group's last night in Washington, CBS correspondent Eric Severeid had told Dunne that the CFA had "put the wind up Thomas." The show hadn't played as planned and Severeid added that he would not be surprised if the whole thing were shut down in a day or two. So far eleven writers had been grilled. Ten refused to cooperate. The eleventh, German poet Bertolt Brecht, writer of *The Threepenny Opera* and one of the influential playwrights of the century, denied Communist connections in an accent so thick that much of what he had to say mystified the committee, and two days later flew to Switzerland via Paris before eventually settling in East Germany. A mere two years after World War II and having lived through fascism, no sensible European was going to hang around and be sucked into something like this, even if it meant giving false testimony.

With eight more witnesses remaining, the committee simply closed up shop. The number of unfriendly witnesses was now reduced to ten, because Brecht had testified. The next witness on the list, Waldo Salt, was not called until 1951. (The Hollywood Ten, then, were Alvah Bessie, Herbert Biberman, Lester Cole, Edward Dmytryk, Ring Lardner Jr., John Howard Lawson, Albert Maltz, Samuel Ornitz, Adrian Scott, and Dalton Trumbo.) The news of the committee's decision to call no one else left the delegation feeling higher than their plane. Hunt and the others "were elated. There was a sense of, 'We've made a difference! We've shaken them to their very toes and by gosh it was worth it!' "

Then they looked at the papers they picked up on their stops west, from Indianapolis and Cincinnati, Peoria and Chicago. The Thomas Committee had been poorly received, but so, too, had the unfriendlies, and the Committee for the First Amendment was caught in the crossfire. "These groups always choose some high sounding name . . . that obscures the real purpose," a Peoria editorial went. "It is odd, isn't it, how persons associated with endeavors seeking to undermine the American government always fall back upon the rights guaranteed in the Constitution, the very institution they are trying to wreck."

The CFA were seeing words in quotes that they had never said, uttered in places they had never been. This backlash against the unfriendlies and those perceived as their defenders destroyed the consensus that until now had united the Committee for the First Amendment.

Huston recalled "a general feeling of shock at the way things had turned out. The way the papers had turned. We had all *kinds* of support, up until the testimony. And then—the whole complexion changed. From then on, opinion was against us."

In retrospect, it is hard to comprehend why the Nineteen and their supporters couldn't have come to an agreement on an honorable position for a practical resolution, one that stuck to the First Amendment, as Dunne suggested, but still allowed those subpoenaed the chance to make their case. An idealistic hope for a better world had attracted many people to the Communist Party, especially in the 1930s. Even though history has shown that the Soviet system was politically bankrupt and murderous, those who joined the Party, while in hindsight certainly guilty of poor judgment, had done nothing illegal. Clearly the strategy of the Nineteen had backfired, their issues lost amid the shouting and invective that alienated even the many in the news media who had no sympathy for Thomas and his ilk.

The St. Louis *Post Dispatch,* which had condemned the hearings, commented, "Usually men who . . . espouse unpopular causes are happy and proud to make open avowals. These men are not in that mold." Instead, the newspaper said, they seemed oddly self-destructive. Thinking there was no one who could sympathize with them, they behaved unsympathetically. Others papers agreed with the *Post Dispatch,* and showed how the now Ten might have fared better had they put their trust in their fellow Americans. "There is no law against being a communist," said the Lewiston (Maine) *Sun.* "They should answer yes or no, and if the answer is in the affirmative, follow up by asking the Congressmen what they are going to do about it." "When a man refuses to answer questions," said the Decatur (Illinois) *Review,* "the public jumps to the conclusion that he has something to hide."

The press fastened on the refusal rather than on the rationale. In upholding their rights, the Ten had circumvented The Question, and often eloquently, but they came out looking like prevaricators. They were all good screenwriters, but they forgot the rule that good screenwriters should have remembered from their scripts—the old American suspicion of anyone who didn't seem to talk straight.

Ring Lardner, a quieter witness with a flash of gallows humor on the stand, did come to a realization of that rule, but too late. (Lardner had joined the Party in 1936. Asked if he was or ever had been a Communist, he replied, "I could answer it, but if I did, I'd hate myself in the morning.") Perhaps all of them had lived too many years in a world where the truth always emerged and the hero was vindicated, a world of their own imagination and craft.

Howard Koch, who had opposed the tactic agreed to by his friends and colleagues, later wrote: "As far as I could judge, they were sincerely and even zealously committed to [their approach]. . . . I was equally convinced—and still am—that the precedent they set in that first Washington hearing tainted the whole liberal movement with unwarranted public suspicion, harming it immeasurably."

Lardner came to agree with him. The witnesses' truculence "made the testimony sound much worse than . . . if we'd just come out and said, 'I won't answer that question because it's a violation of the First Amendment.' It was a tactical mistake." That mistake cost him a year in prison, a thousand-dollar fine, and nearly twenty years on the blacklist. Although he wrote many scripts under an alias, Ring Lardner Jr., who had won an Oscar for the 1942 Katharine Hepburn–Spencer Tracy comedy *Woman of the Year,* was unable to get a screenplay produced under his own name until *The Cincinnati Kid,* in 1965. He won another Oscar in 1970, for the screenplay of *M*A*S*H.*

Contempt citations were lodged against all ten. They had broken no law, except to yell at a chairman soon to be indicted and convicted for padding his payroll and taking kickbacks from his employees. J. Parnell Thomas was sentenced to no more than eighteen months in the federal prison at Danbury, Connecticut, where Lardner and others of the Ten were also sent to serve their year-long sentences. On Lardner's arrival in June 1950, guards asked him to swear that he intended no violence toward Thomas, a rumor that Thomas himself had started. "I was convicted for contempt, not for violence," Lardner told them. "Kill him? My greatest pleasure will be seeing him here with his own kind, petty thieves."

After his conviction, the Lardner family could no longer afford the new house they had just bought in Santa Monica, and while Ring was in prison, his wife Frances moved herself and the children into "this tacky little joint in the middle of Hollywood. It wasn't *that* awful. People live in far worse circumstances. It was just different from what we had been used to."

The time Lardner and the others served was entirely real, but at least one portion was also entirely surreal. Around Christmas, Frances came east to see her husband and stayed with her mother-in-law, Alice, who had a country house not far from Danbury. Alice's chauffeur drove Frances, dressed to look as nice as possible for her husband and wearing her only warm coat, a mink, to the prison. After clearing several security checks, she was escorted across the yard by one of the guards.

"I don't know whether it was the mink coat that impressed this guy, but he treated me like a visiting celebrity—'Mrs. Lardner, on the right we have our baseball diamond. And down there is where they do their work. We're so happy that you could come.' The whole thing was totally crazy! There I was coming to see this poor guy who had been in jail since the previous June, and this man kept saying these things—'And here we have this and there we have that' and 'Mrs. Lardner' and 'Mrs. Lardner' and 'Mrs. Lardner.' It was absolutely crazy because I was scared to death and frightfully self-conscious."

Later in the visit she learned that the guard wanted to become an actor.

For the Committee for the First Amendment, the flight home from Chicago was a quiet one. There was no singing this time, though Danny Kaye did make jokes to keep up their flagging spirits. For the most part, everyone sat reading quietly or looking out the window. The CFA had powerful allies in the network pundits and the Eastern Establishment papers, but their act, quite literally, wasn't playing in Peoria. Theirs was an industry obsessed with mass acceptance; and when mass acceptance turned into merely group acceptance, everyone knew there was trouble ahead.

The experience was sobering for the stars. "Here you had been like a king, a minor god," Evelyn Keyes said, "and you've had all these people out there who *love* you. Well then, you get carried away—you think they're going to love you no matter *what* you do. And here's a solid *block* of these gods and goddesses, and you think: That'll do it. They'll see. All these people who love us, they'll understand, we'll *show* them. But when you've got the United States government and all that power—they think they're pretty big shots too. And if you're going to decide who's the bigger hotshot, I'll have to take the government, won't I? They've got a little more power behind them."

William Wyler greeted the group at the airport in Los Angeles and a meeting of the membership was called. Memories differ as to what happened next. To screenwriter Abraham Polonsky, who worked on the 1947 John Garfield film *Body and Soul* and was later blacklisted, the atmosphere resembled "the middle of a flu epidemic." In Polonsky's recollection, Bogart shouted at Danny Kaye, "You fuckers sold me out!" and left.

Philip Dunne remembered only a simple debriefing. "We all spoke, including Bogie, of what we thought we'd accomplished."

In fact, Bogart signed an ad along with the others who had gone to Washington. They called the hearings a failure, a travesty of justice, an abuse of the defenseless, and a subversion of the courts. He also joined another all-star cast in the taping of round two of *Hollywood Fights Back.* Personally, they had taken a pounding. On the positive side, however, Thomas had backed down by canceling the remainder of the hearings.

The show aired on November 2. Bogart spoke for the delegation, his lines once again written by Jerome Lawrence but sounding as if they came from his gut:

> This is Humphrey Bogart. We sat in the committee room and heard it happen. We saw it—and said to ourselves, "It *can* happen here." We saw American citizens denied the right to speak by elected representatives of the people! We saw police take citizens from the stand like *criminals,* after they'd been refused the right to defend themselves. We saw the gavel of the committee chairman cutting off the words of free Americans. *The sound of that gavel, Mr. Thomas, rings across America!* Because every time your gavel struck, it hit the First Amendment to the Constitution of the United States.

The Motion Picture Association of America, desperate to protect the studios, agreed to meet in emergency session in New York, in three weeks' time. Its members had solemnly promised that there would be no blacklist, but rumors abounded of backstairs deals, of stockholder pressures, of furtive conferences between investors and the studio executives; in short, of clandestine and underground behavior—exactly what those blacklisted were accused of, except the producers' behavior was not based on individual philosophical commitment but on financial resolve. If maintaining their bottom lines meant the destruction of a few hundred careers, well, that was the cost of doing business.

The blacklist would last for more than a dozen years. Livelihoods as well as lives were ruined by merely an unfounded mention that a writer or an actor had once been a Communist or a sympathizer. "The plague years," Stefan Kanfer called the period. No Hollywood studio was willing to make a film about the subject until *The Front* in 1976, written by Walter Bernstein and directed by Martin Ritt. Woody Allen played the title role. Bernstein and Ritt had both been blacklisted, as had most of the cast, including Zero Mostel and Herschel Bernardi. "It is our revenge," Bernstein wrote; even so, he added, the only way Columbia Pictures would agree to finance a movie about the blacklist was to do it as a comedy—although the powerfully written film is as dramatic as it is funny.

In Burbank, behind his gleaming black desk, Jack Warner took stock of his and his studio's situation. The House Un-American Activities Committee was off their backs and there was no danger of a connection to the Ten: Maltz, by choice, had worked from picture to picture. Bessie's option had been dropped in 1946. Trumbo was at MGM, Lawson hadn't been on the payroll for years. Now it was time to deal with Humphrey Bogart.

CHAPTER 19

No Mark of the Squealer

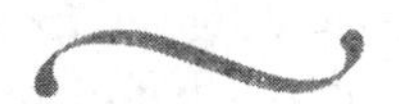

Home from Washington little more than a week, the Bogarts went to New York on November 10 and checked into the Gotham. Their idea was to relax, see some plays, and publicize *Dark Passage.* Despite Jack Warner's desire to have them back in Los Angeles as soon as they finished the promotion, the couple told him they intended to stay in the city as long as possible and would return in December.

Dark Passage, sold to exhibitors at a premium price, had opened in a hundred cities in September to tepid reviews that did not deter an adoring public. Late that month, Royal Crown Cola and Warner Brothers signed a deal for a thousand ads featuring Bacall and a plug for *Dark Passage,* to be run in some six hundred papers nationally. It was said to be the largest advertising tie-in ever between a product and a motion picture. When, in October, the picture opened in another eighty cities, it was still being held over in 91 percent of its first-run engagements, a studio record.

In New York, Warners' chief publicist, Mort Blumenstock, lined up interviews, and columnists scurried to "21" for usable quotes. The trip had all the appearances of a regular publicity junket, but it wasn't. *The Treasure of the Sierra Madre* was due to be released in January, and under normal circumstances the studio would have held what was called a star screening for the national and fan magazines. Instead, two days after Bacall and Bogart arrived, Blumenstock received a telegram from Jack Warner, detailing his apprehensions about proceeding on account of the "WASHINGTON BOGART SITUATION."

There was much to be apprehensive about. The fallout from the HUAC hearings was intense—and not only at Warner Brothers. At RKO, shareholders loudly demanded it fire any of the Ten who were under contract; Paramount was under pressure as well. However, the studio head arguably under the most pressure was Jack L. Warner. The national media were slamming his top star, their denunciations vociferously echoing those of the political right wing. The Los Angeles *Examiner* described the Committee for the First Amendment as "that extremely peculiar group which also includes John Howard Lawson, identified as the holder of a Communist Party card, Humphrey Bogart, and Lauren Bacall." The Waterbury (Connecticut) *American,* writing up the hearings, referred to "Bogart and his fellow agitators." Hearst's New York *Daily Mirror* was blatantly dramatic. "The Thomas Committee is investigating America's foremost enemy, the hater of our people, the foe of our way of life, the poisoner of the minds of our children—Communism!

"Speak, Bogart and Bacall!! Is that your grievance?"

On November 12, William Randolph Hearst, himself a moviemaker (in the 1930s his offices were on the Warners lot), raised the stakes and terrified the studio heads who had been his friends. In a by-lined page-one editorial in his papers, he called for government censorship:

> Under the false pretense that freedom of speech and of the press has been violated by the exposure of Communism in the motion picture industry, a group of Hollywood's "notables" and excitables have formed a so-called "*Committee of the First Amendment*" [*sic*]. . . . Of course the real purpose—in fact **THE ONLY POSSIBLE PURPOSE** is to protect, if not promote, the use of films for the dissemination of Communist propaganda. . . .
>
> In times like these, Communism is tantamount to **TREASON** and should be outlawed as such. . . . **AN INDUSTRY WHICH PUTS ITS BOX OFFICE RETURNS ABOVE THE FLAG AND THE NATION'S SECURITY DESERVES NO CONSIDERATION**. . . . Since the movie magnates are unwilling to keep Communism out of films, it is necessary for the Government to do so.
>
> The need is **FEDERAL CENSORSHIP OF MOTION PICTURES**. The Constitution permits it. The law sanctions it. **THE SAFETY AND WELFARE OF AMERICA DEMAND IT**.

Each day brought, in Dorothy Parker's expression, fresh hell, neatly encapsulated in eye-catching headlines: "HOUSE TO VOTE ON FILM GROUP"; "CONTEMPT CITATION FOR TEN TO BE FORWARDED TO SPEAKER"; "HOUSE TO ACT SOON"; "RKO, PARAMOUNT TO FIRE REDS." Soon after, Twentieth Century–Fox joined the bandwagon, vowing to dismiss anyone refusing to cooperate with HUAC. By the third week of November, Jack Warner was in a panic. His biggest star was sitting in New York giving interviews in which he pointedly refused to back down or disavow the trip to Washington.

"It cost Bogart about $2,000 of undeductible, unrecoverable cash," the *Herald Tribune* said in a Sunday piece titled "The Playbill: Citizen Bogart in Defense of a Principle," "but he considers the results in terms of newsprint and radio time well worth the outlay."

"Our object," Bogart said, "was to exert our influence in defense of a principle—the principle that no man should be forced to tell what political party he belongs to." He didn't know whether the trip would hurt him professionally or not, and he really didn't care. Those who thought liberal Republicans dangerous had called him a Communist, he added—"and a few Communists, whom Hollywood has known about for years without spending $4,000,000 to find out, have called me a reactionary. . . . Anyhow, I think I have a big investment in America, and I think it is my duty to protect it." To the man from the *Trib,* it sounded like the Bogart voice telling rival gangsters to get the hell out of town.

While Bogart talked, Jack Warner sent frantic messages to the staff on Forty-fourth Street. "GET THIS MAN TO MAKE A RETRACTION. . . . WHY SHOULD HE PUT HIMSELF IN THIS SPOT?" The "Bogart situation," he fumed, was becoming worse by the minute. Publicity head Alex Evelove had offered to screen *The Treasure of the Sierra Madre* for *Cosmopolitan,* a flagship publication of the Hearst empire, and had been flatly turned down; the new Hearst policy was to give no breaks to Bogart or to anyone else who had gone to Washington in opposition to HUAC. The upcoming issue of *Life* was to feature yet another swipe at "mistakes these people made." Fox theaters on the West Coast reported a letter-writing campaign in protest of the showing of Bogart films. Worse, box office receipts on *Dark Passage* plummeted. In Long Beach, where the film did not open until after first playing in larger cities, a house that averaged a thousand dollars a day took in only $267 on its opening day, $320 the second, whereupon Warners pulled the picture.

Bogart was pressed to make a retraction not only by the New York staff but also by Steve Trilling, their conversations being a notable exception to the studio's prime directive, printed on all memo forms: "Verbal messages cause misunderstanding and delays. (Please put them in writing.)" The Warner Brothers files lack any details of what Trilling may have said to Bogart and Bacall; yet when, on Thursday the twentieth, he had dinner with Ann Sheridan, their discussions were fully recorded in the cables to J. L. in Burbank. All Trilling committed to paper on the Bogarts was that he had spent several hours with them.

Lauren Bacall does "not remember any specifics" of the conversation at the Gotham, only that "Jack Warner pushed Trilling hard to get Bogie to make a statement to soften the trip to Washington. The studio heads panicked. They thought that everything was going to go up in smoke. Trilling was a nice man but he was an errand boy for Warner, who didn't have the guts to do this himself. Jack Warner was uneasy around actors. He did not know how to deal with them. He thought Bogie was always making fun of him."

Bogart's defiant interview in the *Herald Tribune* appeared on the morning of Sunday the 23rd, on the lead page of the entertainment section under a two-column headline. It coincided perfectly with the meeting of the Motion Picture Association of America to deal with "Communism in the industry" that was scheduled to begin the next day at the Waldorf Astoria Hotel. Also that Monday, the House of Representatives was to vote on the contempt citations brought against the Ten by HUAC. In twenty-four hours, the industry, the media, the public, and the accused would know exactly where the government stood.

That same Sunday, according to FBI records, newsman Ed Sullivan placed a call to director J. Edgar Hoover. Sullivan and Bogart had been professional if not intimate friends for twenty years, beginning with evenings of drinking during the speakeasy days. Sullivan remembered Bogart's acting mentor William Brady, and they shared the same memories of a New York now vanished. No friend of the CFA, Sullivan had nonetheless kept Bogart out of his criticism. "I'm about as much a Communist as is J. Edgar Hoover," the actor told him. After Sullivan ran the statement in his column, he received a flood of hate mail for coupling the director with a dirty Red. Since then Bogart's and Sullivan's discussions had grown more heated.

An apparent explanation for the Sunday call is that, after reading Bogart's piece, Sullivan, in a move symptomatic of the mood gripping the country, wanted to cover himself. Bogart was an old friend—one of his oldest in show business. But these days one couldn't be too careful.

Calls for Hoover were automatically rerouted, usually to his associate and companion Clyde Tolson. In this instance there are neither names nor annotations on the FBI memo describing the conversation with the agitated newsman: "He says that he has talked to Bogart further, that Bogart denies that he is a Communist, that he has nothing to do with Communist activities. . . . Sullivan stated that he would like to know anything that we could tell him about Bogart because he certainly is not going to let Bogart sell him a bill of goods. . . ."

At the close of the conversation, either under questioning or an attack of guilt, the columnist tried to step back from a flat-out condemnation: "He was frank to confess that he did not believe there was anything sinister about Bogart, but that he had probably just been misled."

The next day, Sullivan was back on the phone, again asking if there was anything he should know. The Bureau remained noncommittal. He was referred to press clippings and told not to worry, the director wasn't concerned about the item in his column.

At the same time, a four-page summary on Bogart was on its way to Hoover. The compendium of press coverage going back to Martin Dies concluded only that Bogart had no Communist Party connections in 1940. But the report, predictably, did highlight the trip to Washington and favorable commentary in the *Daily Worker* that identified Bogart as "the leader of the Washington delegation" in articles presenting, as the Bureau put it, "the Communist Party line on the House Committee on Un-American Activities." Like other memos of its kind, this one was overtly non-judgmental yet somehow damning in its implications. It also added more bulk to a growing file and seemed to be confirmation that the Bureau wasn't wrong to keep its eye on Humphrey Bogart. Over the years, his file grew to be more than two inches thick.

On Monday morning, November 24, film industry executives, their lawyers, and their backers gathered at the Waldorf for the meeting billed as the most important ever held by the MPAA; it was attended by the biggest gathering of financial names in the history of motion pictures. There was much to discuss with the money men, who were concerned over investments amounting to some sixty million dollars. The boom times were over. Despite record grosses, costs were up, theater attendance was down. The Associated Press reported the biggest production slump since the Depression days of 1933.

In Washington, the House of Representatives voted 346 to 17 to cite the Ten for contempt of Congress and send their cases to a federal grand jury. Two of the holdouts were from California, Chet Holifield and Helen Gahagan Douglas, the wife of actor Melvyn Douglas.

At the Waldorf the next day, the Motion Picture Association of America announced their intention to discharge forthwith any of the Ten in their employ for having done "a disservice to their employers and to have impaired their usefulness to the industry." The Ten would have no chance of being rehired until they had "purged" themselves of the charges. The MPAA further stated that they would not "knowingly employ a Communist or a member of any party or group which advocates the overthrow of the Government of the United States."

The 180-degree turn from their former stance came after heated argument. Eric Johnston, the presumed defender of the freedom of the screen, instead shouted at the producers to make up their minds—keep these Commies on the payroll and justify it, or fire them. The last holdouts finally went along after their scruples had been soothed by MPAA counsel and former Roosevelt and Truman secretary of state James F. Byrnes, an architect of Cold War policy.

A great deal has been written of the immigrant mentality and Old World mindset of the studio heads (although by now many of them were American-born) that led them to capitulate out of fear of government authority. This was a government, moreover, that had just won a global war and now led half the world. It was also one as yet unweakened by unpopular smaller wars, presidential resignations, and the decline of authority in society.

Another ingredient in the MPAA's decision can be seen in retrospect, though not openly heard in their discussions. In a conversation with Philip Dunne in the early 1950s, Darryl Zanuck, then the head of Twentieth Century–Fox, complained of bowing to outside pressure because the studios needed money to operate. Dunne took that as a reference to the New York banks, the WASP establishment that stayed in the background while the ethnic studio heads did the public hatchet job. "When money is involved," Dunne remarked afterward, "people have no spine whatever." Ed Sullivan had spotted that right away and printed it in his column the week of the meeting: "Wall Street jiggled the strings, thas all."

Whatever the root cause or causes, the MPAA turnaround altered the way Hollywood did business and undermined the liberals. To Dunne, "The motion picture producers betrayed themselves and everybody else. The Waldorf declaration was the stunning blow. Because *they* were the people who did the hiring."

Jack Warner exuberantly welcomed the MPAA's declaration—"AN IM-

PORTANT STAND" he wired Johnston. Warner's support of the agreement meant proof of his loyalty, and it banished the ghosts of *Mission to Moscow* and his liberal past. In addition, it strengthened his hand regarding Bogart, who was sitting alone in New York, far from Huston and the others and, in Warner's mind, an isolated target with few defenses.

Bogart had his private doubts about the Washington trip, though in public he ignored the press's accusations. He was confident in human reason and his anti-Communist disclaimers, even if reason had nothing to do with the HUAC hearings and the national political mood. Ed Sullivan met up with him one night, took him aside, and as Bogart later described it, "bawled the life out of me." Bogart cut him short—"Stop it, Ed!"—and gave his usual response: lose a few Republicans, gain a few Democrats.

"He looked at me as if I had two heads," Bogart wrote. It wasn't a question of Republicans or Democrats, Sullivan stormed. "This is a question of alienating *Americans.* . . . the public is beginning to think you're a Red! Get that through your skull, Bogie!"

Warners continued to apply its own pressure. The Waldorf declaration was issued on Tuesday; the Bogarts were scheduled to leave the following Monday. For the next six days, the studio did all it could to keep the couple away from friends who might influence them. John Huston, who was just finishing the screenplay of *Key Largo* in Florida, planned a few days in New York after he was done. Instead, Jack Warner ordered him back to Burbank, ostensibly to begin pre-production.

In an interview with the *Post*'s Archer Winsten on Friday at "21," Bogart talked about his marriage, his career, his life as a movie star—about everything except politics. When there was a call for him from California, Bacall visibly tensed. She was just so *worried,* she told Winsten after her husband went to the phone. Her mother was out there, and something might have happened to her. Or the dog might have been run over. Bogart's face was grim when he returned to the table. Seven hundred people had been let go at MGM, "Men who've been there twenty-five years. Just like that." Bogart made no mention of the trip to Washington. As for communism, he was against it. The talk then turned to Pittsburgh first baseman Hank Greenberg, who after a dozen years with Detroit was playing his final season with the lowest batting average of his career.

In Los Angeles, Mark Hellinger watched with increasing concern as his best asset turned into his worst liability. In September, the producer had made a deal with David O. Selznick to provide the production facilities, handle the distribution and marketing, and partially finance the

Hellinger-Bogart films. There were plans for Bogart to star in a Hemingway story and an adaptation of the new best-seller *Knock on Any Door,* the tale of a juvenile delinquent as victim of his childhood. Supposedly Marlon Brando was to play the young man, whose credo was "live fast, die young, and leave a good-looking corpse."

The agreement between Hellinger and Selznick was to have taken effect after sixty days, in early November, but at the end of the month the contracts were still being negotiated. Hellinger, underfinanced, needed money immediately. Even on optimum terms, the Selznick preproduction financing was only one-third of a projected million-dollar budget for *Knock on Any Door,* but it was essential. A $300,000 loan had been advanced through two Los Angeles banks with Hellinger's pictures put up as security. The banks were inclined to lend the rest; but because their doing so depended on the final signatures, the extended negotiations left Hellinger without ready money in a labor-intensive industry that requires a steady flow of cash.

A big spender forced onto a starvation diet, he had to turn elsewhere. Mark Hellinger Productions, announced with such fanfare and looking so solid, was actually held together more with promises than money. For the moment, it was surviving with stopgap financing: $25,000 from Bogart, $60,000 borrowed by Hellinger from his father's estate, the advances against the Selznick loan, and whatever could be raised from various creditors. Hellinger was by any measure overextended. His one more or less immediate product, *Naked City,* was not due out for months and had not yet even been previewed.

Selznick, an obsessive micromanager who critiqued every line of the lengthy agreements and sent them back to his tiny staff to rework, had at first been responsible for the delay in closing the deal; but by early November, even he had grown impatient with the pace.

The HUAC hearings and Bogart's stance were an unmentioned part of every conference between Hellinger and Selznick's lawyers. As the haggling dragged on through November, a morals clause was sent back for rewrite, since under its original terms "Mr. Bogart's participation with respect to the recent Un-American Committee hearings" could be cause for termination. While Selznick, a onetime HUAC opponent, was eager to conclude the deal, his top lawyer and corporate assistant, Daniel T. O'Shea, was an ultra-conservative who three years later moved to CBS and ran the tightest blacklist in the entertainment industry.

In the beginning of the contract discussions, Bogart, as star, business associate, and signatory to the agreement, had been a prime bargaining chip. "What we are buying," Selznick told his lawyers at the outset, "is Bogart and Hellinger." The obvious fact that Hellinger was linked to Bogart was evident in his desperate pitch to Jules Buck in October to help persuade Bogart not to make the trip to Washington—"You know that's going to reflect on me!"

It is easy to draw the conclusion that Bogart's politics made Selznick and his backers jittery, but it is impossible to learn all that happened. The Selznick files, which bulge with loquacious conference notes and copious memos for virtually all his career, reveal little about those weeks around the Waldorf declaration and the House vote on the Ten. Everywhere in Hollywood people jumped to display their support of American ideals, but few were willing to put much on paper.

On December 1, Bogart and Bacall boarded the Twentieth Century Limited and headed west amidst jubilation at Warners and the involved banks. Bogart, the New York office wired Burbank, had agreed to recant. Jack Warner had won again. Even though so little was committed to telegrams and memos, the arguments he used seem obvious: the old threat of never working again augmented by the new climate that made dissenters not only unemployable, but treasonable as well. Without a studio, Bogart was a balding actor pushing fifty, with a young wife, denounced in the media as a defender of traitors. Perhaps he could go back to the theater, but when Helen Hayes had once mentioned his doing so a few years before, he'd almost panicked. "My God," he told her, "I wouldn't dare do that!" He had been away too long; the confidence was gone.

On December 3, during a change of trains in Chicago, the Bogarts held a news conference attended by reporters from the AP, the UP, and the INS. With Bacall at his side, Bogart read aloud the prepared statement that had been rushed that day by special delivery to city rooms across the country: He was not a Communist, not a sympathizer, and he detested communism just as "any decent American" did.

"I went to Washington because I thought fellow Americans were being deprived of their Constitutional rights, and for that reason alone. That the trip was ill-advised, even foolish, I am very ready to admit. At the time it seemed the right thing to do.

"I have absolutely no use for Communism nor for anyone who serves that philosophy. I am an American. And very likely, like a good many of you, sometimes a foolish and impetuous American."

He stumbled over the word "impetuous" and hinted at the duress he was under as he added with his best movie snarl, "that word never came outa me."

"Miss Bacall," the United Press reported, "said she agreed with Bogart '100 percent.' "

In a brief question-and-answer period, Bogart added that Communists had " 'adopted' the movie stars who made the trip to Washington." Why was the trip ill-advised? Because the people in Washington were too smart for the Hollywood group. "We went in green and they beat our brains out."

In Los Angeles, the story broke on page one of the *Examiner* and page two of the *Times.* "EXCELLENT," J. L. wired New York. The studio executives and the bankers may have been happy, but Bogart gained only the worst of both worlds as censure rained on him with equal vehemence from liberals and conservatives. "Okay, Mr. Bogart," a typical column ran, "but without wishing to twist the knife in your vitals we might point out just how 'foolish and impetuous' you were. . . ." A Minnesota paper remarked, "Even the brazen Humphrey Bogart said he made a serious mistake in joining the hegira to Washington to help his Red friends." The heads over the editorials said it all: "Running to Cover"; "Mr. Bogart's Mistake"; "Actors Are Wilting"; "Tough Guy Waves Flag"; "We Who Got Fooled."

But woven through the coverage was an almost perceptible undertone of gratification as Middle America took the film colony down a peg. "The group of actors and writers who went to Washington is now realizing that the United States Government is bigger than Hollywood." To the studios, the press comments were like a letter from home saying all was forgiven. Columbus, Ohio; Worcester, Massachusetts; Fergus Falls, Minnesota; Marshalltown, Iowa: the heartland of America embraced the Waldorf policy. The masses would still go to the movies.

Not every paper was so favorable to the retraction. The Toledo *Blade* deplored "the state of hysteria which has developed in the United States when it becomes necessary or advisable for any man to protest that he is not a Communist, simply because he has acted in defense of what he believes to be Constitutional rights."

Congressman Chet Holifield published an open letter that began "Dear Humphrey":

> . . . I do not wish to criticize you . . . I understand how pressure can be applied. From my conversations with you . . . I am sure you believe in the fundamental principles of American justice and fair play. . . .
>
> Seventeen Members of Congress stood alone and dared to fight against the three hundred and forty six Members who bowed to

> pressure. . . . None of us are naive politically. We all realized that political antagonists would misconstrue our actions and include us in the red smear. . . .
>
> I write for the purpose of reassuring you that your trip was neither "ill-advised, even foolish." It may have been impetuous, but it was a spontaneous action grounded firmly in the desire to protect the basic principles which mean the difference between any form of totalitarianism and . . . Democracy.

The Washington Post in a lead editorial titled "Apologia" saw "no reason for Mr. Bogart to apologize":

> The Committee for the First Amendment, organized very hurriedly and compelled by circumstances to function in an altogether impromptu manner, rendered a real service to the industry for which it spoke and the concept of freedom it sought to defend. . . . certainly its conduct contributed far more to the dignity and prestige of Hollywood than the conduct of those men who used the Thomas Committee to point accusing fingers. . . .
>
> Here is illustrated the terrible danger of that committee's irresponsibility. An actor, dependent for his livelihood upon popular acceptance, could be ruined by Representative Thomas—and without any redress whatever. . . . We are rather sorry for Mr. Bogart. He had nothing at all to be ashamed of until he began to be ashamed.

An Indiana columnist summed up the general feeling of those opposed to HUAC: "All right, Humphrey. You can get up off your knees."

Bacall later hinted at pressures to denounce the Ten, and Bogart's absolute refusal. It was Jack Warner himself, knowing perhaps how far matters could be pushed, who came up with a wording acceptable to both sides. No names, no denunciations, no badmouthing the Committee for the First Amendment. All Bogart had to do was say his going to Washington was a mistake.

The statement that had been drawn up over Bogart's name drew rave reviews in intra–Warner Brothers messages that had a smirky ring of victory. "JUST WHAT YOU HAD SUGGESTED," Blumenstock wired J. L. "HE REALLY GOES TO TOWN CALLING HIMSELF MISGUIDED IMPETUOUS AMERICAN DOPE. . . ."

A few details did survive. By mutual agreement, the studio connection was downplayed; this was to be "out and out Humphrey Bogart." Bogart would guide Warners regarding a statement on anything further that came up. J. L., his prime objective met, said yes; anyway, it was better for the screen image if the actor seemed his own man. For Bogart, it meant salvaging some shred of control—no names, no turning on friends—with just a dash of the old gangster code of the movies. He was ready to tough out a public about-face. He would disown his declarations of the past several weeks, look like a fool and maybe a coward, but not an informer. There would be, in the language of *Dead End*, no mark of the squealer.

"THEY ARE PLENTY FRIGHTENED," J. L. wrote in a wire to the New York office shortly after the Bogarts returned to Los Angeles, and he kept putting the screws to them. The New York office had worried about tie-in advertising for Bacall on *Dark Passage*. No problem, J. L. replied. "BOTH BOGART BACALL ARE BENDING BACKWARDS BEYOND THE FLOOR." It was Jack Warner at his most vindictive, repaying Bogart for every slight, every role turned down, every gesture of defiance. Warner also informed the sales department that thanks to Bogart's statement, *Dark Passage* (a remarkably appropriate title, under the circumstances) had "taken a new lease on life."

Hollywood liberals were thrown into shock by the recantation. Marsha Hunt's reaction to Bogart's statement was typical. "At first we were disbelieving. They had had such conviction on the trip. It couldn't be. Someone had taken it upon himself to misquote them or distort what they said. For the most spotlighted pair to just pull the rug out from the whole thing—it was bewildering. But clearly Warner Brothers just descended on them." Paul Henreid would be bitter all his life. "The only man that behaved badly was Bogart. No character, nothing. A shit." Victor Laszlo's revenge on Rick Blaine for winning Ilsa's heart.

Conversely, there was gloating at the Motion Picture Alliance for the Preservation of American Ideals, founded in 1944 by, among others, Clark Gable, Walt Disney, Gary Cooper, Robert Taylor, Ginger Rogers, John Ford, Barbara Stanwyck, Irene Dunne, and John Wayne. The group, devoted to the notion that "the American motion picture is dedicated to the preservation and continuance of the American scene and the American way of life," was a prime lobbyist for the HUAC hearings in Los Angeles. For all the high-powered people among its founders, the Motion Picture Alliance was especially strong among those whom the industry had bypassed, who now had a handy outlet for their resentments. Richard Arlen had been a screen idol when Bogart was an unknown scrambling for roles, but his star had faded long ago. He was a friendly witness at the HUAC hearings in Los Angeles in May but was not big enough to qualify for the main event in Washington. "As for Bogart and his gang," he wrote a colleague, "don't let anybody tell you they are not pink (run, rat, run)."

The pressure on Bogart to distance himself from the Washington hearings came not only from Warner Brothers. In late November Malvin Wald, who had written the story and first draft of *Naked City,* got some bad news from Hellinger. Some months earlier, Hellinger had persuaded Wald to share the writing credit with Albert Maltz, who had been brought in for rewrites and work on the final script. Maltz's name would attract the first-string critics, who often did not review small, independently produced films. (Maltz, who became one of the Hollywood Ten, had not yet been subpoenaed to testify before HUAC and been branded a Communist when Hellinger made the deal to give him a credit.) In return for Wald not demanding a solo credit, with Maltz credited only with "additional dialogue by," Hellinger dangled the promise of adapting Hemingway once the new company was financed. Wald, envisioning himself writing the screenplay for "The Snows of Kilimanjaro," accepted the offer. Now here was Hellinger saying, "Remember that promise I made you? Well, I don't know how to tell you this, but . . ."

The production company appeared to be in jeopardy, Hellinger informed Wald. One of the backers had threatened to pull out; once things were settled, the money from Selznick and the banks would come through. However, things weren't settled, and an out-of-town investment group intended as source of bridge money had turned skittish after Bogart and Bacall confronted HUAC. If Bogart was about to diminish his box office possibilities—what with the American Legion threatening to picket anyone favorable to the Hollywood Ten—well, Hellinger reported the financiers saying, they might just have to withdraw and choose a more "prudent and wise" investment.

Hellinger told Wald he was trying to reach Bogart to give him the news. It didn't take much to see the implications. One investor pulling out could cause others to follow, and probably kill the deal with Selznick. Malvin, the brother of writer and producer Jerry Wald, understood the hazards of the business. Malvin was silently cursing himself for giving up the solo credit on *Naked City* when the phone rang. Hellinger picked it up and motioned for Wald to stay.

Hellinger's voice remained low, quiet, and relentlessly matter-of-fact. "Bogie, it's up to you. We're not strong-arming you, but I know how much you want this and they'll pull out, so what are you going to do?"

Hellinger saw his production company as his chance to outshine Jack Warner, and, Wald said, "now Bogie, innocently, had jeopardized the future of Mark Hellinger. Bogart must have had tremendous guilt feelings about that." The story was kept out of the papers, but it nonetheless made the rounds. Four months later, the *Daily Worker* ran down rumors of a "frantic phone call" to Bogart; the reported details of the call are similar to Malvin Wald's account.

In later years Wald often wondered: did Bogart and Bacall argue out his decision to make the Chicago statement, or did he come to it himself? Did he say, "I can't do this" to Hellinger? Whatever the process, the outcome was clear.

In the months following, Bogart publicly insisted that he'd been used. He complained to the press of being exploited on the front page of the *Daily Worker* and groused to Joe Hyams about being "suckered into it. He was resentful. He'd been had. Though he never said he wouldn't do it again." To his friends, however, Bogart was a tortured man. Jules Buck was at the Hustons' in Tarzana when Bogart turned up one day, alone. "Bogie was embarrassed. I think he really felt he let the side down. He wasn't sucking up—he never sucked up to anybody—he was just explaining, in a halting way, 'John, you must understand the pressure.'

"John said, 'Kid, *I* understand,' in that condescending way."

Forty years later, Huston's long face grew even longer at the recollection of those weeks. "I felt Bogie was out of line. But he was only the first of quite a number."

"Well, what was he going to say to him?" Evelyn Keyes asked. "If you're going to go on being friends—and they were—what are you going to say? It's like when John twisted Bogie's nose; he didn't talk about it. But he let him know how he felt. John did that very well."

At a dinner party, Bogart, troubled and apologetic, took Philip Dunne aside. A longtime Hollywood insider, Dunne could readily imagine the pressure behind the retraction. It was Bogart, after all, who had been the lightning rod through the whole trip. He was the most conspicuous, the only one who year after year had made the *Motion Picture Herald*'s Top Ten list of box office draws. At one point during the trip to Washington, Huston and Dunne had tried to jump in when right-wing Hearst columnist George Sokolsky went after Bogart in print and demanded, Who put you up to this? Give us names! "We're the ones," Dunne and Huston wrote in a letter, enclosing a copy of their petition for redress of grievances with the admonition. "We suggest you read this petition carefully." They were brushed aside. Bogart made better copy.

It was simple, Dunne said. "He was a big star, and we were not. He had much greater pressure. And he had Jack Warner. I had Darryl Zanuck, which is quite a difference. Zanuck could be a bastard, but he was a very fair-minded bastard, and he was my friend in many ways. So when he fired Ring Lardner, because he was ordered to, he called me and said, 'Don't do anything foolish.' I found out later that he thought I was much closer to Ring than I was." Dunne genuinely tried to reassure Bogart that the actor's situation was by no means comparable to his own. Bogart seemed unconvinced.

Within six months of its founding, the Committee for the First Amendment was disintegrating, as member after member quit. Bogart seemed the natural person to blame, but Dunne thought that was wrong. "Obviously those among our group who are ranking stars took the brunt of the campaign of vilification," he wrote Chet Holifield, "but the real blow was the complete collapse of the producers' association."

In later years, Bacall maintained that it was the Committee for the First Amendment that changed perspective, that unbeknownst to her and Bogart, they had been used "to some degree" by the unfriendlies, their focus "subtly altered to defending them individually and collectively." Dunne called that statement "an attempt to cover." Both she and Bogart, he said, had known exactly what they might be risking: that they would be misunderstood, accused of defending traitors, of being part of the Communist conspiracy. They had talked about it at Chasen's and on the plane to Washington. No one, however, had foreseen the price. To Dunne, the CFA's chief problem was that it had only one star of Bogart's magnitude. "He attracted all the fire. If we'd had two or three, it would have been easier, they could have reinforced each other."

Hemingway once said of Mark Hellinger, "He has death sitting on his shoulder." Earlier in 1947, Hellinger had barely survived a coronary. His response was to subsist largely on adrenaline, nitroglycerin tablets, and bourbon. In late November, after visiting with Hemingway in the snows of Idaho, he came home gray-faced, and coughing until he shook. He refused medical attention. On the night of Saturday, the 20th of December, he was rushed by ambulance to Cedars of Lebanon Hospital in West Hollywood. His wife, Gladys, held his hand as he pleaded, with the eyes of a frightened child, "Don't let me die. . . . don't let me die. . . . don't let me die." At 1:45 on Sunday morning, he did.

His funeral was held at All Saints' Episcopal church in Beverly Hills on the Wednesday after his death, Christmas Eve day, 1947. The grandiose affair had celebrities, press, fans, and all the trappings of a religion he didn't follow, the whole thing bearing no more resemblance to Hellinger than did the cosmetics-covered corpse laid out in the massive casket, beneath a glass panel. As Bogart and Bacall entered the church, she looked at their old friend and was sorry she did. "Better to remember him as he was," Bogart told her. He hated funerals, he added. When he died he wanted to be cremated—it was nice and clean and final—his ashes scattered at sea. And maybe a few friends to raise a glass afterward.

Shortly after the organ began to play at the start of the service, a woman started sobbing, rose, and hurried outside. It was Ann Sheridan, the only one besides Hellinger who knew the number for the phone in the bottom drawer of his desk—a phone he never picked up if others were present, with the exception of a few friends who knew of his liaison with the actress.

After delivering a eulogy that had nothing to do with Hellinger, the priest made the sign of the cross over the Jew whose only religion had been show business, declared that only believers in Christ could enter the kingdom of heaven, and sent the congregation out in "a kind of surprised shock," Richard Brooks said. Back on the sidewalk in the bright December sunlight, Hellinger's friends, John Huston among them, felt cheated. It just wasn't Mark. Within minutes, almost all had left. "We should have had a bottle," Bogart said. "That's what would have been right."

A few days later, Selznick exercised his right to cancel their contract in the event of Hellinger's death. It no longer mattered what some out-of-town investor thought of Bogart's trip to Washington. He was back in Burbank, and Jack Warner had him.

As the blacklist spread, the producers called on the craft guilds to help root out ostensible subversives. By the end of December, only the Screen Writers Guild had said no. On December 22, the day after Hellinger's death, the *Christian Science Monitor* published a joint statement of several individuals charging a "reign of fear" in the industry. It cited stories suddenly shelved, the cutting of "hundreds of lines with mildly liberal implications," scripts being "rewritten by businessmen in front office positions," blacklisting, and "self-censorship at every level—in literary agencies, in story departments, in the minds of writers, in conferences, on the set, and in the cutting room." The statement went out over the names of John Huston, Philip Dunne, William Wyler, character actor Shepperd Strudwick—and Humphrey Bogart.

The five, in what the *Monitor* called "a sweeping declaration," spoke of the "present hysterical atmosphere" in Hollywood and charged that the true purpose of the hearings had been to silence liberals. "[This] marks one of the few instances in which top-ranking film workers have been willing to place themselves on record," the paper said.

Before going to press, the *Monitor* bureau chief double-checked that Bogart was actually a signatory. "The appearance of Mr. Bogart's name on the statement is regarded by his co-signers as a move which clarifies his position after a public controversy, including declarations by Mr. Bogart himself, which left an ambiguity as to where he stood. . . . Mr. Bogart now confirms that he has not resigned from the Committee for the First Amendment, and that he is seriously concerned over the present situation in Hollywood."

But no one was any longer paying attention. It was the Chicago release that remained in the public's mind and on the public record. No other paper picked up the *Monitor* story. The hearings were already old news, and the purges were well under way. As part of his damage-control deal with Warners, Bogart himself had long since drafted and sent off a piece to run in the March issue of *Modern Screen*, titled "I'm No Communist." ("Our plane load of Hollywood performers came East to fight against what we considered censorship. . . . We were there solely in the interests of freedom of speech. . . . We may not have been very smart . . . may have been dopes in some people's eyes, but we were American dopes! . . . it would be tragic if . . . actors should withdraw to the political sidelines. That would be downright cowardice. So long as we are opposed completely to Communism and do not permit ourselves to be used. . . .")

In the new Hollywood, you couldn't have it both ways. The choice was to make your peace or join the others in the darkness. Bogart had wanted to do the right thing; but he also wanted his life. His agent Sam Jaffe laid much of the responsibility for the retraction on Bogart's business manager, Morgan Maree, although Bogart never discussed the issue with Jaffe and there is no record of what Maree advised. While Jaffe was not sympathetic to Bogart's decision, he was realistic in his appraisal of it. As far as he was concerned, "Maree told Bogart, 'You better pull out, or you're going to get in trouble.' They were frightened and he backed away. But that was a scary period. I can understand it. What do you do? Fight for the rights of others? Save your own neck? He had a career. It's very hard to be a hero under those circumstances. Heroes get killed, too."

In defense of the First Amendment, a piece of Humphrey Bogart died. His prediction to Richard Brooks that "they're going to kill you *anyway;* when the time comes, they'll *get you*" was prescient. Seeing the right thing through to the finish is often difficult, and in any case wanting to do the right thing doesn't guarantee that one will be able to overcome whatever obstacles are in the way.

When his sense of duty was pressured at a few critical points in his life, Bogart sacrificed his desires and stances for the sake of a deeper commitment. Mark Hellinger's friendship along with Jack Warner's pressure (and perhaps Morgan Maree's) conspired to make him waver, just as he had over leaving Mayo, just as Warner had made him do over a few hundred dollars when he was a contract player. Now he had to contend with his public image as well. The steadfast Bogart character was tough to live up to, which is one reason it was so appealing.

"For all his outward toughness, insolence, braggadocio, and contempt (and those were always part of the character he played, though they were not entirely within Bogie)," Edward G. Robinson wrote, "there came through a kind of sadness, loneliness, and heartbreak (all of which *were* very much part of Bogie the man). I always felt sorry for him—sorry that he imposed upon himself the facade of the character with which he had become identified."

Superficially, by December of 1947, everything was back on track. On the fifteenth, Bogart and Huston began work on *Key Largo,* a story of shattered ideals and loss of faith. But at the personal level, those around him noted a deepened cynicism. "I don't think it ever went away," Jules Buck said of Bogart's shame over the coerced "apology" for the Washington trip. "He could have been more."

"Bogie was a man of principle," Bacall says, "and because he was a man of principle, he never felt it was right for him to go back on anything he said. Perhaps he thought that the studio could put so much pressure on him that he wouldn't be able to work, or that he would not be able to take care of me. But he never felt good about having made that statement."

Richard Brooks saw the effect on his friend as being even greater. The recantation had meant an end to "the illusions of life, that everything is going to be fine, that there's going to be a happy ending. Bogie was never the same again."

CHAPTER 20

The Boris Karloff of the Supper Clubs

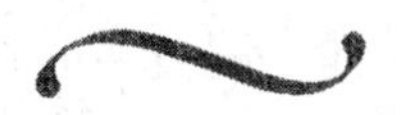

In the aftermath of the Thomas hearings, rumors abounded that the FBI was about to take over the casting of films. Lillian Ross, reporting on Hollywood in early 1948 for *The New Yorker,* found that behind the facade of normalcy, people were skittish as they carefully navigated the new political waters. On the set of *Adventures of Don Juan* at Warner Brothers, Errol Flynn, in royal blue tights as the sixteenth-century swashbuckler, assured Ross that the picture was definitely not subversive. A hovering PR man asked Ross not to bring up politics, a request she encountered all over town; publicity personnel seemed to have been given the added duties of lawyers and intelligence agents.

At the Lakeside Country Club near the Warner studio, Ross had lunch with the director and stars of *Key Largo.* Huston was in a good mood. He had just succeeded in overcoming the studio's objections to his insertion into the script of some lines FDR had delivered during World War II, to be spoken by Bogart: "But we [of the United Nations] are not making all the sacrifice of human effort and human lives to return to the kind of world we had after the last war." Couldn't the hero say the same sort of thing in his own words? the studio asked. Huston insisted on the original. No one remarked on the irony that the studio that had been closest to FDR, that had been an instrument of his policy, now feared even to quote him.

Bogart jumped into the conversation. "Roosevelt was a good politician.

He could handle those babies in Washington. They're too smart for guys like me. Hell. I'm no politician. That's what I meant when I said our Washington trip was a mistake."

Huston was acerbic. "Bogie has succeeded in not being a politician," he told Ross. "Bogie owns a fifty-four-foot yawl. When you own a fifty-four-foot yawl, you've got to provide for her upkeep." Bogart said nothing.

Edward G. Robinson, the *Key Largo* villain who had been listening until now, spoke up. "The great chief died and everybody's guts died with him."

Bogart turned around. "How would you like to see your picture on the front page of the Communist paper of Italy?"

Robinson let out a Little Caesar sneer—"Nyaaah."

Bacall turned to Ross. "The *Daily Worker* runs Bogie's picture and right away he's a dangerous Communist. What will happen if the American Legion and the Legion of Decency boycott all his pictures?"

Bogart didn't want to talk about boycotts. "It's just that my picture in the *Daily Worker* offends me, Baby."

Robinson made more Little Caesar noises. Huston said, "Let's eat."

Key Largo had been scheduled well before the Thomas hearings, and producer Jerry Wald denied to Ross that the fallout from them would have any effect on the production. Bogart, he told her, played a disaffected guy who comes to realize he must fight against evil. All that morning, they rehearsed the scene in which Bogart's character, Frank McCloud, having been taunted for his passivity, is reassured by the gangster's girlfriend: "You were smart, fella. It's better to be a live coward than a dead hero."

Ross's comment was that "Bogart had not yet reached the point where a guy learns he must fight against evil."

The film was based on Maxwell Anderson's 1939 drama about a Spanish Civil War veteran who had quit under fire, and then comes to seek out the sister and aged father of a buddy who remained steadfast to the Loyalist army and died. At the play's end, he is killed while resisting gangsters and so redeems his honor. When the old man is asked the stranger's identity, he answers, "This is my son, who has returned from Spain."

In selling Warners on the project, however, Wald envisioned an action picture more like a recycled *To Have and Have Not* crossed with *The*

Petrified Forest and a bit of *Casablanca.* The Spanish Civil War veteran became a disillusioned World War II major decorated for his valor in the Italian campaign. Just as Rick Blaine had been a symbol of an isolationist America that came through when needed, Bogart as Frank McCloud summed up the restlessness and loss of focus of the immediate post-war years. McCloud, a former newspaperman with high ideals, now drifts through life, "driving taxis, waiting on tables, anything to make a dollar." There was a beefed-up romance for Bacall and a happy ending, with the penitent of the play turned into a variation of Blaine and Harry Morgan—a strong, silent, cynical burnt-out case who regains his compassion and humanity in the final reel.

The supporting cast was a first-class ensemble: Lionel Barrymore, on loan from MGM, as the crippled owner of the off-season hotel taken over by mobsters; Bacall as his widowed daughter-in-law; Claire Trevor as the boozy girlfriend of head mobster Johnny Rocco; and Edward G. Robinson as Rocco. The character was deliberately patterned on Caesare Bandello, "Little Caesar," after Jack Warner had squelched Huston's initial request for Charles Boyer in a screaming phone call. "BOX OFFICE POISON! NEVER! NEVER! NEVER! NEVER!"

"He doesn't need a phone," Huston told *Key Largo* screenwriter Richard Brooks, "the son of a bitch yells so loud."

Robinson had wanted the part—and $12,500 a week to play it. On the other hand, Claire Trevor, who had appeared with Bogart in *Dead End,* so "wanted that part" that she was willing to take less for what she knew was a plum role. Still the studio dallied. Her husband at the time, producer Milton Bren, cornered Bogart one day at the Finlandia baths, where many actors and film executives steamed away tensions and hangovers. Bren persuaded Bogart to call Jack Warner and say he wanted Trevor in the role, and only then was it hers. The rest of the cast was filled with familiar faces from Warner Brothers—Dan Seymour; Marc Lawrence, the sadistic prison guard in *Invisible Stripes;* William Haade from *They Drive by Night*—and a few new faces, including Native American actor Jay Silverheels, who eventually became the Lone Ranger's "faithful Indian companion" Tonto.

Huston's fury over the Thomas hearings had been continuous since their close. When he arrived in Key West in early November to join Brooks, "he was in a twenty-four-hour-a-day rage." Indeed, for a while it looked as though his fury might sabotage the project. Pre-production on *Key Largo* had moved along on schedule since August, but suddenly, nothing was right. It was based on a verse play; Huston said he didn't like free verse. Its hero fought in the Spanish Civil War; so who the hell *cared* about the Spanish Civil War? The larger problem was that Maxwell Anderson was a reactionary who hated Roosevelt, and Huston had had enough of that in Washington.

Was there a place called Key Largo? he growled at Brooks. There was, and Brooks took him there. They located the owner of the empty Largo Hotel, an Irishman who quickly drove Huston nuts. "Mr. How-ston, you want me to bring a cook or something? You going to stay here?"

"And John said, 'Wait. Wait a minute,' in that deep voice of his. 'Show me the storm cellar.' Because in the play, when the hurricane hit, they went down in the storm cellar.

"The Irishman said, 'Mr. How-ston, if you dig three feet below the floor, you're in the ocean. There's no storm cellar!'

"John turned to me, 'What did I tell you? That son of a bitch Anderson, he can't write! He's a liar! Let's go home!' "

Brooks, frustrated, had to remind Huston that the cellar was a dramatic device and not an architectural prerequisite. Houston eventually calmed down and they settled into a routine—Brooks wrote, and Huston edited the pages between excursions to the end of the pier to fish.

Huston's anger over the HUAC hearings and the country's political mood became a part of the script. The gangsters were a metaphor for the right-wing forces bent on compelling obedience to the new political orthodoxy. Asked by Johnny Rocco, "Why'd you stick your neck out?" McCloud answers, no good reason. He'd simply believed some words that Roosevelt said about not returning to the kind of world that had existed after the last war and about "fighting to cleanse the world of ancient evils, ancient ills." The quote is delivered, however, with a quiet, ironic laugh.

As in *The Petrified Forest,* romance blossoms in an atmosphere of violence; the violence is more implied than explicit; the action is more verbal than physical; and the whole piece resembles a play, in that it takes place largely on a confined set. But there was more than merely the dozen years' difference between Archie Mayo's almost statically photographed *Petrified Forest* and John Huston's fluid use of the camera. The director's vision in this case was echoed and augmented by cinematographer Karl Freund, who had photographed Fritz Lang's German Expressionist masterpiece *Metropolis* (1926) and had directed the Boris Karloff classic *The Mummy*

(1932). Freund's genius with lighting and camera angles made the camera an integral part of the narrative.

In one respect, however, Huston did treat the project like a play. The days of rehearsals on the sound stage gave the cast an easy sense of exactly where to be when filming began. "They had freedom," editor Rudi Fehr explained. "They moved around. They invented." No doubt the rehearsals also helped make the company close-knit from the time its members assembled in mid-December. Ramps constructed by the Warner carpenters allowed Lionel Barrymore—elderly, arthritic, and confined to a wheelchair—to be mobile. He quickly became the father figure on the set, in sharp contrast to the curmudgeons he played on the screen. To the surprise of Harry Lewis, a contract player cast as Robinson's top gun, he was not at all like Old Man Potter in *It's A Wonderful Life* or any of the various Scrooges and crabby doctors he'd made a career of, but "an extremely friendly man." Even the stars were drawn to Barrymore, often gathering around him between shots as he told anecdotes about his sister, Ethel, the grande dame of stage and screen, and his brother, John, one of the great Hamlets, who five years before had died a hopeless alcoholic. The three were the royal family of the American theater, and the others "wanted to hear what he had to say about what they did together—the rivalry, the love, everything that went on in that family."

According to a Warner publicity release, "Mr. Barrymore gained something of a reputation as the most relaxed man on the set . . . by nodding slightly in the arms of Lauren Bacall . . . waiting for a scene to be filmed. Bogart remarked that any man who can fall asleep 'when my wife's arms are around him ought to retire.' Barrymore just growled."

It was an easy shoot for Bogart, made comfortable by Huston's familiar direction. The occasional needling about Bogart's recantation was just that, and did not interfere with their friendship. Bogart's role was familiar to him, too, though more subtly muted than usual. Huston and Brooks wrote some touches into the script that reflected Bogart—for instance, making McCloud a man who loves the sea and wants to make his living on it. "My first sweetheart was a boat," he says. The getaway boat on which McCloud settles scores with the gangsters is called the *Santana*.

Bogart's relations with Robinson were easy as well. It was their fifth film together, but the first since *Brother Orchid* in 1940, in which Bogart was cast as a hired thug. Their careers had diverged considerably in the intervening seven years. The end of Robinson's days as a leading man coincided with Bogart's ascent. Robinson wrote in his autobiography *All*

My Yesterdays that he had not expected to be the star. "Why not second billing? At 53 I was lucky to get any billing at all." Bogart, he added, extended every courtesy. When the call came to go to the set, he checked to be sure Robinson was ready, and even went by his trailer to pick him up. He was given the star treatment, Robinson said, because Bogart insisted on it.

To those watching them on the set, the way they played off each other was a lesson in the art of film acting. The underlying tension in *Key Largo* stems essentially from the antagonism of the Bogart and Robinson characters. Huston let the two explore their ideas scene by scene before filming began. Fehr recalled that "he just said to them, 'Show me what you'd like to do here,' and then he improved on that." As the actors worked out the scene in which Robinson slaps Bogart's face, "Huston walked back and forth, and took not just one look but two or three to see what was going to happen next. Who was going to kill whom? No man likes to be slapped without taking action; yet at the end Bogart's character does the smart thing by doing nothing. But that had to be played out. I watched Huston, and when I put the film together, I included three or four cuts, back and forth between the two." Earlier, Robinson gives Bogart what turns out to be an empty gun, hoping to goad him into a one-sided shootout. Bogart's reaction is at the heart of the film. Will he take a stand and pull the trigger, or does he stick to his supposed credo, "I fight nobody's battles but my own"? When he puts down the gun and says, "One Rocco more or less isn't worth dying for," his cowardice seems complete.

Everyone knew that a good deal of the success of the interaction came from the high regard Bogart and Robinson had for each other, the remarks recorded by Lillian Ross notwithstanding. For years, Robinson had fought against insinuations that he was somehow politically tainted. No one ever directly accused him of being a Communist, but rumors and columnists often branded him a dupe. In an attempt to clear his reputation, he had appeared before HUAC that fall, asserting that "my Americanism is unblemished and fine and wonderful, and I am proud of it." Ultimately Robinson would not be blacklisted so much as graylisted; he worked, but less often and in smaller parts, and hence his sardonic feeling that he "was lucky to get any billing at all."

"They were delighted to be in the same picture," Fehr said. "They joked around. Watching them rehearse together was delightful because of their ability to create a scene and come up with a solution if a line didn't play, or if one of them was uncomfortable sitting in a certain position or doing some bit of business."

Despite the commonly accepted story depicting both men as loftily indifferent to matters of status, it took months for their agents and the studio to agree on the placement of names and faces, type size, and other details of billing. Bogart, as the star, naturally got first place, but everything after that was negotiable. Sample layouts were made and given to all parties. At one point, Robinson's agent complained that Bogart's name was too big. At another, Bogart's complained that Robinson's head shot was too big. It wasn't just a question of ego; it was one of money, too. Billing determined earnings, negotiating power, and above all, one's place in the tightly hierarchic structure of studio Hollywood.

It was easier going with Claire Trevor, who to get the part had to agree for first featured billing after Lionel Barrymore rather than a co-star credit. (When there were two stars of the same magnitude, the male was always listed first, a custom as prevalent as the practice that female stars never earned as much as comparable male stars.) Billing, however, is no indicator of performance. As Gaye Dawn, Rocco's girlfriend, whom he hasn't seen for the eight years he'd been in exile, Trevor steals the movie, and everyone knew she was doing it as the film was being made.

In her most compelling scene, Gaye, who has become an alcoholic since last being with Rocco, is forced by the mobster to sing one of her old hits. She has lost her voice, her youth, and her looks to whiskey and is barely holding on to reality. She asks for a drink. If she sings the song, Rocco tells her, he will give her one. Her dialogue sets the stage—"My gowns were gorgeous . . . I wore hardly any makeup . . . no lights, just a baby spot"—then she begins to sing in a threadbare voice, wobbly and off-key: "Moanin' low/My sweet man, I love him so,/Though he's mean as can be,/He's the kind of man needs the kind of woman like me. . . ."

Now let me have that drink, she tells one of Rocco's henchmen. No, Rocco says. But you promised! she pleads. You were rotten, he tells her. She staggers to a table and puts her head down in tears. McCloud pours her a drink, which leads to Rocco's slapping him.

The scene is excruciating and sadistic. Trevor said she was embarrassed when it was made, in part because she was unprepared for the scene to be shot out of schedule. Huston purposely had her film it with only enough warning to get into costume, and thus added an extra dimension.

Yet everyone watching the take knew how special the performance was, and the moment after Huston yelled, "Cut!" they applauded. Harry Lewis turned to the actor next to him and said, correctly, "She's going to get an Academy Award for this."

Gaye Dawn was not in the Anderson play. Huston and Brooks created her, using as a faint model Gaye Orlova, a nightclub friend of the mobster Lucky Luciano, who vowed to follow him if he was deported. All the characters, Brooks said, were "parts of the stories we had heard and exchanged." Rocco embodied society's—and Huston's—attitude about alcoholic women: "One thing I can't stand it's a dame that's drunk. . . . They turn my stomach. No good to themselves or anybody else." There was no dearth of female alcoholics in Hollywood, but Huston almost surely drew on his memory of that night in Caserta, Italy, in 1943: a bar full of men, the fiery Mayo Methot drunk and staggering through a song, her voice as unsteady as her feet. Early in the movie, after the Bacall character has scratched his face in return for his sexual advance, Rocco talks briefly about his girlfriend's early days. "Some little wildcat. I knew one like you a long time ago. Scratched, kicked a bit. A regular hellion. She even stuck a knife in me once. Irish kid . . . a real fireball. Her name was Maggie Mooney. . . . I had her change it to Gaye Dawn."

As he had been in *To Have and Have Not,* Bogart was helpful to Bacall, though he never gave her advice in front of others. "The audience is always a little ahead of you," he told her after taking her aside before she shot a scene one day. "If a guy points a gun at you, the audience knows you're afraid. You don't have to make faces."

Bacall had a difficult scene with Robinson, in which the gangster taunts the young widow with graphic sexual intentions. She responds by spitting in his face, leaving Rocco standing open-mouthed and furious. Huston knew that the language in the scene would cause a problem with the Breen Office. Brooks had explicitly "written all the vile things he was saying to her, but John told me, 'You know we can't say that crap. So think of something else.' " Brooks suggested that Robinson say the lines, but that they be whispered and the audience not hear them. The scene was made more effective because it gives rein to the viewers' fantasies, but it put an additional dramatic burden on Bacall, whose reaction to Robinson is the dramatic focus.

She called *Key Largo* one of her happiest movie experiences. Huston, she said, "was hypnotic. He could convince you to commit murder." The resulting effort was reflected in the reviews, which for the first time praised Bacall not as a personality but as an actress. Trevor said that during filming she felt a little sorry for her, an extraordinary personality playing a quite ordinary young woman, with not much else to do than provide the love interest.

The two women got on well together. Bacall was confident in her position as Mrs. Bogart, and she admired the more experienced Trevor, who was fifteen years older. "Claire and I," Bacall told a studio publicist, "are as chummy as a couple of Republicans."

Huston spent considerable time with Harry Lewis as Toots, the plainly psychotic gang member of whom even his cohorts are afraid. While the other hoods give the impression that they would easily kill the inhabitants of the hotel if necessary, the audience has the feeling that Toots would do it for the sheer pleasure of the cruelty. As Lewis was preparing for a scene in which he laughs maniacally while reading a comic book, Huston knelt beside him and said, "Now I want to talk about what I want you to do in this scene, and how I want this character to feel, and what his mind is like." It was Huston who specified Toots's distinctive wardrobe—light gray suit, black shirt, white suspenders, light hat. (When he wasn't training with Huston to be a psychopath, Lewis liked to spend time with Robinson, talking about Robinson's Romanian grandmother.) The killer is a minor character, although he appears in many scenes; Huston was a perfectionist down to the least detail. But Lewis felt that Huston "had a particular fondness for Toots," and that the director was projecting some of his own darker impulses into the character—the unpredictability, the violence and sporadic cruelty, the total freedom from accepted rules of conduct.

Key Largo was generally well received; but despite its allegorical intentions, what critics and audiences saw was primarily a good crime picture. The enemy was Little Caesar, not Parnell Thomas, no matter how hard Huston and Brooks tried, and the message that ended up being delivered was older than *Racket Busters:* an honest man pitted against the mob and outnumbered is protected by his purity of purpose. The New York *Herald Tribune,* in a typical reaction, summed it up as "a bang-up thriller of the old gangster school."

In the late spring of 1948, not long after *Key Largo* was completed, Bacall joyfully met Bogart at the gate in their yard and told him she was pregnant. Instead of the rapture she expected, he grew very quiet, put an arm around her, and led her into the house. No mention of the baby was made that evening or over dinner. Later that night, the couple had the worst fight of their marriage as Bogart blustered with all the primal fury of a mother-rejected son. He was not about to lose his wife to a child, he screamed.

The next day he wrote a contrite letter to Bacall, apologizing for his behavior. "He didn't know what had gotten into him except his fear of losing me," Bacall wrote. "He was so afraid our closeness and incredible happiness together would be cut into by a child—but of course he wanted us to have a baby more than anything else in the world, he just would have to get used to the idea."

Bacall's pregnancy was providential, not only for personal reasons but for professional ones as well. Her relations with Warner Brothers were under increasing strain, as the studio tried to force her into roles she felt were unsuitable. *Dark Passage* and *Key Largo* were fine, but several others that were offered were not. In the spring of 1947, Michael Curtiz had wanted her for the pop singer lead in *Romance on the High Seas,* a pleasant musical comedy with Oscar Levant, Jack Carson, and Eric Blore, but hardly a role for her. Bacall knew that Judy Garland and Kathryn Grayson had turned it down and that she was at best the third choice. Besides, she told Jack Warner, she was not a singer. She held out against blandishments from Curtiz and threats from Warner, choosing to be suspended rather than take the part. Actresses had no judgment, Curtiz wrote to Steve Trilling, adding with Hungarian hyperbole, "She is a fool to refuse this part, the like of which comes along once in a lifetime."

Band vocalist Doris Day's career was launched by the role, but Bacall was right about her own limitations. The Jule Styne–Sammy Cahn songs with their range of an octave and a half required a trained singer. The demands were far different from having a few usable notes in one's voice, utilized in a straight dramatic role, as she had in the two Howard Hawks films. Besides, after the pairing with Bogart, how would the public have reacted to seeing Slim in the arms of Jack Carson?

Bogart's relations with the studio soured along with Bacall's. For all the arguments over the years, he was still considered one of the Warners family in the paternalistic studio world. Whether he was being a good boy or a bad, he was recognized as a company member who had paid his dues. Bacall, acquired at considerable expense, was an underused outsider and perceived as an ingrate. As far as Jack Warner was concerned, she was a girl who had a lucky break at nineteen and was presuming to tell him how to run his business. "This company is not a department store and I am not going to have you, who have been in only four or five pictures, insulting my intelligence!" Warner screamed at her over the phone during one of their periodic confrontations, before slamming down the receiver.

Bacall had discussed two big parts with the studio—the heroine in *The Fountainhead* (1949), adapted by Ayn Rand from her novel, directed by King Vidor and with Gary Cooper as the co-star; and the part of the gutsy heroine opposite Sydney Greenstreet in the steamy *Flamingo Road* (1949). For the latter, Steve Trilling had favored her over Warner's first choice, Ann Sheridan, but the casting decision was made during the time that Bogart was refusing to distance himself from the Committee for the First Amendment, which may have played a role in the studio's decision. (Joan Crawford ended up with the part.) Whatever the reason, Bacall instead was offered and turned down such smaller-scale efforts as *The Girl from Jones Beach;* she didn't look good in a bathing suit, she said. (Virginia Mayo played the role, beside Ronald Reagan). She challenged the studio to give her better roles. After all, she pointed out, didn't her contract specify that her services were "of a special, unique, extraordinary and intellectual character"? In a series of bitter exchanges, she learned that it was the legal department, not the artist, that decided the meaning of such high-sounding clauses. As in the case of Bette Davis, pursued to England a dozen years before, the true meaning of a long-term contract became painfully clear—except that Davis returned to a healthy business and an expanding studio. Bacall's struggles took place against the background of an industry falling in on itself, in a time of shrinking opportunities.

She repeatedly asked to be released from her contract, but the studio refused. General counsel Roy Obringer pointed out that since her services were indeed so special and unique, they couldn't possibly consider a release. She contemplated a lawsuit; her lawyer told her to forget it. Morally, she was right, he said; legally, she hadn't a leg to stand on.

"I congratulate you, Jack, on your methods of dealing with me," she wrote Warner in July 1948 as she viewed the litter of a once-flourishing career. "It was my mistake to ever believe you when you told me you had confidence in me and my best interests at heart." The quarrel had gone public that spring and was quickly escalated by the local gossip columnists.

After Bacall turned down *Blowing Wild* (tempestuous wife of oil baron tries to rekindle old romance with wildcatter) in June, Hedda Hopper asked the actress if it was true that she was pregnant. In Bacall's later account, she denied the rumor, figuring it was none of Hopper's business. When the columnist asked if she was lying, Bacall hung up after a furious "No!"

Nevertheless, Hopper's column item said, "Lauren Bacall Bogart first denied she was going to have a baby on the advice of her agent and lawyer. . . . Lauren told me she wanted the blessed event kept quiet so she could continue drawing a salary from the studio. . . . should think the Bogarts would be so proud of the coming event that money would be the least of their considerations." It was a year before the two women spoke to each other again.

Bacall was put on suspension for her refusal to do *Blowing Wild.* Bogart claimed he had bet the film's producer, Harry Warner's son-in-law Milton Sperling, that the picture would never be shot and said it was unjust to suspend his wife. (The movie was made with Barbara Stanwyck and Gary Cooper four years later, and was released in 1953 to poor reviews.)

It meant little to the studio that the comedies she turned down were a study in miscasting or that the dramas were turgid and badly received. She was the property of Warner Bros. Pictures, Inc., to do with as it pleased. When in late 1948 a very pregnant Bacall modeled maternity clothes in *Life,* J. L. erupted. Here this girl, he fulminated to Roy Obringer, had refused to make a movie in a bathing suit, but was ready to pose for a national magazine in this condition! A stern letter went to *Life,* reminding its editors to go through Warner Publicity before approaching stars under contract to the studio.

Throughout it all, Bogart backed his wife. In the summer of 1948 he told columnist Harrison Carroll of their decision to put a temporary hold on Bacall's dispute with the studio, as "the baby is the most important thing right now," but the acrimony repeatedly intruded upon what should have been the happiest time of her life. In supporting Bacall, Bogart may have drawn some satisfaction in her being able to retaliate against Warner in a way that he could never do early in his career. As Mrs. Bogart she had the social and financial security he did not have when he came to the studio. Still, the continuing confrontation only fueled his long-standing differences with J. L.

Walking around the Warner lot in dark glasses one day in June, Bogart was overheard to say, "These glasses are handy when you go to see Jack Warner; all he can see is his own reflection." A news story recounting Ida Lupino's wedding two months later reported Bogart almost coming to blows with an unnamed Warner producer after the producer had criticized Bacall for her continual suspensions; that same producer now wanted Bogart for a movie. "Bogey's reply," the paper reported, "is sardonic laughter."

Bogart and Bacall's problems were with a studio for which 1948 was a pivotal year. Much of the heart had gone out of Warner Brothers when

Hal Wallis left, and his brilliance was never replaced, Jack Warner's ostensible assumption of his job notwithstanding. Steve Trilling had been a great casting director and was a capable assistant to Warner, but he was no Hal Wallis. (For that matter, even Hal Wallis, now an independent producer at Paramount, wasn't looking like Hal Wallis.) There was no longer a production intelligence screening every frame of film, critiquing the pace, the lighting, the acting, the direction, and the editing.

Warner Brothers was now a studio in search of an identity. Following the writers' purge, the studio backed away from the social commentary films that had built its reputation and fueled its success, and instead fell back on pleasant minor musicals and recyclings of its older staples. There were a few notable exceptions, including James Cagney's return to the studio in *White Heat,* Jane Wyman in *Johnny Belinda,* and the newly signed Danny Kaye in *The Inspector General,* but the overall quality was down.

In addition, there was financial erosion in the studio system itself. The 1948 United States Supreme Court decision known as the Consent Decree ruled that studios could not simultaneously be producers, distributors, and exhibitors, which meant they had to sell the theater chains that were the built-in outlet for their product and a vital source of cash. At the same time, the new and rapidly expanding television industry offered free entertainment at home. Warner Brothers' profits for 1948 were one half of those for 1947, eleven million dollars as opposed to twenty-two. The unrelenting pressure from New York was transmitted through Harry Warner, who was now in Burbank much of the time. Harry, who had always been afraid of going broke, kept up the refrain: Economize, economize, cut cut cut!

With Harry's move to California, the tensions between the two brothers and the urgency to retrench increased. Art Silver of the trailer department came upon J. L. in a corridor one day and was startled to see tears streaming down his boss's face. "I don't know what I'm going to do," he wept. "Harry keeps on telling me to cut back and I can't withstand him."

Jack Warner, his son said, was always afraid of his brother. Harry still wielded a certain moral, even physical power as the eldest brother and surrogate father in what, despite all its quirkiness, remained a traditional family. Jack Jr. once watched uneasily as his uncle confidently slaughtered and cut up a calf. ("My father could cut up a script and an actor, so *he* had that.") Harry was an overbearing presence, not often withstood, and he disapproved of J. L.'s adulterous lifestyle. But that, his nephew said, was "only gasoline on a fire that was already burning." Harry Warner shared the easterners' business-office view that the westerners—the Burbank studio executives—were self-indulgent profligates "who wasted the money that he had gotten out of the bankers, who were terribly tough to deal with." Each brother had cause to be upset with the other, Jack Jr. felt, but that upset was compounded by their being "stubborn men."

Bogart hoped that his years-old dream of independent filmmaking would be fulfilled when his own company rose from the ashes of Mark Hellinger Productions. In January 1948, Bogart, as vice-president of Hellinger Productions, presided over a special shareholders' meeting, the first step in dissolving the corporation. The company's total assets, including expectancies on released productions, came to a little over half a million dollars, to be distributed among the creditors. Also left was the preliminary outline and incomplete first draft of *Knock on Any Door.*

Bogart, through his lawyer and business adviser Morgan Maree, picked up the project and formed a new company named after his yawl: Santana Productions. The Selznick deal had died with Hellinger. It was Hellinger and his innate production know-how and showmanship that Selznick had wanted. But there was one last bit of glory for the ambitious producer who fancied himself rivaling Jack Warner. Upon its release in March, *The Naked City,* with its sense of the streets and its documentary/newsreel quality, was hailed by critics as a bold new step in movie making, and Jules Dassin was praised for his direction. (In the early 1950s, Dassin was forced into exile in Europe after being named as a Communist during another set of HUAC hearings.) Bogart and Maree went back to Columbia, where Harry Cohn had shown interest the year before, and struck an agreement for partial financing and distribution, as well as use of the studio facilities for production. But Harry Cohn—once described as "the road company version of Jack Warner"—was hardly in David O. Selznick's league. Columbia had always been the lowest rung on the ladder of major studios; its box office gross was less than a third of Warners', and an even smaller fraction of the others'. Nor did the studio apply the care in picture making that Selznick did. (Columbia did, however, avoid two of the major traumas that rocked most studios in the 1940s. Since it owned no theaters, its cash-flow was unaffected by the Consent Decree, and it was the first studio to profit from television, by forming a TV subsidiary, Screen Gems.)

In place of Hellinger as producer, Bogart brought in Robert Lord. Lord had been a Warners' screenwriter of some success in the 1930s—*Black Legion, Bordertown,* and *Gold Diggers of 1935,* as well as the great weeper *One Way Passage* (1932), for which he won an Academy Award for his original story—but he was now at liberty, having priced himself out of the market upon his return from military service. Though a stockholder of Santana along with Bogart and Maree, he was essentially an employee who ran the enterprise from a desk on the Columbia lot on Gower Street, along with an assistant and one or two secretaries; Morgan Maree's office on Wilshire Boulevard was the mailing address and headquarters. Without Selznick and Hellinger, the company was undercapitalized in both money and administrative talent. All the elements that previously had been so right were now quite wrong.

By October 1948, Bogart and Bacall were more involved with the child that was due in a matter of weeks than with fighting Warner Brothers. Bacall's pregnancy had so far been easy—"I gloried in it"—and she didn't intend to jeopardize her well-being or the child's in a no-win battle with the studio. Wearily, she sent off a notice, post-dated, of her willingness to resume her services and report to the studio. But the day after, Bogart, not filming at the time and therefore inclined to long, liquid lunches at Romanoff's, called Burbank. The secretary listened as Bogart, his voice thick and his words uncharacteristically slurred, asked for Jack Warner. Mr. Warner was off the lot, he was told. Bogart asked to speak with Milton Sperling.

"He talked as though he was quite 'drunk,' " the receptionist reported, "and when he used some foul language, he was cut off. Our operator explained that the Telephone Company will cut people off who use bad language. Believe this is what happened."

The following day, Alex Evelove had his staff prepare a five-page summary for J. L. of all comments made about the studio to the press by Bogart and Bacall in the past months, with the suggestion that it be turned over to the legal department. But tempers cooled, at least temporarily. Bacall's letter earned her time off for the rest of her pregnancy and until March 1949. Beneath the surface the rancor was far from subsiding, but at least she would have her baby in peace.

Bacall's obstetrician predicted a delivery date in late December, but the year ended with her still expecting. On January 6, 1949, a few days after Bogart began work in Santana Productions' *Tokyo Joe* at Columbia, Bacall woke up feeling contractions. Because they were still mild, she said nothing to Bogart and sent him off to work with a kiss. Before long, however, the contractions were more regular, and she phoned her doctor, who said to let him know when they were five minutes apart. As she sat there timing them, the gossip columnist Sheila Graham called and asked, "Tell me, is it true Bogie had a child by another woman?" "No," Bacall, astonished, answered; and she hung up.

A few hours later, Bacall's doctor reached Bogart on the set and told him to come to the office and take her to the hospital. As they drove, Bacall told him about Graham's call. "I thought he'd go mad," she wrote. "He called her every name in the book. 'Wait till I get hold of her, I'll fix that insensitive bitch. . . . why the hell didn't she call *me*?' "

"It obviously wasn't true," Bacall added. "But suppose it had been and she'd made that call?"

At Cedars of Lebanon Hospital, Bogart was brought into the labor room to be with his wife. "He wore a green gown to match his face," she wrote. After a few minutes, he said he couldn't bear to see anyone he loved in pain and begged to be excused. Former Warner publicity man Jaik Rosenstein, who now worked for Hedda Hopper, found him pacing in the waiting room. "You goddamn ghoul, what are you doing here," Bogart asked, but it was clear he was glad to see him.

At 11:22 P.M., Bacall gave birth to a healthy six-pound, six-ounce boy. When she was wheeled back into her room, Bogart was waiting for her. "Hello, Baby," he said with tears in his eyes.

Later, he went to Chasen's to celebrate. A photograph shows Dave Chasen, Paul Douglas, and Frank Sinatra as master of ceremonies watching the tired, glassy-eyed, happy father. The next morning, after stopping by the hospital, he showed up on the set beaming. He told writer Steve Fischer with some excitement that he and Betty were now parents of a baby boy and that they had chosen "a very nice name" even though Fischer should not take credit for it. "We're going to name him Steve"—Stephen Humphrey Bogart—in tribute to the movie that had brought his parents together.

At a campaign rally in Los Angeles a few months earlier, Bacall had been seated next to President Harry Truman. During dinner, Truman and Bogart made a $20 wager on whether the baby would be a boy or a girl. Truman bet on a boy, and soon after Stephen's birth, Bogart airmailed a check to the White House, with a note asking the president to please cash it; he wanted it as a keepsake for Steve. Bacall writes that a couple of months later the check arrived with a letter:

Dear Mr. Bogart—

I am returning the check which you sent me endorsed to Mr. Bogart, Jr.

I hope you will buy him a savings bond with it and put it in his educational fund with my compliments.

It is a rare instance when I find a man who remembers his commitments and meets them on the dot.

Harry S. Truman

Presents for the baby arrived from friends and from strangers. Lionel Barrymore sent an engraved sterling silver cup and porringer. A fan on the East Coast sent an 1899 edition of Maud's *The Baby's Record.* Louis Bromfield's gift was a silver cup with the inscription, "To S. H. B. from L. B. From One Capricorn to Another and God Help The World."

Bacall and a nurse brought the baby home in the wake of one of Los Angeles's rare snowfalls—three inches on the flowerbeds and in the palm trees—and Bogart built an enormous snowman on the front lawn as a greeting. With both parents working, they would need a nanny, and Philip Dunne's wife, Amanda, had a friend who knew a highly recommended, no-nonsense Canadian. Bogart, Dunne noticed, seemed apprehensive during the discussion. Out of Bacall's hearing, he questioned her closely: What was she like, this woman? Did she like children? "Will she be *kind*?" It seemed more like a question a mother would ask, not a father of Bogart's vintage. In the needling that spared neither his friends nor his wife, he would at times later reproach Bacall for wanting her career and thereby ostensibly neglecting the house, or himself, or the children. Behind the cutting remarks were the painful memories of his absentee parents and abusive caretakers.

In mid-1948, shortly after the completion of *Key Largo,* Santana Productions had made *Knock on Any Door.* With Hellinger's death, Brando was no longer interested, and he was replaced by twenty-two-year-old John Derek as the doomed Nick Romano, the altarboy turned killer. The film was the first for director Nicholas Ray. But all Derek's hard work, youth, and good looks were not enough in a part that called for a Brando or young Bogart. Bogart's role as Nick's concerned defense attorney was no better than his nice-guy part had been eleven years before in *Marked Woman.* As he describes Nick's life to the court, the audience sees it in flashback: his father dying in prison, his own stint in reform school, his young wife's suicide. "Bogart is so wearing," the critic Pauline Kael wrote, "that you wish he'd stop orating and get out his rod again." But Ray's direction began a notable career, and his 1950 film with Bogart, *In a Lonely Place,* is one of the best movies made by either of them. Ray, who had an affinity for pictures about the disaffected, would go on to direct James Dean in *Rebel Without a Cause* (1955).

Two more Santana films, both strongly derivative of *Casablanca*—*Tokyo Joe* (1949) and *Sirocco* (1951)—came and went quickly. The problem with Santana's pictures was not in the screenplays, which were worked on by very good writers and were based in most cases on serious works; Bogart had an eye for a good literary property. The real drawback was the absence of the kind of integrated production team that supported Bogart at Warner Brothers, where directors, stars, cinematographers, screenwriters, and all their support crews had the benefit of years of working together. Bogart participated actively in all phases of Santana's productions, but he was an actor, not a producer—an actor, moreover, still saddled with obligations to Warners.

The company was also hampered by its lack of clout, which became evident when Bogart tried to acquire the newest hit by playwright Sidney Kingsley, whose *Dead End* had, years before, helped to advance his career. *Detective Story,* with its taut, episodic view of life in an urban precinct station, was the dramatic ancestor of *Hill Street Blues* and innumerable other police dramas. Central to its portraits of "cops, reporters, shyster lawyers, shoplifters, dope pushers," as one critic described it, was Detective James McLeod, an uncompromising policeman driven to destruction by his inner demons: "Evil has a stench of its own," he tells a colleague. "I know. . . . Every day and night of my childhood I saw and heard [my father] abuse and torment my mother. . . . She died in a lunatic asylum. . . . Every time I look at one of these bastards I see my father's face!"

The play, with Ralph Bellamy in the lead, was in tryouts in Philadelphia in late 1948 when Bogart and Maree came backstage to talk with Kingsley about wanting to buy the film rights. Kingsley had no trouble visualizing Bogart as his troubled hero: "He'd have been marvelous." And Bogart wanted Kingsley to direct the picture as he had the play, which would have made the deal more inviting. Santana, though, was not alone in wanting to acquire the property. Paramount, Kingsley said, "bid an enormous amount of money and seventeen and a half percent of the distributor's gross. There had never been a deal like that before."

William Wyler, a backer of the play and director of the filmed version of *Dead End,* wanted Paramount to have the rights, with good reason; the studio wanted him to direct. Bogart and Maree simply could not compete. "I don't think they had the resources to buy the properties he wanted," Kingsley said of Santana and Bogart. "He'd have been *wonderful* in *Detective Story.* I often regret that I didn't somehow say to him, 'All right.' But I couldn't in fairness to my backers accept his offer. According to the Dramatists Guild rules, I had to accept the highest offer.

"I would meet him occasionally and we'd talk. Humphrey at that point was going through a period of aggressiveness. He would tease me about not selling him the rights and sometimes be a little surly—something to the effect of, 'You don't like actors.' I reminded him that the reason he and his partner didn't have *Detective Story* was that they couldn't afford it. I don't think he ever quite forgave me. I never quite forgave myself either, although Willy Wyler did a marvelous film out of it."

Detective Story, released in November 1951, with Kirk Douglas in the lead, became one of the highest-grossing films of the year. It also received four Academy Award nominations, including Best Director, Best Actress, and Best Screenplay. But the success of the film underscored the likelihood that Bogart's dream of independence would never materialize, and that he would spend the rest of his career as somebody else's high-paid employee.

There were clear financial as well as artistic advantages to being his own producer. The tax rate on capital gains was a fraction of that on earned income. He also had a guaranteed salary of at least $133,000 for every picture he made for Santana, in addition to his share of the receipts. At one point in late 1948 Jack Warner had expressed interest in a production deal. After Columbia released the first two Santana pictures, perhaps Warners could take over the third and have Bogart exclusively again. "I don't think it would interfere with his capital gain setup," J. L. told Trilling and Obringer, "inasmuch as he has produced two other pictures on the outside." Obringer negotiated with Maree during much of December, but there were many points of disagreement and in the end nothing came of the idea.

The failure to strike a deal derived purely from business reasons. Warner Brothers wanted at least a one-third investment, half the profits, smaller budgets, and Bogart pictures only. Bogart and Maree did not want that kind of outside control. Their demands were no longer unusual; the general trend, as the power of the studios receded, was for stars to form this kind of private corporation through which they could trade their highly taxed salaries for low-taxed capital gains. Burt Lancaster and John

Wayne were already on the Warner lot with their own companies. Most of the new generation of actors hadn't come out of the Depression and weren't focused primarily on job security. They were as eager as their earlier colleagues for a Hollywood career; but the savviest of them, like Gregory Peck or the vastly successful Montgomery Clift, wanted more control over their films than was allowed by Warner policy. Peck, in particular, was attracted by the kinds of movies Warners made; but when even a personal pitch by J. L. himself couldn't hide the studio's intention to have absolute control, the actor went to Twentieth Century–Fox instead.

With Bogart, Jack Warner took the inability to reach an agreement more personally. Supposedly, Bogart was one of the Warner family. J. L. had *made* Humphrey Bogart, or so he felt, and Bogart, accordingly, owed him gratitude and loyalty. Despite the fact that Bogart's Warner Brothers board–ratified contract granted him the right to have a business and creative life in which the studio had no part, Warner never forgave the actor for demanding those terms. Yet for all of Warner's regarding Bogart as family, the two had never been friends. To begin with, Warner didn't like actors, with the possible exception of such non–Warner Brothers male stars as Cary Grant, Gary Cooper, and Henry Fonda. "My father didn't socialize with actors," Jack Warner Jr. said. On the other hand, actors who were so powerful as to be independent businessmen were another matter. "That was prestige. Gary Cooper could name his own price, his own picture. He didn't depend on my father. He was his own man, and my father could be so charming and captivating to these people."

It was these people, not Bogart, who were invited to the chic dinner parties at Warner's home, where guests dined off antique Chinese porcelain and places were marked by gold-lettered names on placards shaped like Los Angeles trolley cars. To Warner, Bogart had started as "just somebody you put into a part," and J. L. could never quite forget it. "Later on, after all those wonderful pictures, he recognized that Bogart was a tremendous asset to the company. But there was never one hundred percent acceptance. There always had to be a stinger in there."

Bogart, in turn, made no secret of his low personal regard for Warner. One day, Warner took Bogart aside and said, "Bogie, I hear you called me a prick." Bogart replied, "Jack, your hearing is off. I referred to you, because you're so strict and moral, as a prig. *P-R-I-G.* And somebody didn't hear me right." Warner returned to his office and called the Research Department: "Look up the word for *P-R-I-G.*"

Throughout their association, however, there had been a basic if grudging respect and a certain commonality of purpose in "the making of good pictures." Now, in the late 1940s, that commonality seemed gone. The studio's mishandling of Bacall, the HUAC hearings, and the arm-twisting that followed loosened the personal and professional ties of almost a decade and a half.

Following the films that brought Bogart to the height of his career—*To Have and Have Not, The Big Sleep, The Treasure of the Sierra Madre, Key Largo*—he entered a fallow period. The studio seemed tired, too. After *Key Largo,* John Huston left for MGM. Michael Curtiz was getting old. Howard Hawks was long gone. And Jerry Wald would soon depart, driven out, like Hal Wallis, by Jack Warner's jealousy. By the end of the 1940s, only two of the five approved directors specified in Bogart's contract—Curtiz and Delmer Daves—were still at Warner Brothers.

In mid-1949, Bogart began production at Warners on *Chain Lightning,* as a jet pilot who atones for what he considers his part in a buddy's accidental death, and wins back Eleanor Parker. Bacall went back to work opposite Kirk Douglas in *Young Man with a Horn,* based loosely on the life of the great jazz cornetist Bix Beiderbecke and adapted from Dorothy Baker's biographical novel by Bogart's longtime friend Edmund North. She was the second female lead to Doris Day, in a role described by *The New York Times* as a "confused, mentally sick wife. It is a heavy, disagreeable part that would tax the ability of a more accomplished actress, and the fatuous dialogue she has to speak is no help either."

Bogart went east that September for a personal appearance tour of Loew's theaters in New York to publicize Santana's film *Tokyo Joe.* Bacall, who accompanied him, asked whether she could make co-appearances. Absolutely not, Steve Trilling wired in reply, reminding her that she was under contract exclusively to Warner Brothers. Undeterred, once in New York, Bacall asked Mort Blumenstock in the Warner publicity office there. He knew about her request to Trilling and was not fooled. "WITHOUT MENTIONING WIRE LITTLE LADY TELEPHONED ME SEE IF I DIDN'T THINK IT GOOD PUBLICITY FOR HER," Blumenstock cabled back to Burbank. "THIS WAS MOST AGGRAVATING AS HAD ASKED HER WHEN SHE WAS GOING TO COOPERATE. . . . BOGART TOLD ME THEY WERE BOTH TOO WEALTHY TO HAVE TO BOTHER WITH PERSONAL APPEARANCES. REMINDED HER OF THIS AND TOLD HER . . . THAT WE WANTED TO SAVE HER TO APPEAR WITH YOUNG MAN WITH HORN." Warner lawyers shot off legal notices to Loew's, Bacall, and Columbia as Santana's distributor, warning them off. Bacall spent the tour of the movie houses watching from the wings.

Then came the incident that, blown up by the news media, would dominate the front pages for days and drag Bogart-Warner relations to a new low.

There are drastically differing accounts of precisely what occurred the night of Saturday September 25, at the tony New York night spot El Morocco, but the prelude to the incident is clear. The evening started with dinner and many drinks for the Bogarts and a few friends at "21," after which they walked back to the St. Regis Hotel, where Bacall suggested they call it a night. Bogart demurred and went on for more drinks with his old friend Manhattan grocery wholesaler Bill Seeman while Bacall went up to their room alone. "She had some sense," he later told columnist Earl Wilson.

By 2:45 or 3:00 A.M., Bogart and Seeman were at El Morocco, very drunk, with two 22-pound stuffed pandas. During an earlier stop at the Stork Club they had decided the toys would be good company and sent someone out to buy them at Reuben's, an all-night delicatessen that sold such things along with their thick sandwiches. Bogart also sported some new red Stork Club suspenders. A young woman named Robin Roberts, described in the ensuing news reports as someone who "models for a living in the daytime," was at the club with "a big manufacturing person from Philadelphia." Evidently she tried to take one of the pandas and wound up on the floor, a result of Bogart's determination to defend his property. Miss Roberts's friend society girl Peggy Rabe then made a pass at a panda and wound up in the same position. Miss Rabe's escort was gangster Johnny Jelke. Bogart hurled a saucer at Jelke, who in turn smashed a couple of dinner plates on Seeman's shoulder. "No blows were exchanged," club spokesman Leonard MacBain later said. "It was just one of those things."

The following Wednesday at eight A.M.—"too damn early," a sleepy Bogart commented—a city official rapped on the door of the Bogart suite at the St. Regis to serve him with an assault summons, ordering him to appear in Mid-Manhattan Court at ten o'clock on Friday morning. The press had a field day and ran such headlines as "BOGART ROUGHS UP TWO CUTIES." Model Roberts posed on the carpet of her room at the Mayflower Hotel to re-create the exact position of her fall and yanked the bodice of her low-cut dress even lower to disclose three marks purportedly incurred during the alleged altercation "as photographers leered happily. . . . She explained that they were swellings and contusions," *Time* reported. She denied grabbing the panda. Someone told her she could have it, she said. She reached for it and was pushed by Bogart, who yelled,

"Get away from me—I'm a happily married man!" Gossip columnist and El Morocco publicity man Lee Mortimer gleefully claimed he had instigated the fracas.

The media streamed over to the St. Regis, where Bogart met them still unshaven, in his slippers, with a blue bathrobe thrown over a pair of white pajamas. He admitted that he had few recollections of the evening other than a tug-of-war over the panda with "this screaming, squawking young lady. Nobody got hurt, I didn't sock anybody; and if girls were falling on the floor, I guess it was because they couldn't stand up." As for the flying saucer, Bogart allowed as how he might have "picked up a platter sometime or other. I'm apt to be a pretty bad-tempered guy at 3:45 in the morning." In the background, Bacall hummed "Some Enchanted Evening."

The Warner forces on both coasts kept their distance. Normally a high-profile incident such as this would have immediately brought a platoon of publicists from Mort Blumenstock's office on West Forty-fourth Street to run interference for the studio's biggest asset. When it had been a matter of keeping his wife from so much as setting one foot on stage with him, Warners' legal talent had been marshaled. Now that their star had been called into court, the studio counselors weren't making even a brief appearance. It was not a coincidence or slip-up. As soon as the story came out, the New York office wired Burbank for instructions. J. L.'s reply was explicit: Do nothing. "These people must learn that they are not above the law."

Bogart, never at a loss when it came to dealing with the press, toughed it out with wisecracks. "Me hit a woman?" he told Earl Wilson. "Why, I'm too sweet and chivalrous. Besides, it's dangerous." So, Wilson asked, he never hit a woman in his life? "Nope." Bacall gave him a long look. "*Never* . . . Mr. Bogart?" Bogart took a long drag on his cigarette. "Oh, maybe an old wife some time or other."

But he knew that this skirmish could be serious. For all his reputation as a brawler, he had never really been in trouble with the law. Now, approaching fifty, he was being haled before a judge on a possible criminal charge. Not only that, but in New York City, far from his home base, where the studios could fix anything. If they wanted to.

Jack Warner's hanging Bogart out to dry fulfilled a promise he had jokingly made two or three years before, after Bogart had walked off the lot in a contract dispute. When he returned a few weeks later, Warner told him, "Don't worry, everything's going to be all right," and, both relieved, they shook hands. Then as Bogart walked away, Warner called out to him, "Bogie, I just want to tell you something. In the future, if anybody's gonna fuck you, let it be Warner Brothers." And so they did.

At 8 A.M. Friday, *Journal-American* photographer Charles Carson went up to Bogart's suite to take a picture of him before the hearing. Bogart met him at the door, again in bathrobe and slippers, with the unmistakable look of someone rousted out of bed. He was perfectly polite, however, and alone. Bacall was in the next room still asleep, he said. To Carson's surprise, Bogart "was very upset and concerned, because he thought he was going to get into trouble." Carson considered the whole matter ridiculous and told him, " 'Don't worry about it, they won't do anything.' But he was certain he'd get *hung,* at least." They talked a few minutes while Bogart, subdued, sucked on an unlit cigarette. It was hard for Carson to reconcile the film image with the nervous man before him. Carson snapped a picture of Bogart bent over a cup of coffee, minus his toupee. He looked like a tired, worried, middle-aged man.

Bogart changed into a well-pressed gray suit and bow tie and was driven the few blocks to the Mid-Manhattan Court on East Fifty-seventh Street. There were seven hundred or eight hundred people outside, and they cheered him. He managed what the *Daily News* called "a wan smile," squared his shoulders, and marched into the courthouse. He was Bogie again.

Inside, the overflow crowd was handled by a ten-officer detail. Women filled nearly every seat, and a collective sigh went up as the hero of *Casablanca* entered. Warners may not have sent a lawyer, but Bogart had someone better than anyone the studio could have hired—Bacall's Uncle Charlie Weinstein, the onetime assistant corporation counsel for the City of New York and still politically connected. He argued that Miss Roberts's suit was a "publicity stunt by a Hollywood-stricken female" out to "shake down Mr. Bogart" for whatever she could get.

On the stand, Roberts, decked out in a tight-fitting velvet suit with rabbit trim, said that all she had done was touch the panda. Magistrate John R. Starkey ruled that Bogart had been defending his property, said he suspected the actor had been mousetrapped in the cause of club publicity, and dismissed the case. Outside, the star was cheered by delighted fans. Scores of them broke through the police line to shake his hand. Roberts fled to a cab through a gauntlet of boos and catcalls.

El Morocco, in a fine display of impartial justice, banned both Bogart and Roberts from its premises for life. (It was Bogart's second offense, the club spokesman explained. The previous March he had refused to take off his hat and threatened to put his cigarette into the face of the bouncer.) Not to be outdone, Paul Henkel, president of New York's Society of Restaurateurs, representing 250 top restaurants and nightspots, served notice that Humphrey Bogart and also Errol Flynn would get the "bum's rush" the next time they caused trouble. Bogart, unfazed, said Henkel needn't expect him to come to New York carrying a lunch box. "I am confident that such fine catering houses as the Automat, Childs and Schraffts will always welcome me . . . Let Mr. Henkel remember that old adage, 'What's sauce for the goose is sauce for the panda.' "

Asked by Earl Wilson if it was true he was drunk during the incident, Bogart answered, "Who isn't at 3 o'clock in the morning?" "So we get a little stiff once in a while," he told a Los Angeles *Herald-Express* reporter, "this is a free country, isn't it? I can take my Panda any place I want to. And if I want to buy it a drink, that's my business." To New York *Journal-American* columnist Inez Robb, he expressed confidence that "with a little effort on my part, I can probably be barred from Central Park and Ebbets Field. As a matter of fact, the only places I am really socially acceptable now are '21' and Grand Central Station. Put it down to natural charm. I'm loaded with it. And experience, too. It takes a long time to develop a repulsive character like mine. You don't get to be the Boris Karloff of the supper clubs overnight. You've got to work at it."

"You've got to hand it to him," Bacall added. "When he gets barred, he gets barred from the right places."

"At heart," Bogart said, "I'm a lovable character, about as vicious as Margaret O'Brien." But behind the joking there was anger. New York was still a "fun town," he told a reporter back in Los Angeles. "You meet different people. You talk about things. You feel good. Out here you see the same dull crowd at night spots. They sit in the same seats with the same people, bored with everything—including themselves. That's why I step out with pandas. They're not always blabbing about their latest movie."

It was not lost on Bogart that throughout the ordeal his own studio, with its potent legal and public relations forces, had left him on his own. Since he was barely three years into his fifteen-year contract, the point was clear enough. Even worse in terms of how he felt the studio valued him were the roles he was offered. *Chain Lightning* was routine and uninspired. The next year he was put in *Murder, Inc.* Even though the depiction of crime syndicates was realistic, the film looked backward, not forward, with a formula that dated from the Depression. He tried for other properties; most recently he had attempted, through Jerry Wald, to get the studio to buy Budd Schulberg's boxing novel, *The Harder They*

Fall. J. L. agreed to take it, but only on the condition that Bogart indemnify the studio if anything occurred to prevent him from doing the film. By the time *Murder, Inc.*, now renamed *The Enforcer,* went into production, relations were at their nadir.

"Fireworks" were reported from the closed set. "There are those who say it will be Humphrey Bogart's last film on the lot," the Los Angeles *Daily News* reported, "and that one of these mornings he will charge that the studio deliberately set out to make him break his contract."

These were not like the old conflicts, which were rather like an indentured servant rebelling against his master and therefore held no doubt who would prevail. Now, after nearly fifteen years and almost fifty films, Bogart was Warners Brothers' top star. Through talent and perseverance he had worked his way closer toward a kind of equality with J. L., and his situation was not unlike Hal Wallis's at the end: he had become too successful. As a result, the chances that he would fulfill the dozen years remaining on his contract looked slim. By all the evidence, Bogart or J. L.—or both of them—would find a reason to part company.

CHAPTER 21

All the Aspects of a Loser

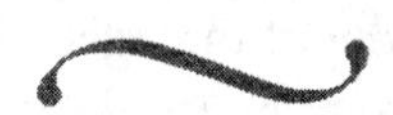

Ext. ROMANOFF's—NIGHT

A big car pulls up to the curb and unloads a party of well-dressed people. The parking boy takes the car. . . . Into the scene, headed for Romanoff's, comes Dix Steele. He is a tightly knit man with an air of controlled, spring-steel tension about him. He wears a well-cut, but well-worn tweed jacket and slacks. Mr. Steele—God help him—is a motion picture writer.

It was Bogart who wanted to play Dixon Steele, the heavy-drinking writer of *In a Lonely Place* whose pent-up anger and paranoia provide the foundation for the plot of one of the best pictures ever made about Hollywood. Screenwriter Edmund North had known Bogart since the 1930s, through times bad and good and three marriages, and had him in mind as he adapted Dorothy Hughes's novel. There is also no question of whom he expected to play Laurel:

> She's about twenty-six, a striking-looking girl with high cheek bones and tawny hair. Sultry and smooth, she is sexy without being cheap-looking. . . . She appraises him coolly as he does her.

But when Warners refused to lend Bacall to Bogart's Santana Productions, the role went to the underestimated actress Gloria Grahame, the wife of Nicholas Ray, the director of the movie. Andrew Solt received the screenplay credit (North was credited with the adaptation), but Ray contributed scenes that reflected his own deteriorating marriage, which ended with the conclusion of filming.

The film noir is about two worldly people who lose a chance for real love because the emotional turmoil of their pasts infects the relationship between them. Steele, a good screenwriter whose drinking and argumentative nature have left him not much in demand, refuses an assignment to adapt a novel that his hardworking agent has lined up for him. Although he has not read the book, he thinks it a potboiler, and in a confrontation in the restaurant's bar accuses the director of continually making the same film. When a strutting producer insults Steele's friend Charlie Waterman, a drunken, washed-up actor who is also at the bar, Dix slugs him several times, immediately establishing his violent side. (Robert Warwick, who played Charlie, had encouraged the young Bogart not to give up during a difficult period early in his stage career, and helped him get parts.)

The agent persuades Steele to go home and read the novel. On his way out, the hatcheck girl tells him it is wonderful and offers to recount the story. He takes her to his bungalow (which is reminiscent of the Garden of Allah, where Bogart lived in the 1930s); and Laurel, who has just moved in across the way, sees them enter. Eventually Steele has heard enough of the plot and gives the girl cab fare home. The next day, her horribly mutilated body is found. Steele, the last person thought to see her alive, is the prime suspect.

Laurel becomes the typist for Dix's screenplay. Soon, despite their hard edges and past hurts, the two fall in love. She believes in his innocence, but his flashes of anger and his beating up of a man in yet another fight feed the doubt placed there by the police investigation. Still, she wants to be with him, and as they are driving one night Steele says: "I was born when she kissed me; I died when she left me; I lived a few weeks while she loved me." He turns to her and asks, "Like it?" / "What is it?" / "I want to put it in the script—I don't know quite where."

After Laurel's doubts about him have overwhelmed her faith in his innocence, he discovers she has secretly arranged to go to New York. Wild over her leaving and her lack of trust, he pushes her onto the bed and grabs her by the throat. When the phone rings, he pulls away, walks into the living room, and eventually answers. It is the police, who have been trying for hours to reach him to say they have a confession for the murder. Steele is expressionless as he hears the news. "A man wants to apologize," he tells Laurel, handing her the phone. She listens, then says flatly, "Yesterday that would have meant so much. Now it doesn't matter. It doesn't matter at all." He walks out while she is on the phone. She goes to door and watches him disappear. "I lived a few weeks while you loved me. Good-bye, Dix."

When *In a Lonely Place* was released in May 1950, many critics called it one of the best pictures of Bogart's career. "Mr. Bogart . . . moves flawlessly through a script which is almost as flinty as the actor himself," *The New York Times* said. "Although Steele is callous, insulting and vicious in his dark, ugly moods, he can be tender and considerate under the influence of love. . . . Mr. Bogart plays the role for all it's worth, giving a maniacal fury to his rages and a hard edge to his expressions of sympathy."

The parallels between Steele and Bogart are striking—the aloofness, the lightning-quick intelligence evident even in hack work, the flashes of humor and warmth, and the unexpected anger. Richard Schickel makes the point that Steele's "WASPish name implies the possibility of a solid background, as do his manners, dress and literate speech."

All of which suggests that Dixon Steele may be the closest Bogart came to portraying his own inner turmoil, his difficulty with women, and his often resentful dependence on an industry that rewarded lavishly and punished fearsomely. Many of the characters and places in the film seem closely modeled on Hollywood figures and landmarks in Bogart's life. Besides the apparent reference to the Garden of Allah, for instance, the bar and restaurant is very like Chasen's, and the self-important producer Steele slugs could pass for Carl Laemmle Jr. There is even a Sam Jaffe figure in Steele's agent, Mel Lippman, "a small, round man with qualities not usually associated with Hollywood agents . . . wisdom and humor and humility and loyalty."

Bogart admired and somewhat envied writers, who fight their battles on paper rather than before the camera. His friend and drinking companion, the drama critic John McClain, felt that Bogart "would much rather have made a more modest living as a writer, where he could have aired his frustrations in print. He was a guy who didn't open up much, but the people he always sought out were writers . . . and they were the people for whom he had the most affection." Yet despite Bogart's enthusiasm for the project, he never liked the film. Perhaps the characterization was too close to the part of himself that he protected with barbs and wisecracks.

Lauren Bacall's long-smoldering feud with Warner Brothers finally ignited during the months that *In a Lonely Place* was being filmed. The studio's refusal to loan her to Bogart's company was only the last in a string of differences. Columbia and Paramount also had asked for her on loanout, and both were turned down. In 1948, Twentieth Century–Fox had wanted her to co-star with Gregory Peck in its big western *Yellow Sky*, directed by William Wellman. Warners said no. The next year, after she returned to work following Stephen's birth, she played in the undistinguished *Bright Leaf* (1950), directed by Michael Curtiz, with Gary Cooper as a tobacco farmer who becomes a vengeful tycoon. By early 1950, Bacall was in open rebellion.

While she and Bogart were in New York in January, Warners asked her to do some publicity for *Young Man with a Horn,* which was to open at Radio City Music Hall the second week in February. Warners needed Bacall's signature on the usual waiver of reimbursement for interviews and photographs, but suddenly they couldn't get it. The *Daily News,* the *Times,* the newspaper syndicates, and every columnist in town were lined up to see her.

She was due back in Burbank on February 9 to begin her next picture, *Stop, You're Killing Me,* a mediocre comedy based on a Damon Runyon story about a racketeer going straight. Mort Blumenstock phoned to work out her travel plans, but the hotel operators informed him they had been forbidden to put through any calls. When he finally did speak with her, both she and Bogart were "adamant," he reported to J. L., that they would not leave until February 12. Steve Trilling wired them approval to stay, but he begged Bacall to report by February 15, as the studio had the entire company standing by. It took four days, many calls, and a telegram to save the elaborate interview schedule from being canceled, but once Bacall had won the postponement of her departure, she cooperated.

Her actions in New York made it obvious that Bacall was doing everything possible to prod Warner Brothers into canceling her contract. One of her interviewers, who asked for anonymity, told Blumenstock that he wasn't going to publish some of the things she said about Warner executives or indicate the language she used. "She is trying her best to infuriate you for reasons we know," Blumenstock told J. L., and added that the reporter wanted never to interview Bacall again.

Bogart supported his wife's defiance with his own. He thought it was useless for her to try to make up with Warner and the other executives; his own experience had taught him that it was the nature of studio executives to fight with actors. Ann Sheridan had left. Joan Crawford, after her Academy Award–winning performance in *Mildred Pierce* (1945), was turned into a money loser within two years. It was a bad time for Warner Brothers and a worse one for its stars.

The Bogarts boarded the Super Chief on the 12th; the next day, in a retaliatory tack of its own, the studio decided to temporarily shelve *Stop, You're Killing Me*—it was finally made in 1952 with Broderick Crawford and Virginia Gibson. Instead, Bacall was cast in *Rocky Mountain* (1950), a tired Civil War story of U.S. and Confederate soldiers fighting off an attack by Indians, opposite a paunchy Errol Flynn sadly unable to disguise the ravages of an alcoholic middle age. She refused, claiming that the part was "essentially nothing more than a 'bit.' . . . To appear in such a role could have no effect but a harmful one upon my career and the value of my services to you." Jack Warner, as stubborn as he was, had met his match. After four months of turndowns and suspensions, the studio finally decided to cut its losses. On July 12, Bacall was released from her contract. She had her wish, but at the expense of a damaged career and lingering bitterness.

The cash price for Bacall's freedom was $50,000. Until the debt was paid, Warners would get 50 percent of her future earnings in motion pictures or other means of entertainment, but she could only appear in films in which Warners' share would be at least $15,000. Bacall further agreed to make weekly reports of her earnings.

For the next four years, Warners accountants were a part of her life. The smallest item—a mention in a column, a notice in the *Hollywood Reporter*—brought a note from J. L. to Obringer: "Roy, Bacall is working." A formal reminder of her obligation was then sent to either Bacall or Morgan Maree. If she signed to do a picture, someone at Warners called the studio to make sure of the start date. By the time she made her final payment of $3,250 in May 1954, Bogart, too, was gone from Warner Brothers.

In late 1950, the Bogarts became radio performers. *Bold Venture* was a weekly adventure show whose half-hour segments were a spin-off of *To Have and Have Not.* The series grew out of an agreement between Santana and the Frederic W. Ziv Company, a packager of syndicated shows ranging from *The Cisco Kid* to bandleader Guy Lombardo. Over the years, there had been numerous network offers for live shows, but Bogart had always turned them down, insisting on a schedule that allowed him to take a vacation when he wanted and make movies when he had to without worrying over the conflicts with a broadcasting timetable. The increasing use of audio tape, however, made it possible to record several programs at once. *Bold Venture* was typical of this new kind of programming, in which recordings and spot sales freed producers from the networks' restrictions. The shows could be sold in any city on a fifty-two-week basis, for any time period, to any sponsor. (For *Bold Venture* about 40 percent of the ads came from beer makers. Apparently the adventure tales appealed to men who bought beer in bars and to women who brought it home in six-packs.)

The series had a Havana locale and a hero with a charter boat. Perhaps in deference to the more conservative social climate and the requirements of a medium even more heavily censored than the movies, Bogart played Bacall's guardian. Warner Brothers had no part of the deal; but Walter MacEwen, the studio's story editor, had an assistant audit the series closely for any infringement by the radio scripts on Warner pictures in which Bogart had appeared. He found none.

The show began airing nationally on 423 stations in the early spring of 1951, with 95 percent of the major markets sold. New York was among the missing 5 percent but the short life of the series had more to do with the decline of radio drama and Bogart's shooting schedule than with the number of markets in which it played. Nevertheless, for the time and effort put in, the couple, who collected a fee as well as a percentage of the profit, did very nicely. Ziv's original estimate was that they would clear an average of $5,000 a week. By the time the last tape aired, they had done much better; their share came close to half a million dollars.

The couple had recorded thirty-six episodes when they announced in March 1951 that they would soon go to Africa and Europe, where Bogart would make what for many is his most beloved film.

C. S. Forester's *The African Queen* had all the aspects of a loser. The novel about a reprobate and a proper lady missionary in East Africa intent on sinking a German gunboat at the onset of World War I had kicked around Hollywood story departments since its publication in 1935. RKO once thought of it for Charles Laughton and his wife Elsa Lanchester, then changed its mind. Story editors at every studio, tied to the movie ideal of youth and conventional beauty, were offended by the plot's premise of sexual attraction between middle-aged spinster Rose Sayer and rum-soaked boatman Charlie Allnut, described by the author as a "Liverpool or London slum rat." "A good literary work which will never achieve desirable screen transition," is about the nicest thing anyone had to say.

Nevertheless, Warner Brothers bought it in 1946 as a possible Bette Davis vehicle, but by 1947 was desperately trying to unload it. One studio's reaction to the offer was, "Not even if Bette went with this!" An RKO reader commented. "It is dated, incredible, quite outside accepted dramatic screen material. . . . Its two characters are neither appealing nor sympathetic enough to sustain interest for an entire picture. . . . Both are physically unattractive and their love scenes and romance are distasteful and not a little disgusting. It's no bargain at any price. No amount of rewriting can possibly salvage this dated yarn." By mid-1950, when John Huston and producer Sam Spiegel bought the novel's film rights for their independent production company, Horizon Pictures, it had gone through many options and at least one screenplay. (In an effort to put forward a more anglicized name, Spiegel's producer's credit in the film was S. P. Eagle.)

At the very least, *The African Queen* seemed a highly unlikely choice for two of the most sought-after stars of the time. But Katharine Hepburn, after reading the copy of the book sent her by Spiegel, easily saw herself as Rose and knew it was a great part. Her only question was, Who would play Allnut? Spiegel suggested Bogart: "He could be a Canadian," thus avoiding the jarring sound of a cockney accent instead of the familiar voice. After Spiegel approached Bogart, Huston and Bogart went to lunch at Romanoff's to talk about it. A typical Bogart-Huston story conference, the director said, went something like:

Huston: Wanna do something?

Bogart: Yeah.

In this instance Huston told him, "The hero is a lowlife, and you are the biggest lowlife in town and therefore most suitable for the part."

Bogart agreed that the part was wonderful and accepted. "He wanted very much to do it," Huston said. "And the idea of doing it with Katie Hepburn—instantly appealing." Hepburn was staying at the home of her friend Irene Selznick; and after lunch, the two men went to see her to talk about the proposed film. Despite Hepburn and Bogart's many years in Hollywood and a few passing introductions at large events, this was the first time they had talked at any length. She was immediately taken by him and felt that "he was the only man who could have played that part."

Hepburn's opinion of Bogart was a departure from the impression he had made twenty years earlier, when they met through their common patron Arthur Hopkins. She had thought of him as "just a nice young man. Sort of a mother's boy. And then all of a sudden—this other quality.

Bogie, who was playing nice boys, became a star when he played wicked ones. And *Spencer* played wicked ones, and became a star when he played priests. It's very interesting—the essential quality in the man." Hepburn would have a key role in yet another transformation of Bogart's image at a time of life when most actors are content to play characters that allow them to settle into a more-or-less permanent professional middle age.

It was obvious from the start that to be credible the movie would have to be shot in Africa, which complicated the financing. Most banks were not keen on the idea of risking money in a location where weather and elaborate logistics could ruin the budget. Romulus Productions, a new London-based company eager to lure Hollywood creative talent overseas, provided most of the movie's backing. In the end, only about $400,000 came from America. Bogart's pay of $125,000 was deferred, in return for which he had 30 percent of the profits. Hepburn's was $65,000 up front with another $65,000 deferred, and 10 percent of the profits.

The great concern for Bogart was the half-year separation from Stephen, and his fears over being away from home were almost instantly realized. Stephen and his nurse, Alice Hartley, had come to the airport to wave good-bye to Bogart and Bacall. As they watched the plane become airborne, Miss Hartley, with the boy in her arms, suffered a stroke and was taken to a hospital. The news reached the Bogarts when they landed in Chicago en route to New York. By the time they were in Manhattan, she had died. Bacall wrote later that her doctor told her she should not return to Los Angeles and instead should go on with her husband. He also recommended a replacement, whom Bacall interviewed at length by telephone from "21." Bacall's mother, who lived in New York, volunteered to go to Los Angeles to watch over her grandson.

"I hate like the devil to take Betty away from our son for such a long time," Bogart told columnist Marie Torre on their arrival in New York. "The kid's only two and we're going to be away at least six months. But I can't see it any other way. My other marriages broke up on account of separations. Betty and I, we've been married six years, and I want to go on. So wherever I go, she goes."

The Bogarts sailed for Le Havre on the *Liberté* in mid-March, then went on to Paris, London, and Rome before flying to Leopoldville in the Belgian Congo, now Zaire. It was Bacall's first trip outside the United States, and she was thrilled—"I was longing to go, to see and do everything"—but Bogart, while happy about the prospect of doing a picture with Hepburn and Huston, was ambivalent about traveling so far. "We've got a comfortable home, a wonderful son, a boat, and nice friends," and that should be enough for anyone, he told a columnist. He would never feel the tug of Europe as Bacall did, though there would be many other trips abroad.

In London they stayed at the elegant Claridge's, where a noontime cocktail party and press conference were held on April 16. Bacall, in a black-and-white-checked Balenciaga suit with black velvet trim, found herself upstaged by the forty-one-year-old Hepburn, who wore an oatmeal-colored pants suit, white turtleneck, brown suede flats, and no makeup other than lipstick. "Drawing a big crowd of note-takers away from the Bogarts," one reporter wrote, "she chattered steadily for about two hours, most of it leg-pulling solemnly printed the next day."

Behind the glamour were the problems of no final script and the continuing difficulties with financing. Hepburn, concerned, asked Bogart what they should do. He told her that working with Huston was always a little like this, but that eventually the money would be there. Hepburn thereupon told her agent that, pay or no pay, she was going to do the picture. Bogart, she decided, was right. "His was a simple approach," she wrote later. "All the elements were there—it will work—don't fuss." She did, however, demand that producer Sam Spiegel pay her hotel bills, as originally agreed. "I didn't mind doing the film for nothing, but I didn't intend to pay for the privilege of doing it."

Hepburn and Bogart's time in London began a friendship that, despite perceptible differences in temperament, grew stronger over the months of working together. Yet Hepburn, like so many others, would feel that she never knew Bogart really well. "But he was very friendly. Very easy. With life. Very sensible. Horse sense especially. I think he was sensitive. Just a really—nice—man. And that's rare in our business."

In mid-May the cast and crew flew from Rome to Leopoldville (now Kinshasa) and on for a five-day stop in Stanleyville (Kinsangani), where Hepburn went with the Bogarts to celebrate their sixth wedding anniversary at a restaurant a few miles out of town. They drove there carrying iced champagne and a tin of caviar wangled from the governor-general, only to find that the manager objected to a bottle party and to the bristly stubble Bogart was cultivating for his part. "The first time in my life I ever go out with Humphrey Bogart," Hepburn later told a reporter, "and I'm thrown out of the joint."

The trip from Stanleyville to the location was a journey back through time—by car, by a trolley-sized four-car train pulled by a wood-burning engine, and by ferry raft propelled by four men with poles. "The train kept catching fire from the sparks and we all helped put the fires out,"

Bogart said later. "Every time we stopped, the natives tried to borrow hot water from the engine for tea. Then we traveled another 150 miles by auto and finally reached our camp on the Ruiki River," a branch of the Congo River so remote it isn't marked in most atlases. "The water is black, damnedest thing you ever saw." (The color was caused by tannic acid from the vegetation.) Huston had chosen the river by an aerial survey for a suitable site. Because the waterway traveled by Rosie and Charlie is almost as integral a part of the film as the two protagonists, Huston wanted a beautiful, unusual, and varied river, with dark water and rapids. The river of choice in Kenya was in a periodic drought stage. The Ruiki, by contrast, was perfect; even though the rapids were not on the river, they were nearby. *Life* photographer Eliot Elisofon, who did a picture story for the magazine, thought it was one of the most beautiful rivers in Africa.

When Bogart, Bacall, and Hepburn arrived at the jungle camp that had been built for the company, Huston was waiting for them in the bar.

"Well, I've found it," he announced merrily and with little exaggeration. "We have almost every known kind of disease, and almost every known kind of serpent."

The filming, like the movie, was adventurous, funny, and frightening. The details are in Bacall's autobiography and Hepburn's memoir, *The Making of "The African Queen."* The local hazards included poisonous snakes, crocodiles, scorpions, invading soldier ants, leprosy, dysentery, and a particularly nasty malady called bilharzia that comes from contact with tainted river water and involves worms working their way under one's skin.

As he had in Mexico while making *The Treasure of the Sierra Madre,* Huston loved every minute of it, his pleasure quotient rising with each new hardship. Not for nothing did Bogart call him The Monster. It is said that one reason Huston picked the Congo, rather than Kenya, the original site of Forester's novel, was because he wanted to go hunting like Hemingway and had been turned down by officials in Nairobi. On rainy days when they couldn't film, Huston would disappear into the jungle with a rifle over his shoulder. "John wanted to shoot an elephant," an assistant director said. "That was what the whole picture was about." (Despite his tough-guy image and his father's interest, Bogart parted company with his friend over the issue of hunting. The night of their arrival, Huston kept them up until one A.M. trying to interest Bacall into coming along on an elephant shoot. Forget it, Bogart said as they fell exhausted into bed. He didn't like killing animals, and besides, John "could not hit his hat.")

The camp had been cleared and built in eight days by eighty-five Congolese workers. There were dormitories, a production building with offices and a two-room suite for Huston, a storage hut with a pit for keeping exposed film cool, a makeup hut with two sets of lavatories and showers, plus a laundry, a kitchen, a dining area, and a bar, where a shot of whiskey cost twenty cents. The Bogarts and Hepburn had their own bungalows, built, like the other buildings, from bamboo and palm without use of a single nail. Cots, camp chairs, and mosquito netting were brought in. Twenty-eight women carried water from a spring a mile away; it was then boiled, filtered, and treated with halizone tablets. Fresh food came from Stanleyville. A small generator provided electricity.

The costumes were meticulous re-creations of the clothing of the period. The hat worn by Hepburn in the early scenes regularly drooped into limpness from the high humidity and needed constant restarching. Bogart's one outfit of striped shirt, pants, cap, sneakers, and bandanna were no problem, but off-set clothes were. Most of what he had brought to wear turned out to be useless in the wet heat that grew mold on almost everything. Hepburn, by contrast, came admirably equipped with loose-fitting cottons and a man's-cut pants suit from Abercrombie and Fitch. The suit fit Bogart remarkably well, and she loaned it to him until a tailor in Stanleyville, who doubled as a piano player at the local hotel, could make safari clothes for him.

Unlike Hepburn, Bogart disliked Africa and refused to settle in as comfortably as possible. "The food was so awful we had to drink Scotch most of the time," he told an interviewer, "and Katie . . . kept saying wouldn't it be mahvelous if we could all stay there forever."

What excited Bogart was the chance to stretch his abilities as an actor. He knew that *The African Queen* was as much a milestone in his upward progression as *The Maltese Falcon* had been a decade earlier. Charlie Allnut was a small man who becomes a big man after being prodded into heroism by the strong-willed Rosie. "Nature, Mr. Allnut, is what we are meant to rise above," she informs him.

Bogart had to rise above his own nature as well. Huston told a reporter not long after making the film, "With his almost aggressive personality, he had trouble being dominated by a woman, and every once in a while he'd know he was slipping. Then he'd stop and button himself up again in the role." Huston later added that this "couldn't have happened more than once or twice. But when he began to play something like 'Bogart-Bacall,' why, I just said, 'Bo-*gie?*' And instantly, he knew what to do."

Charlie Allnut was an apologetic little man, self-conscious in the presence of his alleged betters in the rigid society of World War I. "He knew he wasn't in the same class," Huston said. "He knew what his place was. And yet, he was as good as anybody. The comic quality Bogie got out of that—it was *ideal,* that's all."

Bogart felt he had to get to know Hepburn better before he was comfortable with the three-way arrangement. He and Huston were especially close, and he seemed to need the assurance that their ease in working together would not be interfered with.

"He never did an awful lot of talking, about the performance or anything," Hepburn said. "At first, when I saw John in the jungle, in my house, and would sit talking to him, Bogie would come up and sit. Maybe he thought I was trying to louse up the script, or butt in or something. But then he heard enough to suit him." Once he was at ease, Bogart enjoyed as before the close work and ensemble spirit that were part of a Huston production. "We were a little company, a kind of task force," Bogart said later. "That was one reason why we felt a sense of accomplishment."

From time to time, location difficulties arose. When the *Queen* sprang a leak and sank to the bottom of the Ruiki, everyone—stars, crew, and villagers—pulled on a rope lassoed around the boiler. The locals, Bogart said, had a work chant that sounded something like "hoola-ha." "So with each pull we all sang hoola-ha! I don't know how many hoola-ha's it took to raise the damn thing, but it took two days to get it up and another day to get it back in order." Then came the invasion of soldier ants that literally carpeted the camp, followed by malaria and dysentery. Hepburn lost twenty pounds from her already spare frame and was debilitatingly ill while working the seven-day-a-week schedule. Bogart, Huston, and Bacall, however, seemed immune. Bogart put it down to his sticking to canned goods and booze. "I was practically a vegetarian the entire trip," he told Art Buchwald. "All I ate was baked beans, canned asparagus and Scotch whisky. Whenever a fly bit Huston or me, it dropped dead."

Hepburn wrote, "Those two undisciplined weaklings had so lined their insides with alcohol that no bug could live in the atmosphere . . . a very good joke on me. Especially as privately I had felt so completely superior to that unhealthy pair." Her discipline, however, did not go unnoticed by Bogart. " 'Damn Hepburn! Damn her, she's so goddam cheerful,' Bogie exploded one afternoon. 'She's got ants in her pants, mildew in her shoes, and she's still cheerful. I build a solid wall of whiskey between me and the bugs. She doesn't drink, and she breezes through it all as if it were a weekend in Connecticut!' "

"An odd fellow," she wrote of her co-star. ". . . Very generous and thoughtful. And . . . not a fool in case of trouble. . . . He'd say to me, 'Are you comfortable? Everything O.K.? Need anything?' He was looking out for me." He never seemed to sweat, she noticed, no matter how hot it became. Neither did Bacall. During the time on the Ruiki, Bacall and Hepburn became lifelong friends, and Hepburn enjoyed watching the couple together: "She and Bogie seemed to have the most enormous opinion of each other's charms, and when they fought it was with the utter confidence of two cats locked deliciously in the same cage."

In Stanleyville, she and the others witnessed Bogart's competence in an emergency, when some of the company hired a boat for an excursion on the river. As they cast off from the dock, the guide went below to start the engine. When it didn't start, he lit a match. The fumes inside the hold exploded. The guide, who was badly burned, leaped into the water and threw himself onto the sand in agony, while the burning boat started to float downstream toward a river steamer. Bogart acted like a trained fireman. He told writer Peter Viertel to get the fire extinguisher from the forward bulkhead. Viertel did, but it was empty. Meanwhile, Bogart managed to maneuver close enough to the steamer to throw a line to it. He helped to unload the women, then he stayed aboard to aid in putting out the fire.

Huston once characterized Bogart as someone who would raise hell in the best hotel when his eggs weren't done right but would face a crisis with calm quiet. Hepburn, sounding exactly like Rosie speaking of Charlie toward the end of *The African Queen,* wrote of the incident on the boat: "I had visions of us going up like a firecracker [but] Bogie, completely courageous and cool, finally put it out by smothering it with sand and a blanket. Right down in the fire he was, as far as I could see; and I found myself being very proud of him."

In mid-June, the mail brought a clipping from Bacall's mother. The United Press dispatch datelined June 9, Portland, Oregon, read: "MAYO METHOT, STAGE AND FILM ACTRESS, IS DEAD."

In the years following the divorce, Mayo's drinking had become even more of a problem. Los Angeles friends who loved her had tried to comfort and assist her; Gertie Hatch invited her to come east for a while; a director friend from the early days wanted to bring her back to the theater. Nothing helped.

Miss Methot, the story said, had been living with her mother and had died at Holladay Park Hospital, at age forty-seven, "of complications following surgery." There was no further comment on the cause of death.

"In 1923 she scored a hit as George M. Cohan's leading lady. . . . She appeared in three plays in 1929: 'All the King's Men,' 'Great Day,' and Sidney Howard's 'Half Gods.' Of her portrayal of Ivy Stevens in 'Torch Song' in August, 1930, Brooks Atkinson wrote: 'Mayo Methot gives a splendid performance—vivid in composition, sincere in feeling.' "

After reading the news, Bogart fingered the clipping, thoughtful and taciturn. " 'Too bad,' was all he said. 'Such a waste.' " When Bacall asked him why, he answered that she had real talent and had thrown her life away. Bacall wondered in that moment whether he was sorry not to have stayed with Mayo, and understood years later that "nothing could have been further from his mind."

The company rounded out their African shooting in Uganda, though not before the familiar feeling that Huston was deliberately delaying their departure. "You son of a bitch, you like it here," Bogart exploded at him one day. "I hate it!" Several months after his return to America, Bogart called Huston a "real genius," but added that as usual he also had been "murder to work with" over the final three weeks, "always restless, wanting to quit for some new idea."

Bogart and Bacall finally left Africa in late July and flew to London. Stephen joined them the day after their arrival. News photographers snapped shots of the two-and-half-year-old in his parents' arms, screwing up his small face after a scratchy kiss from his still-stubble-bearded father.

At Shepperton Studios and Worton Hall, a small studio near London, the remaining scenes were filmed. Among them is the early sequence in which Rose and her clergyman brother, played to perfection by Robert Morley, sit down to tea with Charlie. The little man, to his horror, finds his stomach acting up. With the camera fixed on Bogart's face, the accompanying sound is of a stomach growling.

"They got him in close-up, but I provided the background noises," Hepburn later said with some pleasure. "I was an absolute expert on a growling stomach. If mine got empty enough it would growl, and I ruined some of my own takes. So they said, 'Now—you're going to be of some use to us.' "

One of the last scenes to be shot was that of Charlie and Rosie dragging the boat—Charlie in the water, pulling, Rosie poling—through the tall reedy swamp that nearly becomes their grave. The script called for Charlie to come out of the water with his upper torso covered with leeches. Huston, of course, insisted on the real thing, and brought in a leech breeder with a tank of the repellent little creatures. Hepburn remembered her asking Bogart to try one, and his response: "You try it first, kid."

Huston finally agreed to use fake leeches, and settled for one close-up of the real article dangling nicely from the breeder's chest. The crew then struggled to come up with a usable adhesive for the ersatz leeches while Bogart sat patiently, bare to the waist, looking sad and skinny, as one sticking formula after another was tested. "He was funny, sitting there," Hepburn said. "Like a little kid." She remembered above all how thin he was. No one present during the filming had known him long enough to realize just how much the well-built young actor who came to Hollywood twenty years before had deteriorated. His neck had become thin, the once-athletic chest concave, the shoulders resembling those of a welterweight boxer, shrunk and hunched.

The Bogarts spent six weeks in London. After the pleasures of that summer, amplified by the glow of accomplishment and the friendships made with Laurence Olivier, Vivien Leigh, Richard Burton, Emlyn Williams, and T. S. Eliot, they returned to a claustrophobic, fear-ridden Hollywood.

In the days before the Bogarts went abroad in March, the House Committee on Un-American Activities began a new and even more ominous round of hearings, and stepped up its unceasing hunt for names. The friendly witnesses were no longer "vigilantes of crackpot disposition like Adolphe Menjou or frightened executives like Jack L. Warner, but ex-Communists scrambling to save their own careers. . . . A new kind of talkie was born." Among the many who were named was Robert Rossen, who had gone on from the screenwriters stable at Warners to win an Oscar for *All the King's Men* (1949) and who, after years on the blacklist, would direct and co-write *The Hustler* (1961); Zero Mostel, the comic who had acted so powerfully opposite Bogart in *The Enforcer* (1951); Lillian Hellman, who had written the screenplay for, among other films, *Dead End;* and John Garfield, who many felt was hounded into a fatal heart attack.

Little was said that hadn't already been known to the committee; anyway, it was the publicity that HUAC wanted, along with a public ritual of recantation. This time there wasn't even the pretext of investigation into alleged espionage or propaganda or of the formulation of legislation outlawing communism. It was, in writer Walter Goodman's words, "a punitive expedition pure and simple."

The blacklist ruled the film and television industries. Some private "patriotic" organizations offered "clearance" for a fee; others were staffed by people drunk on a power that they had never achieved before. Revenge, too, as in 1947, motivated some. A disappointed screenwriter named Myron C. Fagan, his sole credit acquired for the dialogue in Bogart's 1931 film *A Holy Terror,* became a crusader against the industry that had failed to give him recognition. He littered the lots with his tract *Red Stars in Hollywood.* The pamphlet, offered at $10 for a thousand copies, charged the movie colony was "founded on Reds." In particular, he inveighed against "the rat who masquerades as a good American but who secretly nourishes the Communist's slimy case," and under that heading included Humphrey Bogart and Lauren Bacall.

The Bogarts were in London when actor Sterling Hayden, a member of the Committee for the First Amendment who had gone to Washington in 1947, took the stand to declare that for a brief time he had indeed been a Communist. He had joined after parachuting into wartime Yugoslavia and fighting with Tito's partisans against the Nazis and their allies, the Croatian Fascists, and then had resigned a few months later. Though by 1950 the CFA was inactive, its memory was still a rallying point for those who tried to oppose the claims of blacklisting organizations. The Hayden testimony devalued their opposition. Committee membership now was cited as sufficient grounds for questioning loyalty to the United States.

"It was terrible," Jules Buck said. "You just saw the whole spirit collapse, like gas escaping from a balloon."

Bogart's last political radio appearance had been on behalf of Harry Truman in 1948, on a series sponsored by organized labor. But in pamphlets, in FBI files, and in studio memos, he remained suspect, considered left-wing and unreliable.

Warner Brothers, once the spearhead for New Deal progressivism, now released films featuring John Wayne bashing Reds in *Big Jim McClain* (1952) and docudramas with titles like *I Was a Communist for the F.B.I.* (1951). It was the same at other studios. Darryl Zanuck had tackled bigotry with *Gentleman's Agreement* (1947) and the Philip Dunne–written *Pinky* (1949), and he was about to sign Bogart to play a crusading newspaper editor in *Deadline USA.* But he made his writers excise derogatory references to newspaper chains out of deference to, and fear of, William Randolph Hearst, and questioned use of the word "censorship." He didn't want trouble with the Breen Office, he wrote Sol Siegel, Fox's head of production. Wasn't there another way of saying the same thing? Richard Brooks was in his office at Twentieth Century–Fox when director Elia Kazan (director of *Gentleman's Agreement* and *Pinky*) dropped by and asked, "Has anybody come to see you about being a witness, because you knew all these people who had been subpoenaed?"

"I didn't know their politics," Brooks answered, "so what the hell would they want *me* for?"

"Well, HUAC'll come to you anyway."

"What about you?"

"I just got the word, two guys were here. And Zanuck says, if I don't testify, I might as well figure I'm washed up here [in Hollywood]." Kazan more than testified. He "named everyone he had seen at a Communist meeting."

All aspects of one's life were open to review. Brooks had "gone to John Wexley's house once, the guy who wrote *The Last Mile*. [His compelling play about a killer on death row who takes over the cellblock was made into a film in 1932.] I was invited with about 150 other people. We were raising money for Roosevelt. Well, years afterward these HUAC investigators came around. They showed me the license number of my car, parked outside his house. 'What were you doing there?' they asked. That's *insane!*"

Not long after his encounter with Kazan, Brooks, at a dinner party at Ira Gershwin's, was told someone wanted to see him. In a little hall by the front door was Anne Shirley. The actress, who was married to producer and writer Adrian Scott, apologized for disturbing him. Her husband, one of the Hollywood Ten, had come out of prison with his health broken and his career gone. They wanted to go to England in the hope of starting over, but they had no money. Might he help them out? She would take cash if he didn't want to risk putting his name on a check. Brooks sent money to her the next day. "That's what it was like," Brooks said. "If you put your name on a check, someone came calling." Scott never made another film.

Bogart's contract with Warner Brothers permitted him to act in *Deadline U.S.A.*, to be written and directed by his friend Brooks; and in the early fall he completed the deal with Zanuck. Bogart was not the star of choice: Zanuck had wanted Gregory Peck or Richard Widmark, and the negotiations were arduous and prolonged. After a summer in which everything seemed right, there came a winter in which everything seemed wrong.

Brooks noted in Bogart an increasing sourness unrelated to his usual caustic humor. The two had worked together before, and to Brooks, Bogart "was a real pro, meticulously correct, and always ready and prepared." But now, "He was withdrawing. I don't know if it was already his illness or not, but that could have been part of it." There also were the effects of the months of hard work on *The African Queen,* all the more debilitating for a heavy smoker pushing fifty-three. "There was an impatience" during the shooting, "which was *totally* unlike him."

Bogart's annoyance was not with the part. He liked the role of Ed Hutchins, a journalistic variation on the cynical-yet-idealistic Bogart hero, a crusading editor trying to keep his publisher's heirs from selling the paper and trying to keep his marriage together while fighting a local mobster. (Brooks modeled the family on Joseph Pulitzer and his heirs.) Hutchins makes some fine speeches in which Bogart probably believed: "The *Day* is more than machines. . . . It is 1,500 men and women whose skill, hearts, brains and experience make a great newspaper possible. . . . We—together with 290,000 people who read this paper—have a vital interest in whether it lives or dies. . . . Without competition there can be no freedom of the press. I'm talking about free enterprise—the right of the public to a marketplace of ideas and opinion—not one man's or one leader's or one government's."

Zanuck assembled a strong supporting cast, including Kim Hunter as Hutchins's estranged wife and the regal Ethel Barrymore as his boss, the widow of the paper's founder and former publisher. In an introductory sequence, Hutchins meets with the family and their lawyers in an attempt to convince the widow not to go through with the paper's proposed sale to a mass-market tabloid.

"Your husband created a new kind of journalism," he tells her. "Take a look at the first paper you ever printed. On page one. . . . 'This paper will fight for progress and reform—We never will be satisfied merely to print the news—We never will be afraid to attack wrong, whether by predatory wealth or poverty.' You're not selling the *Day,* you're killing it!"

The complex shot called for Bogart to move as he spoke, while the camera introduces the family and lawyers one by one. After delivering two or three lines, he abruptly stopped and turned to Brooks. "Why do I have to move? Why can't I just stand *there* and do it?" Brooks explained why, and then, after this time managing four or five lines, Bogart stopped again. "It doesn't *feel* right." After six or seven other failed takes, Brooks was concerned; he had never seen Bogart behave this way. Finally Bogart threw up his hands. "I don't know, the thing doesn't seem to work."

That was enough for Ethel Barrymore. "*Humphrey!*" she exclaimed. "*Will you for Christ's sake do it!*"

"Why should I?" he snapped.

"*Because,* Humphrey, the Swiss have no navy!"

That broke Bogart up and relaxed him enough to get through the scene. When he returned to his dressing room, Brooks followed.

"What in the *hell* was that all about?" the director inquired of his friend. "I've never heard of you *doing* anything like that. What's really wrong?"

Bogart explained that some friends had been over the night before, "and we did a little drinking, a lot of talking, and they stayed until three or four in the morning. Instead of going to sleep, I started studying the script. I came in here today and I didn't know the speech. And I'm faking it until I learn the speech. I'm sorry." The sarcastic bravado from the set was gone. To Brooks, he looked worn and wilted.

Such behavior was a repeat of his worst days with Mayo. But this time, uncharacteristically, his querulousness was directed toward his colleagues, with dismal consequences for anyone without the status and authority of Ethel Barrymore.

Kay Thackeray was one of the film business's most respected and professional script supervisors, a tough job that is essential, undervalued, and, because at the time (and even today) it was considered a "woman's job," underpaid. The script supervisor makes sure that everything matches from one shot to the next, allowing the director and editor to make a disjointed operation appear seamless. Thackeray, who had supervised such classics as *Stage Door* and *My Man Godfrey,* had particularly looked forward to working with Bogart and had campaigned for the assignment. She soon came to regret her enthusiasm.

"He was rude; he was sarcastic; he was arrogant. He dictated several letters to me—which is not my job, but I took them down, typed them. He signed them, said, 'Mail them,' and walked away. And then we came to the thing that made it very personal to me."

In a comedy relief scene, the Bogart character, on his way upstairs to meet with Ethel Barrymore, has Miss Barndollar of the research department trotting next to him, with the results of a background check run on his estranged wife's new suitor. The scene begins with a dolly shot, the camera running alongside the two actors. Elevator doors open, the two get in. Question and answer as the elevator rises: "Alcoholic? Swindler? Maybe he's a dope fiend. Check his Army record. Probably a deserter." Barndollar checks her notes: "Silver Star and Purple Heart." The elevator doors were then to open, followed by Bogart's exit line: "That's a rotten report."

The scene was shot several times. The camera stopped at the elevator door, Bogart went in and Barndollar came in right after him. "It was a *long* dolly shot that took a good deal of work," Thackeray said. "I think we worked on it for about two hours until we finally got the shot the director wanted."

When they continued the next day, from *inside* the elevator, something was wrong. The two shots didn't match: this time Bogart had let the woman in first. Thackeray waited a moment and then went over to Brooks. "This has to match—it's a direct cut. He got in first, and then the girl got in and then the door closed," she said.

"And Bogie looked at me and said, 'Well, I *hope* I'm enough of a gentleman to let the lady get in first!' And I said, 'Well, in this instance *you* got in, you were walking ahead'—but he didn't even listen to me."

Without knowing it, Kay Thackeray had touched a sore point. She had implied that Humphrey DeForest Bogart was not a gentleman.

"He turned to Brooks and laughed a nasty, sarcastic laugh. Then they both laughed and looked away and did nothing about it." Later, of course, and after the set had been struck, the film editor noticed the mismatch and upbraided Thackeray, who explained what happened. Still, the editor had to notify the production department because an expensive retake would have to be done. She would be allowed to finish the picture, but would quite likely not be rehired anytime soon.

Later in the filming, Thackeray was doing the usual supervisor's job of cueing an actor if he missed a word. Bogart continued to have trouble remembering his dialogue, and when she threw it in with some inflection, his response was "Are you trying to tell *me* how to read a line?" Then he walked over, snatched the script from her hand, looked at the line, and returned to his spot. From then on, "anytime I threw him a line, I threw it *in absolute monotone without any inflection whatever.* Then on the last scene on the last day he said, 'Thank God I won't have to listen to you anymore.' I said, '*Amen.*' In all fairness to him, there must have been something about me that just antagonized him. Or the whole set! Because he wasn't nice to any of us."

Somehow, the trouble and expense of a retake on the elevator scene was avoided. Thackeray was never sure how they did it; she could never bring herself to see the film.

The Bogarts' Christmas Eve parties had become famous—it was, after all, the night before Bogart's birthday—and Bacall outdid herself on Christmas Eve 1951. There was a great deal of industry excitement over *The African Queen,* which had opened to wonderful reviews and promised to be an enormous commercial as well as critical success. It was also the first hit from which he stood to have a piece of the proceeds. Bogart was often on the phone during the breaks in the shooting of *Deadline U.S.A.* to get the latest figures.

December 24 was also the last day of production, with shooting going into the evening so they could finish. By mutual agreement, the usual wrap party was canceled so everyone could go home as soon as possible. Before people left, Brooks had a prop man go to his car and bring in two or three cases of bourbon, a bottle for each member of the crew. For Thackeray, there was an extra present from Brooks and his wife: a brooch with matching earrings.

The prop man had just put down the last of the boxes when Bogart, who had gone to make another phone call, came back to the sound stage. "Do you want me to bring in anything from *your* car, Bogie?" he asked.

"Hell, no," he snapped. "They make enough money, let 'em buy their own damn gifts!"

"And he strode from the set," Thackeray said. "No 'Merry Christmas, Happy New Year, it's been good knowing you.' It was really nasty. And uncalled for. Nobody had asked for anything, you know."

Bogart's behavior was the antithesis of the working habits of a lifetime. "It was *totally* unlike him," Brooks said forty years later. "Plenty was wrong."

CHAPTER 22

The Toy Department

The *African Queen* was greeted with tremendous enthusiasm, and the public took Rosie and Charlie to their hearts in a way that was quite extraordinary. Something made them do it, Huston wrote Hepburn. "Oh, I guess it really isn't so mysterious; that something is you and Bogie and the story."

In February 1952, the film received Oscar nominations in most of the major categories, including Best Actor, Best Actress, and Best Director, though not Best Picture. Despite the internal devastation in the movie industry, 1951 had been a year of many strong films, including *Detective Story, A Streetcar Named Desire,* director George Stevens's *A Place in the Sun,* and the musical *An American in Paris.*

Bogart, who had not been among the predicted contenders in the *Los Angeles Times*'s pre-nomination handicapping, faced serious competition: Montgomery Clift (*A Place in the Sun*), Fredric March (*Death of a Salesman*), Arthur Kennedy (*Bright Victory*), and the actor he referred to admiringly as "this guy Brando—he'll be doing *Hamlet* when the rest of us are selling potatoes."

Publicly, Bogart always claimed to disdain awards. Privately, he was ambivalent, as his attitude toward Hollywood was ambivalent. He coveted the Oscar as much as anyone yet felt that expressing any desire for it was not in keeping with his self-image. But Oscars are not simply won; they are campaigned for in subtle and overt ways. The Spiegel organization hired a public relations firm to conduct a well-planned and well-directed effort on Bogart's behalf. John Strauss, a publicist specializing in Academy Award campaigns, went to the house in Benedict Canyon to meet with him. Strauss, whose regular clients included James Stewart and Clark Gable, had begun his career as a Warner sales representative in Buffalo, New York, where he drove the snowy streets to sell *Casablanca* to exhibitors. The film was one of his favorites, and Bogart one of his favorite stars. Bogart was polite, but very sensitive about having it known that anybody was working to get him the nomination. "He said, 'I'll do anything I can—but keep my name out of it.' He wanted to keep that tough-guy, didn't-give-a-crap-about-anything image. But he really wanted that Oscar."

The job was a challenge for any publicist, but for Strauss, it was also a pleasant assignment. He felt Bogart's performance was the best of his career and that *The African Queen* was "a great movie. We really thought he had a wonderful chance, and we never veered from that stance in our minds." Strauss and his associates arranged for interviews in such a way that it looked as though the press were asking to interview Bogart. True to their profession, Strauss and the others also "dreamed up items to plant, that might or might not have been out of the whole cloth. The object was always to link Bogart with the words 'Academy Award' and '*The African Queen.*' " But not necessarily with Katharine Hepburn, whom Strauss did not represent: to promote both would have diluted the effort. At that time there were five newspapers in Los Angeles, as well as the two trade papers, *Variety* and the *Hollywood Reporter,* and all of them had at least one show business columnist. To Strauss, having so many outlets competing for fresh material "was a field day."

During the publicity strategy sessions at his home, Bogart smoked heavily and always had a full glass at hand. He was likable, polite, and professional, though Strauss was always aware of "a wall all around him that nobody could quite penetrate." One day a little gate in the wall opened. "How is it going? What are the chances?" Bogart asked. Strauss told him he was doing well. "We feel that you're going to be a sentimental favorite, anyway. But the performance is so incredible, we feel that you have a remarkable chance. Particularly since you didn't get it for *Casablanca.*"

After a while, Bogart warmed to the role of Oscar candidate. "Oscar Spells D-o-u-g-h So Bogie Relents," columnist Erskine Johnson announced, referring to Bogart's percentage of *The African Queen.* "My opinion is different about Academy Awards now that I own a piece of the picture," he quoted the actor as saying.

Bogart was as busy as "a Republican candidate," an amused Nunnally Johnson wrote to their mutual friend Thornton Delehanty in early March of 1952. "To hear Betty talk, you'd think they were headed for the White House. We are all going together to the ceremonial . . . preceded by motorcycles bearing flares and followed by a delegation . . . with a huge banner declaring that Bogart is for the Little Man and against entangling foreign alliances. . . . The ritual is at the Pantages Theatre this year and he has a seat on the aisle in the second row, with four men from . . . the Los Angeles Rams to clear the way to the microphone in case his name is mentioned. Betty and Dorris and I are supposed to keep stamping our feet and yelling, 'We want Bogart!' "

As March 20 approached, Bogart grew increasingly, miserably apprehensive. Finally the Thursday night arrived, and the Bogarts and the Johnsons and Richard Brookes piled into the limousine that Johnson had rented for the occasion. The group sat glumly silent as they drove down Benedict Canyon and turned east on Sunset Boulevard for the four- or five-mile trip to the Pantages on Hollywood Boulevard.

It was Brooks who broke the silence. " 'Well, Bogie, when you win the award, what are you going to say?' He said, 'I'm not going to win, I don't want to talk about it, all right?' I said, 'You never know. They don't give you an aisle seat for nothing.' He said, 'Brando is going to win it, now will you, for Christ's sake, stop talking about it! Cut it out!' So we drove in silence again for a while. Finally Nunnally said, 'Bogie, the guy is trying to help you. How do you know? Let's say you're not to be chosen, but if you are—what are you going to say?' He said, '*I don't know!* I'm not going to win it. I'm not going to say anything! There's nothing for me to say.'

"So," Brooks continued, "Nunnally asked me, 'What would *you* have him say?' Bogie's now looking out the window, he doesn't want to hear it. He's *very* nervous. I said, 'Bogie, it's going to be probably the toughest part you've ever played in your life.' He said, 'Really?' That's the first interest he had. I said, 'You see, they name the five nominees, and the woman is going to say: "And the winner is . . ." And when she calls your name, like everybody else you're going to jump out of your goddamn seat, you're going to *run* down the aisle, you're going to run up on stage, you're going to kiss her and she'll kiss you—and then you'll start to thank every son of a bitch in this town, and then you'll cry and all of that crap. And that's what you *must not do*!

" 'The first thing you do, they call your name, you *get up*! And you *walk* down the aisle. *Do not run!* You get up on stage, *don't run to kiss the broad*! They hand you the Oscar. And this is where the acting comes in, Bogie. You look at the Oscar. You look out at the audience over the Oscar's head. And you wait for a whole minute. Now it's going to seem like a year. You wait for one minute. Or as long as you can. Say nothing. Then: here's your speech: "Well—it's about time." And walk off the stage.'

"He said, '*Goddamn it!* I'll *do* it!'

"We get to the theater and we go inside and sit down. We wait the whole evening and finally, they get to Best Actor. 'And the winner is . . . *Humphrey Bogart*!' Bang! He's *up* out of the goddamn chair, runs down the aisle and up on stage. He kisses the broad, they throw the Oscar at him, and he looks over, tears in his eyes, and thanks about forty people. He thanked Katie. John he thanked *nine* times. Then they lead him off backstage to take pictures.

"So we're driving home in the limousine. He's got the Oscar in his lap. I said, 'For God's sake, what happened? You were not going to *do* all that jazz!' And he said, 'When you get yours, *you* do it!' "

As Greer Garson had read out Bogart's name to a roar of delight, Bacall, four months pregnant with their second child, had leaped excitedly to her feet, and her half-slip had fallen down from her extended waist. Montgomery Clift, a gentlemanly loser, delicately picked up the item from the floor before it became an embarrassment.

Also sitting near the Bogarts that night was young Karl Malden, nominated for Best Supporting Actor for his work in *A Streetcar Named Desire*. A Broadway import, he was so used to New York weather that he carried a topcoat from force of habit. When early in the evening his name was announced as the winner, his first thought was, *What the hell am I going to do with my coat?* Leaning toward Bogart, he asked if he would keep an eye on it. Later, when they were all backstage holding their statuettes, Malden asked him, "What did you do with my coat?"

Bogart answered, smiling, "Forget your coat, hold on to the goddamn *Oscar*."

At a post-ceremony party hosted by Mike Romanoff, Bogart was back in character. He debunked the whole process, claiming a true Best Actor competition would be a kind of "pie-eating contest" in which every actor read the same role, say, Hamlet—and there would be some terrible Hamlets. But there was no doubt of his feelings, and the outpouring of affection from his peers that night left him dazed and tearful. He had made the odyssey from stock bad man to beloved Hollywood figure, and on his own terms. An internal *Time* report called him "one of a handful of old-timers whose acting reputation and box office value is indestructible, and [whose] Hemingwayish philosophy tends to make him, moreover, morally indestructible in that nothing [he] does or says will surprise or scandalize anyone—an enviable spot these days when high-earners in Hollywood are afraid to spit on the sidewalk lest they cut industry grosses by a third."

He was at the peak of his profession, basking in the recognition that had so often eluded him. About the only person not happy for his triumph was his son Stephen, who was still angry over the absence of his parents for so many months. In his memoir *In Search of My Father* he wrote, "I seem to recall that when my father brought home the Oscar, visible symbol of all that he had accomplished in Africa, I wanted to pick it up and hurl it at him."

Bogart spent the weekend after he won the Oscar aboard the *Santana,* where he went about forty-five weekends a year. He drove the hour down to Newport Beach in an open convertible, then relaxed with his friends and crew—to whom he was a superb sailor who happened to be a movie star. George Roosevelt, a nephew of the late president, was a constant sailing companion of Bogart's. "We had teased him for years about *not* winning an Oscar. That weekend, we went out and gave him a bad time." Roosevelt and the others had earlier encouraged Bogart to buy the *African Queen,* "because it was so ugly and awful," and anchor it off the Newport Harbor Yacht Club, to which Bogart belonged and where the *Santana* was moored. Bogart looked into the cost and logistics and was tempted, but restrained himself.

One weekend it was raining so heavily that he decided that he and his friends would just sleep on the boat and pass the time in the club bar. Bogart asked Carl "Pete" Peterson, the *Santana*'s full-time caretaker and a highly regarded skipper, to join them. The club had a reputation for snobbishness, and Roosevelt was with Bogart when "an elderly man came over and said, 'I know you're a member and of course you can have your guests, but you *certainly* cannot bring in your professional captain!' Bogie raised an eyebrow, called for the bill, and, along with his signature, wrote out his resignation from the club. We all went back and continued drinking on the *Santana.* A short while later a very nice man came aboard with the bill in his hand and said, '*Any* time Pete wants to come into the club, he can.' Then he tore up the bill and the resignation and left."

In many ways, Bogart preferred the bonhomie on the *Santana* and the easy pleasures of boating life to the glamour of the film business, and his friendships with his sailing friends were deep and affectionate. He and the crew gave up a weekend of sailing to attend Roosevelt's wedding. In the middle of the reception, Carl Peterson arrived with an enormous package that Bogart insisted Roosevelt open immediately. As the guests looked on, Roosevelt unwrapped a life ring from the *Santana* signed by Bogart and the other shipmates and inscribed, "Love and kisses to Mr. and Mrs. George Roosevelt. Thanks for fucking up the weekend."

"I think 'humble' is not a bad word for him, considering his lifestyle," Roosevelt said. "He could make a joke about himself. And he had a terrific grin. If something amused him and you got a grin out of him, you had it made." Bogart sailed hard during the day ("the number of trophies he won annually was phenomenal"), played cards and drank with his friends in the evening, and had a rule that bedtime was at 9:00 P.M. His idea of a good time was to sail to Todos Santos, an island off the Baja California coast, whose harbor had room for only four or five boats. There he relaxed, swam, and smoked his Chesterfield cigarettes in peace. Mexican fishermen would trade a dozen lobsters for a pack of cigarettes or a few bottles of beer, and the sailors would eat the lobsters for breakfast mixed with scrambled eggs. Bogart was happy to anchor there for a week or more at a time and sail the local waters, or to circle Catalina for ten days at a stretch, stopping each night at a different cove.

Despite the stories that circulated at movie industry parties of women and wild drinking on board, the *Santana* was a thoroughly male preserve. Which suited Bacall, who much preferred Hollywood social gatherings. "Bogie would call her every morning to ask how the last night's party was, and say that we didn't do anything except play cards and go to bed," Roosevelt said. None of the regulars on the *Santana* saw much of Bacall. "She didn't particularly like the boat and she didn't particularly like the crew. We were not her style. We were just sailing people; we were not the president of the United States playing the piano with her sitting on it."

Belmont Bogart would have been proud that his son was appreciated by knowledgeable sailing people. According to Roosevelt, who had a reputation as an excellent helmsman, Bogart "really *understood* the water and how to handle bad weather. My father, who was as old and stuffy as they come and was the Commodore of the New York Yacht Club, called him 'a damn fine sailor.' *That* was a compliment."

As so often happened in Bogart's career, a time of achievement and acclaim was followed by professional stagnation. In January of 1952 he had set his heart on playing in the upcoming screen adaptation of William Inge's Broadway hit *Come Back, Little Sheba,* produced by Hal Wallis for

Paramount. The script was ready and Bogart liked the part of Doc Delahanty, the middle-aged, mild-mannered, alcoholic ex-chiropractor. (Shirley Booth, who had starred in the play as the wife, would win an Oscar for her performance.) There was only one problem. He had done two pictures in his last April-to-April contract year, neither of them for Warners, and he owed his studio a picture. Under the complicated terms of the agreement, Warners was not obliged to submit a script to him until May.

Sam Jaffe talked to Roy Obringer. He knew this film was over the limit, he pleaded, but it wouldn't inconvenience Warner Brothers or keep Bogart from his obligation. All Bogart wanted was an opportunity to do a picture that would start in February and be finished in April, a good month before the earliest submission date for Warners. Jaffe reminded the lawyer that no property had been sent for Bogart's consideration during the past year when he worked on *The African Queen* and *Deadline U.S.A.*

Warners, which had not had a Bogart film since 1950 and regretted having allowed him to make pictures for other studios, was not inclined to be flexible. J. L. and Obringer were especially uninterested in releasing Bogart to make a picture for Hal Wallis, whom they now hated. So they said no. Jaffe, sensing a ploy to make his client break his contract, said philosophically that Bogart would not press the issue. The result was that for almost a year and a half, in the wake of his Academy Award, Bogart made no films for Warners and was off-limits to other studios. The script Warners finally did send him in May was a potboiler about a football coach who forms a winning team that saves a small-town college. His reward is Donna Reed. This time it was Bogart's turn to say no, and he exacted a little revenge as well.

"He still resents not being allowed to do *Come Back, Little Sheba,*" Hedda Hopper told her readers. " 'But there'll come a day of reckoning,' he declares. 'In five years when I have no hair or teeth, Warners will have to keep putting me in pictures.' "

Such comments horrified the boys in Burbank, Harry Warner the most. At his behest, Obringer fired off a letter on behalf of Warner Bros. Pictures, Inc.: "We are at a total loss to understand your attitude," he huffed, reminding the actor that Warners alone was "solely responsible" for giving him the opportunity to reach his present position in the industry, not to mention his "very high rate of compensation." And Obringer was fairly sputtering to set the record straight: "When we entered into our existing contract with you there was no understanding or intention on our part that a part of the deal would involve an obligation on our part to accept your uncooperative services and be limited in the time when you would render such services to when you have no hair or teeth."

In the strange ways of Hollywood, Warners at the same time was conducting meetings with Bogart's lawyer and business manager Morgan Maree to discuss the possible financing and distribution of the next Bogart-Huston picture; the box office success of *The African Queen* spoke more loudly than the howls of wounded corporate egos. But the studio, at J. L.'s request, was also engaged in seeing if there was a way to terminate Bogart's contract. In June, Ralph E. Lewis of the law firm of Freston and Files wrote Obringer that there was not. "The contract is simply a bad contract from the point of view of the studio at the present time, and, legally speaking, this is no obstacle whatever to the validity of the contract. Many contracts turn out worse for one party than he expected it would." But very few ever had for Jack Warner. The Bogart-Warner relationship was looking a lot like the Bogart-Methot marriage.

According to Bogart's contract, turning down the Donna Reed film meant that he would earn $10,000 less for his next Warner film, but he was also now free to make one outside the studio. He signed with MGM to play a Korean War Army doctor in *M.A.S.H. 66* (no relation to Robert Altman and Ring Lardner Jr.'s 1970 comedy *M*A*S*H*).

The screenplay was by Bogart's old friends Allen and Laura Rivkin, and Richard Brooks directed. Bogart and June Allyson as a dewy-eyed rookie nurse made no screen magic, though, and the conventional love scenes were overshadowed by the documentary quality of the helicopter action sequences. The film was not helped by the studio's decision to release the picture under the title *Battle Circus.* "Mr. Brooks' Korea too often reverts to pure redundant Hollywood," the *New York Times* critic wrote.

The exteriors were shot in and around Fort Pickett, an Army base in Virginia; the Army also provided helicopters for the movie and, later in production, quarters for the film company. William Campbell, a young actor who played a medevac helicopter pilot, came back to his hotel after dinner one night to find a note from Humphrey Bogart: "Mr. Campbell, as soon as you get in, I want you to come directly to my room and I don't care what hour it is."

Campbell was apprehensive. He had attracted unwanted attention when, in an interview with a local columnist, he had said something to the effect that it was time the older actors stopped playing younger men. Bogart, asked for a comment, said he was absolutely right. Nevertheless, in the elevator ride to Bogart's floor, Campbell wondered whether the star was about to berate him. He knocked on the door and heard Bogart's voice.

"Who is it?"

"Uh, it's Mr. Campbell, Mr. Bogart."

"Oh yes, Mr. Campbell. Wait a minute."

After what seemed several minutes Bogart called out, "All right, Mr. Campbell."

He walked into a sitting room, and in front of him were Bogart, his hairdresser Verita Peterson, and Keenan Wynn, another member of the cast, seated on the sofa with their legs crossed, each with an arm across the chest and holding a drink. All appeared to be naked.

"Mr. Campbell, come on in, get yourself a drink, get your clothes off, join the party."

Stunned, Campbell replied that he would like to, but he had to fly a helicopter in the morning. Then he turned and got back to his room as fast as he could. The next day when he saw Wynn, with whom he'd done another picture, he was furious.

Wynn laughed. He and the others had been in their rooms getting ready for bed when Bogart had called them in for a nightcap. They'd had a few drinks and decided to put Campbell on. The deep-seated sofa concealed the swimming suits the three wore.

Following the hoax, Campbell developed a warm friendship with Bogart. During their conversations on those evenings after shooting when there was nothing to do but drink, Campbell noticed "a deep sadness" in the older man. Bogart talked about John Garfield, whom Campbell had known, and who had just died from a heart attack at thirty-nine. "He *loved* Garfield. He thought he was a brilliant actor. He said that he always felt that Garfield had gone through two thirds of a career but had never reached that which he wanted." Bogart also talked about what later became known as the Rat Pack. He was getting impatient with the whole scene, with the hangers-on who came to his house to drink and kill time, and, to Campbell's surprise, with Frank Sinatra, whom he seemed to dislike.

"He was not too . . . enamored. At least that's the way *I* picked it up. He didn't tell me this, but there is a case for his feeling about Sinatra based upon Bacall. Because there *was* some relationship there, more on her part than his. And I think Bogart was aware of it."

It was Campbell's impression, too, that Bogart already knew that something was seriously wrong with his health. There was never a long conversation about the subject, but one night over drinks with Wynn and Campbell, Bogart "indicated that he had a big problem and that the prognosis was questionable. He didn't dwell on it, and in retrospect it didn't sound *fatal* in that sense. He had a kind of wistful quality; a kind of sadness."

This was a point in Bogart's career where, like a few other stars at the top, he was, as Campbell said, "bigger than the director, bigger than the picture, bigger than the producer. Everybody is subservient, everybody is busting their ass, and everybody wants to be patted on the head." Campbell described the day the whole company was to move from their hotel to accommodations at Fort Pickett. The commanding general had vacated his house so Bogart could live there. Bogart, however, had no intention of living in someone else's house. "I'm staying at the hotel," he told the assistant director. "Here's what you're going to do. You have my wardrobe in my room at the end of the evening, and ready to go in the morning. I will be dressed and I will be prepared for the first scene. You will pick me up in the limo every morning, and when I hit the set, you better be ready for the first shot." His wishes were observed.

Sometime later over drinks, Campbell asked Bogart about the scene with the assistant director. "He said, 'I know it may sound childish to you, Mr. Campbell, but I'm only paying back for some of the things they did to me when I first went under contract. It doesn't hurt anybody and it makes it comfortable for me. And right now what's most important to me is my comfort. I'm not interested in their comfort. And I'm more comfortable living at the hotel.' "

Campbell had recently worked on *The People Against O'Hara* (1951) with Spencer Tracy, who gave him a piece of advice that he took very much to heart: "Just never forget that when you're doing motion pictures you're in the toy department." Campbell quoted the remark to Bogart, who nodded and said, "He's right."

"What he meant by that was, this is fun and games, this is not serious acting. This has another element to it. Don't listen to people who say that they just *have* to serve their public, because that is a crock. People go into this business for a number of reasons: Big money. Stardom. Patronage. Playing a game. Becoming a superstar. But always watch yourself. I think that Bogart and *all* these guys knew it was the toy department. And I think there was a certain sadness in their knowledge of that, a sense of, What *really* of significance am I offering in the long haul? Bogart and I once had a conversation about character. He said, 'A lot of people don't even understand where we come from; they don't realize we're constantly being tested and that we are in a business that is a total character builder. Every time we finish a job, we're fired. Each time you finish a picture, no matter how big you are, you say to yourself, Holy Christ! I better call the agent tomorrow.' "

On August 23, 1952, again at Cedars of Lebanon Hospital, Bacall gave birth to a six-pound, five-ounce baby girl. She was named Leslie Howard Bogart, in memory of Bogart's old friend and benefactor. *Time's* correspondent first filed a report that the child was a boy. The movie business, though, with its cruelly short memory, had virtually forgotten the onetime idol in the nine years since his death. He appeared in half-faded prints on late-night TV reruns or revivals of *Gone With the Wind.* But he remained alive for Bogart.

In the months between winning the Oscar and the birth of Leslie, the Bogarts moved from the rustic Benedict Canyon house to a $160,000 gracious, roomy, whitewashed brick colonial mansion in Holmby Hills. A large lanai faced the pool and tennis court in back. "The place is so elegant," Bogart told Hedda Hopper, "I'll have to wear black tie every night. When Betty showed me through the place, she pointed out the suites for herself, the babies, the butler and the maid; then she showed me an oversized closet and said, 'That's your room.' "

Bogart's friend David Niven wrote that in buying the house, "Bogie felt he was being conned into joining the Establishment, which he wholeheartedly despised. . . . [But] he grew to be obsessively proud of his new acquisition. He never dressed the part of a Holmby Hills squire and forever slopped about the place attired in a grisly selection of antiquated moccasins, sweaters, windbreakers and dungarees—usually with a battered yachting cap on his head."

Holmby Hills, at the western edge of Beverly Hills, is an even more exclusive enclave than its neighbor. Thick woods protect its large houses from view, and its plantings have the trimmed-but-rustic look that can be afforded only by the truly rich. The narrow winding streets are bordered by steep, wooded embankments that give the impression of country lanes. The Bogarts' neighbors were a mix of first-magnitude business and entertainment figures: A. P. Giannini, the founder of regional branch banking in the United States and head of the giant Bank of America; Lana Turner and her wealthy husband Bob Topping; Charles Correll, the Andy of *Amos and Andy;* producer Walter Wanger and his actress wife Joan Bennett; songwriter Sammy Cahn. The neighbors on one side were the Hoagy Carmichaels, though their visits were infrequent. Contact between the families was limited largely to cherry bombs thrown over the wall by the Carmichael children. Better friends were Judy Garland and her producer husband Sid Luft, whose daughter Lorna played with Stephen, accompanied sometimes by her older sister Liza, Garland's daughter from her previous marriage to director Vincente Minnelli. Also in residence at the new house were Harvey; his mate, Baby; and one of their pups, George. The Bogarts had bought Baby as a companion for Harvey, who was special to them. "Harvey was like a person" to Bacall, Stephen Bogart said.

The dogs' barking at night so annoyed the neighbors that a group headed by Charles Correll, screenwriter Cy Howard, and TV host Art Linkletter lodged a complaint with the city, suggesting that the boxers have their vocal cords removed. Bacall suggested the complainers have their own vocal cords removed. Bogart, his son writes, said of one of the complainers: "The son of a bitch doesn't like dogs? What kind of monster is he? He ought to be glad he can hear the wonderful sound of dogs barking."

In the fall, Bogart tried to acquire the movie rights to Hemingway's *The Old Man and the Sea,* a story he closely identified with and very much wanted to make, with Nicholas Ray as the director. The deal fell through. (Spencer Tracy, with whom he became particularly close following the making of *The African Queen,* starred in it the year after Bogart's death.) Whether it was a matter of professional discontent, domestic discontent, health problems, or the painful readjustments of mid-life, some of those closest to Bogart sensed a massive unease in him. Jules Buck's wife, Joyce, who knew him throughout his career, felt that "a lot of his sarcasm and bitterness came because of late recognition." There had been too many years of being "George Raft's brother-in-law," Richard Brooks said. In addition, there was no way he could know that "this character, the Bogart character, was going to live. He didn't believe any of that. It was all thin ice. Sure, you could get an Oscar. But, he said, if you ask somebody two years later who got it, they won't remember. So what the hell is it?" He knew that at first hand—look at what happened to his friend, the forgotten idol Leslie Howard—and so viewed his career as one of continuing impermanence.

At the Bogart house one night, Spencer Tracy was surprised to see Bogart's Oscar holding a door open. Brooks, who was there, said Tracy was furious. "He saw this thing and he said, 'Boy, that's pretty goddamn pretentious. You're never going to get another one the rest of your life and you've got it as a doorstop! Now what the hell is that supposed to mean? Is that what you think of the acting business?' But Bogie had to denigrate it, you see. He wanted it, and he wanted to be punished for wanting it, too. Both! He knew that New York laughed at this town. As he did."

Once a year, either as a birthday screening on Christmas Day or on Christmas Eve, Bogart would set up a sixteen-millimeter projector and show the 1937 version of *A Star Is Born,* the story of a youthful female star, on her way up, married to a fading, older alcoholic male star, on his way down. "*Every* Christmas," Brooks said. "And he cried." The tears started with the scene in which Fredric March and Janet Gaynor stand on a balcony and look out at the lights of Hollywood. Gaynor says how her career would have been nothing without him and tells him that his career will rise again. No, he replies, it's too late.

After a few years of this, Brooks finally asked, " 'What the hell are you *crying* about, Bogie?' And he answered softly, 'If you *don't* like the movie, don't watch it.' " Unsatisfied, Brooks tried again on another occasion.

"What are you so unhappy about?"

"I'm not unhappy! I'm happy. I'm having a *great* time."

"You sure *seem* unhappy. Why do you knock yourself? You're always putting yourself down. You do it with humor, but nevertheless you do it."

Bogart's answer came quickly. "Well, I expected a lot more from me. And I'm never going to get it."

In the summer of 1952, with a presidential election coming up in the fall, Bogart and Bacall reentered national politics. For the first time, they supported a Republican, the war hero Dwight Eisenhower, who had been furiously courted by the Democrats as well. Many other Democrats were drawn to a Republican moderate at a time when the party's right was symbolized by Senator Joe McCarthy.

Bogart and Bacall appeared at a massive outdoor rally for Ike in Los Angeles, but their allegiance—Bacall's particularly—turned out to be not very deep. It took only one encounter with Governor Adlai Stevenson of Illinois, the Democratic candidate, to make her switch sides. In mid-September, MGM production chief Dore Schary hosted a lawn party for Stevenson and invited six hundred movie people. Bogart stayed home but Bacall attended. Stevenson's wit, charm, and eloquence won him the eager support of many of those there—"comforting evidence," *Time* magazine wrote, "that many a torrid summer romance with Eisenhower had ended in a reconciliation with the Democratic Party." Bacall made her way through the crowd, brimming with enthusiasm. "Bogie hasn't switched yet," she told reporters, "but I'm working on him."

Bacall writes of being warned by a "very well known producer" at the Schary party to keep her mouth shut about her politics. Memories of the Washington trip were still strong, and the studio heavyweights were now almost solidly conservative. New Deal stalwart Jack Warner had become a born-again Republican, wooing the old WASP Los Angeles establishment that had always rejected him.

Eisenhower had disillusioned his liberal supporters by trying to appeal to the McCarthyite wing of the Republican Party instead of repudiating it. He endorsed the HUAC hearings, brought McCarthy aboard his campaign train in Wisconsin, and, in a Milwaukee speech, went the senator one better by accusing successive Democratic administrations—without naming them—of "treason itself."

Even though support of Stevenson was frowned upon by the studio heads, film-industry Democrats had the same enthusiasm that once sparked the Hollywood Democratic Committee. Bacall agreed to travel to San Francisco on Stevenson's behalf. A few days before her trip, Bogart changed sides and joined the Volunteers for Stevenson. The country was fairly "teeming" with the election, Bogart wrote in October to Huston, who was in London preparing their next picture, *Beat the Devil.* "Stevenson is making wonderful speeches, literature [*sic*], intelligent and intellectual. Eisenhower is saying what they tell him to say, which is a sad spectacle because I thought he was going to be a wonderful fellow. Miss Bacall supports whole heartedly, Governor Stevenson, up to the vomiting point."

All the "right people" were on the other side, he continued—"Jack Warner, [actor and later Senator] George Murphy, [ultra-conservative Paramount head] Y. Frank Freeman . . . etcetera etc. I of course am supporting Stevenson because as [screenwriter] Wilson Mizner once said, 'A single golden hair from the head of a beautiful woman is stronger than the trans-Atlantic cable.' " Though there was also, he added, a Prohibition candidate toward whom he leaned slightly, "especially early in the morning."

Bogart went on to tell his friend that the traveling HUAC show had just "blessed" Los Angeles with another visit: "The usual well-known writer that nobody ever heard of bared his soul and exposed members of the Communist Party who have already done their time in jail. . . . As you once said, old boy, and I agree with you, it's a shitty world."

Bacall quickly established a close friendship with Stevenson. In *By Myself* she writes about her undeniable sexual attraction to the candidate, who was divorced, charming, and flirtatious, and who collected an entourage of high-profile supporters. It was one of a number of attractions that Bacall dismisses as flirtations—attractions that included Richard Burton and Leonard Bernstein—indulged, she said, by an understanding, older husband.

Bogart's admiration for the candidate grew so that it more than matched his exasperation and minor jealousies. Bacall writes about his suggestion for a cartoon: Bogart, a child on either side, in the front doorway, looking plaintively out into the rain, and captioned, "Daddy, where's Mommy?" "With Adlai."

That fall both Bogart and Bacall were with Stevenson aboard his campaign train, doing brief turns from the rear platform with other celebrities at whistle stops along the way east. On October 27 they appeared at a huge Stevenson rally at Madison Square Garden. The evening's script was written by Robert Sherwood, who had served earlier Democratic administrations, and who inserted for Bogart a few Duke Mantee lines from *The Petrified Forest.* The Dumont Network carried the event live on television. The broadcast began with the familiar, throaty Bacall voice, off-camera: "Good evening, America! This is Lauren Bacall, Volunteers for Stevenson, speaking to you from Madison Square Garden. . . . Outside the Garden tonight the streets are lined with thousands of people who couldn't get in. . . ."

The celebrities inside included Montgomery Clift, Richard Rodgers and Oscar Hammerstein, Tallulah Bankhead, comedian George Jessel, cartoonist Al Capp, Robert Ryan, and Mercedes McCambridge. After the introductions, actress Benay Venuta turned to one side. "And now, I take great honor introducing that eminent actor, Mr.—Humphrey—Bogart!" Even as she spoke, the crowd went wild. He hadn't worn his toupee. A small tuft of hair was all there was in the center of a shining, bald crown fringed at the sides and back. He was short, he was slight, he wore a bow tie. But the crowd saw Duke Mantee, and they loved him.

He glowered in silent parody. The audience laughed on cue. After all the years away from the stage, he could still work a crowd with absolute assurance. "The cops ain't likely to catch up with me . . . so let's all be quiet and peaceable and have a few laughs together and listen to da music . . . don't let's nobody make any wrong moves, 'cause I'm feelin' kind nervous and jumpy . . . so let's—everybody—stay where dey are."

He drew back his lip in the familiar snarl. The crowd ate it up. Bogart himself broke up laughing as he reverted to his natural voice to make a quick endorsement speech. But masterly as he had been as Duke Mantee, he now seemed uncomfortable and diffident. After three words, he broke off with an embarrassed laugh—"we're a little short of time so I'm going to cut my speech"—and introduced the next speaker, the poet and Lincoln biographer Carl Sandburg.

Bogart and Bacall dashed to Chicago for the final rally, flew home to vote, then at Bacall's insistence and with Bogart's misgivings, flew at Stevenson's invitation to the Illinois capital, Springfield, to follow the election returns. Bacall was optimistic. Bogart, true to form but also knowledgeable in politics, saw "disaster ahead." He was not alone. Stevenson had already drafted his concession statement.

Whatever the hopes that an Eisenhower win might put a stop to McCarthyism, the overall effect of the Eisenhower-Nixon victory on Hollywood was to strengthen the hand of Southern California conservatives, of the Motion Picture Alliance, and the blacklist itself. Jack Warner, who had worked for the Republicans with the same energy he once brought to campaigns for Roosevelt, sent a short telegram to the Bogarts: "THANKS FOR HELPING ELECT EISENHOWER. WITHOUT LOVE. JACK WARNER."

"Betty and I campaigned very hard for Stephenson [*sic*], who is a wonderful man," Bogart wrote Huston that November, "and we are now licking our wounds and paying our election bets. The cry of the Republicans is 'Thank God we got America back' which is to assume that the 27,000,000 who voted for Stevenson have been in some way subversive and will either have to leave the country or go to jail."

Bogart himself was planning to leave the country, though for other reasons. All through the year, he and Huston had corresponded about their next film together. In January 1953, not long before Harry Truman was, in his words, "elevated back to the rank of private citizen" and Dwight David Eisenhower was sworn in as the thirty-fourth president of the United States, Bogart left for Italy and his final collaboration with John Huston.

CHAPTER 23

Beating the Devil

Santana Productions bought the film rights to *Beat the Devil* in 1951. Claud Cockburn's picaresque novel about a group of rogues chasing an unobtainable treasure and of a beautiful woman incapable of telling the truth is a wryly comic twist on the theme of *The Maltese Falcon.* John Huston, a friend of the novelist, who published the book under the pseudonym James Helvick, brokered the low-price sale; Cockburn was ill with tuberculosis and in financial straits. Bogart quickly sent the money for the rights and a draft of the script to Cockburn's home in Ireland.

After reading the proposed script, one of the censors in the Breen Office at the Motion Picture Association of America wrote, "Everyone in the story, with one exception, is a completely amoral person, to whom the question of right or wrong would never occur." Which was, of course, the very quality that had attracted Huston and Bogart to this story of a motley gang of thieves and an English couple who comically double-cross each other in a duplicity-laden hunt for an African uranium mine. Bogart's role as the gang's front man, the appealingly amoral Billy Dannreuther, was sniffily described by the censor as that of "a man with a criminal background, who is currently engaged in some sort of unethical, if not illegal business."

Huston was Bogart's obvious choice for director. "I think [he] is the best director in the whole business," Bogart told Louella Parsons in

March. "Remember *The Maltese Falcon?* That's still one of my favorite pictures. That's why I want John to direct *Beat the Devil*." Huston, though, was hesitant. Bogart's straitjacketed schedule at Warners allowed only a short and specified time for an outside film, and Huston had a prior commitment to Katharine Hepburn. After Huston asked an intermediary to explain to her that the Bogart film would pay him more and enable him to settle his debts, she graciously stepped aside, but there remained the obstacle of Huston being able to finish *Moulin Rouge,* his current project, on time. Nicholas Ray was presented to executives of Romulus, Santana's English partner, as the alternative. Morgan Maree wrote them that Ray was "a very excellent director who also had Bogart's complete confidence." At the same time, though, Maree wrote to Huston to say he was still the first choice, "as you know that Bogart would prefer to work with you than any other person."

Still, Huston procrastinated. To David O. Selznick, who inquired that February about a role for his wife Jennifer Jones, Huston expressed doubts about the property he had urged on Bogart. "The picture," he wrote, "would be more fortunate in getting her than she would be in getting it." Finally Maree had to cable Huston, asking him to make a decision. "As you know, Bogie has been waiting rather impatiently for your answer." Huston agreed and a contract was drawn up to pay him $175,000 for his services as writer, director, and co-producer.

The supporting cast included Peter Lorre and Robert Morley as two of the crooks, in a comic variation of Joel Cairo and the Fat Man. Bogart and Huston both wanted Lorre, who was doing fewer pictures at the time. Although Lorre was half-committed to a play, he far preferred to work with his old friends and was willing to take a 50 percent cut on his standard $50,000 salary. Maree offered $15,000. Paul Kohner, Lorre's agent as well as Huston's, was, as is often the case in Hollywood, working both sides of the street; and he persuaded the actor to take the $15,000 plus first-class living expenses to play O'Hara, one of the five gang members. (O'Hara has the most memorable lines in the film, which has become a cult classic. Much is made of the importance of time as the story progresses, and finally O'Hara says, "Time, time, what is it? The Swiss manufacture it, the French hoard it, Italians want it, Americans say it's money, Hindus say it does not exist. You know what I say? I say time is a crook.")

Bogart and Huston's hardest casting decision was the part of Gwendolen Chelm, the wide-eyed seeming innocent whose comically compulsive lying sets the twisted plot in motion. (Bogart suggested the title be changed to *The Lady Lies.*) Huston's first choice was either Jean Simmons or Audrey Hepburn. Maree offered two him counter-suggestions—Ingrid Bergman, who lived in Italy, where the film was to be shot, and Lauren Bacall. "I talked to Bogie about Betty and he wanted me to assure you that there is absolutely nothing personal in the suggestion that Betty be used. In other words, he is perfectly willing to abide by your judgment as to whether or not she can fit the part, No. 1, and is capable of acting it, No. 2." Huston's reply was succinct: "I don't think that either one is all right for Gwendolen, but as far as Bergman is concerned she is going to have a baby anyway." The role went to Jennifer Jones, whose portrayal of a religious French girl in *The Song of Bernadette* (1943) had made her a star.

Earlier, Huston had written Bacall to say he was considering her for the part of Gwendolen. "Dear Fly in the Ointment," Bogart wrote back, "Because I always open my wife's mail, I read your insidious and immoral proposals to my wife. It is perfectly sure that she is knocked up [awakened]—by me, that is. I therefore instructed Miss Bacall to disregard your blandishments and as your employer I request you not to further fuck up my home, which already has been fucked up by Adlai Stevenson."

Actually, Bacall had recently signed a deal with Twentieth Century–Fox to do a picture a year and she was about to work for the first time in three years, as one of the trio of gold-digging models in Nunnally Johnson's *How to Marry a Millionaire.* (The film, released in 1953, showed her abilities with light comedy and was a comeback, but it was Marilyn Monroe who caught the public's attention and became the sex symbol of the fifties, as Bacall had been in the forties.)

For the second female lead, that of Dannreuther's voluptuous European wife, Huston had "two lively candidates," the Italian Gina Lollobrigida and the French Claude Nollier. Both, he wrote in August, were "beautiful dames. Nollier has a bit of an edge when it comes to talent." But the film, an early example of international deal-making, needed an Italian partner and, therefore, an Italian actress, and so Lollobrigida, the top star in the country, was signed with the agreement that she would receive billing above the title in Europe. Huston and Bogart came to call her Lola Frigidaire, a comment on her statuesque build.

It was necessary for the shooting of *Beat the Devil* to begin in early January 1953 in order for Bogart to be finished by April 5, the date his new contract year at Warners started. Meanwhile, Cockburn's script required considerable rewriting by Tony Veiller, at the time working with

Huston on *Moulin Rouge,* and by Peter Viertel, who had worked without credit on *The African Queen.*

"Got a long letter from Peter," Bogart wrote Huston, "saying that everything is going fine and the script is in wonderful condition, which I presume means that somebody has written a title on a piece of yellow paper."

Bogart the producer was involved in every step of the process. "With an eye to the future residuals of this epic upon which we are about to embark," he wrote Huston in October, "may I as a very timid employer, offer for your consideration, color. . . . It seems to me that if we are going to all the places you plan to go, we'd lose a lot without it. . . . this is entirely up to you as since I've won the Oscar, I have tremendous respect for your opinions, drunk or sober." (*The African Queen* was Bogart's first color film.) Huston replied that he didn't think color would be an improvement, but asked whether Bogart thought the eventual sale to television would be so greatly enhanced as to warrant the extra expense. "That is a question that I, a lowly craftsman, am less able to answer than you big corporation guys. Whatever you and Morgan decide is fine with me." Huston, absorbed in the intricacies of *Moulin Rouge* and its experiments in color photography, as well as in the logistics of a picture in which José Ferrer had to play the crippled Toulouse-Lautrec by having his legs doubled and walking on his knees, was probably sick of the problems that came with the process.

Bogart also wanted to know about his wardrobe. Huston suggested "a brand new Bogart. Not that old thing that's been haunting raincoats and snap-brimmed hats for God knows how long. I'd like to see you as a very Continental type fellow—an extreme figure in a homburg, shoulders unpadded, French cuffs, regency trousers, fancy waistcoats and a walking stick."

"I've [given your suggestions] a great deal of thought," Bogart wrote a week later, "oh, I would say about two or three minutes while I was preparing a highball last night. I agree with you about the trench-coat, etc. but as regards your brilliant conception of my wardrobe, may I say that you're full of shit. May I suggest that you wear the costume you describe. . . . May I also suggest that you rig up some kind of a contrivance that will permit you forever to walk on your knees. . . . As regards the cane, I don't have to tell you what you can do with *that.*"

Costumes were a minor concern compared to the script. Although Bogart realized it was still in draft "and has not yet had the famed Huston touch," nevertheless it seemed to him to "lack the comic flavor the book had. . . . It didn't seem to know what it wanted to be, a comedy, a melodrama or just a yarn. The sort of comic effect of the lady's lies to the gang didn't seem to have the salty impact it had in the book." There were other difficulties, too. Because three companies in different countries—Santana in America, Romulus in Britain, and Roberto Haggiag in Italy—were involved with the picture, the normal problems with finances, regulations, and work permits were tripled. There was also difficulty in insuring the film until there was a final script and in getting coverage for a director who, for all his genius, had become notorious for not meeting deadlines. Maree was blunt with Huston: "I don't think it is necessary for me to tell you that no man can afford to have the financial interests of a country frightened of him to the point where they refuse to guarantee completion of pictures that are made under his direction."

In early January, Bogart left for Rome, this time without Bacall, who was filming *How to Marry a Millionaire.* With Warners' permission, the start of shooting on *Beat the Devil* had been moved to February, but in mid-January, the Breen Office informed Santana that the Veiller-Viertel script was "unacceptable under the provisions of the Production Code." Their disapproval almost ended the project. Huston, irritated at the prospect of yet being involved with another draft, suggested they simply drop the picture, but Bogart dissuaded him, saying, "It's only money." It was Selznick who came up with the writer who saved the film, the young novelist Truman Capote, who had polished the script of the Jennifer Jones picture *Indiscretion of an American Wife.* The movie had been shot in Rome and Capote was still there. He was signed on for $1,500 a week. He "turned out to be magnificent," Bogart told Joe Hyams. "He wrote like fury—has the damnedest and most upside down slant on humor you've ever heard." In an era of conformity and closet gays, Capote proudly displayed his homosexuality. Bogart, the quintessence of macho who called anyone he didn't like a "fag," grew genuinely fond of Capote. They became friends when, to Bogart's surprise, Capote, who was quite solidly built, beat him at arm wrestling—three times in a row.

Just before the start of production, Bogart and Huston were being chauffeured to the location in Ravello. Bogart was in the back seat. "Our Italian driver came to a fork in the road," he later wrote, "which had so many markers he couldn't decide whether to turn left or right. His solution was to go straight ahead until stopped by a stone wall." Bogart's head cracked against the front seat and his teeth bit through his tongue.

The force of the blow also broke his bridge. Huston, he remembered, "started to laugh like a fool."

"What'th the matter," Bogart asked through a mouthful of blood.

"The crazy creep," Huston replied, "drove through a stone wall."

Later Bogart said that Huston "was probably hoping my teeth would fall out so he wouldn't have to go through with the picture."

Bogart sat still while a doctor in Naples stitched up his tongue without anesthetic; the needle, the doctor said, would hurt as much as the stitches, so why bother? "Bogie had guts," Huston said. "Not bravura. Real courage." A week later, he went to work, with a quickly duplicated bridge sent from Los Angeles.

Given the time constraints, there was a necessarily improvised quality to the production. Capote, with Huston as his goad and editor, produced the dialogue at most a day before it was to be shot and sometimes wrote on the set as the actors contributed their thoughts. In the evening, Capote sat with Huston and went through his pages for the day. Bogart sometimes put on a white jacket and mixed martinis for them all.

For Bogart, who was used to learning his lines the morning of shooting anyway, the absence of finished scenes until the last moment was no problem. Julie Gibson, a pretty blond actress and publicist, was a neighbor of Capote's in Rome. Of Bogart she said, "He was taking it in his stride as a professional: This is the script; I have to learn it; I'll do it. John was taking it with tongue in cheek and great glee." Gibson, who had dated Huston briefly while working as the publicist for *Moulin Rouge,* saw the best and worst of Bogart. Production had already started when she asked Huston for a job on the new film, and he told her to come to the company's quarters in the crumbling but beautiful old Hotel Colombo, overlooking the Mediterranean. On the far side of the lobby was a big room with a piano and an old phonograph. A few people danced, others sat and talked. A man looked up at her as she came in; she didn't recognize him as Bogart.

"He looked very tired and very ill. But he walked over, introduced himself and asked me if I'd like to dance. I said I'd love to. He said, 'You're an actress, of course.' I said, 'Well, I've been an actress under contract to Paramount but now I'm working over here.' He walked over to Huston. 'John, this is Paramount's answer to Jean Arthur.' "

In the conversation that followed after Huston left, Bogart talked about Mayo with apparent affection, but he also began to show the side of himself that emerged after several drinks. "He said, 'Women are funny.

Just because of the little triangle they have, they think they can get by with anything.' And suddenly he got very angry. But when he talked about Mayo, his eyes lighted up."

Gibson felt she was dealing with two personalities, a charming man when sober, a vitriolic one when not. Each night for dinner, Gibson, Huston, and Bogart went downstairs in the hotel, where a large table was set for them. "We all had a couple of martinis before dinner, that was our ritual. John usually bought the drinks for everybody." It was then that what she called Bogart's "chemical change" took place. "His face would just get dark, as if he had a mask on." In her second week on the job, after a few martinis, he suddenly turned on her.

"He said, 'I know how all you broads get your jobs. You come up here and flaunt your sex appeal, and you go to be with somebody to get the job, and then you end up *with* the job.' Well, I didn't want to hear any more of this and I walked away. He could find your Achilles heel and he'd go right after it, and he was cruel." She quickly learned not to sit next to him at dinner, because whoever sat by him was the person he needled.

Gibson had brought a girlfriend with her, an attractive American model whom Huston liked. "Bogie grabbed her one evening when we were sitting in the parlor. I saw that look on his face and thought, *uh-oh.* He was saying, 'You come up here and you sleep with the director. . . . ' Well, she started to cry. She liked John and they were having a nice little thing, and he was trying to destroy it. And when Bogie had gotten the result he wanted, he just walked away from her." The model, distraught, ran to Gibson. " 'What's the *matter* with him?' she asked. I said, 'Stay away from him after the third martini, that's all. It's not just you. He does it to everybody. Otherwise, he's perfectly delightful. He's very professional. He's always on time, even if he's sick. He knows his lines, he knows what he's doing, and he's very charming. But when he has that third martini, out come the toads and snakes.' "

Huston was perhaps the one person other than Bacall who could modify Bogart's behavior. "John was always the head of the table," Gibson said. "He was the boss and everybody knew it—including Bogie." The writer and film critic James Agee said that Huston was always able to do anything with or to Bogart. The reason for this control and Bogart's "boy-like subservience" was Bogart's intense desire to be respected by Huston as a man.

Gibson remembered Bogart asking her after the car accident: "What would you think if a director, your own director, after you knock your two front teeth out, sits there and *laughs.* What would you think about that?"

Huston didn't really mean to laugh, Gibson protested.

"Yes, he did," Bogart insisted.

Jules Buck was never certain that Huston really liked Bogart. Gibson felt he did. "John would always say that his favorite actor was his father, but he put Bogie next. 'People don't appreciate him,' he said, 'don't realize what a fine actor he is.' And Bogie respected John—loved John. But Bogie in a way resented John, because John was doing all the things that he would have loved to do. John could get any woman just by turning on the charm. You *had* to love him. He was so much fun and so delightful; he flirted with everything. And Bogie could not do that. That wasn't his personality. Still, he would have liked to be like that."

One evening before dinner, Huston, as usual, was the focus of attention. "He had been really turning on the charm for me. We were doing Irish melodies while Bogie sat there with the blackest look on his face but also getting a kick out of it in a funny way. The next night, John wasn't there. I asked where he was. Bogie turned and gave me that Bogart look and he said, 'You, too! You were taken in by all that phony Irish dialect and that phony Irish charm. You're one of God's followers too—one of God's worshipers.' He edged in closer. 'Well, let . . . me . . . tell . . . you. God went to Salerno to get *laid.*' "

Bogart was one of the most melancholy people she ever met. "I'd look at his face, and in repose, he was a very sad man." Sometimes, after several martinis, he would continue talking, as he had that first night with her, about Mayo, now nearly two years dead. "He would smile and seemed to be reminiscing to himself. There was something in there I hadn't seen before and that I never saw again."

Gibson always felt that the alcohol-induced mood swing had a lot to do with his mother. It seemed at times as though Maud were emerging in her son. The night Bogart had verbally attacked her friend he had said, suddenly icily correct, "You think just because I play all those gangster roles that I don't know how to talk!" Then, Gibson said, "he started becoming very articulate and terribly elegant. And I remembered he was Humphrey Bogart the Third, or whatever it was, and that his mother was a fashionable artist. He got terribly haughty and I thought, That's the way his mother must have been."

Once the shooting in Ravello ended, the company prepared to move to London to film some interior shots and edit the picture. At the party on the last night at the Colombo Hotel, Huston, six-foot-four, and Capote, five-foot-nothing, showed up in identical puce-colored velveteen jackets which had been tailored for the occasion. "That was John's little joke," Gibson said, "and Truman loved it. *Loved* it. But Bogie didn't give a damn about stuff like that." He did, however, make a point of saying good-bye to Gibson, who had not been able to get a work permit for England. She noticed how lined his face was, how the dark circles beneath his eyes were heightened by the lack of color in his skin, and how tired he looked, except when he performed. Then he seemed to have an inner energy.

In the late fall of 1952, Warner Brothers and Bogart discussed developing a screenplay first called *Rock of Gibraltar* and then *The Ferry Boat Story,* which was to be written and directed by Nicholas Ray. Bogart, however, had not committed himself to the project, and during the course of the informal meetings, he decided that he wanted to first do *The Caine Mutiny* for Columbia, which his contract entitled him to accept. Informed of his determination, J. L. and Obringer felt used and angry, feelings more familiar to Bogart than to them. Had they not consented to moving the starting date for *Beat the Devil*? Now here was Sam Jaffe, asking the studio to step aside.

In December, Warner instructed Obringer to tell Jaffe and Bogart the studio would not cooperate this time, and scribbled at the bottom of the memo in large letters, "Do ours first, then *Caine Mutiny*!"

Jaffe answered that Bogart would be happy to be bought out of his agreement for $400,000 and everyone go their separate way. Two days later, Obringer told Jaffe's assistant Herb Brenner that Jack Warner was "so disgusted and fed up with [their] ridiculous proposal" that he did not "even want to talk" about it. The studio was willing, however, to "effect a mutual release of [Bogart's] contract and waive any monies coming to us from the Bacal settlement, which is $28,250. Brenner stated that he did not think the Bacal money meant anything one way or the other."

By this time, the only thing that meant anything to either party was to win the fight. Bogart and Warner were both fed up with what each viewed as the other's obstinacy. The studio's tack was to rely on the letter of its contract. In April, Obringer reminded J. L. that "by May 4, 1953, we must have submitted to HUMPHREY BOGART one story (original or published or unpublished works, in any form), and must designate role at time of approval." If Bogart did not approve within seven days, the picture automatically would be canceled and his compensation for each of the last six of the remaining nine pictures in his contract would be reduced by $10,000, but he would gain the right to make two outside pictures instead of one during his contract year. On May 4, a formal notice was sent to Bogart in care of the Jaffe office, informing him that he was assigned the character of "Brett Thorpe" in a screenplay entitled *The Last Train West.* Jaffe airmailed the script to Bogart in Europe. He turned it down.

Bogart's response was figuratively the same as his response to J. L. nearly ten years earlier, when Warner was pressing him to take the role in *Conflict:* "Turn your dogs on me." The difference was that he could now draw a top salary anywhere. The onetime wheelhorse of the Warner factory was getting his revenge for past abuses and for the treatment Warners had given his wife. Jack Warner could only look on as his biggest star roamed virtually at will, working everywhere on earth, it seemed, except at his studio.

In London on May 21, the Bogarts celebrated their eighth wedding anniversary. They were now part of the international set, as well as of the American expatriate colony that included Huston, who had set up residence in Ireland; columnist Art Buchwald; the great combat photographer Robert Capa, who shot some of the stills for *Beat the Devil;* the writer Irwin Shaw; and Howard Hawks and his new wife Dee Hartford, who wintered in Klosters, along with Peter Viertel and Greta Garbo. Their English friends included Laurence Olivier and Vivien Leigh, and Richard and Sybil Burton.

In Paris, Bill Mauldin, on assignment for *Life* magazine, ran into the Bogarts and Huston; they offered him a ride in their limo. Later, Bogart confided his concern about Huston's constant debt and what Mauldin called his "cavalier attitude about money."

Bogart, in contrast, worried over money, whether or not he needed to. Art Buchwald received a phone call from Bogart one day, asking him to come over to his suite at the Ritz—"I need a witness in case this thing ever goes to court." When Buchwald arrived, there on the bed were Bacall's purchases from Hermes, Givenchy, and Guerlain. Bogart waved a glass of scotch vaguely in the direction of the bed. "My whole interest in *Beat the Devil* has been spent in Paris this morning."

In June Bogart returned to Los Angeles to begin *The Caine Mutiny* for Columbia. Captain Philip Francis Queeg was a role he felt attracted to as soon as he read Herman Wouk's 1951 best-seller. "I liked Captain Queeg," he said of the alternately neurotic and psychotic martinet. "I felt I understood him." Producer Stanley Kramer thought so, too. "I needed somebody who came on with that Bogart kind of confidence and the interior kind of strangeness that he had. It was his own character. He wasn't like Queeg, but he had Queeg-like qualities, including his violence, which I was never a party to, but which must have been intense."

Phil Gersh, the soldier who slept in Bogart's room during the war when he and Mayo were entertaining the troops in Italy, was now an agent in his brother-in-law Sam Jaffe's office. Bogart had called him when the sale of the movie rights was announced and expressed his interest in the role. A few days later, Jaffe and Bogart went to Kramer's office to discuss the film. José Ferrer, Van Johnson, and Fred MacMurray were already lined up, if not actually signed. Bogart brought along a set of steel balls, like those fingered by Queeg during his climactic courtroom breakdown, and rolled them as they spoke. If Bogart had brought the balls for Kramer's benefit, though, the strategy backfired. The studio was supposed the woo the star, not vice-versa. The maximum salary at the time for any major star was $200,000, augmented by a percentage of the gross. Gersh was able to negotiate similar terms in future deals, but not in this one. Kramer reported Bogart's enthusiasm for the part of Queeg to Columbia head Harry Cohn. Cohn afterward called Gersh to say the studio was "not going to pay $200,000 because he knew that Bogart wanted this role."

Bogart always believed that he had been underpaid by Cohn. "Stanley called me," he later wrote. " 'Okay, Bogie, we're rounding up a big name cast. I hope you don't mind taking less money.' " Even though he felt he was being pinched, Bogart accepted the offer, because "for Queeg, I'd take less money." Yet Bacall wrote that Bogart was only putting the best public face on the deal. Privately, he was furious: Why was he always being low-balled? Why didn't this ever happen to Cooper or Grant or Gable? Chances are, it did; the producer's job is to get actors for the least money. Consider what Bogart's company had done with Peter Lorre on *Beat the Devil.* But this time Bogart was the actor, not the producer, and he howled. "Damn it, Harry knows I want to play it and will come down in my price rather than see them give it to somebody else."

The Navy, after considerable nervousness and much back-and-forth with Washington, agreed to lend its facilities in Hawaii to the production—including a destroyer temporarily named the *Caine*—after Kramer told "the admiral in charge of public relations that I was going to make the picture anyhow, so he might as well cooperate. First they couldn't give us anything; eventually they turned over all of Pearl Harbor."

Bogart, Bacall, and Stephen were put up in a suite at the Royal Hawaiian Hotel on Waikiki Beach. Leslie, too young to travel, was left at home with a nurse. Irving Moore, later the director of many *Dallas* and *Dynasty* television episodes, was then a third assistant director. One Sunday morning he watched the couple and their five-and-a-half-year-old son sunning on the hotel beach as the other guests "looked out of the corners of their eyes at the Bogart family. Evidently the little boy said something, because all of a sudden Bogart yelled out, 'Hey, Betty! The kid wants to pee! Take him in the water.' Everybody's head turned and looked. I'm sure he did it purposely."

The cast was not a chummy one. Bogart kept to himself and to his family during the off-hours. The director, Edward Dmytryk, said, "When I worked with Jimmy Stewart, if he was through working at three o'clock, he'd sit on the set. Not Bogart." Van Johnson, according to Moore, "would horse around and kid and joke up until the time the director said, 'Action.' Then he played the character." Fred MacMurray, whose wife had just died, also kept to himself. Kramer said he gave him the role to help him get through his mourning. His part of Lieutenant Tom Keefer was very much against type: Keefer is the villain of the piece and MacMurray normally played all-Americans.

Yet when the cameras rolled, it was a textbook operation by an ensemble of thorough professionals. There was no haggling between the actors over a missed line. The film was the first Bogart had done with Dmytryk, though they had earlier connections. Both had been in the hearing room in Washington in October 1947. Dmytryk was one of the Hollywood Ten. He had served his prison time like the others, and emerged angry and feeling used. "We were the test rats. Nobody else used the First Amendment after we went to jail; we were the sacrifices. And nobody gave a damn." Bitter about the Party and not about to waive his career into the bargain, he had gone back before the House Committee on Un-American Activities after his release and named other Party members. Doing so cleared his name from the blacklist.

But 1947 was something neither talked about. Dmytryk felt that Bogart "just wanted to forget it. I think he realized more quickly than anybody else that it was a Party thing and that these people weren't carrying on a glorious battle for free speech, for Christ's sake. Not in the least. Took me a long time to realize that fully, though. The hard way." Dmytryk found Bogart to be "a very introverted man. He impressed me as very sharp and intelligent, a man who obviously was making no judgments. We didn't become friends instantly; it took a while to get him on open terms."

First Bogart had to test his director. During a rehearsal, he stopped in the middle of a long speech and said, "Jesus Christ, what does *that* mean?" Dmytryk answered as though talking to a child, "Well, I'll tell you Bogie. . . ." From then on there were no problems. A tough, barrel-chested Ukrainian farm boy from western Canada who had run away from home when he was fourteen, Dmytryk was not about to be intimidated. "I took it as being a self-protective attitude, because he wasn't a tough guy by any means. He was capable of discussing anything."

Dmytryk thought Bogart a great actor, "not in the Shakespearean sense; but he was honest, and he was great at putting a human being on the screen. I don't think there was ever a point at which he was acting a line, where he was reading the line for effect. Some actors have tricks in reading. Others, like Bogie and Tracy, never resorted to tricks. There was always a newness, and a freshness."

Claude Akins, who played Horrible, the sailor in the target-practice scene whose sloppy dress incites the captain, found that "Bogart was riveting to work with." Queeg becomes so caught up in chewing out Horrible for having his shirttail out that he allows the *Caine* to steam in a circle and cut its own tow line. "I mean when he looked at you, he looked *at* you. And when he said something to you, it came right out of him and right at you. Which is so much easier to play than with some big stars who give absolutely nothing." While in the Army, Akins had been "eaten out" by officers and knew the real thing. "And I'll tell you, Bogart scared the *shit* out of me. He was Queeg and he was pissed and he was letting me know it! You have so much to play with then, when you get that from somebody. It just kindles you, ignites you, and spurs you along."

Naval officials were uneasy about the picture because it depicted a destroyer captain who was, as one Columbia official put it, "a loony." The service had approved the script, but it had assigned a technical adviser, Commander James C. Shaw, a veteran of Iwo Jima and Guadalcanal, to be on the set at all times to be sure that everything purportedly Navy was done according to regulations. The filming went smoothly until a simple scene in which Queeg talks with his first officer, Steve Maryk (Van Johnson), in his quarters, discussing the strawberries whose disappearance becomes the captain's obsession. Queeg, eating his breakfast, neurotically plays with the toast while he talks, buttering it the way one spreads concrete with a trowel. The mannerism upset Commander Shaw. Granted, he said, Captain Queeg had a mental problem, but that didn't mean that he was not an officer and a gentleman. Any officer out of

Annapolis was presumed to have sufficient manners to break a slice of bread into small pieces before buttering it.

"I am aware of manners and I think this bread I've cut into triangles is small enough without breaking it down smaller," Bogart said. Shaw pronounced it still too big. Bogart became annoyed. He announced that his father was a doctor, that his mother was a famous artist, and that he certainly did have good table manners, even though the character he was playing had a screw loose somewhere. Was the commander saying that Annapolis turned out better gentlemen than Andover?

In a decision worthy of Solomon, the crust was trimmed from the bread, thus reducing the size and satisfying both Bogart and the Navy.

Bogart never mentioned having been in the Navy along with his other credentials. But then he hadn't been an officer, which might have only proved the commander's case.

Stanley Kramer was put to what had become Bogart's standard test, at the end of a dinner early in the production. Around eleven o'clock Kramer said it was time to call it an evening because of the early shooting the next day. Bogart looked at him for a moment and asked what would happen if Kramer weren't there?

" 'I don't know,' " he answered, " 'but it is my duty to see to it that prematurely aging and balding actors are on the set on time.' After that we got on fine. He had this facade of the tough character he played most of the time on film, and he used it to his advantage to keep from revealing any sign of weakness. Underneath he was really quite soft."

Bogart's real character was revealed in his acting. When the camera rolled, Irving Moore felt that "he had an aura of his own. When he walked out there, you were dealing with a star, and you knew it. He had such inner strength."

"Bogart would have hated to be characterized as an intellectual," Kramer added. "That was somehow for him a sign of weakness. Yet his logical approach to performance was very thorough and deep. He was one hell of an actor, and even though acting well was everything to him, he swept his accomplishment aside like it was nothing. He wanted to be sure nobody thought that he worked or took it seriously. As Tracy used to say, 'Take the job seriously and yourself not at all.' "

Later it would be said that Bogart's concept of Queeg allowed no room for development, but the real fault was with the script rather than with the performance. Bogart had his doubts about the Stanley Roberts–Michael Blankfort screenplay and privately sent a copy to Huston in London for his comments. "I think Queeg loses face all too quickly," he wrote back. "I would like to see him . . . in a good light for a while longer. . . . At first he should appear to be the perfect and complete officer. Then something ever so slight should make us wonder briefly. Then something else should cause us to put away our doubts. . . . And then, when we least expect it, those doubts should be sickeningly confirmed."

There were few doubts, though, about the courtroom scene in which the mutineers are tried and Queeg has his most memorable moment. "I played Queeg as a very controlled person when he first took the chair to testify," Bogart later wrote. "He was regular Navy, and he was facing a board largely composed of regular Navy officers. . . . Then, as pressure was applied . . . [he] gradually went to pieces. Queeg was not a sadist, not a cruel man. He was a very sick man. His was a life of frustrations and insecurity. His victories were always small victories." The more Bogart talked and wrote about Queeg, the more the character became almost an alter ego for him to publicly vouch for. "I don't know whether he was a schizophrenic, a manic depressive or a paranoiac—ask a psychiatrist—but I do know that a person who was any one of these things works overtime at being normal. In fact he's super normal until pressured. And then he blows up. I personally know a Queeg in every studio. . . ."

The interior scenes were shot back in Los Angeles, on the Columbia lot. The first to be filmed was the post-trial scene following the not guilty verdict for Maryk. The celebrating officers—Johnson, MacMurray, and the others—await José Ferrer, playing Lieutenant Barney Greenwald, Maryk's defense attorney, who, rather than joining in their revelry, tells them off and reminds them of Queeg's lifetime of service. Ferrer, instead of drinking his champagne, throws it in MacMurray's face.

The actors rehearsed the scene several times. Then came the first take. The door opened, heads turned, and Ferrer walked in, on his knees. "Anybody want to buy a painting?"

There was no joking around with Queeg's courtroom scene. The movie would fall or stand largely on his monologue. Crew members, caught up in their jobs, generally pay attention to lighting cues and other tasks rather than to the performance. On this occasion, though, they were aware that they were seeing something extraordinary. Stanley Kramer watched from the side and knew how right his choice of actor was. "Bogart's performance electrified the crew. There was utter silence and then they applauded. They were suddenly galvanized into a condition which I don't think they had expected, or if they knew about Bogart, at least they hadn't witnessed it firsthand."

The calm, quiet logic of Rick Blaine bent over his chessboard was now the agonized, inverted logic of Queeg, the chess player gone mad. Sometime after the film was released, a New York friend asked Bogart how he had managed to get that manic, paranoid look in his eyes in the close-ups. "Easy," he said. "I'm nuts, you know."

To cleanse himself of Queeg, Bogart went sailing on the *Santana.* At the first jostle from a wave, hundreds of little ball bearings hidden all over the boat by Frank Sinatra rolled out, clattering on the counters and deck. "I could have killed Frankie at first," he told Joe Hyams. "But it was a helluva gag."

The Caine Mutiny, though successful, fell short of the high expectations of the studio and of Stanley Kramer. For the maker of *High Noon, Judgment at Nuremberg, The Defiant Ones, Death of a Salesman,* and *Inherit the Wind,* it has never been a favorite. The initial Pentagon screening was far too well received for his liking: "Their reception made me suspicious of myself." In retrospect, he disagreed with the ending, José Ferrer's summation "that the Navy was inviolate. Maybe we were too much interested in seeing to it that the Navy's skirts were protected." In its review, *Time* called the film "handsome and expert but sometimes a little cold and loud. . . . a proper topside salute to all things Navy."

The cast, however, drew uniformly good reviews, and Bogart's were superb. Whatever the faults of the film, *Time* added that "he brings the hollow, driven, tyrannical character of Captain Queeg to full and invidious life, yet seldom fails to maintain a bond of sympathy with his audience. He deliberately gives Queeg the mannerisms and appearances of an officer of sternness and decision, and then gradually discloses him as a man who is bottling up a scream. . . ." "The massive close-up of Queeg in disintegration is almost as painful and terrifying as it is meant to be."

The Caine Mutiny took up the summer of 1953, and after the completion of filming, Bogart corresponded with Huston about *Beat the Devil,* then in post-production and showing every indication of swallowing all the money put into it. Huston had already declared his reservations—"It is more difficult for me to come to any opinion about it than any picture I've done"—and warned Bogart and Maree not to expect another *African Queen.* It might be "a very fine success," he wrote, but even though it was shot in black and white, "it cost hellishly. However, if the humor comes off—as I pray it will—I believe it will make some very tidy sums. . . . On the other hand, if the joke should fall flat—well, God help us!"

Huston refused to commit to a delivery date for the final cut. He was quoted in an overseas paper as saying he liked the film but that it was not his usual style and was not for one moment to be taken seriously. Afterward, John Woolf of Romulus wrote asking him to please not give the papers ammunition to shoot down the film.

When the print of *Beat the Devil* finally arrived, Bogart screened it for Morgan Maree, Dore Schary of MGM, Don Hartman of Paramount, William Wyler, and Billy Wilder, and found his misgivings confirmed. He cabled Huston that they couldn't tell if it was a straight melodrama or a comedy, and thought that the opening was confusing. Everyone agreed the picture needed *something.* Did he have any suggestions? Huston, on to *Moby Dick,* his next project, had none.

Audiences didn't know what to make of the film, either. When *Beat the Devil* opened in March 1954, it fulfilled almost every fear. In ads, the studio tried to play the picture for laughs:

YOU HAVE SEEN COLOR—DIMENSION—CINEMASCOPE
BUT NOW—WE PROUDLY PRESENT
ON THE SMALL FLAT SCREEN
BEAT THE DEVIL
IN GLORIOUS BLACK AND WHITE.

The joke fell flat. "It should have been called *Beat the Customer,*" one viewer wrote. Exhibitors complained to United Artists that they'd been had. It Baltimore, a theater owner called it "a hodgepodge of nothing," and refunded admission to keep customer good will. A New York City filmgoer said it "should go down as a freak picture in the Museum of Modern Art," obviously the worst insult he could think of. A Detroit-based chain of movie houses canceled its bookings after its management had seen an ad apologizing to patrons from a theater manager who had already shown it.

But *Beat the Devil* was a critical success. *The New Yorker* said the film was "a hugely entertaining work" and "a satire on melodramas dealing with international intrigue," and went on to praise its "bright lunacy that used to be a conspicuous virtue of Evelyn Waugh." *Time* found it "as elaborate a shaggy-dog story as has ever been told. . . . A sort of screwball classic."

Bogart seemed almost lighthearted about the potential losses of a project in which the Santana investment was about $400,000 of his own money. He sent the comments on to Huston in London:

> Enclosed please find several letters from grateful customers and also grateful exhibitors who have been privileged to exhibit and see "the thing." As you can see by the ads, the exhibitors are behind us all the way. I'm afraid too far behind—say about one million dollars. In spite of all this it looks as though we'll just about scrape through and to cheer you up, I met a weird character the other day who almost knocked me down screaming "but I liked it, I liked it!"

Through Joe Hyams's column in the New York *Herald Tribune,* Bogart blasted exhibitors, calling them "the parasite of the film business," who "sit on their asses and criticize creative people who invest their own time, talent and money making a picture that the exhibitor . . . can make money with." Two days later he was on the phone to Hyams, complaining of calls from furious exhibitors and blaming the columnist for "the blast I let you con me into making." Before Hyams could rise to his own defense, Bogart added slyly, "It was a good piece, kid. Looks like we told them off, huh?"

Nearly two decades after its release, critic Charles Champlin wrote that "in its rather quirky way [*Beat the Devil*] is about loyalty, and loyalty is a theme that runs through so much of Huston's work. . . . It's also a celebration of rascals, lowlifes, underdogs and born losers." When Champlin told Jennifer Jones that his favorite of her roles was Gwendolen, "she smiled thinly and said, 'When Johnny was persuading me to do it,' he said, 'Jennifer, they'll remember you longer for *Beat the Devil* than for *Song of Bernadette.* I think the S.O.B. was right.' "

Regardless of the disappointing receipts for *Beat the Devil,* Bogart and Huston talked incessantly about the idea for their next film, an adaptation of Rudyard Kipling's *The Man Who Would Be King.* The project was announced with fanfare, and the co-star in the story of two raffish British soldiers in nineteenth-century Asia was variously announced as Clark Gable or Spencer Tracy. But the venture was continually postponed. First Bogart wasn't available, then Huston was tied up. There were rumored billing problems between Bogart and Tracy. Huston was off doing something else. (He finally made the picture in 1975 with Sean Connery and Michael Caine.) Maybe the real reason for the delay was that the comparative failure of *Beat the Devil* weighed more heavily on both men than they were ready to admit, even to themselves.

The newspapers and fan magazines were full of stories of Bogart's success—the Holmby Hills mansion; two Jaguars in the garage, one for Bacall and one for him; an oceangoing racing yacht; international celebrity; and an unassailable position for Mr. and Mrs. Bogart atop the movie industry's social pyramid. But publicist Walter Shenson found Bogart looking drawn and ill.

In late summer 1953, Shenson, who had worked on *The Caine Mutiny,* came by the house with photographs of Bogart, Bacall, and Stephen taken aboard an aircraft carrier in Hawaii. The ship's captain had given the three of them a private tour, and he sent transparencies to Bogart. Because not many labs at the time were equipped to make prints from transparencies, Bogart had asked Shenson if Columbia could help so that he could send a set to the captain. Since Columbia had got free use of an aircraft carrier, not to mention a three-thousand-sailor crew as unpaid extras, it seemed a pretty good trade. But Harry Cohn, as cheap as they came, said no. Shenson's more sensible boss in publicity told him to go ahead and covered the expense with a bogus lunch.

Bogart invited Shenson in for a drink. While they talked, Bogart, complaining of an upset stomach, ate antacids steadily, little bits of chalky residue gathering at the edges of his mouth. Bogart continually cleared them away by putting two fingers at the corners and pulling down in what had become almost a signature gesture of his screen character. He smiled as he looked at the pictures. "I'll mail these on. I'm going to write the captain and thank him for his cooperation. And I'll keep a set of these things."

At the same time, Warner Bros. Pictures, Inc., was reviewing its options of what to do with Humphrey Bogart. A summary of his contract and appearances in Warner films since the 1946 agreement showed that he had done four pictures for the studio (*The Treasure of the Sierra Madre, Key Largo, Chain Lightning,* and *The Enforcer,* made for United States Pictures but released by Warners) and nine outside, with a tenth under serious consideration. The three scripts Warners had sent Bogart in the past two years for his approval had been rejected. Not only had he not made a picture for Warners in nearly three years, the last two he had made were duds. Meanwhile the studio's supposed major star had won an Academy Award for Horizon-Romulus, a dinky independent, and had just scored a critical and commercial success for Columbia, a lesser Warner Brothers. It was time to admit the obvious.

A headline in the September 22 *New York Times* announced "BOGART, WARNERS END 15-YEAR PACT / STAR RELEASED FROM CONTRACT SIGNED IN 1946, FAILURE TO AGREE ON PICTURES CITED."

The union with Warners, so fruitful for both sides, had lasted longer than many Hollywood marriages, but like so many of them, it was dead long before the divorce. "Mr. Bogart," the story explained, "who starred in some of Warners' biggest money-makers, including *Casablanca,* said he would 'be most happy to do pictures with Warners in the future.' Jack L. Warner, vice president of the studio, wished the actor well and said, 'Our association has been most productive and together we have made some very fine pictures.' " Omitted from the statement were the usual studio wishes that Mr. Bogart, in some happier time, might return to the lot.

The bitterness between the studio and Bogart had become too corrosive. Warners had once again reexamined his contract to see if there was a loophole in their favor. Possibly they found one, perhaps Bogart decided his constant rejection of below-par Warner scripts was no longer worth the aggravation. Even though Warners was paying him for pictures that he wasn't making and Maree advised him against terminating what film people referred to as "an annuity," Bogart wanted out. The agreement absolved both parties of any obligation to one another. It was eighteen years and twelve days since Humphrey Bogart had signed (by proxy) the studio's minimum artist's contract guaranteeing him three weeks' work on *The Petrified Forest.*

For most of those years, he had toiled at the whim of Jack Warner, who treated him hellishly. With his last contract, he gained the independence he had so long sought, but then the studio dealt with his wife cavalierly and nearly destroyed her career. In the past, when it was just a matter of his own contract, Bogart several times had given in to pressure. But when Warners mishandled Bacall, he supported her rebellion. In helping to free her from the studio, he seemed to find the impetus to finally free himself, and at last to beat the devil in his professional life, Jack L. Warner.

CHAPTER 24

The Old Bull

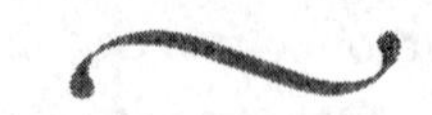

In the seven months since February 1953, in a time before jet travel, Bogart had filmed in Italy, Britain, Hawaii, and Los Angeles. *Beat the Devil* had been especially taxing because of his worries over its cost and whether the picture would make its money back. Earlier in his career, his stamina and recuperative powers would have eased these burdens, but now he was fifty-four, tired, and in uncertain health. Although it was time to visit a doctor, not start another film, Bogart refused to see his physician. Instead, he started *Sabrina* in early September and, four days after signing the Warners release, traveled to New York for location shooting on Long Island. His decision to make the film had been the breaking point with Warners, for whom he had become a star in name only; had he stayed with the studio, *Sabrina* would have been his eighth consecutive outside film. For the first time since early in his film career he was without a long-term contract, but the measure of success for an actor, he always said, was to keep working.

Sabrina, a Cinderella comedy about a chauffeur's daughter who wins the hearts of the two heirs of a rich Long Island family, was hardly the usual Bogart story. It began as a Broadway play by Samuel Taylor starring Joseph Cotten in the role of Linus Larrabee, the stuffy, class-conscious elder brother who hopes to increase the family's already vast wealth through the marriage of his playboy younger brother, David, to the daughter of an industrial magnate. All goes smoothly until Sabrina returns from a year in France, a beautiful and sophisticated young woman instead of the gawky girl who grew up on the estate and earlier attempted suicide because of an unrequited infatuation with David. Now David falls for her, and Linus, to protect the merger-marriage, pretends to woo Sabrina away from David, only to lose his heart to her too. For the film adaptation to be directed by Billy Wilder, Linus was written for Cary Grant, who was the embodiment of suave and ageless elegance. He was also unavailable.

Phil Gersh takes credit for getting Bogart to consider the part. Gersh, who had heard that Audrey Hepburn was to play the title role and William Holden that of the younger brother, saw a draft of the unfinished script and liked what he saw. The young agent occasionally played tennis with Wilder and called to suggest Bogart for the part. "Listen Phil," Wilder told him, "you've got a good forehand and a great service, but you don't know anything about casting. Forget it!"

Two weeks later, Wilder was back in touch. He had been thinking about Bogart and wanted to talk with him. An informal late-afternoon meeting was set up at Gersh's house. Wilder brought Samuel Taylor, who was working with him on the adaptation. As was usual at such meetings, there were cocktails and small talk. At seven-thirty, the film had yet to discussed, but everyone had to leave for other appointments. Bogart said, "Look, Billy, don't tell me the story. I just want you to shake hands with me, that you'll take care of me. I don't have to read the script if I have your handshake." Wilder promised he would take care of him, and they shook hands.

A deal on a handshake. All friendly and sociable, with no indication of the bitterness to come.

Of all the Hollywood talents at the time, none was considered more outstanding than the forty-seven-year-old Wilder. He was a brilliant writer, a brilliant director, and a brilliant producer with a string of classics to his credit: *Ninotchka* (1939), *Double Indemnity* (1944), *The Lost Weekend* (1945), *Sunset Boulevard* (1950), *Stalag 17* (1953). His range was as broad as his talent. He was also known for his cruelty to his collaborators, his needling, and his gratuitous insults. His colleagues either loved him or hated him. In this sense he resembled Bogart too much for the good of either man.

After the first day of shooting, Bogart phoned Gersh from the studio, asking him to come right away. "Billy was shooting Bogart from the back of his neck and the close-ups were on Holden and Hepburn, both of whom were old friends of his. Bogie said, 'I don't even need my hairpiece;

the guy's shooting me from behind.' I told Wilder, 'Billy, you're not keeping faith. You shook hands. I was there.' We raised such hell that Bogie came off very well in the picture."

Wilder's memories, in contrast to Gersh's, were of an impossible star whose on-set tantrums bordered on paranoia. According to Wilder biographer Maurice Zolotow, Bogart started the picture with a grudge, knowing he was second choice to Cary Grant. He resented Wilder's friendship with Holden, resented even the gentle Audrey Hepburn. "She's all right if you like 47 takes," he said. (In a biography of Wilder by Kevin Lally, Wilder claimed that Hepburn "conspired with [Wilder] to hold up completion of the day's work whenever he was running short of screenplay pages.")

Bogart, so accustomed to the camaraderie of Huston and the friendliness of other directors, was discomfited by Wilder's closeness to his co-stars, who were at a high point in their careers. Holden was still basking in his success in *Sunset Boulevard* (1950); his performance in *Stalag 17* (1953) was about to earn him an Oscar. And Hepburn, twenty-two, radiant and fresh from her triumph with Gregory Peck in *Roman Holiday* (1953), was on the verge of an Oscar herself. The director and the two actors made a convivial threesome, and they were joined in Holden's trailer by writer Ernest Lehman, who had taken over the script from Taylor. Evidently no one thought of inviting Bogart. Then again, probably no one observing one of the biggest stars in Hollywood, with one of the world's loveliest women waiting for him at home, would have guessed the wells of insecurity tapped by his exclusion. Bogart was just as likely not to participate if asked. But he *did* want to be asked, and he took refuge in the anger and sarcasm that were his traditional armor.

Holden felt his resentment. The younger actor, studying his lines off-camera and smoking a cigarette while Bogart was filming, saw him uncharacteristically muff his lines during a take. Wilder asked what the trouble was. "It's that fucking Holden back there!" Bogart exploded. "Waving cigarettes around and throwing paper in the air." To Holden, the outburst was a holdover of their personality clash fifteen years before while making *Invisible Stripes;* but there may have been other reasons. Now in his mid-thirties, Holden was still a golden boy whose shining exterior concealed the alcoholism that later killed him, and in the film and on the set, he was a symbol of everything Bogart was not.

Wilder was under pressures of his own, for which he blamed Bogart. "He gave me a rough time. I had lots of rewriting because of the recasting of the part. I was exhausted. I couldn't devote myself to personal contact." But the truth was that Wilder began with an unfinished script and compounded the problem by his abrasive behavior toward his collaborators. (Raymond Chandler—a prickly person himself—felt Wilder was so arbitrary and demeaning during their writing of *Double Indemnity* that he once walked out of a session and refused to work with him any longer, although he did eventually continue.) Ernest Lehman, who had stepped in after Wilder's harshness drove Taylor away, told Zolotow of "a quality of desperation" as they turned out pages. Wilder directed by day, wrote at night, and lived on coffee and cigarettes while trying to keep the script twenty-four hours ahead of shooting. On occasion, Wilder would stall for time by having the lighting director make unneeded adjustments while the next scene came out of the typewriter. The stress drove Lehman to uncontrollable weeping and nervous exhaustion, and the production had to be shut down for two days while he recovered. To Lehman, Wilder was someone who deliberately created a frenetic atmosphere out of "some unconscious need for crises." Several times, Wilder, who suffered from excruciating back pains, went into New York for medical relief at the hands of Dr. Max Jacobson, known as "Dr. Feelgood," a man who eased the strains of his celebrity patients with shots of amphetamines.

Wilder did not appreciate Bogart's mischief-making. Bogart once tried to bait him by saying, "Huston has told me who he thought the ten greatest directors were and you were not on the list. Isn't that Huston a bum?" Wilder didn't bite. "Bogart has a peculiar sense of humor," he said later. "It is both impish and sadistic." They were words Wilder knew; "impish and sadistic" is a description often used by others about him. He himself had learned all about needling from the master, Eric von Stroheim, the prototypical tyrant of the set whom he directed in *Sunset Boulevard.* "I'm in the major leagues [of needlers]," Wilder said of himself. Actors, he declared, were "a special breed between a human being and an amoeba." (Wilder was equally put out by Marilyn Monroe on *The Seven Year Itch* and *Some Like It Hot.* After the second film was released in 1959, he was quoted as saying that "the Directors Guild should award him a Purple Heart.")

Bogart, more tired than he realized, on unfamiliar ground, and feeling rejected, showed the signs of the friendless boy he had been at Trinity forty-five years earlier. He hit out in all directions, even mimicking Wilder's Teutonic accent in front of the company. In these outbursts, Wilder was "a kraut bastard," "a Prussian," and "a Nazi son of a bitch," the worst thing he could think of calling anybody. Wilder, a Jew who grew up in Vienna and whose mother, unbeknownst to Bogart, had died at Auschwitz, was deeply offended.

"I examine your face, Bogie," Wilder retorted in one instance, ". . . your ugly face, and I know that somewhere underneath the sickening face of a shit—is a *real* shit." This kind of exchange on other Bogart films might have passed as macho banter, but here it was heartfelt.

Relations were not improved by Bogart's refusal, even in the face of production delays, to work beyond the 6:00 P.M. cutoff stipulated in his contract. Promptly on the hour Verita Peterson gave him a scotch and water, which he downed and then walked off the set. "You want me to kill him now or later?" Holden at one point asked Wilder. For Bogart, this was one more sign that it was him against the company. In many ways, he was behaving like Dixon Steele.

Wilder spent an evening at Bogart's house, trying to placate him, but on the set their battle continued with ever-growing bitterness. Bogart might be the star, but Wilder was the director and more than Bogart's equal when it came to exercising power and control.

Rumors circulated that the play's ending, in which the Bogart character goes off to Paris and a life with Sabrina, was to change so that she chose Holden. Bogart, sensitive about his age, walked around the set muttering, " 'I'm gonna get fucked. . . . I'm not gonna get the girl.' This was Wilder's most effective thrust," Zolotow wrote. "He deliberately kept Bogart in suspense, torturing him, until the last few days of filming."

Wilder suffered in his own way. After the final shot, Lehman watched him declare the film a wrap, then look up to the heavens and "screech: 'Fuck you!' "

However difficult the filming was for both men, once the cameras rolled, Bogart the artist took over. "He is an extremely competent S.O.B.," Wilder said afterward. "He comes on the set on time, but completely unprepared. But in the time the lights are set . . . he knows his lines." In one breath Wilder would call him "evil, a bore, a coward, a man who would turn and run like a weasel," and in the next characterize him as "a tremendously competent actor with a tremendous presence and an odd quality that comes off. [He is] small of stature, but: rough and tough. He is what every American would like to be."

None of the splenetic behavior on the set shows on the screen. Bogart the tantrum-thrower garnered some of his best reviews as the sober, steady Linus. *The New York Times* called *Sabrina* "the most delightful comedy-romance in years." It was of course Hepburn's film, tailored to her special qualities. "But it is just as much Mr. Bogart's picture, for he is incredibly adroit. . . . the skill with which this old rock-ribbed actor blends the gags and such duplicities with the manly manner of melting is one of the incalculable joys of this show."

Bogart and Wilder were professional enough to know that nobody benefited from a feud in a tightly knit community like Hollywood. "We parted as enemies," Wilder said the next year, "but we finally made up." Evidence suggests that their antagonism was at worst an on-again off-again affair. When a nervous Bogart wanted an expert opinion on the final cut of *Beat the Devil,* it was Wilder, among others, whom he turned to for advice. In the weeks after the filming of *Sabrina* finished, *Daily Variety* mentioned both Wilder and Bogart as part of a group including John Huston, Clark Gable, and William Wyler that was considering going into business with Allied Artists, an umbrella company that would finance productions by big-name independents. And months later, at a party at the Danny Kayes, Bogart appeared to be very friendly with the Wilders. A photograph shows him laughing, with the lovely, smiling Audrey Wilder slung over his shoulders like a sack of potatoes—the same way that Linus Larabee carries Sabrina after her attempted suicide.

In January 1954, Bogart went to Rome to make *The Barefoot Contessa,* written and directed by Joseph Mankiewicz. The filming went well, but the relations were cool between Bogart and the female lead, Ava Gardner, who was then separated from her husband, the Bogarts' friend Frank Sinatra.

The story is a commentary on the people and ways of the movie business without the bite of *In a Lonely Place.* Once again, Bogart plays a broken-down man whose drinking and personality have put his career in jeopardy—and he is the nicest guy in the picture. The millionaire producer (Warren Stevens) is a sadistic bully, the press agent (Edmond O'Brien, who won an Oscar) is a gutless sycophant, and the charming prince with whom the Cinderella dancer should live happily ever after is a castrated count. Bogart is fine as Harry Dawes, the cynical-but-decent director-narrator who saves his career by making a star out of a flamenco dancer from the slums of Madrid, but where *In a Lonely Place* goes for the solar plexus, *The Barefoot Contessa* attempts to be an exposé while going for the handkerchief. One never knows what Dixon Steele will do next; his unpredictable and contradictory nature, so dramatically captured by Bogart, is what drives the picture. Dawes is not so complicated; his flaws are merely the springboard for his redemption. Mankiewicz, who wrote and directed *All About Eve* (1950), arguably the best picture ever made about backstage Broadway, was less successful in portraying off-set Hollywood.

Bacall arrived after shooting was under way, and Howard and Dee Hawks stopped for a while en route to Egypt. William Faulkner was in Rome, too, and the group frequently met for drinks and dinner. Dee Hawks Cramer was standing at a bar one night when "Bogart *slapped* my behind. He kind of looked at me and said, 'Oh kid, you don't have a *chance*! You don't have an *ass*! You're no good for *anything* there!' I was so skinny; 110 pounds of bones. 'Now look at that,' and he points to Betty. He *adored* her figure. Adored her behind. Loved to get his hands on it. He was cute about it; he felt sorry for me. Everybody felt sorry for me—married to the monster."

Bogart's adoration of Bacall did not prevent his fighting with her. "The pitched battles they would have were non-stop," Cramer said. At parties, Bacall's patience with Bogart's baiting of others would wear out; at home, there was recurring resentment of her career—"Actresses!"—though he'd never married anyone who did anything else. He made it clear that, by working, she was neglecting her children, the house, and (while unstated) him most of all. He knew where you were vulnerable, Bacall later told Joe Hyams. She had been needled so often, she said, that she was sure her psyche looked like a dope addict's arm. She always gave as good as she got, however. Cramer could never understand "why they didn't kill each other with those arguments, but they had this marvelous relationship."

In June, Bogart was the subject of a cover story in *Time* magazine. "In spite of being neither young nor handsome, Bogart is a much-sought-after leading man. . . . Few screen personalities are so elastic and subtly adaptable; few stars can so convincingly and smoothly accomplish the trick of fitting the character to themselves. . . . [He] manages to achieve surprising range and depth while still remaining the familiar figure with whom millions expect to renew an acquaintance when they pay at the box office to see a Bogart film."

That September, the house in Holmby Hills was opened up to TV cameras for *Person to Person,* the top-ten-rated interview show produced and hosted by the fabled newsman Edward R. Murrow. The program, a fifties *Lifestyles of the Rich and Famous,* put the definitive imprimatur on celebrityhood. The show was easy for the Bogarts, who shared Murrow's liberal interests. All three belonged to the inner circle of prominent figures in TV, politics, journalism, and the movies. Murrow had first met Bacall while taking a behind-the-scenes role in the Stevenson campaign. An uncompromising journalist, he had set the standard for radio broadcast reporting with his dispatches from London during World War II. Despite such fluff as *Person to Person,* he set equally high standards for television in his special reports, most famously on the deplorable conditions under which migrant workers toiled, and in his devastating March 1954 *See It Now* interview with Senator Joseph McCarthy, which helped to bring down the demagogue. Both Murrow and Bogart were exemplars of the cigarette-smoking, hard-drinking, determinedly manly ideal held up in those days for journalists and movie tough guys.

Bacall, informally dressed in dark slacks and a light blouse, was the star of the telecast. Concealing her nervousness at appearing on live television, she played the camera with the deftness of a veteran, answering prearranged questions with ease. Holding up her wrist to show the bracelet with the gold whistle given her by Bogart in 1945, she delivered a humorous re-creation of the now-famous lines from *To Have and Have Not.* John Horne, a producer on the show and later a television columnist, wrote that Bogart, "who could easily have dominated the situation, played the supporting role in scenes with his wife, deferring to Betty, feeding lines like a straight man. Greater love hath no actor."

Person to Person reinforced the picture of Battling Bogart at last settled down as a comfortable, respectable family man. "The 'bad boy' is becoming a very sedate citizen of the town," Louella Parsons wrote approvingly. He even had kind words for Warner Brothers, remembering his years under contract in the same way he remembered Mayo. "I miss my battles with Jack," he told Parsons. "No one ever gave me such good insults as he did. . . . If he should hand me a script that I like, I'd accept it without a minute's delay. I had some wonderful years at Warner's studio . . . and I realize they were largely responsible for what was to follow in my career."

Stephen and Leslie, wearing pajamas, made cameo appearances during the *Person to Person* show. Stephen remembers his father as a remote parent, neither strictly disciplining nor overtly affectionate. "He was probably scared of me. I was scared of *my* kids, so I could see it—here's a little kid and you think they might break, or you might screw them up for life. So I think he was kind of in awe of this little person running around." There were moments of comradeship, such as the day the *Santana* was moored off Catalina. Stephen swam from the shore to the boat. "I was maybe six or seven. They had Pete [Carl Peterson, the captain] come out in the dinghy and come beside me; but I swam all the way to the boat. And I remember my father was very proud of me."

Joe Hyams accompanied father and son on an overnight train ride to San Francisco to visit Bacall, who was on location for a John Wayne picture, *Blood Alley* (1955). Bogart had asked Hyams, who also had young children, to come along because he was nervous about a night alone with a seven-year-old. After the porter woke the two men in the morning, Hyams saw Bogart move over to where Stephen was sleeping and kiss him on the forehead. Bogart tugged quizzically at one earlobe. Then in a gruff voice, he woke the boy up. Later he said to Hyams, "I guess maybe I had the kid too late in life. I just don't know what to do about him. But I love him. I hope he knows that."

Bacall's mother Natalie was a great influence on Stephen. On her visits from New York, she didn't hesitate to keep him in line. "We used to go swimming. I remember dunking my sister and my grandmother saying, 'If you dunk your sister again I'm going to dunk you!' And *boom* goes the sister, and *boom* goes me. I come up swearing at her and she goes, '*You talk to me like that?*' Later, in the sixties when I had some problems, she was the one that came to talk to me. She was a *great* lady."

Leslie Howard Bogart would remember little of the father who died when she was four. *Life* photographer Philip Stern recorded what seems the essence of their relationship, or lack of it, father and daughter posed at opposite ends of a seesaw. Bogart, sitting in a business suit, looks sadly protective of and yet disconnected from the tiny creature on the other side, who is poised with the delicacy of a Dresden figurine, a look of intensity on her small face.

Bogart was one of the most sought-after talents in the movies, but on those rare occasions when there was no project at hand, his actor's vulnerability quickly surfaced. He hung around Romanoff's for extended lunches in his regular booth, the second from the left as one entered the restaurant. He regarded it as his own; any attempt on Mike Romanoff's part to seat him elsewhere met with stiff resistance. Bogart often asked Phil Gersh along to keep him company, and to pick up the tab as an agency write off. His meal never varied and the waiters knew him so well they would never ask what he wanted or show him a menu. He would have two scotch-and-sodas. (Often after the second he would turn to Gersh and say, "Hey kid, so that's it, huh? No scripts, nobody wants me.

Guess I'm through! Go back to the boat and I'll pack it in.") Then he would have an Omelette Sylvia, a rich concoction of cheese, eggs, and vegetables, with toasted French bread. He would drink a glass of milk with the meal, followed by coffee, and after that, a very good brandy. Then he would go home and take a nap.

The routine was important in a lifestyle that Romanoff, an Eastern European who carried the surname of the Russian Imperial family and knew that nothing was ever what it seemed, characterized as unreal. Romanoff felt that everyone in the movie business suffered from what he called "occupational neurosis," the result of the preposterous wealth they had. The unaccustomed wealth bred uncertainty that it would last, along with a sense that the money was unearned. The result of the uncertainty was the fear that each new picture would be a flop, which would mean the end of making such a preposterous salary. "If they could be examined while asleep, their heartbeats would not be steady."

To Romanoff, who had known Bogart for fifteen years and liked him very much, he was a man in search of an identity other than that of actor. "Bogie is in constant anxiety to be what he calls a character, to distinguish himself away from his occupation. . . . He has never allowed his [own] character to develop. [He] would love nothing better than to be considered a character, even more than a good actor. [He] does not like his career and at the same time he is proud of it."

Bogart and Romanoff had a celebrated friendship—Bogie and Mike trading insults, Bogie and Mike playing chess into the afternoon after the lunch crowd had left and the waiters cleared the tables. "This is his club," Romanoff told a reporter, "just as his yacht is. Where he gets away, where he finds stimulation. . . . He likes getting away from home and certain responsibilities." Every new story about the pair quickly circulated, such as Romanoff insisting that Bogart adhere to the restaurant's dress code by wearing a tie, and Bogart showing up in a nearly invisible one-inch enameled bow tie attached to a pin, made by the wife of his sailing friend George Roosevelt.

Romanoff knew that Bogart, who undertipped, never picked up a lunch tab, never carried money, and had to scrounge a dollar from his agent to pay the parking valet, had also taken care of his mother, paid for a sister in a private sanitarium, given generously to his friend Eric Hatch during a lean time, and worried about providing for the children who came along so late in life. The man whom Romanoff characterized as "the most generous and kindest man" was the same man who at times went out of his way to be a boor.

Bogart's drinking was more controlled than in the days with Mayo. He didn't drink on the set, as Errol Flynn did, but the scotch and water had to be waiting at the end of a day of shooting. (However, Verita Peterson Thompson said that in her makeup case she smuggled in a bottle that he sometimes opened during the day.) There were times, though—between jobs or on a day he wasn't shooting—when drinking became a substitute for meaningful work.

Once during Bogart's last years at Warners, he was in the office of Hal Wallis's assistant Walter MacEwen to read a script. Unsteady and mumbling, the actor kept dropping pages. On another occasion, Bogart, filming at Columbia, turned up in Cohn's office suite plainly drunk. Cohn was out of town, and his inner office door, normally locked, was uncharacteristically ajar. Bogart lurched in and announced, "I want a drink of Harry Cohn's booze." Bogart plunked himself down in Cohn's desk chair, hit the keys on the intercom, and told whoever answered, "You're fired!" or "You get a raise."

In December 1954, Bogart sold Santana Productions to Columbia Pictures for $1,000,000, and was also considering a separate deal proposed by Columbia, to star in a picture a year for six years. Because the million dollars was a capital gain, it was taxed at only 25 percent, which left Bogart with a large lump sum for "Betty and the kids. An actor lives in a world of anxiety and insecurity. He can't spread his big-money years over a lifetime like a businessman, he has to grab the bundle while he can. It is his only defense." He had a copy made of the million-dollar check and hung it on the wall of his den "to have something nice to look at. It's a helluva lot prettier and more impressive to me than a painting worth seven hundred and fifty thousand dollars."

Santana never became the independent developer of young talent that Bogart had hoped it would be. As early as October of 1949, he and Morgan Maree had considered closing it once production was completed on *In a Lonely Place.* But *Tokyo Joe* (American in Tokyo reluctantly becomes a smuggler and blackmailer to protect his family) and *Knock on Any Door,* both released in 1949 and neither a great hit, turned respectable profits. In fact all Santana's films made money, with the exception of *Sirocco* (1951), a story about gunrunners in 1920s Syria, which Bogart himself labeled "a stinker."

One major drawback was that despite its success, Santana still could not compete with the major studios for choice properties. In mid-1954

Bogart wanted to buy *The Desperate Hours,* a best-selling novel about a midwestern family terrorized by a group of criminals who take over their home. But as they had on *Detective Story,* William Wyler and Paramount outbid Santana.

The story, based on actual events, seemed suited for any medium. Paul Newman had had the lead in the successful Broadway run. By way of introduction to his review of the play in *The New York Times,* Brooks Atkinson wrote: "It is a cops-and-jailbirds yarn by Joseph Hayes, who wrote it first in the shape of a taut novel. It is also a movie, though not to be released until next year; and a decade from now it will be a musical drama with a brassy orchestration and a symbolic ballet."

This time, however, though he had lost his bid on the property, Bogart was a free agent. For all the problems on *Sabrina,* Paramount was more than ready for him to do another film for the studio; his name was a guaranteed box office draw, and he got on well with production head Don Hartman. (The two men were in a real estate deal for the development of what Bogart called "a lot of property" near the future Disneyland, forty-five minutes south of Los Angeles.) To Wyler, Bogart as the psychotic gunman Glenn Griffin was perfect, a combination of Babyface Martin and Duke Mantee revisited. Bogart agreed to do the part without prior consultation with his agents Mary Baker, Sam Jaffe, and Phil Gersh. He talked to them from Wyler's office and said, "If I can't buy [it], at least I can play in it."

Another reason for Bogart's interest in *The Desperate Hours* was that it offered the chance to play opposite Spencer Tracy, who was scheduled to have the part of the stalwart father of the family—the test of wills between him and Griffin is the spine of the story. Tracy and Bogart had not appeared together in a film for twenty-five years and wanted to work together again. Each, asked who the top actor in Hollywood was, would, with a twinkle in his eye, put himself first, the other second. Later accounts alleged that Tracy's participation foundered over top billing, but Gersh said that it was never an issue. "Bogie called Tracy in my presence and said, 'Spence, before we kick off, let's do a show together. And if you want first billing, you can have first billing. I don't care about that.' And Spence said, yeah, he'd like to do it, but somehow he backed out." The role was taken by Fredric March.

During the filming, Wyler's meticulous work habits, which required a multitude of takes, was not suited to Bogart's contractual right to stop at 6:00 P.M., so Gersh would come each evening around five-thirty to remind Wyler that it was nearly time to quit for the day. In a version of

Wyler's making Bogart repeatedly practice flipping a knife point into an orange peel while making *Dead End* nearly twenty years earlier, "One evening Willy had Bogart running up and down some stairs. He'd say, 'A little faster, Bogie.' And Bogie would go faster. Then he'd say, 'No, too fast.' It must have been twenty takes." When Bogart became winded, Wyler called a break and Gersh suggested to Bogart, "Go over to Willy and ask him to show you; let *him* run up and down the steps." Bogart smiled wickedly. " 'Yeah, I like that,' and promptly called out, 'Why don't you show me exactly the way you want it?' And Willy Wyler said, 'All right, that's a wrap for the evening.' "

The Desperate Hours was not the huge hit it was expected to be. "Maybe it was because of the 'dignity' label on the film," Bogart told the press, "they didn't let people know it was a gangster film. Maybe it's because of Mom-ism these days and no one cares if Pop is in danger of having his head bashed in."

Nineteen fifty-five was Bogart's busiest year. "After two decades in films and years before that on the Broadway stage, he is at the top of his career," Sheila Graham wrote in her Hollywood column. "Bogey has enough commitments for the next two years. The public loves him, men as well as women and all age groups, and his bank account is fat."

In February, almost immediately after finishing *The Desperate Hours,* he began *The Left Hand of God* at Twentieth Century–Fox. Bogart worked again with Edward Dmytryk, playing an American adventurer impersonating a priest in wartime China. His co-star was Gene Tierney, the beautiful heroine of *Laura* (1944). A few years earlier, Tierney had been emotionally devastated by the birth of her mentally retarded daughter, the result of German measles contracted during a USO tour when she was pregnant.

Although Tierney had appeared in over thirty films, her fragility was evident during shooting. She came to work not knowing her lines, or forgot them on the set, and seemed constantly fearful. Bogart criticized her once before he understood the depth of her trouble, but then he realized how much she resembled his sister Frances. After that, he did all he could to encourage Tierney and find ways to do scenes so her frailty did not show. Over lunch or at the day's end, Bogart talked earnestly with her, gently urging her to get medical attention. Following the end of her relationship with Aly Khan after production on *The Left Hand of God* ended, she would suffer a nervous breakdown and be hospitalized for a year and a half.

A few years earlier, for all his grousing while making *Deadline U.S.A.,*

Bogart had been worried by Ethel Barrymore's disregard of a continual cough. At one point he burst out in concern, "Damn it! Will you see a doctor?" His demeanor with the afflicted was in stark contrast to his deflating of the comfortable. "He was, I think, a very caring man," Dmytryk said.

Soon after the film with Dmytryk was finished, Bogart went to Paramount to make *We're No Angels,* about three Devil's Island convicts on work release who play guardian angels to a befuddled storekeeper and his family. Directed without much flash by Michael Curtiz, it is nonetheless an amusing picture. Bogart is used largely as the straight man to his fellow convicts Peter Ustinov and Aldo Ray, and to a pet adder named Adolph, who conveniently bites the movie's villains at the proper time to kill them and move the story along.

Bogart's best contribution to the film happened off-screen. Joan Bennett, who plays the still-attractive mother of the embattled family, was married to his neighbor Walter Wanger. In 1951 scandal descended on the Wanger household when the producer, no model of fidelity himself, took exception to his wife having an affair with her agent, Jennings Lang. The dispute ended with Wanger accosting Lang in a parking lot and shooting him in the groin. Lang recovered, Wanger served a slap-on-the-wrist few months in jail (the first picture he made after his release was *Riot in Cell Block 11*), but Bennett was blackballed. An actress with sixty-five films to her credit and a woman who made maturity glamorous in *Father of the Bride* (1950), she was suddenly unemployable. By the time *We're No Angels* was shot, she hadn't worked—outside of a low-budget crime movie—in almost three years. Paramount was opposed to using her, but Bogart, who had supported her throughout the domestic mess, told the studio that he wouldn't do the film without her. Bennett said, "He made the stand to show what he thought of the underground movement to stamp me out. . . . I'll never forget Bogie's and Betty's kindness and warmth."

The so-called Rat Pack was formed in the spring of 1955, at the end of a chartered expedition to Las Vegas that spring to see Noël Coward's opening at the Desert Inn. Frank Sinatra organized the trip, and other travelers besides the Bogarts included Mike and Gloria Romanoff, David Niven and his wife Hjordis, agent Irving Lazar and Martha Hyer, songwriter Jimmy Van Heusen and actress Angie Dickinson, Charlie Feldman and model Capucine, the George Axelrods, screenwriter Charles Lederer, and Judy Garland and Sid Luft. After four days of partying, Bacall "surveyed the wreckage of the party" and declared, "You look like a god damn rat pack."

"With that," Nathaniel Benchley wrote, "the group became official." Officers were elected at a dinner back in Beverly Hills at Romanoff's. "Sinatra was named Pack Leader. Betty was Den Mother, Bogie was Director of Public Relations, and Sid Luft was Acting Cage Master." Benchley himself, though not in Las Vegas, became "Honorary Recording Secretary, but since there was little to record the post was a hollow one. It consisted mainly of designing a Pack coat of arms"—a rat gnawing on a human hand—"with Bogie's motto: 'never rat on a rat.' "

During a visit to New York, Bacall told columnist Earl Wilson that the group's aims were "to drink a lot of bourbon and stay up late." Bogart added that "you have to be a little musical" to be a member. Referring to the panda incident, Bogart said that he had retired from nightclub fighting. "I stay out of trouble spots. I go to '21' or to Pavilion. Who can I fight at the Pav—Mrs. Vanderbilt?" The photo accompanying the interview was of Bogart reading in horned-rimmed glasses while lounging in his suite at the St. Regis, his bare feet virtually sticking into the camera lens.

Still on his agenda for the year was *The Harder They Fall,* based on Budd Schulberg's novel about corruption in boxing, and in January 1956 a return to Warner Brothers under the aegis of Milton Sperling's United States Pictures for *Melville Goodwin, U.S.A.,* based on John Marquand's novel. The story had good roles for both Bogart and Bacall, providing them with their first opportunity to work together since *Key Largo.* Sperling was an unpretentious man who had worked his way up even though he was Harry Warner's son-in-law. He had served in combat with the Marines in the Pacific and was a conscientious producer whose good, solid films were well-received and paid their way, including Bogart's 1951 picture *The Enforcer.*

And there were plans to do an adaptation of C. S. Forester's novel *The Good Shepherd* for Columbia. Harry Cohn wished to tie Bogart more closely to the studio; and he did it by dealing with him as an equal and a businessman, which accounts for the sale of Santana Productions. Meanwhile, in Burbank, Jack Warner fumed as he watched the actor he felt he had made a star work for the benefit of other studios, yet J. L. was stubbornly unwilling to acknowledge Bogart as anything but an ungrateful ex-employee. "Sperling claims he talked to Humphrey Bogart, who claims he would like to do a picture for us," was the way Warner spoke of the prospect of Bogart's return in *Melville Goodwin, U.S.A.*

The television networks also wanted Bogart, although he had little use for the medium, which years before he had called "a monster" and "a devourer of talent." Besides, "I look awful on television. Every pore on my face can be seen on those home screens. And you can imagine what I look like on sets with bad reception." Nevertheless, on Memorial Day 1955, Bacall and Bogart appeared in a live television revival of *The Petrified Forest* on *Producers' Showcase,* presented monthly by NBC.

Producers' Showcase was as good a series as the medium offered: adult drama without quarter-hour commercial interruptions. In addition to Bogart as Mantee and Bacall as the young poet Gabrielle Maple, the cast included Henry Fonda as Alan Squier. They were directed by Delbert Mann, who was about to win an Oscar for *Marty.* The production came across as Fonda's show. *The Petrified Forest* had never been an action play, and on the tiny screen the constant, necessary presence of Mantee, coiled and dangerous in the background, was a logistical impossibility. "Duke Mantee should be seen constantly so that . . . the audience as well as his prisoners . . . never forget that he represents destiny," *New York Times* critic Jack Gould wrote the next day. "The limitations of the TV camera . . . [detract] somewhat from the mounting tension embodied in Mantee's figure." Still, Mann's imaginative direction and his use of close-ups of Mantee and Squier, killer and victim, graphically caught the interplay between the two doomed men.

After twenty years away from the stage, Bogart had his doubts not only about live TV but about live performances in general. "Suppose I had laryngitis, suppose I just wasn't feeling up to par. I turn in a bad job and the critics rap me," he said in an interview regarding his TV appearance. "I just don't like the idea of a one-shot. As for a regular weekly series, I'd sooner dig ditches."

At one point he confided his fears to Helen Hayes, in Los Angeles to perform at the Huntington Hartford Theater in Hollywood. Jack Benny had a party for her, and, Hayes remembered, "Bogie was there moaning, 'Oh, to be back doing what you're doing. Oh, to be in the theater again. This is just a lot of nonsense out here.' And he didn't say 'nonsense,' he said something shorter; four letters.

"I said, 'Well, Bogie, there's one way you can do that. Go back and do a play.'

" 'Oh,' he said, 'My God, I wouldn't do that!'

"I said, 'Then why don't you do a play here, at the Huntington Hartford Theater?' And he answered, 'I couldn't do it out here. You know what would happen? These bastards would all go out in the lobby and say, "So that's what came to us as a big, big star—a big important actor of New York. That's what's been posing as a great big performer!" No,' he said, 'I couldn't do that.'

"That was it. He thought they'd scorn him. Which they might have done. Who knows?"

However, Bogart was very much a big star and an important actor. He had earned his third Oscar nomination that spring for *The Caine Mutiny*—though he lost out to Marlon Brando for *On the Waterfront.* That fall, he had three pictures in release. *Life* photographers captured the Bogarts at premieres and at the Nunnally Johnsons' large parties. There was Bogart dancing à trois with Clifton Webb and Marilyn Monroe at a dinner party thrown at Romanoff's by Billy Wilder and Charlie Feldman to celebrate the completion of *The Seven Year Itch.* She wore a red chiffon gown borrowed from her studio, Bogart was adorned in chin stubble from *The Desperate Hours.*

In September, Bogart announced the formation of Mapleton Pictures, to be co-financed and distributed by Allied Artists. While negotiations were still in progress, the new company had already acquired the film rights to the crime series *Underworld, U.S.A.,* then being serialized in the *Saturday Evening Post.* Bogart and Bacall were to be the co-stars, and Walter Wanger was to be the producer.

At the same time, he began work on *The Harder They Fall.* It would be his last film. Producer Jerry Wald, with whom he had made a half-dozen pictures at Warners, had been driven by Jack Warner's jealousy into Harry Cohn's embrace. Bogart was paired with Rod Steiger, one of the group of young performers that included Marlon Brando (who had studied at the Actors Studio in New York) who were adherents of the Method. Bogart reportedly had little use for the technique; he called it the "scratch-your-ass-and-mumble-school-of-acting."

"He talked like that," Steiger said. "Don't forget, here's one generation of actors getting a little upset with this new generation, who were being heralded as maybe being superior, which they weren't. It was just a new way of doing something, a moment of excitement in the theater."

Bogart told his longtime friend Alistair Cooke that the change in Hollywood during the past twenty years "could be measured by the fact that whereas 'I came out here with one suit and everybody thought I was a bum; when Brando came out with one sweatshirt, the town drooled over him.' " Cooke thought his real complaint was that the new generation wore blue jeans and windbreakers.

Bogart was cast as the down-at-the-heels newsman who becomes a flack for the boxing promoters; Steiger, as the corrupt fight manager. Steiger appreciated Bogart's "wonderful sense of humor. He used to kid me about Brando. Somebody tipped me off that he had this phony newspaper made that said, 'BRANDO TEACHES STEIGER.' So I got a headline—I think it said, 'STEIGER COMES TO TOWN. BOGART LEAVES.' He came into my dressing room, a twinkling in his eyes, and he's talking to me and all of a sudden he whips this out. He says, 'I got a present for you.' But as soon as he started to move his arm with the newspaper, I moved *my* arm and they both came out at the same time. He got a big kick out of that."

One day while entertaining some visitors in his dressing room, Bogart said to them, not meanly, "Let's go down to the set and watch Steiger internalize." Of their different approaches to a role, Steiger added, "Bogart came from the school where you did what you thought the character would do in this scene. My school started with Montgomery Clift—he was the purest actor we had on the screen. We believed that if you'd take on the problems of the character, trying to make them your own, the minute you assumed them, you became the character. But good, talented people like Mr. Bogart would get involved, whether they knew it or not. They had their own approach, but they were basically looking for the same things: involvement, identification, a sense of participating in this life that's fictitious."

Steiger's most lasting impression of Bogart was "his independence and his professionalism and his kindness to me" in a picture in which the young actor had the flashier part. "In those days, if you had been working for one of the famous leading ladies—and some of the men—her close-ups would have been over your shoulder and [the audience] would have been lucky if they saw your face. But Bogart always stood alongside the camera and made sure I had my close-up to match his close-ups in the scene. He used to say to me, 'Son of a bitch, you're going to kill me. You're going to kill me.' I said, 'Bo, you got to get better parts. You want to switch? I got the better one.'

"He had what I think we lack today, a sense of honor and professionalism. You didn't bore your other workers with your afflictions during working hours. You might go home and get drunk and drive people crazy with it after six o'clock, but between nine and six you did not bring your personal burdens into the work. He was like the master sergeant who had brought the platoon through the jungle. You respected the wars that he'd been through, and his ability to survive. He was a gentleman, an artistic soldier. There's the story about the young bull and the old bull on the hill. The young bull looks down and he sees all those gorgeous heifers and he goes crazy. He says, 'Let's run down and make love to a couple'—I'm cleaning this up. And the old bull says, 'Let's *walk* down and get 'em all!'

"That was the difference between me and Bogart. He was the old bull. He knew what he was doing. 'Take your time. Don't worry. We'll get 'em all.' "

CHAPTER 25

Sunset and Evening Star

In January 1956, Bogart and Bacall filmed the wardrobe tests for *Melville Goodwin, U.S.A.* Bogart was to play a brass-and-polish Army general; Bacall, a pugnacious press baroness. The prospect of the first Bogart-Bacall film in six years was pleasurable to both Warner Brothers and theater owners. Then a week before production was to begin, Bogart phoned producer Milton Sperling from Palm Springs.

"I can make the picture," he said, "but I'll be dead in six months."

His persistent cough sometimes went on for half an hour, and friends had noticed that he had been having difficulty eating. Sperling had been concerned, as had Amanda Dunne, who, seated next to Bogart at a party one night at Romanoff's, saw that he hadn't touched his food.

She remarked on it "and he said, 'Oh, don't *you* start hounding me about it, too. Everybody's very upset about it.' I said, 'Have you gone to find out about it?' He said, 'No, I'm scared to.' And I told him, 'Oh! You're *just* like my brother! He was afraid, too. He spent about two years thinking that he had something terrible and went to the doctor and it was just some nervous thing.' And he said, '*Oh! Well! I'll go to the doctor tomorrow!*' "

Immediately afterward, Dunne wondered if she had done the right thing—what if it was something serious after all?—and said, "Please, if it's something that you don't have to be put through. . . ." The next day

Bacall was on the phone to say thank you. "We've all tried to get him to go to a doctor. And *he's made an appointment!*"

Greer Garson had given them the name of Dr. Maynard Brandsma, a Beverly Hills internist who specialized in problems of the lungs and throat. After several weeks of tests, there was finally a diagnosis: cancer of the esophagus. Immediate surgery was necessary. Bogart, stunned, asked the doctor about a postponement, at least until the picture was completed. The studio had so much at stake, he explained. "Not unless you want a lot of flowers at Forest Lawn" was Brandsma's reply. He believed there was still time to check the progress of a disease seldom caught so early, but if Bogart insisted on fulfilling his contract and forgoing prompt surgery, "they can all go to your funeral." Brandsma, a caring man who became a good friend during Bogart's illness, was simply being as direct as possible.

Bogart and Bacall "went home dazed, but neither of us panicked. As always, Bogie's attitude was: what has to be done has to be done—no need for dramatics. I took my cue from him."

On February 29, 1956, he entered Good Samaritan Hospital, where the next day he was operated on for nine and a half hours by Dr. John Jones, the surgeon who had pioneered one of the two separate surgeries Bogart required. Jones and his team went first into his chest and then his abdomen. They removed his esophagus, two lymph nodes and a rib, and, in the space where the rib had been, moved the stomach up and sewed it to the tissue that remained at the end of the gullet. He would be left with a scar that ran down his back from his shoulder to his hip. Bacall was waiting in Bogart's room when attendants wheeled in his bed. He was hooked up to a network of tubes, his left arm and hand grotesquely swollen from lying on them in the same position for so many hours.

A telegram arrived at the hospital: "DEAR BOGIE, KNOW YOU WILL BE YOUR GOOD SELF IN THE VERY NEAR FUTURE. MY THOUGHTS ARE WITH YOU FOR A SPEEDY RECOVERY. REGARDS, JACK WARNER." Friends gathered around, attentive and loving. Huston, in the United States for a short while, came to Good Samaritan. He and Bogart laughed and talked about filming *The Man Who Would Be King*. Warners had gone ahead with *Melville Goodwin,* starring Kirk Douglas and, when Bacall dropped out, Susan Hayward. The movie was retitled *Top Secret Affair*. "Betty, I think, was tempted to play it," Sperling said, "but decided to be with her husband—particularly after the operation." On the other hand, the normally ruthless Harry Cohn assured Bogart that *The Good Shepherd* would stay on the books—at a running cost to the studio—and be there for

Bogart when he could come back. According to Eddie Saeta, an assistant director who had been preparing the picture, "Harry kept that picture alive for at least nine months. He spent untold thousands. Cohn, as much of a son of a bitch as he was, he had a heart."

Before there could be any realistic thought of returning to work, Bogart had to undergo many chemotherapy sessions. Sometimes Joe Hyams drove him to the hospital. "The chemo was a bitch—a bitch," Hyams said. "I would ask, 'How'd it go?' and he'd say, 'Shit.' And that would be the end of it. I've said he was one of the bravest men I've ever met; and I think he was. He never complained. He never said, 'Why me?' None of the self-pitying stuff. He just took it."

Bogart, who had already lost thirty pounds, continued to lose more. Eating was an ordeal. The food, no longed encased by the esophagus, simply fell into the stomach that had been moved virtually up into his chest. Still, he remained uncomplaining, and with his usual wry humor he smiled and joked with friends who came by the house.

Kurt Niklas, a longtime waiter at Romanoff's, saw that Bogart was greatly changed when he returned to the restaurant. "He came back much subdued. It was a totally new Bogart. His neck had gotten so thin that the skin was just hanging over the bones." Unlike his employer, Niklas had always considered Bogart "a lightweight . . . a spoiled Hollywood character without particular manners or depth." But as he watched the actor cope with mortality, his respect for him increased. Bogart evinced no false optimism. "He never gave me the impression that he knew he was going to lick it. He acted what he preached: irreverence. When people dropped dead he'd say, 'It's about time the son of a bitch croaked,' and as his own croaking approached, he handled it with dignity." Later, when Bogart no longer had the strength to go to the restaurant, he and Romanoff played chess by phone, Bogart in his bedroom, Romanoff at a table with a little fold-out chess set.

In the months following the surgery, Louis Bromfield died. The once close friends had drifted apart as Bromfield's time was consumed by his farm. Mary Bromfield had died, as had his secretary George Hawkins. Still, for Bogart, another part of his life had fallen away.

In September he felt well enough to join in a birthday celebration for Bacall in Las Vegas, then decided instead to take Stephen out on the *Santana.* They moored in their usual spot at Catalina, and Bogart, shrunken in his clothes, looked wistfully around. Bacall flew to Las Vegas with the rest of the party—Cole Porter, David and Hjordis Niven, the Romanoffs, Martha Hyer, Irving Lazar, and the agent Bert Allenberg and his wife. The party went to hear Sinatra perform and were seated at a long table facing the mike as he sang "Happy Birthday" and a three-tiered cake inscribed to "Happy Birthday Den Mother" was brought out. Bogart called with his greetings. The group was photographed cutting the cake, along with actress Kim Novak, who was there as Sinatra's date.

Bacall returned home to find her husband "edgy and resentful. . . . He was somewhat jealous of Frank—partly because he knew I loved being with him, partly because he thought Frank was in love with me, and partly because our physical life together, which had always ranked high, had less than flourished with his illness." Sinatra had become a constant in their lives. Bogart was "crazy about Frank," Bacall insisted, "loved having him feel that our home was his home." In the months of Bogart's illness, he was a steady visitor. Stephen remembered him as a smiling man in a bright yellow polo shirt and slacks, "a nice, happy person trying to make us feel good."

Bogart's health was the subject of rumors. Joe Hyams dropped by one day and was asked, "What are the ghouls saying about me now?" Hyams told him he was reported to be in a coma. Bogart suggested Hyams write that "I'm down to my last martini. The only thing I'm fighting is to keep my head above the press." On another occasion, infuriated by a bogus report by Hearst columnist Dorothy Kilgallen that he was battling for his life in a hospital that didn't exist, he called in Hyams and dictated an "Open letter to the Working Press" that proved his wit to be intact, despite his physical condition.

> . . . I have read that both lungs have been removed; that I couldn't live for another half hour; that I was fighting for my life in a hospital which doesn't exist out here; that my heart has stopped and been replaced by an old gasoline pump from a defunct Standard Oil station. I have been on the way to practically every cemetery you can name from here to the Mississippi—including several where I am certain they only accept dogs. All of the above upsets my friends, not to mention the insurance companies. . . .
>
> I had a slight malignancy in my esophagus. So that some of you won't have to go into the research department, it's the pipe that runs from your throat to your stomach. The operation for the removal of the malignancy was successful, although it was touch and go for a while whether the malignancy or I would survive.
>
> As they . . . say in Washington, I'm a better man than I ever was—all I need now is about thirty pounds in weight which I am

> sure some of you could spare. Possibly we could start something like a Weight Bank for Bogart and believe me I'm not particular which part of your anatomy it comes from. . . .

On November 26, however, he checked into St. John's Hospital in Santa Monica for what was announced as removal of excess scar tissue but was actually treatment for the cancer, which had metastasized. After a five-day stay, he was sent home. Upbeat hospital press releases pronounced him "doing fine and much stronger." In reality, the doctors held out little hope.

All that could be done in the weeks that followed was to make him as comfortable as possible at home. Friends and film people visited with Bogart in a cozy downstairs sitting area that he and Bacall called the Butternut Room. The Holmby Hills regulars came out in force—the Nivens, the Romanoffs, and Irving Lazar, who surmounted a deeply ingrained fear of illness to be with his friend. Mary Baker was a steady visitor, Truman Capote came by a few times, and Adlai Stevenson made a point of seeing him. Katharine Hepburn and Spencer Tracy arrived around eight-thirty almost every night, after the other visitors had left and Bogart was back upstairs.

Raymond Massey, on a visit to Los Angeles, stopped in, and he and Bogart laughingly reminisced about their misadventures on the set of *Action in the North Atlantic.* Massey, according to Bacall, talked about everything except his friend's illness. "Bogie turned the tables on him by saying, 'Wait till you hear what happened to me—it was awful,' describing his operation in detail and asking Ray if he wanted to see his scar. By the end of the visit it was Ray who needed cheering up." Even Jack Warner came to pay his respects. He was as uncomfortable with Bogart ill as he had been with Bogart healthy, but he tried his best. Screenwriter Henry Ephron, who came with his wife and writing partner Phoebe, later characterized the flow of visitors as a ritual of Hollywood's marking the passing of one of its own; also, it was, in many cases, status seeking—it was important to say that you had been to see Bogart and marvel at his courage.

Bogart would greet his callers sitting in a chair—later a wheelchair—with an iced drink beside him consisting of a dollop of scotch and a lot of water. "People came in with the gossip and joke of the day," Hyams said. "If you didn't know Bogart was a very sick man, you'd think it was kind of a fun party, because everyone was there to brighten up his day. I don't know what *their* day was like, but when they crossed that threshold they were there to pick up his spirits. So I never left really depressed. The only time was when I found out how he'd gotten downstairs."

Since the guests were there to cheer Bogart, he, in turn, wanted to live up to their expectations. As his illness progressed, he grew too weak to walk downstairs and refused to be carried, but he was determined that he would visit with his friends in the Butternut Room rather than upstairs in his sickbed. "He would lie on his couch upstairs at five o'clock," John Huston wrote, "to be shaved and groomed and dressed in gray flannels and scarlet smoking jacket. When he was no longer able to walk, his emaciated body would be lifted into a wheelchair and taken to a dumbwaiter, the roof of which had been removed to give him headroom. His nurses would help him in, and, sitting on a little stool, he would be lowered down to the kitchen where another transfer would be made and, again by wheelchair, he'd be transported through the house into the library and his chair, and there he would be, sherry glass in one hand and cigarette in the other, at five thirty when the guests started to arrive." There were always drinks for the visitors and a bowl kept filled with peanuts.

"Betty organized it," Hyams said, "and she was exemplary. The way she handled his illness, the way she handled the press, the way she handled herself, and the way she handled her children. I thought she was just great—very gallant, very gutsy, a very warm person. If I were dying, I couldn't have asked for anything better."

Alistair Cooke, expecting that the radiation treatments to the esophagus would make it "hard to keep up the usual banter," found instead "there was no strain of any kind, because (I believe) he knew the worst and was resolved to rouse himself for two hours a day to relax with his friends until the end came. We never knew until he died that he had been for many months in the most abominable pain. . . . He remained a genial skeleton, and when I went up there the last time . . . he was just finishing his will. He spoke of it, and of his illness, and the sudden uselessness of money, with an entirely unforced humor and an equally unforced seriousness; neither with complaint nor with a brave absence of complaint."

Bogart's gallantry could not mask his disintegration. "The look of death was on him," Hyams said. Richard Brooks sat with Bogart, not in the controlled party setting below but upstairs, where the devastating effects of his illness were more plainly evident. Bacall writes about Brooks bitterly for not being a regular, for not coming for a long time, for having to be "shamed into it" when he did come.

Brooks later admitted how difficult it was to see his friend in this condition. On one occasion they were playing chess, but Bogart was nauseated. Brooks, out of embarrassment for Bogart and in deference to his own queasiness, said he had to go and they could continue the game the next day. Bogart waved for him to sit down. Brooks lasted about five minutes that "seemed like an hour. And I finally said, 'No, I'll tell you what, Bogie, my mind isn't on the game anymore,' and all that bullshit. Any excuse to go. Because I thought it was embarrassing for *him*."

Brooks got up to go and Bogart smiled wryly up at him and asked quietly, "What's the matter, kid? Can't you take it?"

They were the last words Brooks heard him say. "He was right. I just couldn't take it. And he knew it. It was a twist on the things, never admitting you had pain."

The fact that he was dying was never discussed openly but "he must have known because he was getting weaker," his longtime friend Natalie Schafer said. "He turned to me one day when we were talking alone and he said, 'Keep your eye on Betty. Don't let her get mixed up with these jerks out here.' " To most people, however, he was more upbeat, relying on his career-long belief that actors need to keep working. "If I could just work," he would say, "I'd be okay."

As the illness progressed, there were fewer visits by the children to the upstairs bedroom. "Sometimes they came in to say hello or something," Schafer said, "but they kept it as quiet for him as they could." After Stephen and Leslie had played in the room one day and then gone for their baths, their father said to Bacall, "Don't have them in here too often, Baby." Was it that he wanted them to remember him as he had been, she wondered, or was it simply unbearable to be with them, knowing that he'd never live to see them grow?

At Christmas, Bogart's fifty-seventh birthday, the doctors bluntly told Bacall that Bogart had very little time left; they did not really know how he had managed to stay alive this long. Sometime later, she asked Hepburn if, when Bogart died, Tracy would deliver the eulogy. Tracy, the steadfast friend at the bedside, was so distressed by the impending loss of his friend that he couldn't say yes.

John Huston was at the desk of the St. Regis Hotel in New York in late 1956 and took a long-distance phone call in the lobby. It was Bacall, her voice controlled, with effort. Bogie was going to die, she told him; they didn't know when, but the cancer was terminal. She'd like him to write the eulogy.

Huston talked about that call shortly before his own death, in a low, intense voice. "I . . . I couldn't believe what I was hearing. And I said, yes—of course. She was asking me to *write* something. In case I wasn't there, if I was in Ireland—to write something. To be read. I *tried*, but I couldn't possibly. But when he died—I could."

Huston came back to Los Angeles in January 1957, saw Bogart, and then, distraught at his friend's deterioration in the months since they had last been together, went to his agent Paul Kohner's office on Sunset Boulevard. He was visibly upset by what he had seen. Bogart had seemed to weigh nothing—Huston guessed sixty-five pounds—and his eyes were enormous in his gaunt face.

The evening of Saturday, January 12, Hepburn and Tracy came as usual. At the end of the visit—just long enough, also as usual—Hepburn noticed how thin his hands were. "Bogie was sitting in a wheelchair and I just bent over and kissed him, to go. And Spencer came up to him and said, 'Good night, Bogie.' And he put his hand onto Bogie's shoulder. And Bogie put his hand up over Spencer's, sort of patted it, and said, 'Good-bye, Spence.' "

Hepburn was close to tears as she recalled the scene. "I nearly fainted. When we got outside, Spence said, 'Did you hear what he said?' I said, 'I certainly did.' "

On Sunday, Bacall dropped off Stephen and Leslie at All Saints' Episcopal Church in Beverly Hills for Sunday school, then went home to sit and talk with Bogart. When she returned from picking up the children, Bogart was in what seemed a deep sleep. Dr. Brandsma examined him and told Bacall that her husband would likely not come out of his coma. Brandsma tried to explain the coma to Stephen by saying his father might not wake up. When asked if he understood, the boy ran out of the room. After a while Bacall took him upstairs into Bogart's bedroom "with its awful smell of sickness and decay. We sat on the bed. Mother was more frightened than me. I moved closer. We both took Bogie's hand, and sat there not talking to each other. . . . After a moment I leaned over and kissed my father's cheek. Mother did the same.

"Later that day she found me again in the bedroom, standing by my sleeping father. She asked me why I had come back. 'Because I wanted to,' I said."

At 2:25 on the morning of January 14, Humphrey Bogart died. Bacall cried for the rest of the night. While it was still dark, she called Morgan Maree's son Andy, the leg man for the office, and asked him to make the funeral arrangements. At dawn, she told the children their father was gone.

The news spread quickly. "Bogart dead," Walter Wanger noted in his appointment book. "Called at Betty's 9:45, then back to house." By that time a mass of reporters and newsreel and TV cameras had crowded the treed lawn before the Bogart's long driveway, spilling out onto the road, their cars parked haphazardly.

In New York at the Copacabana Club, Frank Sinatra canceled his two evening performances. He wouldn't be coherent, he told his agent, Abe Lastfogel.

John Huston sat at a desk in the Kohner Agency offices, composing Bogart's eulogy while trying to control his own grief. "He agonized over it," Kohner's secretary, Irene Heymann, said. "He worked on it for hours, trying to have it just so. It was terribly hard on him."

Although Bogart wished to have his ashes scattered over the Pacific, it was illegal to do so at the time. He had told Bacall at Hellinger's burial service and on other occasions that he wanted no funeral, so she and Andy Maree decided on cremation, a memorial service, and a vault for the ashes at Forest Lawn. The arrangements would have amused Bogart. The cemetery provided the entire funeral for the price of the casket, and since the casket was to be burned, Maree's "inclination was to buy the cheapest pine box possible. I had only one concern and that was that Betty might want to visit one of the resting rooms before he was taken to be buried and I didn't want her to see him in too mean a circumstance, so I upgraded my purchase a little—but not enough to make Forest Lawn happy. There were two or three limousines that they had to supply, and the invitations and announcements and all the rest of it. Knowing Bogart, he would have laughed at the fact that they might have taken a loss on his funeral."

The memorial service was held on January 18, at All Saints' Church. Two hundred people filled the pews while thousands milled outside, respectful despite their number. "There weren't any special passes needed for those going to the service," Maree said. "The public more or less parted and let the friends through without too much of the frenzy there would be today." The several news photographers with concealed cameras who tried to sneak in were quickly bundled outside by David Niven and a few others.

Inside were friends, sailing buddies, and Hollywood leaders. Jack Warner was there, as were Harry Cohn and David O. Selznick, with Jennifer Jones beside him. Also Hepburn and Tracy, Gregory Peck, Gary Cooper,

James Mason, Joan Fontaine, Danny Kaye, Ronald Reagan, Dick Powell, Danny Thomas, Edmund Goulding, Charles Boyer, Louis Jourdan, William Wyler, and Richard Brooks. And Billy Wilder, along with his wife and Marlene Dietrich. Nunnally Johnson, in Savannah, Georgia, when his wife Dorris called with the news, rushed back to serve as an usher, with Niven, Romanoff, Leland Hayward, and Irving Lazar.

The service was a simple one. The Reverend Kermit Castellanos included the Ten Commandments among the usual prayers, saying in his brief comments that Bogart had lived by them. He concluded by reading Alfred Tennyson's "Crossing the Bar," with its sailing metaphors for the passage of the soul. In lieu of the coffin, there was a small-scale model of the *Santana,* in a glass case, by the altar rail.

Finally, Huston rose and spoke, in his distinctive, deep, hollow voice about his friend.

> . . . He loved life. Life meant his family, his friends, his work, his boat. He could not imagine leaving any of them, and so until the very last he planned what he would do when he got well. His boat was being repainted. Stephen, his son, was getting of an age when he could be taught to sail, and to learn his father's love of the sea. A few weeks sailing and Bogie would be all ready to go to work again. He was going to make fine pictures—only fine pictures—from here on in.
>
> With the years he had become increasingly aware of the dignity of his profession—Actor, not Star: Actor. Himself, he never took too seriously—his work most seriously. He regarded the somewhat gaudy figure of Bogart, the star, with amused cynicism; Bogart, the actor, he held in deep respect. . . . Those who did not know him well, who never worked with him, who were not of the small circle of his close friends, had another completely different idea of the man than the few who were so privileged. I suppose the ones who knew him but slightly were at the greatest disadvantage, particularly if they were the least bit solemn about their own importance. Bigwigs have been known to stay away from the brilliant Hollywood occasions rather than expose their swelling neck muscles to Bogart's banderillas.
>
> In each of the fountains of Versailles there is a pike which keeps all the carp active, otherwise they would grow over-fat and die. Bogie took rare delight in performing a similar duty in the fountains of Hollywood. Yet his victims seldom bore him any malice,

> and when they did, not for long. His shafts were fashioned only to stick into the outer layer of complacency, and not penetrate through to the regions of the spirit where real injuries are done.
>
> The great houses of Beverly Hills, and for that matter of the world, were so many shooting galleries so far as Bogie was concerned. His own house was a sanctuary. Within those walls, anyone, no matter how elevated his position, could breathe easy. . . . he fed a guest's spirit as well as his body, plied him with good will until he became drunk in the heart as well as the legs. . . .
>
> . . . he was endowed with the greatest gift a man can have: talent. The whole world came to recognize it. . . . He got all that he asked for out of life and more. We have no reason to feel sorrow for him—only for ourselves for having lost him. He is quite irreplaceable.

Many of the mourners cried. "I think there was genuine grief for Bogey's passing," Nunnally Johnson wrote to a friend. "There are a lot of people who detest him, people he had deliberately affronted, and God knows he could do that viciously, but there were many more who were drawn to him because he was a lively fellow. I myself feel the loss terribly."

The service ended with the Twenty-third Psalm and a final prayer, followed by music by Bach and Debussy, one of Bogart's favorite composers. Photographs taken of Bacall outside after the service showed her looking very thin in a black dress. Her facial skin was tight over the bones, an evident effect of the sleepless nights. She had a black-gloved hand on Stephen's shoulder as they walked to the limousine, one of the small boy's hands held to his eyes. "Widow Lauren Bacall tries to comfort son Stephen," the *Life* caption read. Many years later, in a remark reminiscent of his father, Stephen Bogart said that when he saw the caption a few days after the service, "I was really pissed off that they wrote that I was crying. It was a *lie!* I was covering my eyes from the vultures outside. I was eight years old and I wanted the truth! I mean it's bad enough that your father dies, without having your picture in a magazine saying you're crying!"

So many people came to the house to pay their respects that to Bacall it looked as if "everyone in the church had come." There were drinks, and Mike Romanoff sent cassoulet and platters of food along with waiters to serve. "It was like a party—almost."

One person, however, was noticeably absent. Howard Hawks was flying back to Beverly Hills from his years in Europe when Bogart died. Dee

Hawks was crushed by the news of his death, but at least they had come back in time to pay their final respects. "Let's go to the house," she said to her husband.

The man who was above all most responsible for Bogart and Bacall turned cold, his face at once handsome and hostile in its frame of silver-white hair. "They never had me when he was alive," he said frostily. "Why should I go now?"

Comic relief was provided by the American Floral Association. Newspapers had printed Bacall's request that, in lieu of flowers, people send a donation to the American Cancer Society. The florists' group sent her a telegram. Opening what she "thought was another condolence wire, my mouth dropped open: 'Do we say we don't go to see Lauren Bacall movies?' That gave me and all who saw it the one true laugh of the day."

The media regarded Bogart's death as that of a major national figure. *The New York Times* put it on page one, as did the *Los Angeles Times.* Page one of the New York *Herald Tribune* had a feature by Joe Hyams on his friend, and there were editorials and appreciations of Bogart in papers across the country. His film triumphs were ticked off like an honor roll, but the coverage also celebrated the man himself. Political columnists wrote on the passing of a movie star, while wondering aloud why they were paying such attention to a Hollywood actor.

Pundit Max Lerner gave them an answer. Bogart, he wrote, "caught the imagination of the people . . . and he caught and held our affection because he expressed something both in himself and in us that we needed to see expressed. . . . There was always an edge of bravado in both Bogarts—the movie tough guy and the real-life tough guy. It was a nose-thumbing, to-hell-with-it bravado. I think we liked him so much mainly because most of us, in our own actual lives, have so little chance to thumb our noses and consign the fakes, the stuffed men and the hollow men to hell."

In Britain, all nine national newspapers noted his passing in bold, black headlines. *The Times* of London called him a symbol of a mythical American hero—"the masculine counterpart of the girl of easy virtue and the heart of gold." In a Europe where the scars of war were only eleven years old, the sense Bogart evinced of fighting through despair resounded even more deeply than it did with his compatriots. In France, a young generation of directors screened his pictures and saw a hero for their time. In that month's prestigious *Cahiers du Cinéma,* critic André Bazin called him *"l'homme d'après le destin"*—"the man storm-tossed by fate."

In the German press, editorials and commentaries referred to him as *"Der vom Tod Gejagten"*—"the man hunted by death."

In Italy, two Portofino fishermen whom he had befriended while filming *The Barefoot Contessa* slipped a wreath of flowers into the sea.

In New York City, Helen Menken and Grace Lansing Lambert, both still beautiful, met at the Plaza over tea and talked about Humphrey.

According to newspaper stories, there was to be a moment of silence on the Warner Brothers lot at the time of the memorial service, but no one there that day had any recollection of it. Bacall sent a copy of Huston's eulogy to Jack Warner, along with a warm note about the good times that they'd had together. J. L. sent back a note of appreciation and an acknowledgment that they had indeed been good times, but it made no mention of collaboration at some future date.

Humphrey DeForest Bogart's will was probated in February. His estate was reported to be in excess of one million dollars. There were trust funds for Stephen and Leslie, two small bequests for the family cook, May Smith, and his secretary, Kathryn Sloan. Approximately half of the estate and all of his possessions went to Bacall.

The Jaguars were sold. Harvey, old and ill, developed heart trouble and had to be put down. One by one the other boxers died. The crew of the *Santana* cringed at the notion of someone not sailing her as well as Bogart and talked of scuttling the yawl in tribute to its skipper. Instead, at Bacall's request, a couple of the longtime crew members took the plates and dishes and tackle and the rest of the gear, then Bogart's second love was sold. The boat, the ocean, and the pleasure of sailing had provided him escape, relaxation, and a solace that he had known since childhood, when he sailed on *Comrade* with his father. "An actor needs something to stabilize his personality," he once said, "something to nail down what he really is, not what he is currently pretending to be."

Some months later, Max Wilk, whose discovery of *The Maltese Falcon* nearly thirty years earlier had set in motion a chain of events that altered Bogart's career, spotted Bacall off by herself at a party in Bel Air and went over to her. She wouldn't remember him, he began hesitantly, because the last time they had met he was in an Army uniform.

"And where was that?" she asked listlessly.

"At your house. I brought you a dog."

"Oh, God! Harvey! He was the best! We loved him madly."

When she began to cry, Wilk realized they were discussing much more than the dog he had brought by train from Chicago to Los Angeles as a wedding present for Humphrey Bogart and his young bride.

As one travels west toward Burbank along the foothills of the San Gabriel Mountains, Forest Lawn covers acres of hillside with a perpetually green carpet of grass.

In the verdant graveyard the urn holding Bogart's ashes and the gold whistle he had given Bacall was placed in a wall with safe-deposit-sized boxes in the Garden of Memory, a private area behind an iron gate, away from the curious and miles from the ocean where he would have preferred his remains to have been scattered. The plaque reads simply, "Humphrey DeForest Bogart, December 25, 1899—January 14, 1957."

The wilderness surrounding the cemetery is brown for most of the year, the stubby underbrush sere from the absence of rain. Rising in the near distance is the water tower on the Warner lot.

Acknowledgments

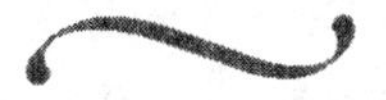

Ann Sperber conducted nearly 200 interviews with people who were connected to Humphrey Bogart. They generously gave her their time, talent, and in many cases their friendship. She was, and I am, deeply grateful to: Harry Ackerman, Junius Adams, Claude Akins, Eddie Albert, Henny Backus, Joy Barlowe, Regina Beaumont, Bruce Bennett, Joan Bennett, Robert Blake, Stephen Bogart, Peter J. Boyer, Richard Brooks, Clarence Bruner-Smith, Joyce Buck, Jules Buck, Isabel Bunker, Murray Burnett, Niven Busch, Sammy Cahn, William Campbell, Hoagy Carmichael Jr., Charles Carson, Ed Clark, Jack Coffey, Norman Corwin, Dee Hawks Cramer, Jane Bryan Dart, Frederick De Cordova, Irene Lee Diamond, Edward Dmytryk, Richard Dorso, Henry Ephron, Julius J. Epstein, Richard Erdman, Rudi Fehr, Geraldine Fitzgerald, Mitch Gamson, Phil Gersh, Julie Gibson, Bill Graf, Arthur Hamlin, Frank Hamlin, Helen Hayes, Paul Henreid, Katharine Hepburn, Irene Heymann, Rose Hobart, Cy Howard, Jean Howard, Marsha Hunt, John Huston, Joe Hyams, Sam Jaffe, Dorris Johnson, Lee Katz, Gene Kelly, Evelyn Keyes, Sidney Kingsley, Leonid Kinsky, Howard Koch, Paul Kohner, Stanley Kramer, Grace Lansing, Ring Lardner Jr., Douglas Laurence, Jerome Lawrence, Paul Lazarus, Kenneth Leffers, Joan Leslie, June Levant, Harry Lewis, Mort Lickter, Cynthia Lindsay, Ida Lupino, Allan McMillan, Delbert Mann, Florence Eldridge March, A. Morgan Maree Jr., Victor Mature, Bill Mauldin, Pat Miller, Irving Moore, Jess Morgan, Richard Morse, Kurt Niklas, William T. Orr, Irving Rapper, Ronald Reagan, Allen Rivkin, Hugh Robertson, Earl Robinson, Henry Rogers, George Roosevelt, Eddie Saeta, Bill Schaefer, Margaret Schaefer, Natalie Schafer, Betty Warner Scheinbaum, Bob Schiffer, Lizabeth Scott, Walter Scott, Walter Seltzer, Gloria Stuart

Sheekman, Walter Shenson, Vincent Sherman, Arthur Silver, Arthur Sircom, Helga Smith, Milton Sperling, Rod Steiger, Gary Stevens, Hope Bromfield Stevens, Marial Hirleman Stevenson, John Strauss, Walter Surovy, Lyle Talbot, Kay Thackeray, Harriet Thompson, Sylvia Sheekman Thompson, Verita Thompson, Regis Toomey, Claire Trevor, Philip Van Renssalaer, Benay Venuta, Peter Viertel, Malvin Wald, Jack Warner Jr., Martin Weiser, Charles Wick, Arthur Wilde, Meta Wilde, Buster Wiles, Max Wilk, and Bob William. I apologize to anyone I have omitted, to whom we are equally thankful.

Ann was particularly grateful to Philip and Amanda Dunne and to Dan and Evelyn Seymour for sharing their recollections and for their wonderful companionship. She also wished to thank Judith Adler-Hennessee, Patricia Bosworth, and Penelope Niven, fellow biographers whose generous dialogue often sustained and encouraged her; Mary Ann Anderson, for her invaluable help and friendship; Charles Champlin for his helpful introductions; Rudy Behlmer for sharing his experience; George M. Carter for the use of helpful matieral; Jane Bloom-Stewart, for her selfless legal advice; Don Swaim, a trusted friend who taught her everything one has to know about computers; Sam Vaughn, for his belief in her work; and Joseph Wershba, for his unfailing encouragement.

Archives are the backbone of this work, and Ann spent years in various ones across the country. We thank Ann G. Schlosser, head of the Cinema-Television Library in the Doheny Library at the University of Southern California, and archives assistant Ned Comstock, who hunted down everything Ann asked for; Stuart Ng and Noelle Carter, of the Warner Bros. Archives, School of Cinema-Television, University of Southern California; Stacey Behlmer, of the Margaret Herrick Library at the Academy of Motion Picture Arts and Sciences; Dace Taub, curator of the Regional History Project, Doheny Library, University of Southern California; Pat Kowalski of the Warner Bros. Corporate Archives; Ann Wilkens, of the Wisconsin Center for Film and Theater Research at the Wisconsin State Historical Society; Janice Madhu, at the George Eastman House in Rochester, New York, and Sid Rosenzweig, for helpful photo research; the Department of Special Collections, Mugar Memorial Library, Boston University; The Harry Ransom Humanites Research Center, The University of Texas at Austin; the Stanford University Libraries, Department of Special Collections; The Harvard Theatre Collection, Harvard College Library; The University of Oregon Library Special Collections; The Theater Collection of the Lincoln Center for the Performing Arts; the Theater Collection of the Firestone Library, Princeton University; the Museum of Broadcasting; the Wisconsin State Historical Society; The Schuyler County (New York) Historical Society; the Museum of the City of New York; and the Ontario County (New York) Historical Society.

Leith Adams, the Warner Bros. Corporate Archivist, was helpful far beyond the boundaries of professional courtesy. His friendship to Ann was a great support to her, as has his kindness been to me.

I thank Linda "Sherlock" Amster, a great friend and a surpassingly great researcher, for untold arcane facts; Lauren Bacall, Milton Barrie, William Barrie, Lita Warner Heller, and Aljean Harmetz, for fresh information; Eivind Boe, for his precise copy editing, and Bruce Giffords, of William Morrow, for his additional contributions; Dennis and Dexter Cirillo, for their warm friendship; William Clark, for handling a thousand calls; David James Fisher, for helping clear the way; David Freeman, for steady insight; Arthur Gelb, for his constant interest; Walter Hill, for a helpful read; John LaHoud, for many minute details; Shirley Lord, for a wonderful recommendation; Sonny Mehta, for a critical introduction; Jonathan Segal, for his support; Ann's great friend Don Swaim, for organizing and transferring the contents of her computer, and without whom I would still be lost in cyberspace; Arthur Ochs Sulzberger, for his abiding concern; Linda and William Tyrer, who let me use their copier but whose friendship cannot be duplicated; and Lisa Sperber joins me in thanking Robert Stein and Edward Weidenfeld, for a happy agreement. Four people dear to me—Terrence Clancy, Dorothy Lax, Harold Barrett Robinson, and Carol Fox Sulzberger—will not read this, but their love remains.

I can only begin to thank my friends of decades Jamie Wolf, for many grace notes, and David Wolf, for being there.

Ann's and my agent, Owen Laster, of the William Morris Agency, brought me to this book. Ann wanted to thank him for getting it off the ground, and I thank him for helping me to land it. Harvey Ginsberg, our editor, has opinions that range from the grandest of concepts to a semicolon and is not hesitant to share them. No author could be better served.

Lisa Sperber, Ann's mother, and Alan Sperber, Ann's brother, trusted me to finish what she began. It cannot have been easy for them, but they could not have made it easier for me. Lisa was a touchstone throughout, and I thank her for all her care. I wish we had met under other circumstances.

For the better part of two years, I was unable to spend evenings and weekends with my wife, Karen Sulzberger, and our sons, Simon and John. My appreciation for their understanding and encouragement is exceeded only by how much I missed being with them.

E. L.

Notes

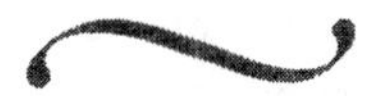

Abbreviations

AMPAS	Academy of Motion Picture Arts and Sciences
AMS	Ann M. Sperber
BU	Boston University
CKF	Charles K. Feldman
CKFC AFI	Charles K. Feldman Collection, Louis B. Mayer Library, American Film Institute
CMC USC	Constance McCormick Collection, University of Southern California
DOSC UT	David O. Selznick Collection, University of Texas
EL	Eric Lax
HDCC WSHS	Hollywood Democratic Committee Collection, Wisconsin State Historical Society
HKC WSHS	Howard Koch Collection, Wisconsin State Historical Society
HRHC	Harry Ransom Humanities Research Center, University of Texas at Austin
JH	John Huston
JLW	Jack L. Warner
JWC	Jack Warner Collection, University of Southern California
MAC BU	Mary Astor Collection, Boston University
MDC WSHS	Melvyn Douglas Collection, Wisconsin State Historical Society
MHC USC	Mark Hellinger Collection, University of Southern California

MMC UO	Mayo Methot Collection, University of Oregon
NB BU	Nathaniel Benchley Collection, Department of Special Collections, Mugar Memorial Library, Boston University
NYT	*The New York Times*
USC WB	USC Warner Bros. Archives, School of Cinema–Television, University of Southern California
WB	Warner Bros.
WSHS	Wisconsin State Historical Society
WWC UCLA	William Wyler Collection, University of California at Los Angeles

All interviews by A. M. Sperber unless otherwise noted.

CHAPTER 1: THE HOUSE AT SENECA POINT

Page

2. *Onnalinda* 142 feet long and other details of boat service: Robert J. Vierhile and William J. Vierhile, *The Canandaigua Lake Steamboat Era, 1827 to 1935* (Naples, N.Y.: Naples Historical Society, 1978).
2. Families would travel by canoe and details of Sunday services: Frank Hamlin, *Summers at the Lake*, private collection.
3. "I should have let . . .": Frank and Arthur Hamlin, interview, 8/14/89.
3. "We were a career family . . .": Humphrey Bogart and Kate Holliday, "Humphrey Bogart's Own Story: I Can't Say I Loved Her," *Ladies' Home Journal*, 7/49.
3. "Dr. Bogart had . . .": Grace Lambert, interview, 7/14/89.
4. "She had a short temper . . .": Ibid.
4. "When the pain began . . .": Bogart/Holliday, "Own Story."
5. "Dr. and Mrs. Bogart stood on the front stairs . . .": Hamlins, interview.
5. Maud wore white boots and deemed black ones "plebeian": Bogart/Holliday, "Own Story."
5. Belmont Bogart known as Bogie, and his personality: Hamlins, interview.
6. "She was essentially a woman . . .": Bogart/Holliday, "Own Story."
6. "Her caress was a kind of blow . . .": Ibid.
6. "I can't truthfully say I loved her": Ibid.
7. "They were abused . . .": Lambert, interview.
7. "Wouldn't *dare* . . . about her servants": Ibid.
10. "He has always thought . . .": Mrs. H. A. Hill to George Greer, letter, 3/6/1871; "I know his whole mind . . .": Josephine Sakler to George Greer, letter, 3/7/1871, Schuyler Country Historical Society, Watkins Glen, N.Y.

10. Belmont on the staffs of Bellevue, St. Luke's, and Sloan's hospitals: Bogart/Holliday, "Own Story."
11. "impending sufferings" and details of wedding and honeymoon: *Ontario County* (N.Y.) *Times,* 7/15/1898.
12. "The Maud Humphrey baby . . .": Bogart/Holliday, "Own Story."
12. Details of Maud Humphrey's publishers, works, and income: Francine Kirsch, "Maude Humphrey," *Upstate* magazine, 3/18/84.
13. "Starving in a garret . . .": Canandaigua *Daily Messenger,* 6/28/39.
13. "cry, drool, get dirty or throw . . .": Betsy Brayer, *New York–Pennsylvania Collector,* 8/78.
13. horsehair furniture and maintained by a legion of Irish maids: Bogart/Holliday, "Own Story."
13. "I know nothing of her background . . .": Ibid.
13. "Born at New York . . . ": the usual surname spelling for Bogart's middle name is "De Forest," and handwritten court documents from 1808 indicate that Belmont's middle name may have had the space. But newspaper accounts of Belmont and Maud, Humphrey's Trinity School records and yearbooks, and his signature on a letter to Louis Bromfield, show no space. Biographies by Bogart's friends Nathaniel Benchley and Joe Hyams use "DeForest," as did *The New York Times* in its obituary (1/15/57). Additionally, although *Lauren Bacall by Myself* has it "de Forest," in a telephone interview with EL (11/5/96), she said DeForest was "one word."
13. Dr. Bogart's objection to Maud's attending an art show: Joe Hyams, *Bogie* (New York: New American Library, 1966; Signet, 1967), p. 23.
14. "a last century man": Nathaniel Benchley, *Humphrey Bogart* (Boston and Toronto: Little, Brown, 1975), p. 11.
14. *Dau's New York Blue Book, 1907 Winter Season 1908* (New York: Dau Publishing Co.).
14. Maud worked late into the night: Bogart/Holliday, "Own Story."
15. Bogart's see-saw academic average but consistently good grades in religion: Trinity School records, New York.
15. "and wasn't happy at home . . .": Doug Storer, *Pictorial Living,* 8/15/65.
15. "a misfit . . . miserable for Bogart": Ibid.
15. "you could tell by the look on his face . . .": Ibid.
16. "I wouldn't be here . . .": Hamlins, interview.
16. Bogart would refer to those months as the happiest of his first forty years: Canandaigua *Daily Messenger,* 4/17/41.
16. Activities of the Seneca Point Gang and correctly uniformed lead soldiers, etc.: Frank Hamlin, *Summers at the Lake,* private collection.
17. "But Humphrey would always rescue me . . .": Lambert, interview.
17. "It was sort of my first experience. . . . In silence": Ibid.

18. "caught my fancy completely when I was two": Bogart/Holliday, "Own Story."
19. Bogart's academic averages and need to repeat year: Trinity School records, New York.
20. "declassed gentleman . . . Hollywood": Richard Schickel, *Schickel on Film* (New York: William Morrow & Co., 1987), p. 219.
20. "in his first forty-five films . . .": Ibid., p. 215.
20. "Bogart can be tough without a gun . . .": Raymond Chandler to Hamish Hamilton, letter, 5/30/46, *Selected Letters of Raymond Chandler*, edited by Frank MacShane (New York: Delta/Dell, 1987), p. 75.
20. "Chin down, loose lower lip . . .": Eric Hatch, letter, 12/2/67, Eric Hatch Collection, BU.
21. "while some of my best friends . . .": Franklin P. Adams to Robert Benchley, "Wednesday" (probably 1917), NB BU.
22. "Every absence . . . hour of the community": Phillips Academy Blue Book, 1914–1915.
22. "Furlow was witty . . .": Arthur Sircom to Nathaniel Benchley, letter 12/31/73, NB BU.
23. "never cracked a book," etc.: Ibid.
23. "They made you learn dates . . .": Hyams, *Bogie,* p. 31.
23. "He lived . . . Andover": Sircom, letter.
23. Letter of dismissal: Dr. Alfred Stearns to Dr. Belmont Bogart, 5/18/18, Phillips Academy archives.
24. "away on business," etc.: Maud Humphrey Bogart to Dr. Alfred Stearns, letter, 5/20/18, Phillips Academy archives.
24. "No, I'm leaving . . . you're ruining your life!": Sircom, letter.

CHAPTER 2: "YOUNG AND HANDSOME AS VALENTINO AND ELEGANT IN COMEDY"

27. Bogart's lip damaged by flying splinter: Hyams, *Bogie,* p. 33.
27. Bogart's lip damaged by escaping prisoner: Stuart Rose, interview, n.d., NB BU.
27. Details of Bogart's physical examinations and service: National Personnel Records Center, Navy Records Branch, St. Louis.
28. "no nearer to an understanding . . .": Hyams, *Bogie,* p. 33.
28. The family moved to 79 East 56th Street and "had social aspirations . . .": Bogart/Holliday, "Own Story."
28. "There was no running . . .": Ibid.
28. Belmont's practice had diminished and poor investments: Rose, interview.

29. Bogart worked for S. W. Strauss and Co.: Hyams, *Bogie,* p. 34.
29. "when I found out . . .": Ibid.
29. Rose's first meeting Bogart and Frances: Rose, interview.
29. Details of Stuart Rose and Frances Bogart's elopement: *Ontario County* (N.Y.) *Times,* 6/11/24.
29. "never found a man . . .": Ibid.
30. "give him a chance": Hyams, *Bogie,* p. 36.
30. "There were some beautiful . . .": Clifford McCarty, *The Complete Films of Humphrey Bogart* (New York: Citadel Press, 1990), p. 8. Originally published 1965 as *Bogey: The Films of Humphrey Bogart.*
30. "full of blood and death": Howard Sharpe, "The Amorous Life Story of a Movie Killer," part 1, *Movieland,* probably 2/43, p. 28.
30. "Bogart once wrote for me": Ibid.
31. "taken ill": Charles Frohman Inc., agency questionnaire, 1928 (no month), Theatre Collection, The Museum of the City of New York.
31. "was unprepared . . .": Benchley, *Humphrey Bogart,* p. 25.
31. "It was awful . . .": Hyams, *Bogie,* p. 36.
31. "The boy's good, isn't he?": Rose, interview.
31. "flashy melodrama": Burns Mantle, N.Y. *Daily News,* 1/4/22; "strangely protuberant": Alan Dale, N.Y. *American,* 1/4/22. Also Benchley, *Humphrey Bogart,* p. 27.
31. "Which way do I face . . .": Benchley, *Humphrey Bogart,* p. 27.
32. "So you wanted . . .": Bogart/Holliday, "Own Story."
32. "I will read you . . .": Howard Sharpe, "The Amorous Life Story of a Movie Killer," part 2, *Movieland,* probably 3/43, p. 33.
32. "observation, integrity, and brains . . .": Rose, interview.
32. "Get this, Bogart . . .": Howard Sharpe, "The Amorous Life Story of a Movie Killer," part 2, *Movieland*.
33. Louella Parsons claimed she heard Bogart utter, "Tennis, anyone?": Louella Parsons, "Bogey," *Modern Screen,* n.d. (probably 1961 or 1962), CMC USC.
33. "It's forty-love . . ." and "spoken every . . .": Benchley, *Humphrey Bogart,* p. 30.
33. "He must have taken a liking to me": Mary Philips MacKenna, interview, n.d., NB BU.
33. "badly swelled head. . . . easily fall in love": Hyams, *Bogie,* p. 40.
34. "I guess I shouldn't have . . .": Ibid., p. 41
34. "Oh, all right, then. . . .": Benchley, *Humphrey Bogart,* p. 37
34. "[Bogart] is as young and handsome . . .": Hyams, *Bogie,* p. 41.
35. "a slim boy . . . disfigurement": Louise Brooks, *Lulu in Hollywood* (New York: Alfred A. Knopf, 1982), pp. 59–60.
36. "If you don't marry . . .": Rose, interview.
36. "everybody in the theater . . . ": Ibid.

36. Episcopal ceremony performed by the Reverend John Kent: Hyams, *Bogie,* p. 42.
36. "We quarreled over the most . . .": Ibid., p. 43.
37. "I tried to make my marriage . . .", Ibid.
37. "By this time you have probably . . .": Benchley, *Humphrey Bogart,* p. 39.
37. "I was to blame . . .": Hyams, *Bogie,* p. 43.
37. "I had had enough women . . .": Ibid., p. 44.
38. Holbrook Blinn's advice: Ibid., p. 45.
38. "a sort of Puritan . . .": MacKenna, interview.
38. "Mary is a mixture . . .": Hyams, *Bogie,* p. 45.
38. "good actors did the best . . . showy counterfeit": Percy Hammond, N.Y. *Tribune,* 1/12/29, NB BU.
39. *A Most Immoral Lady* ran 160 performances: Hyams, *Bogie,* p. 45.
39. "Humphrey Bogart, darkly handsome . . .": *It's a Wise Child* program, New York Theatre Program Corporation, WSHS.
39. "You know, I love . . .": Rose, interview.
39. "For God's sake . . .": MacKenna, interview.
40. "everything that was published . . . did and it was": and Bogart's salary, Rose, interview.
40. "modern couple": Hyams, *Bogie,* p. 46.
40. Farrell and Gaynor the leading romantic team: Ephraim Katz, *The Film Encyclopedia,* 2nd ed. (New York: HarperCollins, 1994), p. 435.
41. "just a bunch of junk . . .": Jonathan Coe, *Humphrey Bogart: Take It and Like It* (London: Bloomsbury, 1991), p. 24.
41. "I can lick *you* . . . friends": Hyams, *Bogie,* p. 47.
41. Johnson's Scaramouch theory and "his detractors . . .": Benchley, *Humphrey Bogart,* p. 5.
42. Bogart's part cut from the prints of *Women of All Nations*: Patricia King Hanson, executive ed., *The American Film Institute Catalog of Motion Pictures Produced in the United States: Feature Films, 1931–1940,* vol. 2 (Berkeley, Calif.: University of California Press, 1993), p. 2,469.
42. "I was too short . . .": Hyams, *Bogie,* p. 48.
42. "The trouble with George . . .": Benchley, *Humphrey Bogart,* p. 49
42. "Then things became really . . . fashion": Bogart/Holliday, "Own Story."
43. Bogart landed parts in five plays: Sharpe, "The Amorous Life Story of a Movie Killer," part 2, *Movieland,* p. 34.
43. Ten people in the audience and figures for 1933 season: Hyams, *Bogie,* p. 49. Also Sharpe, "The Amorous Life Story of a Movie Killer," part 2, *Movieland.*
44. Mel Baker's curious eating habits: Cynthia Lindsay, interview, 5/8/91.
44. "To make my position . . .": Humphrey Bogart to the Players, n.d. (probably 1934 or 1935), the Players' archives, New York.

45. "It was only in that moment . . .": Hyams, *Bogie,* p. 51.
45. "doubled up momentarily . . .": Bogart/Holliday, "Own Story."
45. Belmont Bogart's debts and uncollected fees: Hyams, *Bogie,* p. 51, and Benchley, *Humphrey Bogart,* p. 59.
45. "sank into one of . . .": John Mason Brown, *The Worlds of Robert E. Sherwood, Mirror to His Times, 1896–1939* (New York: Harper & Row, 1965), p. 320.
46. The *Post* reported ticket-buyers wanting seats close enough to see Mantee's beard: Hyams, *Bogie,* p. 52.
47. "Presently, Mitchell . . .": Brooks, *Lulu in Hollywood,* p. 68.

CHAPTER 3: FITTING THE BILL

49. "a practice the brothers . . .": Cass Warner Sperling and Cork Millner, *Hollywood Be Thy Name* (Rocklin, Calif: Prima Publishing, 1994), p. 2.
51. Jerome Lawrence and last performance of *The Petrified Forest:* Jerome Lawrence, interview, 11/2/87. The evening show was the capper on a long theatrical day. "I saw *Awake and Sing* at the Group Theater with Stella Adler, then ran without eating to see Noël Coward in that wonderful Ben Hecht picture that they wouldn't allow to be shown in Ohio [*The Scoundrel*]. And I ran to the final performance of *The Petrified Forest.*"
52. "It was Bogie . . ." and account of visit to studio: Henrietta Kaye, interview, n.d. (probably 1989).
54. Bogart's single-sheet contract: USC WB.
54. "Her spirit and intelligence . . .": *NYT,* 9/23/35.
56. Warner Brothers lost $31 million: Rudy Behlmer, *Inside Warner Bros., 1935–1951* (New York: Viking, 1985), p. 56.
57. "You better save Jack Warner . . .": Lyle Talbot, interview, 10/16/89.
57. "There was an exciting . . .": Carl Schaefer, interview, 9/16/88.
58. "If I don't make it this time . . .": Ibid.
58. "Everyone was exhausted from breathing in the dirt": Henry Blanke to Hal Wallis, Daily Production and Progress Report, 11/5/35, USC WB.
59. "The strength of *The Petrified Forest* . . .": Blanke to Wallis, memo, 12/6/35, USC WB.
59. "Having carried the story logically . . .": Leslie Howard to JLW, n.d., USC WB.
59. "Howard should be notified . . .": Roy Obringer to Hal Wallis, memo, 12/23/35, Rudy Behlmer, *Inside Warner Bros.,* p. 27
61. Maud working at Stonewright Studios, etc.: William Barrie and Milton Barrie, interviews with EL, 8/14/95, 7/11/96.

61. "Be sure and get HUMPHREY BOGART'S contract . . .": JLW to Roy Obringer, 12/9/35 WB legal files, USC WB.
61. Terms of Bogart's contract: Bogart legal file, USC WB.
62. $300 bonus: Gurney, 4/13/37, WB legal files, USC WB.
62. *The Postman Always Rings Twice* "too hot" for Hollywood: *Philadelphia Inquirer*, 2/7/36
63. "This is the first time I've really . . .": Hyams, *Bogie*, p. 59
64. Exceptions to picking up paychecks: Obringer to Bogart, letter, 1/22/43, WB, legal files, USC WB.
64. Al Jolson paid with checks on New York bank . . . : Behlmer, *Inside Warner Bros.*, p. 57
64. "Are we using Humphrey Bogart?" JLW to Hal Wallis, memo, 1/3/36, JWC, USC WB
64. "He'd get a script . . .": Arthur Silver, interview, 11/19/87.
65. "Beneath a thin veneer . . .": Pressbook for *Bullets or Ballots,* USC WB.
66. The day ended at five minutes to midnight: Lee Hugunin to T. C. Wright, Daily Production and Progress Report, 7/6/36, USC WB.
66. "Humphrey Bogart has been making it . . .": Hugunin to Wright, Daily Production and Progress Report, 7/7/36, USC WB.
67. "Midnight dinner on a filthy set": Hugunin to Wright, Daily Production and Progress Report, 7/8/36, USC WB.
67. "This gets away from amusements . . .": Hugunin to Wright, memo, 6/15/36, USC WB.
68. "Would you get me a drink of water, dear?": Hyams, *Bogie,* p. 53
68. Bogart was seated on the floor . . . : Barry Paris, *Louise Brooks* (New York: Anchor/Doubleday, 1989), pp. 375–6; Brooks, *Lulu in Hollywood*, p. 67
68. "Coming from anyone else . . . silence and Scotch": Brooks, *Lulu in Hollywood*, p. 67
68. "Being supremely confident . . .": Ibid, p. 65.
69. "intuitive artistry": N.Y. *Daily News*, 2/26/36.
69. "the gas station strumpet": *NYT*, 2/26/36.
69. "Mary Philips has just arrived . . .": Robert Benchley to Mrs. Robert Benchley, letter, 4/27/36, NB BU.

CHAPTER 4: THE PORTLAND ROSEBUD

70. Mayo a performer since age six: N.Y. *Daily News,* 2/10/24.
70. "Take it": N.Y. *Journal*, 2/13/24; N.Y. *Telegram,* 2/14/24.
71. Bogart and Mayo meeting at the Biltmore: Sidney Skolsky, "Tintypes" *Hollywood Citizen-News*, ca. 7/43. Also Hyams, *Bogie*, p. 60.
72. "She was an alcoholic. . . . liked to laugh": Gloria Stuart, interview, 2/2/90.

72. "clad in a sheath. . . . hid Mayo's slipper": Brooks, *Lulu in Hollywood*, pp. 67–68.
73. Move to North Horn Avenue: Benchley, *Humphrey Bogart*, p. 66; Gertrude Chase, interview, n.d., NB BU; also WB staff and cast listings, *Isle of Fury*, USC WB.
73. Mayo's charge of Percy's cruelty in not letting her rearrange the furniture: in unidentified newsclip and photo, 1938, CMC USC.
73. "Bogie didn't really want to marry Mayo . . .": Mary Baker, interview, n.d., NB BU.
74. "there comes a time in everyone's career . . .": Bette Davis to JLW, letter, 6/21/36, Behlmer, *Inside Warner Bros.*, p. 27.
74. "naughty young lady": London *Daily Mirror*, 10/15/36.
75. "I don't know how he ever, ever married her . . .": Jane Bryan Dart, interview, 9/24/90.
75. "Some of the really tough ladies. . . . poison to one another": Dart, interview.
76. "Jewish," "foreign," "a distinctly American-looking actor": Robert Lord to Hal Wallis, memo, 1936 (date uncertain), USC WB.
78. "*Black Legion* will not stay . . .": Frank S. Nugent, "Second Thoughts on *Black Legion*," *NYT*, n.d.
78. "as much a story in human . . .": N.Y. *Herald Tribune*, 1/6/37.
79. "Celluloid Dynamite": Red Kann, *Motion Picture Daily*, 12/20/26.
79. "nothing about the covert network . . .": Editorial, "Caliban in America"; Paul W. Ward, "Washington Weekly: Who's Behind the Black Legion?," *The Nation*, 6/30/36.
79. "what constituted libel": Morris Evenstein to Hal Wallis, memo, 11/6/36, USC WB.
79. "dynamic and stirring. . . .": N.Y. *Post*, n.d. (1936 or 1937).
79. "His powerful performance . . .": N.Y. *Morning Telegraph*, n.d. (1936 or 1937).
80. "There's no Paul Muni . . .": Warner Bros. Pictures, Inc., News and Feature Service, for release after 1/23/37; *Black Legion* press file, USC WB.
80. Warners sued by KKK: *The Knights of the Ku Klux Klan* v. *Warner Bros. Pictures, Inc. and Vitagraph, Inc.*, petition to the U.S. District Court for the Northern District of Georgia, Atlanta Division.
81. "He was going home . . .": Sidney Kingsley, interview, 12/27/89.
81. "Virtually always, Bogart's various shootouts . . .": Periodical name unknown, CMC USC. Bogart did have a brief dying speech in *San Quentin*, filmed in late 1936 and released in 1937. After being fatally shot by the police on his way to give himself up, he tells his fellow cons to cooperate with the warden, played by Pat O'Brien.
82. The title role of Katherina in *The Taming of the Shrew* was played by

Frieda Inescourt, earlier seen as Bogart's long-suffering wife in *The Great O'Malley.*

82. "If it won't interfere with his . . .": JLW, handwritten answer on memo from Arnow to Warner, 6/26/37, USC WB.
82. Huston, Aherne, Bogart performance of *Henry IV, Part I:* According to Lawrence Grobel in *The Hustons* (New York: Scribner's, 1989, p. 182) the production did not receive good notices.
82. "You could almost make a card index . . ." Ezra Goodman, source unknown.
83. "a little more particular" and "He looks dirty": Wallis to Bacon, memos, 12/22/36, 1/12/37, USC WB.
83. "A self-destructive man . . .": Kingsley, interview.
83. "I'm glad I ain't like you saps . . .": Sidney Kingsley and Lillian Hellman, *Dead End*—bound script, WWC UCLA, Box 63.
83. "liked him and admired . . .": Kingsley, interview.
83. "kind of broken. . . . to the face": Ibid.
84. Goldwyn was bringing the original boys' cast: One of the group that didn't go West with the others was Sidney Lumet, who gave up acting for directing.
84. "there isn't an actor in town . . .": Louella O. Parsons column, Los Angeles *Examiner*, 2/12/37.
84. "He went around town asking . . .", Kingsley, interview.
85. "They were shooting on the waterfront set" and details of Bogart's actions: Baker, interview.
85. Bogart unenthusiastic about marriage to Mayo: Ibid.
85. Kay's death caused by peritonitis: Benchley, *Humphrey Bogart*, p. 49.
85. "She was a victim . . .": Hyams, *Bogie* p. 66.
85. The question of what to do with Pat, Rose's finances, and going to California to be cared for by Bogart: Stuart Rose, interview, n.d., NB BU.
86. Bogart took "full care" of Frances: Baker, interview.
86. "A very heavy expense . . .": Noll Gurney to JLW, letter, 4/13/37, Bogart legal file, USC WB.
87. "You're crazy if you think . . .": Tay Garnett, interview, n.d., NB BU.
87. ". . . the One and Only Weaver Brothers . . .": of no relation to Pete Seeger's Weavers.
88. Order to have Bogart report at 9:45 A.M.: Maxwell Arnow to JLW and Wallis, memo, 9/3/37, *Swing Your Lady* production file, USC WB.
88. Raise to $1,000 a week; Warner Bros. Pictures, Inc., to Humphrey Bogart, letter, 9/7/37, USC WB.
88. $24,000 net over the costs of the negative of *Swing Your Lady.* USC WB.
89. "Wallis was ready to scrap the whole thing . . .": Hal Wallis to Walter McEwen, memo, 4/24/36, USC WB.

90. "would Baker please pick up her interlocutory decree . . .": Baker, interview.
90. "a pleasure to see Miss Mary Philips again . . .": *NYT*, 3/23/38.

CHAPTER 5: "IF IT'S A LOUSE-HEEL, GIVE IT TO BOGART"

91. Mayo borrowed her wedding dress: Gloria Stuart, interview, 2/2/90.
91. Drinking Black Velvets: Ibid.
92. "Mischa Auer took off his pants . . .": Ibid.
92. "It could have been anything . . .": Benchley, *Humphrey Bogart*, p. 30.
92. Bogart and Baker driving off to Mexico and the aftermath of the wedding: Ibid., p. 38.
92. "muttering about what a shit the other was": George Oppenheimer, interview with Nathaniel Benchley, n.d., NB BU.
92. "Whenever Lindsay was at the Reinhardts' . . .": Cynthia Lindsay, interview, 5/8/91.
92. "Sober, Bogart was great . . .": Allen Rivkin, interview, 1/20/90.
93. "He was either perfectly charming . . .": Ibid.
93. "We heard this ruckus . . .": Ibid.
93. "I'm going to hang you!": Nathaniel Benchley, telling the story, had it from George Oppenheimer, who was not present but cited Cynthia Lindsay as his source. Oppenheimer evidently changed the story slightly in the telling, saying it was Bogart, not Mayo, who had the rope around the neck. Lindsay, who was present, says it was Mayo. Lindsay, interview.
93. "We were all laughing . . .": Ibid.
93. "Mayo was a tough broad . . .": Rivkin, interview.
93. "she reached out and slugged him": Ibid.
94. "a plumpish blond lady . . .": Niven Busch, interview, 5/5/89.
94. "Their fights usually ended in bed": Mary Baker, Nathaniel Benchley interview, n.d., probably early 1960s, typed notes, NB BU.
94. "I love a good fight . . .": Hyams, *Bogie*, p. 60.
94. "The Bogarts were always there . . .": Henrietta Kaye, interview, n.d. (probably 1989).
94. Account of the fight at Slapsie Maxie's: Stuart, interview.
95. "some sort of fairy": Rivkin, quoted by Benchley, *Humphrey Bogart*, p. 87.
95. "a great housekeeper": Benchley, interview with Gertrude Hatch Chase, n.d., typed notes, NB BU.
96. "She was devoted to Bogie's mother . . .": Ibid.
96. "When Maud stops working . . .": Bogart/Holliday, "Own Story."
96. "Oh, I almost forgot . . .": Ibid.

96. "She joined its congregation . . .": Ibid.
97. "You'd walk in for dinner . . .": Stuart, interview.
97. "a very jittery lady . . .": Lindsay, interview.
97. "took her out . . . just a little unbalanced": Ibid.
97. "If not, she was in trouble . . .": Baker, transcript of taped interview with Benchley, n.d., NB BU.
97. "Did you hear . . .": Lindsay, interview.
97. "The paper would come out . . .": Stuart, interview.
97. "Bogart adored her . . .": Joe Hyams, interview, 4/10/91.
98. "Yeah, don't pay . . . scary things": Richard Brooks, interview, 9/26/88.
98. "Although Bogart harbored resentment": Baker, transcript of taped interview, n.d., NB BU.
98. "There was a spirit of duty . . .": Bogart/Holliday, "Own Story."
99. "Harry didn't die . . .": Sperling and Miller, *Hollywood Be Thy Name,* p. 313.
99. "You know that saying . . .": Aljean Harmetz, *Round Up the Usual Suspects* (New York: Hyperion, 1992), p. 26.
99. Wallis's black-and-white saddle shoes and everyone snapping to attention when he appeared: Dart, interview.
99. "Production manager": T.C. Wright's full title was "production manager in connection with the administration of the general mechanical operation of the Producer's studio." His contract of 8/8/36 set his salary at $400 a week. WB legal files, USC WB.
100. "Tenny was a good Irishman . . .": William Schaefer, interview, 7/28/88.
100. Obringer's title of Warners' general counsel: Application to the Commissioner of Internal Revenue 11/11/43, WB WB. legal files, USC.
100. Matthews a reputed former FBI man: Arthur Silver, interview, 11/19/87.
101. Twelve thousand Warner Club members and twenty-seven hundred in the West Coast Studio Division: Arthur W. Warnock, Program, The Warners Club West Coast Studio Division Third Annual Dinner Dance, 4/1/37, USC WB.
101. "It was always black tie . . .": Ronald Reagan, interview, 11/15/90.
101. "You're the top . . .": Esther Bernstein, "Ode to the Warner Club," *The Warner Club Yearbook,* Third Annual Dinner Dance, West Coast Studio Division, Thursday Evening, 4/1/37, p. 25.
102. Cagney slapping a Dead End Kid: Lee Server, "An Interview with Huntz Hall," *Filmfax,* n.d.
102. "Nevertheless, Bogie turned in . . .": Louis Bromfield, "Bogie" *Photoplay,* n.d., CMC USC.
102. "We can finish off the wagon . . .": Robert Buckner, Virginia City, script scene 602, p. A33, USC WB.
102. "If it'd been Jack Warner's blood . . .": Richard Gehman, *Bogart* (New York: Gold Medal Books, 1965), p. 122.

103. "that S.O.B., he'll crack . . .": William Holden, interview, n.d., NB BU. Holden's age from "Vital Statistics," *Invisible Stripes* press file, USC WB.
103. "more force than conviction": N.Y. *Herald Tribune*, n.d. (c. 1939).
103. "wasn't exactly right for him": Geraldine Fitzgerald, interview, 12/8/89.
104. "Humphrey Bogart shows . . .": *National Box Office Digest*, 3/1/39.
104. "lastingly impressive": *Hollywood Reporter*, Wed., 3/8/39.
104. "Bogart, wonder of wonders . . .": the N.Y. *Post*, 4/21/39.
104. "Ronald Reagan longed": Reagan, interview.
104. "the director wanted it . . .": Ibid.
104. "I'm as good as some . . .": *Dark Victory*, cutter's script, p. 124, USC WB.
104. "That stable scene . . ." Hal Wallis to Edmund Goulding, memo, 11/3/38. Jonathan Coe, in *Humphrey Bogart: Take It and Like It*, claims that Goulding refused to direct this sequence and that writer Casey Robinson shot it. Coe does not cite his source and Warner production notes contain no references to such a radical change. In fact, this memo strongly suggests it was done by Goulding. Robinson is quoted in Rudy Behlmer in *America's Favorite Movies* (New York: Frederick Ungar, 1982) as saying, "I was practically never present on the stage during the shooting of a movie" (p. 169).
104. "I thanked God . . .": Coe, *Humphrey Bogart: Take It and Like It*, p. 51.
104. "She cried very heavily . . .": Bob Ross to T. C. Wright, memo, 12/3/38, USC WB.
105. Davis claimed she named the Oscar statuette: Katz, *The Film Encyclopedia*, p. 333.
105. "Mush mouth Robinson . . .": Bette Davis Collection, scrapbooks, BU.
105. "take the edge off Judith's . . .": David Lewis, memo, 11/4/38, USC WB.
105. "finely—beautifully": *Dark Victory*, cutter's script, USC WB.
105. "She could have told . . .": *Dark Victory*, changes, 12/3/38, p. 166, USC WB.
105. "he cried at card tricks": Philips, interview, n.d.
105. "Irving, I *can't*": Irving Rapper, interview 7/24/89.
105. "to remember throughout the play . . .": Goulding, memo, 3/22/39, USC WB.
106. "Wallis decided on Bogart": Hal Wallis to Steve Trilling, memo, 2/22/39, USC WB.
106. "By the following Monday . . .": Al Alleborn to T. C. Wright, memo, 3/20/39 ("I do feel Tenny, however, that they will recast the part tomorrow that BOGART is in, and have advised Trilling to check on a man named [Alan] MARSHALL who was tested for this part and whom DAVIS and GOULDING feel is the perfect 'CLEM' "), Behlmer, *Inside Warner Bros.*, p. 86.
106. "important both in name . . ." and related concerns: Alleborn to T. C.

Wright, memo, 3/20/39; Alleborn to Wright, memo, 3/22/39; Goulding to Wallis, memo, 3/22/39; Behlmer, Inside Warner Bros., p. 86.

106. "stalked off the set in a rage": Coe, *Humphrey Bogart: Take It and Like It*, p. 52, citing Charles Higham.

106. Passenger list of Santa Fe Special: Folder, *Warner Bros. Dodge City Special: Meet the Folks,* collection of Jules Buck.

107. "every precaution . . .": S. Charles Einfeld to JLW, memo, 3/12/39, JWC, USC WB.

107. "Really, it was a saloon . . .": Jules Buck, interview, 9/11/88.

107. "Wallace was *big* . . .": Ibid.

107. "Jesus! Did you . . .": Ibid.

108. Note from Bogart to Mayo: MMC UO.

109. "Leland Hayward had just . . .": Sam Jaffe, interview, 8/15/87.

109. "Here was a man that read. . . .": Ibid.

110. "When you see a picture . . .": *NYT*, 2/5/39.

110. "They have only a temp script . . .": Trilling to Wallis, memo, 10/24/39, USC WB.

110. "too uncertain": Trilling to Wallis, memo, 10/19/39, USC WB.

111. "They gave him nothing . . .": Jaffe, interview.

111. "He was kind of a nuisance . . .": Carl Schaefer, interview, 9/16/88.

112. Formation of the Production Code Administration: Thomas Schatz, *The Genius of the System* (New York: Pantheon, 1989), p. 204.

112. Production Code rules: Katz, *The Film Encyclopedia,* p. 1105.

112. "The hard-edged antisocial . . .": Schatz, *The Genius of the System*, pp. 206–207.

112. "The word was, 'If it's a louse-heel . . .' ": Vincent Sherman, interview. 11/5/87.

112. Raft's refusal to play Grasselli, calling it "a Humphrey Bogart part": In a subsequent letter to Warner, Raft reminded him that in their last contract negotiation, "if anyone at your studio ever submitted a script to me in which I was to play a dirty heavy I was to bring the script to you and you would take me out of it. I remarked at the time to you that I was afraid the studio would put me into parts that Humphrey Bogart should play and you told me I would never have to play a Humphrey Bogart part. . . .": George Raft to JLW, letter, 10/17/39, Behlmer, *Inside Warner Bros.*, p. 116.

112. "designed for use in situations . . .": *Dark Victory* press book, ad insert, USC WB.

113. Francis no longer box office: According to *Box Office Digest,* 1937, her films were grossing well below their average.

113. "It was a comedown . . .": Sherman, interview.

113. Kay Francis briefly married to Ken MacKenna: George Eells, *Ginger, Loretta and Irene* Who? (New York: G. P. Puttnam's Sons, 1976).

114. "Miss Francis, Bogart and the writer . . .": Carrol Sax to T. C. Wright, memo, 6/6/38, USC WB.
114. "*And that goes for you, too* . . .": Silver, interview.
115. "It never occurred to us . . .": Bosley Crowther, *NYT*, n.d., 1938.

CHAPTER 6: THE BEGINNING OF A BEAUTIFUL FRIENDSHIP

116. "I was just the writer": John Huston, interview, 5/20/87.
116. "a nodding acquaintance . . . ": Ibid.
117. "Take the spirit out of Burnett . . .": John Huston to Hal Wallis, letter, 3/21/40, USC WB.
118. "His face was swarthy . . .": W. R. Burnett, "High Sierra," *Redbook*, March, 1940; also W. R. Burnett, *High Sierra* (New York: Alfred A. Knopf, 1940).
118. Muni's contract stipulated making of Beethoven biography: Roy Obringer to JLW, memo, 5/23/40, USC WB.
118. "PROVIDED DON'T BECOME . . .": Paul Muni to Hal Wallis, telegram, 3/18/40, Paul Muni legal file, USC WB.
119. Muni's co-producer privileges, etc.: Paul Muni Agreement with Warner Bros. Pictures, Inc., 10/2/37, Muni legal file, USC WB.
119. "sexy, gangster-ennobling . . .": John Wexley to Hal Wallis, memo, 3/21/40, USC WB.
120. "What of the superb romance . . .": Hellinger to Wallis, memo, 3/19/40, USC WB.
120. "SOMETHING WORTHWHILE": Muni to Wallis, 3/18/40, telegram, USC WB.
120. Base the screenplay on the book rather than do conventional treatment: memo, Huston to Wallis, letter, 3/29/40, USC WB.
120. "I NEVER RECEIVED AN ANSWER . . .": Bogart to Wallis, telegram, 5/4/40, USC WB.
121. "such a great actor . . .": W. R. Burnett to Hal Wallis, letter, 3/28/40, USC WB. Burnett, in an interview published in 1986 (Pat McGilligan, *Backstory: Interviews with Screenwriters of Hollywood's Golden Age* [Berkeley, Calif., and Los Angeles: University of California Press, 1986]), told of Huston getting "a little loaded" at a Hollywood party during the time of the first draft and telling Muni "what he thought of him as an actor," ostensibly causing Muni's rejection of the first draft. Muni, however, was touring with *Key Largo* on the East Coast at the time. There may have been an occasion when Huston, smarting from the *Juarez* rewrites and the later rejections of his *High Sierra* drafts, told Muni off, but it would seem to have been at a later date.

121. "For chrissakes . . .": Grobel, *The Hustons,* p. 211.
121. "I never had so much fun . . .": McGilligan, *Backstory,* p. 64, and Grobel, *The Hustons,* p. 211.
121. Hellinger's calling Huston and screaming at Warner: Grobel, p. 211.
122. "Look, you want Raft's . . .": Louis Sobol, *New York Cavalcade,* King Features Syndicate, 11/5/41.
123. "Dear Marty . . . I can count on you . . .": S. Charles Einfeld to Martin Weiser, letter, 7/17/40, USC WB.
123. "the Sheridan truck": Martin Weiser, interview, 11/24/87.
124. "Raft was not . . .": Bruce Bennett, interview, 1/26/90.
124. "out-and-out heavies": Obringer to JLW, memo, 5/23/40, USC WB.
124. "*Everything* was intended . . .": Huston, interview.
125. production number 324 . . . : E. I. De Patie to T. C. Wright, memo, 7/31/40, USC WB.
125. "the air of a man . . .": Schickel, *Schickel on Film,* p. 228.
126. "It was a damn good . . .": Ida Lupino, interview, 8/28/91.
126. "had just a few words . . .": Ibid.
126. "I had heard rumors . . .": Joan Leslie, interview, 1990.
126. Jack Warner's paternal interest in Leslie and the presentation of a new car: Otto Friedrich, *City of Nets* (New York: Harper & Row, 1986), p. 131.
127. "I feel like . . .": Buster Wiles, interview, 3/9/90.
127. cookies concealed between the fingers: Wiles, interview: also Buster Wiles and William Donait, *My Days with Errol Flynn* (Santa Monica, Calif: Roundtable Publishing, 1988), p. 90.
127. Zero belonged to Bogart: Lupino, interview.
127. "I'd open it . . .": Ibid.
127. Bogart's ability to quote Plato, etc., and his correspondence with Holmes: Hyams, *Bogie,* p. 105.
127. "more cocktails than one . . .": Huston, interview.
127. "We were all buddies . . .": Lupino, interview.
128. "It didn't turn out . . .": Ibid.
128. "Bogie was crazy . . ." and "Ida was in love . . .": Rapper, interview.
128. "They should have signed . . . ' ": Wiles, interview.
128. "Mayo could be very nice . . ." Wiles, interview; also Wiles and Donait, *My Days with Errol Flynn.*
128. "a good size" wreath . . . : William Graf, interview, 10/24/90.
129. "I'm having trouble . . .": Lupino, interview.
129. "Listen, doll . . .": Jerry Vermilye, *Ida Lupino, Pyramid Illustrated History of the Movies* (New York: Pyramid Communications, 1977).
129. "Unable finish . . .": *High Sierra,* Daily Production and Progress Report, 9/9/40, USC WB.

129. "toward the finish . . .": Lupino, interview.
129. Memo reversing billing of *High Sierra:* Wallis to JLW, 9/18/40, Behlmer, *Inside Warner Bros.*, pp. 128–129.
130. "Miss Lupino broke . . .": Al Alleborn to T. C. Wright, memo, 9/20/40, USC WB.
130. "he never said . . .": Lupino, interview.
131. "Everyone is on a committee . . .": Robert Benchley to Mrs. Benchley, letter, 4/27/36, Robert Benchley Collection, BU.
132. "read the doctrines of Karl Marx": "Humphrey Bogart," FBI summary, 8/30/40. Schulberg's son Budd was in fact a member of the Young Communist League at the time and was among those named by Leech. Leech's emphasis, however, was on the stars, and none of those allegations held up.
132. names on Leech's "master list . . .": Ibid; also *NYT*, 8/15/40 and 8/21/40; Washington *Times Herald*, 8/15/40 and 8/21/40, et al.
132. "HOLLYWOOD STARS ACCUSED . . .": *NYT*, 8/15/40.
132. Account of Bogart's testimony before Dies: *Investigation of Un-American Propaganda Activities in the United States,* U.S. House Committee on Un-American Activities, 8/16/40 (Washington, D.C.: U.S. Government Printing Office, 1940).
133. "a political belief . . .": *NYT*, 8/16/40.
133. "It would be foolish . . .": *NYT*, 8/16/40.

CHAPTER 7: BIRTH OF A HERO

135. "It didn't seem likely . . .": Ring Lardner Jr., interview, 7/25/90.
135. "a conflict between . . .": Motion Picture Democratic Committee, newsletter, May 22, 1940, MDC WSHS.
136. "It hit me real hard . . .": Ida Lupino, interview, 8/28/91.
136. "It was wonderful . . .": Ibid.
136. "Why We of Hollywood . . .": *NYT*, 10/31/40.
136. "We had driven . . .": Eric Hatch to Howard Gotlieb, letter, 11/1/70, Eric Hatch Collection, BU.
137. "Bogie was drinking . . .": Ibid.
137. "Eric Hatch, Esq." . . . : Humphrey Bogart to Eric Hatch, letter, 1940 (probably late October or early November), Eric Hatch Collection, BU.
137. "a low-budget . . .": David Lewis to Hal Wallis, memo, 10/16/40, USC WB.
138. Raft turned down *Carnival*: Correspondence, 9/40, Raft legal file, USC WB.

138. "It was surrounded by tall bars . . .": Eddie Albert, interview, 2/5/90.
138. "She died as she . . .": Bogart/Holliday, "Own Story."
138. "Cruel as it may sound . . .": Ibid.
139. "Who is the vilest . . .": Ibid.
139. "Here is my heart . . .": MMC UO.
140. Warner Bros. Pictures reimbursed by Warner Bros. Circuit Management: H. Berkowitz to Obringer, letter, McDonald, Martin, Shipman, 12/30/40, USC WB.
140. "Humph-*ree* . . .": Junius Adams, interview, 9/17/90.
141. "The picture brings . . .": Kansas City *Star*, 1/26/41.
142. "Blanke couldn't . . .": Blanke to Wallis, memo, 12/19/40, USC WB.
142. "IT SEEMS TO ME . . .": Bogart to JLW, telegram, 1/16/41, USC WB.
142. Lupino wanting to play in *How Green Was My Valley*: Trilling to Wallis, memo, 1/2/41, USC WB.
142. "LUPINO REFUSES . . .": JLW to Hal Wallis, telegram, 2/4/41, JWC, USC WB.
142. "Bogart's verbal treatment . . .": Vermilye, *Ida Lupino.*
142. "quite a verbal battering": Thomas Wood, *Menace as Usual*, periodical unknown, 1943, CMC USC.
143. "Ahhh, well . . .": Huston, interview.
143. Lupino and Garfield not happy: "Jack" to Mr. Wallis, memo, 1/16/41, USC WB.
143. "the problem of convincing . . .": Blanke to JLW, memo, 1/31/41, USC WB.
143. "straighten out . . .": Blanke to Trilling, memo, 2/3/41, USC WB.
144. "He reads every line . . .": Thomas Wood, *Menace as Usual*, ibid.
144. Warners weighing other options, including loanout to MGM: Trilling to Wallis, memo, 2/25/41, USC WB.
144. "Raft didn't want the competition . . .": Max Wilk, interview, 5/4/87.
144. "AND NOBODY MADE ANY EFFORT . . . WORK WITH ME": Bogart to Wallis, telegram, 3/6/41, USC WB.
145. "did violently rough-house and push . . .": Affadivit, Roy Obringer, Warner Brothers, to Screen Actors Guild, 4/30/41, USC WB.
145. "*Are you kidding* . . .": Bogart to Trilling, letter, 3/17/41, USC WB.
145. "Please be advised . . .": Obringer to Einfeld, memo, cc: Taplinger, Trilling, Wright, Blumenstock, 3/18/41, Bogart legal file, USC WB.
146. "ready, willing and able": Sam Jaffe, Ltd. Agency to Warner Bros. Pictures, Inc., letter, 4/2/41, WB, USC.
146. Lift or continue Bogart's suspension: Roy Obringer to JLW and Hal Wallis, memo, 4/4/41, USC WB.
146. "*Kid Galahad* in a new . . .": Mishkin, *Morning Telegraph,* 5/12/41.
146. "A bit of carnival color . . .": N.Y. *Herald Tribune*, 5/10/41.
146. "apparently, the Strand . . .": N.Y. *Daily News,* 5/10/41.

146. "The Strand customers . . .": N.Y. *Post,* 5/10/41.
146. "badly hampered . . .": *The Wagons Roll at Night,* press file—reviews of 5/10/41, USC WB.
147. What should the studio do about Bogart's suspension: Obringer to JLW, memo, 4/18/41, USC WB.
147. "Put Humphrey Bogart back . . .": JLW to Mr. Obringer, memo, 4/18/41, USC WB.

CHAPTER 8: THE BLACK BIRD

148. "This dumb magazine . . .": Max Wilk, interview, 5/4/87.
148. Paramount ran into casting problems: According to Thomas Schatz (*The Genius of the System,* pp. 79–80), Hammett, then working as a screenwriter for Paramount, had sold the studio an original story based on *The Maltese Falcon.* David O. Selznick, the executive assistant to production head B. P. Schulberg, liked the story and wanted Spade to be played by George Bancroft, who had convincingly played a heavy in the 1927 silent epic *Underworld.* However, Paramount story editor Edward J. Montagne felt that Fredric March was the perfect Spade. Since March was then known only for light comedy, and Paramount was not inclined to offcast its stars, the story was dropped. There was no indication of the final disposition or legal status of the story sold to Paramount. Warners bought the rights from the author and publisher.
148. "Well, we bought it . . .": Max Wilk, interview.
149. "by actually making . . .": Hal Wallis to Harry Joe Brown, memo, 6/27/34, USC WB.
149. "The fact was . . .": John Huston, *An Open Book* (New York: Alfred A. Knopf, 1980).
149. "I decided on a . . .": John Huston to Alan S. Downer, letter, 3/31/47, Warner Bros. Collection, Princeton University.
149. "Why don't we . . .": John Huston, interview, 5/20/87.
150. "he didn't want to work . . .": Ibid.
150. "You are to portray . . .": Warner Bros. Pictures, Inc. to George Raft, letter, 5/26/41, George Raft legal file, USC WB.
150. Raft to be formally ordered to work June 2: JLW to Roy Obringer, memo, 5/28/41, USC WB.
150. "word leaked back from Fox": Steve Trilling to JLW, memo, 6/2/41, Raft legal file, USC WB.
150. "Just to show his authority . . .": Huston, interview.
151. "Dear Jack . . .": George Raft to JLW, letter, 6/6/41, USC WB.
151. "He is very likely . . .": Obringer to Wallis, memo, 5/22/41, USC WB.
151. "Roy had played . . .": William Schaefer, interview, 8/10/88.

151. Raft's reputation: *Katz's Film Encyclopedia, Cinemania '95,* Microsoft Corp.
152. "It was the only . . .": Schaefer, interview.
152. "unquestionably the finest . . .": N.Y. *Post,* 4/21/39, *Dark Victory* press file, USC WB.
152. Fitzgerald's contract: Agreement, Warner Bros. Pictures, Inc. and Geraldine Fitzgerald, 10/1/38, Fitzgerald legal file, USC WB.
153. "a humdinger": Henry Blanke to Hal Wallis, memo, 5/19/41, USC WB.
153. "I didn't have to be . . .": "Bogie—for Real," *NYT,* 4/23/67; also Mary Astor, *A Life on Film* (New York: Delacorte, 1971).
153. Greenstreet's weighing 357 pounds and the studio's needing to make his wardrobe: Al Alleborn to T. C. Wright, memo, 6/17/41, USC WB.
153. "Don't try to get . . .": Wallis to Huston, memo, 6/20/41, USC WB.
153. "I attempted . . .": Huston to Downer, letter, 6/20/41, USC WB.
154. Huston dismissed any indebtedness to Welles, and Huston's method: Ken Whitmore, Warner Brothers Studio Publicity, 1941, USC WB.
154. "real rooms and offices . . .": Ibid.
154. Mary Astor's costume: Daily Production and Progress Report: "Maltese Falcon": Tests, 6–3–41, WB, USC.
154. Descriptions of Spade and O'Shaughnessy: Screenplay, *The Maltese Falcon,* Final, 5/26/41, WB USC.
155. Bogart's costume: Ibid.
155. "the punchy, driving . . .": Wallis to Blanke, memo, 6/12/41, USC WB.
155. "quick and staccato": Huston to Wallis, memo, 6/13/41, USC WB.
155. Wyler's assistance and Blanke's advice: Grobel, *The Hustons,* p. 218.
156. "perfect from the word . . .": Huston, *An Open Book.*
156. "the enchanting . . .": Ibid.
156. "a showgirl, a gentlewoman . . .": John Huston obituary, *NYT,* 8/29/87.
156. "He had affairs with . . .", Meta Wilde, interview, 2/8/90.
156. "The ladies liked Bogie . . .": Huston, interview.
156. "Bogey looked at the world . . .": Mary Astor, *Bogie—for Real,* unedited draft of *NYT* article, MAC BU.
157. "Bogie did his best . . .": Huston, *An Open Book.*
157. "She was always . . .": Huston, interview.
157. "Bogie was *morbidly* . . .": Ibid.
157. Lunch at Lakeside: Ibid.
157. "People from other companies . . . wrong with that": Astor, *Bogie—for Real.*
158. "We had to . . .": Ibid.
158. "Now wait a minute . . .": Ibid.
158. "the audience knows . . .": Huston to Downer, letter, 6/20/41, USC WB.
158. "The camera followed . . .": Meta Carpenter Wilde and Orin Borsten, *A*

Loving Gentleman: The Love Story of William Faulkner and Meta Carpenter (New York: Simon & Schuster, 1976), p. 262.

159. "he was forever surprising . . .": Huston, interview.
159. "was quite brilliant . . .": Astor, *Bogie—for Real.*
160. "he didn't like . . .": Ibid.
160. "Try not to knock . . .": Ibid.
160. "Fine work . . .": Al Alleborn to Tenny Wright, memo, 6/17/41, USC WB.
160. "phony . . . pretty obvious": Wallis to Blanke, memo, 6/17/41, USC WB.
160. "too coy . . .": Wallis to Blanke, memo, 6/24/41, USC WB.
161. "One solid . . .": Blanke to Wallis, memo, 6/30/41, USC WB.
161. "*It's a fake!*": Greenstreet, during post-production, recorded a wild track of that line. The line itself was in the script, however, and the voice, contrary to some current assertions, is Greenstreet's. There are no records as to why the wild track was necessary, but presumably it was related to some problem during the shooting.
162. $54,000 under budget and two days ahead of schedule: Alleborn to Wright, Daily Production and Progress Report, 7/19/41, USC WB.
162. "They feel they can . . .": Alleborn to Wright, memo, 7/19/41, USC WB.
162. "last looks . . .": Blanke to Al Alleborn, memo, 7/30/41, USC WB.
163. "POLHAUS . . .": *The Maltese Falcon,* cutter's script, USC WB.
163. misquoting Shakespeare: The actual line is: "We are such stuff as dreams are made on." *The Tempest,* act IV, scene 1.
163. "Why be so clever . . .": JLW to Mr. Wallis, memo, 9/6/41, USC WB.
163. Title change: Wallis, memo, 8/29/41, USC WB.
164. Specifics on title: Main Title and Lithograph Billing, 7/10/41, USC WB.
164. Billing changes: Corrected Billing, *The Maltese Falcon,* 9/8/41, USC WB.

CHAPTER 9: "DO TOUGH GUYS HAVE *SEX* APPEAL?"

165. "a solid professional . . .": Vincent Sherman, interview, 11/5/87.
165. "Mayo's in the dressing room . . .": Ibid.
166. "His secretary . . .": Herb Cohen, Brooklyn *Eagle,* 10/4/41.
166. "DO TOUGH . . . really gets 'em": *The Maltese Falcon* press book, USC WB.
166. "He doesn't know . . .": Sharpe, "The Amorous Life Story of a Movie Killer," CMC USC.
166. "She gave up . . .": *Movieland,* n.d. (probably after 7/42 and the release of *The Big Shot*), CMC USC.

166. "She had talent . . .": Milton Sperling, interview, 8/13/87.
167. "The fact that she . . .": Marsha Hunt, interview, 2/26/90.
167. "a kind of *zaftig* . . .": Ibid.
167. " 'Flynn said to Bogie . . .": Wiles, interview.
167. "We, Mr. and Mrs. Bogart . . .": Letter to Eric and Gertie Hatch, n.d. (probably August 1941), Eric Hatch Collection, BU.
168. "It was an ongoing . . .": Walter Seltzer, interview, 11/19/90.
168. "He never said . . .": Joy Barlowe, interview, 1/31/90.
168. "He would cheat . . .": Sam Jaffe, interview, 8/15/87.
169. "Well, well . . .": Hyams, *Bogie,* p. 61.
169. "He liked a good . . . Yeah, that's Bogie!": Allan McMillan, interview, 1/16/88.
171. "on rubber heels . . .": Hal Wallis to JLW, memo, 10/8/41, USC WB.
171. "strangely bashful": *NYT,* 10/4/41.
171. "I should think . . .": Blanke to Wallis, memo, 11/13/41, USC WB.
171. "because . . . for the past . . .": Sam Jaffe to JLW, letter, n.d., USC WB.
171. "the white-haired boy . . .": Louis Sobol, *New York Cavalcade,* 11/5/41.
171. "There but for . . .": Leonard Lyons, *"The Lyons Den"* N.Y. *Post,* 10/10/41.
172. "You look like . . .": *All Through the Night,* press file, USC WB.
172. "The editor was acquainted . . .": Malvin Wald to AMS, letter, 12/27/93.
173. "Nazis make swell . . .": MacEwen to JLW and Hal Wallis, memo, 3/12/41, USC WB.
173. "Herr Mannheimer . . .": *All Through the Night,* Rev. Final, 7/31/41, USC WB.
173. "The audience laughed . . .": Sherman, interview.
173. "played off each other . . .": Rudi Fehr, interview, 2/14/90.
174. "create war hysteria" and "If Warner Brothers . . . anti-American": Testimony of Harry M. Warner, president of Warner Bros. Pictures, Inc., Hollywood, Calif., *Hearing Before the Subcommittee of the Committee on Interstate Commerce, Moving-Picture Screen and Radio Propaganda,* U.S. Senate Subcommittee of the Committee on Interstate Commerce, 9/25/41 (Washington, D.C.: U.S. Government Printing Office, 1941), pp. 338–348. Statement of Harry M. Warner, president of Warner Bros. Pictures, Inc., "Regarding Moving Picture Propaganda," U.S. Senate, 9/25/41.
175. "The number one enemy . . .": Humphrey Bogart, *Hollywood Reporter,* n.d.
175. "full participation . . .": Statement of Policy of the Fight for Freedom Committee, Inc., MDC WSHS.
175. "We made speeches . . .": Stuart, interview.
176. "Better shoot it fast . . .": Mary Astor, *Bogie—for Real.*

CHAPTER 10: "IT'S GOING TO BE A LOT OF SHIT LIKE *ALGIERS*"

177. "with the exception . . .": Harmetz, *Round Up the Usual Suspects,* p. 66; also *Hollywood Reporter,* 12/11/41 and 12/12/41.
177. "everyone on the lot was shocked . . .": Mort Lickter, interview, 11/6/90.
177. the drain of actors and technicians: Approximately 40,178 of the movie industry's 240,000 employees and executives joined the Armed Forces: Katz, *The Film Encyclopedia,* p. 1389.
178. "Everyone knows everything . . .": JLW to Jacob Wilk, memo, 12/11/41, JWC, USC WB.
178. "JAPANESE SITUATION . . .": JLW to Jacob Wilk, telegram, 12/9/41, JWC, USC WB.
178. "he felt that . . .": Irene Lee Diamond, interview, 3/6/90.
178. "Lee never hesitated . . .": Ibid.
178. Karnot worked for $1.12 an hour: Harmetz, *Round Up the Usual Suspects,* p. 16.
178. "Hal would give . . .": Ibid.
178. The purchase price of *Everybody Comes to Rick's* was $20,000: Harmetz, *Round Up the Usual Suspects,* p. 18.
178. "sheer hokum . . .": Bob Buckner to Hal Wallis, memo, 1/6/42, USC WB.
178. "a very obvious imitation . . .": Lord to Irene Lee, memo, 12/23/41, USC WB.
178. "It was crap . . .": Vincent Sherman, interview, 11/5/87.
179. "make a good vehicle . . .": Jerry Wald to Irene Lee, memo, 12/23/41, USC WB.
179. "IF HE HASN'T . . .": JLW to Jake Wilk, telegram, JWC, USC WB.
180. "We may want Huston . . .": JLW to Jake Wilk, memo, 1/13/42, JWC, USC WB.
181. "a little good luck": Walter MacEwen to Hal Wallis, memo, 1/7/42, USC WB.
181. "a reprint of any one . . .": Movies by Lee Mortimer, 7/18/42, press file, *The Big Shot,* USC WB.
181. "THE THEATRE AND PUBLICITY . . .": JLW to Bernhard, Kalmenson, Kalmine, Schneider, Blumenstock, Schless, Hummel, telegram, 1/14/42, JWC, USC.
182. "Compared to the deep . . .": Jack Moffitt to Hal Wallis, memo, 3/12/42, USC WB.
182. "Hitler had invaded Austria . . .": Murray Burnett, interview, 11/29/89.
182. "suddenly faced . . . what a setting for a play!" Ibid.
182. "It's a place to go . . .": Ibid.

183. "Unfortunately, all the good . . .": Trilling to Wallis, memo, 2/7/42, USC WB.
183. "the third member . . .": Warner Bros. News and Feature Service, *Hollywood News,* 1/5/42.
183. Announcement of Sheridan, Reagan, and Morgan, *Hollywood Reporter,* 1/7/42.
183. "I never had any inkling . . .": Ronald Reagan, interview, 11/15/90.
183. "the part is a combination . . .": Lord to Wallis, memo, 12/22/41, USC WB.
183. "Bogart and Sheridan shared billing on six pictures": With Bogart and many others, Sheridan also had a cameo in Warner Bros.' *Thank Your Lucky Stars* (1943), and she had an unbilled cameo as a streetwalker in *The Treasure of the Sierra Madre* (1948).
183. Peter Lorre subtly botching breakfast scene: Astor, *A Life on Film.*
184. "waiting for him . . . quieted her down": Hyams, *Bogie,* p. 63.
185. "He was *never* late . . .": John Huston, interview, 5/20/87.
185. Mayo's threat to kill Bogart and setting fire to the house: Hyams, *Bogie,* pp. 63–64; $100,000 life insurance policy: Hyams, *Bogie,* p. 77, and Benchley, *Humphrey Bogart,* pp. 86–87.
186. Details of Wallis's producer contract: Hal Wallis legal file, USC WB.
187. "J. L. insisted nothing had changed": JLW to Bernhard, Schneider, Kalmenson, memo, 12/30/41, JWC, USC WB.
187. Cagney demanded the Epsteins' work on *Yankee Doodle Dandy:* James Cagney, *Cagney by Cagney* (New York: Doubleday, 1976), p. 50; also Harmetz, *Round Up the Usual Suspects,* p. 42.
187. "They are anxious . . .": Nathan to JLW, memo, 2/4/42, USC WB.
187. "You must remember . . .": Julius Epstein, interview, 11/25/87.
187. "we certainly felt . . .": Ibid.
188. "never took Warner seriously . . . feel like a swim": Ibid.
188. "Sometimes it was the same day. . . . It worked": Ibid.
189. *Round Up the Usual Suspects*: Film historian Rudy Behlmer's *America's Favorite Movies: Behind the Scenes* also has thorough details on *Casablanca.*
190. "How about it?": JLW to Mr. Hal Wallis, memo, 4/2/42, JWC, USC WB.
190. "He hasn't done a role . . .": Wallis to JLW, memo, 4/3/42, USC WB.
190. "Both my husbands . . .": Harmetz, *Round Up the Usual Suspects,* p. 55.
190. "Try to get . . .": Julie and Phil Epstein to Hal Wallis, letter, n.d. (early 1942), USC WB. A copy appears in Harmetz, p. 48.
191. Selznick suddenly receptive to a loanout of Bergman: Schatz, *The Genius of the System,* p. 81.
191. "Tell him the story . . . we had Bergman": Epstein, interview.
192. Curtiz naming Ilsa: "I think it was Mike who thought of it." Ibid.

192. Bogart wanted to get aboard his boat: Steve Trilling to Hal Wallis, memo, 5/15/42.
193. "I sincerely hope . . .": R. J. Obringer to Sam Jaffe, letter, 1/5/42, Bogart legal file, USC WB.
193. "It wouldn't work . . .": Jaffe, interview.
193. "REACTION OF AUDIENCE . . .": JLW to Bernhard, Kalmenson, Kalmine, Schneider, Einfeld, Blumenstock, Hummel, telegram, 5/22/42. JWC, USC WB.
194. The Warners dined at the White House: JLW to Marvin McIntyre, the White House, letter, 6/9/42, JWC, USC WB
194. "We talked about . . .": William Schaefer, interview.
194. "The Russians were asking . . .": Ibid.
195. "The purge and the terror . . .": Joseph E. Davies to the Hon. Marvin H. McIntyre, Secretary to the President, letter, 4/4/38, FDR Library.
195. "keep the Soviets aligned with the Allies by all means possible": Joseph E. Davies to Edward R. Murrow, A. M. Sperber, *Murrow: His Life and Times* (New York: Freundlich Books, 1986), p. 296.
195. "The whole subject . . .": Harmetz, *Round Up the Usual Suspects,* p. 119.
196. "I kissed him . . .": Laurence Leamer, *As Times Goes By: The Life of Ingrid Bergman* (New York: Harper & Row, 1986), p. 121; also Benchley, *Humphrey Bogart,* p. 112, and Ingrid Bergman interview notes, NB BU.
196. "When the camera moves . . .": Ibid.
196. Wallis had hoped to cast Philip Dorn: Harmetz, *Round Up the Usual Suspects,* p. 95.
197. "He isn't ideal . . .": Hal Wallis to Mike Curtiz, memo, 4/22/42, USC WB.
197. "The dialogue may be . . .": Wallis to Curtiz, memo, 5/25/42, USC WB.
197. "The only line . . .": Epstein, interview.
197. "He is very . . .": Kathryn R. Sloan to Irving Kovner, letter, 4/4/42.
198. "the chess-like intrigue . . .": Koch to Wallis, memo, n.d., USC WB.
198. "Bogart was anxious . . .": Paul Henreid, interview, 2/20/90.
198. Wallis wrote a scene: Alleborn to Wright, memo, 6/11/42, USC WB.
199. "There's a time . . .": Henreid, interview.
199. "We said, 'There are . . .' ": Epstein, interview.
200. "I've been . . . did it very well." Howard Koch, interview, 10/17/89.
200. "He always had time . . .": Leonid Kinsky, "As Time Goes By," *Movie Digest,* 9/72.
200. "patiently and kindly": Harmetz, *Round Up the Usual Suspects,* p. 203.
200. "Christmas Baby . . .": Lee Katz, interview, 11/25/87.
201. "I don't like them . . .": Ezra Goodman source unknown.
201. "He liked Bergman . . .": Leonid Kinsky, interview, 2/9/90.
201. "One thing about Bogart . . .": Dan Seymour, interview, 2/15/90.

201. Bergman's screening *Maltese Falcon* and nervous: Nathaniel Benchley interviews, n.d., Tape #1, NB BU.
201. Bogart wore three-inch wooden blocks: AP photo, n.d. The caption reads that it is Bogart's feet in the picture, but Bogart's face is not shown.
202. Mayo showing up for lunch in the Green Room: Benchley interview with Bergman, n.d., Tape #1, NB BU.
202. "always looking like . . .": Katz, interview.
202. Mayo refused treatment: Hyams, *Bogie,* p. 81.
202. "You bitch . . .": Bob William, interview, 1/19/90.
202. "Bergman recalled . . . Wallis": Benchley interviews, n.d., Tape #1, p. 10, NB BU.
203. "Bogie just looked . . .": Kinsky, interview.
203. "Mike drove . . . watching the camera": Ibid.
203. "Do it with a full . . .": Hal Wallis, MUSIC NOTES, "CASABLANCA," 9/2/42, USC WB.
203. "I could see their faces . . .": Seymour, interview.
204. "sharp differences about the story's outcome": Alleborn to Wright, memo, 6/29/42, USC WB.
204. "Conferences were taking . . .": Koch, interview.
204. "worried that he wouldn't . . .": Epstein, interview.
204. "Casey Robinson's brainchild": Casey Robinson, "Notes on 'Casablanca,' " 5/20/42, USC WB.
204. "Toward the end . . .": Epstein, interview.
204. "How can I play . . .": Koch, interview.
204. "He kept wanting . . .": Ibid.
205. "midgets from central casting": Katz, interview.
205. "Rick is not just . . .": Robinson to Wallis, memo, 5/20/42, USC WB.
205. "they wound up shouting . . .": William, interview.
205. "arguments with Curtiz . . .": Alleborn to Wright, memo, 7/18/42, USC WB.
205. "finally decid[e] . . .": Ibid.
205. "Story conference between . . .": *Casablanca,* Daily Production and Progress Report, 7/17/42, USC WB.
206. "Are you ready, Ilsa?": Hal Wallis, memo, 6/6/42, USC WB.
206. "a little more guts . . .": Wallis to Curtiz, memo, 7/22/42, USC WB.
206. "Louis, I might have . . .": Wallis to Owen Marks, memo, 8/7/42, USC WB.
207. "That's Hal Wallis . . .": McGilligan, *Backstory,* p. 308.
207. "I have never heard . . .": Wallis to Einfeld, memo, 8/28/42, USC WB.
207. "coming more into prominence . . .": Wallis to JLW, memo, 11/6/42, USC WB.
207. "AS WE CONTEMPLATE . . .": JLW to Hummel, telegram, 11/10/42, JWC, USC WB.

207. "WILL DEFINITELY NOT TOUCH . . .": JLW to Major Bernhard, etc., telegram, 11/12/42, JWC, USC WB.
208. "A SMALL TAG . . .": JLW to Major Bernhard, Kalmenson, etc., telegram, 11/10/42, JWC, USC WB.
208. "Again Warner Bros . . .": *Los Angeles Times,* 12/7/42.
208. "Casablanca! A magic . . .": *Film Daily,* 11/27/42.
209. "I want to show you . . .": Martin Weiser, interview, 11/24/87.

CHAPTER 11: "THE HAPPIEST OF COUPLES"

211. "Miss Bergman is . . .": *Action in the North Atlantic,* press book, USC WB.
211. "rather proud . . .": Sidney Skolsky, "Tintypes" (syndicated), June–August 1943, CMC USC.
212. "You couldn't have . . .": Arthur Silver, interview, 11/19/87.
212. Bogart told Clark that the studio's choice for a name was Jose O'Toole: Raymond Massey to Nathaniel Benchley, n.d., NB BU. Also Hyams, *Bogie,* p. 77.
212. "Bogart had convinced . . .": Dane Clark, interview, 5/23/90.
212. "or the making of . . .": Frank Mattison to T. C. Wright, memo, 1/12/43, USC WB.
212. Louis Bromfield a descendent of Daniel Boone: Hope Bromfield Stevens, interview, 7/25/89.
213. "to make you homesick . . .": Louis Bromfield, letter, 1/5/43.
213. "couldn't have been . . .": Matthew Flam, "Bogie! Tribute to a Movie Tough Guy," N.Y. *Post,* 7/30/92.
213. "Coffee? Hell no! . . .": Ibid.
213. "Well, where are we going today?": Bruce Bennett, interview, 1/26/90.
214. "a sincere . . . things up": Ibid.
214. "Mayo was a . . .": Ibid.
214. "hungover . . . the next night": Ibid.
215. *Passage to Marseille* to begin in May: Trilling to Col. Warner, memo, 3/29/43, USC WB.
215. Greenstreet hated part: Trilling to Wallis, memo, 5/21/43, USC WB.
216. "AFTER ALL, HUMPHREY . . .": JLW to Humphrey Bogart, telegram, 4/6/43, JWC, USC WB.
216. "You shouldn't be . . .": Bennett, interview.
216. "I want a divorce . . .": *Conflict* script, draft, April, 1943, *Conflict* picture file, USC WB. These lines were not used in the film.
216. "We are reluctant . . .": Roy Obringer to Humphrey Bogart, letter, 4/30/43, USC WB.

217. "Let Bogart know . . .": JLW to Hal Wallis, memo, 5/6/43, JWC, USC WB.
217. "DEAR HUMPHREY . . .": JLW to Humphrey Bogart, telegram, 5/4/43, JWC, USC WB.
217. "Hello, Steve . . . Goodbye and good luck": "Telephone conversation between Humphrey Bogart and J. L. Warner that took place on May 6, 1943, between 4 and 4:30 P.M.," Bogart legal file, USC WB.
218. "If you can get . . .": JLW to Hal Wallis, letter, 5/6/43, JWC, USC WB.
218. "AS CAN'T TRUST . . .": JLW to Hal Wallis, telegram, personal and confidential, 6/30/43, JWC, USC WB.
218. "PER 'DAILY NEWS' . . .": JLW to Hal Wallis, telegram, 11/28/43, JWC, USC WB.
218. "WANT YOU INFORM . . .": JLW to Charles Einfeld, telegram, 11/30/43, Behlmer, *Inside Warner Bros.,* p. 233.
218. "STOP GIVING ME DOUBLE TALK . . .": JLW to Hal Wallis, telegram, 11/30/43, Behlmer, *Inside Warner Bros.,* p. 234.
219. Rewrites for Gabin: CKF to JLW, letter, 5/17/43, USC WB.
219. Urged to do *Conflict* as a favor: Steve Trilling to JLW, telegram, 5/15/43, USC WB.
219. "DEAR HUMPHREY . . .": JLW to Humphrey Bogart, telegram, 5/11/43, JWC, USC WB.
219. "Confidentially believe . . .": Roy Obringer and Steve Trilling to JLW 5/11/43, USC WB.
219. "Bogart has not changed . . .": Steve Trilling to JLW, 5/17/43, USC WB.
219. Telegram to Feldman: JLW to CKF, 5/17/43, CKFC AFI.
219. "stew in his own juice": JLW to Steve Trilling, telegram, 5/17/43, JWC, USC WB.
220. "He knew that she . . .": Rose Hobart, interview, 11/11/87.
221. "He *hated* it . . . bloody murder": Ibid.
221. "I got the idea . . .": Dwight Taylor to William Jacobs, memo, 8/3/43, *Conflict* picture files, USC WB.
221. "Have you ever been married . . .": *Conflict* script, 8/5/43, pp. 109–110, USC WB.
221. "We do not want . . .": Steve Trilling to William Jacobs, memo, 8/4/43, USC WB.
222. "quiet gossip . . .": William, interview.
222. " 'Bogart's gal.' . . .": Ibid.
222. "It's just this thing . . .": Verita Thompson, interview, 8/9/88.
222. "He'd tell me . . .": Ibid.
222. "would call me . . . these pigs": Ibid.
222. Verita Thompson was listed only once: for *The Enforcer* (1950), Bogart's last picture for Warners, USC WB.
223. "I didn't know much . . .": Jaffe, interview.

223. "She was upstairs . . .": Stuart, interview.
223. "I don't know . . .": Hyams, *Bogie* p. 81.
223. "My wife is . . .": Ibid., pp. 81–82.
224. "weighed heavily . . .": Verita Thompson and Donald Shepherd, *Bogie and Me* (New York: St. Martin's Press, 1982), pp. 37–38.
224. "Humphrey Bogart suffering . . .": Eric Stacey to T. C. Wright, Daily Production and Progress Report, 9/22/43, USC WB.
224. "He says he likes you . . .", Silver, interview.
224. "You know, you're acting . . .": William Schaefer, interview, 12/1/90.
225. "Drunk as a skunk . . . puke?": Harmetz, *Round Up the Usual Suspects,* p. 199.
225. FDR "delighted" with *Mission to Moscow:* Joseph E. Davies papers, cross-reference, 5/8/43, FDR Presidential Library.
225. Litvinov clapped loudly: Silver, interview.
225. "Russo-American goodwill . . .": Moscow Conference on American and British Cinema, Aug. (probably 1942), JWC, USC WB.
225. "NATURALLY PICTURE IS . . .": JLW to Charlie Einfeld, telegram, 5/5/43, N.Y. wires, 1943, JWC, USC WB.
227. "Excellent character . . .": Humphrey DeForest Bogart, Loyalty and Character Report, 12/7/43, Western Defense Command Report, War Department, FBI File.
227. German propaganda broadcasts: Hyams, *Bogie,* p. 79.
227. "No heat or hot . . .": Mayo Methot Bogart to Buffy Methot, letter, n.d., MMC UO.
228. "Joyeux Noel/Afrique '43 . . .": MMC UO.
228. "It is very . . .": Mayo Methot Bogart to Buffy Methot, letter, n.d., MMC UO.
228. "packed with these . . . great with them": Bill Mauldin, interview, 4/6/90.
228. "We work pretty hard . . .": Mayo Methot Bogart to Buffy Methot, letter, n.d. (probably 1/44), MMC UO. All other letters also MMC UO.
230. Bogart assuring triple amputee: Hyams, *Bogie,* p. 70.
231. "I guess I looked. . . . took the guns away": Gersh, interview.
232. "word was telephoned . . ." John Huston, interview, 5/20/87.
232. "Mayo decided . . .": Ibid.
232. "He was raising . . .": Ibid.
233. Rescheduling of *To Have and Have Not:* Steve Trilling to JLW, 12/9/43, JWC, USC WB.
233. "The place was . . .": Sam Jaffe to Nathaniel Benchley, interview, 1/13/74, NB BU.
233. Bogart rushed out: Sam Jaffe to Nathaniel Benchley, interview notes, n.d., NB BU.
234. "a slut . . . he told me": Sam Jaffe, interview, 6/17/89.

234. "the 'Bogart matter' ": Abe Lastfogel to JLW, telegram, 2/7/44, 6:48 P.M., Bogart legal file, USC WB.
235. "HE ABSOLUTELY REFUSES . . .": Mort Blumenstock to Steve Trilling, telegram, 2/9/44, JWC, USC WB.
235. "BELIEVE HAVE SCARED . . .": Mort Blumenstock to JLW, telegram, 2/10/44, USC WB.
235. "they treated him . . .": Jaffe, interview.
235. "grim and dirty . . .": *Los Angeles Times,* 2/15/44.
235. "AS THERE ARE . . .": Steve Trilling to Humphrey Bogart, telegram, 12/12/44, JL/Tr, JWC, USC WB.

CHAPTER 12: BETTY

236. "to reassure her . . . pay for herself": Earl Robinson, interview, 4/24/91.
237. "a determined . . . very strong": Gloria Nevard, interview, 1/29/93.
237. Weinstein-Bacal shortened to Weinstein: Lauren Bacall, *Lauren Bacall by Myself* (New York: Alfred A. Knopf, 1979), p. 5.
238. Registered as Betty Perske: Letter to AMS from Transcript Coordinator, Julia Richman High School 2/2/93.
238. "I'm Jewish . . .": Lauren Bacall, *By Myself,* p. 31.
238. Bacal attracted to older men: Nevard, interview.
239. "She was darling . . .": Gloria Stuart, interview, 2/2/90.
239. "She was strikingly . . .": Joyce Gates Buck, interview, 9/11/88.
239. "there will be another . . .": George S. Kaufman to "Peggy Bacall," letter, Bacall, *By Myself,* pp. 61–62.
240. "Like Monet forever . . .": David Thomson, *A Biographical Dictionary of Film,* 3rd ed. (New York: Alfred A. Knopf, 1984), p. 323.
241. "a chronic liar . . . ruinous womanizer": Ibid.
241. Wilde began career with Hawks: Meta Wilde and Pat Miller, interview, 1/24/90.
241. "cold and ruthless . . . *Well?*": Meta Wilde, interview, 2/8/90.
241. "Miz Dee . . .": Dee Hawks Cramer, interview.
242. "just a kid . . .": John Kobal, *People Will Talk* (New York: Alfred A. Knopf, 1986), p. 487.
242. Bacal and Robinson paying own way: CKF, Daybooks, Monday 4/5/43, CKFC AFI.
242. Arrangements for Ella Raines: CKF to Grace Dobish, 1/8/43, and CKF wire, 1/28/43, file, NY trips, CKFC AFI.
242. Hawks's own publicity agent to break story: CKF to Al Rockett, 2/3/43, NY trips, CKFC AFI.
242. "She just sounds . . . she's very *pretty.*" Jean Howard, interview, 12/12/91.

243. "everything good and fine about freedom-loving nations": CKF to Eddie Mannix, Motion Picture Producers Association (MPPA), 6/8/42, AFI; Unidentified to CKF, n.d., 3/43 folder, CKFC AFI.
243. American sequence to include *The Lonesome Train,* CKF to Roy Orbinger, 4/23/43, *Battle Cry,* USC WB; also Hawks/Feldman file, CKFC AFI.
243. "Friday: Becall + Robinson," etc.: CKF, Daybooks, CKFC AFI.
243. "It was just natural . . .": Robinson, interview.
243. "She had a good . . .": and Bacall's liking *Porterhouse Lucy,* Robinson, interview.
244. "Mr. Hawks will direct . . .": Trilling to Wright, McGreal, Westmore, Burns, JL/Tr., USC WB.
244. "she was nervous and frightened . . .": Howard, interview.
244. Bacal's budget: Budget re approval of contract between Howard Hawks and Betty Bacal, n.d. (probably May or June 1943), CKFC AFI. Address on S. Reeves Drive: CKF, Daybooks, 5/25/43, "New ap'tm't," CKFC AFI.
245. Appearance before judge to approve contract: No. 485767: Order approving minor's contract as an actress, Joseph W. Vickers, Judge, 6/29/43, Bacall legal file, USC WB.
245. "she was pretty solid . . .": Howard, interview.
245. Feldman gave up on model: CKF to Grace Dobish, 1/8/43, NY trips, correspondence files, CKFC AFI.
245. "a low voice . . .": Joy Barlowe, interview, 1/31/90.
245. "that girl . . .": Kobal, *People Will Talk,* p. 487.
245. "It was a great . . .": Howard, interview.
245. "the most beautiful house . . .": Bacall, *By Myself,* p. 86.
246. Details of Hawks's property on Moraga Drive: "Liabilities Compiled for Collector of Internal Revenue," Noel Singer to Laurence Beilenson, 1/28/47, Description of property as of 12/31/46, folder: Hawks–Nancy Hawks Settlement, 75–17, Dee Cramer–Howard Hawks papers, Hawks legal file, USC WB.
246. "The style was . . . *became* Slim": Cramer, interview.
246. "I knew that Betty . . .": Howard, interview.
246. Too few writers available for *Battle Cry:* CKF to JLW, *Battle Cry*/WB/HF file, CKFC AFI.
246. *Battle Cry* too expensive: Minutes Regulating Meeting of H-F Productions, formerly Charles K. Feldman Common Man Productions, 9/1/43, legal files, CKFC AFI; also see telegrams, 7/28/43 and 7/26/43, JL/Tr, JWC, USC WB
246. Purchase of *To Have and Have Not:* H-F Productions, Minutes, 9/1/43, legal file, CKFC AFI; Mr. Marin to CKF 9/7/43, *Battle Cry* WB/HB, CFK, AFI; H-F Minutes, 9/10/43, CKFC AFI; Roy Obringer to JLW, 9/15/43, JL/Tr, JWC, USC WB.

247. Hawks dunned for back taxes: Treasury Department: Notice of Levy, 6/22/43; Office of the Collector to Warner Bros. Pictures, Inc., 6/30/43; Howard Hawks to Warner Bros. Pictures Inc., 11/8/43; all in Howard Hawks legal file, USC WB.
247. By September 7, *To Have and Have Not* set: Mr. Marin to CKF 9/7/43, *Battle Cry*/WB/HB, CFKC AFI.
247. Warners to share in Bacal's contract: Marin to CKF, 9/7/43, CKFC AFI.
247. Campaign to increase Bacal's visibility: Bacall, *By Myself,* pp. 88–89.
247. Party for Bacal's nineteenth birthday: Bacall, *By Myself,* p. 89.
247. "Charlie was sweet . . .": Robinson, interview.
247. "He did *not* make . . .": Howard, interview.
248. "She had a dilemma . . .": Jules Buck, telephone interview, 9/5/89.
248. Hawks wanted to be more than friends: Bacall, *By Myself,* p. 124.
248. "She was careful . . .": Joyce Gates Buck, interview.
248. "if you look . . . Poor girl": Howard, interview.
248. "Ella was very . . .": Jules Buck, interview, 2/6/93.
249. "but we're not obligated . . .": JLW to Roy Obringer, telegram, 11/4/43, JWC, USC WB.
249. "our various young . . .": Steve Trilling to JLW 12/9/43, *To Have and Have Not* story file, USC WB.
249. Bacall and Bogart meeting on set: *"B 'n' B,"* Mr. and Mrs. Hollywood Series No. 5, ca. 1947, unidentified fan magazine.
249. H-F Productions took over Hawks's contract with Bacal: Minutes, H-F Productions, 1/5/44, legal file, CKFC AFI.
249. "That lynx-eyed . . .": *To Have and Have Not,* temporary script, 10/14/43, p. 206, USC WB. Jules Furthman also wrote Dietrich's *Morocco* (1930) and *Blonde Venus* (1932, with S. K. Lauren).
249. "You must have caught . . .": Ibid., 12/30/43, p. 74.
250. JLW directed Furthman to cut down script: JLW to Trilling, 12/1/43, JL/Tr, telgrams, 1943, JWC, USC WB.
250. Furthman's work done over by Faulkner: Wilde, interview.
250. "the polishing required": Trilling to JLW, 12/18/43, 12/22/43, USC WB.
251. Adams a mystery writer: Cleve F. Adams to Roy Obringer, letter, 1/7/44, USC WB.
251. *Sinner Takes All*: 1937, *NYT* Reviews Index.
251. "(*She sits on his lap* . . . —and *blow*!": "Rec'd 1/10/44—Material by Whitman Chambers," pp. 63–65, typescript, *To Have and Have Not,* production files, USC WB.
251. "*You know you don't have* . . .": *To Have and Have Not,* 1/29/44, Part II, Final. The precise extent of Adams and Chambers contribution is hard to determine, though there is ample evidence at being pleased with the scene. Namely, Adams's memo to Hawks, dated 1/14/44, asking about

collaborating directly with Chambers to save time. "Failing that, my own version of the revised script (that portion of it which is completed) is at your disposal any time. All you gotta do is pucker up your lips and whistle. Remember?" USC WB.

252. "felt he could get this . . .": Trilling to JLW, 12/9/43; JLW to Trilling, 12/13/44, JL/Tr, JWC, USC WB.

252. "We want to be ready . . .": JLW to Steve Trilling, memo, 12/1/43, JL/Tr, JWC, USC.

252. *Report from the Front* spokesman with credibility: Gordon Hollingshead to Steve Trilling, letter, 2/10/44, JL/Tr, JWC, USC.

253. "Will you make . . .": *Report from the Front,* cutter's script, 12/21/44, USC WB.

253. Bogart refused: "Unable to shoot, as Mr. Bogart wanted his wife to be in the scene." Daily Production and Progress Report, USC WB.

253. "We'll have a lot . . .": Bacall, *By Myself,* p. 93.

CHAPTER 13: THE FUN BEGINS

254. "My character's not in this . . .": Dan Seymour, interview, 8/10/90.

254. "Hope we don't . . .": Humphrey Bogart, "You," ca. 6/48, unidentified periodical.

255. "realized one way . . .": Bacall, *By Myself,* p. 94.

255. Academy Awards at Grauman's Chinese Theatre: Stacey Endres and Robert Cushman, *Hollywood at Your Feet: The Story of the World-Famous Chinese Theatre* (Los Angeles: Pomegranate Press, 1992).

255. The Bogarts' dress: Photo, collection of Stacey Endres and Robert Cushman, Academy of Motion Picture Arts and Sciences.

255. Warner beating Wallis to the podium: *Variety,* 3/3/44, p. 5.

255. "there was nothing . . .": Harmetz, *Round Up the Usual Suspects,* p. 322.

256. Applause for Lukas: *Variety,* 3/3/44, p. 5.

256. "Every Wallis movie . . . with the statue" Harmetz, *Round Up the Usual Suspects,* p. 323.

256. "Take it easy, Junior . . .": "Young Star Aided by Studio's Great," *To Have and Have Not* pressbook, p. 11, USC WB.

256. "Moran just didn't . . .": Walter Surovy, interview, 3/6/92. Surovy was listed in the billing as Walter Molnar after Jack Warner insisted he change his name and asked what he would like. Surovy thought of the Hungarian playwright Ferenc Molnár, and hastily suggested his surname, a decision he says he regretted.

257. "An *excellent* suggestion . . .": Bogart, "You."

257. "at first . . . handle it": Seymour, interview.

257. "almost imperceptible": Bacall, *By Myself,* p. 96.
257. It was all so . . .": Wilde, interview.
258. Bogart kissed her: Bacall, *By Myself,* p. 96.
258. "Imagine he's bringing . . .": Eddie Albert, interview, 2/5/90.
258. "The way they did . . .": Seymour, interview.
258. "It was like an explosion . . .": Surovy, interview.
258. "She's wonderful . . .": Cameron Shipp, "The Gentlest," *Movie Life,* n.d., ca. 3/10/46, USC CMC.
258. "She was different . . .": Frederick De Cordova, interview, 11/5/90.
259. "They were really . . .": Joy Barlowe, interview, 1/31/90.
259. "Being European . . .": Surovy, interview.
259. "They would go into . . .": Wilde, interview.
259. "like a smitten . . .": Wilde and Borsten, *A Loving Gentleman,* p. 298.
259. "Bogie was more serious . . .": Barlowe, interview.
259. "Bogie had a lot of power . . .": Ibid.
259. "I might have been in some trouble . . .": Kobal, *People Will Talk,* p. 488.
260. "we'd sit down every . . .": Seymour, interview.
260. "The script was all there . . .": Dee Hawks Cramer, interview, 8/13/88.
260. "A good director . . .": Bill Rice, Warner Bros. Studio, Burbank, Calif., No. 6221, USC WB.
260. "a surprisingly excellent . . .": Humphrey Bogart to Gladys Hall, 5/9/46, Gladys Hall Collection, Margaret Herrick Library, Center for Motion Picture Study, AMPAS.
261. "mood matches": Humphrey Bogart to Gladys Hall, 5/10/46, Gladys Hall Collection, Margaret Herrick Library, Center for Motion Picture Study, AMPAS.
261. "He used to kid . . .": Seymour, interview.
261. Hawks leaving the set: Seymour, interview.
262. Hawks stopping at the same corner: Billy Wilder, *Eine Nahaufnahme von Hellmuth Karasek* (Hamburg: Hoffman u. Campe, 1992), p. 198.
263. "very handsome-looking . . .": Seymour, interview, 2/15/90.
263. Hawks telling her that she meant nothing to Bogart, etc.: Bacall, *By Myself,* p. 99.
263. Bogart threatening to walk and "personal talk . . .": R. J. Obringer to Herbert Freston, memo, 8/23/44, USC WB.
264. Renegotiated deal: R. J. Obringer to Herbert Freston, memo, 8/23/44, USC WB.
264. "would be a good boy . . .": Obringer to Freston, memo, 8/23/44, USC WB.
264. Bacall did her own singing: Trilling to Leo Forbstein, memo, 7/29/44, JL/Tr, A-Z/43/44, p. 6, JWC, USC WB. In fact, in answer to a 1972

query, music head Ray Heindorf stated "Lauren Bacall did her own singing. A voice double was not used." Lois McGrew: Memo to the file, 5/26/72, story file, *To Have and Have Not,* USC WB.

264. "In this connection . . .": Assignment of Employee contract, Betty Bacal—professionally known as Lauren Bacall—Artist, assignment 5/3/44, legal letter 5/8/44, USC WB.
265. Mayo given bracelet watch: Bill Rice, Warner Bros. Studios, n.d., USC WB.
265. "It has been apparent . . .": Louella Parsons, Los Angeles *Examiner,* n.d. (1944), CMC USC.
265. ". . . the star studied Miss Bacall's . . .": Carlisle Jones, Warner Bros. studios, *To Have and Have Not,* press file, USC WB.
265. "It took only one ring . . .": Surovy, interview.
265. "Hello, lover boy . . .": Hyams, *Bogie,* p. 84.
265. "He's out with the cast . . .": Mary Baker to Nathaniel Benchley, n.d., interview, NB BU.
265. Mrs. Bogart creating a disturbance: Ibid.
266. "The *loveliest* young girl . . .": Martin Weiser, interview, 11/24/87
266. "I hope they do . . . a whole campaign": Ibid.
268. "There you will find . . .": Mitch, Warner Bros. Studio, USC WB.
268. "Our pal Bogart . . .": Steve Trilling to JLW, memo, 5/29/44, JL/Tr, JWC, USC WB.
268. "IS THIS WHAT YOU . . .": JLW to Humphrey Bogart, telegram, 5/25/44, JWC, USC WB.
269. "YOU SPEAK OF MY . . .": Humphrey Bogart to JLW, telegram, 5/26/44, JWC, USC WB.
269. Jaffe barred from Warners because he couldn't "control" his actors: Obringer to JLW, memo, 7/11/44, USC WB.
269. Howard and Nancy Hawks's nicknames for each other were Slim and Steve: "My wife called me Steve," Hawks said in Joseph McBride, *Hawks on Hawks* (Berkeley, Calif., and Los Angeles: University of California Press, 1982), p. 34.
269. "Bogart was enchanted . . .": Hyams, *Bogie,* p. 84.
269. "She courted him . . .": Ibid.
269. "all the love . . .": Bacall, *By Myself,* p. 102.
269. "I was older . . .": Ibid, p. 101.
269. Letters from Bogart to Bacall: Ibid, pp. 105–107.
270. "I don't want to break . . .": Hyams, *Bogie,* p. 84.
270. Three-car motorcade: William Schaefer, Preview List, June 29, 1944, USC WB.
270. Warner's unclear where Hawks's jurisdiction ended and its began: Evelove to Obringer, memo, 11/28/44, USC WB.

271. Bacall's salary: Obringer to Ralph Lewis, memo, 21/11/44, USC WB.
271. Bill for $4,900: CKF to Noel Singer re Betty Bacal–WB, letter, 7/26/44, CKF AFI.
271. "JL declined . . .": JLW to Obringer, memo, 2/29/44; also R. J. Obringer to Noel Singer, memo, 8/1/44, USC WB.
271. H-F Productions due 20 percent, etc.: Trilling to Dick Pease, memo, n.d., JL/Tr, JWC, USC WB.
272. "gave him more of a kick . . .": Bacall, *By Myself,* p. 111.
272. "This is why I love . . .": Ibid.
272. Plans for a story with a detective background, etc.: Transcript, telephone conversation, Bogart and Trilling, 4:00 P.M., 7/27/44, USC WB.
272. "a highly censorable . . .": Trilling to JLW, memo, 8/2/44, Hawks legal file, USC WB.
272. "He and Mayo have common . . .": *Life,* 6/12/44.

CHAPTER 14: THE LENGTHY GOOD-BYE

274. Flimsy truce in the Bogart household: Bacall, *By Myself,* p. 118.
274. "I said I'd have . . .": Ibid.
275. Shelving of *Dark Eyes:* Robert F. Buckner to Steve Trilling, memo, Hawks legal file, USC WB.
276. "I believe the public . . .": N.Y. *Herald Tribune,* 2/20/44.
276. "He is regretful . . .": Evelove to JLW and Einfeld, memo, JWC, USC WB.
276. "He could have made . . .": Kenneth Leffers, interview, 1/21/91.
276. "SIT TIGHT": George Hawkins to Mrs. Humphrey Bogart, telegram, 10/25/44, MMC UO.
276. Miniature wedding cake: Leffers, interview.
277. "Mayo and I have decided . . .": Associated Press, 11/1/44; N.Y. *Herald Tribune,* 11/2/44.
277. "He'd be glad . . .": Bacall, *By Myself,* p. 120.
277. "Bogie always knew . . .": Regis Toomey, interview, 8/29/87.
277. Brackett, who was also a gifted and noted science fiction writer, died in 1978 while working on an early draft of George Lucas's *The Empire Strikes Back.*
277. "inspired" and "He brought . . .": Cramer, interview.
278. "We were just . . .": Ibid.
278. "Barlowe, concerned . . . breeze": Barlowe, interview.
278. "Regis Toomey . . . one of the cast": Toomey, interview.
279. "This girl didn't know . . .": Ibid.
280. "a mobilization against . . .": Ad, *Hollywood Reporter,* 9/20/44.
280. "available almost any time": Hollywood Democratic Committee to Democratic National Committee, 10/14/44, HDCC WSHS.

280. "a man named . . . touch with it": Script, "Humphrey Bogart," 10/28/44, CBS, HDCC WSHS.
280. The four major networks were CBS, NBC, ABC, and Mutual.
280. "magnetic quality, so . . .": Norman Corwin, interview, 8/9/88.
280. "cordial and amenable . . .": Ibid.
282. "this wasn't a character . . .": Ibid.
282. Conservative pressure on Durante: The full story was that Durante, a star of radio as well as films, had been threatened by his sponsor. It was a harbinger of the political pressures that became the rule in broadcasting as well as movies during the blacklist period ahead.
282. The Democrat's show ended at 9:55: Corwin, interview.
282. "was rather radical": Ibid.
282. "make public appearances . . .": JLW to Trilling, 10/13/44, telegram, JL/Politics /'44 JWC, USC WB.
282. "KEEP MY NAME . . .": JLW to Evelove, 10/19/44, telegram, JWC, USC WB.
283. "Listen, you Jewish . . .": Bacall, *By Myself,* p. 122.
283. "This time, he says . . .": Louella O. Parsons, L.A. *Herald Examiner,* n.d. (probably ca. 12/4/44).
283. "It's hard to break . . .": Ibid.
283. "I don't want a big . . .": *L.A. Times,* 12/4/44.
283. "Why, any woman . . .": Alistair Cooke, "Epitaph for a Tough Guy," *The Atlantic Monthly,* May 1957.
283. "Mayo will never . . .": Louella Parsons, "The Bewildering Bogarts," n.d. (probably 12/44), Chamberlain and Lyman Brown Theatrical Agency Collection, Lincoln Center, New York.
283. "What can I do . . . very upset": Hedda Hopper, *L.A. Times,* 12/4/44.
284. "I've tried to tell . . .": Ibid.
284. Bogart told Mary Baker that he worried about his and Bacall's age difference: Mary Baker to Nathaniel Benchley, interview, n.d., NB BU.
284. "hypersensitive . . .": Bacall, *By Myself,* p. 126.
285. Godfrey set to take over: Trilling to JLW, memo, 11/18/44, JL/Tr, JWC, USC WB.
285. Bacall had laryngitis: Stacey to Wright, Daily Production and Progress Report, 11/9/44, USC WB.
285. Rains washed out street sets: Stacey to Wright, Daily Production and Progress Report, 11/13/44, USC WB.
285. "Mr. Bogart overslept . . .": Stacey to Wright, Daily Production and Progress Report, 11/24/44, USC WB.
285. "Dec. 14th . . .": Stacey to Wright, Daily Production and Progress Report, 12/14/44, USC WB.
285. "Dec. 15th . . .": Stacey to Wright, Daily Production and Progress Report, 12/15/44, USC WB.

285. "Dec. 20th . . .": T. C. Wright to Obringer—Dick Pease, re *The Big Sleep*—production delays due to Humphrey Bogart, memo, 12/26/44, USC WB.
285. playing to capacity: JLW to Trilling, et al., JL NY wires, memos, 1944, JWC, USC WB.
285. "FUROR CREATED BY NEWCOMER . . .": Blumenstock to Einfeld, telegram 12/1/44, NY wires, JWC, USC WB.
286. "sensational new girl": JLW to Kalmenson, 9/7/44, telegram, JWC, USC WB.
286. "She gave this woman . . .": "What Now, Lauren?" *Silver Screen,* 4/45.
286. "He sensed he had lost . . .": Bacall, *By Myself,* p. 124.
286. "siding together against . . .": Cramer, interview.
286. "The company lost . . .": Stacey to Wright, Daily Production and Progress Report, 12/22/44, USC WB.
286. "There have been several instances . . .": Wright to Obringer—Dick Pease, memo, 12/26/44, USC WB.
287. Vreeland called the Beverly Wilshire: Stacey to Wright, memo, 12/26/44, USC WB.
287. "in very bad condition . . .": Ibid.
287. "The atmosphere . . .": Ibid.
287. "There is absolutely . . .": Ibid.
287. "THANKS FOR NOT . . .": JLW to Humphrey Bogart, telegram, 12/26/44, USC WB.
287. "The company did not . . .": Stacey to Wright, Daily Production and Progress Report, 12/27/44, USC WB.
288. "was very angry . . .": Wilde, interview.
288. "The following rewritten . . .": William Faulkner to James Geller, letter, n.d. (probably early 12/44), USC WB.
288. "It was the sort . . .": Wilde, interview.
288. "Dammit, I didn't know . . .": Raymond Chandler to Hamish Hamilton, letter, 3/21/49, *Selected letters of Raymond Chandler,* pp. 155–6.
289. "You will realize . . .": Raymond Chandler to Hamish Hamilton, 5/30/46, *Selected Letters of Raymond Chandler,* p. 75.
289. "it was the most confusing . . .": Cramer, interview.
289. Adding up the losses: Obringer to Wright, memo, 12/27/44; Pease to Wright, memo, 12/27/44, USC WB.
289. "apparently in good shape": Stacey to Wright, memo, 12/29/44; USC WB.
290. "a direct descendant . . .": Alistair Cooke: "Epitaph for a Tough Guy," *The Atlantic Monthly,* May 1957.
290. "got hit they hurt . . .": Judith Crist, N.Y. *Herald Tribune,* 4/3/66.

CHAPTER 15: THE HAPPIEST TIME

291. "armed truce": L.A. *Examiner,* 1/25/45, CMC USC.
291. "so that we don't . . .": Blumenstock to Einfeld, memo, 12/22/44, USC WB.
292. "Seems everybody . . .": Einfeld to Evelove, memo, 11/16/44, USC WB.
292. "Mr. Bogart's personal . . .": Stacey to Wright, memo, 1/5/45, USC WB.
292. "Bogart's last day . . . a good trip": Arthur Silver, interview, 11/19/87.
293. "I'm in love . . . goddamn right!": Earl Wilson, "*It Happened Last Night,*" N.Y. *Post,* 1/30/45.
293. "I chose this Oxford . . ." and "Mayo's a fine . . .": Inez Robb (INS), L.A. *Examiner,* 1/31/45.
293. "She's a swell . . .": Ibid.
293. "I POINTED OUT . . .": Blumenstock to Einfeld, telegram, 1/31/45, JL/NY wires/45, JWC, USC WB.
294. "anything he wants . . . okay in the program": Gary Stevens, interview, 12/8/92.
294. "he was a definite . . .": Ibid.
294. "That afternoon, Stevens . . . the guy wasn't unhappy": Ibid.
296. "BACALL HANDLING . . .": Blumenstock to Einfeld, telegram, 2/2/45, JL/NY wires/45, JWC, USC WB.
297. "He thought I might . . .": Bacall, *By Myself,* pp. 130–131.
297. "Gary, you've got . . .": Gary Stevens, interview.
297. "He *loved* Peter. . . . Bogart wanted to hear": Ibid.
298. "He couldn't really . . .": Bacall, *By Myself,* p. 112.
298. "worried about her being Jewish . . .": Interview notes, Mary Baker, n.d., NB BU. It was a detail that Benchley, a family friend, omitted from his biography of Bogart. He also omitted any reference to Bacall's origins, aside from her father's name and an oblique reference to "an element of Russia in her ancestry."
298. Gershwin's memories of Maud Humphrey's anti-Semitism: Interview notes, Lee Gershwin, n.d., NB BU.
298. "very respectful . . .": Dan Seymour, interview, 8/10/90.
298. "raised hell . . . let him know": Harmetz, *Round Up the Usual Suspects,* p. 244.
298. "FOR NEWCOMER . . .": Blumenstock to Einfeld and Evelove, telegram, 2/5/45, JL/NY wires/45, JWC, USC WB.
298. "What they do . . .": unidentified, 2/24/45, Brady file, USC WB.
299. "Betty was all excited . . . transported": Nevard, interview.
299. "Christ! You've got . . .": Bacall, *By Myself,* pp. 131.
299. "DEAR LAUREN . . .": JLW, Relay to Lauren Bacall, copy Blumenstock, 2/6/45, JL/NY wires/45, JWC, USC WB.

299. "I think it would . . .": Ibid.
299. "I wanted to be . . .": Bacall, *By Myself,* p. 133.
299. "WE HAVE TRIED . . .": Blumenstock to Einfeld, telegram, 2/5/45, USC WB.
299. "PERSONALLY THINK . . .": Blumenstock to Einfeld, telegram, 2/5/45, JL/NY wires/45, JWC, USC WB.
300. Diamond passed on confidences to the studio: A telegram from Blumenstock to Weinfeld (2/6/45) concerning Bacall's disputed trip to Washington, includes the following instructions: "Matter you asked me to discuss with Bogey calls for great finesse as otherwise any value Diamond has will be destroyed. Matter was given him in confidence and only way you or I could know would be if he told us. Bogey will know that and discount Jack from this point on unless I can get him to open up." JL/NY wires/45, JWC, USC WB.
300. "resident child . . . people": Sylvia Sheekman Thompson, interview, 3/24/90.
301. "The way she moved . . .": Ibid.
301. "She gave me that . . .": Ibid.
301. "butter wouldn't melt . . .": Ibid.
301. "everybody adored Betty . . .": Dorris Bowden Johnson, interview, 8/9/87.
301. "Dear Father Bromberg . . .": Humphrey Bogart, handwritten letter to Louis Bromfield, n.d., NB/BU.
302. "She must make . . .": Louella O. Parsons, L.A. *Examiner,* n.d., CMC USC.
302. Giesler and Mayo Bogart's settlement: Louella O. Parsons, Los Angeles *Examiner,* 3/15/45, CMC USC.
302. "despondent . . . right thing": Hyams, *Bogie,* p. 86.
302. "very nice and . . .": Victor Mature, letter to AMS read by telephone, 10/26/90.
302. "Bogey and I . . .": *L.A. Times,* 5/11/45, CMC USC.
303. "Until Howard got . . .": Slim Keith and Annette Tapert, *Slim: Memories of a Rich and Imperfect Life* (New York: Simon & Schuster, 1990), pp. 94–95.
303. "It was a business deal . . .": Dee Hawks Cramer, interview, 8/13/88.
304. "any limitations or restrictions . . .": Warner Bros. Pictures, Inc., to H-F Productions, 4/12/45, Lauren Bacall legal file, USC WB.
304. "All the documents . . .": R. J. Obringer to Lloyd Wright, Esq., letter, 5/9/45, Lauren Bacall legal file, USC WB.
304. "A situation which . . .": Obringer to Ralph Lewis, memo, 4/30/45, Bacall legal file, USC WB.
304. "Miss Bacal must . . .": R. J. Obringer for Warner Bros. Pictures, Inc., application to the Commissioner of Internal Revenue, and to Hugh L.

Ducker, Regional Head, Salary Stabilization Unit, Los Angeles, approved 12/27/44, USC WB.

304. "Something terrible's going . . .": Earl Wilson, N.Y. *Post,* 5/17/45.
305. "About that blood . . .": John Bainbridge, "Farmer Bromfield," *Life,* 10/11/48.
305. "Really good-looking . . .": Hope Bromfield Stevens, interview, 7/25/89.
305. "Louis loved Mayo . . .": Philip Van Rensselaer, interview, 4/30/91.
306. "Every photographer . . .": Ed Clark, interview, 5/27/88.
306. "Clark, a soft-spoken . . . *Life*": Ibid.
307. "Bacall was coming . . .": Ibid.
307. "Hell, I'd covered . . .": Ibid.
307. flowered wallpaper, ceramic roosters, and Audubon prints: Roy Bongartz, "Malabar Farm: Louis Bromfield's Paradise Lost," *NYT,* 5/19/74.
308. "to visually record . . .", JLW to H. M. Warner, telegram, NY wires, 4/23/45, JL/telegrams/1941–57, JWC, USC WB.
308. "extremely short notice": Gen. George C. Marshall, Chief of Staff, War Department, form letter, 5/14/45, Jules Buck Collection.
308. "HOW LONG HAVE I . . .": HM to JLW, telegram, 4/24/45, JL telegrams, folder 37:19, JWC, USC WB.
309. "That Dachau thing . . .": JLW, European Trip, 1945, Reel 11, folder 61:4, JWC, USC WB.
309. "And [now] . . .": JLW, European Trip, 1945, Record 11, p. 4, JWC USC WB.
309. "Warner Brothers was . . . in doing": JLW, European Trip, 1945, Record 6, pp. 6–7, Reel 10, p. 2 JWC, USC WB.
309. "It was like Times Square . . .": Walter Seltzer, interview, 11/19/90.
309. JLW's end of war telegrams: 8/15/45, JL: NY wires, JWC, USC WB.
310. three thousand Marines: Owen Callin, "Longing for Home Worst GI Morale Problem, Actor Says," unidentified publication, n.d., *The Big Sleep* press file, USCWB.
310. "mutual understanding . . .": The Hollywood Independent Citizens Committee of the Arts, Sciences, and Professions, Statement of Policy, flyer, 8/1/46, Morris-Kenny Collection, WSHS.
310. "You cheap sissy . . ." and "contaminating the air . . .": Humphrey Bogart, "I Stuck My Neck Out," *Saturday Evening Post,* 2/10/45, USC WB.
310. "If you'll write it . . .": Stuart Rose to Nathaniel Benchley, interview, n.d., NB BU.
311. "On the evening of . . . interesting people that way": Bogart, "I Stuck My Neck Out."
313. "He died in . . .": Ibid.
313. "away from subject . . .": Finlay McDermid to Steve Trilling, memo, 8/29/45, JL/Tr/A-Z/'45, JWC, USC WB.
313. "was everything that IATSE . . .": Friedrich, *City of Nets,* p. 247.

314. Account of the IATSE/CSU split and strike: Friedrich, *City of Nets,* pp. 247–248.
315. "which is most progressive . . .": Mikhail Kalatozov, Special Representative of the Soviet Motion Picture Industry, to 3/20/44, JL/Tr-H, 1944, JWC, USC WB.
315. "They turned the fire hoses . . .": Rose Hobart, interview, 11/11/87.
315. LeRoy Prinz knocked unconscious: LeRoy Prinz, deposition, 10/8/45, Studio Strike folder, JWC, USC WB.
316. "And on the street . . . Oh, were they wild!": Silver, interview.
316. "perpetrated by . . . civil liberties": Telegram to Jack and Harry Warner, Studio Strike folder, JWC, USC WB.
316. "strikers' siege resembled Stalingrad": Steve Trilling to Jake Wilk, letter, 10/23/45, and Strike 1945, JWC, USC WB.
316. Warners protested only trying to keep doors open: memo of conversation between Steve Trilling and Jack Dales, SAG, 10/19/45, JWC, USC WB.
317. Blayney Matthews and background checks: telegram to Warner Bros., 10/8/45, photocopy with note: "original given to Blayney Matthews"; also original with notations, some names underlined and notated with check marks, NY wires, 1945, JWC, USC WB.
317. Wilde refused to work against strikers: Meta Wilde, interview, 2/8/90, and *Strike Notes,* Strike folder, 6:10, 1945, JWC, USC WB.
317. "The Dove of Peace . . .": Steve Trilling to Zelma Brookov, letter, 11/3/45, P.S. to Jake Wilk, USC WB.

CHAPTER 16: AFTER THE WAR

318. Warner Bros. assessment that Shumlin had much to learn: Bob Buckner to Steve Trilling, letter, 1/22/45, JL/Tr, JWC, USC WB.
318. "It was wrong . . .": "In Defense of My Wife," *Photoplay,* n.d. (probably ca. summer 1946), p. 99, CMC USC.
319. "You can keep . . .": Des Moines *Register,* 8/24/45.
319. "Betty wouldn't take . . .": Dan Seymour, interview, 8/10/90.
319. "Let the audience . . .": JLW to Buckner, memo, 6/15/45, JL/Trilling files, JWC, USC WB. Shumlin in turn complained about his assistant director, Art Lueker, and tried to take him off the picture. Lueker in turn was under orders to contact Trilling and Wright "if any of Shumlin's demands strike them as unreasonable or impractical or probably both." Buckner to Trilling, memo, 7/24/45, USC WB.
319. Account of bullet going through Harry Warner's window: Seymour, interview.
319. "A great part . . .": Robert Buckner to Herman Shumlin, 10/31/45, *Confidential Agent* picture file, USC WB.

320. New York wanted rough cuts to interest magazines: Evelove to JLW, 9/11/45, JL/Tr/A-Z/'45, JWC, USC WB.
320. "*Stop everything*... that was ever made": Arthur Silver, interview, 11/19/87.
320. "Bacall fails...": *Variety,* 11/2/45, *Confidential Agent* press file, USC WB.
320. "Confidentially, it stinks...": *Hollywood Review,* 11/12/45, *Confidential Agent* press file, USC WB.
320. "Engrossing... unmitigated bore": 11/3/45; "savagely exciting... range of expression": N.Y. *Herald Tribune,* 11/3/45: *Confidential Agent* press file, USC WB.
321. "pushed too far...": *Time,* 11/19/45, *Confidential Agent* press file, USC WB.
321. "I have my points": Herman Shumlin to Bob Buckner, letter, 11/3/45, *Confidential Agent* picture file, USC WB.
321. "Miss Bacall starts...": Bosley Crowther, *NYT,* 11/3/45, *Confidential Agent* press file, USC WB.
321. "Extraordinary inept...": Brooklyn *Eagle,* 11/3/45, *Confidential Agent* press file, USC WB.
321. "The noise she makes...": Bosley Crowther, *NYT,* 11/3/45.
321. "I watched Betty's...": Humphrey Bogart, "In Defense of My Wife."
321. "went out of their way...": Ibid.
321. "Thank God...": Bacall, *By Myself,* p. 148.
321. "The fault is not...": John McManus, *PM Reviews,* n.d., USC WB.
322. "They are calling her...": unidentified Chicago newspaper, n.d., *Confidential Agent* press file, USC WB.
322. "She is unique...": N.Y. *Post,* 11/3/45, *Confidential Agent* press file, USC WB.
322. "I also as the author...": Graham Greene to the London *Sunday Telegraph,* letter, 1/18/79, reprinted in Graham Greene, *Yours Etc., Letters to the Press* (Toronto: Lester & Orphen Dennys, 1989), p. 188.
322. "There's still promise...": *L.A. Times,* 11/10/45, *Confidential Agent* press file, USC WB.
322. Screening on Okinawa amid wreckage of tanks: Doug Kennedy to Steve Trilling, memo, ca. 12/45, JL/Tr/A-Z/'45, JWC, USC WB.
323. "which she definitely...": CKF to JLW, letter, 11/16/45, USC WB.
323. Hawks paid $10,323 for additional shooting: Warner Bros. Pictures, Inc., to Howard Hawks, 1/18/46, Hawks legal file, USC WB.
323. "You got a... in the saddle": *The Big Sleep,* cutter's script, USC WB.
323. "Whether you understand...": Archer Winston, N.Y. *Post,* n.d. (probably 8/24/46).
323. "Miss Bacall is okay...": *Showman's Trade Review,* 8/17/46, USC WB.
323. "The love song...": Cecilia Ager, *PM,* n.d., USC WB.

323. It took Bacall years to get even halfway: Bacall, *By Myself,* p. 196.
324. Happiest time of Bacall's life: Ibid., p. 201.
324. "In his earlier . . .", Gloria Stuart, interview, 2/2/90.
324. "He was a changed . . .": Sam Jaffe, interview, 8/25/87.
324. "improved by Betty's . . .": John Huston, interview, 5/20/87.
324. "Betty was *marvelous* . . .": Dorris Bowdon Johnson, interview, 8/9/87.
324. "going V-R-R-R-O-O-M-M-M . . .": Philip and Amanda Dunne, interview, 8/7/87.
325. "a kind of *Thin Man* . . .": Joe Hyams, interview, 4/10/91.
325. "They *liked* each other . . .": Evelyn Keyes, interview, 8/26/87.
325. "We had a hard . . .": Max Wilk, interview, 5/4/87.
326. Surprise birthday party: Bacall, *By Myself,* p. 199.
326. Bogart paid $50,326 for *Santana:* Sarah Pileggi, "Lady with a Past" *Sports Illustrated,* 7/20/81, p. 59.
326. "a delight to the seaman's . . .": John Vigor, "Bogie's Boat," *Cruising World,* June 1991; see also James Murray, "All Right, Louie, Drop the Jib," *Sports Illustrated,* 4/30/56; and Sarah Pileggi, "Lady with a Past."
326. "an enchanting mess . . .": Thornton Delehanty, "Bogart Gets a Shakedown," N.Y. *Herald Tribune,* 12/16/45.
327. "Bogie was in love": Bacall, *By Myself,* p. 153.
327. "I don't use . . .": James Murray, "All Right, Louie."
327. "He didn't like . . .": Jaffe, interview.
328. "If he comes home . . .": transcript, *Lux Radio Theatre,* 10/14/46, USC WB.
328. "Sid—May You . . .": Endres and Cushman, *Hollywood at Your Feet: The Story of the World-Famous Chinese Theatre.*
328. " 'Who's he?' . . .": Richard Dorso, interview, 12/6/90.
329. "We want a Bogart picture": Dorso, interview.
329. "Two of our most . . .": Trilling to Warner, 12/4/45, USC WB.
329. Warners offered him much to be critical of: Proposed scripts for Bogart included *Nobody Lives Forever; Manhattan Fury;* a new Burnett story called *Tomorrow's Another Day; Alma Mater,* the story of a football coach; and a period piece entitled *When Old New York Was Young.* The Burnett story, unrecognizably rewritten, became a low-budget vehicle for Steve Cochrane and died. *Nobody Lives Forever* went to John Garfield. *Alma Mater* became *Trouble Along the Way,* with John Wayne, and the period piece hung around until 1950, when it resurfaced as a Gordon MacRae–June Haver musical, *The Daughter of Rosie O'Grady.* Jerry Wald lobbied Bogart for the lead in *Task Force,* Warners' love letter to the U.S. Navy's role in World War II. Bogart was interested until he learned from studio scuttlebutt that he'd be playing second lead to an aircraft carrier. Gary

Cooper eventually took the role, but the picture sank under the weight of too much hardware and not enough story.

329. a "plum": Evelove to JLW, memo, 11/30/45, USC WB.

330. "because of her earlier . . .": Evelove to JLW, memo, 12/18/44, USC WB.

330. *Lux Radio Theatre,* 10/14/46: tape heard at Museum of Television and Radio, New York.

330. "Now we are in it together . . .": Invitation, dinner in honor of Dr. Harlow Shapley, December 10, 6:30, private collection.

330. "liberal thinkers, writers . . .": Cameron Shipp, "The Gentlest," unident. (probably *Movie Life*), ca. 3/10/46, CMC USC.

330. "Danger!! Alcohol and Bogart . . .": *Louella Parsons in Hollywood,* L.A. *Examiner,* 11/2/47.

331. "immobilized" by "redbaiting": HICCASP, Report of Campaign Activities, Morris-Kenny Collection, WSHS.

331. "Isn't this a *stupid* . . .": Lizabeth Scott, interview, 11/7/90.

331. "warm, charming . . .": Ibid.

331. "He said to the crew . . .": Ibid.

331. Bogart brought lunch pail from home and took a nap: Philip Gersh, interview, 8/1/87.

331. "Not that he didn't want . . .": Scott, interview.

331. "If you ever . . .": Richard Brooks, interview, 9/26/88. *The Brick Foxhole* was eventually filmed under the title *Crossfire* (1947), directed by Edward Dmytryk and starring Robert Young, Robert Ryan, Robert Mitchum, and Gloria Grahame. The victim was changed from a homosexual to a Jew.

332. "the box office value . . .": Humphrey Bogart to JLW, telegram, 5/26/44, Bogart legal file, USC WB.

332. "From his own experience . . .", Brooks, interview.

332. Bogart first gave *The Dark Road* to Wald: Jerry Wald to JLW, 11/26/45, JL/Tr, "W" 1945, JWC, USC.

332. "He is always . . .": Ibid.

333. Bogart said he'd take any female star: Warner Bros. Studio, "Production Memo," n.d., USC WB.

333. "I can just hear . . .": Harrison Carroll, unidentified, 12/21/46, *Dark Passage* press file, USC WB.

333. "The proposition was . . .": Thornton Delehanty, N.Y. *Herald Tribune,* 9/29/46.

333. longest agreement; *NYT,* 12/23/46.

334. Ratification of contract: E. K. Hessberg, Asst. Secretary of Warner Bros. Pictures, Inc., Certification of Warner Bros. Board of Directors, 12/17/46, USC WB.

334. Bogart's 1946 salary of $467,361 the highest in the world for an actor:

United Press International, 2/6/49, Aljean Harmetz Collection. Bette Davis's $328,334 salary was the highest that year for an actress. The highest salary in the film business was $985,300, earned by Twentieth Century–Fox executive Charles P. Skouras (UPI, 2/6/49, Aljean Harmetz Collection).

334. "the screenplay. . . .": Agreement, 12/19/46, p. 55, Bogart legal file, USC WB.

334. "Awaiting a new . . .": Producers: Script Progress Reports, 8/45-12/45, JL/Tr, JWC, USC WB.

334. "Awaiting John Huston": Ibid.

CHAPTER 17: "A LOATHSOME CHARACTER"

335. "Wait till you see . . .": *Time* file, 1954 cover article: "Extra-curricular activities," *Time* morgue.

335. "He's a man prepared . . .": Stanley Karnow, *Time* file, received 5/1/54, *Time* morgue.

336. "claiming to be an American": According to his wife of a late marriage, B. Traven said he was born in Chicago. Larry Rohter, *NYT*, 6/25/90.

336. Traven's real name Ret Marut: Ibid. Traven's widow, Rosa Elena Luján, told Larry Rohter that the one-hundredth anniversary of Traven's birth was "an appropriate time" to divulge what she knew. The story adds that besides Hal Croves, Traven assumed the identity of Traven Torsvan, supposedly born in Chicago on May 3, 1890. Among the other surnames he supposedly used as an alias were Arnold, Barker, Feige, Kraus, Lainger, Wienecke, and Ziegelbrenner. His widow told Rohter that he "lived something like 10 lives."

336. "non-capitalist countries": Paul Kohner, Inc., to Alfred A. Knopf, Inc., letter, 7/25/38, private papers of Paul Kohner, Los Angeles.

336. Traven's books have sold 25 million copies in more than thirty languages: *NYT*, 6/25/90.

336. "They coveted gold . . .": Emanuel Geibel (1815–1884), "Die Goldgräber" ("The Golddiggers").

336. "I guess I had that coming . . .": Ibid.

337. "top acting possibilities . . .": Thornton Delehanty, N.Y. *Herald Tribune,* 9/26/46.

337. "Huston had urged Warners . . .": All the details of *The Treasure of the Sierra Madre*'s coming to Warner Bros. are based on the correspondence of Paul Kohner and B. Traven. Private papers of Paul Kohner, Los Angeles.

337. "go down as one of . . .": Paul Nathan to JLW, memo, 4/11/42, USC WB.

338. Legal department's worries over copyright: R. J. Obringer to Morris Ebenstein, memo, 6/30/42, USC WB.
338. "All the time I was in . . .": John Huston to J. H. McCallum, Harcourt, Brace and Co., letter, 3/21/46, JH, AMPAS.
338. "scripts were drafted . . .": Several screenwriters wrote versions of *The Treasure of the Sierra Madre,* including Robert Rossen, later writer-producer of *All the King's Men* and *The Hustler,* then known mostly for his work on *Marked Woman* and *The Roaring Twenties.* Other writers considered were Howard Koch and Emmet Lavery, and Vincent Sherman was mentioned as a possible director.
338. Hemingway sold rights to Hellinger: Agreement, Ernest Hemingway and Mark Hellinger Productions, DOSC UT.
338. Bogart to star in one picture a year: Announcement, n.d., MHC USC.
338. Bogart to be a director and shareholder: Minutes of the Board of Directors, Mark Hellinger Productions, 1945–1948, MHC USC.
339. Ben Hecht's interest: Martin Gang to Mark Hellinger, letter, 2/10/47, MHC USC.
339. Minimum per-picture fee of $199,999: Artist's Contract between Mark Hellinger Productions and Humphrey Bogart, cc, n.d., 1947, 58 pp., MHC USC.
339. Hellinger's fear of fresh catastrophe: Richard Brooks, "Swell Guy," *The Screen Writer,* 3/48.
340. "like a kid" and "a very valuable part of my life": Stephen Humphrey Bogart and Gary Provost, *In Search of My Father* (New York: Dutton, 1995), p. 194.
340. "even a no-talent bastard . . .": Ibid.
340. "He had this *enormous* . . .": Jules Buck, interview, 9/11/88.
340. "nice guests and good hosts . . .": Evelyn Keyes, interview, 8/26/87.
341. "Bogie liked to drink . . .": John Huston, interview, 5/20/87.
341. "They acted like a couple . . .": Keyes, interview.
341. "these were John and . . . Band-Aided feet": Evelyn Keyes, interview. Joe Hyams writes that this happened in 1949 at a post-Oscar celebration after Huston and his father won awards for *The Treasure of the Sierra Madre.* Hyams, *Bogie,* p. 127.
341. Huston never locked door and Croves by his bedside: Grobel, *The Hustons,* p. 286.
342. "to confer with the author . . .": Kenneth Cox to W. L. Guthrie, memo, 2/1/47, *The Treasure of the Sierra Madre,* Location File, USC WB.
342. Kohner was convinced Traven and Croves were the same man, and Crove's confession: Grobel, *The Hustons,* pp. 290–291.
342. "as close alongside . . .": B. Traven to John Huston, Esq., letter, 9/2/46, Behlmer, *Inside Warner Bros.,* pp. 279–280.

342. "Croves" promised to send comments along, plans for expedition and details of lost wallet: H. C. (Hal Croves) to John Huston, letter, 2/2/47, JH, AMPAS.
342. "a sort of duel . . .": Traven to Huston, letter, 1/4/47, JH, AMPAS.
342. "From that moment on . . .": Huston to Traven, letter, 12/30/46, JH, AMPAS.
342. "and Dobbs, recognizing Gold Hat . . .": Traven to Huston, letter, 12/30/46, JH, AMPAS.
343. "I was just thinking . . .": H. C. to Huston, letter, 2/4/47, JH, AMPAS.
343. "Bogart will be a great . . .": Traven to Huston, letter, 1/4/47, JH, AMPAS.
343. "You know as well . . .": B. Traven to John Huston, Esq., letter, n.d., JH, AMPAS.
343. "Howard steals the picture . . .": H. C. to Huston, letter, 2/12/47, JH, AMPAS.
343. "First he is . . .": Bob Fender, WB Publicity, n.d., USC WB.
344. Script cleared with censors in Mexico: W. L. Guthrie to John Huston, 2/5/47, *The Treasure of the Sierra Madre,* Location Folder, USC WB.
344. The Mexican government found nothing offensive: Michael Sokol to W. L. Guthrie, memo, 2/21/47, Location Department, USC WB.
345. "like a moth to light . . .": Robert Blake, interview, 11/13/90.
345. Huston "made him do it several times.. . . .when you were near him you were safe": Blake, interview.
347. "As many of the party . . .": Daily Production and Progress Report, 4/7/47, USC WB.
347. "We had nice . . .": Bob Fender, *By Humphrey Bogart,* Warner Bros. Studios, n.d., WB and Carl Combs, Warner Bros. Studio, n.d., and publicity folder, USC WB.
347. "He's just a mite . . .": Eileen Creelman, "Picture Plays and Players: Humphrey Bogart and Lauren Bacall Talk of 'The Treasure of the Sierra Madre,' " N.Y. *Sun,* 11/24/47, USC WB.
347. Practical joke on Fender: Ibid.
348. "You know that he . . .": Blanke to Page, memo, 2/4/47, USC WB.
348. Bogart's baldness exacerbated by hormone treatments: Hyams, *Bogie,* p. 124.
348. "growing a fine . . .": Grayson to Blanke, memo, 5/2/47, USC WB.
349. "We have a lad . . .": Charles Bonniwell to "Dear Ed," 4/17/47, *The Treasure of the Sierra Madre,* location folder, USC WB.
349. Contact with Bogart: Karl S. Guthke, *B. Traven: The Life Behind the Legends* (Chicago: Lawrence Hill Books, 1987), p. 345.
349. "wonderful understanding . . . Break for lunch!": Bruce Bennett, interview, 1/26/90.
350. "He didn't usually. . . . somebody's fingers": Huston, interview.

351. "it was like Big Daddy . . .": Keyes, interview.
351. "Badges? . . . I don't got . . .": *The Treasure of the Sierra Madre,* dialogue script, script file, USC WB.
351. "goatish kind of jig": *The Treasure of the Sierra Madre,* Rev. final, 1/10/47, p. 36, script folder, USC WB.
352. "As soon as the word. . . . the *intensity*": Helga Smith, interview, 12/12/89.
352. "If you're shooting . . .": Bennett, interview.
353. Performance of his career: *Time,* 2/2/48, *The Treasure of the Sierra Madre,* press file, USC WB.
353. "a loathsome character . . .": *Hollywood Reporter,* 1/6/48.
353. "THIS IS DEFINITELY . . .": JLW to Ben Kalmenson, telegram, 8/1/47, USC WB.
353. "Croves" listed as an adviser: *The Treasure of the Sierra Madre,* Daily Production and Progress reports, 6/21/47 and 6/23/47, USC WB. Hal Croves is not listed as an adviser in the film credits.
353. "paying me a lousy $100 . . .": *Life,* 2/n.d./48, *The Treasure of the Sierra Madre,* press file, USC WB.
353. "This could have happened . . .": Paul Kohner, interview, 9/2/87.

CHAPTER 18: MR. BOGART GOES TO WASHINGTON

354. "carried on crusades . . .": *NYT,* 4/3/55.
354. "to the lowest . . .": Stefan Kanfer, *A Journal of the Plague Years* (New York: Atheneum, 1973), p. 13.
355. "Russian-born": Frank Hughes, Chicago *Daily Tribune,* 11/23/46.
355. "one of the greatest propaganda . . .": Frank Hughes, Chicago *Daily Tribune,* 11/17/46.
355. "top priority": Willard Edwards, Chicago *Daily Tribune,* 11/27/46.
355. "to tell what they know . . .": L.A. *Herald Express,* 5/14/47.
356. "the greatest hotbed . . . overthrow of the government": Quoted by Friedrich, *City of Nets,* p. 299.
356. Rankin's view of Jews and "the Jewish gentleman . . . being called a gentleman?": Friedrich, *City of Nets,* p. 299; quoted from Walter Goodman, *The Committee: The Extraordinary Career of the House Committee on Un-American Activities* (New York: Farrar, Straus & Giroux, 1968), pp. 42, 172–174.
356. Thomas's desire to seem less obviously Catholic or Irish: In his petition to the court, Feeney/Thomas pleaded that "your petitioner believes he can get recognition and business under the name of Thomas that he could not get under the name of Feeney." Friedrich, *City of Nets,* p. 299. Also the St. Louis *Post Dispatch,* 12/1/48.

356. "The charge is often made . . .": Gordon Kahn, *Hollywood on Trial* (New York: Boni and Gaer, 1948), p. 24. Also Chicago *Tribune,* 5/29/47, JWC, USC WB.
356. Warner named Phil and Julie Epstein: Associate Press, readback of testimony of May 1947; *Hollywood Citizen News,* 10/20/47, JWC, USC WB.
356. "make himself the American Stalin": Chicago *Tribune,* 6/2/47.
356. "amazed. . . . this dangerous situation": Ibid.
357. Nixon announced subpoenas about to be served: *Hollywood Citizen News,* 5/28/47, *L.A. Times* 5/29/47.
357. "It will be sensational": *Hollywood Citizen News,* 7/30/47; *Hollywood Reporter,* 7/31/47.
357. McCarthy's and Thomas's lists specious: For an interesting account, see Friedrich, *City of Nets,* p. 300.
357. "Nobody can tell . . .": Larry Ceplair and Steven Englund, *The Inquisition in Hollywood: Politics in the Film Community, 1930–1960* (Garden City, N.Y.: Anchor/Doubleday, 1980), p. 259.
358. "the place . . . than at the commissary": Philip Dunne, interview, 8/7/87.
358. "The whole town . . .": John Huston, interview, 5/20/87.
358. "premature anti-fascism": Jack Warner Jr., interview, 11/12/90.
358. "Obviously the Constitution . . .": Philip Dunne, "The Constitution Up Close and Personal," *Constitution* magazine, vol. 4, no.3, 1992.
358. "Betty was all for it . . .": Huston, interview.
358. Charles Feldman gave $10,000, and stipulations: Jules Buck, telephone interview, 10/18/91.
358. "$50 (no name)": Donations list, records of the Committee for the First Amendment.
359. "Down the block," using Lennart's phone, and "By the way . . .": Philip and Amanda Dunne, interview, 8/7//87.
359. "I said to Eddie . . .": Katharine Hepburn, interview, 3/20/89.
360. "AT WALLACE HOOPLA . . .": L.A. *Herald-Express,* 10/27/47, J.L. clip file, 10/27/47, L.A. papers, JWC, USC WB
360. "They could attack . . .": Hepburn, interview.
360. Wilder's favorite co-writer: "If I ever lost this guy," Wilder once said, "I'd feel like Abercrombie without Fitch." Katz, *The Film Encyclopedia,* p. 364.
360. "*The words of Parnell Thomas are . . .*": *The Screen Writer,* 12/47.
360. "The Hollywood People . . .": Ad, N.Y. *Herald Tribune,* 10/27/46, Hollywood Ten, Morris-Kenny Collection, WSHS.
360. "The damn thing . . .": Philip Dunne, interview.
360. "What we objected to . . .": Gene Kelly, interview, 12/13/90.
360. noting license plate numbers: Philip Dunne, interview.

361. "circus" atmosphere: *Hollywood Citizen News*, 10/17/47.
361. "the Hollywood investigation . . .": *NYT*, 10/26/47.
361. Press setup in hearing room: Associated Press, *NYT*, 10/18/47.
361. Thomas sat on phone book and pillow: Friedrich, *City of Nets*, p. 311. Also red pillow, Kanfer, *A Journal of the Plague Years*, p.42.
361. "a Congress-eye view . . .": *Daily Variety*, 10/20/47, J. L. clip file, 10/20/47, L.A. papers, JWC, USC WB
361. "It's obvious he should . . .": Jack Warner Jr., interview.
362. Warner originally named sixteen writers: Alvah Bessie, Guy Endore, Julius and Philip Epstein, Sheridan Gibney, Gordon Kahn, Howard Koch, Ring Lardner Jr., Emmet Lavery, John Howard Lawson, Albert Maltz, Clifford Odets, Richard Rossen, Irwin Shaw, Dalton Trumbo, John Wexley. He amended this list to the committee by saying that Endore, Gibney, and the Epsteins had "never written any subversive elements" (Friedrich, *City of Nets*, p. 312). The Epsteins, Gibney, and Lavery were known for their criticism of communism: Ceplair and Englund, *The Inquisition in Hollywood*, p. 259.
362. "AS UNDER NO . . .": telegrams, 10/21/47, 10/22/47, 10/23/47, JWC, USC WB.
362. "I want to make a correction. . . . a fantasy": JLW, *Hearings Regarding the Communist Infiltration of the Motion Picture Industry Before the Committee on Un-American Activities*, U.S. House Committee on Un-American Activities, 10/20/47 (Washington, D.C.: U.S. Government Printing Office, 1947).
362. "If making *Mission to Moscow* . . .": *Hearings Regarding the Communist Infiltration of the Motion Picture Industry*. Also Robert Carr, *The House Committee on Un-American Activities, 1945–1950* (Ithaca, N.Y.: Cornell University Press, 1952), p. 61.
362. "Stripling asked . . . war effort": Ibid.
363. "I think he got angry . . .": Jack Warner Jr., interview.
363. "Jesus . . . there to laugh": Ibid.
363. "HAPPY EVERYTHING OVER . . .": JLW to Blumenstock, telegram, 10/21/47, JWC, USC WB.
363. "EVERYTHING WORKED OUT . . .": JLW to Kalmenson, telegram, 12/21/47, JWC, USC WB.
363. "agents of a foreign country": N.Y. *Daily News*, 10/21/47, Hollywood Ten, Morris-Kenny Collection, WSHS.
364. "arm to the teeth": David Caute, *The Great Fear* (New York: Simon & Schuster, 1978), pp. 492–493.
364. "Farce is tragedy . . .": Kanfer, *A Journal of the Plague Years*, p. 3.
364. "Bing Crosby? . . .": United Press International, *Hollywood Citizen News*, 10/24/47, J. L. clip file, 10/24/47, L.A. papers, JWC, USC WB.

364. "make democracy work": *Washington Daily News,* 10/23/47, Morris-Kenny Collection, WSHS.
364. Lawson admitted Communist affiliation in 1934: Friedrich, *City of Nets,* p. 322.
365. "headline publicity . . .": Philip Dunne, interview.
365. CFA meeting at William Wyler's house: There is a split in recollections as to whether this famous phone call took place at Wyler's home or at Ira Gershwin's. Both were favored meeting places. Most witnesses, however, place the meeting at Wyler's.
365. "They said, 'the following . . .' ": Philip Dunne, interview.
365. "We decided to bring . . .": Kelly, interview.
365. "We must go": Bacall, *By Myself,* p. 211.
365. "It's wrong. . . . up his hands": Dee Hawks Cramer, interview, 8/13/88.
365. "Jack Warner, despite . . . throats": Jack Warner Jr., interview.
366. "How can you go on this trip . . .": Jules Buck, interview, 9/11/88.
366. "Just one of . . .": Huston, interview.
366. "We said, 'All right . . .' ": N.Y. *Herald Tribune,* 11/23/47.
366. Actress Marsha Hunt: Hunt was a former Powers model whose movie career began in the mid-1930s. She played in a number of MGM films in the 1940s, and should not be confused with another Marsha Hunt, who appeared in British films in the 1980s.
366. "a kind of tense . . .": Marsha Hunt, interview, 2/26/90.
366. "In all the good . . .": Richard Brooks, interview, 9/26/88.
366. Roster for trip to Washington: *L.A. Times,* 10/25/47.
367. "We needed him . . .": Henry Rogers, interview, 8/9/87.
367. "essential": Philip Dunne, interview.
367. Hughes and knockdown fee for charter: Ibid.
367. "I think it was John . . .": Ibid.
367. "What the hell . . .": Jerome Lawrence, interview, 11/2/87.
367. The writers at secretaries' desks and other preparations: Lawrence, interview.
368. "This is Humphrey. . . . Americans shall think": Committee for the First Amendment: *Hollywood Fights Back,* 10/26/47, Jerome Lawrence Collection.
368. "Most of our troops . . .": Philip Dunne, interview.
369. Ring Lardner quotation: Ring Lardner Jr., *The Lardners: My Family Reconsidered* (New York: Harper & Row, 1976), p. 325.
369. "It was not *quite* . . .": Hunt, interview.
369. "we share your feelings . . .": Ceplair and Englund, *The Inquisition in Hollywood,* p. 282.
369. "are embarrassed . . .": Ibid., p. 280.
369. "The Motion Picture Association . . .": Philip Dunne, *Take Two: A Life in Movies and Politics* (New York: McGraw-Hill, 1980), p. 58.

369. The Progessive Citizens of America convocation held October 25 to bolster the spirits of the Nineteen: Ceplair and Englund, *The Inquisition in Hollywood*, p. 282.
369. CFA's premise based on Constitutional rights: Philip Dunne, *Take Two*, p. 197.
370. "We requested that if there . . .": Huston, interview.
370. "We are against communism . . .": L.A. *Herald-Express*, 10/26/47.
370. "It was stupid . . .": Paul Henreid, interview, 2/20/90.
371. "He had a very attractive voice . . .": Buck, interview.
371. "we clustered around . . .": Hunt, interview.
371. "We were on a high . . .": Buck, interview.
371. "a mingling . . .": Hunt, interview.
371. "It wasn't fun and games . . .": Marion Stevenson, interview, 6/4/92.
372. "She'll get him to keep his mouth . . .": Henry Rogers, *Walking the Tightrope* (New York: William Morrow & Co., 1980), pp. 84–85.
372. "That was the compromise . . .": Philip Dunne, interview.
372. "They had been standing . . .": Hunt, interview.
372. "We came in . . . were worn out": Buck, interview.
372. "We do not represent . . .": N.Y. *Daily News*, 10/27/47.
373. "We feel . . . next move": Ibid.
373. "That just isn't right": N.Y. *Sun*, 10/27/47.
373. "SURPRISE WITNESS . . .": Ibid.
374. "so our actors . . . have been sustained": Philip Dunne, interview.
374. "If you *are* . . .": Huston, interview.
374. "Phil Dunne and John Huston were more or less . . .": Ring Lardner Jr., interview, 7/25/90.
374. "insisted that we. . . . didn't work": Ibid.
375. "not only was he parked . . .": Philip Dunne, interview.
376. "Thomas pulled a fast . . .": Ibid.
376. Thirty-one Capitol policemen and exploding flood lamp: *PM*, 10/28/47.
377. "both Thomas and Lawson were doing . . .": Philip Dunne, interview.
377. "a fishwife brawl": *Daily Variety*, 10/28/47.
377. "This isn't what . . .": Edward Dmytryk, interview, 4/4/91.
377. "Who's going to be . . .": Philip Dunne, interview.
377. Bogart rose out of his seat and other reactions: photo, *Life*, 11/24/47.
377. "That bank of camera lights . . .": Evelyn Keyes, interview, 8/26/87.
378. Lawson and contempt motion and litany of "fronts": L.A. *Daily News*, 10/28/47.
378. "Mr. Lawson . . . screamed . . .": N.Y. *Herald Tribune*, 10/28/47.
378. "We stuck to the same . . .": Philip Dunne, interview.
378. "a censorship of fear . . . a communist?" and Bacall's question: *PM*, 10/28/47.

378. "God, I'm a dumb . . .": Elise Morrison, *Innocents Abroad in the Nation's Capitol*, 11/3/47, publication data unknown, private archive.
378. "As politicians . . .": *Life*, 11/10/47.
379. "We muddled through": Otis L. Guernsey Jr., "The Playbill: Citizen Bogart in Defense of Principle," N.Y. *Herald Tribune*, 11/23/47, Section V, p. 1.
379. "this whole procedure. . . . Tell a joke, Danny": Sidney Olson, *Life*, 11/24/47.
379. "These were political . . .": Keyes, interview.
379. "Lost Liberals": *Life*, 11/24/47.
379. "Unless this evidence is presented . . .": Eric Johnston, prepared speech, 10/27/47, Morris-Kenny Collection, WSHS.
379. "an exposed Communist . . .": Ceplair and Englund, *The Inquisition in Hollywood*, p. 285.
380. "The mistake we made . . .": Ibid.
380. "a kind of disbelief . . .": Hunt, interview.
380. "The procedures adopted . . .": Petition for Redress of Grievances Presented, October 28, 1947, to the Congress by Members of the Committee for the First Amendment, Philip Dunne private papers, Los Angeles.
381. Nixon had vanished: Philip Dunne, interview.
381. "I want to read you . . .": Kanfer, *The Plague Years*, p. 73. While Rankin said that Kaye's birthname was Kimirsky, it was actually was Kami*n*ski.
381. "Perhaps I'm the girl . . . end with us. . . .": Lauren Bacall, "Why I Came to Washington," *Washington Daily News*, 10/29/47, copyright 1947, *Washington Daily News*. Details of the writing of the article are contained in the sidebar, "A Note About This Story." "Every word of the story is hers," the paper assured its readers. "No ghost-writer or press agent had anything to do with it."
382. Bogart stuck his head in: Ibid.
382. Comments monitored by FBI: Special Agent in charge, Philadelphia, to Director, FBI, 11/3/47, FBI files.
382. "I discount those": Transcript, interviews broadcast over Radio Station WIP, Philadelphia, 10: 00 P.M., 10/29/47, FBI files, Special Agent in Charge, Philadelphia to Director, FBI, 11/3/47.
382. "Don't you believe . . .": Hunt, interview.
382. Sullivan column and "He took a slap . . .": Rogers, interview.
382. "There! It's over . . .": Hunt, interview.
382. "You're right. No congressman's . . .": Huston, interview.
383. Brecht's accent was so thick it "mystified the committee": photo caption, *Life*, 11/24/47.
383. "were elated . . .": Hunt, interview.
383. "These groups. . . .": Peoria (Illinois) *Journal-Transcript*, 10/28/47.
383. "a general feeling of shock . . .": Huston, interview.

384. "Usually men who . . ." St. Louis *Post Dispatch,* 10/30/47.
384. "There is no law against . . .": Lewiston (Maine) *Sun,* 10/28/47.
384. "When a man refuses . . .": Decatur (Illinois) *Review,* 11/2/47.
384. "I could answer . . .": Friedrich, *City of Nets,* p. 329.
385. "As far as I could judge . . .": Howard Koch, "To Whom It May Concern," p. 7., n.d., Howard Koch Collection, WSHS.
385. "made the testimony . . .": Ring Lardner Jr., interview.
385. Lardner and others of the Ten swore no vengence on Thomas: Lester Cole, *Hollywood Red: The Autobiography of Lester Cole* (Palo Alto, Calif.: Ramparts Press, 1981), pp. 314–319; also Friedrich, *City of Nets,* p. 426.
385. "I was convicted . . . petty thieves": Friedrich, *City of Nets,* p. 426; also Lardner, *The Lardners: My Family Reconsidered,* p. 322.
385. "this tacky little joint . . .": Frances Lardner, interview, 7/25/90.
386. "I don't know . . .": Ibid.
386. "Here you had been like . . .": Keyes, interview.
386. "the middle . . . sold me out!": Nancy Lynn Schwartz, *The Hollywood Writers' Wars* (New York: Alfred A. Knopf, 1982), p. 281.
387. "We all spoke . . .": Philip Dunne, interview.
387. "This is Humphrey Bogart . . .": *Hollywood Fights Back,* ABC Radio broadcast, 11/2/47. Script in Jerome Lawrence's private collection.
387. Columbia Pictures would make *The Front* only if it was a comedy: Walter Bernstein, *Inside Out* (New York: Alfred A. Knopf, 1996), p. 278.
388. Bessie's option dropped: Warner Bros., Personnel List, 3/10/47, JWC, USC WB.

CHAPTER 19: NO MARK OF THE SQUEALER

389. "the couple . . . December": Trilling to JLW, telegram, 11/17/47, USC WB.
390. "WASHINGTON BOGART SITUATION": JLW, to Kalmenson, Blumenstock, Western Union telegram, 11/12/47, NY wires, outgoing, 11/47–12/47, JWC, USC WB.
390. "that extremely peculiar . . .": George Dixon, "Washington Scene," L.A. *Herald Examiner,* 10/30/47.
390. "Bogart and his fellow . . .": Waterbury (Connecticut) *American,* 10/28/47.
390. "The Thomas Committee . . .": N.Y. *Daily Mirror,* 10/29/47.
390. "Under the false . . .": L.A. *Examiner,* 11/12/47; also N.Y. *Journal American,* other Hearst papers.
391. "It cost Bogart . . .": Otis L. Guernsey Jr., "The Playbill: Citizen Bogart in Defense of a Principle," N.Y. *Herald Tribune,* 11/23/47.
391. "Our object . . . to protect it": Ibid.

391. "GET THIS MAN . . .": JLW to Major Perkins and Blumenstock, telegram, 11/21/47 JWC, USC WB.
392. Trilling spent hours with the Bogarts: Trilling to JLW, telegram, 11/21/47, NY wires, outgoing/incoming, November–December 1947, JWC, USC WB.
392. "not remember any specifics . . .": Lauren Bacall, telephone interview with EL, 11/2/96.
392. "Communism in the industry": *Weekly Variety,* 11/25/47
393. "He says that he has . . .": office memorandum, 11/24/47, sender and receiver not identified, Bogart's FBI file.
393. "He was frank . . .": Ibid.
393. Sullivan back on the phone: Ibid.
393. "the leader of the Washington . . .": Humphrey DeForest Bogart, Summary Memorandum, 11/24/47, FBI files.
393. Bogart's FBI file at least two inches thick: this is the measurement of papers released under the Freedom of Information Act.
393. Biggest gathering of financial names: *Weekly Variety,* 11/25/47.
394. Discharge any of the Ten: They added the words "or suspend without a compensation," a euphemism framed to get around possible violations of labor laws.
394. "knowingly employ a Communist . . .": Statement, 11/25/47, Motion Picture Association, issued by Eric Johnston, printed in *Weekly Variety,* 11/26/47, "Film Industry's Policy Defined."
394. "Wall Street jiggled . . .": N.Y. *Mirror,* 11/29/47, quoted by John Cogley, *Report on Blacklisting,* 2 vols., New York, Fund for the Republic, 1956 p. 23.
394. "The motion picture producers . . .": Dunne, inerview.
395. "bawled the life . . .": Humphrey Bogart, "I'm No Communist," *Modern Screen,* 3/48, CMC USC WB; also FBI files.
395. "Men who've been there . . .": Archer Winsten, "Movies" N.Y. *Post,* 11/29/47.
396. *Knock on Any Door* was eventually made by Columbia in 1949, with John Derek as the boy and Bogart as his lawyer. *Let No Man Write My Epitaph* (1960) was the sequel.
396. $300,000 loan: Bankers Trust Company and the Security-First National Bank, Robert E. Kopff, of Gang, Koop & Tyre, to A. Morgan Maree and Mark Hellinger, 11/12/47, MHC USC WB.
396. "Mr. Bogart's participation . . .": Robert Koop to A. Morgan Maree and Mark Hellinger, 11/24/47, USC WB.
397. "What we are buying . . .": D.O.S. to Mr. O'Shea, Mr. Scanlon, "Immediate and Confidential," 9/10/47, Mark Hellinger–DOS, DOSC, HRHRC, UT.
397. "You know that's going to . . .": Jules Buck, interview, 9/11/88.

397. "My God, I wouldn't . . .": Helen Hayes, interview, 7/30/90.
397. "any decent American" and "I have absolutely . . .": The full statement reads: "My recent trip to Washington, where I appeared with a group of motion picture people, has become the subject of such confused and erroneous interpretation that I feel the situation should be clarified./I am not a Communist./I am not a Communist sympathizer./I detest Communism just as any other decent American does./I have never in my life been identified with any group which was even sympathetic to Communism./My name will not be found on any Communist front organization nor as a sponsor of anything Communistic./I went to Washington because I thought fellow Americans were being deprived of their Constitutional rights, and for that reason alone./That the trip was ill-advised, even foolish, I am very ready to admit. At the time it seemed the thing to do./I have absolutely no use for Communism nor for anyone who serves that philosophy./I am an American./And very likely, like a good many of the rest of you, sometimes a foolish and impetuous American. (signed) Humphrey Bogart."
397. "that word never . . .": United Press, Chicago, 12/3/47, reported in Washington *Times Herald,* 12/4/47, FBI files.
398. "Miss Bacall . . .": Ibid.
398. " 'adopted' the movie . . ." and "We went in green . . .": Chattanooga, (Tennessee) *Times,* 12/4/47.
398. "EXCELLENT": JLW to Blumenstock, telegram, 12/3/47, JWC, USC, WB.
398. "Okay, Mr. Bogart . . .": Tulsa (Oklahoma) *Tribune,* 12/4/47.
398. "Even the brazen . . .": Fergus Falls (Minnesota) unidentified, 12/5/47.
398. "The group of actors . . .": Worcester (Massachusetts) *Telegram,* 11/25/47.
398. "the state of hysteria . . .": Toledo (Ohio) *Blade,* 12/8/47.
398. "Dear Humphrey . . .": Chet Holifield, MC, House of Representatives, to Humphrey Bogart, 12/9/47, Philip Dunne private papers. Unbeknownst to Bogart, Dunne wrote about half the letter, including the parts dealing with what Dunne later called the "ferocious pressures" brought to bear on the actor.
399. "no reason for Mr. Bogart . . .": *Washington Post,* 12/4/47.
399. "All right, Humphrey . . .": Kennesaw M. Landis II, "The Terror Must Be Fierce in Hollywood," publication data unknown, 12/9/47, Morris-Kenny Collection, WSHS.
399. "JUST WHAT YOU . . .": Blumenstock to JLW, telegram, 12/1/47, NY wires, JWC, USC WB.
399. "out and out . . .": Ibid.
400. J. L. said yes: JLW to Blumenstock, Western Union, 12/1/47, NY wires, ibid., JWC, USC WB.

400. "THEY ARE PLENTY . . .": JLW to Blumenstock, telegram, 12/11/47, New York wires, 11/47–12/47, JWC, USC WB.
400. "taken a new lease . . .": JLW to Kalmenson, Kalmine, Blumenstock, memo, 12/9/47, WB, USC WB.
400. "At first we were . . .": Marsha Hunt, interview, 2/26/90.
400. "The only man . . .": Paul Henreid, interview, 2/20/90.
400. Motion Picture Alliance founders and "The American motion picture . . .": Friedrich, *City of Nets,* pp. 167–168.
401. "As for Bogart . . .": Richard Arlen, letter, Theater Collection, New York Public Library.
401. Hellinger persuaded Wald, and "Remember that promise . . .": Malvin Wald, interview, 11/20/90.
401. One of the backers threatened to pull out: MHC USC WB. Money from Selznick would come in: DOSC, HRHRC, UT.
401. "However . . . HUAC": Malvin Wald, interview, 9/7/88.
401. "about to diminish box office possibilities": Malvin Wald, interview, 11/20/90.
401. "Bogie, it's up to you . . .": Wald, interviews, 9/7/88, 11/20/90.
402. "now Bogie . . .": Wald, interview, 9/7/88.
402. "frantic phone call": *Daily Worker,* 3/2/48, FBI files.
402. "suckered into it . . .": Joe Hyams, interview, 4/10/91.
402. "Bogie was embarrassed. . . . condescending way": Jules Buck, interview, 8/12/93.
402. "I felt Bogie . . .": John Huston, interview, 5/20/87.
402. "Well, what was he going . . .": Evelyn Keyes, interview, 8/26/87.
402. "We're the ones . . .": Philip Dunne, *Take Two,* pp. 200–201.
402. "He was a big star . . .": Philip Dunne, interview, 8/7/87.
403. "Obviously those among . . .": Philip Dunne to Congressman Chet Holifield, 12/17/47, Philip Dunne private papers.
403. "to some degree" and "subtly altered . . .": Bacall, *By Myself,* p. 216.
403. "an attempt to cover": Philip Dunne, interview.
403. "He attracted all . . .": Ibid.
403. "Don't let me die . . .": Richard Brooks, repeating what Gladys Hellinger told him, interview, 9/26/88.
404. "Better to remember him as he was" and Bogart's wishes for his own funeral: Bacall, *By Myself,* p. 219.
404. "a kind of surprised . . . would have been right": Richard Brooks, "Swell Guy," *The Screen Writer,* vol. 3, no. 10 (3/48), pp. 13, 17; and Brooks, interview.
404. Selznick and right to cancel: DOS, conference notes, 9/26/47, DOSC, HRHRC, UT.
404. "reign of fear . . . in the cutting room": "Five Film Figures Report—

Hollywood 'Reign of Fear,' " *Christian Science Monitor,* 12/22/47, Morris-Kenny clip files, WSHS.

405. "a sweeping declaration. . . . themselves on record": Ibid.
405. "The appearance of Mr. Bogart's . . .": Ibid.
405. "Our plane load . . .": Humphrey Bogart, "I'm No Communist."
405. Bogart did not discuss the issue with Jaffe and Jaffe's belief that Maree was ultimately responsible for Bogart's recantation. Also, "What do you do? . . .": Sam Jaffe, interview, 8/15/87.
406. "For all his outward . . .": Edward G. Robinson, *All My Yesterdays: An Autobiography,* with Leonard Spigelgass (New York: Hawthorn Books, 1973), p. 181.
406. "I don't think . . .": Buck, interview.
406. "Bogie was a man . . .": Lauren Bacall, telephone interview with EL, 11/5/96.
406. "the illusions of life . . .": Richard Brooks, interview, 9/26/88.

CHAPTER 20: THE BORIS KARLOFF OF THE SUPPER CLUBS

407. Account of lunch at Lakeside: Lillian Ross, "Onward and Upward with the Arts," *New Yorker,* 2/21/48.
409. "driving taxis . . .": *Key Largo,* dialogue script, USC WB.
409. "He doesn't need . . .": Richard Brooks, interview, 9/26/88.
409. "wanted that part": Claire Trevor, interview, 6/6/92.
409. Trevor took less: Phil Friedman to Obringer, "Deal contract for Claire Trevor—*Key Largo,*" memo, 12/15/47, *Key Largo* production file, USC WB. Also M. C. Levee, manager for Miss Claire Trevor, to Steve Trilling, letter, 12/26/47, *Key Largo* production file, USC WB.
409. Bren browbeat Bogart: Trevor, interview.
409. "He was in . . . let's go home!": Brooks, interview.
411. "They had freedom . . .": Rudi Fehr, interview, 2/14/90.
411. "an extremely . . .": Harry Lewis, interview, 1/28/90.
411. "wanted to hear . . .": Ibid.
411. "Mr. Barrymore gained . . .": *Key Largo* press file, Production Notes on *Key Largo,* USC WB.
412. "Why not second . . .": Robinson, *All My Yesterdays,* p. 254.
412. Bogart's courtesy to Robinson: Ibid.
412. Bogart and Robinson's acting a lesson: Lewis, interview.
412. "he just said . . . between the two": Fehr, interview.
412. "my Americanism is unblemished . . .": Robinson, *All My Yesterdays,* p. 263.

412. "They were delighted . . .": Fehr, interview.
413. Trevor said she was embarrassed, etc.: Grobel, *The Hustons*, p. 312.
414. "She's going to get . . .": Lewis, interview.
414. "parts of the stories . . .": Brooks, interview. Brooks also wrote in a statement for a legal dispute: ". . . as a substitute for the two molls in the [Maxwell Anderson] play we developed a single character, Gaye. Huston and I discussed at some length a number of women who had been mistresses of ganglords and notorious public figures. We agreed that, in most cases, time and fashion had passed these women by. Most of them, unable to maintain an aura of glamour and success, had taken to whiskey or drugs as a substitute for their former beauty and talent. Rocco's mistress was supposed to represent happier days of long ago—now faded. She also was to be the foil for Rocco's sadism. Gaye Dawn (in film) was a natural consequence based on real life and from out of our combined experience." Behlmer, *Inside Warner Bros.*, p. 295.
414. "One thing I can't . . .": *Key Largo,* dialogue script, USC WB.
414. "Some little wildcat . . .": Ibid.
414. "The audience is always . . .": Grobel, *The Hustons,* p. 313.
414. "written all the vile . . .": Brooks, interview.
414. "one of her happiest movie experiences . . .": Bacall, *By Myself,* p. 220.
414. "was hypnotic . . .": Grobel, *The Hustons,* p. 313.
415. Trevor felt somewhat sorry for Bacall: Ibid., p. 313.
415. "Claire and I are as. . . .": Carl Combs, *Key Largo* press file, USC WB.
415. "Now I want to . . .": Lewis, interview.
415. "had a particular fondness . . ." : Ibid.
415. "a bang-up thriller . . .": Otis Guernsey Jr., N.Y. *Herald Tribune,* 7/17/48.
416. Worst confrontation and Bacall's intuition: Hyams, *Bogie,* pp. 97–98; Bacall, *By Myself,* pp. 166–167.
416. "He didn't know . . .": Bacall, *By Myself,* p. 167.
416. "She is a fool . . .": Curtiz to Trilling, letter, 4/25/47, USC WB.
416. "This company is not . . .": Memorandum of telephone conversation between JLW and Lauren Bacall, 4/15/48—4:00 P.M., p. 1 USC WB.
417. Bacall and agents discussed two big parts with the studio: Mrs. Betty Bogart, p.k.a. (professionally known as) Lauren Bacall, to Warner Bros. Pictures, Inc., 6/18/48, USC WB.
417. "I congratulate you, Jack . . .": Betty Bogart to JLW, letter, 7/27/48, USC WB.
417. Quarrel escalated by gossip columnists: Roy Obringer to Ralph Lewis, memo, 4/29/48, USC WB.
417. Account of call from Hopper and "No!": Bacall, *By Myself,* p. 222.
417. "Lauren Bacall Bogart . . .": *L.A. Times,* 7/1/48.

418. "Bogart claimed he bet the producer . . .": Obringer to Milton Sperling, memo, 8/25/48, USC WB.
418. Stern letter to *Life*: JLW to Roy Obringer, memo, 10/5/48, and R. J. Obringer to *Life* magazine, 10/5/48, USC WB.
418. "the baby is the most . . .": L.A. *Herald-Express,* 8/24/48; Obringer to Milton Sperling, memo, 8/25/48, USC WB.
418. "These glasses are handy . . .": Glendale *News Press,* 6/7/48; Evelove to Warner, summary of Bogart-Bacall comments, 10/12/48, USC WB.
418. "Bogey's reply . . .": *Hollywood Citizen News,* 8/23/48; Evelove to Warner, 10/12/48.
419. "I don't know what . . .": Arthur Silver, interview, 11/19/87.
419. "My father. . . . stubborn men": Jack Warner Jr., interview, 11/12/90.
420. Special shareholders' meeting of Mark Hellinger Productions: The small group, all of them officers, were all present: Hellinger's widow Gladys Glad, Morgan Maree, Bogart, and Bogart's lawyer Martin Gang.
420. "the road company version . . .": Richard Dorso, interview, 12/6/90.
421. "I gloried in it": Bacall, *By Myself,* p. 168.
421. "He talked as though . . .": "Matt" to JLW, 10/11/48, USC WB.
421. Account of waking up with contractions and Graham's phone call: Bacall, *By Myself,* p. 169.
422. "I thought he'd go mad . . . made that call": Ibid.
422. "He wore a green . . .": Ibid.
422. "You goddamn ghoul . . .": Hyams, *Bogie,* p. 99.
422. "Hello, Baby": Bacall, *By Myself,* p. 170.
422. "a very nice name . . . Steve": Bernard Eisenschitz, *Humphrey Bogart* (Paris: Le Terrain Vague, 1967), p. 106.
422. Their son to be called Steve after *To Have and Have Not*: Bacall, *By Myself,* p. 169.
422. Bogart's bet with Harry Truman and letter: Ibid., pp. 171–172.
423. Gifts for Stephen: Avery Carroll, magazine unknown, ca. 1949, CMC USC.
423. "Will she be *kind?*": Amanda Dunne, interview, 8/7/87.
424. "Bogart is so wearing . . .": Pauline Kael, *5001 Nights at the Movies,* (New York: Henry Holt, 1982), p. 310.
424. Bogart participated in all phases of production: Eisenschitz, *Humphrey Bogart,* pp. 89–90.
424. "Evil has a stench . . .": *Detective Story,* script by Philip Jordan and Robert Wyler, WWC UCLA Theatre Collection.
424. Bogart told Kingsley that he wanted to buy *Detective Story*: Sidney Kingsley, interview, 12/27/89.
424. "He'd have been . . .": Ibid.
424. "bid an enormous . . .": Ibid.

425. "I don't think they had . . .": Ibid.
425. "I don't think it would . . .": JLW to Steve Trilling, cc: R. Obringer, memo, 12/18/48, Bogart legal file, USC WB.
425. Warners wanted at least a one-third investment, etc.: R. J. Obringer to JLW, memo, 12/13/48 and Obringer to JLW, memo, 12/22/48, Bogart legal file, USC WB.
426. "My father didn't socialize . . .": Jack Warner Jr., interview.
426. "just somebody you put . . .": Ibid.
426. "Later on, after all . . .": Ibid.
426. "Bogie, I hear . . .": Ibid.
427. "confused, mentally sick wife . . .": *NYT,* 2/10/50.
427. "Absolutely not, Steve Trilling wired . . .": Steve Trilling to Mrs. Betty Bogart p.k.a. Lauren Bacall, 9/30/49, USC WB.
427. "WITHOUT MENTIONING WIRE . . .": Blumenstock to Obringer, telegram, 10/4/49.
428. "She had some sense": N.Y. *Post,* 9/29/49.
428. The twenty-two-pound pandas were bought at Reuben's: *Time,* 10/10/49, CMC USC.
428. "a big manufacturing . . .": *Time,* 10/10/49.
428. "No blows were exchanged . . .": UP, L.A. *Daily News,* 9/28/49.
428. "BOGART ROUGHS UP . . .": Ibid.
428. "as photographers . . .": *Time,* 10/10/49.
428. Red suspenders acquired at Stork club and "Get away from me . . .": Bacall, *By Myself,* p. 176.
429. "this screaming, squawking . . .": N.Y. *World-Telegram,* 9/28/49.
429. "Me hit a woman? . . .": Earl Wilson, N.Y. *Post,* 9/29/49.
429. "Don't worry. . . . let it be Warner Brothers": Silver, interview.
430. "was very upset . . .": Charles Carson, interview, 5/16/87.
430. "a wan smile": N.Y. *Post,* 10/1/49.
430. Bogart's second offense: Earl Wilson, N.Y. *Post,* 9/28/49.
431. "bum's rush": United Press, L.A. *Herald-Express,* 11/11/49. "21," one of Bogart's favorite restaurants, did not join in the foolishness, and he and Bacall had lunch there following the dismissal of the court case.
431. "I am confident . . .": Ibid.
431. "Who isn't at 3 o'clock . . .": Earl Wilson, N.Y. *Daily News,* 9/28/49.
431. "So we get a little . . .": Virginia MacPherson, L.A. *Herald Evening Express,* 11/10/49.
431. "With a little . . . the right places": Inez Robb, N.Y. *Journal-American,* 10/20/49.
431. "At heart . . .": L.A. *Examiner,* 10/1/49, CMC USC.
431. "fun town. . . . their latest movie": L.A. *Herald Evening Express,* 10/10/49.
432. "Fireworks . . . break his contract": L.A. *Daily News,* 10/5/50.

CHAPTER 21: ALL THE ASPECTS OF A LOSER

433. "*Ext. Romanoff's . . .*" : *In a Lonely Place* (script), Edmund North Collection, Theater Collection, UCLA.
433. "*She's about twenty-six . . .*": Ibid.
434. Ray's deteriorating marriage ended with completion of *In a Lonely Place*: Vincent Curcio, *Suicide Blonde* (New York: William Morrow & Co., 1989), pp. 84–85.
435. "Mr. Bogart Moves . . .": *NYT*, 5/18/50.
435. "WASPish name implies . . .": Schickel, *Schickel on Film*, p. 237
435. "a small, round man . . .": Curcio, *Suicide Blonde*, pp. 84–85.
435. "would much rather . . .": John McClain, N.Y. *Journal American* 1/18/57.
435. Bogart didn't like *In a Lonely Place*: Hyams, *Bogie*, p. 128.
436. Fox wanted Bacall for *Yellow Sky*: Mrs. Betty Bogart (Lauren Bacall) to Warner Bros. Pictures, Inc., letter, 6/18/48, USC WB.
436. Bacall due in Burbank Feb. 9: Roy Obringer to Sam Norton, Famous Artists Corp., letter, 2/6/50, USC WB
436. Blumenstock told no calls could be put through Bacall: Blumenstock to JLW, telegram, 2/3/50, USC WB.
436. "adamant": Blumenstock to JLW, memo, 2/3/50, USC WB.
436. Trilling begged they return by February 15: Trilling to Bacall, telegram, 2/4/50, USC WB.
436. Problems with Bacall's interview schedule: Blumenstock to JLW, telegrams, 1/30/50 and 2/1/50, USC WB.
436. "She is trying . . .": Blumenstock to JLW (confidential), telegram, 2/3/50, USC WB.
437. "essentially nothing more . . .": letter, Betty Bogart (p.k.a. Lauren Bacall) to Warner Bros. Pictures, Inc., 5/12/50, Bacall legal file, USC WB.
437. Details of Bacall's contract cancellation agreement: JLW to Roy Obringer, 7/10/50 and "*Cancellation of Contract and Mutual Release*," 7/12/50, Bacall legal file, USC WB.
437. Bacall's final payment of $3,250: notation of check received, 5/24/54, Bacall legal file, USC WB.
437. *Bold Venture*'s appeal to male and female beer drinkers: Gene Shefrin, David O. Alber Associates, Inc. to Jean Sulzberger, *Time*, 3/21/51.
438. MacEwen's assistant audited *Bold Venture*: Walter MacEwen to Roy Obringer, memo, 4/30/51, USC WB.
438. Estimate that Bogarts would average $5,438 week: Walter Ames, *L.A. Times*, 1/11/51.
438. "A good literary work . . .": Virginia Denman to William Fadiman, 8/26/47, RKO Collection, Theater Collection, UCLA.

439. Warner Bros. bought *The African Queen*: Agreement between Cecil Scott Forester and Warner Bros. Pictures, Inc., 4/19/46, USC WB.

439. "Not even if Bette . . .": RKO Pictures, Inc., WJF, V.R.D., 7/29/47, RKO Collection, UCLA.

439. "It is dated . . .": Lee Phillips: reader's report, 7/28/47, and Virginia Denman to William Fadiman, 8/26/47, RKO Collection, UCLA.

439. *The African Queen* and its various options: Screenwriter John Collier optioned it from Warners; in June 1950 he transferred his option to Horizon Pictures. Horizon bought the rights from Warner Bros. 8/9/50, along with the temporary screenplay written by Collier for Warners in 1947. USC WB.

439. "He could be . . .": Katharine Hepburn, *The Making of "The African Queen"* (New York: Alfred A. Knopf, 1987), p. 7.

439. "The hero is a lowlife . . .": Hyams, *Bogie*, p. 128.

439. "He wanted very much . . .": John Huston, interview, 5/20/87.

439. "He was the only man . . .": Katharine Hepburn, interview, 3/20/89.

439. "Just a nice . . .": Ibid.

439. "only about $400,000 . . . America": Howard Thompson, *NYT*, 3/2/52.

439. Bogart and Hepburn's payment for doing *The African Queen:* Grobel, *The Hustons*, p. 366.

439. Bacall's doctor said she should continue with Bogart and her mother's volunteering to go to Los Angeles: Bacall, *By Myself*, p. 179.

439. "I hate like the devil . . .": Marie Torre, N.Y. *World-Telegram*,. 3/17/51.

440. "I was longing . . .": Bacall, *By Myself*, p. 179.

440. "We've got a comfortable . . .": Torre, N.Y. *World-Telegram*.

441. "Drawing a big crowd . . .": *Time*, 4/21/51.

441. "Hepburn, concerned. . . . don't fuss." Hepburn, interview.

441. "I didn't mind . . .": Hyams, *Bogie*, p. 130.

441. "But he was . . .": Ibid.

441. "The first time in my life . . .": Leonard Lyons, N.Y. *Post*, 8/2/51.

441. "The train kept . . . you ever saw": N.Y. *World-Telegram*, 9/18/51.

442. Ruiki's black water from tannic acid: Edwin Schallert, probably *L.A. Times*, n.d., 1952, CMC USC.

442. "Well, I've found it . . .": Benchley, *Humphrey Bogart*, p. 190.

442. "John wanted to shoot . . .": Grobel, *The Hustons*, p. 367.

443. "could not hit his hat": Bacall, *By Myself*, p. 184.

443. Camp built by eighty-five people in eight days: Ibid., p. 184.

443. Hepburn gave Bogart her suit: Hepburn, interview.

443. "The food was so awful . . .": N.Y. *World-Telegram*, 9/18/51.

443. "With his almost aggressive . . .": Huston interview, by Stanley Karnow, received 5/1/54, *Time* morgue.

443. "couldn't have happened . . .": Huston, interview, 5/20/87.

444. "He knew he wasn't . . .": Ibid.
444. "He never did an awful . . .": Hepburn, interview.
444. "We were a little . . .": *NYT*, 3/2/52.
444. "so with each pull . . .": Art Buchwald, *Herald Tribune,* European Edition, 8/6/51.
444. "I was practically . . .": Ibid.
444. "Those two undisciplined . . .": Hepburn, *The Making of "The African Queen,"* p. 118.
444. "Damn Hepburn! . . .": Hyams, *Bogie,* p. 130.
445. "An odd fellow. . . . in case of trouble": Ibid., p. 30.
445. "He'd say to me. . . . out for me": Ibid., p. 8.
445. "She and Bogie . . .": Ibid., p. 34.
445. "Bogart acted like a trained . . . putting out the fire": Joe Hyams, interview. Also in Benchley, *Humphrey Bogart,* p. 194.
445. Huston said Bogart would raise hell over eggs not done right but face a crisis calmly: Huston, interview, *Time* morgue.
445. "I had visions . . .": Hepburn, *The Making of "The African Queen,"* p. 30.
445. Details of Mayo Methot's death: UP, 6/9/51.
446. "Too bad. . . . from his mind": Bacall, *By Myself,* p. 190.
446. "You son of a bitch . . .": Huston, interview, *Time* morgue.
446. "real genius. . . . new idea": *NYT*, 3/2/52.
446. "they got him . . .": Hepburn, interview.
447. "You try it . . .": Hepburn, *The Making of "The African Queen,"* p. 125.
447. "He was funny . . .": Ibid., p. 125.
447. "vigilantes of crackpot . . .": Caute, *The Great Fear,* p. 501.
448. "a punitive expedition . . .": Goodman, *The Committee,* p. 309.
448. "founded on Reds" and "the rat who . . .": Myron C. Fagan, *Red Stars in Hollywood: Their Helpers . . . Fellow Travelers . . . and Co-Conspirators* (St. Louis: Patriotic Tract Society, 1948), text of speech delivered 4/12/48.
448. "It was terrible . . .": Jules Buck, interview, 9/11/88.
449. Zanuck's concern over using "censorship": Darryl F. Zanuck to Sol Siegel, memo, 2/2/51, and DZ to Siegel, Brooks, Mandaville, 9/19/51.
449. "Has anybody. . . . washed up here [in Hollywood]": Richard Brooks, interview, 9/26/88.
449. "named everyone he had seen . . .": Friedrich, *City of Nets,* p. 366.
449. "gone to John Wexley's. . . . someone came calling": Ibid.
450. "was a real. . . . been part of it": Ibid.
450. "There was an impatience . . .": Ibid.
450. "why do I have to move. . . . I'm sorry": Brooks, interview.
451. Kay Thackeray's account of difficulties: Kay Thackeray, interview, 9/22/88.

453. "Do you want me . . . asked for anything, you know": Ibid.
453. "It was *totally* . . .": Brooks, interview.

CHAPTER 22: THE TOY DEPARTMENT

454. "Oh, I guess . . .": John Huston to Katharine Hepburn, 1/8/52, JH, AMPAS.
454. "this guy Brando . . .": *NYT*, 3/2/52.
455. Bogart polite but sensitive: John Strauss, interview, 2/6/91.
455. "He said, 'I'll . . .' ": Ibid.
455. "a great movie . . .": Ibid.
455. "very circumspect. . . . field day": Ibid.
455. "Oscar Spells D-o-u-g-h . . .": Erskine Johnson, "*In Hollywood*," 3/4/52.
456. "A Republican candidate . . .": *The Letters of Nunnally Johnson,* selected and edited by Dorris Johnson and Ellen Laventhal (New York: Alfred A. Knopf, 1981), p. 75.
456. Account of ride in limo and Bogart's reaction: Richard Brooks, interview, 9/26/88.
457. Clift picked up Bacall's dropped half-slip: *Time* morgue, 3/21/52.
457. "What did you. . . . goddamn *Oscar*." Judith Michaelson, *Los Angeles Times Calendar*, 1/20/91.
457. "one of a handful . . .": *Time* morgue, 3/21/52.
458. "I seem to recall . . .": S. Bogart and Provost, *In Search of My Father*, p. 270. He adds that the award is now on a shelf in his home.
458. "We had teased. . . . ugly and awful," George Roosevelt, interview, 4/13/91.
458. "an elderly man. . . .": Ibid.
459. "Love and kisses . . .": Ibid.
459. "I think 'humble' . . ." and account of sailing trips: Ibid.
459. "the number of trophies . . .": Ibid.
459. Bacall preferred Hollywood gatherings and "Bogie would call . . . sitting on it": Ibid.
459. "really *understood* . . .": Ibid.
460. Warners not obligated to submit a script until May 1952: Obringer to JLW, memo, 9/24/51, USC WB.
460. Warners sent no scripts for Bogart: Obringer to JLW, memo, 1/4/52, USC WB.
460. "He still resents . . .": Hedda Hopper, *L.A. Times*, 5/19/92.
460. "We are at a total loss . . .": R. J. Obringer, Assistant Secretary, for Warner Bros. Pictures, Inc., to Humphrey Bogart, letter, 7/7/52, Bogart legal file, USC WB. Also R. J. Obringer to H. M. Warner, memo,

7/7/52, apologizing for not understanding Warner wanted a letter sent immediately after Bogart's quote appeared on 5/19/52, USC WB.

461. "The contract is simply . . .": Ralph E. Lewis to Roy J. Obringer, letter, 6/11/52, Bogart legal file, USC WB.
461. "Mr. Campbell, as soon . . .": William Campbell, interview, 11/30/87.
462. "Who is it?. . . . warm friendship with Bogart": Ibid.
462. Bogart talked about Garfield: Ibid.
462. Garfield's death at thirty-nine: "Those close to him said it was the blacklisting that really killed him." Katz, *The Film Encyclopedia*, p. 507.
462. "He *loved* Garfield. . . . aware of it": Campbell, interview.
463. "bigger than the director . . .": Ibid.
463. "Spencer Tracy, who. . . . call the agent tomorrow": Ibid.
464. *Time* report that baby was a boy: memo, 8/23/52, *Time* morgue, 1952 folder.
464. "The place is so elegant . . .": Hedda Hopper, *L.A. Times,* 5/19/52.
464. "Bogie felt he . . .": David Niven, *Bring on the Empty Horses* (New York: Putnam, 1975), p. 239.
465. "Harvey was like . . .": Stephen Bogart, interview, 9/23/87.
465. "The son of a bitch . . .": S. Bogart and Provost, *In Search of My Father,* p. 247.
465. "a lot of his . . .": Joyce Gates Buck, interview, 9/26/88.
465. "He saw this thing. . . . never going to get it": Brooks, interview.
467. "comforting evidence . . .": *Time,* 9/22/52.
467. "Bogie hasn't switched . . .": Ibid.
467. "very well known producer": Bacall, *By Myself,* p. 199.
467. "Stevenson is making . . . shitty world": Bogart to Huston, letter, 10/8/52, JH, AMPAS.
468. Bogart's suggested cartoon about Stevenson: Bacall, *By Myself,* pp. 200–201.
469. "disaster ahead": Ibid., p. 202.
469. "Betty and I campaigned . . .": Bogart to Huston, letter, 11/26/52, JH, AMPAS.

CHAPTER 23: BEATING THE DEVIL

470. "Everyone in the story . . .": Motion Picture Association of America, Inc., to Jess Morgan, Santana Productions, 2/13/53.
470. "a man with . . .": Ibid.
470. "I think [he] is the best . . .": Louella O. Parsons, "In Hollywood," N.Y. *Journal-American,* 3/23/52.
471. "a very excellent . . .": Morgan Maree to James Woolf, Romulus Films, letter, 1/29/52.

471. "as you know . . .": Morgan Maree to John Huston, telegram, 1/29/52.
471. "The picture would be more fortunate": John Huston to David O. Selznick, letter, 2/8/52, DOSC UT; also see Grobel, *The Hustons,* p. 383.
471. "As you know . . .": Maree to Huston, telegram, 4/4/52.
471. Huston was paid $175,000 to write, direct, and co-produce: Grobel, *The Hustons,* p. 401.
471. Kohner persuaded Lorre to settle for less: Paul Kohner to John Huston, letter, 11/6/52, Paul Kohner private papers.
472. Bogart's suggestion to change the title to *The Lady Lies*: memo, Santana Productions, 10/8/52.
472. "I talked to Bogie . . .": Maree to Huston, letter, 4/8/52.
472. "I don't think . . .": Huston to Maree, letter, 4/15/52.
472. "Dear Fly in the . . .": Bogart to Huston, letter, 10/8/52; Grobel, *The Hustons,* p. 396.
472. "two lively candidates . . .": Huston to Maree, letter, 8/17/52.
472. Billing above the title in Europe and "Lola Frigidaire": Grobel, *The Hustons,* p. 402.
472. Had to begin shooting in early January to be done by start of Warner contract year: Maree to Huston, letter, 10/9/52.
473. "Got a long letter . . .": Bogart to Huston, letter, 10/8/52, JH, AMPAS.
473. "With an eye . . .": Bogart to Huston, 10/8/52; Grobel, *The Hustons,* p. 396.
473. "That is a question . . .": Huston to Bogart, letter, 11/19/52; Grobel, *The Hustons,* pp. 396–397.
473. "a brand new Bogart . . .": Ibid.
473. "I've [given your suggestions] a great . . .": Bogart to Huston, letter, 11/26/52; Grobel, *The Hustons,* p. 397.
473. "and has not yet had . . .": Ibid.
474. "I don't think . . .": Maree to Huston, letter, 11/2/52.
474. "unacceptable under the provisions . . .": MPAA to Jess Morgan, 2/13/53.
474. "It's only money": Grobel, *The Hustons,* p. 401.
474. Capote signed for $1,500 a week: Ibid., p. 402.
474. He "turned out . . .": Humphrey Bogart as told to Joe Hyams, "Movie Making Beats the Devil," *Cue,* 8/16/54.
474. Capote won at arm wrestling: Grobel, *The Hustons,* p. 407.
474. "Our Italian driver . . .": Humphrey Bogart, "Around the World in 80 Reels," N.Y. *Herald Tribune,* 3/24/54.
475. "started to laugh. . . . with the picture": Bogart and Hyams, "Movie Making Beats the Devil."
475. "Bogie had guts . . .": Hyams, *Bogie,* p. 134.
475. Bogart mixed martinis in a white jacket: Grobel, *The Hustons,* p. 403.
475. "He was taking . . .": Julie Gibson, interview, 2/21/90.

475. "He looked very tired. . . . his eyes lighted up": Ibid.
476. "We all had a couple. . . . toads and snakes": Ibid.
476. "Huston was perhaps . . . including Bogie": Ibid.
476. "boy-like subservience": James Agee interview, 4/27/54, *Time* morgue.
476. "What would you think. . . . get *laid*": Gibson, interview.
477. "I'd look. . . . stuff like that": Ibid.
478. "Do ours first . . .": JLW to Obringer, memo, 12/10/52, USC WB.
478. Jaffe's offer "ridiculous . . . one way or the other": Obringer to Warner-Trilling, memo, 12/12/52, USC WB.
478. "by May 4, 1953 . . .": Obringer to JLW, memo, 4/14/53, USC WB.
479. "cavalier attitude . . .": Bill Mauldin, interview, 4/6/90.
479. "I need a witness . . .": Art Buchwald, "We Lost the War," N.Y. *Herald Tribune*, 6/7/53.
479. "I liked Captain Queeg . . .": *American Weekly*, 6/27/54.
479. "I needed somebody . . .": Stanley Kramer, interview, ca. 1990.
480. Bogart rolled the steel balls: Ibid.
480. The maximum salary was $200,480 and "not going to pay . . .": Philip Gersh, interview, 8/1/87.
480. "Stanley called me . . .": *American Weekly*, 6/27/54.
480. "Damn it, Harry . . .": Bacall, *By Myself*, p. 211.
480. "the admiral in charge . . .": Kramer, interview.
481. "One Sunday morning . . . purposely": Irving Moore, interview, 1/11/91.
481. Van Johnson "would horse . . .": Ibid.
481. "We were the test rats . . .": Edward Dmytryk, interview, 4/4/91.
481. "But 1947 . . . The hard way": Ibid.
481. "a very introverted . . . discussing anything": Ibid.
482. "not in the Shakespearian . . . freshness": Ibid.
482. "Bogart was riveting . . .": Claude Akins, interview, 4/4/89.
482. "a loony": Walter Shenson, interview, 2/12/90.
482. "The mannerism upset . . . good table manners": Ibid.
483. "Was the commander saying that Annapolis turned out out better gentlemen than Andover?": *Time*, 6/7/54, p. 68.
483. "I don't know . . .": Kramer, interview.
483. "he had an aura . . .": Moore, interview.
483. "Bogart would have hated . . .": Kramer, interview.
484. "I think Queeg loses face . . .": Huston to Bogart, letter, 6/10/53, JH, AMPAS.
484. "I played Queeg . . .": *American Weekly*, 6/27/54.
484. "Queeg was not a sadist. . . . every studio": Ibid.
484. "The actors . . . 'buy a painting?' ": Akins, interviews.
484. "Bogart's performance electrified the crew . . .": Kramer, interview.
485. "Easy. I'm nuts . . .": *American Weekly*, 6/27/54.

485. "I could have killed . . .": Hyams, *Bogie,* pp. 154–155.
485. "Their reception . . .": Kramer, interview.
485. "that the Navy . . .": Ibid.
485. "handsome and expert . . .": *Time,* 6/28/54.
485. "He brings the hollow. . . . bottling up a scream": *Time,* 6/7/54.
485. "The massive closeup . . .": *Time,* 6/28/54.
485. "It is more difficult..": Huston to Maree, letter, 6/10/53, JH, AMPAS.
486. Huston quoted in overseas paper: *Empire News,* 9/6/53.
486. John Woolf wrote an anxious letter: Woolf to Huston, 9/7/53, JH, AMPAS.
486. "It should have been called . . .": Special Collections, AMPAS Library; also Grobel, *The Hustons,* p. 415.
486. "a hodgepodge of nothing" and refunds: Ben Joel Jr. to Milton E. Cohen, United Artists, n.d., Special Collections, AMPAS Library.
486. "should go down . . .": Ben Joel Jr. to Milton E. Cohen, United Arists, Report from Theater Manager, n.d., Special Collections, AMPAS Library.
486. "a hugely entertaining . . .": *New Yorker,* 3/20/54
486. "as elaborate a shaggy-dog . . .": *Time,* 3/8/54.
487. "the parasite of the film business . . .": Hyams, *Bogie,* p. 136.
487. "the blast I let you . . .": Ibid.
487. Charles Champlin on *Beat the Devil* and Jennifer Jones story: Charles Champlin, DGA Memorial, 9/12/87; also Grobel, *The Hustons,* p. 415.
488. Bogart asked Columbia to make prints: Shenson, interview.
488. two fingers pulling at corner of mouth: Ibid.
488. "I'll mail these on . . .": Ibid.
488. Summary of Bogart's contract and pictures: 7/29/53, USC WB.
489. "BOGART, WARNERS. . . .": *NYT,* 9/22/53.
489. "Mr. Bogart . . .": *NYT,* 7/29/53.

CHAPTER 24: THE OLD BULL

491. Cary Grant unavailable: Maurice Zolotow, *Billy Wilder in Hollywood* (New York: Putnam, 1977), p. 198.
491. "Listen, Phil . . .": Philip Gersh, interview, 8/1/87.
491. Wilder's reconsideration of Bogart and account of the meeting: Ibid.
491. "Billy was shooting . . .": Ibid.
492. Bogart resented Hepburn: Zolotow, *Billy Wilder in Hollywood,* pp. 251–252.
492. "She's all right..": Ibid.
492. "conspired with him . . .": Kevin Lally, *Wilder Times* (New York: Henry Holt, 1996), pp. 236–7.

492. "It's that fucking Holden . . .": Benchley, *Humphrey Bogart,* notes, interview with William Holden, NB BU.
492. "He gave me a rough . . .": Ezra Goodman, interview, 4/29/54, *Time* morgue.
493. Chandler's refusal to work with Wilder: Frank MacShane, *The Life of Raymond Chandler* (New York: Penguin Books, 1978), pp. 108–109.
493. "quality of desperation" and stalling because scene not ready: Zolotow, *Billy Wilder in Hollywood,* p. 183.
493. "some unconscious need . . .": Ibid.
493. Wilder's back pains and "Dr. Feelgood": Ibid., p. 106.
493. "I'm in the major leagues" and "a special breed . . .": Goodman, interview.
493. "the Directors Guild should . . .": David Freeman, "Sunset Boulevard Revisited," *New Yorker,* 6/21/93, p. 78.
494. "I examine your face . . .": Zolotow, *Billy Wilder in Hollywood,* p. 253.
494. "I'm gonna get fucked . . .": Ibid., pp. 254–255.
494. "screech: 'Fuck you!' ": Ibid., p. 187.
494. "He is an extremely . . .": Goodman, interview.
494. "the most delightful . . . joys of this show": *NYT,* 9/23/54.
495. "We parted as enemies . . .": Goodman, interview.
495. Photo of Bogart with Audrey Wilder over his shoulders: Benchley, *Humphrey Bogart,* p. 206.
496. "Bogart *slapped* my behind . . .": Dee Hawks Cramer, interview, 8/13/88.
496. Bacall's psyche looked like a dope addict's arm: Hyams, *Bogie,* p. 102.
496. "why they didn't . . .": Cramer, interview.
496. "In spite of being . . .": *Time,* 6/7/54.
497. "who could easily . . .": John Horne, " 'Person to Person' Brings the 1950's Back to Life," *NYT,* 7/2/78.
497. "The 'bad boy'. . . . in my career": Louella O. Parsons, Motion Picture Editor, International News Service, "Strange Things Are Happening to Hollywood's 'Bad Boy.' " 12/27/53.
497. "He was probably . . .": Stephen Bogart, interview, 9/28/87.
497. "I was maybe six or seven . . .": Ibid.
498. "I guess maybe . . .": Hyams, *Bogie,* p. 101.
498. "We used to go swimming . . .": S. Bogart, interview.
498. Bogart's routine at Romanoff's: Gersh, interview.
499. "occupational neurosis. . . . not be steady": Goodman, interview.
499. "Bogie is in constant . . .": Ibid.
499. One-inch enameled bow tie: George Roosevelt, interview, 4/13/91; and Benchley, *Humphrey Bogart,* p. 205.
499. Bogart helped Hatch through a lean time: Ibid., p. 174.

500. Thompson alleged a bottle in his trailer: Thompson and Shepherd, *Bogie and Me,* p. 131.
500. Bogart unsteady and dropping pages: Richard Nash, interview, probably 1990.
500. Bogart in Harry Cohn's office: William Graf, interview, 10/24/90.
500. "Betty and the kids. . . . seven hundred and fifty thousand dollars": Hyams, *Bogie,* p. 148.
500. Considered closing Santana as early as October 1949: *NYT,* 10/28/49.
501. "If I can't buy . . .": Hyams, *Bogie,* p. 144.
501. "Bogie called Tracy . . .": Gersh, interview.
501. Gersh having to come to the set and Wyler's having Bogart run up stairs: Ibid.
502. "Maybe it was because . . .": *Time,* 12/19/55.
502. "After two decades . . .": Sheilah Graham, "Hollywood," 11/4/55.
503. "He was, I think . . ." and account of Bogart's treatment of Tierney: Dmytryk, interview, 4/4/91.
503. "He made the stand . . .": Joan Bennett and Louis Kibbee, *The Bennett Playbill* (New York: Holt, Reinhart and Winston, 1970), p. 306.
504. Rat Pack members and "surveyed the wreckage . . . rat pack": Benchley, *Humphrey Bogart,* p. 216.
504. "With that, the group . . .": Ibid.
504. "to drink a lot of bourbon . . .": Earl Wilson, "It Happened Last Night," N.Y. *Post,* 10/5/55.
504. "Sperling claims he talked . . .": Jack Warner to Steve Trilling, memo, 4/4/55, USC WB.
505. "I look awful . . .": N.Y. *Herald Tribune,* 11/6/55.
505. "Duke Mantee should be seen . . .": *NYT,* 5/31/55.
505. "Suppose I had . . .": N.Y. *Herald Tribune,* 11/6/55.
505. "Bogie was there moaning . . .": Helen Hayes, interview, 7/30/90.
506. "scratch-your-ass . . .": Hyams, *Bogie,* p. 145.
506. "could be measured . . .": Alistair Cooke, "Epitaph for a Tough Guy," *Atlantic Monthly,* May 1957.
507. "wary. . . . big kick out of that": Rod Steiger, interview, 1/30/90.
507. "Let's go down . . .": Richard Erdman, interview, 2/16/90.
507. "Bogart came from. . . . We'll get 'em all": Steiger, interview.

CHAPTER 25: SUNSET AND EVENING STAR

509. "I can make the picture . . .": Milton Sperling, interview, 8/13/87.
509. "She remarked. . . . *made an appointment!*": Amanda Dunne, interview, 8/7/87.
510. "Not unless you want . . .": Bacall, *By Myself,* p. 228.

510. "they can all go . . .": Ibid.
510. "went home dazed . . .": Ibid., pp. 228–229.
510. "DEAR BOGIE . . .": JLW to Humphrey Bogart, telegram, 3/6/56, USC WB.
510. "Betty, I think . . .": Sperling, interview.
511. "Harry kept that picture . . .": Eddie Saeta, interview, 11/6/90.
511. "The chemo was a bitch . . .": Joe Hyams, interview, 4/10/91.
511. "He came back . . .": Kurt Niklas, interview, 4/8/91.
511. Chess games with Romanoff by phone: Niklas, interview.
511. Details of Sinatra show and birthday cake: Bacall, *By Myself,* pp. 240–241.
512. "edgy and resentful . . .": Ibid., p. 241.
512. "crazy about Frank . . . was his home": Ibid.
512. "a nice, happy . . .": S. Bogart, interview, 9/28/87.
512. "What are the ghouls . . . the press": Bacall, *By Myself,* p. 253.
512. "I have read . . .": Ibid., pp. 242–243.
513. "doing fine and much stronger": U.P., N.Y. *Herald Tribune,* 12/7/56.
513. "Bogie turned the tables . . .": Bacall, *By Myself,* p. 248.
513. "People came in . . .": Ibid.
514. "He would lie . . .": John Huston, *An Open Book,* pp. 249–250.
514. "Betty organized it . . .": Hyams, interview.
514. "hard to keep. . . . absence of complaint": Alistair Cooke, "Epitaph for a Tough Guy."
514. "shamed into it": Bacall, *By Myself,* p. 248.
515. "seemed like an hour . . .": Richard Brooks, interview, 9/26/88.
515. "he must have known . . .": Natalie Schafer, interview, 3/18/90.
515. "If I could just . . .": S. Bogart and Provost, *In Search of My Father,* p. 289.
515. "Don't have them in . . .": Bacall, *By Myself,* p. 250.
515. Huston's call from Bacall asking him to write the eulogy: Huston, *An Open Book,* p. 249.
515. "I . . . I couldn't believe . . .": Huston, interview.
516. Huston visibly upset: Irene Heymann, interview, 10/26/90.
516. "Bogie was sitting. . . . I certainly did": Katharine Hepburn, interview, 3/20/89.
516. "with its awful smell . . .": S. Bogart and Provost, *In Search of My Father,* p. 298.
516. Bogart's death at 2:25 A.M.: Death Certificate, State of California, Department of Public Health.
517. "Bogart dead . . .": Walter Wanger, appointment book, 1957, Walter Wanger Collection, WSHS.
517. Mass of reporters: Charles Wick, interview, 2/1/90.
517. Sinatra canceled performances: Earl Wilson, N.Y. *Post,* 1/15/57.

517. "He agonized over it . . .": Heymann, interview.
517. "The arrangements would have amused Bogart . . . his funeral": A. Morgan Maree Jr., interview, 11/29/90.
517. 3,000 people estimated outside the church: *L.A. Times,* 1/19/57.
517. "There weren't any . . .": Maree, interview.
517. News photographers bundled outside: Niven, *Bring on the Empty Horses,* p. 244.
518. Huston eulogy: Bacall, *By Myself,* p. 266.
519. "I think there was . . .": *The Letters of Nunnally Johnson,* p. 147.
519. Debussy one of Bogart's favorite composers: Bacall, *By Myself,* p. 267.
519. "Widow Lauren Bacall . . .": *Life,* 1/28/57.
519. "I was really . . .": S. Bogart, interview.
519. "everyone in the. . . . party—almost": Bacall, *By Myself,* p. 267.
519. "Let's go . . . I go now?": Cramer, interview.
520. "thought was another condolence . . .": Bacall, *By Myself,* pp. 267–8.
520. "caught the imagination . . .": Max Lerner, "Death and the Heroes," 285. *Post,* 1/18/57.
520. "the masculine counterpart . . .": Reuters, N.Y. *Post,* 1/15/57.
520. "*l'homme d'après* . . .": Eisenschitz, *Humphrey Bogart,* p. 20.
521. Two Portofino fishermen: N.Y. *Journal-American,* 3/12/57.
521. Helen Menken and Grace Lambert met at the Plaza: Grace Lambert, interview, 7/14/87.
521. Details of Bogart's will: *L.A. Times,* 2/5/57, and UP, N.Y. *Herald Tribune,* 2/5/57.
521. "An actor needs . . .": Hyams, *Bogie,* p. 154.
521. "some months later . . . his young bride": Max Wilk, interview, 5/4/87.

BIBLIOGRAPHY

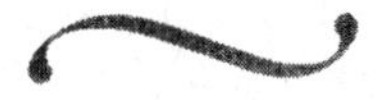

Astor, Mary. *My Story: An Autobiography.* Garden City, N.Y.: Doubleday, 1959.

———. *A Life on Film.* New York: Delacorte, 1971.

Bacall, Lauren. *Lauren Bacall: By Myself.* New York: Alfred A. Knopf, 1980.

Barfour, Alan G. *Humphrey Bogart. Pyramid Illustrated History of The Movies.* New York: Pyramid Communications, 1973.

Behlmer, Rudy. *America's Favorite Movies: Behind the Scenes.* New York: Frederick Ungar, 1982

———. *Inside Warner Bros., 1935–1951.* New York: The Viking Press, 1985.

Benchley, Nathaniel. *Humphrey Bogart.* Boston and Toronto: Little, Brown & Co., 1975.

Bergman, Ingrid, and Alan Burgess. *Ingrid Bergman: My Story.* New York: Delacorte, 1980.

Bernstein, Walter. *Inside Out: A Memoir of the Blacklist.* New York: Alfred A. Knopf, 1996.

Bessie, Alvah. *Inquisition in Eden.* New York: Macmillan, 1965.

Bishop, Jim. *The Mark Hellinger Story: A Biography of Broadway.* New York: Appleton-Century-Crofts, 1952.

Bogart, Humphrey, and Kate Holliday. "Humphrey Bogart's Own Story: I Can't Say I Loved Her." *Ladies' Home Journal,* 7/49.

Bogart, Stephen Humphrey, and Gary Provost. *In Search of My Father.* New York: Dutton, 1995.

Brooks, Louise. *Lulu in Hollywood.* New York: Alfred A. Knopf, 1982.

Brown, John Mason. *The Worlds of Robert E. Sherwood, Mirror to His Times, 1896–1939.* New York: Harper & Row, 1965.

Carr, Robert K. *The House Committee on Un-American Activities, 1945–1950.* Ithaca, N.Y.: Cornell University Press, 1952

Ceplair, Larry, and Steven Englund. *The Inquisition in Hollywood: Politics in the Film Community, 1930–1960.* Garden City, N.Y.: Anchor Press/Doubleday, 1980.

Chandler, Raymond *Raymond Chandler Speaking.* Edited by Dorothy Gardiner and Kathrine Sorley Walker, London: Hamish Hamilton, 1962.

———. *Selected Letters of Raymond Chandler.* Edited by Frank MacShane. New York: Delta/Dell, 1987.

Coe, Jonathan. *Humphrey Bogart: Take It and Like It.* London: Bloomsbury, 1991.

Cole, Lester. *Hollywood Red: The Autobiography of Lester Cole.* Palo Alto, Calif.: Ramparts Press, 1981.

Curcio, Vincent. *Suicide Blonde.* New York: William Morrow & Co., 1989.

Davidson, Bill. *Spencer Tracy: Tragic Idol.* New York: E. P. Dutton, 1987.

Davies, Joseph E. *Mission to Moscow.* New York: Simon & Schuster, 1941.

Davis, Bette. *The Lonely Life: An Autobiography.* New York: G. P. Putnam's Sons, 1962.

Deutsch, Armand. *Me and Bogie and Other Friends and Acquaintances from a Life in Hollywood and Beyond.* New York: G. P. Putnam's Sons, 1991.

Dmytryk, Edward. *It's a Hell of a Life but Not a Bad Living.* New York: Times Books, 1978.

Dunne, Father George H. *Holly Labor Dispute: A Study in Immorality.* Los Angeles: Conference Publishing Co., n.d.

Dunne, Philip. *Take Two: A Life in Movies and Politics.* New York: McGraw-Hill, 1980.

———. "The Constitution Up Close and Personal." *Constitution Magazine,* Fall 1992.

Eells, George. *Ginger, Loretta and Irene* Who? New York: G. P. Putnam's Sons, 1976.

Eisenschitz, Bernard. *Humphrey Bogart.* Paris: Le Terraín Vague, 1967.

———. *Nicholas Ray: An American Life.* Translated by Tom Milne. London: Faber & Faber, 1993.

Endres, Stacey, and Robert Cushman. *Hollywood at Your Feet: The Story of the World-Famous Chinese Theatre.* Los Angeles: Pomegranate Press, 1992.

Ephron, Henry. *We Thought We Could Do Anything: The Life of Screenwriters Phoebe and Henry Ephron.* New York: W. W. Norton & Co., 1977.

Freeman, David. *A Hollywood Education.* New York: G. P. Putnam's Sons, 1986.

Friedrich, Otto. *City of Nets: A Portrait of Hollywood in the 1940s.* New York: Perennial Library/Harper & Row, 1986.

Gabler, Neal. *An Empire of Their Own: How the Jews Invented Hollywood.* New York: Crown Publishers, 1988.

Gehman, Richard. *Bogart: An Intimate Biography.* New York: Fawcett–Gold Medal, 1965.

Goodman, Ezra. *The Fifty-Year Decline and Fall of Hollywood.* New York: Simon & Schuster, 1961.

———. *Bogey: The Good-Bad Guy.* New York: Lyle Stuart, 1965.

Goodman, Walter. *The Committee: The Extraordinary Career of the House Committee on Un-American Activities.* New York: Farar, Straus & Giroux, 1968.

Grobel, Lawrence. *The Hustons.* New York: Charles Scribner's Sons, 1989.

Guthke, Karl K. *B. Traven: The Life Behind the Legends.* Chicago: Lawrence Hill Books, 1987.

Hamlin, Frank. *Summers at the Lake.* Unpublished. Private collection.

Hanson, Patricia King, executive ed. *The American Film Institute Catalog of Motion Pictures Produced in the United States: Feature Films, 1931–1940.* 2 vols. Berkeley, Calif.: University of California Press, 1993.

Harmetz, Aljean. *Round Up the Usual Suspects: The Making of "Casablanca"—Bogart, Bergman, and World War II.* New York: Hyperion, 1992.

Hayden, Sterling. *Wanderer.* New York: Alfred A. Knopf, 1963.

Hellman, Lillian. *Scoundrel Time.* Boston: Little, Brown & Co., 1976.

Hepburn, Katharine. *The Making of "The African Queen": Or How I Went to Africa with Bogart, Bacall and Huston and Almost Lost My Mind.* New York: Alfred A. Knopf, 1987.

———. *Me: Stories of My Life.* New York: Alfred A, Knopf, 1991.

Huston, John. *An Open Book: John Huston.* New York: Alfred A. Knopf, 1980.

Hyams, Joe. *Bogie: The Biography of Humphrey Bogart.* New York: New American Library, 1966; Signet, 1967.

Johnson, Nunnally. *The Letters of Nunnally Johnson.* Edited by Dorris Johnson and Ellen Leventhal. New York: Alfred A. Knopf, 1981.

Kael, Pauline. *5001 Nights at the Movies.* New York: Henry Holt & Co., 1982.

Kahn, Gordon. *Hollywood on Trial: The Story of the Ten Who Were Indicted.* New York: Boni & Gaer, 1948.

Kanfer, Stefan. *A Journal of the Plague Years.* New York: Atheneum, 1973.

Katz, Ehraim. *The Film Encyclopedia.* Second Edition. New York: HarperPerennial/HarperCollins, 1994.

Kazan, Elia. *Elia Kazan: A Life.* New York: Alfred A. Knopf, 1988.

Kelley, Kitty. *His Way: The Unauthorized Biography of Frank Sinatra.* New York: Bantam Books, 1992.

Keyes, Evelyn. *Scarlett O'Hara's Younger Sister: My Lively Life In and Out of Hollywood.* Secaucus, N.J.: Lyle Stuart, 1977.

Kobal, John. *People Will Talk.* New York: Alfred A. Knopf, 1986.

Koch, Howard. *As Time Goes By: Memoirs of a Writer.* New York and London: Harcourt Brace Jovanovich, 1979.

Lally, Kevin. *Wilder Times: The Life of Billy Wilder.* New York: Henry Holt & Co., 1996.

Lardner, Ring, Jr. *The Lardners: My Family Reconsidered.* New York: Harper & Row, 1976.

Lax, Eric. *Woody Allen: A Biography.* New York: Alfred A. Knopf, 1991.

Leamer, Laurence. *As Time Goes By: The Life of Ingrid Bergman.* New York: Harper & Row, 1986.

McBride, Joseph. *Hawks on Hawks.* Berkeley, Calif., and Los Angeles: University of California Press, 1982.

McCarty, Clifford. *The Complete Films of Humphrey Bogart.* New York: Citadel Press, 1990. Originally published as *The Films of Humphrey Bogart,* 1965.

McGilligan, Pat. *Backstory: Interviews with Screenwriters of Hollywood's Golden Age.* Berkeley, Calif., and Los Angeles: University of California Press, 1986.

MacShane, Frank. *The Life of Raymond Chandler.* New York: Penguin Books, 1978.

Madsen, Axel. *John Huston: A Biography.* Garden City, N.Y.: Doubleday & Co., 1978.

MHQ: The Quarterly Journal of Military History, Summer 1989.

Michael, Paul. *Humphrey Bogart: The Man and His Films.* New York: Bobbs Merrill, 1966.

Monaco, James, and the editors of *Baseline. The Movie Guide.* New York: Perigee Books/Putnam, 1992.

Mosley, Leonard. *Zanuck: The Rise and Fall of Hollywood's Last Tycoon.* Boston: Little, Brown & Co., 1984.

Nash, Jay Robert, ed. in chief, and Stanley Ralph Ross, executive ed. *The Motion Picture Guide, 1927–1983.* Chicago: Cinebooks, 1986.

Navasky, Victor S. *Naming Names.* New York: The Viking Press, 1980.

New York Times Directory of the Film, The. New York: Arno Press/Random House, 1971.

New York Times Theatre Reviews, The; 1920–1940. 10 vols. New York: The New York Times and Arno Press, 1971.

Niven, David. *The Moon's a Balloon.* New York: G. P. Punnam's Sons, 1972.

———. *Bring on the Empty Horses.* New York: G. P. Putnam's Sons, 1975.

Paris, Barry. *Louise Brooks.* New York: Anchor/Doubleday, 1989.

Pettigrew, Terrence. *Bogart: A Definitive Study of His Film Career.* London and New York: Proteus, 1981.

Phillips, Cabell. *The 1940s: Decade of Triumph and Trouble.* New York: Macmillan, 1975.

Reagan, Ronald, and Richard C. Hubler. *Where's the Rest of Me?* New York: Hawthorn, 1965.

Robinson, Edward G., with Leonard Spiegelgass. *All My Yesterdays: An Autobiography.* New York: Hawthorn, 1973.

Roffman, Peter, and Jim Purdy. *The Hollywood Social Problem Film: Madness, Despair, and Politics from the Depression to the Fifties.* Bloomington, Ind.: Indiana University Press, 1981.

Rogers, Henry. *Walking the Tightrope.* New York: William Morrow & Co., 1980.

Ross, Lillian. *Reporting.* New York: Simon & Schuster, 1969.

Ruddy, Jonah, and Jonathan Hill. *Bogey: The Man, the Actor, the Legend.* New York: Tower, 1965.

Schatz, Thomas. *The Genius of the System: Hollywood Filmmaking in the Studio Era.* New York: Pantheon, 1989.

Schickel, Richard. *Schickel on Film: Encounters—Critical and Personal—with Movie Immortals.* New York: William Morrow & Co., 1989.

Schwartz, Nancy Lynn. *The Hollywood Writers' Wars.* New York, Alfred A. Knopf, 1982.

Sharpe, Howard. "The Amorous Life of a Movie Killer." *Movieland,* ca. 2/43 (part 1) and 3/43 (part 2).

Sperber, A. M. *Murrow: His Life and Times.* New York: Freundlich Books, 1986.

Sperling, Cass Warner, and Cork Millner. *Hollywood Be They Name.* Rocklin, Calif.: Prima Publishing, 1994.

Steele, Donna. *Wings of Pride: TWA Cabin Attendants, a Pictorial History, 1935–1985.* Marceline, MO.: Walsworth Publishing Co., 1985.

Thompson, Verita, with Donald Shepherd. *Bogie and Me: A Love Story.* New York: St. Martin's Press, 1982.

Thomson, David. *A Biographical Dictionary of Film.* Third Edition. New York: Alfred A. Knopf, 1994.

U.S. House Committee on Un-American Activities. *Investigation of Un-American Propoganda Activities in the United States,* 8/16/40. Washington, D.C.: U.S. Government Printing Office, 1940.

———. *Hearings Regarding the Communist Infiltration of the Motion Picture Industry Before the Committee on Un-American Activities,* 10/20/47. Washington, D.C.: U.S. Government Printing Office, 1947.

U.S. Senate Subcommittee of the Committee on Interstate Commerce. *Hearing Before the Subcommittee of the Committee on Interstate Commerce, Moving-Picture Screen and Radio Propaganda,* 9/25/41. Washington, D.C.: U.S. Government Printing Office, 1941.

Vermilye, Jerry. *Ida Lupino. Pyramid Illustrated History of the Movies.* New York: Pyramid Communications, 1977.

Vierhile, Robert J. and William J. *The Canandaigua Lake Steamboat Era, 1827 to 1935.* Naples, N.Y.: The Naples Historical Society, 1978.

Viertel, Peter. *Dangerous Friends: At Large with Huston and Hemingway in the Fifties.* New York: Doubleday, 1992.

Wallis, Hal, and Charles Higham. *Starmaker: The Autobiography of Hal Wallis.* New York: Macmillan, 1980.

Walsh, Raoul. *Each Man in His Time.* New York: Farrar, Straus & Giroux, 1974.

Warner, Jack, with Dean Jennings. *My First Hundred Years in Hollywood: An Autobiography.* New York: Random House, 1965.

Warner, Jack, Jr. *Bijou Dream.* New York: Crown, 1982.

Wilde, Meta Carpenter, and Orin Borsten. *A Loving Gentleman: The Love Story of William Faulkner and Meta Carpenter.* New York: Simon & Schuster, 1976.

Wiles, Buster, and William Donait. *My Days with Errol Flynn.* Santa Monica, Calif.: Roundtable Publishing, 1988.

Wilk, Max. *The Wit and Wisdom of Hollywood.* New York: Atheneum, 1971.

Zolotow, Maurice. *Billy Wilder in Hollywood.* New York: G. P. Putnam's Sons, 1977.

Humphrey Bogart's Broadway Plays

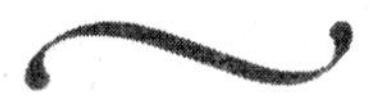

The year in parentheses is that of the first performance. Performance totals are unavailable for some plays. Casts and credits are based on playbills and newspaper reviews.

Drifting (1922), a melodrama in six scenes, by John Colton and D. H. Andrews; produced by William A. Brady; directed by John Cromwell. Opened January 2 at The Playhouse; 63 performances.

Cast: Alice Brady (Mrs. Cassie Cook), H. Mortimer White (Deacon Cook), Burr Curruth (Dr. Hepburn), Barry Fitz Patrick (Willie Bates), H. D. Bogart (Ernie Crockett), Florence Short (Mrs. Polly Voo Frances), Blanche Wallace (Foo Chow Lizzie), Winifred Lawshe (Rangoon Rose), Leward Meeker (Molyneaux), Maxwell Driscoll (Flock), Franklin Fox (Monsieur Repin), Robert Warwick (Bad Lands McKinney), Lumsden Hare (Dr. Li Shen Kueng), Selene Johnson (Lady Bramish), Leonard Cary (Cyril Trenwyth), Marguerite de Marhanne (Woman of Tung Kow), Millie Beland (Chu Che La Lu), Jack Grattan (Tommy Hepburn), Allen Atwell (Wang), Frank Backus (Komisky), H. Mortimer White (the Jhanzi Kahn), Harry Davies (Captain Jack John Michaeljohn), William Blaisdell (Ramires).

Up the Ladder (1922), a play in four acts, by Owen Davis; produced by William A. Brady; staged by Lumsden Hare. Opened March 6 at The Playhouse.

Cast: George Farren (Henry Smith), Nannette Comstock (Mary, His Wife), Doris Kenyon (Jane, Their Daughter), Anna Marston (Lucy), Albert Hackett (Jerry), Paul Kelly (John Allen), Edward Donnelly (Joe Henley), Mary

Brandon (Rosalind Henley), Robert Middlemass (Dick Wilmers), Adele Klaer (Eva Wilmers), Claude Cooper (Bert Muller), Mary Jeffery (Mrs. Muller), Humphrey Bogart (Stanley Grant) [Bogart replaced George Le Guere, who originated the role], Grace Heyer (Ellen), Frederick Brennan (Dr. Maynard), George Fitzgerald (Butler).

Swifty (1922), a comedy in three acts, by John Peter Toohey and W. C. Percival; produced by William A. Brady; directed by John Cromwell. Opened October 16 at The Playhouse.

Cast: Frances Howard (Miriam Proctor), Hale Hamilton (Swifty Morgan), Humphrey Bogart (Tom Proctor), William Holden (Jefferson Proctor), Robert Ayrton (Milton), Margaret Mosier (Alice), Grace Goodhall (Mrs. Kimball), Elmer Nicholls (Chauffeur), Helen Scott (Helen Kimball), Guy Hitner (First Detective), John O. Hewett (Second Detective).

Meet the Wife (1923), a comedy in three acts, by Lynn Starling; produced by Rosalie Stewart and Bert French; staged by Bert French. Opened November 26 at the Klaw Theatre; 232 performances.

Cast: Mary Boland (Gertrude Lennox), Charles Dalton (Harvey Lennox), Eleanor Griffith (Doris Bellamy), Clifton Webb (Victor Staunton), Humphrey Bogart (Gregory Brown), Ernest Lawford (Philip Lord), Patricia Calvert (Alice), Charles Bloomer (William).

Nerves (1924), a play in three acts, by John Farrar and Stephen Vincent Benét; produced by William A. Brady; directed by William A. Brady Jr. Opened September 1 at the Comedy Theatre; 16 performances.

Cast: Marie Curtis (Mrs. Hill), Kenneth MacKenna (Jack Coates), Paul Kelly (Ted Hill), Winifred Lenihan (Peggy Thatch), Reed Brown (Paul Overman), Henry Whittemore (Frank Smith), John McCauley (Arthur Greene), Humphrey Bogart (Bob Thatch), Barbara Kitson (Mary), Mary Phillips (Jane), John Gray (Carter, the Butler), Cynthia Hyde (Janet), Walter Baldwin (Rook), Kyra Alanova (Jean), Edward H. Weaver (Matthew Anderson), T. C. Durham Jr. (Orderly).

Hell's Bells (1925), a comedy in three acts, by Barry Connors; produced by Herman Gantvoort; directed by John Hayden. Opened January 26 at Wallack's Theatre; 120 performances.

Cast: Olive May (Mrs. Buck), Shirley Booth (Nan Winchester), Humphrey Bogart (Jimmy Todhunter), Tom H. Walsh ("Jap" Stillson), Eddie Garvey (D. O. O'Donnell), Joseph Greene (Horace E. Pitkins), Camilla Crume (Mrs. Amos Todhunter), Virginia Howell (Abigail Stillson), Violet Dunn (Gladys Todhunter), Ernest Pollock (Chief of Police Pitkins), Fletcher Harvey (Dr. Bushnell),

James Cherry (Halligan), Clifton Self (Swartz), Converse Tyler (Riordan), George Spelvin (Mahoney).

Cradle Snatchers (1925), a comedy in three acts, by Russell Medcraft and Norma Mitchell; produced by Sam H. Harris; directed by Sam Forrest; settings by Clark Robinson. Opened September 7 at The Music Box; 332 performances.

Cast: Mary Boland (Susan Martin), Edna May Oliver (Ethel Drake), Margaret Dale (Kitty Ladd), Myra Hampton (Anne Hall), Billie Shaw (Elinor), Mary Murray (Francine), Lillian Gerald (Jackie), Raymond Hackett (Henry Winton), William Corbett (George Martin), George Lessey (Roy Ladd), Joseph Holicky (Howard Drake), Humphrey Bogart (Jose Vallejo), Raymond Guion (Oscar Nordham), Gerald Phillips (Paul).

Saturday's Children (1927), a comedy in three acts, by Maxwell Anderson; directed by Guthrie McClintic; settings by Jo Mielziner; produced by the Actors' Theatre, Inc. Opened January 26 at the Booth Theatre; 310 performances.

Cast: Ruth Hammond (Florrie Sands), Richard Barbee (Willie Sands), Lucia Moore (Mrs. Halevy), Ruth Gordon (Bobby), Frederick Perry (Mr. Halevy), Humphrey Bogart (Rims O'Neil) [Bogart took over the role originated by Roger Pryor, who became ill], Bulah Bondi (Mrs. Gorlick).

Baby Mine (1927), a farce in three acts, by Margaret Mayo; settings by Livingston Platt; revived by John Turek. Opened June 9 at Chanin's Forty-sixth Street Threatre; 12 performances.

Cast: Roscoe "Fatty" Arbuckle (Jimmy Jenks), Lee Patrick (Zoe Hardy), Humphrey Bogart (Alfred Hardy), W. J. Paul (Hardy's Secretary), Floy La Pointe (Aggie), Zelma Tiden (Maggie O'Flarety), Anna Kostant (Rosa Gatti), M. Tello Webb (Finnigan), W. J. Brady (Michael O'Flaherty), Jerome Jordan (Donaghey).

A Most Immoral Lady (1928), a comedy in three acts, by Townsend Martin; produced by William A. Brady Jr. and Dwight Deere Wiman; staged by Dwight Deere Wiman; settings by Jo Mielziner. Opened November 26 at the Cort Theatre; 160 performances. Bogart, who reportedly took over a role after the production began, is not listed in any archival playbill. Alice Brady starred.

The Skyrocket (1929), a comedy in three acts by Mark Reed; produced by Gilbert Miller and Guthrie McClintic; directed by Guthrie McClintic; settings by Jo Mielziner. Opened January 11 at the Lyceum Theatre.

Cast: Mary Phillips (Del Ewing), J. C. Nugent (Mr. Ewing), Humphrey Bogart (Vic Ewing), Clara Blandick (Mrs. Ewing), Lotta Linthicum (Mrs. Bemis), Howard Freemen (Homer Bemis), Morris Lee (Oishi; a Butler), Franklin

Fox (Frank Greer), William Broussard (Reggie MacSweeney), Dorothy Bigelow (Kitty Marsh), Gwyneth Gordon (Lillian).

It's a Wise Child (1929), a comedy in three acts by Laurence E. Johnson; produced and directed by David Belasco; settings by Joseph Wickes. Opened August 6 at the Belasco Theatre; 378 performances.

Cast: Helen Lowell (Mrs. Stanton), Olga Krolow (Alice Peabody), Leila Bennett (Bertha), George Walcott (Bill Stanton), Humphrey Bogart (Roger Baldwin), Mildred McCoy (Joyce Stanton), Minor Watson (James Stevens), Harlan Briggs (G. A. Appleby), Sidney Toler (Cool Kelly), Porter Hall (Otho Peabody).

After All (1931), a comedy in three acts, by John Van Druten; produced by Dwight Deere Winman, by arrangement with Sydney W. Carroll; directed by Auriol Lee; settings by Raymond Sovey. Opened December 3 at the Booth Theatre; 20 performances.

Cast: Helen Haye (Mrs.Thomas) [Haye, who appeared in seven Broadway productions between 1920 and 1934, has been credited by some Bogart biographers as being the more famous Helen Hayes], Walter Kingsford (Mr. Thomas), Edmund George (Ralph Thomas), Margaret Perry (Phyllis Thomas), Minna Phillips (Mrs. Melville), Lillian B. Tonge (Alice), Phillip Leigh (Mr. Melville), Humphrey Bogart (Duff Wilson), Dorothy Matthews (Greta), J. Kerby Hawkes (Cyril Greenwood), Patricia Calvert (Doris Melville).

I Loved You Wednesday (1932), a play in a prologue and three acts, by Molly Ricardel and William Du Bois; produced by Crosby Gaige; staged by Worthington Miner; settings by Raymond Sovey. Opened October 11 at the Sam H. Harris Theatre; 63 performances.

Cast: Frances Fuller (Victoria Meredith), Edward La Roche (Jardinier), Humphrey Bogart (Randall Williams), Henry O'Neill (Philip Fletcher), Jane Seymour (Dr. Mary Hansen), Harry Gresham (Tom), Robert Henderson (Freddy), Henry Bergman (Eddie), Mary Alice Collins (Jennifer), Henry Fonda (Eustace), Anna Lubowe (Hat Check Girl), Eddie Sexton (Ralph), Ken Harvey (Gene), Philip Van Zandt (Fritz), Rose Hobart (Cynthia Williams), Fred Irving Lewis (Wyn Terrell), Robert Wallsten (Jack), Marjorie Jarecki (Irene), Ralph Simone (Dino), Arline Francis (Peggy), Jean Briggs (Viola), Guy Hamilton (Nichols).

Chrysalis (1932), a play in three acts and ten scenes, by Rose Albert Porter; produced by Martin Beck in association with Lawrence Langner and Theresa Helburn; directed by Theresa Helburn; settings by Cleon Throckmorton. Opened November 15 at the Martin Beck Theatre; 23 performances.

Cast: Lily Cahill (Elizabeth Cose), Osgood Perkins (Michael Caverhill; Her

Brother), Margaret Sullavan (Lyda Cose), Gilberte Frey (Mary), Fan Bourke (Blondie), Elisha Cook Jr. (Honey Rogers), June Walker (Eve Haron), Elia Kazan (Louis), Humphrey Bogart (Don Ellis), Hazel Hanna (Mrs. Reilly), Jessie Graham (Mrs. Thomas), Kathleen Comegys (Mrs. Haron), Frank Layton (Nat Davis), Lalive Brownell (Miss Haskell), Russell Thayer (Guard), Henry D. Southard (Pete, a Convict), Alvin Barrett (Cook), Arling Alcine (Flaggerty), Thurston Hall (Judge Halman), Georgie Lee Hall, Jean Macintyre, Mary Orr, Henrietta Kaye, Kathleen Comegys, Phyllis Laughton, Florence Heller, Wilhelmina Barton, Beta Rothafel, Kathryn McClure (Girls in Rose Manor).

Our Wife (1933), a comedy in three acts, by Lillian Day and Lyon Mearson; produced by Thomas J. R. Brotherton and Abe H. Halle; staged by Edward Clarke Lilley; settings by Golding Studios. Opened March 2 at the Booth Theatre; 20 performances.

Cast: Rose Hobart (Margot Drake), Humphrey Bogart (Jerry Marvin), Michelette Burani (Concierge), June Walker (Barbara Marvin), June Walker (Barbara Marvin), Miriam Battista (Elisabetta), Edward Raquello (Antonio di Mariano), Raymon O'Brien (First Agente), Juan Varro (Second Agente).

The Mask and the Face (La Maschera e il Volto) (1933), a comedy in three acts, by Luigi Chiarelli; adapted from the Italian by W. Somerset Maugham; produced by the Theatre Guild; directed by Philip Moeller (production committee: Theresa Helburn and Helen Westley); setting by Lee Simonson. Opened May 8 at the Guild Theatre; 40 performances.

Cast: Shirley Booth (Elisa Zanotti), Donald McClelland (Giorgio Alamari), Dorothy Patten (Marta Setta), Leo G. Carroll (Cirillo Zanotti), Alice Reinhart (Wanda Sereni), Ernest Cossart (Marco Millotti), Charles Campbell (Piero Pucci), Judith Anderson (Savina Grazia), Stanley Ridges (Count Paulo Grazia), Humphrey Bogart (Luciano Spina), Manart Kippen (Andrea), William Lovejoy (Giacomo), Jon Marion (Teresa).

Invitation to a Murder (1934), a melodrama in three acts, by Rufus King ("the author acknowledges some indebtedness to Marcel Strauss in connection with the play"); produced by Ben Stein; staged by A. H. Van Buren; setting by Robert Barnhart. Opened May 17 at the Masque Theatre; 37 performances.

Cast: William Valentine (Walter Channing), Daphne Warren Wilson (Estelle Channing), Humphrey Bogart (Horatio Channing), James Shelburne (Martin), Juan Varro (Pedro), Sherling Oliver (Peter Thorne), Gale Sondergaard (Lorinda Channing), Walter Abel (Doctor Linton), Jane Seymour (Jeanette Thorne), Edgar Charles (Mr. Dickson), Robert Burton (Detective Sergeant Selbridge).

The Petrified Forest (1935), a play in two acts, by Robert Emmett Sherwood; produced by Gilbert Miller and Leslie Howard, in association with Arthur Hopkins; staged by Arthur Hopkins. Opened January 7 at the Broadhurst Theatre; 181 performances.

Cast: Leslie Howard (Alan Squier), Peggy Conklin (Gabby Maple), Charles Dow Clark (Gramp Maple), Humphrey Bogart (Duke Mantee), Frank Milan (Boze Hertzlinger), Walter Vonnegut (Jason Maple), Blanche Sweet (Mrs. Chisholm), Robert Hudson (Mr. Chisholm), John Alexander (Joseph), Ross Hertz (Jackie), Esther Woodruff Leeming (Paula), Tom Fadden (Ruby), Robert Porterfield (Herb), Slim Thompson (Pyles), Aloysius Cunningham (Commander Klepp), Guy Conradi (Hendy), Frank Tweeddell (Sheriff), Milo Boulton (a Telegrapher), James Doody (Another Telegrapher), Eugene Keith (A Deputy), Harry Sherwin (Another Deputy).

FILMOGRAPHY

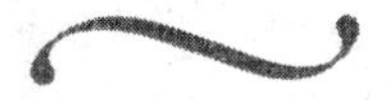

Some films have varying running lengths, all of which are listed. With five exceptions, Bogart's films were shot in black and white; color pictures are noted.

The Dancing Town (1928). Paramount Pictures. Two-reeler short with Helen Hayes.

Broadway's like That (1930). Vitaphone, distributed by Warner Bros. 10 minutes. Directed by Murray Roth; screenplay by Stanley Rauh; musical direction by Harold Levey.

Cast: Ruth Etting, Humphrey Bogart, Joan Blondell.

A Devil with Women (1930). Fox. 76 minutes. Directed by Irving Cummings; associate producer, George Middleton; screenplay by Dudley Nichols and Henry M. Johnson, based on the novel *Dust and Sun* by Clements Ripley; cinematography by Arthur Todd; music by Peter Brunelli; edited by Jack Murray; art direction by William Darling; sound by E. Clayton Ward and Harry M. Leonard.

Cast: Victor McLaglen (Jerry Maxton), Mona Maris (Rosita Fernandez), Humphrey Bogart (Tom Standish), Luana Alcaniz (Dolores), Michael Vavitch (Morloff), Soledad Jimenez (Jiminez), Mona Rico (Alicia), John St. Polis (Don Diego), Robert Edson (General Garcia).

Up the River (1930). Fox. 92 minutes. Directed by John Ford; screenplay by Maurice Watkins; cinematography by Joseph August; staged by William Collier Sr.; edited by Frank Hull; sound by W. W. Lindsay.

Cast: Spencer Tracy (St. Louis), Claire Luce (Judy), Warren Hymer (Dannemora Dan), Humphrey Bogart (Steve), William Collier Sr. (Pop), Joan Marie Lawes (Jean), George MacFarlane (Jessup), Gaylord Pendleton (Morris), Sharon Lynn (Edith LaVerne), Noel Francis (Sophie), Goodee Montgomery (Kit), Robert Burns (Slim), John Swor (Clem), Robert E. O'Connor (the Warden), Louise MacIntosh (Mrs. Massey), Richard Keene (Dick), Johnnie Walker (Happy), Pat Somerset (Beauchamp), Morgan Wallace (Frosby), Edythe Chapman (Mrs. Jordan), Althea Henly (Cynthia), the Keating Sisters (May and June), Joe Brown (Deputy Warden), Wilbur Mack (Whiteley), Harvey Clark (Nash), Carol Wines (Daisy Elmore), Adele Windsor (Minnie), Mildred Vincent (Annie).

Body and Soul (1931). Fox. 83 minutes. Directed by Alfred Santell; screenplay by Jules Furthman, from the unproduced and unpublished play *Squadrons* by Elliott White Springs and A. E. Thomas, based on the short story "Big Eyes and Little Mouth" by Elliott White Springs, published in *Nocturne Militaire* (1927); cinematography by Glen MacWilliams; music by Peter Brunelli; edited by Paul Weatherwax; art direction by Anton Grot; sound by Donald Flick; songs: "Oh, How I Hate to Get Up in the Morning," words and music by Irving Berlin; "Dark Town Strutters' Ball," words and music by Shelton Brooks.

Cast: Charles Farrell (Mal Andrews), Elissa Landi (Carla), Myrna Loy (Alice Lester), Humphrey Bogart (Jim Watson), Donald Dillaway (Tap Johnson), Craufurd Kent (Major Burke), Pat Somerset (Major Knowles), Ian Maclaren (General Trafford-Jones), Dennis D'Auburn (Lieutenant Meggs), Harold Kinney (Young), Bruce Warren (Sam Douglas).

Bad Sister (1931). Universal. 71 minutes. Directed by Hobart Henley; produced by Carl Laemmle Jr.; screenplay by Raymond L. Schrock and Tom Reed, dialogue by Edwin H. Knopf, based on the story "The Flirt" (1913) by Booth Tarkington; cinematography by Karl Freund; edited by Ted Kent; sound by C. Roy Hunter. First filmed by Universal in 1922 as *The Flirt*, also directed by Henley.

Cast: Bette Davis (Laura Madison), Conrad Nagel (Dick Lindley), Sidney Fox (Marianne Madison), ZaSu Pitts (Minnie), Slim Summerville (Sam), Charles Winninger (John Madison), Emma Dunn (Mrs. Madison), Humphrey Bogart (Valentine Corliss), Bert Roach (Wade Trumbull), David Durand (Hedrick Madison).

Women of All Nations (1931). Fox. 72 minutes. Directed by Raoul Walsh; produced by Archibald Buchannan; screenplay by Barry Conners, based on characters created by Laurence Stallings and Maxwell Anderson; cinematography by

Lucien Andriot; music by Reginald H. Bassett; edited by Jack Dennis; art direction by David Hall; sound by George H. Leverett.

Cast: Victor McLaglen (Sergeant Flagg), Edmund Lowe (Sergeant Quirt), El Brendel (Olson), Greta Nissen (Elsa), Fifi Dorsay (Fifi), Marjorie White (Pee Wee), T. Roy Barnes (Captain of Marines), Bela Lugosi (Prince Hassan), Humphrey Bogart (Stone), Joyce Compton (Kiki), Jesse DeVorska (Izzie), Charles Judels (Leon), Marion Lessing (Gretchen), Ruth Warren (Ruth). Bogart's character was cut from the final print.

A Holy Terror (1931). Fox. 53 minutes. Directed by Irving Cummings; scenario by Ralph Block, dialogue by Alfred A. Cohen and Myron Fagan, based on the novel *Trailin'* (1920) by Max Brand; cinematography by George Schneiderman; edited by Ralph Dixon; sound by Donald Flick.

Cast: George O'Brien (Tony Bard), Sally Eilers (Jerry Foster), Rita LaRoy (Kitty Carroll), Humphrey Bogart (Steve Nash), James Kirkwood (William Drew), Stanley Fields (Butch Morgan), Robert Warwick (Thomas Bard; alias Thomas Woodbury), Richard Tucker (Tom Hedges), Earl Pingree (Jim Lawler), Jay Wilson (Cowboy), Charles Whitaker (Johnson).

Love Affair (1932). Columbia. 68 minutes. Directed by Thornton Freeland; adaptation and dialogue by Jo Swerling; continuity by Dorothy Howell; based on the August 1930 *College Humor* story by Ursula Parrott; cinematography by Ted Tetzlaff; edited by Jack Dennis; sound by Charles Noyes.

Cast: Dorothy Mackaill (Carol Owen), Humphrey Bogart (Jim Leonard), Jack Kennedy (Gilligan), Barbara Leonard (Felice), Astrid Allwyn (Linda Lee), Bradley Page (Georgie), Halliwell Hobbes (Kibbee), Hale Hamilton (Bruce Hardy), Harold Minjir (Antone).

Big City Blues (1932). Warner Bros. 65 minutes. Directed by Mervyn LeRoy; screenplay by Ward Morehouse and Lillie Hayward, based on the play *New York Town* (1932) by Ward Morehouse; cinematography by James Van Trees; edited by Ray Curtis; music by Ray Heindorf and Bernard Kaun.

Cast: Joan Blondell (Vida Fleet), Eric Linden (Bud Reeves), Jobyna Howland (Serena Cartlich), Inez Courtney (Faun), Evalyn Knapp (Jo-Jo), Guy Kibbee (Hummel), Gloria Shea (Agnes), Walter Catlett (Gibbony), Ned Sparks (Stackhouse), Humphrey Bogart (Adkins), Lyle Talbot (Sully), Josephine Dunne (Jackie), Grant Mitchell (Station Agent), Thomas Jackson (Quelkin), Sheila Terry (Lorna), Tom Dugan (Red), Betty Gilette (Mabel), Edward McWade (Baggage Master).

Three on a Match (1932). Warner Bros. 64 minutes. Directed by Mervyn LeRoy; scenario by Lucien Hubbard; dialogue by Kubec Glasmon and John Bright, based on a story by Kubec Glasmon and John Bright; cinematography by Sol

Polito; edited by Ray Curtis; art direction by Robert Haas; music direction by Leo F. Forbstein.

Cast: Joan Blondell (Mary Keaton), Warren William (Robert Kirkwood), Ann Dvorak (Vivian Revere), Bette Davis (Ruth Wescott), Lyle Talbot (Michael Loftus), Humphrey Bogart (Harve), Allen Jenkins (Dick), Edward Arnold (Ace), Virginia Davis (Mary as a Child), Dawn O'Day [later known as Anne Shirley] (Vivian as a child), Betty Carse (Ruth as a child), Buster Phillips (Robert Kirkwood Jr.), Sheila Terry (Pianist-Singer), Grant Mitchell (Mr. Gilmore), Glenda Farrell (Girl in Reform School), Frankie Darro (Bobby), Blanche Frederici (Miss Blazer), Hardie Albright (Phil), Herman Bing (Professor Irving Finklestein), Jack LaRue (Henchman), Spencer Charters (Street Cleaner), Ann Brody (Mrs. Goldberg), Mary Doran (Prisoner), Selmer Jackson (Radio Announcer).

Midnight (1934). All-Star Productions, distributed by Universal. 80 minutes. Produced and directed by Chester Erskine; screenplay by Chester Erskine, based on the play by Paul and Claire Sifton, produced in New York by the Theatre Guild (1930); cinematography by William Steiner and George Webber; sets by Sam Corso; edited by Leo Zochling; sound by C. A. Tuthill; makeup by Eddie Senz.

Cast: Sidney Fox (Stella Weldon), O. P. Heggie (Edward Weldon), Henry Hull (Bob Nolan), Margaret Wycherly (Mrs. Weldon), Lynne Overman (Joe "Leroy" Biggers), Katherine Wilson (Ada Biggers), Richard Whorf (Arthur Weldon), Humphrey Bogart (Gar Boni), Granville Bates (Henry McGrath), Cora Witherspoon (Elizabeth McGrath), Moffat Johnston (District Attorney Plunkett), Henry O'Neill (Edgar V. Ingersoll), Helen Flint (Ethel Saxon), Katherine Wilson (Ada Biggers).

The Petrified Forest (1936). Warner Bros. 83 minutes. Directed by Archie Mayo; executive producer, Hal B. Wallis; associate producer, Henry Blanke; screenplay by Charles Kenyon and Delmer Daves, based on the play by Robert E. Sherwood; cinematography by Sol Polito; music direction by Leo F. Forbstein; score by Bernhard Kaun; edited by Owen Marks; assistant director, Dick Mayberry; art direction by John Hughes; costumes by Orry-Kelly; special effects by Warren E. Lynch, Fred Jackman, and Willard Van Enger; sound by Charles Lang.

Cast: Leslie Howard (Alan Squier), Bette Davis (Gabrielle Maple), Genevieve Tobin (Mrs. Edith Chisholm), Dick Foran (Boze Hertzlinger), Humphrey Bogart (Duke Mantee), Joseph Sawyer (Jackie), Porter Hall (Jason Maple), Charley Grapewin (Gramp Maple), Paul Harvey (Mr. Chisholm), Eddie Acuff (Lineman), Adrian Morris (Ruby), Nina Campana (Paula), Slim Thompson (Slim), John Alexander (Joseph).

Bullets or Ballots (1936). First National Picture/Warner Bros. 81 minutes. Directed by William Keighley; associate producer, Louis F. Edelman; executive producers, Jack L. Warner and Hal B. Wallis; screenplay by Seton I. Miller, based on an original story by Martin Mooney and Seton I. Miller; cinematography by Hal Mohr; music by Heinz Roemheld; edited by Jack Killifer; assistant director, Chuck Hansen; art direction by Carl Jules Weyl; special effects by Fred Jackman, Fred Jackman Jr., and Warren E. Lynch; sound by Oliver S. Garretson.

Cast: Edward G. Robinson (Johnny Blake), Joan Blondell (Lee Morgan), Barton MacLane (Al Kruger), Humphrey Bogart (Nick "Bugs" Fenner), Frank McHugh (Herman), Joseph King (Captain Dan McLaren), Richard Purcell (Driscoll), George E. Stone (Wires), Joseph Crehan (Grand Jury Spokesman), Henry O'Neill (Bryant), Henry Kolker (Hollister), Gilbert Emery (Thorndyke), Herbert Rawlinson (Caldwell), Louise Beavers (Nellie), William Pawley (Crail), Ralph Remley (Kelly), Frank Faylen (Gatley), Wallace Gregory (Lambert), Frank Bruno (Ben).

Two Against the World (1936). First National/Warner Bros. 64 minutes. Directed by William McGann; executive producers, Jack L. Warner and Hal B. Wallis; associate producer, Bryan Foy; screenplay by Michael Jacoby, based on the play *Five Star Final* (1930) by Louis Weitzenkorn; cinematography by Sid Hickox; music by Heinz Roemheld; edited by Frank Magee; dialogue director, Irving Rapper; assistant director, Carrol Sax; art direction by Esdras Hartley; special effects by Fred Jackman Jr. and Rex Wimpy; sound by C. A. Riggs.

Cast: Humphrey Bogart (Sherry Scott), Beverly Roberts (Alma Ross), Henry O'Neill (Jim Carstairs), Linda Perry (Edith Carstairs), Carlyle Moore Jr. (Billy Sims), Virginia Brissac (Mrs. Marion Sims), Helen MacKellar (Martha Carstairs), Clay Clement (Mr. Banning), Claire Dodd (Cora Latimer), Hobart Cavanaugh (Tippy Mantus), Harry Hayden (Martin Leavenworth), Robert Middlemass (Bertram C. Reynolds), Douglas Wood (Malcolm Sims), Bobby Gordon (Herman O'Reilly), Paula Stone (Miss Symonds), Frank Orth (Tommy the Bartender), Howard Hickman (Dr. McGuire), Ferdinand Schumann-Heinke (Sound Mixer), Paul Regan (Maxey), Milton Kibbee (Second Writer), Pietro Sosso (Butler), Jack McHugh (Newsboy), Charles Evans (Newsboy), Elliott Gordon (News Commentator), Edward Peil Sr. (Coroner), Emmett Vogab (Radio Announcer), Bill Ray (Radio Announcer), George Fisher (Radio Announcer).

China Clipper (1936). First National/Warner Bros. 85 minutes. Directed by Ray Enright; associate producer, Louis F. Edleman; executive producers, Jack L. Warner and Hal B. Wallis; screenplay by Frank Ward; additional dialogue by Norman Reilly Raine; cinematography by Arthur Edeson; music by Bernhard Kaun and W. Franke Harling; edited by Owen Marks; dialogue direction by Gene Lewis; assistant director, Lee Katz; art direction by Max Parker; costumes by Orry-Kelly; aerial photography by Elmer G. Dyer and H. F. Koenekamp; special effects by Fred Jackman, Willard Van Enger, and H. F. Koenekamp; sound by Everett A. Brown.

Cast: Pat O'Brien (Dave Logan), Beverly Roberts (Jean Logan), Ross Alexander (Tom Collins), Humphrey Bogart (Hap Stuart), Marie Wilson (Sunny Avery), Joseph Crehan (Jim Horn), Joseph King (Mr. Pierson), Addison Richards (B. C. Hill), Ruth Robinson (Mother Brunn), Henry B. Walthall (Dad Brunn), Carlyle Moore Jr., (Radio Operator), Lyle Moraine (Co-pilot), Dennis Moore (Engineer on Clipper), Wayne Morris (Navigator), Alexander Cross (Bill Andrews), William Wright (Pilot), Kenneth Harlan (Department of Commerce Inspector), Anne Nagel (Secretary), Marjorie Weaver (Secretary), Milburn Stone (Radio Operator), Owen King (Radio Operator), Jean [Skippy] Logan (Department of Commerce Inspector), Hal K. Dawson (Airplane Designer), Thomas Pogue (Speaker), Jack Hatfield (Reporter).

Isle of Fury (1936). Warner Bros. 60 minutes. Directed by Frank McDonald; associate producer, Bryan Foy; executive producers, Jack L. Warner and Hal B. Wallis; screenplay by Robert Andrews and William Jacobs, based on the 1932 novel *Narrow Corner* by W. Somerset Maugham; cinematography by Frank Good; music by Howard Jackson; edited by Warren Low; assistant director, Frank Heath; art direction by Esdras Hartley; costumes by Orry-Kelly; special effects by Fred Jackman, Willard Van Enger, and H. F. Koenekamp; sound by Charles Lang.

Cast: Humphrey Bogart (Val Stevens), Margaret Lindsay (Lucille Gordon), Donald Woods (Eric Blake), Paul Graetz (Captain Deever), Gordon Hart (Anderson), E. E. Clive (Dr. Hardy), George Regas (Otar), Sidney Bracy (Sam), Tetsu Komai (Kim Lee), Miki Morita (Oh Kay), Houseley Stevenson Sr. (the Rector), Frank Lackteen (Old Native), George Piltz (Native).

Black Legion (1937). Warner Bros. 83 minutes. Directed by Archie Mayo; associate producer, Robert Lord; executive producers, Jack L. Warner and Hal B. Wallis; screenplay by Abem Finkel and William Wister Haines, based on a story by Robert Lord; cinematography by George Barnes; music by Bernhard Kaun; edited by Owen Marks; assistant director, Jack Sullivan; art direction by Robert Haas; costumes by Milo Anderson; special effects by Fred Jackman Jr. and H. F. Koenekamp; sound by C. A. Riggs.

Cast: Humphrey Bogart (Frank Taylor), Dick Foran (Ed Jackson), Erin O'Brien-Moore (Ruth Taylor), Ann Sheridan (Betty Grogan), Robert Barrat (Brown), Helen Flint (Pearl Davis), Joseph Sawyer (Cliff Moore), Addison Richards (Prosecuting Attorney), Eddie Acuff (Metcalf), Clifford Soubier (Mike Grogan), Paul Harvey (Billings), Samuel S. Hinds (Judge), John Litel (Tommy Smith), Alonzo Price (Alexander Hargrave), Dickie Jones (Buddy Taylor), Dorothy Vaughn (Mrs. Grogan), Henry Brandon (Joe Dombrowski), Charles Halton (Osgood), Pat C. Flick (Nick Strumpas), Francis Sayles (Charlie), Paul Stanton (Dr. Barham), Harry Hayden (Jones), Egon Brecher (Elder Dombrowski), Ed Chandler, Robert E. Homans (Policemen), William Wayne (Counterman), Frederick Lindsley (*March of Time* voice), Fred MacKaye, Frank Nelson, John Hiestand, Ted Bliss (Radio Announcers), Larry Emmons (Man in Drugstore), Don Barclay (Drunk), Emmett Vogan (News Commentator), John Butler (Salesman), Frank Sully (Helper), Max Wagner (Truck Driver), Carlyle Morre Jr., Dennis Moore, Mike Kibbee (Reporters), Lee Phelps (Guard), Wilfred Lucas (Bailiff), Jack Mower (County Clerk).

The Great O'Malley (1937). Warner Bros. 71 minutes. Directed by William Dieterle; associate producer, Harry Joe Brown; executive producers, Jack L. Warner and Hal B. Wallis; screenplay by Milton Krims and Tom Reed, based on the story "The Making of O'Malley" by Gerald Beaumont; cinematography by Ernest Haller; music by Heinz Roemheld and Leo F. Forbstein; edited by Warren Low; dialogue direction by Irving Rapper; assistant director, Frank Shaw; art director by Hugh Reticker; costumes by Milo Anderson; special effects by James Gibbons, Fred Jackman Jr., and H. F. Koenekamp; sound by Francis J. Scheid.

Cast: Pat O'Brien (James Aloysius O'Malley), Sybil Jason (Barbara Phillips), Humphrey Bogart (John Phillips), Ann Sheridan (Judy Nolan), Freida Inescort (Mrs. Phillips), Donald Crisp (Captain Cromwell), Henry O'Neill (Defense Attorney), Craig Reynolds (Motorist), Hobart Cavanaugh (Pinky Holden), Gordon Hart (Doctor), Mary Gordon (Mrs. O'Malley), Mabel Colcord (Mrs. Flaherty), Frank Sheridan (Fr. Patrick), Lillian Harmer (Miss Taylor), Felmar Watson (Tubby), Frank Reicher (Dr. Larson), Armand "Curly" Wright (Vegetable Peddler), George Humbert (Junkman), Jerry Mandy (Italian Umbrella Salesman).

Marked Woman (1937). First National/Warner Bros. 96 minutes. Directed by Lloyd Bacon; executive producer, Hal B. Wallis; associate producer, Louis F. Edelman; screenplay by Robert Rossen and Abem Finkel; cinematography by George Barnes; music by Bernhard Kaun and Heinz Roemheld; edited by Jack Killifer; assistant director, Dick Mayberry; art direction by Max Parker; costumes by Orry-Kelly; special effects by James Gibbons and Robert Burks; sound by Everett Brown; words and music for the songs "My Silver Dollar Man" by Harry Warren and Al Dubin, and "Mr. and Mrs. Doaks" by M. K. Jerome and Jack Scholl.

Cast: Bette Davis (Mary Dwight Strauber), Humphrey Bogart (David Graham), Lola Lane (Gabby Marvin), Eduardo Cianelli (Johnny Vanning), Rosalind Marquis (Florrie Liggett), Mayo Methot (Estelle Porter), Jane Bryan (Betty Strauber), Allen Jenkins (Louie), John Litel (Gordon), Ben Welden (Charlie Delaney), Damian O'Flynn (Ralph Krawford), Henry O'Neill (Arthur Sheldon), Raymond Hatton (Lawyer at Jail), Carlos San Martin (Headwaiter), William B. Davidson (Bob Crandall), Kenneth Harlan (Eddie), Robert Strange (George Beler), James Robbins (Bell Captain), Arthur Aylesworth (Mr. Johnny Truble), John Sheehan (Vincent), Sam Wren (Mac), Edwin Stanley (Detective Ferguson),

Alan Davis (Henchman), Allen Mathews (Henchman), Guy Usher (Detective Casey), Gordon Hart (Judge at First Trial), Pierre Watkin (Judge at Second Trial), Herman Marks (Joe), Wilfred Lucas (Foreman of Jury), Wendell Niles (News Commentator), Clayton Moore Jr. (Elevator Boy), Harry Hollingsworth (Doorman), Mary Doyle (Nurse), Lyle Moraine (First Reporter), Billy Wayne (Second Reporter), Max Hoffman Jr. (Third Reporter), Emmet Vogan (Court Reporter).

Kid Galahad (1937). Warner Bros. 100 or 105 minutes. Directed by Michael Curtiz; executive producers, Jack L. Warner and Hal B. Wallis; associate producer, Samuel Bischoff; screenplay by Seton I. Miller, based on the 1936 novel by Francis Wallace; cinematography by Tony Gaudio; music by Heinz Roemheld and Max Steiner; edited by George Amy; dialogue direction by Irving Rapper; assistant director, Jack Sullivan; art direction by Jules Weyl; gowns by Orry-Kelly; music direction by Leo F. Forbstein; special effects by James Gibbons and Edwin B. DuPar; sound by Charles Lang; song *"The Moon Is in Tears Tonight,"* music and lyrics by M. K. Jerome and Jack Scholl.

Cast: Edward G. Robinson (Nick Donati), Bette Davis (Fluff [Louise Phillips]), Humphrey Bogart (Turkey Morgan), Wayne Morris (Ward Guisenberry), Jane Bryan (Marie Donati), Harry Carey (Silver Jackson), William Haade (Chuck McGraw), Soledad Jiminez (Mrs. Donati), Joe Cunningham (Joe Taylor), Ben Welden (Buzz Barett), Joseph Crehan (Brady), Veda Ann Borg (the Redhead), Frank Faylen (Barney), Harland Tucker (Gunman), Bob Evans (Sam), Hank Hankinson (Burke), Bob Nestell (O'Brien), Jack Kranz (Denbaugh), George Blake (Referee).

San Quentin (1937). First National/Warner Bros. 65 or 70 minutes. Directed by Lloyd Bacon; executive producers, Jack L. Warner and Hal B. Wallis; associate producer, Samuel Bischoff; screenplay by Peter Milne and Humphrey Cobb, based on a story by Robert Tasker and John Bright; cinematography by Charles Hickox; music by Heinz Roemheld, Charles Maxwell, and David Raskin; music direction by Leo F. Forbstein; edited by William Holmes; assistant director, Dick Mayberry; art direction by Esdras Hartley; costumes by Howard Shoup; special effects by James Gibbons and H. F. Koenekamp; sound by Everett A. Brown; song "How Could You?," music and lyrics by Harry Warren and Al Dubin.

Cast: Pat O'Brien (Captain Stephen Jameson), Humphrey Bogart (Joe "Red" Kennedy), Ann Sheridan (May Kennedy), Barton MacLane (Captain Druggin), Joseph Sawyer (Sailor Boy Hansen), Veda Ann Borg (Helen), James Robbins (Mickey Callahan), Joseph King (Warden Taylor), Gordon Oliver (Captain), Garry Owen (Dopey), Marc Lawrence (Venetti), Emmett Vogan (Lieutenant), William Pawley (Convict), Al Hill (Convict), Max Wagner (Prison Runner), George Lloyd (Convict), Ernie Adams (Fink).

Dead End (1937). United Artists. 90, 93, or 95 minutes. Directed by William Wyler; produced by Samuel Goldwyn; associate producer, Merritt Hulburd; screenplay by Lillian Hellman, based on the play by Sidney Kingsley; cinematography by Gregg Toland; edited by Daniel Mandell; music by Alfred Newman; dialogue direction by Edward P. Goodnow; assistant director, Eddie Bernaudy; art direction by Richard Day; set decoration by Julia Heron; costumes by Omar Kiam; special effects by James Basevi; sound by Frank Maher.

Cast: Sylvia Sidney (Drina Gordon), Joel McCrea (Dave Connell), Humphrey Bogart (Baby Face Martin), Wendy Barrie (Kay Burton), Claire Trevor (Francey), Allen Jenkins (Hunk), Marjorie Main (Mrs. Martin), Billy Halop (Tommy), Huntz Hall (Dippy), Bobby Jordan (Angel), Leo Gorcey (Spit), Gabriel Dell (T. B.), Bernard Punsley (Milty), Charles Peck (Philip Griswold), Minor Watson (Mr. Griswold), James Burke (Officer Mulligan), Ward Bond (Doorman), Elisabeth Risdon (Mrs. Connell), Esther Dale (Mrs. Fenner), George Humbert (Mr. Pascagli), Marcelle Corday (Governess), Alan Bridge, Robert Homans (Policemen), Thomas Jackson (Detective), Donald Barry (Intern), Charles Halton (Whitey).

Stand-in (1937). Walter Wanger Productions, Inc., released through United Artists. 91 minutes. Directed by Tay Garnett; produced by Walter Wanger; screenplay by Gene Towne and Graham Baker, based on the 1937 *Saturday Evening Post* serial by Clarence Budington Kelland; cinematography by Charles Clarke; music by Heinz Roemheld; edited by Otto Lovering and Dorothy Spencer; assistant director, Charles Kerr; art direction by Alexander Toluboff; costumes by Helen Taylor; sound by Paul Neal.

Cast: Leslie Howard (Atterbury Dodd), Joan Blondell (Lester Plum), Humphrey Bogart (Douglas Quintain), Alan Mowbray (Koslofski), Marle Shelton (Thelma Cheri), C. Henry Gordon (Ivor Nassau), Jack Carson (Potts), Tully Marshall (Fowler Pettypacker), J. C. Nugent (Pettypacker Jr.), William V. Mong (Cyrus Pettypacker), Art Baker (Director of Photography), Charles Middleton (Actor Dressed as Abraham Lincoln), Esther Howard (Landlady), Olin Howard (Hotel Manager), Charles Williams (Boarder), Pat Flaherty (Bouncer at Nightclub), Harry Myers (Bank Board Member), Anne O'Neal (Elvira's Mother), Theodore von Eltz (Sir Geoffrey in *Sex and Satan*), Harry Woods (Studio Employee).

Swing Your Lady (1938). Warner Bros. 72 or 79 minutes. Directed by Ray Enright; executive producers, Jack L. Warner and Hal B. Wallis; associate producer, Samuel Bischoff; screenplay by Joseph Schrank and Maurice Leo, based on the 1936 play by Kenyon Nicholson and Charles Robinson; cinematography by Arthur Edeson; music by Adolph Deutsch; edited by Jack Killifer; dialogue direction by Jo Graham; assistant director, Jesse Hibbs; art direction by Esdras Hartley; costumes by Howard Schoup; sound by Charles Lang; musical numbers created by Bobby Connolly; songs "Mountain Swingaroo," "Hillbilly from Tenth Avenue," "Swing Your Lady," "The Old Apple Tree," and "Dig Me a Grave in Missouri," music and lyrics by M. K. Jerome and Jack Scholl.

Cast: Humphrey Bogart (Ed Hatch), Frank McHugh (Popeye Bronson), Louise Fazenda (Sadie Horn), Nat Pendleton (Joe Skopapoulos), Penny Singleton (Cookie Shannon), Allen Jenkins (Shiner Ward), Leon Weaver (Waldo Davis), Frank Weaver (Ollie Davis), Elviry Weaver (Mrs. Davis), Ronald Reagan (Jack Miller), Daniel Boone Savage (Noah Webster), Hugh O'Connell (Smith), Tommy Bupp (Rufe Horn), Sonny Bupp (Len Horn), Joan Howard (Mattie Horn), Sue Moore (Mabel), Olin Howland (Hotel Proprietor), Sammy White (Specialty Dancer), Eddie Acuff (Roscoe Turner), Irving Bacon (Photographer), Vic Potel (Clem), Roger Gray (First Hillbilly), John "Skins" Miller (Second Hillbilly), Foy Van Dolsen, Frank Pharr (Hillbillies), George Over (Telegraph Operator), Georgia Simmons (Mountain Woman), June Gittleson (Fat Waitress).

Crime School (1938). First National/Warner Bros. 86 minutes. Directed by Lewis Seiler; executive producers, Jack L. Warner and Hal B. Wallis; associate producer, Bryan Foy; screenplay by Crane Wilbur and Vincent Sherman, based on a story by Crane Wilbur; cinematography by Arthur Todd; music by Max Steiner; edited by Terry Morse; dialogue direction by Vincent Sherman; assistant director, Fred Taylor; art direction by Charles Novi; gowns by N'Was McKenzie; sound by Francis J. Scheid.

Cast: Humphrey Bogart (Mark Braden), Gale Page (Sue Warren), Billy Halop (Frankie Warren), Huntz Hall (Goofy), Leo Gorcey (Spike Hawkins), Bernard Punsley (Fats Papadopolos), Gabriel Dell (Bugs Burke), George Offerman Jr. (Red), Weldon Heyburn (Cooper), Cy Kendall (Morgan), Charles Trowbridge (Judge Clinton), Spencer Charters (Old Doctor), Donald Briggs (New Doctor), Frank Jacquet (Commissioner), Helen MacKellar (Mrs. Burke), Al Bridge (Mr. Burke), Sibyl Harris (Mrs. Hawkins), Paul Porcasi (Nick Papadopolos), Frank Otto (Junkie), Ed Gargan (Officer Hogan), James B. Carson (Schwartz), Milburn Stone (Joe Delaney), Harry Cording (Second Guard).

Men Are Such Fools (1938). Warner Bros. 66 or 70 minutes. Directed by Busby Berkeley; executive producers, Jack L. Warner and Hal B. Wallis; associate producer, David Lewis; screenplay by Norman Reilly Raine and Horace Jackson, based on the novel by Faith Baldwin; cinematography by Sid Hickox; music by Heinz Roemheld; music direction by Leo F. Forbstein; edited by Jack Killifer; dialogue direction by Jo Graham; assistant director, Chuck Hansen; art direction by Max Parker; gowns by Howard Shoup; sound by Stanley Jones; orchestration by Ray Heindorf.

Cast: Wayne Morris (Jimmy Hall), Priscilla Lane (Linda Lawrence), Humphrey Bogart (Harry Galleon), Hugh Herbert (Harvey Bates), Penny Singleton

(Nancy), Johnnie Davis (Tad), Mona Barrie (Beatrice Harris), Marcia Ralston (Wanda Townsend), Gene Lockhart (Bill Dalton), Kathleen Lockhart (Mrs. Dalton), Donald Briggs (George Onslow), Renie Riano (Mrs. Pinkle), Claude Allister (Rudolf), Nedda Harrigan (Mrs. Nelson), Eric Stanley (Mr. Nelson), James Nolan (Bill Collyer), Carole Landis (June Cooper), Jean Benedict, Fern Barry, Rosella Towne (Secretaries), Leyland Hodgson (Ronald Ainsworth), Bruce Warren (Charlie Allen), Lois Lindsay (Anita), Diana Lewis (Telephone Operator), John Harron (Toni Bellamy), Ken Niles (Radio Announcer).

The Amazing Dr. Clitterhouse (1938). First National/Warner Bros. 87 minutes. Directed by Anatole Litvak; produced by Gilbert Miller; executive producers, Jack L. Warner and Hal B. Wallis; associate producer, Robert Lord; screenplay by John Wexley and John Huston, based on the 1937 play by Barré Lyndon; cinematography by Tony Gaudio; music by Max Steiner; music direction by Leo F. Forbstein; edited by Warren Low; dialogue direction by Jo Graham; assistant director, Jack Sullivan; art direction by Jules Weyl; costumes by Milo Anderson; sound by C. A. Riggs; technical adviser, Dr. Leo Schulman:

Cast: Edward G. Robinson (Dr. Clitterhouse), Claire Trevor (Jo Keller), Humphrey Bogart (Rocks Valentine), Allen Jenkins (Okay), Donald Crisp (Inspector Lane), Gale Page (Nurse Randolph), Henry O'Neill (Judge), John Litel (Prosecuting Attorney), Thurston Hall (Grant), Maxie Rosenbloom (Butch), Bert Hanlon (Pal), Curt Bois (Rabbit), Ward Bond (Tug), Vladimir Sokoloff (Popus), Billy Wayne (Candy), Robert Homans (Lieutenant Johnson), Irving Bacon (Jury Foreman), Georgia Caine (Mrs. Updyke), Romaine Callender (Butler), Mary Field (Maid).

Racket Busters (1938). Warner Bros./Cosmopolitan. 65 or 71 minutes. Directed by Lloyd Bacon; executive producers, Jack L. Warner and Hal B. Wallis; associate producer, Samuel Bischoff; screenplay by Robert Rossen and Leonardo Bercovici; cinematography by Arthur Edeson; music by Adolph Deutsch; edited by James Gibbon; assistant director, Dick Mayberry; art direction by Esdras Hartley; gowns by Howard Schoup; sound by Robert B. Lee; music direction by Leo F. Forbstein; orchestration by Hugo Friedhofer.

Cast: Humphrey Bogart (Pete Martin), George Brent (Denny Jordan), Gloria Dickson (Nora Jordon), Allen Jenkins (Horse Wilson), Walter Abel (Thomas Allison), Henry O'Neill (Governor), Penny Singleton (Gladys), Anthony Averill (Crane), Oscar O'Shea (Pop Wilson), Elliott Sullivan (Charlie Smith), Fay Helm (Mrs. Smith), Joseph Downing (Joe), Norman Willis (Gus), Don Rowan (Kimball), Nary Currier (Mrs. Allison), Wedgewood Nowell (Businessman), Bruce Mitchell (Deputy), Jack Goodrich (Clerk).

Angels with Dirty Faces (1938). First National/Warner Bros. 97 minutes. Directed by Michael Curtiz; produced by Samuel Bischoff; executive producers,

Jack L. Warner and Hal B. Wallis; screenplay by John Wexley and Warren Duff, based on a story by Rowland Brown; cinematography by Sol Polito; music by Max Steiner, edited by Owen Marks; dialogue direction by Jo Graham; assistant director, Sherry Shourds; art direction by Robert Haas; gowns by Orry-Kelly; music direction by Leo F. Forbstein; orchestration by Hugo Friedhofer; sound by Everett A. Brown; technical adviser, Father J. J. Devlin.

Cast: James Cagney (Rocky Sullivan), Pat O'Brien (Jerry Connolly), Humphrey Bogart (James Frazier), Ann Sheridan (Laury Ferguson), George Bancroft (Mac Keefer), Billy Halop (Soapy), Bobby Jordan (Swing), Leo Gorcey (Bim), Gabriel Dell (Pasty), Huntz Hall (Crab), Bernard Punsley (Hunky), Joseph Downing (Steve), Edward Pawley (Edwards), Adrian Morris (Blackie), Frankie Burke (Rocky as a Child), William Tracy (Jerry as a Child), Marilyn Knowlden (Laury as a Child), Oscar O'Shea (Kennedy), William Pawley (Bugs), Theodore Reid, Charles Sullivan (Gunmen), John Hamilton (Police Captain), Earl Dwire (Priest), William Worthington (Warden), and the St. Brendan's Church Choir.

King of the Underworld (1939). A Warner Bros. Picture; Jack L. Warner in charge of production. 69 minutes. Directed by Lewis Seiler; associate producer, Bryan Foy; screenplay by George Bricker and Vincent Sherman, based on the *Liberty Magazine* serial *Dr. Socrates* by W. R. Burnett; cinematography by Sid Hickox; music direction by Leo F. Forbstein; music by Heinz Roemheld; edited by Frank Dewar; dialogue direction by Vincent Sherman; assistant director, Frank Heath; art direction by Charles Novi; costumes by Orry-Kelly; sound by Everett A. Brown.

Cast: Humphrey Bogart (Joe Gurney), Kay Francis (Dr. Carol Nelson), James Stephenson (Bill Stevens), John Eldredge (Dr. Niles Nelson), Jessie Busley (Aunt Margaret), Arthur Aylesworth (Dr. Sanders), Raymond Brown (Sheriff), Harland Tucker (Mr. Ames), Ralph Remley (Mr. Robert), Charley Foy (Slick), Murray Alper (Eddie), Joe Devlin (Porky), Elliott Sullivan (Mugsy), Alan Davis (Pete), John Harmon (Slats), John Ridgely (Jerry), Richard Bond (Intern), Pierre Watkin (District Attorney), Charles Trowbridge (Dr. Ryan), Edwin Stanley (Dr. Jacobs), Herbert Heywood (Clem), Paul MacWilliams (Anesthetist), Richard Quine (Student).

The Oklahoma Kid (1939). Warner Bros. 85 minutes. Directed by Lloyd Bacon; executive producers, Jack L. Warner and Hal B. Wallis; associate producer, Samuel Bischoff; screenplay by Warren Duff, Robert Buckner, and Edward E. Paramore, based on a story by Edward E. Paramore and Wally Klein; cinematography by James Wong Howe; music direction by Leo F. Forbstein; music by Max Steiner; edited by Owen Marks; assistant director, Dick Mayberry; art direction by Esdras Hartley; costumes by Orry-Kelly; sound by Stanley Jones.

Cast: James Cagney (Jim Kincaid, the Oklahoma Kid), Humphrey Bogart (Whip McCord), Rosemary Lane (Jane Hardwick), Donald Crisp (Judge Hardwick), Hugh Sothern (John Kincaid), Harry Stephens (Ned Kincaid), Charles Middleton (Alec Martin), Edward Pawley (Doolin), Ward Bond (Wes Handley), Lew Harvey (Curley), Trevor Bardette (Indian Jack Pascoe), John Miljan (Ringo), Arthur Aylesworth (Judge Morgan), Irving Bacon (Hotel Clerk), Joe Devlin (Keely), Wade Boteler (Sheriff Abe Collins).

Dark Victory (1939). Warner Bros. Pictures, Inc.; Jack L. Warner in charge of production. A First National Picture. 105 minutes. Directed by Edmund Goulding; associate producer, David Lewis; screenplay by Casey Robinson, based on the play by George Emerson Brewer Jr. and Bertram Bloch; cinematography by Ernest Haller; music direction by Leo F. Forbstein; music by Max Steiner; edited by William Holmes; assistant director, Frank Heath; art direction by Robert Haas; costumes by Orry-Kelly; sound by Robert B. Lee; song "Oh, Give Me Time for Tenderness," music and lyrics by Elsie Janis and Edmund Goulding.

Cast: Bette Davis (Judith Traherne), George Brent (Dr. Frederick Steele), Humphrey Bogart (Michael O'Leary), Geraldine Fitzgerald (Ann King), Ronald Reagan (Alec Hamm), Henry Travers (Dr. Parsons), Cora Witherspoon (Carrie Spottswood), Dorothy Peterson (Miss Wainwright), Virginia Brissac (Martha), Charles Richman (Colonel Mantle), Herbert Rawlinson (Dr. Carter), Leonard Mudie (Dr. Driscoll), Fay Helm (Miss Dodd), Lottie Williams (Lucy), Jack Mower (Veterinarian).

You Can't Get Away with Murder (1939). First National/Warner Bros. 78 minutes. Directed by Lewis Seiler; associate producer, Samuel Bischoff; screenplay by Robert Buckner, Don Ryan, and Kenneth Gamet, based on the play *Chalked Out* by Warden Lewis and Jonathan Finn; cinematography by Sol Polito; music by Heinz Roemheld; edited by James Gibbon; dialogue direction by Jo Graham; assistant director, William Kissel; art direction by Hugh Reticker; costumes by Milo Anderson; sound by Francis J. Scheid.

Cast: Humphrey Bogart (Frank Wilson), Billy Halop (Johnnie Stone), Gale Page (Madge Stone), John Litel (Attorney Carey), Henry Travers (Pop), Harvey Stephens (Fred Burke), Harold Huber (Scrappa), Joseph Sawyer (Red), Joseph Downing (Smitty), George E. Stone (Toad), Joseph King (Principal Keeper), Joseph Crehan (Warden), John Ridgely (Gas Station Attendant), Herbert Rawlinson (District Attorney), William Worthington (First Specialist), Alexander Leftwich (Second Specialist), Ila Rhodes (Secretary), Stuart Holmes (Doctor), Frank Darien (Anxious Little Man), Sidney Bracy (Bartender), Rosella Towne (Girl in Box), Edgar Edwards (Trainer).

The Roaring Twenties (1939). Warner Bros. Pictures, Inc.; Jack L. Warner in charge of production. 106 minutes. Directed by Raoul Walsh; executive producer, Hal B. Wallis; associate producer, Samuel Bischoff; screenplay by Jerry Wald, Richard Macaulay; and Robert Rossen, based on a story by Mark Hellinger; cinematography by Ernest Haller; music direction by Leo F. Forbstein; music by Heinz Roemheld and Ray Heindorf; edited by Jack Killifer; dialogue direction by Hugh Cummings; assistant director, Dick Mayberry; art direction by Max Parker; costumes by Milo Anderson; special effects by Byron Haskin and Edwin B. DuPar; sound by Everett A. Brown.

Cast: James Cagney (Eddie Bartlett), Priscilla Lane (Jean Sherman), Humphrey Bogart (George Hally), Gladys George (Panama Smith), Jeffrey Lynn (Lloyd Hart), Frank McHugh (Danny Green), Paul Kelly (Nick Brown), Elisabeth Risdon (Mrs. Sherman), Edward Keane (Pete Henderson), Joe Sawyer (Sargent Pete Jones), Joseph Crehan (Mr. Fletcher), George Meeker (Masters), John Hamilton (Judge), Robert Elliott (First Detective), Eddie Chandler (Second Detective), Abner Bieberman (Lefty), Vera Lewis (Mrs. Gray), Elliott Sullivan (Eddie's Cellmate), Bert Hanlon (Piano Accompanist), Murray Alper (First Mechanic), Dick Wessel (Second Mechanic), George Humbert (Restaurant Proprietor), Ben Welden (Tavern Proprietor), John Deering (Commentator), Ray Cooke (Orderly), Norman Willis (Bootlegger), Pat O'Malley (Jailer).

The Return of Dr. X (1939). First National/Warner Bros. 60 minutes. Directed by Vincent Sherman; executive producers, Jack L. Warner and Hal B. Wallis; associate producer, Bryan Foy; screenplay by Lee Katz, based on the story "The Doctor's Secret" by William J. Makin in the July 30, 1938, issue of *Detective Fiction Weekly;* cinematography by Sid Hickox; music by Bernhard Kaun; edited by Thomas Pratt; dialogue direction by John Langan; assistant director, Dick Mayberry; art direction by Esdras Hartley; costumes by Milo Anderson; makeup by Perc Westmore; sound by Charles Lang.

Cast: Humphrey Bogart (Marshall Quesne, alias Dr. Xavier), Wayne Morris (Walter Barnett), Rosemary Lane (Joan Vance), Dennis Morgan (Dr. Michael Rhodes), John Litel (Dr. Francis Flegg), Lya Lys (Angela Merrova), Huntz Hall (Pinky), Charles Wilson (Detective Ray Kincaid), Vera Lewis (Miss Sweetman), Howard Hickman (Chairman), Olin Howland (Undertaker), Arthur Aylesworth (Guide), Jack Mower (Detective Sergeant Moran), Creighton Hale (Hotel Manager), John Ridgely (Stanley Rodgers), Joseph Crehan (Editor), Glenn Langan (Intern), William Hopper (Intern).

Invisible Stripes (1939). Warner Bros. Pictures, Inc.; Jack L. Warner in charge of production. A Warner Bros.–First National Picture. 81 minutes. Directed by Lloyd Bacon; executive producer, Hal B. Wallis; associate producer, Louis F. Edelman; screenplay by Warren Duff, from a story by Jonathan Finn, based on the 1938 book by Warden Lewis E. Lawes; cinematography by Ernest Haller; music by Heinz Roemheld; edited by James Gibbon; dialogue direction by Irving Rapper; assistant director, Elmer Decker; art direction by Max Parker; costumes by Milo Anderson; special effects by Byron Haskin.

Cast: George Raft (Cliff Taylor), Jane Bryan (Peggy), William Holden

(Tim Taylor), Humphrey Bogart (Chuck Martin), Flora Robson (Mrs. Taylor), Paul Kelly (Ed Kruger), Lee Patrick (Molly), Henry O'Neill (Parole Officer Masters), Frankie Thomas (Tommy), Moroni Olsen (Warden), Margot Stevenson (Sue), Marc Lawrence (Lefty), Joseph Downing (Johnny), Leo Gorcey (Jimmy), William Haade (Shrank), Tully Marshall (Old Peter), Chester Clute (Mr. Butler), Jack Mower (Guard in Charge), Frank Mayo (Guard at Gate), George Taylor (Pauly), Frank Bruno (Smitty), John Irwin (Prisoner).

Virginia City (1940). Warner Bros. Pictures, Inc.; Jack L. Warner in charge of production. A Warner Bros.–First National Picture. 115 or 121 minutes. Directed by Michael Curtiz; executive producer, Hal B. Wallis; associate producer, Robert Fellows; screenplay by Robert Buckner; cinematography by Sol Polito; music direction by Leo F. Forbstein; music by Max Steiner; edited by George Amy; dialogue direction by Jo Graham; assistant director, Sherry Shourds; art direction by Ted Smith; special effects by Byron Haskin and H. F. Koenekamp; sound by Oliver S. Garrettson and Francis J. Scheid.

Cast: Errol Flynn (Kerry Bradford), Miriam Hopkins (Julia Hayne), Randolph Scott (Vance Irby), Humphrey Bogart (John Murrell), Frank McHugh (Mr. Upjohn), Alan Hale (Olaf "Moose" Swenson), Guinn "Big Boy" Williams (Marblehead), John Litel (Marshall), Douglas Dumbrille (Major Drewery), Moroni Olsen (Dr. Cameron), Russell Hicks (Armistead), Dickie Jones (Cobby), Frank Wilcox (Union Soldier), Russell Simpson (Gaylord), Victor Kilian (Abraham Lincoln), Charles Middleton (Jefferson Davis), Monte Montague (Stage Driver), George Regas (Halfbreed), Thurston Hall (General Meade), Brandon Tyman (Trenholm), Ward Bond, Reed Howes, Norman Willis, Walter Miller (Sergeants).

It All Came True (1940). A Warner Bros.–First National Picture. 97 minutes. Directed by Lewis Seiler; executive producers, Jack L. Warner and Hal B. Wallis; associate producer, Mark Hellinger; screenplay by Michael Fessier and Lawrence Kimble, based on the 1936 story "Better than Life" by Louis Bromfield; cinematography by Ernest Haller; music by Heinz Roemheld; edited by Thomas Richards; dialogue direction by Robert Foulk; assistant director, Russ Saunders; art direction by Max Parker; music direction by Leo F. Forbstein; orchestration by Ray Heindorf; gowns by Howard Schoup; special effects by Byron Haskin and Edwin B. DuPar; sound by Dolph Thomas; dance direction by Dave Gould; songs "Angel in Disguise," words and music by Kim Gannon, Stephen Weiss, and Paul Mann, and "The Gaucho Serenade," words and music by James Cavanaugh, John Redmond, and Nat Simon.

Cast: Ann Sheridan (Sarah Jane Ryan), Jeffrey Lynn (Tommy Taylor), Humphrey Bogart (Grasselli/Chips Maguire), ZaSu Pitts (Miss Flint), Una O'Conner (Maggie Ryan), Jessie Busley (Norah Taylor), John Litel (Mr. Roberts), Grant Mitchell (Mr. Salmon), Felix Bressart (Mr. Boldini), Charles Judels

(Leantopopulos), Brandon Tynan (Mr. Van Diver), Howard Hickman (Mr. Prendergast), Herbert Vigran (Monks), Tommy Reilly, the Elderbloom Chorus, Bender and Daum, White and Stanley, the Lady Killers Quartet.

Brother Orchid (1940). Warner Bros. Pictures, Inc.; Jack L. Warner in charge of production. A Warner Bros.–First National picture. 88 minutes. Directed by Lloyd Bacon; executive producer, Hal B. Wallis; associate producer, Mark Hellinger; screenplay by Earl Baldwin, based on the May 21, 1938, *Collier's* magazine story by Richard Connell; cinematography by Tony Gaudio; music direction by Leo F. Forbstein; music by Heinz Roemheld; edited by William Holmes; dialogue direction by Hugh Cummings; assistant director, Dick Mayberry; art direction by Max Parker; costumes by Howard Shoup; makeup by Perc Westmore; special effects by Byron Haskin; Willard Van Enger and Edwin DuPar; montages by Don Siegel and Robert Burks; sound by C. A. Riggs.

Cast: Edward G. Robinson (Little John Sarto [Brother Orchid]), Ann Sothern (Flo Addams), Humphrey Bogart (Jack Buck), Donald Crisp (Brother Superior), Ralph Bellamy (Clarence Fletcher), Allen Jenkins (Willie the Knife), Charles D. Brown (Brother Wren), Cecil Kellaway (Brother Goodwin), Morgan Conway (Philadelphia Powell), Richard Lane (Mugsy O'Day), Paul Guilfoyle (Red Martin), John Ridgely (Texas Pearson), Joseph Crehan (Brother MacEwen), Wilfred Lucas (Brother MacDonald), Tom Tyler (Curley Matthews), Dick Wessel (Buffalo Burns), Granville Bates (Pattonsville Superintendent), Paul Phillips (French Frank), Don Rowan (Al Muller), Nanette Vallon (Fifi), Tim Ryan (Turkey Malone), Joe Caites (Handsome Harry), Pat Gleason (Dopey Perkins), Tommy Baker (Joseph), G. Pat Collins (Tim O'Hara), John Qualen (Mr. Pigeon), Leonard Mudie, Charles Coleman (Englishmen), Edgar Norton (Meadows).

They Drive by Night (1940). Warner Bros. Pictures, Inc.; Jack L. Warner in charge of production. A Warner Bros.–First National picture. 93 minutes. Directed by Raoul Walsh; executive producer, Hal B. Wallis; associate producer, Mark Hellinger; screenplay by Jerry Wald and Richard Macaulay, based on the 1938 novel *Long Haul* by A. I. Bezzerides; cinematography by Arthur Edeson; music direction by Leo F. Forbstein; music by Adolph Deutsch; edited by Thomas Richards; dialogue direction by Hugh MacMullen; assistant director, Elmer Decker; art direction by John Hughes; costumes by Milo Anderson; makeup by Perc Westmore; special effects by Byron Haskin, H. F. Koenekamp, James Gibbons, John Holden, and Edwin DuPar; montages by Don Siegel and Robert Burks; sound recording by Oliver S. Garretson; orchestration by Arthur Lange.

Cast: George Raft (Joe Fabrini), Ann Sheridan (Cassie Hartley), Ida Lupino (Lana Carlsen), Humphrey Bogart (Paul Fabrini), Gale Page (Pearl Fabrini), Alan Hale (Ed Carlsen), Roscoe Karns (Irish McGurn), John Litel (Harry McNamara), George Tobias (George Rondolos), Henry O'Neill (District Attorney),

Paul Hurst (Pete Haig), Charles Halton (Farnsworth), John Ridgley (Hank Dawson), George Lloyd (Barney), Joyce Compton (Sue Carter), Charles Wilson (Mike Williams), Pedro Regas (McNamara's Helper), Norman Willia (Neves), Joe Devlin (Fatso), William Haade (Driver), Vera Lewis (Landlady), John Hamilton (Defense Attorney), Dorothea Kent (Sue), Lillian Yarbo (Chloe), Eddy Chandler (Truck Driver), Mack Gray (Mike), Max Wagner (Sweeney), Wilfred Lucas (Bailiff), Joe Hamilton (Defense Attorney), Howard Hickman (Judge).

High Sierra (1941). A Warner Bros.–First National Picture. 100 minutes. Directed by Raoul Walsh; executive producer, Hal B. Wallis; associate producer, Mark Hellinger; screenplay by John Huston and W. R. Burnett, based on the novel by W. R. Burnett; cinematography by Tony Gaudio; music direction by Leo F. Forbstein; music by Adolph Deutsch; edited by Jack Killifer; dialogue direction by Irving Rapper; art direction by Ted Smith; gowns by Milo Anderson; makeup by Perc Westmore; special effects by Byron Haskin and H. F. Koenekamp; sound by Dolph Thomas; orchestration by Arthur Lange.

Cast: Ida Lupino (Marie Garson), Humphrey Bogart (Roy Earle), Alan Curtis (Babe Kozak), Arthur Kennedy (Red Hattery), Joan Leslie (Velma), Henry Hull (Doc Banton), Barton MacLane (Jake Kranmer), Henry Travers (Pa Goodhue), Elisabeth Risdon (Ma Goodhue), Jerome Cowan (Healy), Cornel Wilde (Louis Mendoza), Minna Gombell (Mrs. Baughman), Paul Harvey (Mr. Baughman), John Eldredge (Lon Preiser), Donald MacBride (Big Mac), Isabel Jewell(Blonde), Willie Best (Algernon), Spencer Charters (Ed), George Meeker (Pfiffer), Robert Strange (Art), Sam Hayes (Announcer), Arthur Aylesworth (Auto Court Owner), Wade Boteler (Sheriff), Erville Alderson (Farmer), Cliff Saum (Shaw), Eddy Chandler (Policeman), Richard Clayton (Bellboy), Louis Jean Heydt (Tourist), Dorothy Appleby (Margie), Gary Owen (Joe), Eddie Acuff (Bus Driver), Harry Hayden (Druggist), Carl Harbaugh (Fisherman), Pard the Dog (Zero the Dog).

The Wagons Roll at Night (1941). A Warner Bros.–First National Picture. 84 minutes. Directed by Ray Enright; executive producers, Jack L. Warner and Hal B. Wallis; associate producer, Harlan Thompson; screenplay by Fred Niblo Jr. and Barry Trivers, based on the novel *Kid Galahad* by Francis Wallace; cinematography by Sid Hickox; music by Heinz Roemheld; edited by Frederick Richards; assistant director, Jesse Hibbs; art direction by Hugh Reticker; special effects by Byron Haskin and H. F. Koenekamp; orchestration by Ray Heindorf.

Cast: Humphrey Bogart (Nick Coster), Sylvia Sidney (Flo Lorraine), Eddie Albert (Matt Varney), Joan Leslie (Mary Coster), Sig Rumann (Hoffman the Great), Cliff Clark (Doc), Charley Foy (Snapper), Frank Wilcox (Tex), John Ridgely (Arch), Clara Blandick (Mrs. Williams), Aldrich Bowker (Mr. Williams), Garry Owen (Gus), Jack Mower (Bundy), Frank Mayo (Wally), Tom Wilson, Al Herman, George Riley, Cliff Saum (Barkers), Eddie Acuff (Man), George

Gube (Deputy Sheriff), Jimmy Fox (Customer), Grace Hayle (Mrs. Grebnick), Beverly Quintanilla, Barbara Quintanilla (Baby), Richard Elliott (Mr. Paddleford), John Dilson (Minister), Ted Oliver (Sheriff), Fay Helm (Wife), Anthony Nace (Husband), Freddy Walburn, Buster Phelps, Bradley Hall, Tom Braunger, Robert Winkler, Harry Harvey Jr., George Ovey (Boys).

The Maltese Falcon (1941). A Warner Bros.–First National Picture. 100 minutes. Directed by John Huston; executiver producer, Hal. B. Wallis; associate producer, Henry Blanke; screenplay by John Huston, based on the novel by Dashiell Hammett; cinematography by Arthur Edeson; music direction by Leo F. Forbstein; music by Adolph Deutsch; edited by Thomas Richards; dialogue direction by Robert Foulk; assistant director, Claude Archer; art direction by Robert Haas; gowns by Orry-Kelly; makeup by Perc Westmore; sound by Oliver S. Garretson; orchestration by Arthur Lange.

Cast: Humphrey Bogart (Sam Spade), Mary Astor (Brigid O'Shaughnessy), Gladys George (Iva Archer), Peter Lorre (Joel Cairo), Barton MacLane (Lieutenant Dundy), Lee Patrick (Effie Perine), Sydney Greenstreet (Casper Gutman), Ward Bond (Detective Tom Polhaus), Jerome Cowan (Miles Archer), Elisha Cook Jr. (Wilmer Cook), James Burke (Luke), Murray Alper (Frank Richman), John Hamilton (District Attorney Bryan), Emory Parnell (Mate of the *La Paloma*), Walter Huston (Captain Jacobi), Robert Homas (Policeman), Creighton Hall (Stenographer), Charles Drake, Bill Hopper, Hank Mann (Reporters), Jack Mower (Announcer).

All Through the Night (1942). A Warner Bros.–First National Picture. 107 minutes. Directed by Vincent Sherman; produced by Jerry Wald; executive producer, Hal B. Wallis; screenplay by Leonard Spigelgass and Edwin Gilbert, based on an original story by Leonard Q. Ross (Leo Rosten) and Leonard Spigelgass; cinematography by Sid Hickox; music by Adolph Deutsch; edited by Rudi Fehr; assistant director, William Kissel; art direction by Max Parker; special effects by Edwin DuPar; sound by Oliver S. Garretson; orchestration by Frank Perkins; songs "All Through the Night," words and music by Johnny Mercer and Arthur Schwartz, and "Cherie, I Love You So," words and music by Lillian Goodman.

Cast: Humphrey Bogart (Gloves Donahue), Conrad Veidt (Hal Ebbing), Kaaren Verne (Leda Hamilton), Jane Darwell (Ma Donahue), Frank McHugh (Barney), Peter Lorre (Pepi), Judith Anderson (Madame), William Demarest (Sunshine), Jackie Gleason (Starchie), Phil Silvers (Waiter), Wallace Ford (Spats Hunter), Barton MacLane (Marty Callahan), Edward Brophy (Joe Denning), Martin Kosleck (Steindorff), Jean Ames (Annabelle), Ludwig Stossel (Mr. Miller), Irene Seidner (Mrs. Miller), James Burke (Forbes), Ben Welden (Smitty), Hans Schumm (Anton), Charles Cane (Spence), Frank Sully (Sage), Sam McDaniel (Deacon).

The Big Shot (1942). A Warner Bros.–First National Picture. 82 minutes. Directed by Lewis Seiler; produced by Walter MacEwen; original screenplay by Bertram Millhauser, Abem Finkel, and Daniel Fuchs; cinematography by Sid Hickox; music by Adolph Deutsch; edited by Jack Killifer; dialogue direction by Harold Winston; assistant director, Art Lueker; art direction by John Hughes; gowns by Milo Anderson; makup by Perc Westmore; sound by Stanley Jones; orchestration by Jerome Moross.

Cast: Humphrey Bogart (Duke Berne), Irene Manning (Lorna Fleming), Richard Travis (George Anderson), Susan Peters (Ruth Carter), Stanley Ridges (Martin Fleming), Minor Watson (Warden Booth), Chick Chandler (Dancer), Joseph Downing (Frenchy), Howard da Silva (Sandor), Murray Alper (Quinto), Roland Drew (Faye), John Ridgely (Tim), Joseph King (Toohey), John Hamilton (Judge), Virginia Brissas (Mrs. Booth), William Edmunds (Sarto), Virginia Sale (Mrs. Miggs), Ken Christy (Kat), Wallace Scott (Rusty).

Across the Pacific (1942). A Warner Bros.–First National Picture. 97 minutes. Directed by John Huston; produced by Jerry Wald and Jack Saper; screenplay by Richard Macaulay [final scenes by Vincent Sherman, uncredited], based on the Saturday Evening Post serial Aloha Means Goodbye by Robert Carson; cinematography by Arthur Edeson; music by Adolph Deutsch; edited by Frank Magee; dialogue direction by Edward Blatt; assistant director, Lee Katz; art direction by Robert Haas and Hugh Reticker; gowns by Milo Anderson; makeup by Perc Westmore; special effects by Byron Haskin and Willard Van Enger; montages by Don Siegel; sound by Everett A. Brown; orchestration by Clifford Vaughan.

Cast: Humphrey Bogart (Richard Thomas Leland), Mary Astor (Alberta Marlow), Sydney Greenstreet (Dr. Lorenz), Charles Halton (A. V. Smith), Victor Sen Yung (Joe Totsukio), Roland Got (Sugi), Lee Tung Foo (Sam Wing On), Frank Wilcox (Captain Morrison), Paul Stanton (Colonel Hart), Lester Matthews (Canadian Major), John Hamilton (Court-martial President), Tom Stevenson (Tall Thin Man), Roland Drew (Captain Harkness), Monte Blue (Dan Morton), Chester Gan (Captain Higoto), Richard Loo (First Officer Miyuma), Keye Luke (Steamship Office Clerk), Kam Tong (T. Oki), Spencer Chan (Chief Engineer Mitsudo), Rudy Robles (Filipino Assassin), Bill Hopper (Orderly), Philip Ahn (Informer in Theater), Frank Mayo (Trial Judge Advocate), Garland Smith, Dick French, Charles Drake, Will Morgan (Officers), Roland Drew (Captain Harkness), Jack Mower (Major), Eddie Drew (Man), Frank Faylen (Barker), Ruth Ford (Secretary), Eddie Lee (Chinese Clerk), Dick Botiller (Waiter), Beal Wong (Usher), James Leong (Nura), Paul Fung (Japanese Radio Operator), Gordon De Main (Dock Official), Peter Lorre [uncredited] (Waiter).

Casablanca (1942). A Warner Bros.–First National Picture. 102 minutes. Directed by Michael Curtiz; produced by Hal B. Wallis; screenplay by Julius J. and

Philip G. Epstein and Howard Koch, based on the unproduced play *Everybody Comes to Rick's* by Murray Burnett and Joan Alison; cinematography by Arthur Edeson; music by Max Steiner; music direction by Leo F. Forbstein; edited by Owen Marks; dialogue direction by Hugh MacMullen; assistant director, Lee Katz; art direction by Carl Jules Weyl; set decoration by George James Hopkins; gowns by Orry-Kelly; makeup by Perc Westmore; special effects by Lawrence Butler and Willard Van Enger; montages by Don Siegel and James Leicester; sound by Francis J. Scheid; orchestration by Hugo Friedhofer; songs "As Time Goes By," music and lyrics by Herman Hupfield, and "Knock on Wood," "That's What Noah Done," and "Muse's Call," music and lyrics by M. K. Jerome and Jack Scholl; technical adviser, Robert Aisner; narrated by Lou Marcelle.

Cast: Humphrey Bogart (Richard Blaine), Ingrid Bergman (Ilsa), Paul Heinreid (Victor Laszlo), Claude Rains (Captain Louis Renault), Conrad Veidt (Major Heinrich Strasser), Sydney Greenstreet (Señor Farrari), Peter Lorre (Ugarte), S. Z. Sakall (Carl), Madeleine LeBeau (Yvonne), Dooley Wilson (Sam), Joy Page (Annina Brandel), John Qualen (Berger), Leonid Kinsky (Sascha), Helmut Dantine (Jan Brandel), Curt Bois (Pickpocket), Marcel Dalio (Emil, the Croupier), Corinna Mura (Singer), Ludwig Stossel (Mr. Leuchtag), Ilka Gruning (Mrs. Leuchtag), Charles La Torre (Officer Tonelli), Frank Puglia (Arab Vendor), Dan Seymour (Abdul), Oliver Prickett (Blue Parrot Waiter), Gregory Gaye (German Banker), Oliver Blake (German Banker), George Meeker (Friend), William Edmunds (Contact), Torben Meyer (Banker), Gino Corrado (Waiter), George Dee (Casselle), Norma Varden (Englishwoman), Michael Mark (Vendor), Leo Mostovy (Fydor), Richard Ryen (Heinz), Martin Garralaga (Headwaiter), Olaf Hytten (Prosperous Man), Leon Belasco (Dealer), Paul Porcasi (Native), Hans von Twardowski (German Officer), Albert Morin (French Officer), Creighton Hale (Customer), Henry Rowland (German Officer), Louis Mercier (Smuggler).

Action in the North Atlantic (1943). A Warner Bros.–First National Picture. 126 minutes. Directed by Lloyd Bacon; produced by Jerry Wald; screenplay by John Howard Lawson, additional dialogue by A. I. Bezzerides and W. R. Burnett, based on the novel by Guy Gilpatric; cinematography by Ted McCord; music by Adolph Deutsch; edited by Thomas Pratt and George Amy; dialogue direction by Harold Winston; assistant director, Reggie Callow; art direction by Ted Smith; set decoration by Clarence I. Steensen; costumes by Milo Anderson; makeup by Perc Westmore; special effects by Jack Cosgrove and Edwin B. DuPar; montages by Don Siegel and James Leicester; sound by C. A. Riggs; orchestration by Jerome Moross.

Cast: Humphrey Bogart (First Mate Joe Rossi), Raymond Massey (Captain Steve Jarvis), Alan Hale (Boats O'Hara), Julie Bishop (Pearl), Ruth Gordon (Mrs. Jarvis), Sam Levene (Chips Abrams), Dane Clark (Johnny Pulaski), Peter Whitney (Whitey Lara), Dick Hogan (Cadet Robert Parker), Minor Watson (Rear

Admiral Hartridge), J. M. Kerrigan (Caviar Jinks), Kane Richmond (Ensign Wright), William von Brincken (German Submarine Captain), Chick Chandler (Goldberg), George Offerman Jr. (Cecil), Don Douglas (Lieutenant Commander), Art Foster (Pete Larson), Ray Montgomery (Aherne), Glenn Strange (Tex Mathews), Creighton Hale (Sparks), Elliott Sullivan (Hennessy), Alec Craig (McGonigle), Ludwig Stossel (Captain Ziemer), Dick Wessel (Cherub), Frank Puglia (Captain Carpolis), Iris Adrian (Jenny O'Hara), Irving Bacon (Bartender), James Flavin (Lieutenant Commander).

Thank Your Lucky Stars (1943). A Warner Bros.–First National Picture. 127 minutes. Directed by David Butler; produced by Mark Hellinger; screenplay by Norman Panama and Melvin Frank, and James V. Kern, based on an original story by Everett Freeman and Arthur Schwartz; cinematography by Arthur Edeson; edited by Irene Morra; dialogue direction by Herbert Farjean; assistant director, Phil Quinn; art direction by Anton Grot and Leo K. Kuter; set decoration by Walter F. Tilford; gowns by Milo Anderson; makeup by Perc Westmore; special effects by H. F. Koenekamp; sound by Francis J. Scheid and Charles David Forrest; dance numbers created and staged by Leroy Prinz; songs by Arthur Schwartz and Frank Loesser; orchestral arrangements by Ray Heindorf; vocal arrangements by Dudley Chambers; musical adaptation by Heinz Roemheld; orchestrations by Maurice de Packh.

Cast: Humphrey Bogart (Himself), Eddie Cantor (Himself and Joe Simpson), Bette Davis (Herself), Olivia de Havilland (Herself), Errol Flynn (Himself), John Garfield (Himself), Joan Leslie (Pat Dixon), Ida Lupino (Herself), Dennis Morgan (Tom Randolph), Ann Sheridan (Herself), Dinah Shore (Herself), Alexis Smith (Herself), Jack Carson (Himself), Alan Hale (Himself), George Tobias (Himself), Edward Everett Horton (Farnsworth), S. Z. Sakall (Dr. Schlenna), Hattie McDaniel (Gossip), Ruth Donnelly (Nurse Hamilton), Don Wilson (Announcer), Willie Best (Soldier), Henry Armetta (Angelo), Joyce Reynolds (Girl with a Book), Spike Jones and His City Slickers.

Sahara (1943). A Columbia Picture. 97 minutes. Directed by Zoltan Korda; produced by Harry Joe Brown; screenplay by John Howard Lawson and Zoltan Korda; adaptation by James O'Hanlon from an original story by Philip MacDonald, based on an incident in the Soviet film *The Thirteen*; cinematography by Rudolph Maté; music by Miklos Rozsa; edited by Charles Nelson; assistant director, Abby Berlin; art direction by Lionel Banks; associate art director, Eugene Lourie; set decoration by William Kiernan; sound by Lodge Cunningham; musical direction by Morris W. Stoloff.

Cast: Humphrey Bogart (Sergeant Joe Gunn), Bruce Bennett (Waco Hoyt), J. Carroll Naish (Giuseppe), Lloyd Bridges (Fred Clarkson), Rex Ingram (Tambul), Richard Nugent (Captain Jason Halliday), Dan Duryea (Jimmy Doyle), Carl Harbord (Marty Williams), Patrick O'Moore (Ozzie Bates), Louis

Mercier (Jean Leroux), Guy Kingsford (Peter Stegman), Kurt Krueger (Captain Von Schletow), John Wengraf (Major Von Falken), Hans Schumm (Sergeant Krause), Frank Lackteen (Arab Guide), Frederick Worlock (Radio Newscaster Voice).

Passage to Marseille (1944). A Warner Bros.–First National Picture. 110 minutes. Directed by Michael Curtiz; produced by Hal B. Wallis; screenplay by Casey Robinson and Jack Moffitt, based on the novel *Men Without Country* by Charles Nordhoff and James Norman Hall; cinematography by James Wong Howe; music by Max Steiner; edited by Owen Marks; dialogue direction by Herschel Daugherty; assistant director, Frank Heath; art direction by Carl Jules Weyl; set decoration by George James Hopkins; costumes by Leah Rhodes; makeup by Perc Westmore; special effects by Jack Cosgrove, Edwin B. DuPar, Byron Haskin, E. Roy Davidson, and Rex Wimpy; montages by James Leicester; sound by Everett A. Brown; music direction by Leo F. Forbstein; orchestration by Leonid Raab; song "Someday I'll Meet You Again," music and lyrics by Max Steiner and Ned Washington; technical adviser; Sylvain Robert.

Cast: Humphrey Bogart (Matrac), Claude Rains (Captain Freycinet), Michele Morgan (Paula), Philip Dorn (Renault), Sydney Greenstreet (Major Duval), Peter Lorre (Marius), George Tobias (Petit), Helmut Dantine (Garou), John Loder (Manning), Victor Francen (Captain Malo), Vladimir Sokoloff (Grand-père), Eduardo Cianelli (Chief Engineer), Corinna Mura (Singer), Konstantin Shayne (First Mate), Stephen Richards (Lieutenant Hastings), Charles La Torre (Lieutenant Lenoir), Hans Conried (Jourdain), Monte Blue (Second Mate), Billy Roy (Mess Boy), Frederick Brunn (Bijou), Louis Mercier (Second Engineer), Donald Stuart (Military Driver), Walter Bonn (Prison Official), Carmen Baretta (Petit's Wife), Diane Dubois (Petit's Daughter), Jean Del Val (Raoul), Alex Papanao (Lookout), Peter Miles (Jean), Raymond St. Albin (Medical Officer), Peter Camlin (French Sergeant), Anatol Frikin (Crazy Convict), Frank Puglia (Older Guard), Harry Cording (Chief Guard), Adrienne d'Ambricourt (Mayor's Wife), Fred Essler (Mayor).

Report from the Front (1944). Prepared by the Red Cross Drive Committee of the Motion Picture Industry, distributed by National Screen Service. 3 minutes.

Cast: Humphrey Bogart and Mayo Methot in film clips of their three-month tour entertaining American troops in Africa and Italy. Bogart narrates scenes of actual battle and appeals to the audience to make generous donations to the Red Cross at the conclusion of the short.

To Have and Have Not (1944). A Warner Bros.–First National Picture. 100 minutes. Produced and directed by Howard Hawks; screenplay by Jules Furthman and William Faulkner, based on the 1937 novel by Ernest Hemingway; cinematography by Sid Hickox; music by Franz Waxman; music direction by

Leo F. Forbstein; edited by Christian Nyby; assistant director, Jack Sullivan; art direction by Charles Novi; set decoration by Casey Roberts; costumes by Milo Anderson; makeup by Perc Westmore; special effects by E. Roy Davidson and Rex Wimpy; sound by Oliver S. Garretson; orchestration by Leonid Raab; songs "How Little We Know," music and lyrics by Hoagy Carmichael and Johnny Mercer, "Hong Kong Blues," music and lyrics by Hoagy Carmichael and Stanley Adams, "Am I Blue?," music and lyrics by Harry Akst and Grant Clarke; technical adviser, Louis Comien.

Cast: Humphrey Bogart (Harry Morgan), Walter Brennan (Eddie), Lauren Bacall (Marie), Dolores Moran (Helene de Brusac), Hoagy Carmichael (Cricket), Walter Molnar (Paul de Brusac), Sheldon Leonard (Lieutenant Coyo), Marcel Dalio (Gerard), Walter Sande (Johnson), Dan Seymour (Captain Renard), Aldo Nadi (Renard's Bodyguard), Paul Marion (Beauclerc), Patricia Shay (Mrs. Beauclerc), Emmett Smith (Emil, the Bartender), Eugene Borden (Quartermaster), Elzie Emanuel, Harold Garrison (Urchins), Major Fred Farrell (Headwaiter), Pedro Regas (Civilian), Adrienne d'Ambricourt, Marguerita Sylva (Cashiers), Margaret Hathaway, Louise Clark, Suzette Harbin, Gussie Morris, Kanza Omar, Margaret Savage (Waitresses), Hal Kelly (Detective), Jean de Briac (Gendarme), Chef Joseph Milani (Chef), Oscar Lorraine (Bartender), Ron Rondell (Ensign), Audrey Armstrong (Dancer), Marcel de la Brosse (Sailor), Edith Wilson (Woman), Jeanette Gras (Rosalie), Jack Chefe (Guide), George Soul (French Officer), Sir Lancelot (Horatio the Dog).

Conflict (1945). A Warner Bros.–First National Picture. 86 minutes. Directed by Curtis Bernhardt; produced by William Jacobs; screenplay by Arthur T. Horman and Dwight Taylor, based on an original story by Robert Siodmak and Alfred Neumann; cinematography by Merritt Gerstad; music by Frederick Hollander; edited by David Weisnart; dialogue direction by James Vincent; assistant director, Elmer Decker; art direction by Ted Smith; set decoration by Clarence I. Steensen; costumes by Milo Anderson; makeup by Perc Westmore; sound by Oliver S. Garretson; music direction by Leo F. Forbstein; orchestration by Jerome Moross.

Cast: Humphrey Bogart (Richard Manson), Alexis Smith (Evelyn Turner), Sydney Greenstreet (Dr. Mark Hamilton), Rose Hobart (Kathryn Mason), Charles Drake (Professor Norman Holdsworth), Grant Mitchell (Dr. Grant), Patrick O'Moore (Detective Lieutenant Egan), Ann Shoemaker (Nora Grant), Frank Wilcox (Robert Freston), Edwin Stanley (Phillips), James Flavin (Detective Lieutenant Workman), Mary Servoss (Mrs. Allman), Doria Caron (Nurse), Ray Hanson, Billy Wayne (Cab Drivers), Ralph Dunn (Highway Patrolman), John Harmon (Hobo), Bruce Bilson (Bellboy), Marjorie Hoshelle (Telephone Operator), Francis Morris (Receptionist), George Carleton (Harris), Oliver Prickett, Harlan Briggs (Pawnbrokers), Wallis Clark (Professor Berens), Jack Morris (Desk Clerk), Emmett Vogan (Luggage Salesman).

Hollywood Victory Caravan (1945). Produced for the War Activities Committee and the Treasury Department by Paramount Pictures. War Activities Committee release No. 136. 20 minutes. Directed by William Russell; produced by Louis Harris; supervising producer, Bernard Luber; screenplay by Melville Shavelson; song "We've Got Another Bond to Buy," music and lyrics by Jimmy McHugh and Harold Adamson.

Cast: Robert Benchley, Humphrey Bogart, Joe Carioca, Carmen Cavallero and his orchestra, Bing Crosby, William Demarest, Dona Drake, Bob Hope, Betty Hutton, Alan Ladd, Diana Lynn, Noreen Nash, Franklin Pangborn, Olga San Juan, Barbara Stanwyck, Charles Victor, the U.S. Maritime Service Training Station Choir. Bogart makes an appeal for Victory Loan Bonds.

Two Guys from Milwaukee (1946). A Warner Bros.–First National Picture. 90 minutes. Directed by David Butler; produced by Alex Gottlieb; original screenplay by Charles Hoffman and I. A. L. Diamond; cinematography by Arthur Edeson; music by Frederick Hollander; edited by Irene Morra; dialogue direction by Felix Jacoves; assistant director, Jesse Hibbs; art direction by Leo K. Kuter; set decoration by Jack McConaghy; costumes by Leah Rhodes; makeup by Perc Westmore; special effects by Harry Barndollar and Edwin B. DuPar; montages by James Leicester; sound by Stanley Jones; orchestration by Leonid Raab; song "And Her Tears Flowed like Wine" by Charles Lawrence, Joe Greene, and Stan Kenton.

Cast: Dennis Morgan (Prince Henry), Jack Carson (Buzz Williams), Joan Leslie (Connie Reed), Janis Paige (Polly), S. Z. Sakall (Count Oswald), Patti Brady (Peggy), Tom D'Andrea (Happy), Rosemary DeCamp (Nan), John Ridgely (Mike Collins), Pat McVey (Johnson), Franklin Pangborn (Theater Manager), Francis Pierlot (Dr. Bauer), Lauren Bacall (Herself), Humphrey Bogart (Himself).

The Big Sleep (1946). A Warner Bros.–First National Picture. 114 minutes. Produced and directed by Howard Hawks; screenplay by William Faulkner, Leigh Brackett, and Jules Furthman, based on the 1939 novel by Raymond Chandler; cinematography by Sid Hickox; music by Max Steiner; music direction by Leo F. Forbstein; edited by Christian Nyby; assistant director, Robert Vreeland; art direction by Carl Jules Weyl; set decoration by Fred M. MacLean; costumes by Leah Rhodes; special effects by E. Roy Davidson, Warren E. Lynch, William McGann, Robert Burks, and Willard Van Enger; sound by Robert B. Lee; orchestration by Simon Bucharoff.

Cast: Humphrey Bogart (Philip Marlowe), Lauren Bacall (Vivian Rutledge), John Ridgely (Eddie Mars), Martha Vickers (Carmen Sternwood), Dorothy Malone (Bookshop Owner), Peggy Knudsen (Mona [Mrs. Eddie] Mars), Regis Toomey (Bernie Ohls), Charles Waldron (General Sternwood), Charles D. Brown (Norris), Bob Steele (Canino), Elisha Cook Jr. (Harry Jones), Louis

Jean Heydt (Joe Brody), Sonia Darrin (Agnes), James Flavin (Captain Cronjager), Thomas Jackson (District Attorney Wilde), Dan Wallace (Owen Taylor), Tom Rafferty (Carol Lundgren), Theodore Von Eltz (Arthur Gwynn Geiger), Joy Barlowe (Taxi Driver), Tom Fadden (Sidney), Ben Welden (Pete), Trevor Bardette (Art Huck), Joseph Crehan (Medical Examiner), Carole Douglas (Librarian), Paul Webber (Gangster in Parking Lot), Tanis Chandler, Deannie Best (Waitresses), Lorraine Miller (Hat Check Girl), Shelby Payne (Cigarette Girl).

Dead Reckoning (1947). A Columbia Picture. 100 minutes. Directed by John Cromwell; produced by Sidney Biddell; screenplay by Oliver H. P. Garrett and Steve Fisher, adapted by Allen Rivkin from an original story by Gerald Adams and Sidney Biddell; cinematography by Leo Tover; music by Marlin Skiles; music direction by Morris W. Stoloff; assistant director, Seymour Friedman; art direction by Stephen Goosson and Rudolph Sternad; set decoration by by Louis Diage; costumes by Jean Louis; makeup by Clay Campbell; hairstyles by Helen Hunt; sound by Jack Goodrich; song "Either It's Love or It Isn't" by Allan Roberts and Doris Fisher.

Cast: Humphrey Bogart (Rip Murdock), Lizabeth Scott (Coral Chandler), Morris Carnovsky (Martinelli), Charles Cane (Lieutenant Kincaid), William Prince (Johnny Drake), Marvin Miller (Krause), Wallace Ford (McGee), James Bell (Father Logan), George Chandler (Louis Ord), William Forrest (Lieutenant Colonel Simpson), Ruby Dandridge (Hyacinth), Lillian Wells (Pretty Girl), Charles Jordan (Mike, the Bartender), Robert Scott (Bandleader), Lillian Bronson (Mrs. Putnam), Maynard Holms (Desk Clerk), William Lawrence (Stewart), Dudley Dickerson (Waiter), Syd Taylor (Morgue Attendant), George Eldredge (Policeman), Chester Clute (Martin), Joseph Crehan (General Steele), Gary Owen (Reporter), Alvin Hammer (Photographer), Pat Lance (General's Aide), Frank Wilcox (Desk Clerk), Stymie Beard (Bellboy), Matty Fain (Ed), John Bohn, Sayre Dearing (Croupiers), Harry Denny, Kay Garrett (Dealers), Jack Santoro (Raker), Joe Gilbert (Croupier), Sam Finn (Raker), Dick Gordon (Dealer), Ray Teal (Motorcycle Policeman), Hugh Hooker (Bellboy), Chuck Hamilton, Robert Ryan (Detectives), Grady Sutton (Maître d'Hotel), Jesse Graves (Waiter), Byron Foulger (Night Attendant), Tom Dillon (Priest), Isabel Withers (Nurse), Wilton Graff (Surgeon), Paul Bradley (Man), Alyce Goering (Woman).

The Two Mrs. Carrolls (1947). A Warner Bros.–First National Picture. 99 minutes. Directed by Peter Godfrey; produced by Mark Hellinger; screenplay by Thomas Job, based on the play by Martin Vale; cinematography by Peverell Marley; music by Franz Waxman; music direction by Leo F. Forbstein; edited by Frederick Richards; assistant director, Claude Archer; art direction by Anton Grot; set decoration by Budd Friend; costumes by Edith Head and Milo Anderson; makeup by Perc Westmore; special effects by Robert Burks; sound by C. A. Riggs; orchestration by Leonid Raab.

Cast: Humphrey Bogart (Geoffrey Carroll), Barbara Stanwyck (Sally Carroll), Alexis Smith (Cecily Latham), Nigel Bruce (Dr. Tuttle), Isobel Elsom (Mrs. Latham), Patrick O'Moore (Charles Pennington), Ann Carter (Beatrice Carroll), Anita Bolster (Christine), Barry Bernard (Mr. Blagdon), Colin Campbell (MacGregor), Peter Godfrey, Creighton Hall (Race Track Touts), Leyland Hodgson (Inspector).

Dark Passage (1947). A Warner Bros.–First National Picture. 106 minutes. Directed by Delmar Daves; produced by Jerry Wald; screenplay by Delmar Daves, based on the novel by David Goodis; cinematography by Sid Hickox; music by Franz Waxman; edited by David Weisbart; music direction by Leo F. Forbstein; assistant director, Dick Mayberry; art direction by Charles H. Clarke; set decoration by William Kuehl; costumes by Bernard Newman; makeup by Perc Westmore; special effects by H. F. Koenekamp; sound by Dolph Thomas; orchestration by Leonid Raab.

Cast: Humphrey Bogart (Vincent Parry), Lauren Bacall (Irene Jansen), Bruce Bennett (Bob Rapf), Agnes Moorehead (Madge Rapf), Tom D'Andrea (Sam), Clifton Young (Baker), Douglas Kennedy (Detective), Rory Mallinson (George Fellsinger), Houseley Stevenson (Dr. Walter Coley), Bob Farber, Richard Walsh (Policemen), Clancy Cooper (Man on Street), Pat McVey (Taxi Driver), Dude Maschemeyer (Man on Street), Tom Fadden (Waiter), Shimen Ruskin (Driver-Watchman), Tom Reynolds (Hotel Clerk), Lennie Bremen (Ticket Clerk), Mary Field (Lonely Woman), Michael Daves, Deborah Daves (Children), John Arledge (Lonely Man), Ross Ford (Bus Driver), Ian MacDonald (Policeman), Ramon Ros (Waiter), Craig Lawrence (Bartender).

Always Together (1948). A Warner Bros.–First National Picture. 78 Minutes. Directed by Frederick de Cordova; produced by Alex Gottlieb; original screenplay by Phoebe and Henry Ephron and I. A. L. Diamond, cinematography by Carl Guthrie; music by Werner Heymann; edited by Folmer Blangsted; dialogue direction by John Maxwell; assistant director, James McMahon; art direction by Leo K. Kuter; set decoration by Jack McConaghy; wardrobe by Travilla; makeup by Perc Westmore; special effects by William McGann and Edwin B. DuPar; montages by James Leicester; sound by C. A. Riggs; orchestration by Leonid Raab.

Cast: Robert Hutton (Donn Masters), Joyce Reynolds (Jane Barker), Cecil Kellaway (Jonathan Turner), Ernest Truex (Mr. Bull), Donn McGuire (McIntyre), Ransom Sherman (Judge), Douglas Kennedy (Doberman). Unbilled appearances by Humphrey Bogart, Jack Carson, Errol Flynn, Dennis Morgan, Janis Paige, Eleanor Parker, and Alexis Smith as inhabitants of a fantasy world in Jane Barker's mind.

The Treasure of the Sierra Madre (1948). A Warner Bros.–First National Picture. 126 minutes. Directed by John Huston; produced by Henry Blanke; screenplay by John Huston, based on the novel by B. Traven; cinematography by Ted McCord; music by Max Steiner; edited by Owen Marks; music direction by Leo F. Forbstein; assistant director, Dick Mayberry; art direction by John Hughes; set decoration by Fred M. MacLean; makeup by Perc Westmore; special effects by William McGann and H. F. Koenekamp; sound by Robert B. Lee; orchestration by Murray Cutter; technical advisers, Ernesto A. Romero and Antonio Arriga.

Cast: Humphrey Bogart (Fred C. Dobbs), Walter Huston (Howard), Tim Holt (Curtin), Bruce Bennett (Cody), Barton MacLane (McCormick), Alfonso Bedoya (Gold Hat), A. Santo Ragel (Presidente), Manuel Donde (El Jefe), Jose Torvay (Pablo), Margarito Luna (Pancho), Jacqueline Dalya (Flashy Girl), Bobby Blake (Mexican Boy), John Huston (White Suit), Jack Holt, Clifton Young, Ralph Dunn (Men in Flophouse), Spencer Chan (Proprietor), Julian Rivero (Barber), Harry Vejas (Bartender), Pat Flaherty (Customer), Guillermo Calleo (Storekeeper), Ann Sheridan [uncredited] (Streetwalker), Manuel Donde, Ildefonso Vega, Francisco Islas, Alberto Valdespino (Indians), Mario Man Cillo (Young Man), Martin Garralaga (Railroad Conductor), Ernesto Escoto (First Bandit), Ignacio (Second Bandit), Robert Canedo (Lieutenant).

Key Largo (1948). A Warner Bros.–First National Picture. 101 minutes. Directed by John Huston; produced by Jerry Wald; screenplay by John Huston and Richard Brooks, based on the 1939 play by Maxwell Anderson; cinematography by Karl Freund; music by Max Steiner; edited by Rudi Fehr; assistant director, Art Leuker; art direction by Leo K. Kuter; set decoration by Fred M. MacLean; costumes by Leah Rhodes; makeup by Perc Westmore; special effects by William McGann and Robert Burks; sound by Dolph Thomas; orchestration by Murray Cutter; song "Moanin' Low," music and lyrics by Ralph Rainger and Howard Dietz.

Cast: Humphrey Bogart (Frank McCloud), Edward G. Robinson (Johnny Rocco), Lauren Bacall (Nora Temple), Lionel Barrymore (James Temple), Claire Trevor (Gaye Dawn), Thomas Gomez (Curley Hoff), Harry Lewis (Toots Bass), John Rodney (Deputy Clyde Sawyer), Marc Lawrence (Ziggy), Dan Seymour (Angel Garcia), Monte Blue (Sheriff Ben Wade), William Haade (Ralph Feeney), Jay Silverheels (John Osceola), Roderic Redwing (Tom Osceola), Joe P. Smith (Bus Driver), Alberto Morin (Skipper), Pat Flaherty, Jerry Jerome, John Phillips, Lute Crockett (Ziggy's Henchmen), Felipa Gomez (Old Indian Woman).

Knock on Any Door (1949). A Santana Production, released by Columbia Pictures. 100 minutes. Directed by Nicholas Ray; produced by Robert Lord; associate producer, Henry S. Kesler; screenplay by Daniel Taradash and John Monks Jr., based on the novel by William Motley; cinematography by Burnett Guffey;

music by George Antheil; music direction by Morris W. Stoloff; edited by Viola Lawrence; assistant director, Arthur S. Black; art direction by Robert Peterson; set decoration by William Kiernan; gowns by Jean Louis; makeup by Clay Campbell; hairstyling by Helen Hunt; sound by Frank Goodwin; orchestration by Ernest Gold; technical advisers, National Probation and Parole Association.

Cast: Humphrey Bogart (Andrew Morton), John Derek (Nick Romano), George Macready (Kerman), Allene Roberts (Emma), Susan Perry (Adele Morton), Mickey Knox (Vito), Barry Kelley (Judge Drake), Cara Williams (Nelly), Jimmy Conlin (Kid Fingers), Sumner Williams (Jimmy), Sid Melton (Squint), Pepe Hern (Juan), Dewey Martin (Butch), Robert A. Davis (Sunshine), Houseley Stevenson (Junior), Vince Barnett (Bartender), Thomas Sully (Officer Hawkins), Florence Auer (Aunt Lena), Pierre Watkin (Purcell), Gordon Nelson (Corey), Argentina Brunetti (Ma Romano), Dick Sinatra (Julian Romano), Carol Coombs (Ang Romano), Joan Baxter (Maria Romano), Evelyn Underwood, Mary Emery, Franz Roehn, Betty Hall, Jack Jahries, Rose Plumer, Mabel Smaney, Joy Hallward, John Mitchum, Sidney Dubin, Homer Dickinson, Netta Packer (Jury), Ann Duncan, Lorraine Comerford (Teenagers), Chuck Hamilton, Ralph Volkie, Frank Marlo (Bailiffs), Joe Palma, Dick Bartell, Eddie Randolph, Eda Reiss Merin, Joan Danton (Reporters), Donald Kerr (Court Clerk), Myron Healey (Assistant District Attorney), Jane Lee, Dorothy Vernon (Women), Gary Owen (Larry), Chester Conklin (Barber), George Chandler (Cashier), Theda Barr (Girl), Wesley Hopper (Boss), Sid Tomack (Duke), Frank Hagney, Peter Virgo (Suspects), George Hickman, Saul Gross, Al Hill, Phillip Morris (Detectives), Helen Mowery (Miss Holiday), Jody Gilbert (Gussie), Curt Conway (Elkins), Edwin Parker, Al Ferguson (Guards).

Tokyo Joe (1949). A Santana Production, released by Columbia Pictures. 88 minutes. Directed by Stuart Heisler; produced by Robert Lord; associate producer; Henry S. Kesler; screenplay by Cyril Hume and Bertram Millhauser, adapted by Walter Doniger, based on a story by Steve Fisher; cinematography by Charles Lawton Jr.; music by George Antheil; edited by Viola Lawrence; music direction by Morris W. Stoloff; dialogue direction by Jason Lindsey; assistant director, Wilber McGaugh; art direction by Robert Peterson; set decoration by James Crowe; costumes by Jean Louis; makeup by Clay Campbell; hairstyling by Helen Hunt; sound by Russell Malmgren; orchestration by Ernest Gold; song "These Foolish Things (Remind Me of You)," music and lyrics by Jack Strachy, Harry Link, and Holt Marvel.

Cast: Humphrey Bogart (Joe Barrett), Alexander Knox (Mark Landis), Florence Marly (Trina), Sessue Hayakawa (Baron Kimura), Jerome Courtland (Danny), Gordon Jones (Idaho), Teru Shimada (Ito), Hideo Mori ((Kanda), Charles Meredith (General Ireton), Rhys Williams (Colonel Dahlgren), Lora Lee Michael (Anya), Kyoko Kamo (Nani-san), Gene Gondo (Kamikaze), Harold Goodwin (Major Loomis), James Cardwell (MP Captain), Frank Kumagai

(Truck Driver), Tetsu Komai (Takenobu), Otto Han (Hara), Yosan Tsuruta (Goro).

Chain Lightning (1950). A Warner Bros.–First National Picture. 94 minutes. Directed by Stuart Heisler; produced by Anthony Veiller; screenplay by Liam O'Brien and Vincent Evans, based on an original story by J. Redmond Prior; cinematography by Ernest Haller; music by David Buttolph; edited by Thomas Reilly; assistant director, Don Page; art direction by Leo K. Kuter; set decoration by William Wallace; gowns by Leah Rhodes; makeup by Perc Westmore; special effects by William McGann, Harry Barndollar, H. F. Koenekamp, and Edwin B. DuPar; sound by Francis Scheid; orchestration by Maurice de Packh; song "Bless 'Em All," music and lyrics by J. Hughes, Frank Lake, and Al Stillman.

Cast: Humphrey Bogart (Matt Brennan), Eleanor Parker (Jo Holloway), Raymond Massey (Leland Wallis), Richard Whorf (Carl Troxell), James Brown (Major Hinkle), Roy Roberts (General Hewitt), Morris Ankrum (Ed Bostwick), Fay Barker (Mrs. Willis), Fred Sherman (Jeb Farley).

In a Lonely Place (1950). A Santana Production, released by Columbia Pictures. 94 minutes. Directed by Nicholas Ray; produced by Robert Lord; associate producer, Henry S. Kesler; screenplay by Andrew Solt, adapted by Edmund North from the novel by Dorothy Hughes; cinematography by Burnett Guffey; music by Geoge Antheil; edited by Viola Lawrence; music direction by Morris W. Stoloff; assistant director, Earl Bellamy; art direction by Robert Peterson; set decoration by William Kiernan; costumes by Jean Louis; makeup by Clay Campbell; hairstyling by Helen Hunt; sound by Howard Fogetti; orchestration by Ernest Gold; technical adviser, Rodney Amateau.

Cast: Humphrey Bogart (Dixon Steele), Gloria Grahame (Laurel Gray), Frank Lovejoy (Brub Nicolai), Carl Benton Reid (Captain Lochner), Art Smith (Mel Lippman), Jeff Donnell (Sylvia Nicolai), Martha Stewart (Mildred Atkinson), Robert Warwick (Charlie Waterman), Moris Ankrum (Lloyd Barnes), William Ching (Ted Barton), Steven Geray (Paul), Hadda Brooks (Singer), Alice Talton (Frances Randolph), Jack Reynolds (Henry Kesler), Ruth Warren (Effie), Ruth Gillette (Martha), Guy Beach (Swan), Lewis Howard (Junior), Mike Romanoff (Himself), Arno Frey (Joe), Pat Barton (Second Hatcheck Girl), Cosmo Sardo (Bartender), Don Hamin (Young Driver), George Davis (Waiter), Billy Gray (Young Boy), Melinda Erickson (Tough Girl), Jack Jaharies (Officer), David Bond (Dr. Richards), Myron Healey (Post Office Clerk), Robert Lowell (Airline Clerk).

The Enforcer (1951). A United States Picture for Warner Bros. 87 minutes. Directed by Bretaigne Windust [and, uncredited, Raoul Walsh]; produced by Milton Sperling; original screenplay by Martin Rackin; cinematography by Robert Burks; music by David Buttolph; edited by Fred Allen; assistant director,

Chuck Hansen; art direction by Charles H. Clarke; set decoration by William Kuehl; sound by Dolph Thomas; orchestration by Maurice de Packh.

Cast: Humphrey Bogart (Martin Ferguson), Zero Mostel (Big Babe Lazich), Ted De Corsia (Joseph Rico), Everett Sloane (Albert Mendoza), Roy Roberts (Captain Frank Nelson), Lawrence Tolan (Duke Malloy), King Donovan (Sergeant Whitlow), Bob Steele (Herman), Adelaide Klein (Olga Kirshen), Don Beddoe (Thomas O'Hara), Tito Vuolo (Tony Vetto), John Kellogg (Vince), Jack Lambert (Philadelphia Tom Zaca), Patricia Joiner (Angela Vetto), Susan Cabot (Nina Lombardo), Mario Siletti (Louis, the Barber), Alan Foster (Shorty), Harry Wilson (B. J.), Pete Kellett, Barry Reagan (Interns), Dan Riss (Mayor), Art Dupuis (Keeper), Bud Wolfe (Fireman), Creighton Hale (Clerk), Patricia Hayes (Teenager), Robert Strong Duncan (Sergeant), Perc Landers (Police Sergeant), Tom Dillon (Policeman), Joe Maxwell (Doctor), Howard Mitchell (Chief), Brick Sullivan (Police Chauffeur), Greta Granstedt (Mrs. Lazick), Louis Lettieri (Boy), Monte Pittman (Intern), Chuck Hamilton, Jay Morley (Policemen), Richard Bactell (Clerk), Karen Kester (Nina as a Child), Eula Guy (Landlady).

Sirocco (1951). A Santana Production, released by Columbia Pictures. 98 minutes. Directed by Curtis Bernhardt; produced by Robert Lord; associate producer, Henry S. Kesler; screenplay by A. I. Bezzerides and Hans Jacoby, based on the novel *Coup de Grâce* by Joseph Kessel; cinematography by Burnett Guffey; music by George Antheil; edited by Viola Lawrence; assistant director, Earl Bellamy; music direction by Morris W. Stoloff; art direction by Robert Peterson; set decoration by Robert Priestly; makeup by Clay Campbell; hairstyling by Helen Hunt; sound by Lodge Cunningham; orchestration by Ernest Gold.

Cast: Humphrey Bogart (Harry Smith), Marta Toren (Violette), Lee J. Cobb (Colonel Feroud), Everett Sloane (General LaSalle), Gerald Mohr (Major Leon), Zero Mostel (Balukjian), Nick Dennis (Nasir Aboud), Onslow Stevens (Emir Hassan), Ludwig Donath (Flophouse Proprietor), David Bond (Achmet), Vincent Renno (Arthur), Martin Wilkins (Omar), Peter Ortiz (Major Robbinet), Edward Colmans (Colonel Corville), Al Eben (Sergeant), Peter Brocco (Barber), Jay Novello (Hamal), Leonard Penn (Rifat), Harry Guardino (Lieutenant Collet).

The African Queen (1951). A Horizon-Romulus Production, released through United Artists. Color by Technicolor. 105 minutes. Directed by John Huston; produced by S. P. Eagle [Sam Speigel]; screenplay by James Agee and John Huston, based on the novel by C. S. Forester; cinematography by Jack Cardiff; music by Alan Gray, played by the Royal Philharmonic Orchestra conducted by Norman Del Mar; edited by Ralph Kemplen; assistant director, Guy Hamilton; art direction by Wilfred Shingleton; associate art director, John Hoesil; production managers, Leigh Aman and T. S. Lyndon-Hatnes; Miss Hepburn's costumes by Doris Langley Moore; other clothes by Connie De Pinna; makeup by George Frost; second-unit photography by Ted Scaife; special effects by Cliff Richardson; sound by Scott Mitchell; sound editor, Eric Wood; camera operator, Ted Moore; hairdresser, Eileen Bates; wardrobe mistress, Vi Murray; continuity by Angela Allen.

Cast: Humphrey Bogart (Charlie Allnut), Katharine Hepburn (Rose Sayer), Robert Morley (Rev. Samuel Sayer), Peter Bull (Captain, *Louisa*), Theodore Bikel (First Officer, *Louisa*), Walter Gotell (Second Officer, *Louisa*), Gerald Onn (Petty Officer, *Louisa*), Peter Swanwick (First Officer, *Shona*), Richard Marner (Second Officer, *Shona*).

Deadline—U.S.A. (1951). A Twentieth Century–Fox Picture. 87 minutes. Directed by Richard Brooks; produced by Sol C. Siegel; original screenplay by Richard Brooks; cinematography by Milton Krasner; music by Cyril Mockridge and Sol Kaplan; edited by William B. Murphy; assistant director, Dick Mayberry; art direction by Lyle Wheeler and George Patrick; set decoration by Thomas Little and Walter M. Scott; wardrobe direction by Charles Le Maire; costumes by Eloise Jenssen; music direction by Lionel Newman; makeup by Ben Nye; special effects by Ray Kellogg; sound by E. Clayton Ward and Harry M. Leonard; orchestration by Edward Powell and Bernard Mayers.

Cast: Humphrey Bogart (Ed Hutchinson), Ethel Barrymore (Mrs. John Garrison), Kim Hunter (Nora), Ed Begley (Frank Allen), Warren Stevens (George Burrows), Paul Stewart (Harry Thompson), Martin Gabel (Thomas Reinzi), Joe De Santis (Herman Schmidt), Joyce MacKenzie (Kitty Garrison Geary), Audrey Christy (Mrs. Willebrandt), Fay Baker (Alice Garrison Courtney), Jim Backus (Jim Cleary), Carleton Young (Crane), Selmer Jackson (Williams), Fay Roope (Judge), Parley Baer (Headwaiter), Betty Francine (Telephone Operator), John Doucette (Hal), Florence Shirley (Miss Barndollar), Kasia Orzazewski (Mrs. Schmidt), Raymond Greenleaf (Lawrence White), Tom Powers (Wharton), Thomas Browne Henry (Fenway), June Eisner (Bentley), Richard Monohan (Copy Boy), Harry Tyler (Headline Writer), Irene Vernon (Mrs. Burrows), William Forrest (Mr. Greene), Edward Keane (Mr. Blake), Clancy Cooper (Captain Finlay), Tom Powers (Wharton), Ashley Cowan (Lefty), Howard Negley (Police Sergeant), Joe Mell (Lugerman), Luther Crockett (National Editor), Larry Dobkin (Hansen), Everett Glass (Doctor), Tudor Owen (Watchman), Ann McCrea (Sally), Willis B. Bouchey (Henry), Paul Dubov (Mac), Harris Brown (Al Murray), Philip Terry (Lewis Schaefer), Joseph Sawyer (Whitey), Alex Gerry (Attorney Prentiss), Joseph Crehan (White's City Editor).

U.S. Savings Bonds Trailer (1952). Metro-Goldwyn-Mayer. Bogart introduced the new Series E Savings Bonds in a trailer attached to the July 25–26 newsreels.

Battle Circus (1953). A Metro-Goldwyn-Mayer Picture. 90 minutes. Directed by Richard Brooks; produced by Pandro S. Berman; screenplay by Richard Brooks, based on an original story by Allen Rivkin and Laura Kerr; cinematography by John Alton; music by Lennie Hayton; edited by George Boemler; assistant director, Al Jennings; art direction by Cedric Gibbons and James Basevi; set decoration by Edwin B. Wallis and Alfred E. Spencer; makeup by William Tuttle; special effects by A. Arnold Gillespie; recording supervisor, Douglas Shearer; orchestration by Robert Franklyn; technical advisers, Lieutenant Colonel K. E. Van Buskirk and Lieutenant Mary Couch.

Cast: Humphrey Bogart (Major Jed Webbe), June Allyson (Lieutenant Ruth McCara), Keenan Wynn (Sergeant Orvil Statt), Robert Keith (Lieutenant Colonel Hillary Whalters), William Campbell (Captain John Rustford), Perry Sheehan (Lieutenant Laurence), Patricia Tiernan (Lieutenant Rose Ashland), Jonathan Cott (Adjutant), Adele Longmire (Lieutenant Jane Franklin), Ann Morrison (Lieutenant Edith Edwards), Helen Winston (Lieutenant Graciano), Sarah Selby (Captain Dobbs), Danny Chang (Danny), Philip Ahn (Korean Prisoner), Steve Forrest (Sergeant), Jeff Richards (Lieutenant), Dick Simmons (Captain Norson).

Beat the Devil (1954). A Santana-Romulus Production, released through United Artists. 93 minutes. Directed by John Huston; associate producer, Jack Clayton; screenplay by John Huston and Truman Capote, based on the novel by James Helvick; cinematography by Oswald Morris; music by Franco Mannino; edited by Ralph Kemplen; art direction by Wilfred Shingleton; sound by George Stephenson and E. Law; musical direction by Lambert Williamson.

Cast: Humphrey Bogart (Billy Dannreuther), Jennifer Jones (Gwendolen Chelm), Gina Lollobrigida (Maria Dannreuther), Robert Morley (Petersen), Peter Lorre (O'Hara), Edward Underdown (Harry Chelm), Ivor Barnard (Major Ross), Bernard (Major Ross), Bernard Lee (CID Inspector), Marco Tunni (Ravello), Mario Perroni (Purser), Alex Pochet (Hotel Manager), Aldo Silvani (Charles), Guilio Donnini (Administrator), Saro Urzi (Captain), Juan de Landa (Hispano-Suiza Driver), Manuel Serano (Arab Officer), Mimo Poli (Barman).

The Caine Mutiny (1954). A Stanley Kramer Company Production, released through Columbia Pictures. Color by Technicolor. 125 minutes. Directed by Edward Dmytryk; produced by Stanley Kramer; screenplay by Stanley Roberts, additional dialogue by Michael Blankfort, based on the novel by Herman Wouk; cinematography by Franz Planer; music by Max Steiner; production design by Rudolph Sternad; edited by William Lyon and Henry Batista; assistant director, Carter DeHaven Jr.; art direction by Cary Odell; set decoration by Frank Tuttle; costumes by Jean Louis; makeup by Clay Campbell; hairstyles by Helen Hunt; second-unit photography by Ray Cory; special effects by Lawrence Butler; sound by Lambert Day; songs "I Can't Believe That You're in Love With Me" by

Jimmy McHugh and Clarence Gaskill, "Yellowstain Blues" by Fred Karger and Herman Wouk; color consultant, Francis Cugat; technical adviser, Commander James C. Shaw, USN.

Cast: Humphrey Bogart (Captain Philip Francis Queeg), José Ferrer (Lieutenant Barney Greenwald), Van Johnson (Lieutenant Steve Maryk), Fred MacMurray (Lieutenant Tom Keefer), Robert Francis (Ensign Willie Keith), May Wynn (May Wynn), Tom Tully (Captain DeVriess), E. G. Marshall (Lieutenant Commander Challee), Arthur Franz (Lieutenant Paynter), Lee Marvin (Meatball), Warner Anderson (Captain Blakely), Claude Akins (Horrible), Katharine Warren (Mrs. Keith), Jerry Paris (Ensign Harding), Steve Brodie (Chief Budge), Todd Karns (Stilwell), Whit Bissell (Lieutenant Commander Dickson), James Best (Lieutenant Jorgensen), Joe Haworth (Ensign Carmody), Guy Anderson (Ensign Rabbit), James Edwards (Whittaker), Don Dubbins (Urban), David Alpert (Engstrand).

Sabrina (1954). A Paramount Picture. 113 minutes. Produced and directed by Billy Wilder; screenplay by Billy Wilder, Samuel Taylor, and Ernest Lehman, based on the play *Sabrina Fair* by Samuel Taylor; cinematography by Charles Lang Jr.; music by Frederick Hollander; edited by Arthur Schmidt; assistant director, C. C. Coleman Jr.; art direction by Hal Pereira and Walter Tyler; set decoration by Sam Comer and Ray Moyer; costumes by Edith Head; makeup by Wally Westmore; special effects by John P. Fulton and Farciot Edouart; sound by Harold Lewis and John Cope.

Cast: Humphrey Bogart (Linus Larrabee), Audrey Hepburn (Sabrina Fairchild), William Holden (David Larrabee), Walter Hampden (Walter Larrabee), John Williams (Thomas Fairchild), Martha Hyer (Elizabeth Tyson), Joan Vohs (Gretchen Van Horn), Marcel Dalio (Baron), Marcel Hillaire (the Professor), Nella Walker (Maude Larrabee), Francis X. Bushman (Mr. Tyson), Ellen Corby (Miss McCardle), Marjorie Bennett (Margaret, the Cook), Emory Parnell (Charles, the Butler), Kay Riehl (Mrs. Tyson), Nancy Kulp (Jenny, the Maid), Hay Kuter (Houseman), Paul Harvey (Doctor), Emmett Vogan, Colin Campbell (Board Members), Harvey Dunn (Man with Tray), Marion Ross (Spiller's Girl), Charles Harvey (Spiller), Greg Stafford (Man with David), Bill Neff (Man with Linus), Otto Forest (Elevator Operator), David Ahdar (Ship Steward), Rand Harper.

The Barefoot Contessa (1954). A Figaro Incorporated Production, released through United Artists. Color by Technicolor. 128 minutes. Directed by Joseph L. Mankiewicz; original screenplay by Joseph L. Mankiewicz; production supervised by Forrest E. Johnston; production associates, Franco Magli and Michael Waszynski; cinematography by Jack Cardiff; music by Mario Nascimbene; edited by William Hornbeck; assistant director, Pietro Mussetta; art direction by Arrigo Equini; gowns by Fontana; sound by Charles Knott.

Cast: Humphrey Bogart (Harry Dawes), Ava Gardner (Maria Vargas), Edmond O'Brien (Oscar Muldoon), Marius Goring (Alberto Bravano), Valentina Cortesa (Eleanore Torlato-Favrini), Rossano Brazzi (Vincenzo Torlato-Favrini), Elizabeth Sellars (Jerry), Warren Stevens (Kirk Edwards), Franco Interlenghi (Pedro), Mari Aldon (Myrna), Bessie Love (Mrs. Eubanks), Diana Decker (Drunken Blonde), Bill Fraser (J. Montague Brown), Alberto Rabagliati (Nightclub Owner), Enzo Staiola (Busboy), Haria Zanoli (Maria's Mother), Renato Chiantoni (Maria's Father), John Parrish (Mr. Black), Jim Gerald (Mr. Blue), Riccardo Rioli (Gypsy Dancer), Tonio Selwart (the Pretender), Margaret Anderson (the Pretender's Wife), Gertrude Flynn (Lulu McGee), John Horne (Hector Eubanks), Robert Christopher (Eddie Blake), Anna Maria Paduan (Chambermaid), Carlo Dale (Chauffeur).

We're No Angels (1955). A Paramount Picture. In VistaVision. Color by Technicolor. 103 minutes. Directed by Michael Curtiz; produced by Pat Duggan; screenplay by Ranald MacDougall, based on the play *La Cuisine des Agnes* by Albert Husson; cinematography by Loyal Griggs; music by Frederick Hollander; edited by Arthur Schmidt; assistant director, John Coonan; dialogue assistant, Norman Stuart; art direction by Hal Pereira and Roland Anderson; set decoration by Sam Comer and Grace Gregory; costumes by Mary Grant; makeup by Wally Westmore; special effects by John P. Fulton; sound by Hugo Grenzbach and John Cope; songs "Sentimental Moments" by Frederick Hollander and Ralph Freed, "Ma France Bien-Aimée" by G. Martini and Roger Wagner; color consultant, Richard Mueller.

Cast: Humphrey Bogart (Joseph), Aldo Ray (Albert), Peter Ustinov (Jules), Joan Bennett (Amelie Ducotel), Basil Rathbone (Andre Trochard), Leo G. Carroll (Felix Ducotel), John Baer (Paul Trochard), Gloria Talbott (Isabelle Ducotel), Lea Penman (Madame Parole), John Smith (Arnaud), Louis Mercier (Celeste), George Dee (Coachman), Torben Meyer (Butterfly Man), Paul Newlan (Port Captain), Ross Gould (Foreman), Victor Romito, Jack Del Rio (Gendarmes), Joe Ploski (Customs Inspector).

The Left Hand of God (1955). A Twentieth Century–Fox Picture. Cinemascope. Color by Technicolor. 87 minutes. Directed by Edward Dmytryk; produced by Buddy Adler; screenplay by Alfred Hayes, based on the novel by William E. Barrett; cinematography by Franz Planer; music by Victor Young; edited by Dorothy Spencer; assistant director, Ben Kadish; art direction by Lyle Wheeler and Maurice Ransford; set decoration by Walter M. Scott and Frank Wade; wardrobe direction by Charles Le Maire; costumes by Travilla; makeup by Ben Nye; hairstyles by Helen Turpin; special effects by Ray Kellogg; sound by Eugene Grossman and Harry M. Leonard; orchestration by Leo Shuken and Sidney Cutner; color consultant, Leonard Doss; technical adviser, Frank Tang.

Cast: Humphrey Bogart (Jim Carmody), Gene Tierney (Anne Scott), Lee

J. Cobb (Mieh Yang), Agnes Moorehead (Beryl Sigman), E. G. Marshall (Dr. David Sigman), Jean Porter (Mary Yin), Carl Benton Reid (Reverend Cornelius), Victor Sen Yung (John Wong), Benson Fong (Chun Tien), Richard Cutting (Father O'Shea), Leon Lontoc (Pao Ching), Don Forbes (Father Keller), Noel Toy (Woman in Sarong), Peter Chong (Feng Tso Lin), Marie Tsien (Woman in Kimono), Stephen Wong (the Boy), Sophie Chin (Celeste), George Chin (Li Kwan), Walter Soo Hoo (Hospital Orderly), Henry S. Quan (Orderly), Doris Chung (Nurse), Moy Ming (Old Man), George Lee (Mi Lu), Beal Wong (Father), Stella Lynn (Pao Chu), Robert Burton (Reverend Marvin), Soo Yong (Midwife), May Lee.

The Desperate Hours (1955). A Paramount Picture. In VistaVision. 112 minutes. Produced and directed by William Wyler; associate producer, Robert Wyler; screenplay by Joseph Hayes, based on his novel and play; cinematography by Lee Garmes; music by Gail Kubik; edited by Robert Swink; assistant director, C. C. Coleman Jr.; art direction by Hal Pereira and Joseph MacMillan Johnson; set decoration by Sam Comer and Grace Gregory; costumes by Edith Head; makeup by Wally Westmore; special effects by John P. Fulton and Farciot Edouart; sound by Hugo Grenzbach and Winston Leverett.

Cast: Humphrey Bogart (Glenn Griffin), Fredric March (Dan Hilliard), Arthur Kennedy (Jesse Bard), Martha Scott (Eleanor Hilliard), Dewey Martin (Hal Griffin), Gig Young (Chuck), Mary Murphy (Cindy Hilliard), Richard Eyer (Ralphie Hilliard), Robert Middleton (Sam Kobish), Alan Reed (Detective), Bert Freed (Winston), Ray Collins (Masters), Whit Bissell (Carson), Ray Teal (Fredericks), Michael Moore (Detective), Don Haggerty (Detective), Ric Roman (Sal), Pat Flaherty (Dutch), Beverly Garland (Miss Swift), Louis Lettieri (Bucky Walling), Ann Doran (Mrs. Walling), Walter Baldwin (Patterson).

The Harder They Fall (1956). A Columbia Picture. 109 minutes. Directed by Mark Robson; produced by Philip Yordan; screenplay by Philip Yordan, based on the novel by Budd Schulberg; cinematography by Burnett Guffey; music by Hugo Friedhofer; edited by Jerome Thoms; assistant director, Milton Feldman; music direction by Lionel Newman; art direction by William Kiernan and Alfred E. Spencer; makeup by Clay Campbell; hairstyles by Helen Hunt; sound by Lambert Day; orchestration by Arthur Morton; technical adviser, John Indrisano.

Cast: Humphrey Bogart (Eddie Willis), Rod Steiger (Nick Benko), Jan Sterling (Beth Willis), Mike Lane (Toro Moreno), Max Baer (Buddy Brannen), Jersey Joe Wolcott (George), Edward Andrews (Jim Weeyerhause), Harold J. Stone (Art Leavitt), Carlos Montalban (Luis Agrandi), Nehemiah Persoff (Leo), Felice Orlandi (Vince Fawcett), Herbie Faye (Max), Rusty Lane (Danny McKeogh), Jack Albertson (Pop), Val Avery (Frank), Tommy Herman (Tommy), Vinnie DeCarlo (Joey), Pat Comiskey (Gus Dundee), Matt Murphy (Sailor Rigazzo), Abel Fernandez (Chief Firebird), Marion Carr (Alice), J. Lewis Smith (Brannen's Manager), Everett Glass (Minister), William Roerick (Lawyer), Lillian Carver (Mrs. Harding), Jack Daly, Richard Norris, Don Kohler, Ralph Bramble, Charles Tannen, Mark Scott, Russ Whiteman, Mort Mills, Stafford Repp, Sandy Saunders, Emily Belser (Reporters), Paul Frees (Priest), Joe Herra, Frank Hagney (Referees), Diane Mumby, Elaine Edwards (Vince's Girlfriends), Tina Carver (Mrs. Benko), Anthony Blankley, Penny Carpenter (Nick's Children), Pan Dane (Shirley), Joe Greb.

Humphrey Bogart made cameo appearances in three additional films:

In This Our Life (1942). A Warner Bros./First National picture. Directed by John Huston; screenplay by Howard Koch, from the play by Ellen Glasgow; starring Bette Davis, George Brent, Charles Coburn, Billie Burke, Lee Patrick, Olivia de Havilland, Dennis Morgan.

The Road to Bali (1952). Color. Paramount Pictures. Directed by Hal Walker; screenplay by Frank Butler, Hal Kanter, and William Morrow; story by Harry Tugend; starring Bing Crosby, Bob Hope, Dorothy Lamour.

The Love Lottery (1953). Color. Ealing Studios. Directed by Charles Crichton; screenplay by Harry Kurnitz; starring David Niven, Ann Vernon, Herbert Lom.

Bogart can be heard in the 1954 version of *A Star Is Born*, starring his friend and neighbor Judy Garland. According to Allen Eyles in *The Movie Makers: Bogart*, as a good-luck gesture while Garland was in the sound studio recording some additions to the soundtrack, Bogart dubbed in the voice of a drunk in a café, asking that "Melancholy Baby" be played.

INDEX

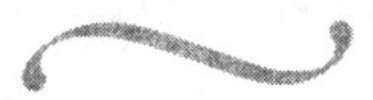

ABC (American Broadcasting Company), 368, 371
Abel, Walter, 92
Academy Awards, 73, 93, 117, 171, 385, 414, 421, 425, 437, 492, 506
  African Queen and, 454–458, 465–466, 488
  Casablanca and, 209, 255–256
Academy of Motion Picture Arts and Sciences, 56
Ackerman, Harry, 167
Across the Pacific (film), 160, 180, 182–187, 192, 193–194
Action in the North Atlantic (film), 210, 211–212, 214, 513
Adams, Cleve F., 251
Adams, Elmer, 315
Adams, Franklin P., 21
Adams, Junius, 140
Adventures of Don Juan (film), 407
Adventures of Robin Hood, The (film), 203
African Queen, The (film), 438–447, 450, 453–458, 473
  Academy Awards and, 454–458, 465–466, 488
  financing of, 440, 441
  location difficulties in, 444
African Queen, The (Forester), 438, 442, 460, 461
After All (Van Druten), 43
Agee, James, 476
Ager, Cecilia, 323
Aherne, Brian, 82
Akins, Claude, 482
Akins, Zoë, 105
Albert, Eddie, 138, 146
Alexander, John, 51
Alexander, Katherine, 36
Alexander Hamilton (film), 17
Alexander Hamilton (Hamlin), 17
Algiers (film), 179, 182, 190, 191, 208
Ali Khan, 240, 502
Alison, Joan, 176, 182, 190
All About Eve (film), 496
Alleborn, Al, 127, 130, 160, 162, 205, 206
Allen, Woody, 240, 387
Allenberg, Bert, 511–512
Allied Artists, 495, 506
All My Yesterdays (Robinson), 411–412
All Quiet on the Western Front (film), 63
All-Star Productions, 44
All Through the Night (film), 165, 172–173, 175, 180, 191
Allyson, June, 461
Aloha Means Goodbye (magazine series), 176
Altman, Robert, 461

Always in My Heart (film), 181
Amazing Dr. Clitterhouse, The (film), 116–117, 166, 358
Amazing Dr. Clitterhouse, The (radio adaptation), 166–167
Ambler, Eric, 231–232
America First, 135, 175
American Federation of Labor (AFL), 314
American in Paris, An (film), 454
American Jewish Committee, 298
American Legion, 401, 408
Americans for Democratic Action, 360
Anderson, Jack, 375
Anderson, Maxwell, 36, 118, 408, 410, 414
Andover (Phillips Academy), 10, 19, 21–25
Angels with Dirty Faces (film), 102
anti-Semitism, 21, 172, 182, 247–248, 298, 340, 355, 356, 381
Arbuckle, Roscoe (Fatty), 36
Arden, Eve, 153
Arlen, Richard, 400–401
Army, U.S., 185, 212, 226–235, 338
Arnow, Max, 88
Arthur, Jean, 275, 475
As Good as Married (film), 84
Associated Press (AP), 276, 277, 306, 357, 393, 397
Astaire, Fred, 63, 88
Astor, Mary, 180, 181, 183–184
  in *Maltese Falcon,* 152–164, 170, 171
Atkinson, Brooks, 43, 46, 54, 71, 90, 446, 501
Auer, Mischa, 72–73, 92, 265
Axelrod, George, 503–504

Babbitt (film), 49
Baby Mine (Mayo), 36
Baby's Record (M. H. Bogart, ill.), 12, 423
Bacal, Natalie, 236, 237, 244–245, 265, 271, 306, 307, 395, 445
  Stephen Bogart's relationship with, 440, 498
Bacall, Lauren (Betty Joan Bacal), 235–239, 241–260, 262–272, 283–285, 291–307, 318–330, 334, 389, 395, 408, 427–431, 436–438, 464–469, 496–498, 503–506
  appearance of, 236, 237, 238, 242, 243, 246, 253, 264, 265, 305, 306, 325, 441
  background of, 237–238
  in *Big Sleep,* 272, 277, 278, 285, 290, 292, 322–323
  comic flair of, 238–239, 472
  in *Confidential Agent,* 303, 318–324
  contracts of, 244, 245, 247, 249, 270–271, 303–304, 323–324, 437
  in *Dark Passage,* 332–333, 400, 416
  determination of, 237–238, 239, 247, 257, 299, 321, 436–437
  as fashion model, 236, 238, 239, 248, 418
  in film reviews, 285–286, 320–323, 414
  foreign travels of, 440–447, 479, 495
  in Hawaii, 480–481, 488
  HB's affair with, 258–259, 263, 265, 267–270, 272, 274, 276, 277, 278, 283, 284, 291
  HB's attraction to, 253, 256–259
  HB's correspondence with, 269–270, 416
  HB's engagement to, 293–302
  and HB's failing health and death, 509–522
  HB's first meeting with, 249
  HB's marriage to, 304–307
  HB's Oscar and, 456, 457
  HB's recantation and, 397–400, 402
  HB's relationship with, 304–305, 324–327, 340, 341, 416, 468, 496
  Hellinger's funeral and, 404
  in *How to Marry a Millionaire,* 472, 474
  Jewish background of, 237, 238, 247–248, 283, 298, 307
  in *Key Largo,* 409, 411, 414–415, 416
  "The Look" of, 246, 255, 266, 271, 322
  Melville Goodwin, U.S.A. and, 504, 509, 510
  memoir of, *see Lauren Bacall by Myself*
  New York junket of, 291–292, 296–299
  political activism of, 358, 359, 360, 365, 366, 368, 370, 372, 375, 377, 378, 380, 381–382, 390, 392, 403, 448, 466–469, 497
  pregnancies and childbirths of, 415–418, 421–423, 457, 464
  radio appearances of, 329–330, 368, 437–438

roles refused by, 328, 329, 416–418, 437
sailing of, 272, 353
screen tests of, 237, 239, 242, 244, 247, 249, 251, 253, 270
sense of humor of, 257, 305, 321
Sinatra and, 462, 512
sixth wedding anniversary of, 441
Slim Hawks's influence on, 246, 263
theater acting of, 237, 238–239
in *To Have and Have Not,* 235, 247, 249, 253–260, 263–268, 270, 271, 275, 285–286, 321
voice of, 245
Warner Bros.' relations with, 247, 249, 270–271, 285, 299, 319, 322–323, 324, 329, 389, 416–417, 421, 436–437, 478, 479, 489, 521
Background to Danger (film), 232
Bacon, Lloyd, 83, 211
Bad Men of Missouri (film), 145, 146
Bad Sister (film), 41, 73
Baker, Dorothy, 427
Baker, Mary, 44, 86, 94, 97, 269, 298, 513
HB's career and, 109, 140, 334, 501
HB'S marriages and, 73, 84–85, 91, 92, 108, 185, 265
Baker, Mel, 44, 91, 92, 223
Ball, Lucille, 136, 368
Ball of Fire (film), 274
Bandello, Caesare (Little Caesar), 409, 415
Bankhead, Tallulah, 82, 468
Barefoot Contessa, The (film), 495–496, 521
Barlowe, Joy, 259, 278
Barnes, Howard, 104, 141
Barrie, Milton, 61
Barrie, Wendy, 84
Barrie, William, 61
Barrymore, Ethel, 368, 411, 450, 451–452, 503
Barrymore, John, 81, 82, 152, 225, 411
Barrymore, Lionel, 70, 71, 409, 411, 413, 423
Barthelmess, Richard, 62–63, 69
Bartlett, Cy, 381
Batista, Fulgencio, 252
Battle Circus (film), 461–463
Battle Cry (film), 243, 244, 246, 247, 271, 303
Battle of San Pietro, The (documentary), 232
Bazin, André, 520
Beal, John, 381
Beat the Devil (film), 467, 469–480, 485–487, 490, 495
casting for, 471–472
script problems with, 472–474
Bedoya, Alphonse, 344, 351
Beebe, Lucius, 41
Beiderbecke, Bix, 427
Belasco, David, 39
Belden, Charles, 149
Belgian Congo, 440–446
Bellamy, Ralph, 424
Benchley, Nathaniel, 31, 37, 41, 72, 85–86, 201, 504
Benchley, Robert, 21, 68, 69, 131, 300, 326
Benét, Stephen Vincent, 33
Bennett, Bruce, 124, 213–214, 344, 349, 352
Bennett, Constance, 65
Bennett, Jeannette, 213, 216
Bennett, Joan, 110, 464, 503
Benny, Jack, 338, 505
Bergman, Ingrid, 152, 173, 472
Casablanca and, 191–192, 195–196, 198, 200–201, 202, 204, 206, 209, 211
Berkeley, Busby, 49, 89, 291
Berle, Milton, 293, 294
Berlin, Irving, 225
Berlin Diary (Shirer), 177–178
Bernardi, Herschel, 388
Bernstein, Leonard, 468
Bernstein, Walter, 387–388
Bessie, Alvah, 357, 364, 380, 383, 388
Biberman, Herbert, 357, 383
Big City Blues (film), 43
Big Jim McClain (film), 448
Big Shot, The (film), 181
Big Sleep, The (Chandler), 272, 278, 285, 288–289
Big Sleep, The (film), 272, 274, 277–279, 284–290, 292, 310, 322–323, 327, 427
Hawks's cutting of, 288
release of, 319, 329
reviews of, 323
Birth of a Nation (film), 137
Black, Lesley, 156
Black Legion (film), 76–80, 86, 421

blacklist, blacklisting, 367, 369, 370, 374, 376, 385, 387–388, 396, 404, 448–450, 469
Black Mask, 148
blacks, 131, 169, 298, 307
in *Casablanca,* 196–197
Blake, Bobby, 345–346
Blanke, Henry, 59, 142, 143, 316, 348
Maltese Falcon and, 149, 152, 156, 160, 161, 162, 171
Blankfort, Michael, 484
Blinn, Holbrook, 38
Blondell, Joan, 39, 43, 55–56, 81, 87
Blore, Eric, 416
Blowing Wild (film), 417, 418
Blue, Monte, 184
Blumenstock, Mort, 234–235, 292–293, 296, 298, 299, 300, 363, 389–390, 399, 427, 429, 436
Blythe, Ann, 303
Body and Soul (film; 1931), 41
Body and Soul (film; 1947), 41, 81
Bogart, Adam Watkins (grandfather), 8–10, 13, 19
Bogart, Belmont DeForest (father), 1–5, 7–11, 13–14, 16, 17, 53, 442
death of, 45, 47
drug addiction of, 4, 5, 8, 11, 28, 42
family background of, 8–10, 19
financial problems of, 28, 45, 47, 270
HB's relationship with, 8, 18, 21–25, 28, 31, 32, 45
health problems of, 42–43, 45
marriage of, 4, 11, 14, 19, 42–43, 96
sailing of, 18, 459
Bogart, Catherine (Catty; Kay; sister), 2, 3, 7, 42
death of, 45, 85
Bogart, Frances, *see* Rose, Frances Bogart
Bogart, Gisbert in den, 8
Bogart, Humphrey DeForest (Bogie):
as abused child, 4, 7–8, 15, 327, 423
acting debut of, 31
acting interest developed by, 16–17, 32
agents switched by, 108–109
appearance of, 4, 14, 15, 16, 19, 20, 23, 26, 27, 32, 35, 45, 46, 51, 54, 60, 82–83, 91, 109, 125, 222, 305, 348, 441, 447, 468, 478, 488, 511
baldness of, 222, 348, 468
birth of, 2, 13–14
in car accident, 474–477
CFA and, 365–368, 370–372, 375, 377–382, 386–387, 390–392, 395–403, 405, 417
chess playing of, 44, 45, 511, 515
Communist allegations and, 130–134, 226–227, 392–393, 395, 448
confidence of, 68–69, 141, 397, 480
contract suspensions of, 145–147, 217
death of, 465, 509–522
death scenes of, 81, 82
depression of, 223, 275, 286
as director, 30
divorces of, 37, 47, 84, 85, 89–90
drinking of, 34–35, 37, 39, 44, 45, 47, 52–53, 92–95, 107, 127, 137, 157, 168, 213, 214, 224–225, 230–233, 286–287, 293–296, 304, 324–326, 339–341, 392, 421, 428, 431, 443, 444, 445, 462, 475–476, 477, 500
education of, 14–16, 19, 21–24
family background of, 1–14, 19, 52–53, 298, 423, 483
as father, 497–498
fears and insecurity of, 15, 29, 284, 293, 296–298, 452, 492, 497–500
in fight for better roles, 109, 118, 122–124, 142, 144–147, 171, 216–219, 268–269, 328, 329
film contracts of, 43, 53, 54, 61–62, 67, 86, 89, 110, 111, 192–193, 215, 226, 264, 269, 333–334, 431, 432, 460–461
in film reviews, 60, 78, 79–80, 103, 104, 141, 146, 170, 323, 352–353, 435, 495
financial problems of, 44, 86, 88, 115, 284
as gentleman, 19–20, 76, 452, 483
gossip and rumors about, 80–81, 222, 265, 422, 512
greatest personal crisis of, 284–290, 292
handwriting of, 62, 137
health problems of, 450, 462–463, 474–475, 488, 490, 509–515
Hellinger Productions and, 338–339, 395–397, 401–402, 420
hormone treatments of, 348
horseback riding of, 29

humor of, 20, 214, 221, 289, 347, 435, 462, 493
income of, 32, 40, 47, 54, 61, 62, 84, 86, 88, 89, 109, 193, 264, 271, 329, 333, 334, 440, 453, 480
independence of, 18, 339, 425, 489
intelligence of, 109, 127, 144, 214, 311, 435, 481
line learning of, 345–346, 475
lip scar of, 27, 35, 266
love affairs of, 71–73, 84, 168, 201, 222–223, 233, 234; *see also* Bacall, Lauren
marriages of, *see* Bacall, Lauren; Menken, Helen; Methot, Mayo; Philips, Mary
naming of, 13
in Navy, 24–28, 483
Oscar of, 454–458, 465–466, 488
pessimism of, 331, 332, 340, 366
political activism of, 134, 136, 175, 180, 279–282, 310–313, 330, 365–368, 370–372, 375, 377–382, 386–387, 466–469
professionalism of, 108, 113, 165, 200, 201, 277, 345, 450, 455, 475, 507–508
radio appearances of, 81–82, 136, 280–282, 292, 293–294, 310, 329–330, 368, 382, 437–438, 448
romantic image of, 106, 109, 159–160, 166, 196, 201, 211, 290, 335
sadness of, 156–157, 462–463, 477
sailing of, 18, 23, 108, 174, 215, 265, 272, 301–302, 304–305, 326–327, 350, 353, 458–459, 485, 521
Santana Productions and, 420–421, 423–427, 433–437, 469–478, 500–501
sarcasm and caustic remarks of, 41, 130, 157, 340–341, 431, 451–453, 465, 475–476
self-mythologizing of, 15, 16
sexuality of, 17–18, 39, 68–69, 75, 94, 109, 123, 166
speech impediment of, 82, 87
stabbing of, 184–185, 202
as stage manager, 30–33
start of film career of, 38–42
star treatment of, 166, 169, 171
temper and violence of, 82, 94–95, 129–130, 142, 168, 227, 284, 294–296, 324, 435, 480, 493–494
theater acting of, 31–39, 43–47, 50, 51, 62, 397, 505–506
in theater reviews, 32, 33, 34, 38, 43, 45, 46–47
tough-guy image of, 7, 20, 166, 227, 289, 290, 442, 455, 474
turning points in career of, 40, 47, 159–160, 171, 440, 443
TV appearances of, 496–497, 505
Victorian spirit of duty in, 45, 47, 86, 96–98, 270
war tour of, 226–235, 249, 252
writing of, 30, 310–313, 405, 512–513
Bogart, Julia A. (grandmother), 9, 10
Bogart, Leslie Howard (daughter), 464, 480–481, 497, 498, 500, 515, 516, 521
Bogart, Maud Humphrey (mother), 1–8, 11–17, 22–25, 62, 298
appearance of, 3, 5, 6, 7, 11
as artist, 2, 3, 4, 6, 8, 11–15, 18, 53, 61, 96, 423, 477
blindness of, 12
death of, 138–139
drinking and drug addiction of, 4, 5, 8
family background of, 11–12, 13
HB's relationship with, 6–7, 28, 32, 61, 138–139, 270, 477
health problems of, 4, 22, 138
in Hollywood, 96–97, 108, 138–139, 270
husband's death and, 45
marriage of, 4, 11, 14, 19, 42–43, 96
Methot's relationship with, 96, 108, 139
pregnancies of, 1–2, 13–14
Bogart, Stephen Humphrey (son), 465, 480–481, 488, 500, 512, 521
birth of, 422–423
father's relationship with, 458, 497–498, 511, 515, 516, 519
parents' separation from, 440, 458
Boland, Mary, 32, 34
Bold Venture (radio show), 437–438
Bolger, Ray, 255
Bond, Ward, 162
Boone, Daniel, 212
Booth, Shirley, 34, 300, 460

Bordertown (film), 53, 58, 126, 421
Boyer, Charles, 179, 242, 303, 318–321, 368, 409, 518
Brackett, Leigh, 277, 288, 303
Brady, Alice, 20, 30, 31, 33, 38–39
Brady, William, Jr., 21, 29, 33, 35–36, 39, 47
Brady, William A., Sr., 17, 20–21, 30–33, 70, 392
Brando, Marlon, 396, 423, 454, 456, 506, 507
Brandsma, Maynard, 510, 516
Brecht, Bertolt, 357, 383
Breen, Joseph I., 112, 207
Breen Office, *see* Production Code Administration
Bren, Milton, 409
Brennan, Walter, 260, 261
Brenner, Herb, 478
Brent, George, 105–106, 183, 326
Brewster, Owen, 367
Brick Foxhole, The (Brooks), 331, 332
Bride's Book, The (M. H. Bogart, ill.), 6, 12
Bright Leaf (film), 436
Bright Victory (film), 454
Bringing Up Baby (film), 63, 111, 241
Brix, Herman, *see* Bennett, Bruce
Broadway's Like That (film), 39
Bromberg, J. Edward, 130
Bromfield, Hope, 305, 306
Bromfield, Louis, 102, 113, 212–213, 276, 292, 296, 300, 330, 423, 511
  HB's marriage and, 301–302, 305–306
Bromfield, Mary, 306, 511
Brooklyn, N.Y., 8, 24, 26, 31, 172
Brooks, Geraldine, 366
Brooks, Louise, 35, 47, 68–69, 72
Brooks, Richard, 98, 331–332, 339, 366, 404, 406, 461, 465, 466
  Deadline U.S.A. and, 449–453
  HB's death and, 514–515, 518
  HB's Oscar and, 456–457
  Key Largo and, 409, 410, 411, 414, 415
Brother Orchid (film), 119, 411
Broun, Haywood, 32, 33, 35
Brown, John Mason, 45–46
Brown, Lyman, 37
Brute Force (film), 338
Bryan, Jane, 75–76, 103
Buchwald, Art, 444, 479
Buck, Joyce, 358, 465
Buck, Jules, 107, 231–232, 248, 340, 365–366, 372–373, 397, 402, 448, 477
Buckner, Robert, 179, 319
Bullets or Ballots (film), 65, 81
Bunker, Isabel, 71
Burbank, Battle of, 316
Burke, Billie, 43
Burnett, Mrs. Murray, 182
Burnett, Murray, 176, 182, 190
Burnett, W. R., 117–121, 141, 149, 329
Burton, Richard, 447, 468, 479
Burton, Sybil, 479
Busch, Niven, 94
Byrnes, James F., 394

Cabinet of Dr. Caligari, The (film), 154, 199
Cagney, James, 55, 57, 65, 111, 112, 123, 177, 187, 256, 281, 328, 419
  Communist allegations and, 130, 131
  HB's films with, 76, 101–102, 103
  HB vs., 80, 86, 142, 346
Cahn, Sammy, 416, 464
Cain, James M., 62–63
Caine, Michael, 487
Caine Mutiny, The (film), 478–485, 506
Caine Mutiny, The (Wouk), 479
Calhern, Louis, 300
Call Bulletin (San Francisco), 208–209
Calloway, Cab, 169
Camille (film), 126, 364
Campbell, William, 461–463
Canandaigua, N.Y., 2, 3, 4, 8–10
Canandaigua Lake, 1–4, 6, 18, 19
Cantor, Eddie, 381
Capa, Robert, 479
Capp, Al, 468
Capra, Frank, 187, 380–381
Capote, Truman, 474, 475, 477–478, 513
Captain Blood (film), 55
Capucine, 503–504
Carmichael, Hoagy, 260–261, 264, 465
Carpenter, Elliot, 197
Carpenter, Meta, *see* Wilde, Meta
Carroll, Harrison, 418
Carson, Charles, 430
Carson, Jack, 416
Casablanca, 207, 208–209, 227, 243

Casablanca (film), 20, 35, 99, 106, 182–183, 187–193, 195–212, 215, 218, 225, 270, 285, 327, 424, 455, 489
All Through the Night vs., 172, 173
casting for, 190–192, 196–197, 199–200
ending of, 204–208
filming of, 195–206
Key Largo vs., 409
music in, 67, 203–204
Oscars and reviews of, 209, 255–256
script for, 187–190, 196, 200, 204–206
Castellanos, Rev. Kermit, 518
Catalina Island, 67–68, 108, 167, 459, 511
Cayenne, 215, 220
CBS (Columbia Broadcasting System), 81, 136, 396
CBS Shakespeare Theater (radio show), 81–82
Celler, Emanuel, 356
censorship, 49, 111–112, 175, 220, 250, 275, 344, 390, 449
HUAC hearings and, 365, 369, 370, 378, 379
see also Production Code Administration
CFA, *see* Committee for the First Amendment
Chain Lightning (film), 427, 431, 488
Challenge of the Post War World to the Liberal Movement, The (forum), 330
Chambers, Whitman, 251
Champlin, Charles, 487
Chandler, Raymond, 20, 100, 272, 278, 285, 288–289, 301, 493
Chase, Gertrude Hatch, 72, 95, 96, 136–137, 167, 445
Chasen, Dave, 422
chess, 197–198, 220, 221, 511, 515
Chicago *Tribune,* 354–355, 356
child abuse, 4, 7–8, 15, 327, 423
China Clipper (film), 65, 66
Christian Science Monitor, 404–405
Chrysalis (Porter), 43, 52
Churchill, Winston, 12, 209, 219, 309, 312
Churchill family, 11–12
Cincinnati Kid, The (film), 385
Citizen Kane (film), 63, 154, 171
civil rights, 131, 279, 310, 316, 358–360, 369–370
Clark, Bennett C., 174
Clark, Dane, 212
Clark, Ed, 306–307
Clark, Fred, 329
Claudia (play), 244
Clift, Montgomery, 426, 454, 457, 468, 507
Clock Struck Three, The (film), 149
Cobb, Lee J., 317
Cockburn, Claud, 470, 472
Cohan, George M., 70, 71, 187, 446
Cohn, Harry, 308, 328, 420, 480, 500, 504, 506, 510–511, 517
Colbert, Claudette, 240, 243, 246, 281
Cold War, 313, 354–388
see also House Un-American Activities Committee
Cole, Lester, 357, 383
Cole, Rev. Dr. Lawrence T. (Bunny), 15
Collier, Bill, 41
Collier's, 285
Collins, Richard, 357
Columbia Pictures, 63, 237, 239, 308, 388, 436, 500
HB's work for, 43, 213–215, 272, 327–328, 478–485, 488, 500, 504, 506–508, 510–511
Hellinger Productions and, 338–339
Santana Productions and, 420–421, 425, 427
Come Back, Little Sheba (Inge), 459–460
Committee for the First Amendment (CFA), 358–360, 365–387, 390–392, 395–403, 405, 417, 448
flight to Washington by, 370–372
HB's recantation and, 397–403, 405–406, 411
radio show of, 367–368, 371
Committee of 56, 131
Committee on Un-American Activities, California version of, 317
see also House Un-American Activities Committee
Communists, Communist Party, 130–134, 194–195, 225–227, 331, 336, 359, 370, 374
HB's recantation and, 397–398
HUAC investigations of, 130–134, 355–388, 390, 392–401, 409–410, 412, 420, 447–449, 467–468, 481

Communists, Communist Party *(continued)*
McCormick and, 354–355
MPAA meeting on, 392, 394–395
Studio Strike and, 314, 316, 317
concentration camps, 308–309, 494
Conference of Studio Unions (CSU), 313–317
Confessions of a Nazi Spy (film), 173, 174–175, 358
Confidential Agent (film), 303, 309, 318–324
Conflict (film), 215–221, 244
Congress, U.S., 174, 195, 308, 355
see also House of Representatives, U.S.; House Un-American Activities Committee; Senate, U.S.
Congress of Industrial Organizations (CIO), 131, 314
Conklin, Peggy, 51
Connery, Sean, 487
Conover Agency, 237, 245
Consent Decree, 419, 420
Constitution, U.S., 311, 358, 359, 369, 372, 382, 383
Conte, Richard, 366
Cook, Elisha, Jr., 153
Cooke, Alistair, 290, 506–507, 514
Cooper, Gary, 130, 174, 239, 262, 274, 282, 364, 400, 417, 418, 426, 436, 517
Correll, Charles, 464, 465
Cortez, Ricardo, 149
Corvette K-225 (film), 248
Corwin, Norman, 280–282, 330, 367–368
Cosmopolitan, 391
Cosmopolitan Pictures, 70
costumes and wardrobe, 17, 57, 80, 82–83, 101, 155, 473
Cotten, Joseph, 490
Cotton Club, 169
Cover Girl (film), 237, 301
Coward, Noël, 503
Cowan, Jerome, 153
Cradle Snatchers (Medcraft and Mitchell), 33, 34, 36
Craig, May, 378
Cramer, Dee Hartford Hawks, 241, 245–246, 263, 277, 286, 303, 365, 479, 496, 519–520
Crawford, Broderick, 437
Crawford, Joan, 131, 417, 437
Crime School (film), 103, 111
Crist, Judith, 290
Cromwell, John, 29, 31, 331, 333, 364
Crosby, Bing, 364
Croves, Hal, *see* Traven, B.
Crowther, Bosley, 110
Crum, Bartley, 281
Cuba, 252
Cummings, Don, 227
Curtiz, Michael, 81, 137, 297, 333, 416, 427, 436, 503
Casablanca and, 190, 192, 197, 198, 200, 202–205, 209, 256
Passage to Marseille and, 215, 224

Dachau, 308–309
Daily Variety, 60, 375, 495
Daily Worker, 393, 402, 408
Dale, Alan, 32, 34
Dalio, Marcel, 199, 203, 257, 260
Dancing Town, The (film), 38, 39
Dangerous (film), 73
Daniels, Bebe, 55, 149
Dark Eyes (play), 274–275
Dark Journey (film), 199
Dark Passage (film), 332–333, 338, 348, 389, 391, 400, 416
Dark Road, The (Goodis), 332
Dark Victory (film), 41–42, 103–106, 110, 111, 112, 152, 159, 189
Einfeld's watching of, 122, 123
Darnell, Linda, 175–176
Dart, Justin, 75
Dassin, Jules, 420
Daves, Delmer, 333, 427
Davies, Joseph E., 194, 195, 225, 309, 362
Davis, Bette, 41–42, 50, 53, 86, 113, 123, 149, 195, 243, 257, 266, 417, 439
in *Bordertown,* 53, 58, 126
in *Dark Victory,* 41–42, 103–106, 112, 152
HB's films with, 41–42, 43, 51, 53–54, 58–61, 73–76, 81, 103–106, 112, 203
lawsuit lost by, 74, 75
in *Marked Woman,* 73–77
in *Now, Voyager,* 178, 198
Oscars of, 73, 117
Petrified Forest and, 53–54, 58–61
political activities of, 131, 310

Dawn Patrol, The (film), 105
Day, Doris, 416, 427
Dead End (film), 83–86, 101, 110, 400, 447
Dead End (Kingsley), 83, 424
Dead End Kids, 84, 102, 111
Deadline U.S.A. (film), 448–453, 460, 502–503
Dead Reckoning (film), 328, 331
Dean, James, 290, 424
Death of a Salesman (film), 454
De Cordova, Fred, 258–259
de Gaulle, Charles, 208, 209
de Havilland, Olivia, 152, 215
Delehanty, Thornton, 60, 326, 333, 337, 456
Delmont, Betty Lou, 348
Demarest, William, 165, 173
DeMille, Cecil B., 30, 279
Democratic National Committee, 280
Democrats, Democratic Party, 3, 134, 136, 355–356, 380, 395
  in election of 1944, 279–282, 310, 311
  in election of 1952, 466–469
Depression, Great, 39, 43–44, 55–56, 59, 62, 63, 113, 431
Derek, John, 423
Desperate Hours, The (film), 501–502, 506
Desperate Hours, The (Hayes), 501
Detective Story (film), 424–425, 454
Detective Story (Kingsley), 424
Devil with Women, A (film), 40–41
Dewey, Thomas E., 74, 279–280, 282
Diamond, I.A.L. (Izzy), 360
Diamond, Jack, 300
Diana, princess of Wales, 12
Dickinson, Angie, 503–504
Dies, Martin, 130–134, 227, 282, 355, 366, 393
Dietrich, Marlene, 143, 246, 249, 270, 275, 518
Dillinger, John, 46, 57
Disney, Walt, 282, 314, 363–364, 400
Dmytryk, Edward, 357, 377, 383, 481–482, 502, 503
Dodge City (film), 106–107
Don Juan (film), 49
Dorn, Philip, 196
Dorso, Richard, 328
Double Indemnity (film), 491, 493
Douglas, Helen Gahagan, 175–176, 394
Douglas, Kirk, 238, 425, 427, 510
Douglas, Melvyn, 130, 131, 136, 175–176, 368, 381, 394
Douglas, Paul, 422
Downing, Joseph, 83
Drake, Charles, 244
Dr. Ehrlich's Magic Bullet (film), 117
Drifting (Colton and Andrews), 31, 33, 35
Dr. Socrates (film), 113
drug addiction, 4, 5, 8, 11, 28, 42
Dunne, Amanda Duff, 359, 423, 509–510
Dunne, Irene, 240, 400
Dunne, Philip, 131, 324, 394, 402–405, 448
  HUAC hearings and, 357–360, 365–379, 381, 383, 384, 387
Durante, Jimmy, 282
Dvorak, Ann, 43

Edeson, Arthur, 154, 158–159, 197, 206
Einfeld, S. Charles, 122–123, 140, 207, 218, 225, 270, 271, 291–292, 296, 299, 300, 319, 358, 366
Eisenhower, Dwight D., 308, 380, 466, 467, 469
elections:
  of 1940, 134, 136, 137
  of 1944, 279–282, 310, 311
  of 1946, 330–331, 354, 358
  of 1952, 466–469
Eliot, T. S., 447
Elisofon, Eliot, 442
Ellington, Duke, 169
El Morocco panda incident, 428–431
Empire Strikes Back, The (film), 277
Enforcer, The (film), 431–432, 447, 488, 504
Engstead, John, 246
Enright, Ray, 137, 145, 258
Ephron, Henry and Phoebe, 513
Episcopalians, 2–3, 14–15, 36, 39
Epstein, Julius, 172, 356, 362, 378
  Casablanca and, 182, 187–189, 191, 192, 197, 199–200, 204, 206, 209, 256
Epstein, Philip, 172, 323, 356, 362, 378
  Casablanca and, 182, 187–189, 191, 197, 206, 209, 256
Evelove, Alex, 265, 267–268, 276, 282, 391, 421

Everybody Comes to Rick's (Burnett and Alison), 176, 179, 182, 189–190

Fagan, Myron C., 448
Fairbanks, Douglas, Jr., 66, 136
Famous Players–Lasky, 240
Farewell, My Lovely (Chandler), 301
Farewell, My Lovely (film), 290
Farmer, Frances, 242
Farnsworth, Arthur, 75
Farrar, John, 33
Farrell, Charles, 40, 41
fascism, 303, 377, 383
 in *Black Legion,* 76–80
 see also Nazi Germany, Nazism
Father of the Bride (film), 503
Faulkner, William, 156, 241, 250, 260, 270, 277, 288, 496
Fazenda, Louise, 87
FBI (Federal Bureau of Investigation), 130, 132, 317, 360, 382, 392–393, 407, 448
Fehr, Rudi, 172, 173, 411, 412
Feldman, Charles K., 216, 219, 236, 237, 239–249, 303, 358, 503–504, 506
 Bacall and, 241–245, 322–323
Fender, Bob, 347, 349
Ferrer, José, 473, 480, 484, 485
Fields, W. C., 110
Fight for Freedom Committee, 175, 176, 180
Fighting 69th, The (film), 177
Film Daily, 208
First Amendment, 358, 372, 374, 384, 385, 387, 481
Fischer, Steve, 422
Fitts, Buron, 100, 132
Fitzgerald, Ella, 196
Fitzgerald, Geraldine, 103, 152, 195–196
Flamingo Road (film), 417
Flynn, Errol, 55, 81, 106, 143, 167, 174, 177, 203, 226, 266, 291, 313, 328, 407, 500
Fonda, Henry, 43, 87, 88, 131, 136, 150, 426, 505
Fontaine, Joan, 518
Foran, Dick, 62, 78
Forbstein, Leo, 203
Ford, John, 41, 400
Foreign Correspondent (film), 174
Forester, C. S., 329, 438, 442, 504
42nd Street (film), 55, 211, 270
For Whom the Bell Tolls (film), 191, 206
For Whom the Bell Tolls (Hemingway), 191
Fountainhead, The (film), 417
Fox, William, 56
Fox Film Corporation, 40–42, 122
Foy, Bryan, 64–65
Foy, Eddie, 64
France, 218
 in World War II, 135, 182, 203, 208
Francen, Victor, 220
Francis, Kay, 88, 113–115, 122
Franco, Francisco, 131, 376
Frankenstein (film), 63
Frankfurter, Felix, 372
Franklin, Benjamin, 12, 312
Franklin, Sidney, 255
Franklin House, 8–9, 10
Franklin Street (Sheekman), 238–239
Frazier, George, 293
Frederic W. Ziv Company, 437–438
Freeman, Y. Frank, 467
Freund, Karl, 410–411
Front, The (film), 387–388
Fugitive, The (film), 332
Fugitive, The (TV series), 332
Furlow, Floyd, 22
Furthman, Jules, 249, 250, 252, 270, 277, 288

Gabin, Jean, 179, 216–219
Gable, Clark, 177, 190, 193, 215, 282, 400, 455, 487, 495
gangster roles:
 in film, 50–54, 57–61, 65, 74–75, 76, 83–85, 101, 116–128, 141, 173, 335, 409, 410
 in theater, 44, 45–47, 50, 51
Garbo, Greta, 88, 239, 270, 271, 275, 364, 479
Garden of Allah, 68–69, 73, 300–301, 318, 434
Gardner, Ava, 495
Garfield, John, 41, 69, 123–124, 136, 281, 313, 337, 462
 HUAC hearings and, 368, 378, 379, 447
 in *Out of the Fog,* 142, 143
Garland, Judy, 280, 281, 360, 368, 416, 465, 504
Garland, Robert, 47

Garnett, Tay, 87
Garson, Greer, 321, 457, 510
Gates, Joyce, 239, 248
Gaye, Gregory, 199
Gaynor, Janet, 40, 466
Gehman, Richard, 103
Geller, James, 288
Gentleman's Agreement (film), 448, 449
Gentle People, The (Shaw), 141
George, Gladys, 81, 153
George, Grace, 20–21, 30, 31, 38
George Washington Slept Here (film), 183
Germany, 336
  in World War I, 24, 438
  see also Nazi Germany, Nazism
Gersh, Phil, 231, 233, 480, 491–492, 498–499, 501–502
Gershwin, Ira, 360, 366, 449
Gershwin, Lee, 298
Giannini, A. P., 464
Gibson, Julie, 475–478
Gibson, Virginia, 437
Giesler, Jerry, 283, 291, 293, 302
Girl from Jones Beach, The (film), 417
Girl of the Golden West (play), 17
Girls About Town (film), 113
Gish, Lillian, 70
Glad, Gladys, 339, 403
Gleason, Jackie, 172, 368
Gleason, Russell, 92
Goddard, Paulette, 360, 368
Godfrey, Peter, 285, 303
God Is My Co-pilot (script), 268–269
God's Country and the Woman (film), 74
Gold Diggers of 1933 (film), 55–56
Gold Diggers of 1935 (film), 421
Golden, John, 51
Golden Boy (film), 81
Goldwyn, Samuel, 30, 83–84, 106, 280
Gone With the Wind (film), 80, 111, 179
Goodis, David, 332
Goodman, Walter, 448
Good Shepherd, The (Forester), 504, 510–511
Gould, Jack, 505
Goulding, Edmund, 104, 105, 518
Graham, Sheila, 422, 502
Grahame, Gloria, 433
Grand Hotel (film), 179
Granite State, USS, 24
Grant, Cary, 63, 262, 274, 426, 491, 492
Grauman's Chinese Theatre, 327–328
Gray, Mack, 144
Grayson, Charles, 341, 348
Grayson, Kathryn, 416
Great Britain, in World War II, 135, 136, 173–174, 175, 207
Great Day (Youmans), 71
Great Lie, The (film), 171
Great O'Malley, The (film), 76
Great Train Robbery, The (film), 48
Greenaway, Kate, 12
Greenberg, Hank, 395
Greene, Graham, 303, 318, 319, 322
Greenstreet, Sydney, 180, 215, 219, 417
  in *Across the Pacific,* 180, 183, 186
  in *Casablanca,* 196, 199, 200
  in *Maltese Falcon,* 153, 155, 156, 158–159, 161, 170, 171
Grobel, Lawrence, 121, 163
Gromyko, Andrei, 309
Group Theatre, 141
Gurney, Noll, 86

Haade, William, 409
Haggiag, Roberto, 474
Hall, James Norman, 215
Halliday, John, Jr., 39
Halliday, John, Sr., 39
Halliday, Mary, 37, 39
Hamilton, Hamish, 289
Hamilton, Neil, 30–31
Hamlin, Arthur, 16
Hamlin, Frank, 5, 16
Hamlin, Mary, 17
Hammerstein, Oscar, 468
Hammett, Dashiell, 148, 149, 151, 153, 154, 162, 163, 180–182
Handy, W. C., 169
Hannegan, Robert, 280
Harburg, E. Y., 281
Harder They Fall, The (film), 504, 506–508
Harder They Fall, The (Schulberg), 431–432
Hardwicke, Sir Cedric, 82
Hark, Ralph, 227, 230
Harlem, 169–170
Harmetz, Aljean, 99, 189, 190, 192, 195–196, 200, 255, 256
Harper's Bazaar, 236, 239, 307
Harriman, Averill, 281
Hartford, Dee, *see* Cramer, Dee Hartford Hawks

Hartley, Alice, 440
Hartman, Don, 486, 501
Hatch, Eric, 71–72, 136–137, 167
Hatch, Gertrude, *see* Chase, Gertrude Hatch
Havoc, June, 366, 377, 381
Hawaii, 480–483, 488
Hawkins, George, 276, 292, 296, 305, 306, 511
Hawks, Athole Shearer, 241
Hawks, Dee Hartford, *see* Cramer, Dee Hartford Hawks
Hawks, Howard Winchester, 144, 179, 240–254, 269, 274–275, 303, 333, 427, 479, 496
  Bacall and, 235, 239, 241–251, 257, 262–265, 270–271, 272, 274, 286, 303–304, 318, 323, 520
  background of, 240
  Big Sleep and, 272, 277, 279, 285–289, 292, 323
  coldness of, 241, 262, 263, 519–520
  HB's blowup with, 263–264
  HB's death and, 519–520
  HUAC hearings and, 365
  tax problems of, 247, 249
  To Have and Have Not and, 235, 246–254, 259–264, 270, 271
Hawks, Nancy Gross (Slim), 239, 246, 251, 262–263, 269, 270, 303
Hawks-Feldman Productions, 241–249, 270–271, 303–304
Hayden, Sterling, 448
Hayes, Helen, 38, 43, 368, 397, 505–506
Hays, Will H., 112
Hayward, Leland, 54, 88, 108–109, 193, 518
Hayward, Louis, 128
Hayward, Susan, 510
Hayworth, Rita, 152, 237, 240, 242, 281, 301, 360
Hearst, Inez Robb, 293, 296
Hearst, William Randolph, 70, 147, 355, 390, 391, 449
Hecht, Ben, 339
Heflin, Van, 368
Heine, Heinrich, 192
Hellinger, Mark, 35, 119–121, 143, 303, 305, 325, 326, 338–340, 401–404
  Brooks and, 331–332
  CFA and, 365–366
  death of, 403–404, 420, 423, 517
  HB's deal with, 338–339, 395–397, 401–402
  High Sierra and, 119–121, 124, 126, 339
  The Roaring Twenties and, 119
Hellman, Lillian, 84, 178, 180–182, 447
Hell's Bells (Connors), 34, 300
Hemingway, Ernest, 191, 246–247, 252, 262, 327, 338, 396, 403, 442, 465
Henkel, Paul, 431
Henreid, Liesel, 370
Henreid, Paul, 196, 198, 199, 203, 206, 400
  HUAC hearings and, 366, 368, 370
Henry IV, Part I (Shakespeare), 82
Hepburn, Audrey, 472, 491–492, 494–495
Hepburn, Katharine, 63, 88, 242, 280, 359–360, 385, 471
  in *African Queen*, 439–447, 454, 455, 457
  HB's death and, 513, 515, 516, 517
Heymann, Irene, 517
Hickox, Syd, 292
High Sierra (Burnett), 117–118
High Sierra (film), 116–130, 139–144, 149
  actors considered for, 118–125
  billing in, 129–130, 133
  filming of, 126–129, 132, 133, 136
  HB's hero image created in, 141
  HB's tests for, 122, 124–125
  reviews of, 140–141
Hilliard, Harriet, 139
His Girl Friday (film), 274
Hitchcock, Alfred, 170, 174
Hitler, Adolf, 131, 135–136, 172, 182, 195, 309, 312, 376
Hitler-Stalin Pact, 135
Hobart, Rose, 220–221, 315, 317
Hoffman, Abbie, 377
Holden, William, 103, 368, 491–492, 494
Holifield, Chet, 380, 394, 398–399, 403
Hollingshead, Gordon, 253
Hollywood, Calif., 49–69, 71–227, 239–292, 300–305, 307–388, 395–427, 431–440, 447–468, 484–522
  alleged Communist takeover of, 354–355
  HB's arrival in, 40–42

HB's second attempt in, 43
politics in, 130–134, 172–176, 279–282, 307, 313–317, 330–331, 354–388
Hollywood Bowl, 224–225
Hollywood Democratic Committee (HDC), 279, 310, 367, 378, 467
Hollywood Fights Back (radio show), 367–368, 371, 387
Hollywood for Roosevelt, 280
Hollywood Hotel (radio show), 147
Hollywood Independent Citizens Committee of the Arts, Sciences, and Professions (HICCASP), 310, 316, 330, 331, 358, 367
Hollywood Motion Picture Review, 170
Hollywood Reporter, 60, 104, 106, 170, 175, 183, 225, 323, 353, 437, 455
Hollywood Review, 320
Hollywood Ten, 377, 383–386, 388, 390–394, 399, 401, 449, 481
House vote on, 392–394, 397
Hollywood Victory Committee, 226, 255
Holmby Hills, 464–465, 496, 497
Holmes, Oliver Wendell, 127
Holocaust, 308–309, 494
Holt, Jack, 345
Holt, Tim, 345, 346, 347, 349
Holy Terror (film), 42, 448
Honolulu Classic, 350, 353
Hoover, J. Edgar, 392–393
Hope, Bob, 253
Hopkins, Arthur, 45–46, 50, 71, 439
Hopkins, David, 371
Hopkins, Harry, 371
Hopkins, Miriam, 84, 88, 106
Hopper, Hedda, 247, 283, 417–418, 422, 460, 464
Horizon-Romulus, 488
Horn Blows at Midnight, The (film), 338
Horne, John, 497
Horne, Lena, 169, 196, 255, 298
House of Representatives, U.S., 392–394, 397
House Un-American Activities Committee (HUAC), 310
Communist influence in Hollywood investigated by, 130–134, 355–388, 390, 392–401, 409–410, 412, 420, 447–449, 467–468, 481
Dies and, 130–134, 282, 355, 366, 393
Howard, Cy, 465
Howard, Frances, 31
Howard, Jean, 239–240, 242, 244–247
Howard, Leslie, 81, 87, 118, 191, 219, 464, 465
in *Petrified Forest* (film), 50, 53, 58–61
in *Petrified Forest* (play), 46, 50, 51
Howe, James Wong, 215
Howell, Miriam, 44
How Green Was My Valley (film), 142, 171
How to Marry a Millionaire (film), 472, 474
Huckleberry Finn (film), 197
Hughes, Dorothy, 433
Hughes, Howard, 119, 239, 246, 247, 367
Hughes, John, 344
Hugunin, Lee, 66, 67
Humphrey, John (grandfather), 12
Humphrey, Maud, *see* Bogart, Maud Humphrey
Hunt, Marsha, 166–167, 366, 368–372, 380, 382, 383, 400
Hunter, Kim, 450
Huntington Hartford Theater, 505–506
Huston, Anjelica, 351
Huston, John, 143, 206, 241, 333–353, 427, 484, 493, 495
Across the Pacific and, 183–186
African Queen and, 439, 440, 442–447, 454, 457
in Army, 185, 231–232, 338
Bacall and, 324, 340, 472
background of, 117
Beat the Devil and, 467, 469–478, 485–487
Christian Science Monitor statement and, 404–405
HB's death and, 514–519
HB's friendship with, 157, 338, 340–341, 350–351, 402, 411, 467–468, 477, 510, 516
on HB's "morbid faithfulness," 157, 168
High Sierra and, 116–121, 124, 127, 141, 149
HUAC investigation and, 357–358, 366–375, 381, 382, 383–384, 409–410
Key Largo and, 395, 406–415

Huston, John *(continued)*
Maltese Falcon and, 149–150, 163, 170, 171, 471
Treasure of the Sierra Madre and, 334, 335, 337, 338, 341–353, 442
Watch on the Rhine and, 180–182
Huston, Tony, 351
Huston, Walter, 82, 117, 136, 160, 181
in *Treasure of the Sierra Madre,* 337, 343, 345, 351
Hutton, Betty, 255
Hyams, Joe, 31, 33, 36, 45, 47, 348, 402, 474, 485, 487, 496, 498
on Frances, 97–98
on HB-Bacall relationship, 269
on HB-Methot marriage, 92, 108, 184, 185, 265
and HB's failing health and death, 511–514, 520
Hyer, Martha, 503–504, 511–512

I Am a Fugitive from a Chain Gang (film), 80, 118
I Loved You Wednesday (Ricardel and Du Bois), 43
"I'm No Communist" (Bogart), 405
In a Lonely Place (film), 424, 433–436, 500
In a Lonely Place (Hughes), 433, 495
Indiscretion of an American Wife (film), 474
Inge, William, 459–460
In Search of My Father (S. H. Bogart), 458
Inspector General, The (film), 419
Intermezzo (film), 191
Internal Revenue Service, 304, 339
International Alliance of Theatrical Stage Employees (IATSE), 313–317
Invisible Man, The (film), 63
Invisible Stripes (film), 103, 151, 492
Invitation to a Murder (King), 44–45
Ireland, 479
Isle of Fury (film), 66–67, 73
isolationism, 173, 174–175
"I Stuck My Neck Out" (Bogart), 310–313
It All Came True (film), 102, 110, 112, 119
Italy, 414
HB in, 227–233, 252, 469, 474–478, 495–496, 521
It Happened One Night (film), 240
It's A Wonderful Life (film), 411
I Was a Communist for the F.B.I. (film), 448
I Was a Male War Bride (film), 241, 247

Jack Bleeck's Artists and Writers Restaurant, 35, 80, 298
Jacobs, William, 221
Jacobson, Max, 493
Jaffe, Sam, 109, 110–111, 144, 152, 165, 171, 219, 223, 231, 233–235, 287, 324, 327, 333, 405, 435, 480, 501
in contract negotiations, 193, 264, 334, 460, 478–479
HB's suspensions and, 145, 146, 269
life insurance and, 185
Japan, 131, 176, 178
Japanese-Americans, rounding up of, 186
Jazz Singer, The (film), 37, 49, 56, 64
Jefferson, Thomas, 312
Jefferson House, 9, 10
Jelke, Johnny, 428
Jessel, George, 468
Jews, 21, 131, 172, 173, 182, 199, 203, 220, 340, 404, 494
see also anti-Semitism; Bacall, Lauren, Jewish background of
Jezebel (film), 111, 117, 149, 178
Johnny Belinda (film), 93, 419
Johnson, Dorris Bowdon, 301, 456, 518
Johnson, Erskine, 455
Johnson, Nunnally, 41, 94, 301, 326, 456, 472, 506, 518, 519
Johnson, Van, 480, 481, 482, 484
Johnston, Eric, 369, 375–376, 379–380, 394–395
Jolson, Al, 49, 64
Jones, Chuck, 330
Jones, Jennifer, 471, 472, 474, 487, 517
Jones, John, 510
Jourdan, Louis, 518
Journey Through the Harz Mountains (Heine), 192
Juarez (film), 117, 120
Juarez, Benito, 117

Kael, Pauline, 424
Kahn, Gordon, 357
Kalmenson, Benjamin, 363
Kanfer, Stefan, 364, 387

Karnot, Stephen, 179
Katz, Lee, 200, 202, 203
Kaufman, George S., 239, 360
Kaye, Danny, 280, 281, 419, 495, 518
CFA and, 360, 366, 368, 370–371, 372, 377–379, 381, 386
Kaye, Henrietta, 52–53, 94
Kazan, Elia, 142, 449
Keighley, William, 329
Keller, Helen, 36
Kelly, Gene, 280, 281, 360, 365, 366, 368, 372, 375, 378, 379
Kelly, Grace, 240
Kennedy, Arthur, 183, 454
Kent, John, 36
Keyes, Evelyn, 325, 340–341, 342, 347, 351, 402
HUAC hearings and, 366, 377, 379, 386
Key Largo (Anderson), 118, 408, 410, 414
Key Largo (film), 122, 172, 395, 406–416, 427, 488
Kid Galahad (film), 81, 105, 137, 146
Kilgallen, Dorothy, 512
Kilgore, Harley M., 368
"Killers, The" (Hemingway), 338
Killers, The (film), 338, 339
King of the Underworld (film), 101, 113–115, 117
Kingsley, Sidney, 83, 84, 424–425
Kinsky, Leonid, 199, 200, 201, 203, 204
Kipling, Rudyard, 487
Kirby, Frank E., 24
Kline, Wally, 183
Knock on Any Door (film), 396, 420, 423–424, 500
Knox, Alexander, 357–358
Kober, Arthur, 68
Koch, Howard, 189, 197, 200, 204, 206, 209, 256, 357, 364–365, 385
Kohner, Paul, 337, 342, 353, 471, 516
Korda, Alexander, 214
Korda, Zoltan, 214
Kovner, Irving, 197
Kramer, Stanley, 479–480, 481, 483, 484–485
Krueger, Kurt, 213
Ku Klux Klan (KKK), 77, 80, 279

labor, labor movement, 131, 279, 313–317
see also specific unions
Ladd, Alan, 289
Ladies' Man (film), 113
Laemmle, Carl, Jr., 435
LaFollette, Suzanne, 225
Lakeside Country Club, 157–158
Lamarr, Hedy, 179, 190, 241, 327
Lambert, Grace Lansing, 3–4, 7, 17–18, 521
Lamond, John, 71
Lancaster, Burt, 328, 368, 425–426
Lanchester, Elsa, 438
Lane, Lola, 75–76
Lane, Priscilla, 89, 107
Lane, Rosemary, 107
Lang, Fritz, 410
Lang, Jennings, 503
Lansing, Grace, *see* Lambert, Grace Lansing
Lansing, Harry, 3–4
Lardner, Alice, 385
Lardner, Frances, 385–386
Lardner, Ring, Jr., 32, 135, 357, 369, 374, 383–386, 403, 461
Lasky, Jesse L., 30
Lasky Feature Play Company, 30
Lastfogel, Abe, 234, 517
Last Mile, The (Wexley), 449
Last Train West, The (screenplay), 479
Laughton, Charles, 215, 438
Lauren Bacall by Myself (Bacall), 249, 263, 268, 349, 442, 468, 480
Lawrence, Jerome, 51, 121, 367–368, 387
Lawrence, Marc, 409
Lawson, John Howard, 212, 357, 363, 364, 376–378, 383, 388, 390
Lazar, Irving (Swifty), 359, 503–504, 511–512, 513, 518
LeBeau, Madeleine, 203–204
Lederer, Charles, 503–504
Lee, Irene, 178–179
Leech, John L., 131–132
Leffers, Ken, 276
Left Hand of God, The (film), 502–503
Legion of Decency, 111, 408
Lehman, Ernest, 492, 493, 494
Leigh, Vivien, 199, 447, 479
Lend-Lease Act, 174
Leonard, Sheldon, 261
Lerner, Max, 520
LeRoy, Mervyn, 43
Leslie, Amy, 34
Leslie, Joan, 126, 138, 258

Levant, Oscar, 416
Levee, Mike, 118
Levene, Sam, 175–176
Leviathan, USS, 26
Lewis, Al, 40
Lewis, Harry, 411, 415
Lewis, Ralph E., 304, 461
Lewis, Sinclair, 49
Life, 225, 272–273, 286, 293, 306–307, 353, 378, 379, 391, 418, 442, 498, 506, 519
Life (film), 30
Life of Emile Zola, The (film), 118
Life on Film, A (Astor), 153
Light in the Piazza (film), 189
Lights of New York, The (film), 49, 64
Linden, Eric, 43
Lindfors, Viveca, 333
Lindsay, Ben, 92
Lindsay, Cynthia, 92, 93, 97
Lindstrom, Peter, 192
Linkletter, Art, 465
Little Caesar (film), 52, 56
Litvak, Anatole, 142, 143, 358
Litvinov, Maxim, 225
Litvinov, Mme., 315, 362
Loew's, Inc., 355, 427
Lollobrigida, Gina, 472
Lombard, Carole, 246
London, 62, 136, 441, 446–447, 448, 479
London Can Take It (film), 173
Lonesome Train, The (Robinson), 243
Longworth, Alice Roosevelt, 74
Look, 285
Lord, Robert, 179, 183, 420–421
Lorre, Peter, 153, 156, 160–161, 172, 183, 297, 303, 316, 471, 480
  in *Casablanca,* 196, 198, 199
Los Angeles, Calif., social tensions in, 279
Los Angeles *Examiner,* 302, 390, 398
Los Angeles *Herald-Express,* 355, 359–360, 361, 431
Los Angeles Times, 171, 208, 209, 219, 247, 322, 356, 454
Love Affair (film), 43
Loving Gentleman, A (Wilde), 158
Loy, Myrna, 88, 368
Luce, Claire, 41
Luciano, Charles (Lucky), 74
Lueker, Art, 320
Luft, Lorna, 465
Luft, Sid, 465, 504
Lukas, Paul, 255, 256
Lupino, Ida, 215, 266, 341, 418
  in *High Sierra,* 124, 126–130, 133, 136, 141, 142–143
  in *Out of the Fog,* 141–143
  in *They Drive by Night,* 124, 126, 129
  work with HB supposedly refused by, 128–129, 142–143, 145
Lux Radio Theatre, 329–330
Lyons, Leonard, 171

M (film), 156
Macauley, Richard, 184
MacBain, Leonard, 428
McCambridge, Mercedes, 468
McCarey, Leo, 364
McCarthy, Joseph R., 331, 357, 466, 467, 497
McClain, John, 435
McCormick, Robert Rutherford, 354–355
McCoy, Frank, 159
McCrea, Joel, 84
MacEwen, Walter, 173, 181, 438, 500
Mackaill, Dorothy, 43
MacKenna, Kenneth, 29–30, 33, 38, 40, 113
  Philips's marriage to, 30, 90
MacKenna, Mary Philips, *see* Philips, Mary
MacKenzie, Aeneas, 179, 183
McLaglen, Victor, 41, 42
MacLane, Barton, 111, 162, 344
MacLeish, Archibald, 360
McMillan, Allan, 169–170
MacMurray, Fred, 480, 481, 484
Mad Honeymoon, The (play), 70
Mad Hopes, The (Brent), 43
Magnificent Obsession (film), 240
Main Street (film), 49
Making of "The African Queen," The (Hepburn), 442
Malabar Farm, 113, 213, 300, 304–307
Malden, Karl, 457
Male Animal, The (film), 150
Maltese Falcon, The (film; 1931), 149
Maltese Falcon, The (film; 1941), 149–164, 180, 201, 290, 443
  Across the Pacific vs., 183, 184
  billing of, 163–164
  budget of, 151, 171, 172

casting for, 149–153
innovations of, 153–154
reviews of, 166, 170–171
Wallis's criticism of, 155
Maltese Falcon, The (Hammett), 148, 151, 153, 154, 162, 163, 180, 470, 471, 521
Maltz, Albert, 357, 364, 366, 380, 383, 388, 401
Mankiewicz, Joseph, 495, 496
Mann, Delbert, 505
Manpower (film), 143–145
Man's Past, A (film), 199
Man Who Came Back, The (film), 40
Man Who Came to Dinner, The (film), 187
Man Who Played God, The (film), 73
Man Who Would Be King, The (film), 487, 510
Man Who Would Be King, The (Kipling), 487
Mapleton Pictures, 506
March, Fredric, 88, 109, 130, 131, 360, 368, 454, 466, 501
March of Time, The (news series), 207
Maree, A. Morgan, 108, 132, 264, 334, 405, 406, 437, 461, 489
Santana Productions and, 420, 421, 424, 425, 471, 473, 474, 485, 486, 500
Maree, Andy, 516–517
Marked Woman (film), 73–77, 82–83, 423
Mark Hellinger Productions, 338–340, 395–397, 401–402, 404, 420
Marks, Owen, 215
Marquand, John, 504
Marshall, George, 308
Martin, Joseph William, 381
Marut, Ret, *see* Traven, B.
Marx, Groucho, 131, 136, 280, 281, 360
*M*A*S*H* (film), 385, 461
M.A.S.H. 66, see Battle Circus
Mask and the Face, The (Chiarelli), 43
Mason, James, 518
Massey, Raymond, 81, 212, 326, 513
Matthews, Blayney, 100, 185, 287, 291, 315–316, 317, 352
Mature, Victor, 302
Maugham, W. Somerset, 43, 50
Mauldin, Bill, 228–229, 479
Maxwell, Elsa, 247
Mayer, Louis B., 190, 239–240, 355, 357, 364
Mayo, Archie, 58, 410
Mayo, Virginia, 417
Meet the Wife (Starling), 32, 33
Melville Goodwin, U.S.A. (film), 504–505, 509, 510
Men Are Such Fools (film), 89
Menjou, Adolphe, 364, 447
Menken, Helen, 82, 298, 521
as actress, 34, 35, 37
HB's affair with, 168, 222, 233, 234
HB's marriage to, 34–37, 85
Men Without Country (Nordhoff and Hall), 210
Mercer, Johnny, 264
Meredith, Burgess, 81, 238
Methot, Beryl Evelyn Wood (Buffy), 70, 95–96, 108, 140, 227–231, 233, 276, 283, 284, 302
Methot, Jack, 70, 93
Methot, Mayo June, 70–76, 89–98, 106–108, 136, 212–215, 227–235, 253, 272–277, 302–305, 324, 340, 475–476
Bacall and, 264–265, 272, 283, 285
broken foot of, 268, 272
death of, 445–446
drinking of, 71, 72, 74, 92, 94, 95, 107–108, 140, 165, 168–169, 184, 202, 223, 224, 230–232, 274, 275, 414, 445–446
fortieth birthday of, 264–265
guns and, 223, 231, 252
HB's career and, 87, 107–108, 140, 157, 166–169, 201–202, 214
HB's conflicts with, 92–95, 107–108, 115, 128, 140, 157, 165–169, 184–185, 202, 212, 214, 215, 220–224, 227–234, 256, 265, 272–276, 283–284, 287
HB's divorce from, 283, 286, 291, 292–293, 302–303
HB's marriage to, 75, 85, 89–92, 307
HB's reconciliation with, 276–277
HB's sense of obligation to, 270, 276–277, 284, 302
HB's separations from, 276, 283–284, 406
jealousy of, 128, 140, 157, 167, 184–185, 201–202, 223, 275
Lupino and, 128–129
Maud's relationship with, 96, 108, 139

Methot, Mayo June *(continued)*
mental illness of, 140, 202, 223–224
in New York City, 139–140, 233–235
suicidal behavior of, 223–224, 284
on war tour, 227–233, 249, 414
Metro-Goldwyn-Mayer (MGM), 63, 124, 144, 190, 193, 196, 241, 337, 355, 388, 409, 427
Feldman and, 239–240
firings at, 395
HB's work for, 461–463
Hellinger Productions and, 338–339
political conservatism at, 279, 282
Mexico, 336–337, 338, 341–344, 347–351, 442
Midnight (film), 44
Mielziner, Jo, 29, 33, 63
Mildred Pierce (film), 437
Milestone, Lewis, 110, 357
Milland, Ray, 326
Miller, Gilbert, 50
Milton Berle Show (radio show), 292, 293–294
Minnelli, Liza, 465
Minnelli, Vincente, 465
Mission to Moscow (Davies), 194
Mission to Moscow (film), 194–195, 209, 225–226, 309, 355, 395
HUAC hearings and, 356, 361–363, 365
Mitchell, Thomas, 47
Mitchum, Robert, 290
Mizner, Wilson, 467
Modern Screen, 405
Moffitt, Jack, 215
Monogram, 263
Monroe, Marilyn, 239, 472, 493, 506
Montgomery, Robert, 130
Moore, Gary, 310
Moore, Irving, 481, 483
Moran, Dolores, 249, 250, 256, 267
Morgan, Dennis, 146, 183
Morgan, Mayo June Methot, *see* Methot, Mayo June
Morgan, Michele, 190, 220
Morgan, Percy T., Jr., 71, 72, 73
Morley, Robert, 471
Morris, Wayne, 81, 89
Mortimer, Lee, 429
Mostel, Zero, 388, 447
Most Immoral Lady, A (Martin), 39
Motion Picture Academy, 105
Motion Picture Association of America (MPAA), 369, 375–376, 387, 392–395
Motion Picture Alliance for the Preservation of American Ideals, 282, 317, 355, 363, 364, 400, 469
Motion Picture Daily, 79
Motion Picture Democratic Committee, 131, 135
Motion Picture Herald, 170, 402
Motion Picture Producers and Distributors of America, 111–112
Motion Picture Relief Fund, 107, 166
Motion Pictures on the Fighting Front (Army short), 255
Moulin Rouge (film), 471, 473, 475
Mountain Music (film), 87
movie palaces, 21, 139–140
Muni, Paul, 53, 55, 110, 112, 113, 118–123
HB vs., 79, 80, 122
High Sierra and, 118–122
Juarez and, 117, 120
Warner Bros. relations severed by, 121–123
Murder, Inc., see Enforcer, The
Murder, My Sweet (film), 301
Murderers' Row, 55, 123
Murphy, George, 256, 467
Murrow, Edward R., 195, 496–497
Muse, Clarence, 197, 281
music, 87, 92, 312, 416
in *Casablanca,* 67, 203–204
politics and, 280, 282
Mussolini, Benito, 131
Mutiny on the Bounty (film), 215
My Little Chickadee (film), 110

Nadi, Aldo, 261
Naked City, The (film), 338, 366, 396, 401, 420
Naples, 228–229, 231, 232–233
Narrow Corner, The (film), 66
Nathan, Paul, 187
Nation, 330
National Labor Relations Board, 316
Navy, U.S., 24–28, 174, 480, 482–485
Nazi Germany, Nazism, 131, 135–136, 141, 142, 219, 227, 312, 448, 493–494
in films, 172–176, 182, 189, 199, 203–204, 215, 220

Nazimova, Alla, 68
NBC (National Broadcasting Company), 81, 136
Nelson, Harmon Oscar (Ham), 105
Nelson, Ozzie, 139
Nerves (Farrar and Benét), 33
Netherlands, 8, 14, 135
Nevard, Gloria, 237, 238, 299
New Deal, 3, 55–56, 131, 174, 194, 280–282, 367
Newman, Paul, 501
New York, N.Y., 10, 12–17, 20–26, 28–40, 42–55, 96, 233–236, 238, 291–300, 521
  HB's returns to, 42–43, 139–140, 169–170, 233–235, 292–300, 389–392, 395, 427–431, 436–437, 440, 468–469
  speakeasies in, 32, 34–35, 37
  theater in, 17, 21, 31–36, 38–39, 43–51, 54–55, 62–63, 69, 70, 71, 83
New York *American,* 32, 34, 60, 80
New York *Daily Mirror,* 382, 390
New York *Daily News,* 60, 146, 354, 430, 436
New Yorker, 407–408, 486
New York *Herald,* 32, 37, 51
New York *Herald Tribune,* 60, 78, 103, 104, 141, 146, 170, 320, 326, 333, 337, 368, 378, 415, 487, 520
  HB's interview in, 391, 392
New York *Journal-American,* 430, 431
New York *Mirror,* 79–80
New York *Post,* 46, 79, 103, 104, 152, 170, 171, 322, 395
New York *Sun,* 60, 376
New York Times, 115, 119, 136, 138, 285, 436, 489, 520
  Communist allegations as viewed by, 133, 134
  film reviews of, 60, 78, 79, 89, 110, 140–141, 146, 170, 171, 209, 225, 320–321, 353, 427, 435, 461, 494, 495
  HUAC hearings and, 361, 369
  theater reviews of, 33, 34, 39, 43, 46, 54, 501
New York *World,* 32, 33, 34
New York *World-Telegram,* 47, 60
nickelodeons, 14, 21
Night Train to Munich (Night Train) (film), 199
Niklas, Kurt, 511
Nineteen, Unfriendly, 357, 364–366, 369, 373–374, 376–380, 383–384, 403
Ninotchka (film), 111, 275, 491
Niven, David, 105, 106, 464, 503–504, 511–512, 513, 517, 518
Niven, Hjordis, 503–504, 511–512, 513
Nixon, Richard, 331, 357, 381
Nollier, Claude, 472
Nordhoff, Charles, 215
North, Edmund, 427, 433, 434
Novak, Kim, 512
Now, Voyager (film), 99, 128, 178, 189, 198, 218
Nugent, Elliott, 150
Nugent, Frank S., 60
Nye, Gerald, 174

O'Brien, Edmond, 495
O'Brien, George, 42
O'Brien, Pat, 65, 66, 76, 102, 130
Obringer, Roy, 59, 61, 100, 193, 216, 219, 425, 460–461, 478
  Bacall and, 304, 417, 418, 437
  HB's suspensions and, 146, 147, 269
  Maltese Falcon and, 150, 151, 152
  To Have and Have Not and, 248, 264
Office of War Information, U.S., 208, 220, 252
Of Human Bondage (film), 50, 53, 73
Of Mice and Men (film), 110–111
Oklahoma Kid, The (film), 101, 103
Old Acquaintance (film), 248–249
Old Maid, The (film), 105–106, 178
Old Man and the Sea, The (Hemingway), 465
Oliver, Edna May, 34
Olivier, Laurence, 152, 447, 479
Olson, Sidney, 379
One Way Passage (film), 87, 113, 421
Ontario County Times, 11, 13
On the Waterfront (film), 506
On with the Show (film), 49
"Open letter to the Working Press" (Bogart), 512–513
Ophuls, Marcel, 220
Oppenheimer, George, 42, 92
Orlova, Gaye, 414
Ornitz, Samuel, 357, 383

O'Shea, Daniel T., 396
Our Wife (Day and Mearson), 43
Out of the Fog (film), 141–143

Paderewski, Ignace, 312
Page, Gale, 111
Page, Joy, 200
Paramount Pictures, 38, 63, 84, 87, 109, 113, 124, 390, 391, 436, 475
  Detective Story and, 424–425
  For Whom the Bell Tolls and, 191, 206
  HB's work for, 490–495, 501–502, 503
  Maltese Falcon and, 148
  Wallis at, 419, 460
Parker, Dorothy, 300, 391
Parker, Eleanor, 427
Parks, Larry, 357
Parsons, Louella, 33, 84, 147, 262, 265, 283–284, 286, 302, 323, 470–471, 497
Passage to Marseille (film), 210, 215–220, 224, 226, 249
Patrick, Lee, 153, 154
Pearson, Drew, 375
Peck, Gregory, 426, 436, 449, 492, 517
Pendleton, Nat, 87
Pepe le Moko (film), 179
Pepper, Claude, 368
Perez Herrera, Raul, 348
Person to Person (TV show), 496–497
Peterson, Carl (Pete), 458–459, 498
Peterson, Verita, *see* Thompson, Verita Peterson
Petrified Forest, The (film), 49–54, 56–62, 78, 86, 216, 468, 489
  Key Largo vs., 409, 410
  production problems with, 58–59
  reviews of, 60
Petrified Forest, The (Sherwood), 45–51, 54, 57, 60, 62, 333
Petrified Forest, The (TV revival), 505
Philips, Mary, 37–40, 68, 72, 73, 105, 302
  as actress, 33, 37, 40, 44, 51, 54–55, 62–63, 69, 84, 90
  drinking of, 37, 44
  HB's divorce from, 84, 85, 89–90, 168
  HB's marriage to, 33, 38, 42, 47, 53, 54, 62–63, 69, 73, 84, 85
  MacKenna's marriage to, 30, 90
Phillips, Cabell, 361
Phillips Academy (Andover), 10, 19, 21–25
Pichel, Irving, 357
Pinky (film), 448, 449
Place in the Sun, A (film), 454
Players, the, 37, 44
PM, 322, 323
Polonsky, Abraham, 386
Porter, Cole, 511–512
Postman Always Rings Twice, The (Cain), 62–63, 69
Powell, Adam Clayton, 196
Powell, Dick, 131
Powell, William, 88, 177, 326, 518
Prang, Louis, 12
Preminger, Otto, 176
Price, Vincent, 238
Prinz, LeRoy, 315
Prizzi's Honor (film), 158
Producers' Showcase (TV show), 505
Production Code Administration (PCA; Breen Office), 49, 74, 112, 250, 338, 414, 449
  Beat the Devil and, 470, 474
  Casablanca and, 190, 191–192
Progressive Citizens of America, 358, 369
Prouty, Olive Higgins, 178
Public Enemy, The (film), 80
Pulitzer, Joseph, 450

Rabe, Peggy, 428
Racket Busters (film), 101
radio, 81–82, 136, 147, 166–167, 189, 193, 329–330
  Bold Venture and, 437–438
  CFA broadcasts on, 367–368, 371, 387
  election of 1944 and, 280–282, 310, 311
Raft, George, 76, 84, 103, 111, 122, 152, 171–172, 179, 190, 232, 465
  It All Came True and roles refused by, 110, 112, 124, 138, 142, 150–152, 165, 181
  Maltese Falcon and, 149–152
  Manpower and, 143–145
  New York junket of, 124–125
  in *They Drive by Night*, 124, 144, 149
  work with HB refused by, 144–145
Rain (play), 51

Rainer, Luise, 241
Raines, Ella, 237, 242, 248
Rainier, Prince, 240
Rains, Claude, 81, 136
  in *Casablanca,* 198, 199, 200, 206, 207, 256
Rand, Ayn, 417
Rand, Sally, 51
Rankin, John, 355–356, 360, 381
Rappe, Virginia, 36
Rapper, Irving, 105, 128
Rat Pack, 503–504
Ray, Aldo, 503
Ray, Nicholas, 423–424, 433–434, 465, 471, 478
Raymond, Gene, 34
Reagan, Ronald, 89, 101, 104, 183, 330, 344, 364, 417, 518
Rebel Without a Cause (film), 333, 424
Red Cross, 252–253
Red Stars in Hollywood (Fagan), 448
Reed, Donna, 460, 461
Reinhardt, Betty, 92
Reinhardt, John, 92
Report from the Front (propaganda short), 252–253
Republicans, Republican Party, 3, 134, 136, 279–282, 311, 355, 356, 367, 380, 395
  in election of 1952, 466, 467, 469
Return of Dr. X, The (film), 102, 139, 165
Revere, Paul, 312–313
Ridgely, John, 249, 285
Rin Tin Tin (film), 56
Riot in Cell Block 11 (film), 503
Ritchie, Robert, 241
Ritt, Martin, 387
Rivera, Diego, 344
Rivkin, Allen, 92–93, 95, 461
Rivkin, Laura, 461
RKO, 50, 53, 63, 367, 390, 391
  African Queen and, 438, 439
Road Show (film), 137
Roaring Twenties, The (film), 101, 103, 110, 119, 125, 179
Robb, Inez, 431
Roberts, Robin, 428–430
Roberts, Stanley, 484
Robinson, Casey, 189, 197, 204, 205, 207, 209, 215, 282
Robinson, Earl, 236–237, 241, 242, 243, 247, 281
Robinson, Edward G., 64, 76, 122, 123, 142, 144, 166, 177, 289, 337, 346, 406
  in *Bullets or Ballots,* 65
  CFA and, 359, 360
  HB vs., 79, 80
  in *Key Largo,* 409, 411–415
  in *Kid Galahad,* 81, 105
  in *Manpower,* 145
  mobster roles and, 51–55, 57, 112, 116, 409, 411–415
  politics of, 136, 359, 360, 408, 412
  on radio, 81–82
Rocky Mountain (film), 437
Rodgers, Richard, 468
Rogers, Ginger, 63, 88, 275, 279–280, 400
Rogers, Henry, 367, 371, 382
Rogers, Will, 329
Romance on the High Seas (film), 416
Roman Holiday (film), 492
Romanoff, Gloria, 503–504, 511–512, 513
Romanoff, Mike, 457, 498–499, 503–504, 511–512, 513, 518, 519
Romulus Productions, 440, 471, 474, 486
Roosevelt, Eleanor, 194, 309
Roosevelt, Elliott, 367
Roosevelt, Franklin D., 3, 43, 55, 134, 136, 151, 331, 379, 407–408, 449
  death of, 307, 310, 408
  in election of 1944, 279–282, 310
  HUAC hearings and, 356, 362, 367
  Key Largo and, 407, 410
  McCormick's attack on, 354
  Mission to Moscow and, 194–195, 225, 356, 362
  World War II and, 174, 178, 194–195, 208, 225, 307, 308, 407
Roosevelt, George, 458–459, 499
Roosevelt, James, 330
Roosevelt, Theodore, 137
Rose, Frances Bogart (Pat), 2, 3, 7, 31, 39, 502
  divorce of, 86
  elopement of, 29
  HB's caring for, 85–86, 97–98
  as manic-depressive, 42, 85–86, 88, 97–98, 115, 223, 270
Rose, Stuart, 27, 29, 36, 40, 85–86, 310
  on HB's acting, 31, 32
  HB's friendship with, 29, 39

Rosenbloom, Maxie, 94
Rosenstein, Jaik, 169, 223, 422
Ross, Lillian, 407–408, 412
Rossellini, Roberto, 192
Rossen, Robert, 357, 447
Rosten, Leo (Leonard Ross), 172
Round Up the Usual Suspects (Harmetz), 189, 190, 192, 195–196, 200, 255, 256
Rubin, Jerry, 377
Ruined Lady, The (play), 30–31, 38
Runyon, Damon, 436
Russell, Rosalind, 81, 131, 242, 274
Ryan, Robert, 368, 468

Sabrina (film), 103, 490–495, 501
Sabrina (Taylor), 490
Saeta, Eddie, 511
Sahara (film), 213–215
sailing, 23, 265, 301–302, 304–305
  racing and, 272, 350, 353
  see also Santana; Sluggy
Sakall, S. Z., 199, 214–215
Salt, Waldo, 357, 383
Salute to Roosevelt (radio special), 136
Sandburg, Carl, 469
Santa Fe Special, 106–107
Santana (yawl), 18, 326–327, 350, 353, 411, 458–459, 485, 497–498, 511, 521
Santana Productions, 420–421, 423–427, 433–437, 500–501
  Beat the Devil and, 469–478, 485–487
  sale of, 500, 504
Santa Olivia, USS, 28
Satan Met a Lady (film), 149
Saturday Evening Post, 176, 310–313, 506
Saturday's Children (Anderson), 36–37
Scarface (film), 118, 119, 120, 179, 241
Schaefer, Carl, 57, 111
Schaefer, William, 100, 151–152, 163, 194, 195, 256
Schafer, Natalie, 300, 515
Schary, Dore, 466–467, 486
Schatz, Thomas, 112
Scheid, Francis, 197
Schenck, Joseph, 56, 355
Schenck, Nicholas, 355
Schettler, Herbert S., 306
Schickel, Richard, 20, 435
Schulberg, Ad Jaffe, 109
Schulberg, B. P., 109, 132
Schulberg, Budd, 109, 431–432, 504
Schultz, Dutch, 119
Schwab's Drugstore, 96
Schwartz, Arthur, 301
Schwartz, Jerome Lawrence, *see* Lawrence, Jerome
Scott, Adrian, 301, 357, 383, 449
Scott, Hazel, 196
Scott, Lizabeth, 331
Scott, Randolph, 248
Scott, Zachary, 344
Scottsboro boys, 131
Screen Actors Guild, 65–66, 71, 130, 132, 226, 314, 316, 364
Screen Gems, 420
Screen Writers Guild, 131, 314, 316, 376, 404
script supervisors, 451–453
Sea Hawk, The (film), 174
See It Now (TV show), 497
Seeman, Bill, 428
Seiler, Lewis, 114, 181
Seltzer, Walter, 168
Selznick, David O., 173, 191, 196, 208, 209, 239, 339, 366, 401, 471, 474, 517
  Hellinger's deal with, 395–397, 404, 420
Selznick, Irene, 439
Selznick, Myron, 54, 86, 88, 151, 193
Senate, U.S., 174–175, 176
  War Investigating Committee of, 367
Seneca Point, N.Y. (the Point), 2–8, 16–18, 23
Seneca Point Gang, 16–17
Sergeant York (film), 174–175, 177
Set Your Clock at U-235 (Corwin), 330
Seventh Heaven (film), 40
Seventh Heaven (Strong), 35, 37
Seven Year Itch, The (film), 493, 506
Severeid, Eric, 383
sex, sexuality, 49, 74
  in *Big Sleep,* 278–279
  censorship and, 49, 74, 112
  in *Confidential Agent,* 319–320
  of HB, 17–18, 39, 68–69, 75, 94, 109, 123, 166
  in *Postman Always Rings Twice,* 62, 69
Seymour, Dan, 200, 201, 203, 254, 257, 258, 260–263, 298, 409
Shakespeare, William, 81–82, 127

Shanghai Express (film), 249
Shaw, Artie, 368
Shaw, Irwin, 141, 479
Shaw, James C., 482–483
Shearer, Norma, 241
Sheekman, Arthur, 91, 94, 95, 175, 223, 238, 300
Sheekman, Sylvia, 300–301
Shenson, Walter, 488
Sheridan, Ann, 106, 123, 131, 222, 247, 266, 275, 337, 392, 437
  Casablanca and, 183, 190, 191–192
  Hellinger's liaison with, 404
Sherman, Vincent, 102–103, 112, 165–166, 173, 179, 181
  Across the Pacific and, 185, 186
  King of the Underworld and, 113–114
Sherwood, Robert, 45, 48, 54, 57, 60, 62, 65, 468
Shirer, William, 177–178
Shirley, Anne, 301, 449
Shoot the Piano Player (Goodis), 332
Shumlin, Herman, 181, 318–321
Sidney, Sylvia, 84, 138, 141
Siegel, Sol, 449
Silver, Arthur, 114, 224, 292, 298, 316, 320, 419
Silverheels, Jay, 409
Silver Screen, 286
Simmons, Jean, 472
Sinatra, Frank, 360, 368, 422, 462, 485, 495, 503–504, 512, 517
Singleton, Penny, 87
Sircom, Arthur, 23, 24
Sirocco (film), 424, 500
Skelton, Red, 255
Skolsky, Sidney, 211
Skyrocket, The (Reed), 38
Slapsie Maxie's, 94–95
Sloan, Alfred P., 357
Sloan, Kathryn, 197, 521
Sluggy (powerboat), 108, 174, 215, 268, 272, 274
"Sluggy Hollow," 95
Small's Paradise, 170
Smith, Alexis, 219
Smith, Helga, 352
Smith, May, 95, 521
"Snows of Kilimanjaro, The" (Hemingway), 338
Sokolsky, George, 402
Solt, Andrew, 433–434
Soma, Tony, 35, 44, 47
Some Like It Hot (film), 493
Sondergaard, Gale, 130
Song and Dance Man, The (play), 70
Song of Bernadette, The (film), 472, 487
Sorrell, Herbert, 314
Sorrow and the Pity, The (film), 220
Sothern, E. H., 34
Soviet Union, 275, 309, 313, 373
  in film, 194–195, 211, 225–226, 355, 361–363
  in World War II, 135, 175, 194–195, 225–227
Sperling, Milton, 166, 418, 421, 504–505, 509, 510
Spiegel, Sam, 439, 441
Spiegel organization, 454–455
Spigelglass, Leonard, 172
Spring Thaw (play), 90
Stacey, Eric, 224, 279, 285, 286, 287
Stag at Bay, The (play), 51
Stalag 17 (film), 491, 492
Stalin, Joseph, 131, 135, 195, 355
Stand-In (film), 87, 108
Stanfell, Alfred, 41
Stanislavsky, Konstantin, 103
Stanwyck, Barbara, 242, 274, 275, 303, 400, 418
Star Is Born, A (film; 1937), 296, 466
Starkey, John R., 430
Stearns, Alfred, 21–24, 32
Steiger, Rod, 506–508
Steinbeck, John, 41, 110
Stella Dallas (film), 178
Stern, Philip, 498
Stevens, Gary, 292–297
Stevens, George, 454
Stevens, Risë, 257
Stevens, Warren, 495
Stevenson, Adlai, 466–469, 472, 497, 513
Stevenson, Marion Hirlman, 371
Stewart, Donald Ogden, 363
Stewart, James, 88, 177, 455, 481
Stewart, Rosalie, 32
Stokes, Frederick A., 12
Stone, Lewis, 337
Stonewright Studios, 61
Stop, You're Killing Me (film), 436, 437
Storer, Doug, 15
Story of Louis Pasteur, The (film), 118
Strand, the, 139–140, 146, 171
Strauss, John, 455
Streetcar Named Desire, A (film), 454, 457

strikes, 96, 130, 313–317, 328
Stripling, Robert E., 361–363
Stroheim, Eric von, 493
Stromboli (film), 192
Strudwick, Shepperd, 404–405
Stuart, Gloria, 72, 97, 175, 223, 300
  Bacall and, 238, 239, 301
  on domestic violence, 94–95
  HB-Methot wedding and, 91, 92
Studio Strike, 313–317, 328
Sturges, Preston, 331
Styne, Jule, 416
Sullivan, Ed, 106, 171, 382, 392–395
Sullivan, Jack, 261–262, 267
Sunset Boulevard (film), 491, 492, 493
Surovy, Walter, 256–259
Swifty (Toohey and Percival), 31–32
Swing Your Lady (film), 87–90
S. W. Strauss and Company, 29

Taft, Robert A., 280
Talbot, Lyle, 57
Taylor, Dwight, 221
Taylor, Glen H., 368
Taylor, Robert, 126, 177, 364, 400
Taylor, Samuel, 490–493
television, 328, 419, 420, 473, 496–497, 505
Temple, Shirley, 131, 171
Tennyson, Alfred, Lord, 518
Thackeray, Kay, 451–453
Thank Your Lucky Stars (film), 42, 214–215
theater, 17, 20–21, 446
  Depression and, 43–44
They Drive by Night (film), 58, 119, 123–126, 144, 179
  budget of, 151
  success of, 129, 142, 146, 149
Thief of Baghdad, The (film), 125
Thin Man, The (Hammett), 180
This Is the Army (film), 225
Thomas, Danny, 518
Thomas, Elbert D., 368
Thomas, J. Parnell, 131, 356, 357, 360, 361, 367, 368, 373, 375–377, 383, 385, 387, 399, 415
Thompson, Slim, 51
Thompson, Verita Peterson, 222–224, 462, 494, 500
Thomson, David, 240
Three on a Match (film), 43, 54, 57
Thurber, James, 150
Tierney, Gene, 502
Tiger Shark (film), 144
Time, 352–353, 428, 457–458, 464, 467, 485, 486, 496
Timpson family, 167–168
Tobin, Genevieve, 58, 62
Todos Santos, 459
Toeplitz, Ludovic, 73
To Have and Have Not (film), 210, 233, 234, 235, 246–268, 271, 427, 437, 497
  Confidential Agent vs., 319, 320, 321
  previews of, 270, 275
  publicity shots for, 266–268
  release of, 272, 285–286, 291, 332
  script problems and, 250, 254
  whistle scene in, 251–252, 258
To Have and Have Not (Hemingway), 246–247, 252
To Have and Have Not (radio show), 329–330
Tokyo Joe (film), 421, 424, 427, 500
Tolson, Clyde, 393
Tone, Franchot, 141
Tony's, 35, 47, 52
Toomey, Regis, 277, 278, 279
Topping, Bob, 464
Torre, Marie, 440
Touch of Brimstone, A (play), 51, 54–55, 62
Toumanova, Tamara, 190
Townsend, James, 54
Tracy, Spencer, 463, 517
  as actor, 41, 385, 440, 465, 482, 483, 487, 501
  HB's friendship with, 41, 465–466, 513, 515, 516
trailers, 292, 320
Traven, B. (Ret Marut; Hal Croves), 336–338, 341–344, 349, 351, 353
Treasure of the Sierra Madre, The (film), 78, 334–338, 389, 427, 488
  casting for, 343–344, 345
  first attempt at making of, 337–338
  HB's immersion in role in, 352
  locations for, 344, 347, 442
  reviews of, 352–353
Treasure of the Sierra Madre, The (Traven), 336–338, 351
Trevor, Claire, 84, 116, 166
  in *Key Largo,* 409, 413–415
Trilling, Steve, 106, 110, 143, 145, 152,

244, 268, 269, 272, 329, 392, 416, 417, 419, 425, 427, 436
Casablanca and, 183, 200
Conflict and, 215–217, 219, 221
Studio Strike and, 316, 317
To Have and Have Not and, 235, 249–252, 270
Trinity School, 14–16, 19, 22
Truffaut, François, 332
Truman, Harry S., 280, 300, 328, 422–423, 448, 469
Trumbo, Dalton, 179, 330, 357, 363, 380, 383, 388
Turner, Lana, 69, 266, 281, 464
Twentieth Century–Fox, 56, 63, 110, 142, 150, 218, 240, 256, 308, 355, 391, 394, 426, 436
Bacall at, 472, 474
Deadline USA and, 448–453
20th Century Pictures, 56
"21," 52, 140, 293, 294, 389, 395, 428, 431, 440
Two Against the World (film), 65
Two-Faced Woman (film), 275
Two Guys from Milwaukee (film), 329
Two Mrs. Carrolls, The (film), 303, 318

Underground (film), 196
Underworld, U.S.A. (crime series), 506
Unfriendly Nineteen, *see* Nineteen, Unfriendly
United Artists, 83–85, 137, 174, 486
United Nations, 242–243, 281, 407
United Press (UP), 397, 398, 445
United States Pictures, 504
Universal, 41, 63, 110, 143, 248
Up the Ladder (Davis), 31
Up the River (film), 41
Uris, Leon, 243
USO, 226, 234–235, 502
Ustinov, Peter, 503

Valiant, The (film), 110, 122
Van Heusen, Jimmy, 503–504
Variety, 51, 170, 320, 323, 361, 455
Veidt, Conrad, 172, 199
Veiller, Tony, 472–473, 474
Venuta, Benay, 468
Verdict, The (film), 316
Verne, Kaaren, 173
Vickers, Martha, 278–279
Vidor, King, 417
Viertel, Peter, 445, 473, 474, 479
Vincent, Allen, 93
Virginia City (film), 102, 110, 202
Vitaphone Corporation, 39
Volunteers for Stevenson, 467, 468–469
Voorhis, Jerry, 331
Vreeland, Bob, 287
Vreeland, Diana, 239

Wagons Roll at Night, The (film), 137–138, 145, 146, 258
Wald, Jerry, 143, 179, 212, 332–333, 360, 401, 427, 431, 506
Key Largo and, 408–409
Wald, Malvin, 172, 401–402
Waldorf declaration, 394–395, 397, 398
Wallace, Bob, 107
Wallace, Henry, 359–360
Wallis, Hal, 56, 64, 78, 88, 89, 99–100, 138, 144, 146, 181, 331, 338
All Through the Night and, 173, 191
Casablanca and, 99, 183, 187–191, 196–198, 205–209
on *Dark Victory,* 104
Goulding's correspondence with, 104, 105
HB loanout refused by, 110
HB's appearance criticized by, 82–83
High Sierra and, 118–120, 122, 129, 141
Lee and, 178–179
Maltese Falcon and, 149–150, 151, 153, 155, 156, 160, 161, 163, 171
Old Maid and, 105, 106
Out of the Fog and, 142, 143
Passage to Marseille and, 215, 217, 218–219
Petrified Forest and, 53, 54, 58–61
political films and, 173, 179, 183, 187–191, 196–198, 205–209
as producer, 99, 119, 186–191, 196–198, 205–208, 218, 419, 459–460
Satan Met a Lady and, 149
Warner's competition with, 218, 255–256, 427, 432
Walsh, Raoul, 42, 143, 338
High Sierra and, 124–127, 129, 141
Walsh, Richard, 314
Wanger, Walter, 30, 87, 110, 179, 360, 366, 464, 503, 506, 517

War Department, U.S., 226–227, 234, 308
Warner, Albert, 48–49, 64, 355
Warner, Ann, 194
Warner, Harry, 48–49, 56, 64, 102–103, 308, 319, 355, 460, 504
  death of, 99
  Jack's relationship with, 98–99, 419–420
  television and, 328
  World War II and, 174–175
Warner, Jack, Jr., 99, 361–363, 419–420, 426
Warner, Jack L., Sr., 48–50, 53, 56–62, 74, 82, 98–103, 115, 120, 122, 126, 186–188, 212, 355, 467
  Across the Pacific and, 193–194
  Bacall and, 247, 249, 270–271, 285, 299, 319, 322–323, 324, 329, 389, 416–417, 421, 436–437, 478, 479, 489, 521
  background and career start of, 48–49, 64
  Casablanca and, 200, 204, 207, 208
  Conflict and, 215–219
  Dachau and, 308–309
  election of 1944 and, 279, 280, 282
  Fitzgerald's relationship with, 152, 195
  Harry's relationship with, 98–99, 419–420
  Hawks's intimidation of, 261–262, 287–288
  HB's recantation and, 397–400, 403, 406
  HB's relationship with, 57, 61–62, 64, 66, 84, 86, 88, 98, 110, 114, 142, 146, 147, 215–219, 224, 234, 263–264, 268–269, 287, 295, 324, 329, 332, 333, 388–392, 397–400, 403, 404, 406, 418, 421, 425–430, 432, 436, 460, 478–479, 489, 497, 504, 510, 513, 517, 521
  Hellinger Productions and, 401–402
  High Sierra and, 121, 129
  HUAC and, 356, 361–363, 365, 369, 388–392, 447
  Key Largo and, 409
  Maltese Falcon and, 149–152, 156, 162, 163–164, 180
  Out of the Fog and, 142, 143
  Petrified Forest and, 50, 53, 57–62
  political films and, 173, 177–178, 180–182, 187, 194–195, 225, 356, 361–363, 365, 395
  Raft's contract and, 152, 171–172
  Roosevelt and, 194–195, 225, 356
  Studio Strike and, 313, 315, 316, 317
  To Have and Have Not and, 246–247, 249, 252, 261–264, 270, 285
  Treasure of the Sierra Madre and, 337, 338, 344, 351
  Waldorf declaration and, 394–395
  Wallis's competition with, 218, 255–256, 427, 432
  Watch on the Rhine and, 180–182, 187
Warner, Rea, 99
Warner, Rose, 48
Warner, Sam, 48–49
Warner Bros. Pictures, Inc., 17, 48–67, 73–87, 98–130, 137–166, 180–181, 183–187, 190–221, 234–235, 242–305, 313–353, 406–421, 425–433, 447–449, 478, 500, 504–505, 509, 510, 521
  Bacall loanouts refused by, 433, 436
  Bacall released from contract by, 437
  Bacall's contract taken over by, 303–304, 323–324
  Bacall suspended by, 418
  B pictures of, 64–67, 89, 225
  Burbank studio of, 55, 56
  Cost Department of, 289
  Green Room of, 116
  HB loaned out by, 82–87, 144, 213–215, 328
  HB loanout refused by, 110–111, 460
  HB's biography by, 13, 29
  HB's contract suspended by, 145–147, 217, 269, 272, 327
  HB's contracts with, 53, 54, 61–62, 67, 86, 89, 110, 111, 192–193, 215, 226, 264, 269, 333–334
  HB's departure from, 437, 488–489
  HB's importance to, 328–329
  HB's lack of standing at, 109–115
  H-F Productions and, 242–249, 270–271, 303–304
  HUAC hearings and, 356, 361–363, 365, 369, 388–392
  Jack's control of, 99
  lawsuits of, 74, 75, 80, 86, 113
  management style of, 98–100
  Muni's contract with, 118, 121–122

need for stars at, 328–329
as New Deal studio, 55–56
1948 as pivotal year for, 418–419
publicity department of, 76, 80, 107, 111, 112, 122–123, 140, 147, 154, 166, 180, 181, 183, 204, 208–209, 218, 220, 265–268, 271–272, 300, 319–320, 349, 418
research department of, 80, 426
Santana Productions and, 425–426
security at, 100–101
skinflint reputation of, 55, 56, 57, 63–64
Studio Strike and, 313–317
Warner Club, 101
Warner Family, 98, 416, 426
Warners Hollywood Theater, 208, 285
War of the Worlds (radio broadcast), 189
Warren, Gloria, 181
Warren, Ralph, 44
Warwick, Robert, 434
Washington, George, 12, 312, 354
Watch on the Rhine (film), 180–182, 187, 195, 209, 218, 225, 318
Watch on the Rhine (Hellman), 178
Waters, Ethel, 169, 170
Watkins, Maurine, 41
Watkins, N.Y., 9, 10
Watts, Richard, Jr., 60
Wayne, John, 239, 240, 242, 328, 400, 425–426, 448
Webb, Clifton, 32, 52, 283, 506
Weinstein, Charlie, 430
Weinstein, Sophie, 271
Weisbart, Dave, 316
Weiser, Martin, 122–123, 140, 208–209, 266–268
Welles, Orson, 63, 82, 154, 189, 345
Wellman, William, 436
Wells, H. G., 59
Wells, Joe, 170
We're No Angels (film), 503
West, Mae, 110
Wexley, John, 449
Weyl, Carl, 172, 215
Wharton, Edith, 105
What Price Glory? (play), 33
What's New, Pussycat? (film), 240
Whistler, James McNeill, 12, 96
White, Pearl, 17
White Heat (film), 419
Why We Fight (propaganda series), 187
Widmark, Richard, 449
Wilde, Arthur, 224–225
Wilde, Meta, 156, 158, 162–163, 241, 250, 257–258, 259, 262, 288, 317
Wilder, Audrey, 495, 518
Wilder, Billy, 360, 486, 491–495, 506, 518
Wiles, Buster, 127, 128, 167
Wilk, Jacob, 48, 49, 148, 180, 317, 325, 326
Mission to Moscow and, 194–195
Watch on the Rhine and, 178, 182
Wilk, Max, 148, 325–326, 521–522
William, Bob, 202, 205, 222, 245
William, Warren, 149
Williams, Andy, 264
Williams, Emlyn, 447
Willkie, Wendell, 136
Willow Brook, 1–8, 18
Wilson, Arthur (Dooley), 197, 199, 209
Wilson, Earl, 286, 292–293, 304, 428, 429, 431, 504
Winchell, Walter, 286
Winsten, Archer, 79, 104, 152, 322, 335, 395
Winwood, Estelle, 87
Woman of the Year (film), 385
Women of All Nations (film), 42
Wood, Sam, 272, 282, 363
Woolf, John, 486
Woollcott, Alexander, 32, 35
World Films, 30
"World Moves On, The" (Hellinger), 119
Worlds of Robert E. Sherwood, The (Brown), 45–46
World War I, 16, 24–28, 176, 177, 229, 438
World War II, 135–136, 219, 225–235, 255, 282, 307, 338, 367, 394, 448, 497
end of, 309–310
in film, 172–215, 220, 225–226, 242–244, 246, 409, 410
Holocaust and, 308–309
wage controls and, 264, 304
Wouk, Herman, 479
Wright, Tennant Campbell (Tenny), 99–100, 114, 149, 285, 287, 289, 353
Wuthering Heights (film), 111, 152
Wyatt, Jane, 358, 366

Wyler, William, 83, 85, 155, 486, 495, 501–502, 518
 Christian Science Monitor statement and, 404–405
 Detective Story and, 424–425
 HUAC hearings and, 357, 360, 365, 369, 375, 381, 386
Wyman, Jane, 419
Wynn, Keenan, 281, 462

Yankee Doodle Dandy (film), 187, 203, 225
Yellow Sky (film), 436
You Can't Get Away with Murder (film), 110
Youmans, Vincent, 71
Young, Collier, 341
Young, Robert, 368
Young, Roland, 42, 51, 55, 90
Young Man with a Horn (film), 427, 436

Zanuck, Darryl F., 56, 110, 142, 218, 240, 308, 394, 403
 Deadline U.S.A. and, 448–450
Zolotow, Maurice, 492, 493, 494